ACCOUNTING
FOR NON-ACCOUNTING STUDENTS

Pearson

At Pearson, we have a simple mission: to help people
make more of their lives through learning.

We combine innovative learning technology with trusted
content and educational expertise to provide engaging
and effective learning experiences that serve people
wherever and whenever they are learning.

From classroom to boardroom, our curriculum materials, digital
learning tools and testing programmes help to educate millions
of people worldwide – more than any other private enterprise.

Every day our work helps learning flourish, and
wherever learning flourishes, so do people.

To learn more, please visit us at **www.pearson.com/uk**

ACCOUNTING
for Non-Accounting Students

Ninth Edition

John R. Dyson
Ellie Franklin

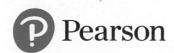

Harlow, England • London • New York • Boston • San Francisco • Toronto • Sydney • Dubai • Singapore • Hong Kong
Tokyo • Seoul • Taipei • New Delhi • Cape Town • São Paulo • Mexico City • Madrid • Amsterdam • Munich • Paris • Milan

Pearson Education Limited

Edinburgh Gate
Harlow CM20 2JE
United Kingdom
Tel: +44 (0)1279 623623

Web: www.pearson.com/uk

First edition published in Great Britain under the Pitman Publishing imprint in 1987 (print and electronic)
Second edition published 1991 (print)
Third edition published 1994 (print)
Fourth edition published under the Financial Times Pitman Publishing imprint in 1997 (print)
Fifth edition published 2001 (print)
Sixth edition published 2004 (print and electronic)
Seventh edition published 2007 (print and electronic)
Eighth edition published 2010 (print and electronic)
Ninth edition published 2017 (print and electronic)

© Pearson Education Limited 1987, 1991, 1994, 1997, 2001 (print)
© Pearson Education Limited 2004, 2007, 2010, 2017 (print and electronic)

The Financial Times. With a worldwide network of highly respected journalists, *The Financial Times* provides global business news, insightful opinion and expert analysis of business, finance and politics. With over 500 journalists reporting from 50 countries worldwide, our in-depth coverage of international news is objectively reported and analysed from an independent, global perspective. To find out more, visit www.ft.com/pearsonoffer.

ISBN: 978-1-292-12897-9 (print)
        978-1-292-12904-4 (PDF)
        978-1-292-12898-6 (ePub)

British Library Cataloguing-in-Publication Data
A catalogue record for the print edition is available from the British Library

Library of Congress Cataloging-in-Publication Data
Names: Dyson, J. R. (John R.), author. | Franklin, Ellie, author
Title: Accounting for non-accounting students / John R. Dyson, Ellie Franklin.
Description: Ninth Edition. | New York : Pearson, 2017 | Revised edition of
    Accounting for non-accounting students, 2010.
Identifiers: LCCN 2016057004| ISBN 9781292128979 (Print) | ISBN 9781292129044
    (PDF) | ISBN 9781292128986 (ePub)
Subjects: LCSH: Accounting.
Classification: LCC HF5636 .D97 2017 | DDC 657—dc23
LC record available at https://lccn.loc.gov/2016057004

10 9 8 7 6 5 4 3 2 1
21 20 19 18 17

Print edition typeset in 10/12pt Sabon LT Pro by SPi Global
Printed and bound by L.E.G.O. S.p.A., Italy

NOTE THAT ANY PAGE CROSS-REFERENCES REFER TO THE PRINT EDITION.

Brief contents

Contents

Supporting resources

Visit **www.pearsoned.co.uk/dyson** to find valuable online resources:

Companion website for students
- Multiple choice questions to help test your learning
- Extra question material
- Links to relevant sites on the web
- Glossary explaining key terms mentioned in the book

For instructors
- Complete, downloadable Lecturer's Guide
- PowerPoint slides that can be downloaded and used for presentations
- Answers to extra question material in the Companion Website
- Extra case studies and guidelines on using them with students

Also: The Companion website provides the following features:
- Search tool to help locate specific items of content
- E-mail results and profile tools to send results of quizzes to instructors
- Online help and support to assist with website usage and troubleshooting

For more information please contact your local Pearson Education sales representative or visit www.pearsoned.co.uk/dyson

Preface

Why study accounting?

This book provides a solid introduction to accounting for those students who are required to study it as part of a non-accounting course. It is also of benefit to those managers in business, government or industry whose work involves them in dealing with accounting information.

Non-accountants are often puzzled why they are required to take a course in accounting, and even more so when they have to take a demanding examination at the end of it. The fact is that these days, no matter what your job, you need to have some knowledge of accounting matters. The main reason for this is that for different specialists to talk to each other they have to speak in a language that everyone understands. In business (in its widest sense) that language is money and that happens to be the accountants' language. The use of a common language enables all the various activities that take place within a business to be translated into monetary terms and for all reports to be prepared on the same basis. So if you need to know what is going on in other departments (as you almost certainly will), you will find it much easier if you speak the language of accounting.

The book's purpose

The problem with many accounting textbooks is that they are written primarily for accounting students. As a result, they go way beyond what a non-accountant needs. This book is different. The subject is not covered superficially but it avoids going into the technical detail that is of relevance only to accountants. Nevertheless, by the time you get to the end of the book you will have gained a perfectly adequate knowledge and understanding of accounting that will enable you to talk to accountants with great confidence and which will help you to do your job much more effectively.

Some guidance for lecturers

The book is divided into four parts. Part 1 introduces students to the world of accounting, Part 2 deals with financial accounting, Part 3 with financial reporting and Part 4 with management accounting.

As you will probably be aware, many further and higher education institutions now operate a modular structure for the delivery of their courses. This book is particularly useful if your own institution does the same. Some accounting syllabi for non-accounting students combine both financial accounting and management accounting in one module while others split them between separate modules. The book is designed so that it can easily be adapted irrespective of whether you combine them or split them.

It is highly unlikely, of course, that the contents of the book will match precisely the syllabus requirements of your own course. There are bound to be topics to which you give more or less emphasis and there will be others that are not covered at all in the book. Nevertheless, the book has now been widely used throughout the UK and in many overseas countries for over 25 years. From the feedback that has been received, the contents appear to continue to meet the main requirements of most introductory accounting courses for non-accounting students.

There is one topic, however, that splits opinion right down the middle: double-entry bookkeeping. Some lecturers are absolutely convinced that non-accounting students need to have a grounding in this topic if they are to understand where the information comes from, what problems there are with it and how it can be used. Other lecturers are adamant that it is totally unnecessary for non-accounting students.

As opinion is so evenly divided on this subject we have decided to retain double-entry bookkeeping in the main part of the book. If you do not include the topic in your syllabus it can be easily left out by skipping the whole of Chapter 3 (Recording data) and possibly parts of Chapter 4 (Sole trader accounts). You could then pick up the thread of the book in Chapter 5 (Company accounts), provided you are sure that your students know something about a trial balance, a statement of profit or loss , and a statement of financial position.

In this edition we have taken the opportunity to revise and update the eighth edition. There are no structural changes made to this edition but a number of chapters have been significantly rewritten or updated:

1 Chapter 2 (Accounting rules and regulations),
2 Chapter 7 (Statement of cash flows), and
3 Chapter 10 (Interpretation of accounts).

By their nature, substantial additions and revisions have had to be made to two other chapters: Chapter 11 (Contemporary issues) and Chapter 20 (Emerging issues). It has not been too difficult to select contemporary financial issues for Chapter 11 because the various accounting bodies have a clearly established development programme and the financial reporting world has been sufficiently dynamic to present us with ample examples to choose from for discussion.

It has proved much more difficult to select emerging management accounting issues for the Chapter 20. Management accounting is not as fast moving as financial accounting and, as yet, there is no such body as a 'management accounting standards board' driving the discipline forward. The main source comes from accountants pursuing academic research in universities but as yet there is no consensus on what changes are needed. When preparing this chapter, therefore, we examined the syllabi of several accounting bodies and also took note of various suggestions made by reviewers. These two sources enabled us to select some likely emerging management issues over the next few years.

The old feature of interspersing the text with news clips has been retained. News clips are brief extracts or summaries of recent newspaper articles that are of relevance to the particular chapters in which they are placed. They are intended to demonstrate that the accounting matters discussed in the various chapters are not theoretical but that they are of practical importance and relevance in the real world.

The news stories introduced into an earlier edition at the beginning of each chapter have been replaced with more recent ones. As before, broad questions on each of these stories may then be found towards the end of the chapter. Students are strongly encouraged to have a go at answering these questions even though some of the issues covered may sometimes appear to be somewhat beyond non-accountants. However, it would be surprising if this were to be the case since most of them were first published in newspapers intended for a general audience.

As publicly traded companies in the European Union (EU) are now required to prepare their financial statements in accordance with International Accounting Standards (IASs), various amendments have had to be made throughout the text. Most notably this has resulted in the update of the terminology in the financial accounting part of the textbook. This has caused a problem for a book aimed at non-accountants as financial statements have become more and more difficult to understand. However, strenuous attempts have been made to keep the text as simple and as relevant as possible.

An additional complexity is that non-listed companies in the UK can adopt UK accounting standards while listed companies must adopt international ones. A similar problem may arise in other EU countries if non-listed companies are allowed to adopt their own accounting standards.

This problem was particularly acute when choosing the names of the financial statements to be used throughout the text. As far as published accounts are concerned, we have limited our discussion to IAS-prepared statements as these are of relevance to *all* EU-based students as well as to students based in other non-EU countries.

Some guidance for college and university students

If you are using this book as part of a formal course, your lecturer should have provided you with a work scheme. The work scheme will outline just how much of the book you are expected to cover each week. In addition to the work done in your lecture you will probably have to read each chapter at least twice.

As you work through a chapter, you will come across a number of 'activities'. Most of them require you to do something or to find something out. The idea of these activities is to encourage you to stop your reading of the text at various points and to think about what you have just read.

There are few right and wrong answers in accounting so we want you to gain some experience in deciding for yourself what you would do if you were faced with the type of issues covered in the activities.

You are also recommended to attempt as many of the questions that follow each chapter as you can. The more questions that you do, the more confident you will be that you really do understand the subject matter. However, avoid looking at the answers (there are some at the back of the book) until you are absolutely certain that you do not know how to do the question. If the answer is not at the back of the book, ask your lecturer to download it for you from the *Lecturer's Guide*.

Some guidance for students studying on their own

If you are studying accounting without having the opportunity of having face-to-face tuition, we suggest that you adopt the following study plan.

1 Organise your private study so that you have covered every topic in your syllabus at least two weeks before your examination. A proven method is to divide the number of weeks (or perhaps days!) you have available by the number of topics. This gives you the *average* time that you should spend on each topic. Allow for some topics requiring more time than others but don't rush though a topic just because you are behind your timetable. Instead, try to put in a few extra hours that week.

2 Read each chapter slowly. Be careful to do each activity and to work through each example. Don't worry if you do not understand each point immediately. Read on to the end of the chapter.

3 Read the chapter again, this time making sure that you understand each point. If necessary, go back and re-read and repeat until you do understand the point.

4 Attempt as many questions at the end of each chapter as you can, but do not look at the answers until you have completed the question or you are certain that you cannot do it. The questions are generally graded so the more difficult ones come towards the end. If you can do them all without too much difficulty, then you can move on to the next chapter with great confidence. However, before you do, it is not a bad idea to re-read the chapter again.

More guidance for all students

At this early stage of your accounting career we want to emphasise that accounting involves much more than being good at doing simple arithmetic (contrary to popular opinion, it is not highly mathematical). The solution to many accounting problems often calls for a considerable amount of personal judgement and this means that there is bound to be an element of subjectivity in whatever you decide to do.

The simplified examples used in this book illustrate some complicated issues and problems in the real world that are not easily solved. You should, therefore, treat the suggested answers with caution and use them as an opportunity to question the methodology adopted. This will mean that when you are presented with some accounting information in your job, you will automatically subject it (rightly) to a great deal of questioning. That is as it should be because, as you will shortly discover, if you were an accountant and you happened to be asked '*What do 2+2 make?*' you might well reply by asking another question: '*What do you want it to make?*'

Puzzled? Intrigued? Then read on – and good luck with your studies.

An explanation

In order to avoid tedious repetition and tortuous circumlocution, the masculine pronoun has generally been adopted throughout this book. No offence is intended to anyone, most of all to our female readers, and we hope that none will be taken.

Guided tour

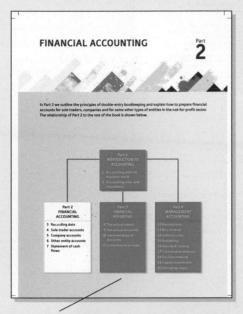

Part openers contain a diagram to help you find your way around the book.

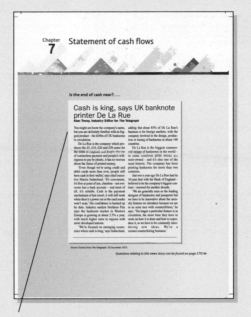

Chapter openers feature a topical news article relating chapter content to the real world, and there are shorter News clips throughout.

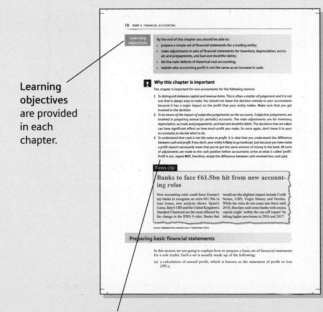

Learning objectives are provided in each chapter.

Why this chapter is important explores the applications and benefits of chapter content for the non-accountant.

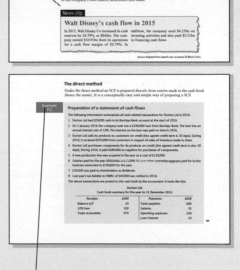

Examples are spread throughout the chapter.

Activities test student understanding at regular intervals throughout the chapter.

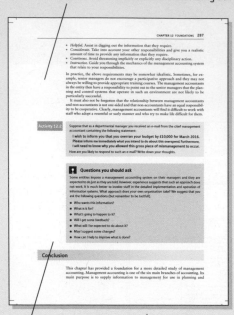

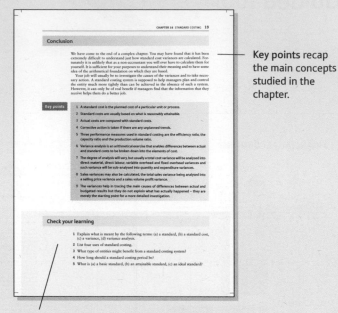

Key points recap the main concepts studied in the chapter.

Questions you should ask are questions business managers might ask to assist in the decision-making process.

Check your learning tests absorption of chapter content and offers a useful revision aid.

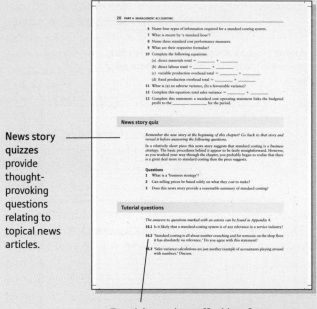

News story quizzes provide thought-provoking questions relating to topical news articles.

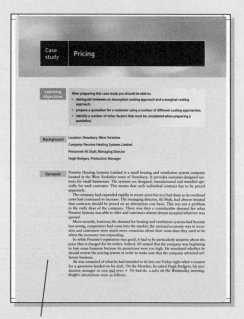

Tutorial questions offer ideas for assignments or class discussion.

Case studies appear at the end of parts.

Visit the Companion Website at www.pearsoned.co.uk/dyson to find further practice questions, study material and links to relevant sites on the World Wide Web. See page vii for full contents.

Acknowledgements

We are grateful to the following for permission to reproduce copyright material:

Figures

Figure 11.1 from http://www.actionfraud.police.uk/fraud-protection/false-accounting-fraud, June 2016, Open Government Licence v3.0; Figure 20.2 adapted from 'Using the balanced scorecard as a strategic management system', *Harvard Business Review* (Kaplan, R.S. and Norton, D. P. 1996), with permission from Harvard Business School Publishing; Figure 20.3 from 'A framework for functional coordination', *Atlanta Economic Review*, 23(6), pp.8–11 (Fox, H. 1973), with permission from the Federal Reserve Bank of Atlanta.

Text

Extract on page 11 adapted from 'In search of the right note', *Financial Times*, 24/08/2015 (Agnew, H.), © The Financial Times Limited. All Rights Reserved; Extract on page 44 from 'Principles of good regulation', https://www.fca.org.uk/about/principles-good-regulation, The Finance Conduct Authority, accessed 15 April 2016; Extract on page 48 adapted from 'Blockchain promises back-office ledger revolution', *Financial Times*, 13/10/2015 (Kaminska, I.), © The Financial Times Limited. All Rights Reserved; Extract on page 52 adapted from 'Toshiba scraps dividend after finding accounting irregularities', *Financial Times*, 08/05/2015 (Inagaki, K.), © The Financial Times Limited. All Rights Reserved; Extract on page 77 adapted from 'ANZ flags increase in bad debts amid commodity price slump', *Financial Times*, 24/03/2016 (Wells, P.); Extract on page 78 adapted from 'Banks to face €61.5bn hit from new accounting rules, says report', *Financial Times*, 01/09/2015 (Agnew, H. and Noonan, L.), © The Financial Times Limited. All Rights Reserved; Extract on page 84 adapted from 'Fractional ownership: Appreciation of depreciation shapes an industry', *Financial Times*, 16/11/2015 (Moscrop, L.); Extract on page 87 after '£2bn wiped off Tesco's value as profit overstating scandal sends shares sliding – as it happened', *The Guardian*, 22/09/2014 (Wearden, G.); Extract on page 88 after 'Debt, defaults, and devaluations: why this market crash is like nothing we've seen before', *The Telegraph*, 17/04/2016 (Khan, M.), © Telegraph Media Group Ltd 2016; Extract on page 109 adapted from 'IASB rule change to bring more transparency to balance sheet', *Financial Times*, 20/01/2016 (Burgess, K. and Agnew, H.), © The Financial Times Limited. All Rights Reserved; Extract on page 116 adapted from 'Prudential to pay special dividend after beating expectations', *Financial Times*, 09/03/2016 (Ralph, O.), © The Financial Times Limited. All Rights Reserved; Extract on page 119 adapted from 'BHS seeks to offload pension deficit worth £571m', *Financial Times*, 07/03/2016 (Vandevelde, M., Cumbo, J. and Evans, J.), © The Financial Times Limited. All Rights Reserved; Extract on page 133 from 'Accountability to parliament for taxpayers' money, https://www.nao.org.uk/press-releases/accountability-to-parliament-for-taxpayers-money, National Audit Office, accessed 23 February 2016; Extract on page 142 adapted from 'Kids Company trustees 'negligent'', *Financial Times*, 01/02/2016 (Viña, G.), © The Financial Times Limited. All Rights Reserved; Extract on page 145 adapted from 'Public sector needs to do a better job with assets', *Financial Times*, 15/04/2016 (Wolf, M.), © The Financial Times Limited. All Rights Reserved; Extract on page 151 adapted from 'Cash is king for the future, says UK banknote printer De La Rue', *The Telegraph*, 30/12/2015 (Tovey, A.), © Telegraph Media Group Ltd 2016; Extract on page 152 adapted from 'Colt Defense files for bankruptcy after debt restructuring deal misfires', *Financial Times*, 15/06/2015 (Paton, E.), © The Financial Times Limited. All Rights Reserved; Extract on page 154 adapted from 'Theo Pahpitis quote', The Guardian online, accessed 23 March 2016, Starting a new business: how to avoid failure, by Rahul Thakrar Monday 22 February 2016 http://www.theguardian.com/small-business-network/2016/feb/22/starting-a-new-business-how-to-avoid-failure; Extract on page 188 adapted from 'Brussels in corporate transparency push', *Financial Times*, 15/04/2014 (Agnew, H.); Extract on page 190 adapted from Bank annual reports too long or 'complex', *Financial Times*, 08/06/2014 (Fleming, S. and Agnew, H.); Extract on page 201 adapted from 'FTSE 100 bosses face fresh revolt over pay', *Financial Times*, 16/08/2016 (Oakley, D.), © The Financial Times Limited. All Rights Reserved; Extract on page 208 adapted from 'Toshiba says it inflated profits by nearly \$2bn over seven years', *Financial Times*, 07/09/2015 (Inagaki, K.), © The Financial Times Limited. All Rights Reserved; Extract on page 218 adapted from 'Auditors' fears increase over Hong Kong companies', *Financial Times*, 23/08/2015 (Hughes, J.), © The Financial Times Limited. All Rights Reserved; Extract on page 226 adapted from 'Investors mine Big Data for cutting-edge strategies', *Financial Times*, 30/03/2016 (Wigglesworth, R.), © The Financial Times Limited. All Rights Reserved; Extract on page 259 adapted from 'Ten UK companies fell short of FRC reporting standards', *Financial Times*, 14/10/2014 (Agnew, H.); Extract on page 261 from 'Tesco to be investigated by FCA over accounting scandal', *The Guardian*, 01/10/2014 (Farrell, S); Extract on page 264 adapted from 'Audit firms called to account for cosy tenures', *Financial Times*, 14/06/2015 (Marriage, M.), © The Financial Times Limited. All Rights Reserved; Extract on page 265 adapted from 'Schroders dumps PwC as its auditor after 57 years', *Financial Times*, 27/03/2016 (Devine, A.), © The Financial Times Limited. All Rights Reserved.

Abbreviations

AAT	Association of Accounting Technicians
ABB	Activity-based budgeting
ABC	Activity-based costing
ABCM	Activity-based cost management
ABM	Activity-based management
AC	Average cost
ACCA	Association of Chartered Certified Accountants
AMT	Advanced manufacturing technology
ARR	Accounting rate of return
ASB	Accounting Standards Board
ASC	Accounting Standards Committee
ASSC	Accounting Standards Steering Committee
BB	Beyond budgeting/Better budgeting
BBC	British Broadcasting Corporation
CA	Chartered Accountant/Companies Act
CE	Capital employed/expenditure
CI	Capital investment
CIMA	Chartered Institute of Management Accountants
CIPFA	Chartered Institute of Public Finance and Accountancy
Cr	Credit
DCF	Discounted cash flow
Dr	Debit
EA	Environmental accounting
ED	Exposure draft
EMA	Environmental management accounting
EPS	Earnings per share
EU	European Union
FA	Financial accounting
FASB	Financial Accounting Standards Board
FCA	Financial Conduct Authority
FIFO	First in, first out
FRC	Financial Reporting Council
FRS	Financial Reporting Standard
FTSE	Financial Times and London Stock Exchange
GAAP	Generally accepted accounting principles
GBV	Gross book value
HCA	Historic cost accounting
HP	Hire purchase
IAS	International Accounting Standard
IASB	International Accounting Standards Board
IASC	International Accounting Standards Committee

ICAEW	Institute of Chartered Accountants in England and Wales
ICAI	Institute of Chartered Accountants in Ireland
ICAS	Institute of Chartered Accountants of Scotland
IFAC	International Federation of Accountants
IFRS	International Financial Reporting Standard
IFRSF	International Financial Reporting Standards Foundation
IRR	Internal rate of return
JIT	Just-in-time
KPI	Key performance indicator
LCC	Life cycle costing
LIFO	Last-in, first-out
LLP	Limited liability partnership
LSE	London Stock Exchange
LTD	Limited
MA	Management accounting
MV	Market value
NBV	Net book value
NCF	Net cash flow
NPV	Net present value
PBIT	Profit before interest and tax
PFI	Private finance initiative
PI	Performance indicator
PLC	Public limited company
PLCC	Product/project life cycle costing
R&D	Research and development
RI	Residual income
ROCE	Return on capital employed
SBU	Strategic business unit
SC	Standard cost/costing
SCE	Statement of changes in equity
SCF	Statement of cash flows
SFP	Statement of financial position
SI	Statutory Instrument
SMA	Strategic management accounting
SME	Small and medium-sized enterprise
SPL	Statement of profit or loss
SRE	Statement of retained earnings
SSAP	Statement of Standard Accounting Practice
TB	Trial balance
TOC	Theory of constraints
TQM	Total quality management
UK	United Kingdom
VA	Value added
VCA	Value chain analysis
WACC	Weighted average cost of capital
ZBB	Zero base budgeting

INTRODUCTION TO ACCOUNTING

This book is divided into four main parts, as shown below. Part 1 contains two chapters. In Chapter 1 we provide some background about accounting, the accountancy profession and the organisations that accountants work for. In Chapter 2 we outline the rules and regulations that accountants are expected to follow when preparing accounting statements.

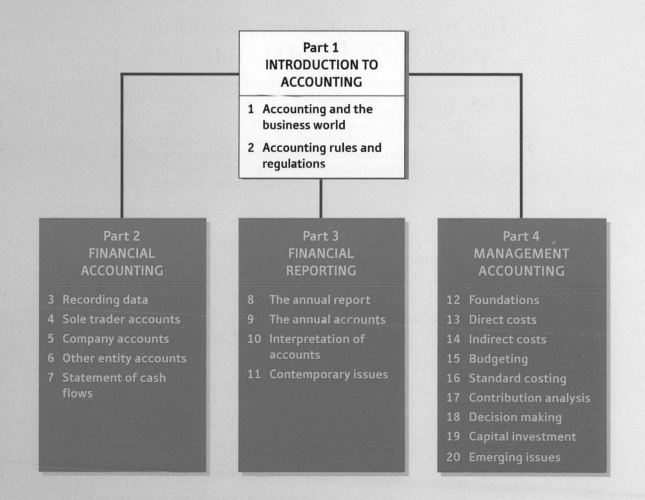

**Part 1
INTRODUCTION TO
ACCOUNTING**

1 Accounting and the business world

2 Accounting rules and regulations

**Part 2
FINANCIAL
ACCOUNTING**

3 Recording data
4 Sole trader accounts
5 Company accounts
6 Other entity accounts
7 Statement of cash flows

**Part 3
FINANCIAL
REPORTING**

8 The annual report
9 The annual accounts
10 Interpretation of accounts
11 Contemporary issues

**Part 4
MANAGEMENT
ACCOUNTING**

12 Foundations
13 Direct costs
14 Indirect costs
15 Budgeting
16 Standard costing
17 Contribution analysis
18 Decision making
19 Capital investment
20 Emerging issues

Accounting and the business world

News clip

The most common routes to the top job in FTSE 100 companies

The general career backgrounds of today's FTSE 100 CEOs remain similar to those analysed in previous years' studies with 52% having a financial background.

Phil Sheridan, the UK Managing Director at Robert Half, said: 'Finance has again proven itself to be the route to the top of Britain's biggest businesses as the ability to provide strong financial leadership and commercial acumen continues to be a key asset of FTSE 100 CEOs. **Professionals with an education or background in finance are highly sought after by organisations and demand continues to outweigh supply in today's job market.'**

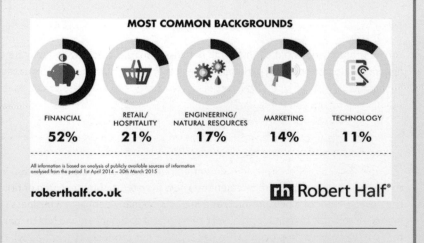

MOST COMMON BACKGROUNDS

FINANCIAL	RETAIL/ HOSPITALITY	ENGINEERING/ NATURAL RESOURCES	MARKETING	TECHNOLOGY
52%	**21%**	**17%**	**14%**	**11%**

All information is based on analysis of publicly available sources of information analysed from the period 1st April 2014 – 30th March 2015

roberthalf.co.uk

rh Robert Half®

Source: Extract adapted and graphics reproduced from The 2015 Robert Half FTSE 100 CEO Tracker report, with the permission of the copyright owner.

Questions relating to this news story can be found on page 22. ➡

About this chapter

This chapter sets the scene for the rest of the book.

The chapter begins with what accounting is and an explanation of why it is vital for you as a non-accountant to study accounting. It then gives a brief explanation of the nature and purpose of accounting and of its historical development. This is followed by an outline of the main branches of accounting and how one becomes an accounting professional. The last main section of the chapter gives a brief overview of the main forms and structures used to set up and run businesses and other enterprises.

Learning objectives

By the end of this chapter you should be able to:

- summarise the nature and purpose of accounting;
- outline its history;
- explain why you need to know something about it in the context of your main subject of study and your career aspirations;
- identify the main branches of accounting;
- list the principal UK accountancy bodies;
- describe the most important types of public and private entities.

 ## Why accounting is important

News clip

The importance of financial education

The importance of financial literacy and specifically the need to promote financial education has been recognised as an important contributor to improved financial inclusion and individuals' financial well-being, as well as a support to financial stability. The relevance of financial education policies is acknowledged at the highest global policy level and has received endorsement by the G20 Leaders and APEC Finance Ministers.

Source: Adapted from the abstract of *Financial Education for Youth, an OECD Report,* April 2014.

You've probably got hold of this book because you're a student. You may be doing a certificate, diploma or degree course in perhaps business, marketing, human resource management, economics, banking, engineering, languages, law, management or one of the sciences, to name but a few possibilities. And then you find to your horror that you have to do some accounting. Why?

OK, we'll try to explain. You probably have a vague idea that accounting has something to do with numbers and profits and tax and, er, *stuff* but you are certainly not sure what that has to do with the subject you're studying. And you resent it.

Right. You might be surprised then to find out that accounting information has to do with many things in a business (from procurement of a new IT systems, through hiring or firing staff, to financing the development of a new product) and impacts on many people in a business (from the marketing manager who has to manage an advertising budget to a banker who has to make lending decisions to a small jewellery shop owner who has to price her products appropriately). Not to mention that we all use accounting in our personal affairs – managing the income that we get from our employer or business and allocating that to various items of spending, calculating and paying our taxes and saving and investing to grow our personal wealth.

Accounting information is just information. And like all information it can be useful for making decisions – if you get hold of it, understand it and act on it.

Accounting (the process by which accounting information is generated) is basically about recording business transactions and summarising them in a way which is useful to people who need to know that information to make decisions – like shareholders and managers (e.g. the marketing managers, the human resource managers and the production managers). Perhaps just like you hope to be. 'So what?' you might well ask. 'If I need it or want it, I'll just ask the accountants to get it for me.' That's fine, but if you were a manager, would you really be quite happy to accept at face value *all* that the accountants gave you? Would you know what it meant, how reliable it was, what you were supposed to do with it or what are the right decisions to be made on the basis of it? We suspect that if you really think about the repercussions of *not* questioning what your accountants gave you, you would be (to say the least) a little unhappy. Maybe even a bit worried, especially if you were legally responsible for it all (and under UK law, the directors are responsible for the accounting records and the preparation of accounts by the businesses they manage).

The point we are making is that accountants provide a service for other people. Most accountants are probably highly qualified, experienced and good at their job, but as accountants they should not make the *decisions*. That is the manager's job – it could be your job and you will know much more about your business than any accountant. Rest assured that there is no doubt that you will be able to make even *better* decisions: (a) if you have some knowledge and some understanding of the nature of accounting information and (b) if you know what it can and what it cannot do in helping you plan and control your business.

So in a sentence, if you know something about accounting, you will become a *better* manager. By the end of this book you will be well on the way to becoming one.

This first chapter sets the scene for what follows. It is important because it provides you with the necessary background information to enable you to become a better manager.

Nature and purpose

We begin our accounting studies by giving a brief explanation of what accounting *is* and what it *does*. We will then tell you something of what it *doesn't* do. For our purposes we will use the following definition of accounting:

> Accounting is a service provided for those who need information about an entity's financial performance, its assets and its liabilities.

This definition contains a number of features that require some explanation:

- *Service*. Accounting is of assistance to other people – if nobody wanted the service, there would be no such thing as accounting.
- *Information*. The information traditionally collected by accountants is restricted to what can be quantified and translated into monetary terms.
- *Entity*. An entity is a jargon term used by accountants to describe any type of organisation, e.g. a person running his (or her) own business or a company.
- *Financial performance*. The financial performance is usually judged by matching incomes received with expenditure incurred over a period of time (usually one year) to calculate profit made in that period.
- *Assets*. In accounting, an asset is regarded as being a resource acquired by an entity as a result of a past event and that will result in a future economic benefit for the entity. For example, the purchase of plant and machinery will provide a benefit over very many years and thereby help the entity generate income in those years.

- *Liabilities*. A liability in accounting is defined as an obligation arising from a past event. For example, you may have bought some furniture but you don't have to start paying for it until next year. So for the time being, what you owe is a debt or an obligation, i.e. a liability.

The above summary shows that accounting information is somewhat restricted:

- It relates to only one entity (although it is possible to aggregate accounting information for groups of entities).
- It has to be quantifiable.
- It must be capable of being converted into monetary terms.
- It relates to an arbitrary period of time.
- A distinction is made between economic benefits that relate to past, current and future periods.

Non-accountants are often surprised when they realise that accounting information is restricted in such ways. This gives rise to what is sometimes called the *expectations gap*, i.e. when users expect accounting to do more than it can.

The expectations gap often causes considerable misunderstanding between accountants and the public, especially when an 'accounting scandal' erupts from time to time. Such scandals are often the result of genuine accounting problems but the public tend to think that they can all be put down to fraud. There have been many examples of high-profile financial fraud and accounting scandals in recent times. In 2008, Lehman Brothers, a global financial services firm, went bankrupt (curiously only in 2007 it had been voted Number 1 'Most Admired Securities Firm' by *Fortune* Magazine). It allegedly hid billions of loans disguised as sales. Closer to home, in early autumn 2014, we saw billions wiped off Tesco's value as the profit overstating scandal broke: Tesco had been artificially manipulating payments to and from suppliers. Questionable accounting practices certainly come to the fore in such high-profile cases.

We now move on to give you a review of the historical development of accounting. We do so in the next section.

Activity 1.1 Look up the definition of accounting in three different sources. Copy the definitions into your notebook. Then outline your ideas about how accounting and accounting information, as defined in the sources you referred to, could be helpful to you in the job or career you aspire to be in (in, say, 5 or 10 years time). Maybe you plan to run your own business, or to be involved in product design, or work in an advertising agency, or invest on the stock market while working for a big bank? Whatever your dream is – explain how accounting and accounting information might be used in your professional and personal life and what benefits would that bring to you.

Historical development

The word *account* in everyday language is often used as a substitute for an *explanation* or a *report* of certain actions or events. If you are an employee, for example, you may have to explain to your employer just how you have been spending your time or if you are a manager you may have to report to the owner on how the business is doing. In order to explain or to report, you will, of course, have to remember what you were doing or what happened. As it is not always easy to remember, you may need to keep some written record. In effect, such records can be said to provide the basis of a rudimentary accounting system.

In a primitive sense, man has always been involved in some form of accounting. It may have gone no further than a farmer measuring his worth simply by counting the number of cows or sheep that he owned (Figure 1.1).

His possessions	A year ago	Now	Change
Cows	••••••••••	•••••••••••••••	+5
Hens [• = 10]	••••••••••	•••••••	−30
Pigs	••••••••••	••••	−2
Sheep [• = 10]	••••••	•••••••	+20
Land [• = 1 acre]	••••	••••	No change
Cottage	•	•	No change
Carts	•••	•	−2
Ploughs	•	••	+1

Figure 1.1 Accounting for a farmer's wealth

Activity 1.2

A-a-a-a-h! Counting! Is that what accounting is all about?

So how many sheep do you count in this flock?

Figure 1.2 How many sheep can you (ac)count in this flock?

Accounting may be about counting, but that is not quite so straightforward as you may think. Are rams sheep? Or do we need to introduce categories to be able to (ac) count for what we have got here – 2 sheep, 1 ram and 3 lambs? And after how many days does a lamb become a sheep? We can make up an arbitrary rule (say, 3 months) so on the last day of that period there are 2 sheep, 1 ram and 3 lambs in the field but as soon as the clock ticks over to the next day there is all of a sudden a 150% increase in the population of sheep – 1 ram and 5 sheep, no lambs! If one of them dies – do we still (ac)count for it? If yes, why yes? If no, why not? (Ac)counting is full of judgements and not as straightforward as you may think!

The growth of a monetary system enabled an even more sophisticated method to be developed. It then became possible to calculate the increase or decrease in individual wealth over a period of time and to assess whether a farmer with perhaps 10 cows and 50 sheep was wealthier than one who had 60 pigs. Figure 1.3 illustrates just how difficult it would be to assess the wealth of a farmer in a non-monetary system.

Even with the growth of a monetary system, it took a very long time for formal documentary systems to become commonplace, although it is possible to trace the origins of modern bookkeeping back to at least the twelfth century. We know that from about that time, traders began to adopt a system of recording information called *double-entry*

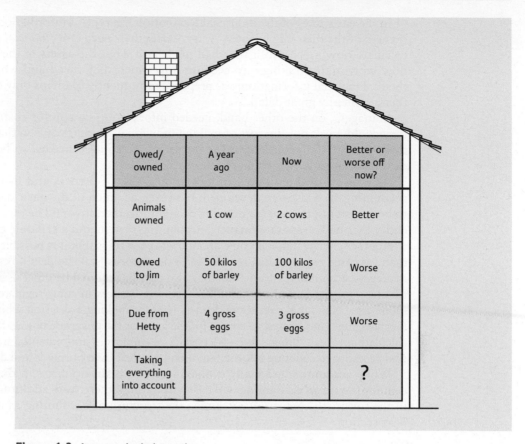

Owed/ owned	A year ago	Now	Better or worse off now?
Animals owned	1 cow	2 cows	Better
Owed to Jim	50 kilos of barley	100 kilos of barley	Worse
Due from Hetty	4 gross eggs	3 gross eggs	Worse
Taking everything into account			?

Figure 1.3 An owner's vital questions

bookkeeping. By the end of the fifteenth century, double-entry bookkeeping was widely used in Venice and the surrounding areas (the first-known book on the subject was published in 1494 by an Italian mathematician called Pacioli, who is often referred to as 'The Father of Accounting'). Modern bookkeeping systems are still based on principles established in the fifteenth century, although they have had to be adapted to suit modern conditions.

There are two main reasons why a recording system devised in medieval times has lasted for so long:

- It provides an accurate record of what has happened to a business over a given period of time.
- Information extracted from the system can help the owner or the manager to operate the business much more effectively.

In essence, the system provides the answers to three basic questions that both owners and managers want to know. They are as follows:

- What profit has the business made?
- How much does the business owe?
- What does the business have and how much is owed to it?

The medieval system dealt largely with simple agricultural and trading entities. In the eighteenth century, however, the United Kingdom underwent the *Industrial Revolution*. Economic activity gradually moved away from growing things to making or manufacturing them and the size of some businesses grew so much that managers had to be employed to run them on behalf of the owners.

In the early days of the Industrial Revolution the type of information supplied to the owners of the then 'big business' was to meet their needs for *financial* purposes, i.e. to calculate how much profit they had made and what the assets of their business were now worth (after taking into account how much they owed and what was owed to them). Financial information was prepared infrequently (perhaps only once a year) and then not in any great detail.

Managers, on the other hand, needed information largely for *costing* purposes, so they could work out the cost of making individual products and so that they can price these products appropriately. The information required needed to be in much more detail and prepared much more frequently.

As a result of the different information needs of owners and managers, separate accounting systems were developed. However, as much of the basic data was common to both systems, they were gradually brought together. It would be rare now to find any entity that had a separate financial accounting system and a separate costing system.

Another change that has come about over the years is that it is possible to identify more than two user groups (often referred to in the press as 'stakeholders'). Besides owners and managers, accounting information may also now be required by other users such as regulators (e.g. for the purpose of granting operating licences in some regulated industries and monitoring standards over time), lenders (e.g. for making a decision whether to lend to a business and what interest to charge for the loan) or the government (e.g. for the purpose of calculating taxes). Other stakeholders such as employees and potential investors also may find accessing accounting information useful for their own purposes and decision making.

While accounting gradually evolved into two main branches in the late nineteenth century (*financial* accounting and *cost* accounting), there were additional developments in the twentieth century. We examine the structure of accounting as it is today in the next section.

Branches of accounting

The work that accountants now undertake ranges far beyond that of simply preparing financial and cost statements. It is possible to identify at least six main branches of accounting and a number of important sub-branches. We will deal with each of them broadly in the order that they have developed over the past 100 years, i.e. financial accounting, management accounting, auditing, taxation, financial management, and insolvency. You will see from Figure 1.4 how they all fit together.

Financial accounting

Until about the middle of the nineteenth century, the nature, purpose and development of accounting described in the last two sections were mainly about the type of accounting that we would now describe as *financial* accounting. We do not, therefore, need to add much more to our outline except to give you a more formal definition of financial accounting. We will adopt that used by the Chartered Institute of Management Accountants (CIMA). It is as follows:

Classification and recording of the monetary transactions of an entity in accordance with established concepts, principles, accounting standards and legal requirements and their presentation in [financial statements], during and at the end of an accounting period. (CIMA, Official Terminology, 2005)

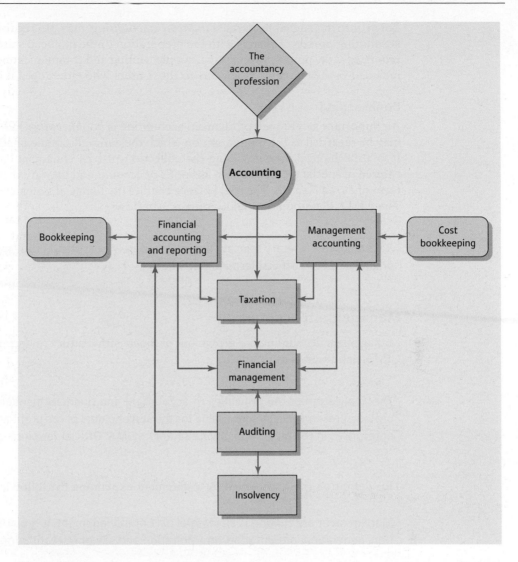

Figure 1.4 The main branches of accounting

'Concepts, principles, accounting standards and legal requirements' are the rules and regulations that govern accounting. We shall be dealing with them in Chapter 2. The financial statements, namely, the statement of profit or loss and other comprehensive income, statement of changes in equity, statements of financial position and statements of cash flows, are dealt with in Part 2 of this book. A statement of profit or loss and other comprehensive income (we will refer to it for short as 'statement of profit or loss') is a calculation of what profit or loss you might have made over a period of time. A statement of changes in equity shows how much of a dividend is paid to shareholders out of the profit for the period and any other contributions to or from shareholders. A statement of financial position (also known as a balance sheet) is a summary of what you own and what you are owed at the end of the period, and a statement of cash flows is a summary of what cash you have received and what cash you have paid in that particular period. The statement of profit or loss, statement of changes in equity, statements of financial position and statements of cash flows are known collectively as the *financial statements*.

A distinction is sometimes made between *financial accounting* and *financial reporting*. We do so in this book mainly for practical reasons in order to break the information down into manageable parts. *Financial accounting* may be regarded as being the accounting process that ends with the preparation of the financial statements. *Financial reporting* is the process of analysing, supplementing and communicating the information included in the financial statements to those users who either need it or want it.

Bookkeeping

An important sub-branch of financial accounting is *bookkeeping*. Indeed, bookkeeping may be regarded as the foundation on which the entire discipline of accounting is built. It is a mechanical task involving the collection of basic financial data. The data are entered in special records known as *books of account* and they are then extracted in the form of a *trial balance*. The trial balance enables the financial statements to be prepared. The CIMA definition of bookkeeping is as follows:

> Recording of monetary transactions, appropriately classified, in the financial records of an entity. (CIMA, Official Terminology, 2005)

Management accounting

Management accounting has grown out of nineteenth-century financial accounting. The CIMA definition is as follows:

> The application of the principles of accounting and financial management to create, protect, preserve and increase value for the stakeholders of for-profit and not-for-profit enterprises in the public and private sectors. (CIMA, Official Terminology, 2005)

This definition is accompanied by a statement explaining the following:

> Management accounting is an integral part of management. It requires the identification, generation, presentation, interpretation and use of relevant information to . . . :

There then follows a list of various functions of management accounting. The list includes strategy development, planning, control, funding, governance and information supply.

Cost bookkeeping

CIMA does not give a specific definition of cost bookkeeping but it does define the verb 'to cost':

> To ascertain the cost of a specified thing or activity. (CIMA, Official Terminology, 2005)

So by combining this definition of 'cost' with the definition of 'bookkeeping' given earlier, we can arrive at a suitable working definition of cost bookkeeping:

> The recording of monetary transactions, appropriately classified, in the financial records of an entity in order to ascertain the cost of a specified thing or activity.

Auditing

CIMA defines an audit as follows:

> Systematic examination of the activities and status of an entity, based primarily on investigation and analysis of its systems, controls and records. (CIMA, Official Terminology, 2005)

So auditing is the process of carrying out that investigation.

Not all entities have their accounts audited but it is a legal requirement for some entities, e.g. large limited liability companies.

Auditors are usually trained accountants who specialise in checking whether the accounts are credible, i.e. whether they can be believed. There are two main types of auditors – external and internal auditors.

1 *External auditors*. External auditors are entirely independent. They come from outside the entity, they are not employees of it and they do not answer to its managers. When they have finished their work, they report their findings to the owners (or any agents they may have appointed to act on their behalf such as the managers themselves (an issue known as '*the agency problem*'). External auditors formally report their opinion on whether the financial accounts represent what is called '*a true and fair view*' of the entity's affairs. They may do some detailed checking of its records in order to be able to come to such a view but normally they would be selective (meaning that they do their checking on a sample basis).

   The public often believe that the job of an auditor is to discover whether any fraud has taken place. This is not so. This misconceived perception forms part of the '*expectations gap*' discussed earlier in the chapter as well as the news clip below.

News clip

In search of the right note

KPMG's UK chairman Simon Collins talks about a tricky issue for the accounting industry globally: an 'expectation gap' in relation to what audit does, or does not, cover: 'We need a consensus between companies presenting information, those using it, those regulating it and ourselves providing assurance on it.' This 'gap' extends to what an audit can find hidden in accounts: 'Audit is not a guarantee of detecting fraud or predicting company failure. It gives an opinion at the time on the truth and fairness of financial statements,' he says. The Swiss firm in KPMG's global network is in the spotlight over its role for the past 16 years as auditor to FIFA, football's governing body, now at the centre of a corruption probe. Then there are the issues closer to home: the UK firm is being investigated by the regulator, the Financial Reporting Council, for its audit of the controversial insurance company Quindell; KPMG was also criticised last year by the Treasury Committee for failing to uncover a £1.5 billion black hole in the Co-operative Bank's finances, revealed after the mutual organisation tried to buy up Lloyds bank branches in 2013.

Source: Adapted from *The Financial Times*, 24 August 2015.

2 *Internal auditors*. Some entities employ internal auditors. Internal auditors are appointed by the managers of the entity; they are employees of the entity and they answer to its management. Internal auditors perform routine tasks and undertake some detailed checking of the entity's accounting procedures. Their task may also go beyond the financial accounts, e.g. they may examine the entity's planning and control procedures (including those regarding detection of fraud) and conduct 'value-for-money' tests.

External auditors and internal auditors usually work together very closely. Nevertheless, they do have separate roles and responsibilities.

Sometimes external auditors may rely on the work performed by the internal auditors but as they are employees of the entity they may not be entirely independent and so subject to the same pressures as other employees, such as job security, pay and promotion prospects. Such factors may impair their objectivity and independence and so cast doubt over the rigour of their work.

Nonetheless even external auditors are not completely independent. In the case of a public company, for example, the directors *recommend* the appointment of the company's auditors to the shareholders. As the shareholders usually accept those whom the directors suggest, the directors are in a strong position if they want to dismiss the auditors. The auditors can then appeal directly to the shareholders but the shareholders usually back the directors.

Taxation

Taxation is a highly complex and technical branch of accounting. Those accountants who are involved in tax work are responsible for calculating the amount of tax payable both by business entities and by individuals. It is not necessary for anybody or any entity to pay more tax than is required by the law. It is, therefore, perfectly legitimate to search out all the legal means of minimising the amount of tax that might be demanded by the government. This is known as *tax avoidance*. The non-declaration of sources of income on which tax might be payable is known as *tax evasion*. Tax evasion is a very serious offence and it could lead to a long prison sentence. The borderline between tax avoidance and tax evasion is a narrow one and tax accountants have to steer a fine line between what is lawful and what is not.

Financial management

Financial management is a relatively new branch of accounting and it has developed rapidly over the past 40 years. Financial managers are responsible for setting financial objectives, making plans based on those objectives, obtaining the finance needed to achieve the plans and generally safeguarding all the financial resources of the entity. They are much more likely to be involved in the general *management* of an entity than are other types of accountant. Their responsibilities involve them in drawing on a much wider range of disciplines (such as economics, statistics and mathematics) than is traditional in other branches of accounting and they use more non-financial and more qualitative data.

Insolvency

One other highly specialist branch of accounting that you may sometimes read about is that connected with *insolvency*, i.e. bankruptcies and liquidation. This branch of accounting is extremely specialised. It has a long history but it is not one that most accountants will have had either anything to do with or indeed know much about.

Bankruptcy is a formal legal procedure. The term is applied to individuals when their financial affairs are so serious that they have to be given some form of legal protection from their creditors. The term *liquidation* is usually applied to a company when it gets into serious financial difficulties and its affairs have to be 'wound up', i.e. arrangements made for it to go out of existence in an orderly fashion.

Companies do not necessarily go immediately into liquidation if they get into financial difficulties. An attempt will usually be made either to rescue them or to protect certain types of creditors. In these situations, accountants sometimes act as *administrators*. Their appointment freezes creditors' rights. This prevents the company from being put into liquidation during a period when the administrators are attempting to manage the company. By contrast, *receivers* may be appointed on behalf of creditors. The creditors' loans may be secured on certain property. The receivers will try to obtain the income from that property or they may attempt to sell it. If you would like to find out more about bankruptcy and liquidation, you can do some exploring of the UK Government's pages (gov.uk) dedicated to the subject.

We hope that you never come into contact with insolvency practitioners and so we will move on swiftly to have a look at another topic, namely, the structure of the accountancy profession.

The accountancy profession

News clip

How to choose the perfect accountant

So how do you hire the right accountant? Check his or her qualifications. Legally, anyone can call themselves an accountant – you don't need any training, qualifications or experience to be one. 'There are unqualified accountants out there and if anything goes wrong with them, you have no comeback,' said Aidan Clifford, advisory services manager with the Association of Chartered Certified Accountants (ACCA), Ireland.

Source: Extract from *Sunday Independent*, 7 December 2014.

In order to become a professional accountant it is necessary to show technical competence by passing a set of rigorous examinations as well as gaining some relevant work experience over a designated period of time.

There are six major accountancy bodies operating in the United Kingdom which grant the 'qualified accountant' badge. They are as follows:

- Institute of Chartered Accountants in England and Wales (ICAEW)
- Institute of Chartered Accountants in Ireland (ICAI)
- Institute of Chartered Accountants of Scotland (ICAS)
- Association of Chartered Certified Accountants (ACCA)
- Chartered Institute of Management Accountants (CIMA)
- Chartered Institute of Public Finance and Accountancy (CIPFA).

The Irish Institute (ICAI) is included in the UK list because it has a strong influence in Northern Ireland.

Although all six major professional accountancy bodies have a Royal Charter, it is still customary to refer only to members of ICAEW, ICAI and ICAS as *chartered accountants* (CAs). Such chartered accountants have usually had to undergo a period of training in a practising office, i.e. one that offers accounting services directly to the public. This distinguishes them from members of the other three bodies because their auditing experience enables them to become approved (in the legal sense) auditors. Much practice work is involved, not just in auditing but also in tax. After qualifying, many CAs go to work in commerce or industry. ACCA members may also obtain their training in practice but relevant experience also counts towards their qualification. CIMA members usually train and work in industry, while CIPFA members specialise almost exclusively in central and local government.

Apart from the six major bodies, there are a number of important (although far less well-known) smaller accountancy associations and societies, e.g. the Association of International Accountants (AIA), the Association of Certified Public Accountants, the Institute of Cost and Executive Accountants and the Institute of Financial Accountants. Such bodies offer some form of accountancy qualification but they have not yet managed to achieve the status or the prestige of the six major bodies. They are usually referred to as *secondary bodies*.

There is also another very important accountancy body, the Association of Accounting Technicians (AAT). The association was formed in 1980 as a professional organisation especially for those accountants who *assist* qualified accountants in preparing accounting information. In order to become an accounting technician, it is necessary to take (or be exempt from) the association's examinations. The AAT's examinations are less technical and perhaps more practical than those of the six major bodies but they are not easy.

The overall organisation of the accountancy profession is shown in Figure 1.5.

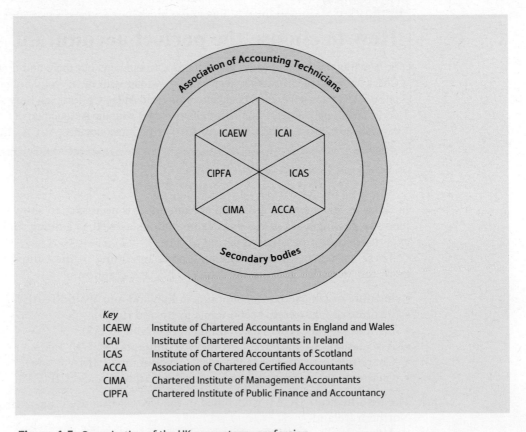

Key
ICAEW	Institute of Chartered Accountants in England and Wales
ICAI	Institute of Chartered Accountants in Ireland
ICAS	Institute of Chartered Accountants of Scotland
ACCA	Association of Chartered Certified Accountants
CIMA	Chartered Institute of Management Accountants
CIPFA	Chartered Institute of Public Finance and Accountancy

Figure 1.5 Organisation of the UK accountancy profession

Public and private entities

The main aim of this section is to introduce you to the two main types of entities with which we shall be primarily concerned in this book – *sole traders* and *companies*. Before we can do this, we need to explain a little bit about the economic structure of the United Kingdom.

In order to simplify our analysis, we will classify the UK economy into two broad groupings – the *profit-making sector* and the *not-for-profit sector*. Within each of these sectors it is then possible to distinguish a number of different types of entities (see Figure 1.6). We begin by examining the profit-making sector.

The profit-making sector

The profit-making sector is extremely diverse but it is possible to recognise three major subdivisions. These are the manufacturing sector, the trading sector and the service sector.

The *manufacturing sector* is involved in purchasing raw materials and component parts, converting (or incorporating) them into finished goods and then selling them to customers. Examples of manufacturing enterprises include Rolls-Royce, Shell, Airbus and any other well known UK companies in the chemicals, glass, iron and steel and textile industries.

The *trading sector* purchases finished goods and then sells them to their customers without any further major conversion work normally being done on them. Trading enterprises are found in the retailing and wholesaling sectors. The sector includes entities

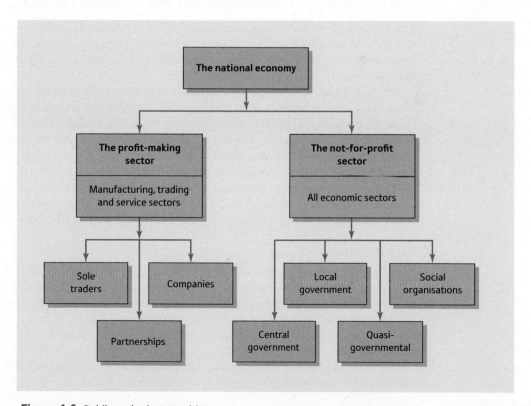

Figure 1.6 Public and private entities

such as builders' merchants, shops and supermarkets, for example, Tesco, Marks & Spencer and Amazon.

The *service sector* provides advice or assistance to customers or clients, e.g. hairdressing, legal and travel services. Unlike the manufacturing and trading sectors, the service sector does not usually deal in physical or tangible goods, for example, Channel 4 (a TV channel), WPP (one of the biggest advertising agencies) or Deloitte (an accountancy and professional services firm). There are some exceptions: the hotel and restaurant trade (such as Hilton or Pizza Hut), for example, is normally classed as part of the service sector even though it provides major tangible services such as accommodation, food and drink.

The accounting systems required of manufacturing, trading and service sector entities are all slightly different, although they are based on similar principles and procedures. Manufacturing entity accounts are the most complex, trading entity accounts are fairly straightforward, while service entity accounts are usually quite simple.

Until about 40 years ago the manufacturing sector was of major significance in the United Kingdom. It is now much less important and the service sector has largely taken its place.

The products or the services offered by the manufacturing, trading or service sectors may be different but the way that they are organised is still very similar. Within each sector you will find three main types of entities: *sole traders, partnerships* and *companies*. The basic distinction between them reflects their ownership, how they are financed and what the law requires of them.

Sole traders

The term 'sole trader' is rather misleading for two reasons:

- 'sole' does not necessarily mean that only one person is involved in the entity;
- manufacturing and service entities may also be organised as sole traders.

The term really reflects the *ownership* of the entity; the main requirement is that only one individual should own it. The owner would normally also be the main source of finance and he or she would be expected to play a reasonably active part in its management.

Sole trader entities are not incorporated, they usually operate on a very informal basis, and some private matters relating to the owner are often indistinguishable from those of the business. Sole trader accounts are fairly straightforward and there is no specific legislation that covers the accounting arrangements. We shall be using sole trader accounts in Chapters 3 and 4 in order to demonstrate some basic accounting techniques. There is no distinction between the person who is the sole trader and the business itself in the eyes of the law. It is thus said that a sole trader has *unlimited liability*. What this means is that if the business is sued or owes money to creditors, it is the sole trader himself or herself who is legally responsible to settle these obligations.

Partnerships

A partnership entity is very similar to a sole trader entity except that there must be at least *two owners* of the business. Partnerships often grow out of a sole trader entity, perhaps because more money needs to be put into the business or because the sole trader needs some help. It is also quite common for a new business to begin as a partnership, e.g. when some friends get together to start a home-decorating service or to form a car-repair business.

The partners should agree among themselves how much money they will each put into the business, what jobs they will do, how many hours they will work and how the profits and losses will be shared (which may be different to the proportion of money they originally put into the business). In the absence of any agreement (whether formal or informal), partnerships in the United Kingdom are covered by the Partnership Act 1890 and its amendments (you can find out more about it on the UK Government pages).

The partners in a partnership, just like sole traders, have unlimited liability. Since 2001 there has been a new type of partnership called a *Limited Liability Partnership* (LLP). An LLP has a separate legal personality from that of its owners (like a company) and so it protects the partners from personal bankruptcy.

Partnership accounts are very similar to those of sole traders and we shall not be dealing with them in this book.

Companies

A company is another different type of business organisation which is incorporated. What that means its 'birth' or 'incorporation' is registered at Companies House. There are many different forms of companies but basically a company is an entity that has a separate existence from that of its owners, it is a separate legal 'person' in the eyes of the law. We are going to be primarily concerned with *limited liability companies*. The term 'limited liability' means that the owners of such companies are required to finance the business only up to an agreed amount. Once they have contributed that amount, they cannot be called on to contribute any more, even if the company gets into financial difficulties.

If you are interested in finding out more about how to start up your own company, you can find more information on the Companies House website.

Activity 1.3

Imagine that you are thinking of setting up a T shirt printing venture – you will be sourcing plain T shirts from China and printing London images and slogans on them before selling them on to tourists and visitors to the UK capital. Insert in the following table one advantage and one disadvantage of operating your business as: (a) a sole trader; (b) a partnership and (c) a limited liability company. Discuss your ideas with others in your group. Are you able to reach a consensus about which option is best?

Type of entity	Advantage	Disadvantage
(a) Sole trader		
(b) Partnership		
(c) Limited liability company		

As there is a risk that limited liability companies may not be able to pay what they owe, Parliament has had to give some legal protection to those parties who may become involved with them. The details are contained within the Companies Act 2006. We will be dealing with company accounts in some detail in Chapters 5–9.

The not-for-profit sector

By 'not-for-profit' we mean those entities whose primary purpose is to provide a service to the public rather than to make a profit. We will consider this sector under four main headings: (1) central government; (2) local government; (3) quasi-governmental bodies and (4) social organisations.

Within the three governmental groups, there is a wide variety of different types of entity. Governmental accounting is extremely specialised and it would require a book of its own to deal with it. We shall not be covering it in any depth.

Central government

Central government is responsible for services such as macro-economic policy, education, defence, foreign affairs, health and social security. These responsibilities are directly controlled by Cabinet ministers who answer to Parliament at Westminster for their actions. In 1999, some of these central government responsibilities were 'devolved', i.e. they became the direct responsibility of elected bodies in Northern Ireland, Scotland and Wales.

Local government

Devolution is not new in the United Kingdom. For well over a century central government has also devolved many of its responsibilities to local authorities, i.e. smaller units of authority that have some geographical and community coherence. Councillors are elected by the local community. They have responsibility for those services that central government has delegated or devolved, for example, the local administration of education, housing, the police and social services.

Quasi-governmental bodies

Central government also operates indirectly through quasi-governmental bodies such as colleges and universities and the British Broadcasting Corporation (BBC). Such bodies are nominally independent of central government, even though their main funds normally come from central government and their senior managers may be appointed by government ministers.

Social organisations

This category covers a wide range of cultural, educational, recreational and social bodies. Some are formally constituted and professionally managed, such as national and international charities (e.g, the British Red Cross or Cancer Research), while others are local organisations run by volunteers on a part-time basis, for example, bridge and rugby clubs, parent–teacher associations (PTAs) or investment clubs.

Overview

Entities come in many different shapes and sizes but all of them need to account for their activities: to work out how much profit they have generated (and what taxes they may have to pay on that profit) and what assets and liabilities they have. All of them also rely on accounting information for decision making: e.g. to cost products and set pricing strategies, to chose between alternative projects or different sources of funding. That is usually the job of the accountant (and each organisation will ordinarily have one or a whole team of accountants) but business benefits and operations are enhanced if more people within the organisation have an understanding and appreciation of financial and accounting information. That is why it is important that you study accounting – it will benefit you as well as the organisations that you will join or have joined.

Questions you should ask

Even though you will probably not be working for the accounting function, whichever role you are in, you are likely to have interactions with the accounting team. It will greatly help your work and their work, as well as the organisation, if you understand more about what, how and why they do what they do. So let's consider what might be helpful for you to know and find out about the accountants in your organisation and their work.

At the outset there are not many technical questions that you might want to ask them. Your questions are more likely to be about the accountants themselves and the organisation of the accounting function. The following is a sample of the types of general question that as a non-accountant you might like to put to your own entity's accountants.

Knowing the answers to these questions will make your work easier as you will understand better how your role fits within the bigger organisation:

- How many accountants do we employ?
- Which ones am I likely to have interaction with and in what context?
- What are the different accountants responsible for?
- How is the accounting function organised?
- What information might the accountants want from me?
- What is it to be used for?
- When is it wanted? What happens if there are delays or missed deadlines?
- What can the accountants do to help me do a better job?
- What am I supposed to do with information I receive from the accountant?
- How can managers and accountants become a better team? How can we work better together?

Conclusion

The main aim of this chapter has been to introduce non-accountants to the world of accounting. The chapter has stressed that the main purpose of accounting is to provide financial information to those parties that need it.

Information must be useful if it is to have any purpose but as a non-accountant you may feel reluctant to question any accounting information that lands on your desk. You may also not understand why the accountant is always asking you what appears to be irrelevant questions and so you respond with any old nonsense. You then perhaps feel a bit guilty and a little frustrated; you would like to know more but you dare not ask. We hope that by the time you have worked your way through this book, you will have the confidence to ask and, furthermore, that you will understand the answer. Good luck!

Now that the world of accounting has been outlined, we can turn to more detailed subject matter. The first task is to learn the basic rules and regulations governing accounting. These are covered in Chapter 2.

Key points

1 To account for something means to give an explanation or to report on it.

2 Owners of an entity want to know (a) how well it is doing, i.e. has it made a profit; (b) what it owes and (c) how much it has and how much is owed to it.

3 Accounting is important for non-accountants because: (a) they must make sure their own entity complies with any legal requirements and (b) an accounting system can provide them with information that will help them do a better job.

4 There are different users (or 'stakeholders') in accounting information: investors (both existing and potential), lenders, suppliers and other trade creditors, employees, customers, governments and their agencies and the public.

5 The six main branches of accounting are auditing, financial accounting and reporting, financial management, management accounting, taxation and insolvency.

6 Sub-branches of accounting include bookkeeping (a function of financial accounting) and cost bookkeeping (a function of management accounting).

7 There are six major professional accountancy bodies in the United Kingdom: the Institute of Chartered Accountants in England and Wales (ICAEW), the Institute of Chartered Accountants in Ireland (ICAI), the Institute of Chartered Accountants of Scotland (ICAS), the Association of Chartered Certified Accountants (ACCA), the Chartered Institute of Management Accountants (CIMA) and the Chartered Institute of Public Finance and Accountancy (CIPFA).

8 The Association of Accounting Technicians (AAT) is an important secondary accountancy body. Its members primarily provide technical assistance to professionally qualified accountants although they themselves are often in senior positions.

9 There are two economic sectors within the UK economy: the profit-making sector and the not-for-profit sector. Within each sector business operations can be classified into manufacturing, trading or service entities. Individual entities may then be organised as sole traders, partnerships or companies.

10 The not-for-profit sector includes central government and local government operations, quasi-governmental bodies and social organisations. Government operations are extremely complex and the accounting requirements are highly specialised. Social organisations are also diverse. They include various associations, charities, clubs, societies and sundry voluntary organisations. Their accounting requirements are similar to those in the profit-making sector.

Check your learning

The answers to these questions can be found within the text.

1 What is accounting?

2 What is meant by the word 'account'?

3 What is meant by an 'entity'?

4 What name is given to the system that accountants use to record information?

5 What are the three basic questions that the owner of a business might ask?

6 What is an asset?

7 What economic event happened in the United Kingdom during the eighteenth century?

8 What happened to the ownership and management of businesses during the nineteenth century?

9 Why did managers in nineteenth-century industrial entities require more detailed information?

10 List three user groups of accounting information.

11 What are the six main branches of accounting?

12 Of which main branch of accounting does cost accounting form a part?

13 What is the difference between 'bookkeeping' and 'cost bookkeeping'?

14 Explain the difference between 'bankruptcy' and 'liquidation'.

15 List the six major UK professional accountancy bodies.

16 What function does the Association of Accounting Technicians fill?

17 Name three subdivisions of the profit-making sector of the United Kingdom.

18 Name real businesses which belong to these different subdivisions.

19 What is meant by 'limited liability'?

20 Name one quasi-governmental body.

21 Complete the following sentences:

    1 The word _____ in everyday language means an explanation or a report.

    2 Traders in the fifteenth century began to adopt a system of _____ to record information.

    3 The owners of a business want to know how much _____ a business has made.

    4 An _____ is a term used to describe any type of organisation.

22 State whether each of the following statements is true or false:

    1 An auditor's job is to find out whether a fraud has taken place. *True/false*

    2 Management accounts are required by law. *True/false*

    3 Tax avoidance is lawful. *True/false*

    4 A statement of financial position is a list of assets and liabilities. *True/false*

    5 Companies have to go into liquidation if they get into financial difficulties. *True/false*

News story quiz

Remember the news story at the beginning of this chapter? Go back to that story and re-read it before answering the following questions.

Questions

1 Are you surprised by the findings of the report into the background of Britain's top companies CEOs (Chief Executive Officers)? What do you expect is the required experience and background of a CEO of a big business?

2 Why do you think it is important for a CEO of a big business to have a sound understanding of finance and accounting?

3 Do you think the same applies for those CEO's who work for small-and medium-sized businesses?

Tutorial questions

The answers to questions marked with an asterisk can be found in Appendix 4.

1.1 'Accountants stifle managerial initiative and enterprise.' Discuss.

1.2 Do you think that auditors should be responsible for detecting fraud?

1.3 The following statement was made by a student: 'I cannot understand why accountants have such a high status and why they have so much influence.' How would you respond to such assertions?

1.4* 'It is necessary for non-accountants to know about accounting.' Discuss.

1.5* Describe two main purposes of accounting.

1.6* What statutory obligations require a public limited company to prepare management accounts?

1.7 State briefly the main reasons why a company may employ a team of accountants.

1.8* What statutory obligations require limited liability companies to prepare financial accounts?

1.9 Why does a limited liability company have to engage a firm of external auditors?

1.10 What is the difference between tax avoidance and tax evasion? Are either of these activities justified?

1.11 Assume that you are a personnel officer in a manufacturing company and that one of your employees is a young engineering manager called Joseph Sykes. Joseph has been chosen to attend the local university's business school to study for a diploma in management. Joseph is reluctant to attend the course because he will have to study accounting. As an engineer he thinks that it will be a waste of time for him to study such a subject.

Required:
Draft an internal memorandum addressed to Joseph explaining why it would be of benefit to him to study accounting.

1.12 Clare Wong spends a lot of her time working for a large local charity. The charity has grown enormously in recent years and the trustees have been advised to overhaul their accounting procedures. This would involve its workers (most of whom are volunteers) in more bookkeeping and there is a great deal of resistance to this move. The staff have said that they are there to help the needy and not to get involved in bookkeeping.

Required:
As the financial consultant to the charity, prepare some notes that you could use in speaking to the voluntary workers in order to try to persuade them to accept the new proposals.

Website

Further practice questions, study material and links to relevant sites on the World Wide Web can be found on the website that accompanies this book. The site can be found at www.pearsoned.co.uk/dyson

Accounting rules and regulations

A principles-based versus rules-based approach

Can principles overrule the rules?

In the words of Franklin D. Roosevelt, 'Rules are not necessarily sacred, principles are.' During his reign, this central figure in world events navigated a period of worldwide economic crisis, introduced the regulation of Wall Street by the Securities and Exchange Commission and spearheaded a variety of reform programs.

Flash forward to today and President Roosevelt may have had a lot of influence over the current debate on principles-based accounting standards.

Five years ago ICAS (the Institute of Chartered Accountants in Scotland) issued a publication called *Principles not Rules: A Question of Judgement*; it was published to help find a resolution to the principles versus rules debate within international accounting standard setting. The report at the time concluded that a principles-based approach to standard setting was essential to serve the needs of business and the public interest. Following the onset of the financial crisis, the need for well-written principles-based accounting standards has gained further backing.

A recent member survey by ICAS determined strong support for a principles-based framework for financial reporting. Nearly 92 per cent of respondents expressed a preference for principles, supported by additional guidance or rules. However, 67 per cent expressed concerns that international financial reporting standards (IFRS) have become more and not less rules-oriented over the past five years.

Hugh Shields, Chair of the ICAS Corporate Reporting Taskforce, warned of an overwhelming belief that the financial crisis will lead to more rules, when the aftermath clearly demonstrates the need for more principles. 'There is a danger that we will breed accountants who like to tick boxes. We must not lose the ability to make judgements. If principles are well written, it is much more difficult to do things that would fail a "smell" test', he said. He urged the profession 'to come to the table with action and to be guided not dominated by technical accounting'.

Source: Extracted from *Accountancy Age,* 24 January 2012

Questions relating to this news story can be found on page 42 ➡

About this chapter

In this chapter we outline the conventional accounting rules that are commonly adopted in practice and the legislation that governs accounting. We then examine the role of the United Kingdom's Financial Reporting Council along with the International Accounting Standards Board in the preparation of financial statements. The chapter closes with a review of the attempts made to develop a framework of accounting based on generally accepted principles.

Learning objectives	By the end of this chapter you should be able to: • identify the most important accounting rules and conventions; • summarise the UK legal requirements covering financial reporting and; outline the role of the Financial Reporting Council in that process; • examine the legal authority that the International Accounting Standards Board has in UK financial reporting.

 ## Why this chapter is important

This chapter is important for non-accountants for the following reasons:

1 It underpins almost the entire contents of this book. So if you are to understand what account-ants do and why they do it, you must be familiar with the rules and regulations that they adopt.
2 You need to have some familiarity with the legal requirements governing accounting in the United Kingdom as you may be required to contribute to the way the organisation you work for meets these legal requirements.
3 Similarly it is necessary to have some knowledge of the quasi-legal role that the Financial Reporting Council and the International Accounting Standards Board play in UK financial reporting.
4 Understanding the difference between principles and rules is important not just in the context of accounting. It is likely to be of use to you in whatever area of business you join.

The rules of the game – why have them?

Most games have an agreed set of rules. Rules define the game and they provide a struc-ture that every player is expected to follow. If you are a footballer, for example, you are expected to follow the rules that apply to football. Without them football (as we know it) would just become a totally uncoordinated and chaotic kick-about. It is the same with accounting – it has its own 'rules of the game'.

Unlike football or any other game, no one actually sat down and devised a set of accounting rules at the outset. What happened was that over a long period of time enti-ties (mainly sole traders) gradually adopted similar procedures for recording their trans-actions and assessing how the business had performed at a regular and fixed interval. In other words, such procedures eventually became generally accepted and they became the rules that virtually everyone adopted. The development of accounting rules over the centuries to where we are today is shown in Figure 2.1.

There was nothing indisputable about such rules. The accounting rules that evolved were man-made and you could argue against them. You were also free to choose whether to adopt them or follow your own rules. If you did, of course, you might cause a great deal of confusion (just as you would in football if you adopted your own rules) but that would be up to you.

Many accountants these days do not like to describe conventional accounting proce-dures as 'rules' because that gives the impression that they are prescriptive. So you will come across a bewildering number of different terms such as assumptions, axioms, concepts, objectives, policies, postulates, principles, practices and procedures. It is quite easy to have an argument about each of these descriptions. For example, if you are told that 'this procedure is a *principle* of accounting', it sounds as though there is a moral code underpinning how that procedure should be dealt with, like being told that 'murder

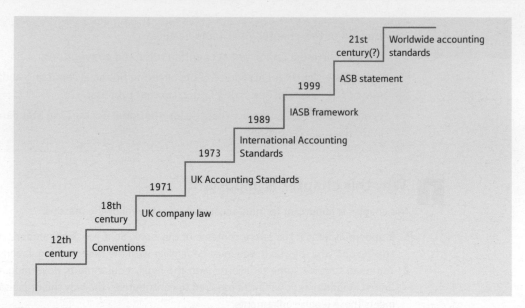

Figure 2.1 The development of accounting rules

is wrong' and 'hanging is the answer', whereas in accounting all we are really saying is that 'this is the way that we usually do it', i.e. it is a convention.

We do not believe that it is necessary to get bogged down in such arguments, so, in this book, for convenience and to avoid repetition, we will generally refer to conventional accounting practices as 'accounting rules'. The fundamental question is why do we need some rules? Surely there is nothing more to accounting than the equivalent of taking away 2 from 6 and making sure that the answer is 4? If accounting is ultimately about working out the profit of an entity during a trading period, is there anything more to it than working out that income of 6 minus costs of 2 will give you a profit of 4? In practice it is not quite as simple as such as an example might suggest.

In order to explain why, we need to re-examine what we mean by 'accounting'. In Chapter 1 we gave you the following definition:

> Accounting is a service provided for those who need information about an entity's financial performance, its assets and its liabilities.

Such a definition is fairly broad one and it perhaps raises more questions than it answers. Some of the questions that might be asked are as follows.

1 What is an 'entity' and what are its boundaries?
2 Who wants the information: customers, employees or the owners and are their needs the same?
3 What information is required? Should it be reported on a numerical basis such as x numbers of cows or sheep or on a extended value basis?
4 How often should the information required be collected and reported?
5 Some factors are hard to quantify such as 'good' reputation so should they be ignored or should an estimate be made of their apparent value?

It is in response to such questions that over the centuries common procedures have evolved. The practices continue to evolve to meet the needs of a fast-moving highly technological age. The questions may remain the same and we sometimes come up with new answers.

Activity 2.1 Consider a supermarket, a bank, an airline or any other business.

- What rules and regulations does it have to comply with in the course of carrying out its business?
- What purpose do such rules and regulations serve?
- How do they compare with accounting rules and regulations?

Conventional accounting rules

Dozens of conventional rules have been adopted over the centuries but it is possible to identify fairly clearly the most common ones. We have selected 14 rules for our purposes. For convenience, we have grouped them into three categories: (1) boundary rules; (2) measurement rules; and (3) ethical rules (see Figure 2.2). We start with what we call 'boundary' rules, i.e. where we draw the line at what should be reported.

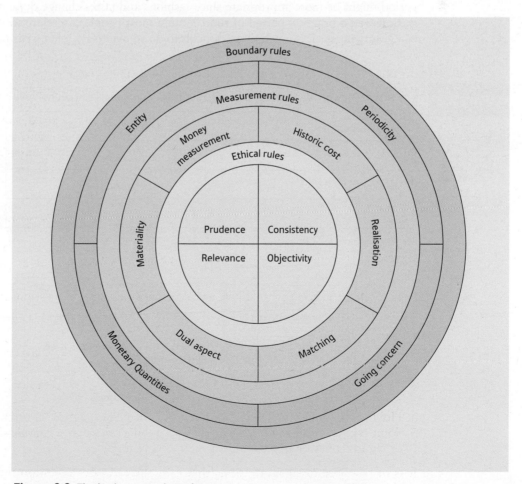

Figure 2.2 The basic accounting rules

Boundary rules

There are four important boundary rules: entity, periodicity or period of account, going concern and monetary quantities.

Entity

It is customary to keep strictly separate the affairs of a business from the private affairs of its owners by setting up, for example, separate personal and business bank accounts. In practice, it is not always easy to distinguish precisely between what is 'business' and what is 'private', especially in the cases of sole trader and partnership entities. The close interrelationship between what are effectively two separate entities is shown in Figure 2.3.

Periodicity (or Period of Account)

If a company is set up today, then the year end of that company would be 12 months from today. The year end does not have to coincide with the calendar year end of 31 December or the tax year end: the year end can be any date. What that means is that the accounting period is accepted to be 12 months. This is an arbitrary period of time especially in the case of entities that have an unlimited life. In the western agrarian world, it does reflect the four seasons of the year although this time period is now of little relevance to manufacturing and service entities. Indeed, in the fashion industry, for example, a much shorter accounting period might be more appropriate since fashions and tastes change quite quickly. A year is, however, a practical period of time because most people can relate to what happened last year, whereas it is much more difficult to do so over (say) a five-year period.

Activity 2.2	List three advantages and disadvantages of preparing financial accounts only once a year.

Advantages	Disadvantages
1	1
2	2
3	3

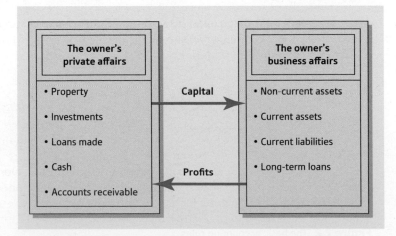

Figure 2.3 The entity rule: separation of business and private affairs

Going concern

In accounting, an entity is said to be a *going concern* if it is assumed that it will continue in business for the foreseeable future for at least the next 12 months from the accounting year end. If this is not the case, then different accounting procedures would be adopted. Even so how is it possible to determine with any certainty whether an entity is a 'going concern' especially when business is bad, such as in a recession? Ultimately there is judgement involved in making such an assessment.

News clip

Is Rangers International Football Club a going concern?

Rangers International Football Club needs £2.5m of external funding before the end of the season after revealing losses of £7.5m for the year ending 30 June.

The business remains dependent on additional financing to cover losses. The business is still working towards recovery. There was an increase in season-ticket sales during the summer, but it is forecast that the first tranche of external funding 'will be required in December 2015'.

The going concern status of the business – its ability to trade for the next 12 months – is not affected by the funding requirements, since the board has received assurance from certain shareholders that they will provide financial support to the club.

Source: Adapted from www.bbc.co.uk, 5 November 2015.

Monetary quantities

Accounting information is usually restricted to that which can be easily quantified in monetary terms. Non-monetary considerations (such as how long the business has been in existence or the length of service of the staff) are usually ignored even though such factors are surely worth something to a long-established entity compared with a newly created business?

Measurement rules

Measurement rules determine how data should be recorded. There are six important ones. They are: (1) money measurement; (2) historic cost; (3) realisation; (4) matching; (5) dual aspect and (6) materiality.

Money measurement

We discussed in Chapter 1 that the first questions accountants grapple with is 'What counts?' (remember the sheep?). Next comes the question of what monetary value needs to be attributed to that which counts, how can that which counts be measured in money terms? Unfortunately it gets even more complicated as money values are not static, for example, the value of money changes over a period of time. During inflationary periods the value of money goes down, i.e. the same quantity of money buys fewer goods and services than the year before. Deflationary periods can also occur but they are quite rare and they are usually quite short. In inflationary and deflationary circumstances it is misleading to compare one year's results with that of another without allowing for the effect of the value of money either going up or going down.

Historic cost

Assets (such as cars) and liabilities (such as amounts owed to a creditor) are usually valued at their historic cost, i.e. at the price paid or received for them when they were originally exchanged. The historic cost is a fact and does not change over time even though the assets and liabilities themselves may change their value, owing to such factors as inflation, as wear and tear and obsolescence (in the case of assets) or non-recoverability (in the case of liabilities).

Realisation

When goods are sold or purchased or sold on credit terms, it is customary practice to treat them as being exchanged at the point when the legal title to the goods is transferred, i.e. when they are *realised*. In modern manufacturing and trading conditions that point is not necessarily obvious and this remains a complex issue that the accountancy profession still has to deal with.

Activity 2.3	Imagine that you have just acquired a Porsche sports car. When would the Porsche car manufacturer have recorded the sale, i.e. when is the sale 'realised'?

1   On you placing the order.
2   On you picking up the car and driving it away from the showroom.
3   On you paying the final instalment towards the financing of the car.
4   On expiration of a 12-month warranty period.

Matching

The matching rule is illustrated in Figure 2.4.

This rule is closely related to the realisation rule. Accounts are not usually prepared on the basis of cash received and cash paid during (say) a 12-month period because there is often a delay between the receipt and the payment of cash depending on the credit period given. This means that a comparison based on cash received/cash paid may be misleading when one year is compared with another. When preparing the accounts at

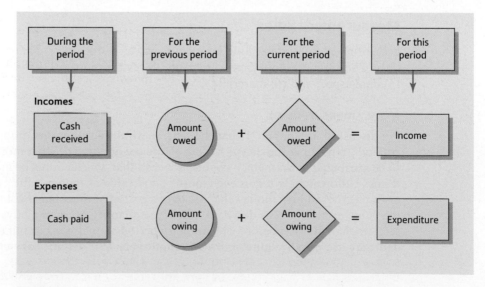

Figure 2.4 The matching rule

the end of a year, therefore, it is necessary to allow for what was *owed to* the entity (i.e. *'receivable'*) and *owing* (i.e. *'payable'*) by it at both the beginning and the end of the year, e.g. opening and closing debtors and creditors. This procedure often involves making an estimate of the amounts due to be received and sometimes the amounts due to be paid. Any estimate, of course, can be incorrect because it is based on the information available at the time. If this proves to be the case, then the accounts for that year will be incorrect.

Dual aspect

Any transaction involves someone giving something and someone else receiving it e.g. a bank gives a company a loan in the form of cash. Each transaction has a dual effect – on one hand, the company received cash, but on the other, it has a liability as eventually it has to pay the loan back to the bank. So the basic rule is: *every transaction has two effects* (even if it is an *internal* transaction). As a result, a recording system known as *double-entry bookkeeping* has evolved. This system has many practical advantages and most entities (apart from perhaps very small ones) now adopt it.

Materiality

The adoption of many of the conventional accounting procedures can result in a tremendous amount of work, for example, in estimating the amount of doubtful debts. However, if the eventual results of that extra work are likely to be immaterial or insignificant, i.e. they do not have any meaningful effect on the overall results, then there does not appear to be much point in sticking strictly to the 'rules'. It would not be customary, for example, to estimate the value of small amounts of stationery at the year end and include them in 'assets'. But what does 'small' mean in this context? Stationery worth £200 may be material to a one-person business but mean nothing to a multinational company. So materiality is a matter of context; it requires judgement and different people will come to a different conclusion.

Ethical rules

Ethical rules relate to the moral code or principles expected to be adopted in the preparation of accounts. There are four main ethical rules: they are (1) prudence; (2) consistency; (3) objectivity and (4) relevance.

Prudence

This is perhaps a rule which has helped to preserve the cautious, careful and pernickety perception of the typical old-fashioned accountant. The rule states that if there is some doubt over the treatment of a particular transaction, then income should be underestimated and expenditure overestimated. By following this rule the overall profit is likely to be lower and so there is less danger of taking too much cash out of the business.

Consistency

The same accounting policies and rules should be followed in successive accounting periods unless there is a fundamental change in circumstances that makes such a change justifiable. It is not usually acceptable, for example, to adopt a different accounting method simply because the profit for a particular accounting period is low.

Objectivity

This rule requires accountants and managers to avoid personal bias and prejudice when selecting and applying the accounting rules. This is not always easy, of course, but an important part of your college or university education is to train you to argue both sides of a case irrespective of just how you feel. This training helps you to deal with problems objectively without letting your own personal feelings overwhelm a particular decision.

Relevance

Financial statements should not include matters that prevent users from learning what they need to know. The overall picture may be obscured if too much information or too much detail is given so the information provided must be *relevant*. In the jargon of the accountancy profession this means that financial statements should give a true and fair view of the financial affairs of the entity.

You are going to come across all the rules that we have discussed in this section in one form or another throughout the rest of the book but we now need to examine which professional and statutory requirements cover accounting. We turn to this topic in the next section.

Sources of authority

The application of the rules summarised in the previous section in an increasingly sophisticated banking, commercial, industrial, political, technological and social society began to cause problems for accountants and the users of financial statements as the twentieth century progressed. A number of fire-fighting solutions were then put forward in all attempt to deal with the numerous problems that began to erupt. During the 1960s, it became obvious that the system had begun to break down and that something needed to be done.

What did happen was that the UK accountancy profession began to develop what are called *accounting standards*. It was not long before *international accounting standards* also began to be developed. Such standards now play a very important part in the UK regulatory framework and we shall be examining them in detail in the later sections of this chapter.

Parliament also played its part in an attempt to come up with some solutions to the financial reporting problem. It takes time to get legislation through Parliament but even so it managed to pass seven Companies Acts in 22 years (between 1967 and 1989). It then took another 17 years before another Companies Act was passed in 2006 (a massive one as it turned out). We will have a look at it a little later in the chapter.

There is also another source of authority: the London Stock Exchange (LSE). The LSE is regulated by the Financial Conduct Authority (FCA). The FCA is an independent non-governmental body which is accountable to the Treasury and to Parliament. It was set up by the Financial Services Act 2012. It is responsible for the UK financial services industry and its powers are wide-ranging. They include rule-making, investigatory powers and enforcement powers.

The LSE plays a very important part in financial reporting but much of it is irrelevant for our purposes. This means that there are three main sources of authority governing accounting regulation in the United Kingdom that we need to examine: (1) the Companies Act 2006; (2) UK accounting standards and (3) international accounting standards (IASs). These three sources are examined in some detail in the following sections. The relationship between them is shown in Figure 2.5.

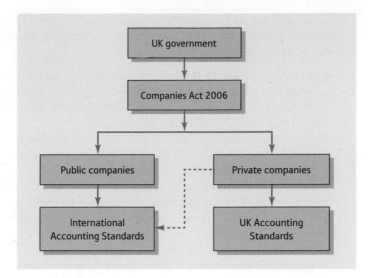

Figure 2.5 Sources of authority

Activity 2.4 Do you think that by law shareholders should have complete freedom of information, i.e. the right to be given all the information that they want about a company in which they hold shares? What practical problems might arise if this were the case?

The Companies Act 2006

There are no specific legal or statutory requirements dealing with sole trader and partnership accounts in the Companies Act or elsewhere. This means that the owners and managers of such entities may keep accounting records that suit them (if any) and prepare periodic accounts when and in what form they wish. However, if they are registered for Value Added Tax they will need to keep adequate records that satisfy the somewhat severe requirements of Her Majesty's Revenue and Customs (HMRC). Similarly, as the owners of a business they will need to include any profit due to them on their own personal self-assessment tax return. As a result of such considerations most entities have to keep some basic accounting records and to compile a simple profit and loss account once a year. The precise form and content of such records and accounts are up to them.

As we mentioned in Chapter 1, a new form of partnership, limited liability partnerships (LLP), was introduced in 2001. The 2006 Companies Act also covers some aspects of this type of entity but as we are not covering LLPs in this book, we do not need to go into the details.

We are going to be mainly concerned with the limited liability company type of entity. The legislation dealing with the formation, management, operation (including the accounting requirements) and reporting of such entities is now contained in the Companies Act of 2006. The Act is extremely detailed and complex and it is the largest Act ever passed by Parliament. No doubt you will be relieved to know that for your purposes (at least at this stage of your career) most of it is way beyond this book.

We will try to give you the answer to explain what you need to know as plainly and as simply as we can. The following is an extremely brief summary of what you need to know about the Companies Act 2006:

1 The Act deals with the entire operation and management of companies so it encompasses much more than simply 'the accounts'. The 'Accounts and Records' are covered in Part 15. This part forms a relatively small section of the entire Act and much of it is based on earlier legislation.

2 It classifies companies into 'small', 'medium' and 'large'. This classification is based on a requirement to satisfy two out of three criteria: turnover, assets and number of employees. The respective quantitative amounts are given in the Act but they are subject to amendment from time to time by Statutory Instrument (SI), which we will come back to later.

3 A company has a duty to keep what are referred to as 'adequate accounting records'. This means that (a) the company's transactions can be shown and explained; (b) the financial position of the company can be disclosed at any time (c) and its accounts must comply with either the Act or with European Union (EU) requirements.

4 A company must keep a daily record of money received and paid and a record of its assets and liabilities.

5 Companies dealing in equity stocks and shares (apart from retail traders) have to keep a record of their purchases and sales during a financial year and details of their suppliers and customers, and their year-end stocks.

6 The Act makes a distinction between (a) publicly traded companies and (b) a non-publicly traded companies. A publicly traded company is basically a company that is permitted to offer its shares to the public on a regulated market, i.e. a Stock Exchange. In the United Kingdom, you should be able to recognise such companies fairly easily because they have to put PLC, plc, or public limited company after their name. Similarly, non-publicly traded companies must put LTD, ltd or limited after their name.

7 PLCs in member states of the European Union must use what are called *International Accounting Standards* (IASs) when preparing *consolidated* accounts, i.e. when all the accounts forming part of a family of closely connected companies are combined. The accounts are then known as the *group* accounts. This requirement applies to every one of the 28 member countries of the European Union.

8 In preparing their accounts non-publicly traded companies in the United Kingdom have a choice. They can use either (a) the accounting requirements of the Companies Act 2006 plus UK Accounting Standards or (b) just IASs.

The 'Annual Accounts' section of the Act (in Part 15) is much broader in scope than was the case in earlier Companies Acts, the precise detail being left to the Secretary of State to determine. The form, content and terminology of accounts, for example, are not set out in the legislation (as they were in the 1985 and 1989 Companies Acts). This does not mean that companies are free to decide these things for themselves. Instead the details are decided by the Secretary of State and he or she issues his instructions in the form of an SI. This is known as *secondary legislation*.

SIs enable the Secretary of State to make changes to *primary* legislation without needing to put another Bill before Parliament. Such a procedure is perfectly legitimate because parliamentary time is short and the government's legislative programme is usually very full. The SI procedure enables changes to be made to non-controversial matters contained in legislation when circumstances change, e.g. the definition of 'small', 'medium' and 'large' companies. Turnover and assets totals (in sterling) can get out of date very quickly, so it makes sense if they are kept up to date on a regular basis without having to introduce even more legislation.

An SI dealing with the form and content of accounts was issued about 18 months after the Companies Act 2006 received the Royal Assent. As it turned out, the requirements were almost identical to those detailed in the 1985 and 1989 Companies Acts. This is a good example of the Act (despite its size) not having a major impact on conventional accounting practices – at least for those companies that did not have to switch to IASs.

We now turn to examine the second main source of accounting authority: UK Accounting Standards.

UK Accounting Standards

It would be helpful if we first define what is meant by an 'accounting standard'. The Companies Act 2006 gives us a definition although it is not a particularly clear one. According to the Act, accounting standards are as follows:

> statements of standard accounting practice issued by such body as may be prescribed by regulations. (CA 2006, S464(1))

In less legalistic language this means that: statements of standard accounting practice (SSAPs) are authoritative pronouncements that explain how to deal with specific accounting problems such as the valuation of closing stocks or the treatment of research expenditure. The regulations referred to above usually come in the form of SIs. In the United Kingdom, there is currently one such prescribed body called the Financial Reporting Council (FRC). Many other countries have a similar body. A brief history of the FRC now follows.

During the 1960s a number of contentious company mergers and takeovers took place. These events received a great deal of publicity and they both annoyed and puzzled the general public in equal measure. What was particularly puzzling to the public was that at the beginning of the week one set of accountants could decide that a company had made a profit and then by the end of that week another set of accountants would decide that it had actually made a loss. 'How was it possible', many people asked, 'for different accountants to arrive at such conflicting results when they both used the same information?' It then began to dawn on the public that there was much more to accounting than simply adding up a lot of figures. And when reality struck home, there was outrage. The figures could be 'fiddled': accountants were not saints after all!

The Institute of Chartered Accountants in England and Wales (ICAEW) was the first professional body to act. In 1970, it founded what was initially called the Accounting Standards Steering Committee (ASSC). It was renamed as the Accounting Standards Committee (ASC) in 1976 but in 1990 it was replaced by the Accounting Standards Board (ASB). By 1996, all the other five major professional accountancy bodies had become ASB members. Throughout this entire period the basic role of the ASSC/ASC/ASB remained unchanged, i.e. to develop definitive standards for financial reporting. The FRC assumed responsibility for accounting standards in 2012.

One of the FRC's main aims is to establish and to improve standards of financial accounting and reporting for the benefit of users, preparers and auditors of financial information. It aims to do so by achieving a number of objectives. In summary, they are as follows:

1 To develop accounting principles.
2 To provide a framework to resolve accounting issues.
3 To issue accounting standards.
4 To amend existing accounting standards.
5 To address promptly any urgent accounting issues.
6 To work with other accounting standard setting bodies and institutions.

Standards developed by the FRC (and its predecessors) are called *Financial Reporting Standards* (FRSs). By the Spring of 2016, 36 FRSs had been issued. In addition, 11 old standards, known as *Statements of Standard Accounting Practice* (or SSAPs) were still mandatory although they will eventually be phased out. The accounting problems covered in FRSs include acquisitions and mergers (FRS 6), goodwill and intangible assets (FRS 10) and life assurance (FRS 27). SSAPs that have not yet been withdrawn cover topics such as stocks and long-term contracts (SSAP 9) and accounting for pension costs (SSAP 24). The SSAPs still in existence give you some indication that they deal with issues that are either less controversial or more difficult to deal with.

We now turn to have a look at the third main source of accounting regulation in the United Kingdom: International Accounting Standards.

International Accounting Standards

International Accounting Standards are issued by what is now called the International Accounting Standards Board (IASB). The IASB was originally created in 1973 as the International Accounting Standards Committee (IASC) but it changed its name in 2001. The main aim of the IASC was to make financial statements much more comparable on an international basis. It was hoped to achieve this aim by issuing International Accounting Standards (IASs).

> Our mission is to develop, in the public interest, a single set of high-quality, understandable and international financial reporting standards (IFRSs) for general purpose financial statements.

News clip

Chairman Hans Hoogervorst presents IASB's mission statement

At a stakeholder event in Toronto, Canada, in early 2015 the Chairman of the IASB Hans Hoogervorst spoke about the IASB mission: 'Our mission is to develop IFRS that bring transparency, accountability and efficiency to financial markets around the world. Our work serves the public interest by fostering trust, growth and long-term financial stability in the global economy.' Mr Hoogervorst went on to explain that the transparency was to be achieved by enhancing the quality and international comparability of financial information, accountability would improve by reducing the information gap between the providers of capital and the people to whom they have entrusted their money and economic efficiency would be enhanced by helping investors to identify opportunities and risks across the world. These three aspects together would then make up the contribution of IFRSs to the public good.

Source: Adapted from http://www.iasplus.com 16 April 2015 (accessed 7 March 2016).

The IASB's aim is similar.

It operates through a body called the International Financial Reporting Standards Foundation (IFRS Foundation). The IFRS Foundation is an independent, private, not-for-profit sector organisation governed by 22 trustees from a number of different countries and professional backgrounds. It is funded by a voluntary system of donors from international accounting firms, business associations and organisations and central banks. The IFRS Foundation appoints the IASB's board of 14 members who are recruited from many wide-ranging backgrounds. It also finances, governs and oversees the IASB.

The IASB works closely with national standard setting bodies (such as the FRC in the United Kingdom) to ensure that accounting standards throughout the world are as comparable as possible. The number of countries either permitting or requiring the use of its standards continued to grow to 120 by the beginning of 2016. The big breakthrough came in 2002 when the European Union decided that as from 2005 publicly traded companies should adopt its standards. The next big hurdle facing the IASB is to encourage the United States to adopt its standards. Discussions have been taking place for some years. The indications are that the United States is 'mindful' to do so (using diplomatic language) but to date the discussions have not been successful. We return to this point later in the chapter.

The IASB's standards are called *International Financial Reporting Standards* (IFRSs). Between 2001 and the Spring of 2016, 15 IFRSs had been issued and were still effective. The topics that they deal with include such matters as insurance contracts (IFRS 4) and operating segments (IFRS 8). In addition, 26 of the original International Accounting Standards (IASs) were still in use in the Spring of 2016. The problems that they deal with range from the presentation of financial statements (IAS 1) to one coping with agriculture activity (IAS 41). Many of these accounting standards are highly technical and are certainly way beyond what you need to know until you become a very senior manager.

Now that we have given you some idea of the importance and status of both the FRC and the IASB in accounting regulation, we are in a position to examine what these two bodies have done to improve their performance. We do so in the next section.

An accounting framework

Until 2005, IASs and IFRSs were not a significant feature of UK financial reporting and SSAPs and FRSs took priority in the preparation of financial statements. The then ASB certainly did not ignore the work of the IASB and the two bodies had a close working relationship but the ASB then had a legal and professional status in the United Kingdom which the IASB did not have. That all changed in 2005 once the European Union decided to adopt International Accounting Standards. As a member of the European Union the United Kingdom was bound to accept the decision.

There were two basic differences between UK Accounting Standards and International Accounting Standards:

1 They did not always deal with the same accounting problems. This was perhaps because what was a contentious issue in the United Kingdom was not necessarily so in the rest of the world (and vice versa).

2 If the ASB and the IASB did issue an accounting standard dealing with the same problem, the IASB's solution tended to be more generalised (possibly because it had to be acceptable in so many different and disparate countries). This was an advantage for the United Kingdom because it meant that compliance with a UK standard almost automatically meant compliance with the equivalent IAS one.

The ASB and the IASB did have one thing in common when framing their respective accounting standards: they were largely fire-fighting exercises dealing with what happened to be a problem at that particular time. This meant that there was often little consistency in the way that the various issues were tackled. It eventually became apparent that accounting standards should be built on a basic framework or foundation. This would then enable solutions to different problems to be based on the same basic principles or rules. As a result, accounting standards would have a common theme running through them.

Academic accountants had argued for years that there was a need for such a framework. They referred to it as a *conceptual* framework which no doubt frightened the more practically trained accountants to death. Nevertheless, both the ASB and the IASB and similar standard setting bodies in many other countries were working on such a project. The IASB was the first to publish its ideas in a document called *Framework for the Preparation and Presentation of Financial Statements* (note that it did not include the word 'concept' in its title). The ideas in it relied very heavily on work done on the same subject in the United States as well as in Australia and Canada. We shall refer to it as the *Framework* from now on.

The ASB took a great deal longer to produce its own framework. It was not until 1999 that it published what it called *Statement of Principles for Financial Reporting*. It is very similar to the Framework. As it is, in effect, a more up-to-date version of it, we will use the Statement to summarise what we need for this chapter. The relevant points are as follows:

1 The *objective* of financial statements is: to provide information about the reporting entity's financial performance and financial position that is useful to a wide range of users when assessing the stewardship of the entity's management and for making economic decisions.

2 The *users* of financial statements are: (i) investors; (ii) lenders; (iii) suppliers and other trade creditors; (iv) employees; (v) customers; (vi) governments and their agencies; and (vii) the public. These users are depicted in Figure 2.6.

3 The *reporting entity* is a cohesive economic unit, its boundary being determined by what it can control both directly and indirectly.

4 The *qualitative characteristics* of financial information are summarised below. Note how they relate very closely to the four ethical accounting rules we discussed earlier in the chapter, i.e. prudence, consistency, objectivity and relevance.

  (a) *Relevance.* Financial statements should meet the needs of users and be *timely*, i.e. not to be so out of date that they have become irrelevant for decision-making purposes. This characteristic, in effect, presupposes the incorporation of the *materiality* concept because information that is not helpful for decision-making is irrelevant.

  (b) *Reliability.* Users should be able to rely on the information contained within the financial statements. It should be free from material error, represent faithfully what it is supposed to represent, be free from bias (i.e. it should be *neutral*), and be compatible with the substance of transactions and not simply just because it is lawful. It should also be complete provided that it is material, and a *prudent* approach should be adopted when it is unclear how a particular transaction should be accounted for. So materiality, prudence and also objectivity are all inherent in this characteristic.

  (c) *Comparability.* Financial statements containing the results for comparative periods should be prepared on a consistent basis. In other words, they should be prepared on the same basis each year. Comparability is almost the same concept as our consistency rule.

  (d) *Understandability.* Financial statements should be capable of being understood by those users who have some knowledge of accounting, business activities and economic affairs and who are willing to study the financial statements diligently. The financial statements themselves should not, however, be so simple that the information becomes meaningless.

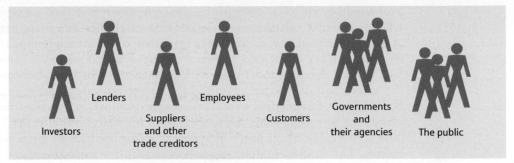

Investors   Lenders   Suppliers and other trade creditors   Employees   Customers   Governments and their agencies   The public

Figure 2.6 The main users of financial statements
Source: Statement of Principles for Financial Reporting, ASB 1999.

5 The *elements* of financial information are the 'building blocks' used in the construction of the financial statements. They include what assets and liabilities the entity owns, what interest the owners have in the entity, what contributions the owners have made and what has been paid out to them.

6 The Statement recognises that assets and liabilities need to be *measured* so that they can be included in the financial statements. They can be included at either their historical cost or at their current value. Historical cost is the more usual. Current cost is a method that relates to the loss an entity would suffer if the entity was deprived of an asset. So it is sometimes called 'deprival value' or 'loss to the business'. We shall not be dealing with current value accounting in this book.

7 Financial statements should be presented clearly, effectively, simply and straightforwardly. When you reach Chapters 8 and 9 of this book you may begin to question whether the authors of the Companies Act 2006 and the compilers of accounting standards were aware of this requirement.

You might also think that despite the fuss that we have made in this chapter about the need to develop a workable framework, the outcome so far has not been very impressive. Both the Framework and the Statement are quite vague in their requirements and perhaps they lack a more prescriptive approach.

News clip

Consistent application of standards is important

Underlying the consistent application of IFRS is the fundamental need for people from different cultures, who speak different languages, to understand fully the requirements of IFRS Standards. A challenge in this context is that countries have different accounting histories: some have an investor-based approach to accounting and corporate reporting, others have a system that is based on central planning, while others again have systems largely based on tax reporting. In many countries, the principle-based nature of the Standards is entirely unfamiliar.

Accounting standards are only as successful as their application in practice – even the best-written standards can be poorly applied.

Source: Adapted from 'Supporting implementation through education' by Liz Fisher, published by IASB at http://www.iasplus.com on 3 March 2016.

You would be right but if the profession went down that road we would be moving to what is called a *rules-based* approach to accounting. The main problems with this approach are that: (1) it is difficult to formulate rules that accommodate every eventuality and (2) ways will always be found of getting round whatever rules are formulated. So a culture develops and creates a climate whereby the attitude becomes 'if it's not in the rules, you can do what you like'. As we indicated earlier in the chapter, the United States has adopted a *rules-based* approach, while EU countries all use a *principles-based* approach. This approach allows for individual circumstances to be taken into account but it can result in apparent inconsistencies in the accounts of different entities. This fundamental difference between the European Union and the United States methods of accounting is the main reason why the United States has been reluctant to adopt IASs but political considerations have, no doubt, also played a part.

Activity 2.5	In the United Kingdom, the applicable Accounting Standards are based on generally accepted *principles*. Some other countries, such as the United States, prefer a *rules-based system*. Which approach do you favour?

1 (a) principles-based   [ ]   (b) rules-based   [ ]   (tick one).
2 Give three reasons for your choice.

! Questions you should ask

This is an important chapter. It not only prepares you for what follows in the rest of the book but it outlines a number of accounting issues that will face you when you become a manager in the real world. We suggest that among the long list of questions that you might well ask are the following:

- Are we subject to the Companies Act 2006?
- Do we adopt International Accounting Standards or UK (or own country's) standards?
- What accounting rules do we follow in the preparation of our financial statements?
- Are we without doubt a going concern?
- How do we determine what is an immaterial item or immaterial error in our financial statements?
- To what extent does neutrality override the need to be prudent?

Conclusion

In this chapter we have identified 14 conventional accounting rules and introduced you to the accounting provisions of the Companies Act 2006 along with the additional semi-statutory requirements specified by the Financial Reporting Council and the International Accounting Standards Board.

The chapter enables you to grasp the fundamentals of what accountants do, why they do it and what the law requires them to do. In subsequent chapters we will show you how to prepare financial statements based on what is required. By knowing why and how they are prepared, you will find that they will be of much greater benefit to you in making and taking the types of decision that your job requires.

Key points

1 In preparing financial statements, accountants use a number of conventional accounting rules (sometimes called principles); these rules have evolved over many centuries.

2 Such rules may be classified into boundary rules (entity, periodicity, going concern and monetary quantities); measurement rules (money measurement, historic cost, realisation, matching, dual aspect and materiality) and ethical rules (prudence, consistency, objectivity and relevance).

3 The main source of legislation affecting accounting matters in the United Kingdom is the Companies Act 2006; the Act is primarily concerned with companies and limited liability partnerships.

4 The Act delegates much of the detail involving the preparation and reporting of financial statements to the International Accounting Standards Board (for publicly quoted group companies) and the UK Financial Reporting Council (for other companies).

5 The IASB issues International Financial Reporting Standards (IFRSs) and the FRC issues Financial Reporting Standards (FRSs) to help companies deal with contentious and difficult accounting matters. Other countries have their own accounting standards boards but many of them also use IASs.

6 Financial statements in the United Kingdom have always been prepared on a custom and practice basis but both the IASB and the FRC have issued a framework outlining the principles that entities are expected to follow in preparing such statements. Both frameworks are similar and they incorporate in one form or another all the 14 rules detailed in the first part of this chapter.

Check your learning

1 In an accounting context name three other terms that are similar in meaning to 'rules'.

2 Identify three categories of accounting rules.

3 What accounting rule is used to describe a defined period of time?

4 What is a going concern?

5 What is matching?

6 What does dual aspect mean?

7 When is a transaction not material?

8 What criteria are used to determine whether items are relevant?

9 Name three important sources of authority governing accounting matters affecting UK companies.

10 What do the following initials stand for?: (a) FRC; (b) IASB; (c) SSAP; (d) IAS; (e) FRS; (f) IFRS.

11 What is an accounting standard?

12 What is a conceptual framework?

13 What is the objective of financial statements?

14 List seven user groups of accounting information.

15 What is a reporting entity?

16 List the qualitative characteristics of financial information.

News story quiz

Remember the news story at the beginning of the chapter? Go back to that story and re-read it before answering the following questions.

This article relates back to the financial crisis that in 2007/8 struck the banking system in Britain and in many other countries. However, the points raised in the article continue to be relevant today as world economies (e.g. Greece and China), and the businesses which operate in them, continue to face challenges.

Questions

1 What are the advantages and disadvantages of a rules-based and a principles-based approach to regulation and in turn, accounting matters?

2 Why is a principles-based approach to regulation necessary particularly in times of economic turmoil?

3 Why is principles-based approach to regulation better serving the public interest? Is it doing a good job?

Tutorial questions

The answers to questions marked with an asterisk can be found in Appendix 4.

2.1 Do you think that when a set of financial accounts is being prepared, neutrality should override prudence?

2.2 'The law should lay down precise formats, contents and methods for the preparation of limited liability company accounts.' Discuss.

2.3 The Financial Reporting Council bases its Financial Reporting Standards on what is sometimes called a 'conceptual framework'. How far do you think that this approach is likely to be successful?

In questions 2.4, 2.5 and 2.6 you are required to state which accounting rule the accountant would most probably adopt in dealing with the various problems.

2.4* (a) Electricity consumed in Period 1 and paid for in Period 2.
(b) Equipment originally purchased for £20,000 which would now cost £30,000.
(c) The company's good industrial relations record.
(d) A five-year construction contract.
(e) A customer with a poor credit record might go bankrupt owing the company £5000.
(f) The company's vehicles, which would only have a small scrap value if the company goes into liquidation.

2.5* (a) A demand by the company's chairman to include every detailed transaction in the presentation of the annual accounts.
(b) A sole-trader business which has paid the proprietor's income tax based on the business profits for the year.
(c) A proposed change in the methods of valuing stock.
(d) The valuation of a litre of petrol in one vehicle at the end of accounting Period 1.
(e) A vehicle which could be sold for more than its purchase price.
(f) Goods which were sold to a customer in Period 1 but for which the cash was only received in Period 2.

2.6* (a) The proprietor who has supplied the business capital out of his own private bank account.
(b) The sales manager who is always very optimistic about the creditworthiness of prospective customers.
(c) The managing director who does not want annual accounts prepared as the company operates a continuous 24-hour-a-day, 365-days-a-year process.
(d) At the end of Period 1, it is difficult to be certain whether the company will have to pay legal fees of £1000 or £3000.
(e) The proprietor who argues that the accountant has got a motor vehicle entered twice in the books of account.
(f) Some goods were purchased and entered into stock at the end of Period 1, but they were not paid for until Period 2.

2.7 The following is a list of problems which an accountant may well meet in practice:

   (a) The transfer fee of a footballer.

   (b) Goods are sold in one period but the cash for them is received in a later period.

   (c) The proprietor's personal dwelling house has been used as security for a loan which the bank has granted to the company.

   (d) What profit to take in the third year of a five-year construction contract.

   (e) Small stocks of stationery held at the accounting year end.

   (f) Expenditure incurred in working on the improvement of a new drug.

Required:

   1 Which accounting rule would the accountant most probably adopt in dealing with each of the above problems?

   2 State the reasons for your choice.

2.8 *FRS 18* (accounting policies) states that profits shall be treated as realised and included in the profit and loss account only when the cash due 'can be assessed with reasonable certainty' (para. 28). How far do you think that this requirement removes any difficulty in determining in which accounting period a sale has taken place?

2.9 The adoption of the realisation and matching rules in preparing financial accounts requires a great deal of subjective judgement.

Required:

   (a) Write an essay examining whether it would be fairer, easier and more meaningful to prepare financial accounts on a cash received/cash paid basis.

2.10 Consider the Principles of Good Regulation – for both the regulator and business as explained by the Financial Conduct Authority (the regulator of financial institutions in the United Kingdom). Discuss:

   (a) to what extent do you think that the same principles apply to the company and the industry you wish to work for when graduating from university?

   (b) to what extent these principles should apply to the way accounting and financial reporting is performed at the company and in the industry you wish to work for?

   (c) as a manager, what might you need to do to be able to operate within the principles personally?

   (d) what might the implications be if you personally, or the business you work for, or the regulator within your industry do not operate within the principles?

The principles of the regulator are as follows:

1. Efficiency and economy	We [the Regulator] are committed to using our resources in the most efficient and economical way. As part of this [we are open to] value-for-money reviews of our operations.
2. Proportionality	We must ensure that any burden or restriction that we impose on a person, firm or activity is proportionate to the benefits we expect as a result. To judge this, we take into account the costs to firms and consumers.

3. Sustainable growth	We must ensure that there is a desire for sustainable growth in the economy of the United Kingdom in the medium or long term.
4. Consumer responsibility	Consumers should take responsibility for their decisions.
5. Senior management responsibility	A firm's senior management is responsible for the firm's activities and for ensuring that its business complies with regulatory requirements. This secures an adequate but proportionate level of regulatory intervention by holding senior management responsible for the risk management and controls within firms. Firms must make it clear who has what responsibility and ensure that its business can be adequately monitored and controlled.
6. Recognising the differences in the businesses carried on by different regulated persons	Where appropriate, we exercise our functions in a way that recognises differences in the nature of, and objectives of, businesses carried on by different persons subject to requirements imposed by or under [applicable laws].
7. Openness and disclosure	We should publish relevant market information about regulated persons or require them to publish it (with appropriate safeguards). This reinforces market discipline and improves consumers' knowledge [for e.g. about their financial matters].
8. Transparency	We should exercise our functions as transparently as possible. It is important that we provide appropriate information on our regulatory decisions, and that we are open and accessible to the regulated community and the general public.

The principles for businesses are as follows:

1. Integrity	A firm must conduct its business with integrity.
2. Skill, care and diligence	A firm must conduct its business with due skill, care and diligence.
3. Management and control	A firm must take reasonable care to organise and control its affairs responsibly and effectively, with adequate risk management systems.
4. Financial prudence	A firm must maintain adequate financial resources.
5. Market conduct	A firm must observe proper standards of market conduct.
6. Customers' interests	A firm must pay due regard to the interests of its customers and treat them fairly.
7. Communications with clients	A firm must pay due regard to the information needs of its clients and communicate information to them in a way which is clear, fair and not misleading.
8. Conflicts of interest	A firm must manage conflicts of interest fairly, both between itself and its customers and between a customer and another client.

9. Customers: relationships of trust	A firm must take reasonable care to ensure the suitability of its advice and discretionary decisions for any customer who is entitled to rely upon its judgement.
10. Clients' assets	A firm must arrange adequate protection for clients' assets when it is responsible for them.
11. Relations with regulators	A firm must deal with its regulators in an open and co-operative way and must disclose to the appropriate regulator appropriately anything relating to the firm of which that regulator would reasonably expect notice. Source: The Finance Conduct Authority, https://www.fga.org.uk/about/operate/principles, accessed 15 April 2016

Website

Further practice questions, study material and links to relevant sites on the World Wide Web can be found on the website that accompanies this book. The site can be found at www.pearsoned.co.uk/dyson

FINANCIAL ACCOUNTING

In Part 2 we outline the principles of double-entry bookkeeping and explain how to prepare financial accounts for sole traders, companies and for some other types of entities in the not-for-profit sector. The relationship of Part 2 to the rest of the book is shown below.

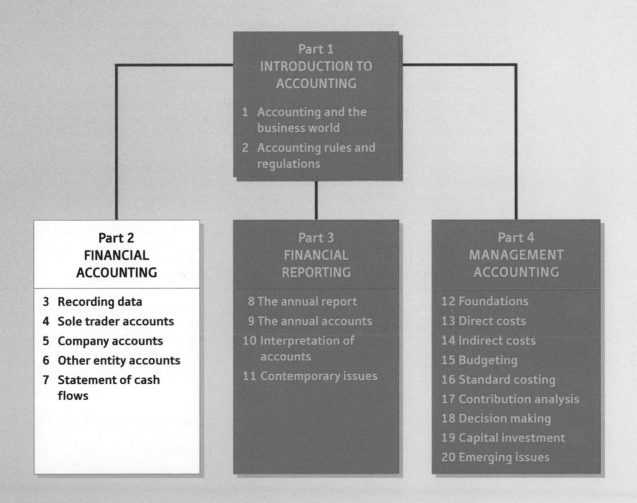

**Part 1
INTRODUCTION TO
ACCOUNTING**

1 Accounting and the business world

2 Accounting rules and regulations

**Part 2
FINANCIAL
ACCOUNTING**

3 Recording data
4 Sole trader accounts
5 Company accounts
6 Other entity accounts
7 Statement of cash flows

**Part 3
FINANCIAL
REPORTING**

8 The annual report
9 The annual accounts
10 Interpretation of accounts
11 Contemporary issues

**Part 4
MANAGEMENT
ACCOUNTING**

12 Foundations
13 Direct costs
14 Indirect costs
15 Budgeting
16 Standard costing
17 Contribution analysis
18 Decision making
19 Capital investment
20 Emerging issues

Recording data

Is this the end of traditional bookkeeping?

Blockchain promises back-office ledger revolution

By Izabella Kaminska

Blockchain technology could represent the most radical departure from longstanding financial bookkeeping practices since Luca Pacioli formally codified the Medicis' double-entry accounting system in the fifteen century, say bankers and investors.

In the process, the world of back-office systems and ledgers is being flung into the heart of a technological arms race that promises much in the way of solutions but is increasingly divided over which particular version of the blockchain technology to bet on.

Originally devised as a computer protocol by the pseudonymous Satoshi Nakamoto to keep his decentralised cryptocurrency bitcoin faithfully in check, bankers justify their enthusiasm for blockchain by pointing to its potential to cut up to $20bn of costs from the financial sector, mostly by eliminating the clunky processes that govern payments and settlements behind the scenes.

'It's not intended to be a currency but an efficient way to record transactions, which is ultimately what interests us,' says Nicolas Granatino, of Andurance Ventures, the VC fund associated with commodity fund manager Pierre Andurand and one of a slew of funds looking to invest in the sector.

Visa, Nasdaq and Citi Ventures, for example, are lending support to a US start-up called Chain which aims to help exchanges such as Nasdaq enter the private share-dealing market. Duncan Niederauer, former chief executive of the New York Stock Exchange, meanwhile, has invested in Symbiont, which is developing a platform that uses generic blockchains.

In September, a group of nine investment banks, including Goldman Sachs, JP Morgan and Credit Suisse, announced their intent to develop common standards for blockchain by way of a collective investment in a New York-based start-up called R3CEV. That number of banks has since grown to 22.

FT   *Source:* Extracted from *The Financial Times,* 13 October 2015.

Questions relating to this news story can be found on page 68. ➡

About this chapter

In Chapter 2 we outlined some fundamental accounting rules. We indicated that some 'rules' are merely conventions, i.e. they have become generally accepted over a long period of time by custom and practice. You may recall that one convention that we dealt with in Chapter 2 is called the *dual aspect rule*. There is no iron law either of man or of nature that requires this rule to be adopted. It is merely a highly practical and useful one that has been shown to work over many centuries.

The dual aspect rule is a logical method of recording accounting data that enables: (1) an accurate record to be kept of an entity's activities on a regular basis and (2) an entity to assess its performance over and at the end of a defined period of time. We cover the practical application of the dual aspect rule in this chapter.

Learning objectives

By the end of this chapter you should be able to:
- explain what is meant by the 'accounting equation';
- define the terms 'debit' and 'credit';
- write up some simple ledger accounts;
- extract a trial balance;
- identify six errors not revealed in a trial balance.

Why this chapter is important

This chapter is important for non-accountants for three main reasons.

1 *To learn the language of accounting.* The chapter will enable you to become familiar with the language and terminology used by accountants. This means that it will then be much easier for you to discuss with them any issues arising from the reports that they prepare for you.

2 *To check the reliability of information presented to you.* The chapter gives you a basic knowledge of the fundamental recording systems used by all types of entities throughout the world. You will then be able to assess the reliability of any accounting information based on the data that have been included in the system. You will also be more aware of what information has *not* been recorded. This will enable you to take into account what is missing from the accounts when considering the usefulness of any information your accountants give you.

3 *To discuss matters with your accountants.* Accounting information is based on a considerable number of questionable assumptions. These may not always be valid. If you are familiar with the language and nuances of fundamental accounting procedures, you will be able to have a more helpful discussion with your accountants about the type of information that you need to do your job.

The accounting equation

The system that accountants use to record financial data is known as *double-entry bookkeeping*. The system recognises that every transaction has a twofold effect. So if I loan you £100, a twofold effect arises because: I give you some money and you receive it. But the transaction also has a twofold effect on *both of us*.

(a) The effect on you: (1) your cash goes up by £100 and (2) what you owe me also goes up by £100.

(b) The effect on me: (1) my cash goes down by £100 and (2) what I am owed by you goes up by £100.

If an entity (say., 'me') uses this twofold effect to record *twice* each of the transactions that take place between 'me' and another entity (say, 'you'), then I am using some form of double-entry bookkeeping. The most commonly used system has evolved over at least the past 600 years and it is now used on a worldwide basis. Before we describe how it works, however, we must first make sure that you are clear about three important accounting terms. They are as follows:

- *Assets:* These are possessions or resources *owned and controlled* by an entity. They include physical or tangible possessions such as property, plant, machinery, stock and cash. They also include intangible assets, i.e. non-physical possessions such as copyright and patent rights, as well as debts owed to the entity such as trade and other debtors and receivables.
- *Capital:* This is the term used to describe the amount that the owners have invested in an entity. In effect, 'capital' is the amount owed by the entity to its owners.
- *Liabilities:* These are the opposite of assets. They are the amounts owed *by* an entity to outside parties. They include loans, bank overdrafts, creditors and payables, i.e. amounts owing to parties for the supply of goods and services to the entity that still have to be paid for.

There is a close relationship among assets, capital and liabilities. It is frequently presented in the form of what is called the 'accounting equation' (see Figure 3.1):

$$\text{Assets} = \text{Capital} + \text{Liabilities}$$

The equation tells us in clear and simple terms that what the entity owns (or possesses) was obtained using a combination of contributions from the entity's owners and borrowings from other people. In other words, the resources the business controls are equal to the sources of funding used to acquire these resources. This is another form of the same equation.

$$\text{Resources} = \text{Sources of funding}$$

We will illustrate the use of the accounting equation with a simple example. Let us assume that you have decided to go into business. You do so by transferring £2000 in cash from your own private bank account. The entity rule means that we are not interested in your private affairs, so we only want to keep track of how the business deals with your £2000.

The business now has £2000 invested in it. This is its starting capital (and what it owes back to the investor) but it also has £2000 in cash. The cash is an asset. So the £2000 asset equals the £2000 of capital. Or in equation form:

Assets		Capital
Cash £2000	=	Capital £2000

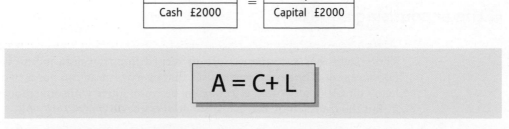

Figure 3.1 The accounting equation

The equation captures the twofold effect of the transaction: the assets of the business have been increased by the capital contributed by the owner.

Now suppose that you then decide to deposit £1500 of the cash into a business bank account. The effect on the equation is:

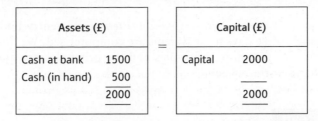

Assets (£)			Capital (£)	
Cash at bank	1500		Capital	2000
Cash (in hand)	500			____
	2000			2000

As you can see, there has simply been a change on the *assets* side of the equation.

Suppose now that you borrow £500 in cash from one of your friends to help finance the business. The assets will be increased by an inflow of £500 in cash, but £500 will be owed to your friend. The £500 owed is a liability and your friend has become a creditor of the business. The business has total assets of £2500 (£1500 at the bank and £1000 in cash). Its capital is £2000 and it has a liability of £500. The equation then reads:

Assets (£)			Capital (£)			Liabilities (£)	
Cash at bank	1500		Capital	2000		Creditor	500
Cash (500 + 500)	1000			____			____
	2500			2000			500

If £800 of goods were then purchased in cash for subsequent resale to the entity's customers, the equation would read:

Assets (£)			Capital (£)			Liabilities (£)	
Stocks	800		Capital	2000		Creditor	500
Cash at bank	1500			____			____
Cash (1000 − 800)	200			2000			500
	2500						

Again there has been a change on the assets side of the equation when £800 of the cash (an asset) was used to purchase £800 of goods for resale (i.e. stocks), another asset.

The equation is now becoming somewhat complicated but it does enable us to see the effect that *any* transaction has on the entity. The vital point to remember about the accounting equation is:

If an adjustment is made to one side of the equation, you *must* make an identical adjustment *either* to the other side of the equation *or* to the same side.

This maxim reflects the basic rule of double-entry bookkeeping:

Every transaction must be recorded twice.

We will explain how the recording is done in the next section.

Double-entry bookkeeping

We are going to explain how a *handwritten* double-entry bookkeeping system works, even though these days most systems are computerised. We do so because both systems use the same accounting principles and the principles are much easier to follow in a simple handwritten system.

Scrutiny of bookkeeping practices increases

Toshiba withdrew its earnings guidance and scrapped its year-end dividend pay-out on Friday, saying it had found improper accounting on some of its infrastructure projects.

Investor scrutiny on bookkeeping practices by Japanese companies has also increased following a $1.7bn accounting scandal at medical equipment maker Olympus in 2011.

Source: Extracted from *The Financial Times*, 8 May 2015.

Just as the accounting equation reflects the twofold effect of every transaction, so does a double-entry bookkeeping system. This means that each transaction must be recorded twice. A change to the accounting system is called an *entry* and so we talk about making entries in the accounts (remember that an *account* is simply a history or a record of a particular type of transaction). Accounts used to be kept in various bound books referred to as ledgers and all the *ledgers* used in a particular accounting system are known collectively as the *books of account*.

The effect of entering a particular transaction once in one ledger account and again in another ledger account causes the balance on each of the two accounts either to go up or to go down (like the accounting equation). So a transaction can either *increase* or *decrease* the total amount held in an account. In other words, an account either *receives* (i.e. accepts) an additional amount or it *gives* (i.e. releases) it. This receiving and giving effect has given rise to two terms from Latin that are commonly used in accounting:

debit: *meaning to receive, or value received;*

credit: *meaning to give, or value given.*

Accountants judge the twofold effect of all transactions on particular accounts from a receiving and giving point of view and each transaction is recorded on that basis. So when a transaction takes place, it is necessary to ask the following two questions:

• Which account should *receive* this transaction, i.e. which account should be debited?
• Which account has *given* this amount, i.e. which account should be credited?

Accounts have been designed to keep the debit entries separate from the credit entries. This helps to emphasise the opposite, albeit equal, effect that each transaction has within the recording system. In a handwritten system, the separation is achieved by recording the debit entries on the left-hand side of the page and the credit entries on the right-hand

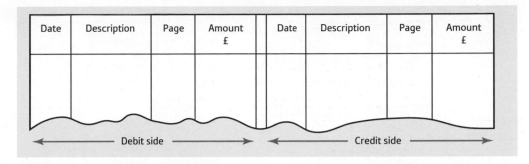

Figure 3.2 Example of a ledger account

side. Each account is normally kept on a separate page in a ledger (i.e. a book of account). A traditional handwritten ledger account is illustrated in Figure 3.2.

In the next section we will show you how particular transactions are recorded in ledger accounts.

Activity 3.1	In one sentence describe what is meant by each of the following terms: (a) An account is _____ (b) A ledger is _____ (c) Debit means _____ (d) Credit means _____

Working with accounts

There are four specific purposes behind this section, as follows:

1 to outline what type of transactions are included in an account;
2 to show how they are entered in an account;
3 to explain what is meant by a debit balance and a credit balance;
4 to demonstrate what happens at the end of an accounting period.

We should stress that we are not trying to turn you into a bookkeeper. We just think that you need to know something about how accounting information is recorded and summarised before it is presented to you as a manager. If you possess that knowledge, then we believe that information will be much more useful to you in deciding what to do with it.

Choice of accounts

There is no specified or statutory list of accounts that *must* be used. Much will depend on the size and nature of the entity and whether it is in the private or public sector. Sometimes it is not clear, even to accountants, what account to use so they then adopt the maxim *if in doubt, open another account*. It really does not matter how many accounts are used – they can always be dropped if some of them become superfluous.

Some of the more common types of accounts that you may come across in your career are summarised below. Figure 3.3 also shows you how they are all so closely interlinked.

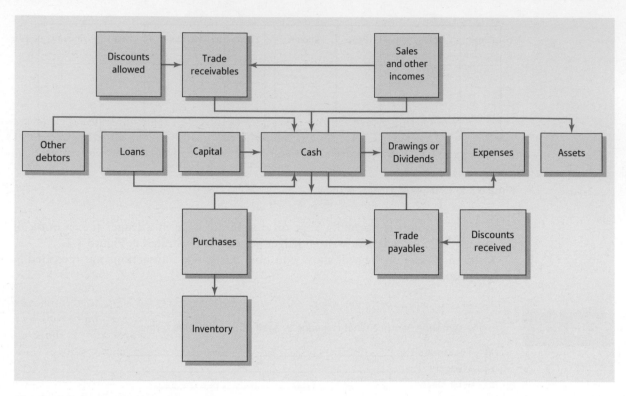

Figure 3.3 Interlinking of accounts

Capital

The *capital account* records what the owner has contributed (or given) to the entity out of private resources in order to start the business and keep it going. In other words, it shows what the business owes the owner. In large businesses, where there is more than one owner, this account shows what the business owes in total to its shareholders as a group.

Cash at bank

The *cash at bank account* records what money the entity keeps at the bank. It shows what has been put in (e.g. cash and cheques) and what has been taken out (e.g. cheque and direct debit payments).

Cash in hand

The *cash in hand account* works on similar lines to the cash at bank account, except that it records the physical cash received (such as notes, coins and cheques) before they are paid into the bank. The cash received may be used to purchase goods and services or it may be paid straight into the bank. From a control point of view, it is best not to pay for purchases directly out of cash receipts but to draw an amount out of the bank specifically for sundry cash purchases. Any large amount should always be paid through the bank account.

Creditors/payables

Creditor accounts record what the entity owes its suppliers for goods or services purchased or supplied on credit (see also *trade creditors*). The creditors accounts are also known as *payables*.

Debtors/receivables

Debtor accounts record what is owed to the entity by its customers for goods or services sold to them on credit (see also *trade debtors*). The debtors accounts are also known as *receivables*.

Discounts allowed

Discounts allowed are cash discounts granted to the entity's customers for the prompt settlement of any debts due to the entity. The amount of cash received from debtors who claim a cash discount will then be less than the total amount for which they have been invoiced.

Discounts received

Discounts received relate to cash discounts given by the entity's suppliers for the prompt payment of any amounts due to them. So the amount paid to the entity's creditors will be less than the invoiced amount.

Drawings or dividends

The term *drawings* has a special meaning in accounting. The *drawings account* is used to record what cash (or goods) the owner of an unincorporated business has withdrawn from the business for his personal use. In the case of a company, we talk about *dividends* which represent the money paid to the shareholders out of the company profits. These are essentially the same.

Petty cash

The *petty cash account* is similar to both the cash at bank account and the cash account. It is usually limited to the recording of minor cash transactions, such as bus fares or tea and coffee for the office. The cash used to finance this account will normally be transferred from the bank account.

Sales

The *sales account* records the value of goods sold to customers during a particular accounting period. The account includes both cash and credit sales. It does not include receipts from (say) the sale of a motor car originally purchased for use within the business.

Inventory

Inventory includes goods which have not been sold at the end of an accounting period. In accounting terminology, this would be referred to as the *closing inventory*. The closing inventory at the end of one period becomes the *opening inventory* at the beginning of the next period. In the United Kingdom, inventory is often referred to as *stock*.

Purchases

The term *purchases* has a restricted meaning in accounting. It relates to those goods that are bought primarily with the intention of selling them (normally at a profit). The purchase of some motor cars, for example, would not usually be recorded in the *Purchases Account* unless they have been bought with the intention of selling them to customers. Goods not intended for resale are usually recorded in separate accounts. Some purchases may also require further work to be done on them before they are eventually sold.

Trade creditors/payables

Trade creditor accounts are similar to creditor accounts except that they relate specifically to what is owed to suppliers for purchases of stock on credit. The trade creditors accounts are also known as *trade payables*.

Trade debtors/receivable

Trade debtor accounts are similar to debtor accounts except that they also relate specifically to what is owing for sales made to customers on credit. The trade debtors accounts are also known as *trade receivables*.

Trade discounts

Trade discounts are a form of special discount. They may be given for placing a large order, for example, or for being a loyal customer. Trade discounts are deducted from the normal purchase or selling price. They are not recorded in the books of account and they will not appear on any invoice.

Other income

Other income accounts such as interest on cash deposits, rental income or dividend income would be set up as such income was earned by an entity.

Expenses

Expense accounts such as rent, advertising, wages and many more would be set up to record the various expenses incurred by an entity.

Assets

Individual *asset accounts* will be set up to record the acquisition of other assets (in addition to the cash and inventory mentioned above), such as motor vehicles, land, fixtures and fittings. In the case of both expenses and assets, cash is paid out ordinarily. The difference is that an expense is used up (so that cash pays for the consumption of a service, for example, accountant fees) whereas an asset is something that the business is able to get benefit from in future periods (e.g. computers and accounting software installed on them).

Once the bookkeeper has chosen the accounts in which to record all the transactions for a particular accounting period, it is then necessary to decide which account should be debited and which account should be credited. We examine this problem in the next subsection.

Activity 3.2

Which two ledger accounts would you use in recording each of the following transactions?

(a) cash sales
(b) rent paid by cheque
(c) wages paid in cash
(d) a supplier of goods paid online by PayPal
(e) goods sold on credit to Ford.

Entering transactions in accounts

When entering a transaction in an account always make sure that you do the following:

Debit the account which receives.

And

Credit the account which gives.

Example 3.1 illustrates the use of this rule. It contains some common ledger account entries. It is not always easy to think of the receiving and of the giving effect of each transaction. You will find that it is very easy to get them mixed up and to then reverse the entries. If we look at Entries 6 and 7 in Example 3.1, for example, it is difficult to understand why the Sales Account should be credited. Why is the Sales Account the giving account? Surely it is *receiving* an amount and not giving anything? In one sense

Example 3.1	**Examples of some common ledger account entries**

Entry 1

The proprietor contributes some cash to the business.

> *Debit*: Cash in Hand Account   *Credit*: Capital Account

Reason: The Cash in Hand Account receives some cash given to the business by the owner. His Capital Account is the giving account and the Cash Account is the receiving account.

Entry 2

Some cash in the till is paid into the business bank account.

> *Debit*: Cash at Bank Account   *Credit*: Cash in Hand Account

Reason: The Cash in Hand Account is the giving account because it is releasing some cash to the Cash at Bank Account.

Entry 3

A van is purchased for use in the business; it is paid for by cheque.

> *Debit*: Van Account   *Credit*: Cash at Bank Account

Reason: The Cash at Bank Account is giving some money in order to pay for a van, so the Cash at Bank Account must be credited as it is the giving account.

Entry 4

Some goods are purchased for cash.

> *Debit*: Purchases Account   *Credit*: Cash in Hand Account

Reason: The Cash in Hand Account is giving up an amount of cash in order to pay for some purchases. The Cash in Hand Account is the giving account, so it must be credited.

Entry 5

Some goods are purchased on credit terms from Fred.

> *Debit*: Purchases Account   *Credit*: Fred's Account

Reason: Fred is supplying the goods on credit terms to the business. As he is the giver, his account must be credited.

Entry 6

Some goods are sold for cash.

> *Debit*: Cash in Hand Account   *Credit:* Sales Account

Reason: The Cash Account receives the cash from the sale of goods and the Sales Account is credited because it is the giving or supplying account.

Entry 7

Some goods are sold on credit terms to Sarah.

> *Debit*: Sarah's Account   *Credit:* Sales Account

Reason: Sarah's Account is debited because she is receiving the goods, and the Sales Account is credited because it is supplying (or giving) them.

it is receiving something, but then that applies to any entry in any account. So in the case of the sales account, regard it as a *supplying* account because it gives (or releases) something to another account.

<table>
<tr><td>**Activity 3.3**</td><td colspan="4">Is there anything wrong with the following abbreviated bank account?</td></tr>
</table>

Debit		£	Credit		£
		000			000
10.3.16	Wages paid	1000	6.6.16	Interest received	500

If you find this concept difficult to understand, think of the effect on the opposite account. A cash sale, for example, results in cash being increased. The cash in hand account must, therefore, be the *receiving* account and it must be debited. Somebody (say, Mr Jones) must have given the cash, but a cash sale is credited straight to the sales account as the *supplying* account. If the sales had been sold to Mr Jones on credit, his account would have been debited (because his account is the *receiving* account) and credited to sales (again because it is the *supplying* account).

<table>
<tr><td>**Activity 3.4**</td><td>

State which account should be debited and which account should be credited in respect of each of the following transactions:

(a) cash paid to a supplier
(b) office rent paid by cheque
(c) cash sales
(d) dividend received by electronic bank transfer.

</td></tr>
</table>

A ledger account example

This section illustrates the procedure adopted in entering various transactions in ledger accounts. It brings together the basic material covered in the earlier part of this chapter. It also demonstrates the use of various accounts as well as the debiting and crediting effect of different types of transactions.

<table>
<tr><td>**Example 3.2**</td><td>

Joe Simple: a sole trader

The following information relates to Joe Simple, who started a new business on 1 January 2017:

1.1.17 Joe started the business with £5000 in cash.
3.1.17 He paid £3000 of the cash into a business bank account.
5.1.17 Joe bought a van for £2000 paying by cheque.
7.1.17 He bought some goods, paying £1000 in cash.
9.1.17 Joe sold some of the goods, receiving £1500 in cash.

Required
Enter the above transactions into Joe's ledger accounts.

</td></tr>
</table>

Answer to
Example 3.2

Joe Simple's books of account

Cash in hand account (£)

1.1.17	Capital (1)	5000	3.1.17	Cash at bank (2)	3000
9.1.17	Sales (5)	1500	7.1.17	Purchases (4)	1000

Capital account (£)

1.1.17	Cash in hand (1)	5000

Cash at bank account (£)

3.1.17	Cash in hand (2)	3000	5.1.17	Van (3)	2000

Van account (£)

5.1.17	Cash at bank (3)	2000

Purchases account (£)

7.1.17	Cash in hand (4)	1000

Sales account (£)

9.1.17	Cash in hand (5)	1500

Tutorial notes

1 The numbers in brackets after each entry refer to the example notes; they have been inserted for tutorial guidance only.

2 The narration relates to that account in which the equal and opposite entry may be found.

After entering all the transactions for a particular period in appropriate ledger accounts, the next stage in the exercise is to calculate the balance on each account at the end of an accounting period. We show you how to do this in the next section.

Balancing the accounts

During a particular accounting period, some accounts (such as the cash at bank and cash in hand accounts) will include a great many debit and credit entries. Some accounts may be made up of mainly debit entries (e.g. the purchases account) or largely credit entries (e.g. the sales account). It would be somewhat inconvenient to allow the entries (whether mainly debits, credits or a mixture of both) to build up without occasionally striking a balance. Furthermore, the owner will almost certainly want to know not just what is in each account, but also its overall or *net* balance (i.e. the total of all the debit entries less the total of all the credit entries). So in order to meet these requirements, it will be necessary to calculate the balance on each account on a regular basis.

Balancing an account requires the bookkeeper to add up all the respective debit and credit entries, take one total away from the other and arrive at the net balance.

Accounts may be balanced fairly frequently, e.g. once a week or once a month, but some entities may only do so when they prepare their annual accounts. In order to keep a tight control on the management of the business, it is advisable to balance the accounts at reasonably short intervals. The frequency will depend on the nature and the size of the entity but once a month is probably sufficient for most entities.

The balancing of the accounts is part of the double-entry procedure and the method is quite formal. In Example 3.3 we show how to balance an account with a *debit* balance (i.e. when the total debit entries exceed the total credit entries).

Example 3.3 demonstrates how an account with a debit entry is balanced. In Example 3.4 we illustrate a similar procedure, but this time the account has a *credit* balance.

Example 3.3

Balancing an account with a debit balance

Cash in hand account (£)

1.1.17	Sales (1)	2000	10.1.17	Jones (1)	3000
15.1.17	Rent received (1)	1000	25.1.17	Davies (1)	5000
20.1.17	Smith (1)	4000			
31.1.17	Sales (1)	8000	31.1.17	Balance c/d (2)	7000
	(3)	15000		(3)	15000
1.2.17	Balance b/d (4)	7000			

Note: The number shown after each narration relates to the tutorial notes.

Tutorial notes

1 The total debit entries equal £15,000 (2000 + 1000 + 4000 + 8000). The total credit entries equal £8000 (3000 + 5000). The net balance on this account, therefore, at 31 January 2017 is a *debit balance* of £7000 (15,000 − 8000). Until both, the debit and the credit entries, have been totalled, of course, it will not usually be apparent whether the balance is a debit one or a credit one. However, it should be noted that there can never be a credit balance in a cash account, because it is impossible to pay out more cash than has been received.

2 The debit balance of £7000 is inserted on the *credit* side of the account at the time that the account is balanced (in this case, at 31 January 2017). This then enables the total of the credit column to be balanced so that it agrees with the total of the debit column. The abbreviation 'c/d' means carried down. In this example the debit balance is carried down in the account in order to start the new period on 1 February 2017.

3 The £15,000 shown as a total in both the debit and the credit columns demonstrates that the columns balance (they do so, of course, because £7000 has been inserted in the credit column to make them balance). The totals are double-underlined in order to signify that they are a final total.

4 The balancing figure of £7000 is brought down ('b/d') in the account to start the new period on 1 February 2017.

Example 3.4

Balancing an account with a credit balance

Scott's account (£)

31.1.17	Cash at bank (1)	20000	15.1.17	Purchases (1)	10000
31.1.17	Balance c/d (2)	5000	20.1.17	Purchases (1)	15000
	(3)	25000		(3)	25000
			1.2.17	Balance b/d (4)	5000

Note: The number shown after each narration relates to the tutorial notes below.

Tutorial notes to Example 3.4

1 Apart from the balance, there is only one debit entry in Scott's account: the cash at bank entry of £20,000. The total credit entries amount to £25,000 (10,000 + 15,000). Scott has a *credit balance,* therefore, in his account as at 31 January 2017 of £5000 (10,000 + 15,000 − 20,000). With many more entries in the account it would not always be possible to tell immediately whether the balance was a debit one or a credit one.

2 The credit balance of £5000 at 31 January 2017 is inserted on the *debit* side of the account in order to enable the account to be balanced. The balance is then carried down (c/d) to the next period.

The £25,000 shown as the total for both the debit and the credit columns shows that the account balances. This has been made possible because of the insertion of the £5,000 balancing figure on the debit side of the account.

3 The balancing figure of £5000 is brought down (b/d) in the account in order to start the account in the new period beginning on 1 February 2017.

Activity 3.5

Write down in your notebook what is meant by

(a) an account having a debit balance
(b) an account having a credit balance.

The next stage after balancing each account is to check that the double-entry procedure has been completed throughout the entire bookkeeping system. This is done by compiling what is known as a *trial balance*.

The trial balance

A trial balance (TB) is a working paper compiled at the end of a specific accounting period. It does not form part of the double-entry procedure. It has three main purposes: (1) to check that all of the transactions for a particular period have been entered correctly in the ledger system; (2) to confirm that the balance on each account is correct and (3) to assist in the preparation of the financial statements.

The trial balance lists each debit and each credit balance in columns side by side. The total of each column is then added up. If the two totals agree, we can be reasonably confident that the double-entry procedures have been carried out correctly. There are, however, some errors that do not show up. We will explain what they are later in the chapter.

We show how to prepare a trial balance in Example 3.5.

Example 3.5

Edward – compilation of a trial balance

Edward started a new business on 1 January 2017. The following transactions took place during his first month in business.

1.1.17   Edward commenced business with £10,000 in cash.

3.1.17   He paid £8000 of the cash into a business bank account.

6.1.17   He bought a van on credit from Perkin's garage for £3000.

9.1.17   Edward rented shop premises for £1000 per quarter; he paid for the first quarter immediately by cheque.

12.1.17 He bought goods on credit from Roy Limited for £4000.

15.1.17 He paid shop expenses amounting to £1500 by cheque.

18.1.17 Edward sold goods on credit to Scott and Company for £3000.

21.1.17 He settled Perkin's account by cheque.

24.1.17 Edward received a cheque from Scott and Company for £2000; this cheque was paid immediately into the bank.

27.1.17 Edward sent a cheque to Roy Limited for £500.

31.1.17 Goods costing £3000 were purchased from Roy Limited on credit.

31.1.17 Cash sales for the month amounted to £2000.

Required

(a) Enter the above transactions in appropriate ledger accounts, balance off each account as at 31 January 2017 and bring down the balances as at that date.

(b) Extract a trial balance as at 31 January 2017.

Answer to Example 3.5(a)

Cash in hand account (£)

1.1.17	Capital (1)	10000	3.1.17	Cash at bank (2)	8000
31.1.17	Sales (12)	2000	31.1.17	Balance c/d	4000
		12000			12000
1.2.17	Balance b/d	4000			

Capital account

		£			£
			1.1.17	Cash in hand (1)	10000

Cash at bank account

		£			£
3.1.17	Cash in hand (2)	8000	9.1.17	Rent payable (4)	1000
24.1.17	Scott and Company (9)	2000	15.1.17	Shop expenses (6)	1500
			21.1.17	Perkin's Garage (8)	3000
			27.1.17	Roy Limited (10)	500
			31.1.17	Balance c/d	4000
		10000			10000
1.2.17	Balance b/d	4000			

Van account (£)

6.1.17	Perkin's Garage (3)	3000			

Perkin's Garage account (£)

21.1.17	Cash at bank (8)	3000	6.1.17	Van (3)	3000

Rent payable account (£)

9.1.17	Cash at bank (4)	1000			

Purchases account (£)

12.1.17	Roy Limited (5)	4000			
31.1.17	Roy Limited (11)	3000	31.1.17	Balance c/d	7000
		7000			7000
1.2.17	Balance b/d	7000			

Roy Limited account (£)

27.1.17	Cash at bank (10)	500	12.1.17	Purchases (5)	4000
31.1.17	Balance c/d	6500	31.1.17	Purchases (11)	3000
		7000			7000
			1.2.17	Balance b/d	6500

Shop expenses account

		£			£
15.1.17	Cash at bank (6)	1500			

Sales account (£)

			18.1.17	Scott & Company (7)	3000
31.1.17	Balance c/d	5000	31.1.17	Cash in hand (12)	2000
		5000			5000

Scott and Company account

		£			£
18.1.17	Sales (7)	3000	24.1.17	Cash at bank (9)	2000
			31.1.17	Balance c/d	1000
		3000			3000
1.2.17	Balance b/d	1000			

Tutorial notes

1 The number shown after each narration has been inserted for tutorial guidance only in order to illustrate the insertion of each entry in the appropriate account.

2 There is no need to balance an account and carry down the balance when there is only a single entry in one account (see Edward's capital account).

3 Note that some accounts may not have a balance (e.g. Perkin's Garage account).

Answer to Example 3.5(b)

Trial balance at 31 January 2017

	Dr(£)	Cr (£)
Cash in hand	4000	
Capital		10000
Cash at bank	4000	
Van	3000	
Rent payable	1000	
Purchases	7000	
Roy Limited		6500
Shop expenses	1500	
Sales		5000
Scott and Company	1000	
	21500	21500

Tutorial notes

1   The total debit balance agrees with the total credit balance and so the trial balance balances, thus confirming that the transactions appear to have been entered in the books of account correctly.

2   The total amount of £21,500 shown in both the debit and credit columns of the trial balance does not have any significance except to prove that the trial balance balances.

Trial balance errors

A trial balance confirms that the books of account balance arithmetically. This means that the following procedures have all been carried out correctly:

- for every debit entry there appears to be a credit entry – a cardinal rule in double-entry bookkeeping;
- the value for each debit and credit entry has been entered in different accounts;
- the balance on each account has been calculated, extracted and entered correctly in the trial balance;
- the debit and credit columns in the trial balance are the same.

As we indicated earlier, there are, however, some errors that are not disclosed by the trial balance. They are as follows.

- *Omission*: a transaction could have been completely omitted from the books of account.
- *Complete reversal of entry*: a transaction could have been entered in (say) Account A as a debit and in Account B as a credit, when it should have been entered as a credit in Account A and as a debit in Account B.
- *Principle*: a transaction may have been entered in the wrong *type* of account, e.g. the purchase of a new delivery van may have been debited to the purchases account instead of to the delivery vans account.
- *Commission*: a transaction may have been entered in the correct type of account but in the wrong *personal* account, e.g. in Bill's account instead of in Ben's account.
- *Compensating*: an error may have been made in (say) adding the debit side of one account and an identical error made in adding the credit side of another account; the two errors would then cancel each other out.
- *Original entry*: a transaction may have been entered incorrectly in both accounts, e.g. as £291 instead of as £921.

Such errors may only be discovered if some transactions are double-checked later on in the period. They may also become apparent when the financial statements are prepared and the results are compared with previous periods. Similarly, some errors may also come to light if they affect creditor and debtor balances and suppliers and customers begin to complain about unpaid or incorrect invoices. Notwithstanding these possible errors, the compilation of a trial balance is still useful because:

- the arithmetical accuracy of the entries made in the books of account can be confirmed;
- the balance owed or owing on each account can easily be extracted;
- the preparation of the financial statements is simplified.

Activity 3.6	State whether each of the following errors would be discovered as a result of preparing a trial balance.

    (a) £342 has been entered in both ledger accounts instead of £432.   *Yes/No*

    (b) The debit column in Prim's account has been overstated by £50.   *Yes/No*

    (c) £910 has been put in Anne's account instead of Agnes's.   *Yes/No*

Computerisation

The manual process described above continues to be used by some small business. By and large, however, companies now use computer software (such as SAGE, PeopleSoft, Oracle, SAP and others) to maintain and store their accounting records. The principles of double-entry bookkeeping underpin the way records are kept in those systems and as managers you need to understand what the process is and how errors can arise at each stage so that you can critically evaluate accounting information presented to you and spot errors. You will also need to consider the security of the information and its integrity. In the past few years cloud accounting has become increasingly popular. This is where accounting records are kept in 'the cloud' and can be accessed from anywhere (just like you keeping your files on Dropbox or Google Docs).

News clip

Cloud accounting gathering momentum

The UK subscriber numbers of the cloud accounting services provider Xero reaches 100,000. 'This means that the scale of Xero's customer base is now approaching the size of the installed base of the United Kingdom's largest legacy accounting software product, and that adoption of cloud and mobile-centric products like Xero has now become the norm among small businesses,' said managing director Gary Turner.

Source: Adapted from *Accountancy Age*, 30 September 2015.

 Questions you should ask

As a non-accountant it is highly unlikely that you will become involved in the detailed recording, extraction and summary of basic accounting information. Your particular responsibility as a senior manager will be to ensure that the following points are ensured:

• adequate accounting records are kept;

• they are accurate;

• appropriate financial statements (as required by any legislation) can be prepared from such records.

As a minimum you should ensure that the accounting records are capable of dealing with all cash received and paid by the entity and that they contain details of all its assets and liabilities.

In order to satisfy yourself about these requirements you should ask the following questions.

- Do we use a double-entry bookkeeping system?
- If not, why not?
- Is it a manual or a computerised one?
- Does the system include a cash book in which all cash in hand and cash at bank transactions are entered?
- Is the balance shown in the cash book checked regularly against the balance disclosed in the bank statements sent by our bank?
- Is a separate account kept for each identifiable group of non-current assets, current assets and current liabilities?
- What is included in such groups?
- Is a balance calculated regularly for each of the accounts?
- How often is a trial balance prepared?
- What steps are taken to ensure that errors not disclosed in a trial balance are minimised?
- What is the system for the separation of duties affecting the recording of the accounting information and the preparation of the trial balance?
- Does a senior manager (not involved with the accounting function) receive a copy of the trial balance? What checks do they perform or what questions do they ask when they review the trial balance?

Conclusion

This book is specifically aimed at non-accountants. In this chapter we have deliberately avoided going into too much detail about double-entry bookkeeping. In your managerial role you will almost certainly be supplied with information that has been extracted from a ledger system. In order to assess its real benefit to you, we believe that it is important that you should know something about where it has come from, what it means and what reliability can be placed on it.

The chapter has, therefore, covered the following features of a double-entry bookkeeping system:

- the accounting equation;
- the type of accounts generally used in practice;
- the meaning of the terms 'debit' and 'credit';
- the definition of the terms 'debtor' and 'creditor';
- the method of entering transactions in ledger accounts;
- the balancing of ledger accounts;
- the compilation of a trial balance.

Key points	
	1 The accounting equation is represented by the formula: assets = capital + liabilities. It underpins the dual aspect rule and it forms the basis of a conventional accounting recording system.
	2 An account is an explanation, a record or a history of a particular event.
	3 A book of account is known as a ledger.
	4 A transaction is the carrying out and the performance of a particular business activity or event.
	5 All transactions have a two-fold effect.
	6 A double-entry system records that two-fold effect.
	7 A debit means that a transaction is received into an account.
	8 A credit means that a transaction is given by an account.
	9 Debits are entered on the left-hand side of an account.
	10 Credits are entered on the right-hand side of an account.
	11 For every debit entry, there must be a credit entry.
	12 Accounts are balanced periodically.
	13 The accuracy of the bookkeeping is tested by preparing a trial balance.
	14 The trial balance does not reveal all possible bookkeeping errors.

Check your learning

1 What is the accounting equation?

2 What is the basic rule of double-entry bookkeeping?

3 What is an account?

4 What is a ledger?

5 What is meant by the terms 'debit' and 'credit'?

6 What factor would indicate whether or not a new account should be opened?

7 What distinguishes a cash in hand account from a cash at bank account?

8 What are the following accounts used for: (a) capital; (b) trade creditors; (c) trade debtors; (d) stock; (e) sales; (f) purchases and (g) dividends?

9 What is the difference between a discounts allowed account and a discounts received account?

10 What must there be for (a) every debit and (b) every credit?

11 What is (a) a debit balance and (b) a credit balance?

12 What is a trial balance?

13 Name three main functions that it fulfils.

14 List six bookkeeping errors that a trial balance does not detect.

News story quiz

Remember the news story at the beginning of this chapter? Go back to that story and reread it before answering the following questions.

The way in which accounting records are kept has remained essentially the same for over five centuries but is that way of keeping records still fit for purpose?

Questions

1 Why do you think the way accounting records are kept is still the same as that adopted by the merchants of Venice in the fifteenth century?

2 What do you think is the role of computers in the maintenance of accounting records? Do we still need accountants if most of the accounting nowadays is processed on a computer?

3 What do you think would be your responsibility as managers for the integrity of accounting information and the security of computer systems?

Tutorial questions

The answers to questions marked with an asterisk can be found in Appendix 4.

3.1 Do you think that non-accounting managers need to know anything about double-entry bookkeeping?

3.2 Is Freda right?

'My accountant has got it all wrong', argued Freda. 'She's totally mixed up all her debits and credits.'
'But what makes you say that?' queried Dora.
'Oh! I've only to look at my bank statement to see that she's wrong,' responded Freda. 'I know I've got some money in the bank, and yet she tells me I'm in debit when she means I'm in credit.'

3.3 'Double-entry bookkeeping is a waste of time and money because everything has to be recorded twice.' Discuss.

3.4* Adam has just gone into business. The following is a list of his transactions for the month of January 2017:

(a) Cash paid into the business by Adam.
(b) Goods for resale purchased on cash terms.
(c) Van bought for cash.
(d) One quarter's rent for premises paid in cash.
(e) Some goods sold on cash terms.
(f) Adam buys some office machinery for cash.

Required
State which account in Adam's books of account should be debited and which account should be credited for each transaction.

3.5* The following is a list of Brown's transactions for February 2017:

(a) Transfer of cash to a bank account.
(b) Cash received from sale of goods.
(c) Purchase of goods paid for by cheque.
(d) Office expenses paid in cash.
(e) Cheques received from customers from sale of goods on cash terms.
(f) A motor car for use in the business paid for by cheque.

Required
State which account in Brown's books of account should be debited and which account should be credited for each transaction.

3.6 Corby is in business as a retail distributor. The following is a list of his transactions for March 2017:

(a) Goods purchased from Smith on credit.
(b) Corby introduces further capital in cash into the business.
(c) Goods sold for cash.
(d) Goods purchased for cash.
(e) Cash transferred to the bank.
(f) Machinery purchased, paid for in cash.

Required
State which account in Corby's books of account should be debited and which account should be credited for each transaction.

3.7 Davies buys and sells goods on cash and credit terms. The following is a list of her transactions for April 2017:

(a) Capital introduced by Davies paid into the bank.
(b) Goods purchased on credit terms from Swallow.
(c) Goods sold to Hill for cash.
(d) Cash paid for purchase of goods.
(e) Dale buys goods from Davies on credit.
(f) Motoring expenses paid by cheque.

Required
State which account in Davies' books of account should be debited and which account should be credited for each transaction.

3.8 The following transactions relate to Gordon's business for the month of July 2016:

(a) Bought goods on credit from Watson.
(b) Sold some goods for cash.
(c) Sold some goods on credit to Moon.
(d) Sent a cheque for half the amount owing to Watson.
(e) Watson grants Gordon a cash discount.
(f) Moon settles most of his account in cash.

(g) Gordon allows Moon a cash discount that covers the small amount owed by Moon.

(h) Gordon purchases some goods for cash.

Required

State which account in Gordon's books of accounts should be debited and which account should be credited for each transaction.

3.9 Harry started a new business on 1 January 2017. The following transactions cover his first three months in business:

(a) Harry contributed an amount in cash to start the business.

(b) He transferred some of the cash to a business bank account.

(c) He paid an amount in advance by cheque for rental of business premises.

(d) Bought goods on credit from Paul.

(e) Purchased a van paying by cheque.

(f) Sold some goods for cash to James.

(g) Bought goods on credit from Nancy.

(h) Paid motoring expenses in cash.

(i) Returned some goods to Nancy.

(j) Sold goods on credit to Mavis.

(k) Harry withdrew some cash for personal use.

(l) Bought goods from David paying in cash.

(m) Mavis returns some goods.

(n) Sent a cheque to Nancy.

(o) Cash received from Mavis.

(p) Harry receives a cash discount from Nancy.

(q) Harry allows Mavis a cash discount.

(r) Cheque withdrawn at the bank in order to open a petty cash account.

Required

State which account in Harry's books of account should be debited and which account should be credited for each transaction.

3.10* The following is a list of transactions which relate to Ivan for the first month that he is in business:

1.9.16	Started the business with £10,000 in cash.
2.9.16	Paid £8000 into a business bank account.
3.9.16	Purchased £1000 of goods in cash.
10.9.16	Bought goods costing £6000 on credit from Roy.
12.9.16	Cash sales of £3000.
15.9.16	Goods sold on credit terms to Norman for £4000.
20.9.16	Ivan settles Roy's account by cheque.
30.9.16	Cheque for £2000 received from Norman.

Required

Enter the above transactions in Ivan's ledger accounts.

3.11*Jones has been in business since 1 October 2016. The following is a list of her transactions for October 2016:

1.10.16	Capital of £20,000 paid into a business bank account.
2.10.16	Van purchased on credit from Lang for £5000.
6.10.16	Goods purchased on credit from Green for £15,000.
10.10.16	Cheque drawn on the bank for £1000 in order to open a petty cash account.
14.10.16	Goods sold on credit for £6000 to Haddock.
18.10.16	Cash sales of £5000.
20.10.16	Cash purchases of £3000.
22.10.16	Miscellaneous expenses of £500 paid out of petty cash.
25.10.16	Lang's account settled by cheque.
28.10.16	Green allows Jones a cash discount of £500.
29.10.16	Green is sent a cheque for £10,000.
30.10.16	Haddock is allowed a cash discount of £600.
31.10.16	Haddock settles his account in cash.

Required

Enter the above transactions in Jones's ledger accounts.

3.12 The transactions listed below relate to Ken's business for the month of November 2016:

1.11.16	Started the business with £150,000 in cash.
2.11.16	Transferred £14,000 of the cash to a business bank account.
3.11.16	Paid rent of £1000 by cheque.
4.11.16	Bought goods on credit from the following suppliers:

Ace	£5000
Mace	£6000
Pace	£7000

10.11.16	Sold goods on credit to the following customers:

Main	£2000
Pain	£3000
Vain	£4000

15.11.16	Returned goods costing £1000 to Pace.
22.11.16	Pain returned goods sold to him for £2000.
25.11.16	Additional goods purchased from the following suppliers:

Ace	£3000
Mace	£4000
Pace	£5000

26.11.16	Office expenses of £2000 paid by cheque.
27.11.16	Cash sales for the month amounted to £5000.

28.11.16	Purchases paid for in cash during the month amounted to £4000.	
29.11.16	Cheques sent to the following suppliers:	
	Ace	£4000
	Mace	£5000
	Pace	£6000
30.11.16	Cheques received from the following customers:	
	Main	£1000
	Pain	£2000
	Vain	£3000
30.11.16	The following cash discounts were claimed by Ken:	
	Ace	£200
	Mace	£250
	Pace	£300
30.11.16	The following cash discounts were allowed by Ken:	
	Main	£100
	Pain	£200
	Vain	£400
30.11.16	Cash transfer to the bank of £1000.	

Required

Enter the above transactions in Ken's ledger accounts.

3.13* The following transactions relate to Pat's business for the month of December 2016:

1.12.16	Started the business with £10,000 in cash.	
2.12.16	Bought goods on credit from the following suppliers:	
	Grass	£6000
	Seed	£7000
10.12.16	Sold goods on credit to the following customers:	
	Fog	£3000
	Mist	£4000
12.12.16	Returned goods to the following suppliers:	
	Grass	£1000
	Seed	£2000
15.12.16	Bought additional goods on credit from Grass for £3000 and from Seed for £4000.	
20.12.16	Sold more goods on credit to Fog for £2000 and to Mist for £3000.	
24.12.16	Paid office expenses of £5000 in cash.	
29.12.16	Received £4000 in cash from Fog and £6000 in cash from Mist.	
31.12.16	Pat paid Grass and Seed £6000 and £8000, respectively, in cash.	

Required

(a) Enter the above transactions in Pat's ledger accounts.

(b) Balance off the accounts as at 31 December 2016.

(c) Bring down the balances as at 1 January 2017.

(d) Compile a trial balance as at 31 December 2016.

3.14* Vale has been in business for some years. The following balances were brought forward in his books of account as at 1 January 2016:

	Dr (£)	Cr (£)
Bank	5000	
Capital		20000
Cash	1000	
Dodd		2000
Fish	6000	
Furniture	10000	
	22000	22000

During the year to 31 December 2016 the following transactions took place:

1 Goods bought from Dodd on credit for £30,000.
2 Cash sales of £20,000.
3 Cash purchases of £15,000.
4 Goods sold to Fish on credit for £50,000.
5 Cheques sent to Dodd totalling £29,000.
6 Cheques received from Fish totalling £45,000.
7 Cash received from Fish amounting to £7000.
8 Office expenses paid in cash totalling £9000.
9 Purchase of delivery van costing £12,000 paid by cheque.
10 Cash transfers to bank totalling £3000.

Required

(a) Compile Vale's ledger accounts for the year 31 December 2016, balance off the accounts and bring down the balances as at 1 January 2017.

(b) Extract a trial balance as at 31 December 2016.

3.15 Brian started in business on 1 January 2017. The following is a list of his transactions for his first month of trading:

1.1.17	Opened a business bank account with £25,000 obtained from private resources.
2.1.17	Paid one month's rent of £2000 by cheque.
3.1.17	Bought goods costing £5000 on credit from Linda.
4.1.17	Purchased motor car from Savoy Motors for £4000 on credit.
5.1.17	Purchased goods costing £3000 on credit from Sydney.
10.1.17	Cash sales of £6000.
15.1.17	More goods costing £10 000 purchased from Linda on credit.

20.1.17	Sold goods on credit to Ann for £8000.
22.1.17	Returned £2000 of goods to Linda.
23.1.17	Paid £6000 in cash into the bank.
24.1.17	Ann returned £1000 of goods.
25.1.17	Withdrew £500 in cash from the bank to open a petty cash account.
26.1.17	Cheque received from Ann for £5500; Ann also claimed a cash discount of £500.
28.1.17	Office expenses of £250 paid out of petty cash.
29.1.17	Sent a cheque to Savoy Motors for £4000.
30.1.17	Cheques sent to Linda and Sydney for £8000 and £2000, respectively. Cash discounts were also claimed from Linda and Sydney of £700 and £100, respectively.
31.1.17	Paid by cheque another month's rent of £2000.
31.1.17	Brian introduced £5000 additional capital into the business by cheque.

Required
(a) Enter the above transactions in Brian's ledger accounts for January 2017, balance off the accounts and bring down the balances as at 1 February 2017.
(b) Compile a trial balance as at 31 January 2017.

3.16 An accounts clerk has compiled Trent's trial balance as at 31 March 2017 as follows:

	Dr (£)	Cr (£)
Cash at bank	2000	
Capital	50 000	
Discounts allowed		5 000
Discounts received	3 000	
Dividends received	2 000	
Drawings		23 000
Investments		14000
Land and buildings	60000	
Office expenses	18000	
Purchases	75000	
Sales		250000
Suspense (unexplained balance)		6000
Rates		7000
Vans	20000	
Van expenses		5000
Wages and salaries	80000	
	310 000	310 000

Required
Compile Trent's corrected trial balance as at 31 March 2017.

3.17 Donald's transactions for the month of March 2017 are as follows:

Item	£
Cash receipts	
Capital contributed	6000
Sales to customers	3000
Cash payments	
Goods for sale	4000
Stationery	500
Postage	300
Travelling	600
Wages	2900
Transfers to bank	500
Bank receipts	
Receipts from trade debtors	
Smelt	3000
Tait	9000
Ure	5000
Bank payments	
Payments to trade creditors:	
Craig	2800
Dobie	5000
Elgin	6400
Rent and rates	3200
Electricity	200
Telephone	100
Salaries	2000
Miscellaneous expenses	600
Other transactions	
Goods purchased from:	
Craig	3500
Dobie	7500
Elgin	7500
Goods returned to Dobie	400
Goods sold to:	
Smelt	4000
Tait	10 000
Ure	8 000
Goods returned by Ure	900

Item	£
Discounts allowed:	
Smelt	200
Tait	500
Ure	400
Discounts received:	
Craig	50
Dobie	100
Elgin	200

Required
(a) Enter the above transactions in appropriate ledger accounts.
(b) Balance each account as at 31 March 2017.
(c) Extract a trial balance as at that date.

Website

Further practice questions, study material and links to relevant sites on the World Wide Web can be found on the website that accompanies this book. The site can be found at www.pearsoned.co.uk/dyson

Sole trader accounts

Another tale of woe

ANZ flags increase in bad debts amid commodity price slump

Shares in ANZ Banking Group slumped more than 5 per cent and are leading peers lower after the Australian lender flagged an increase in bad debts.

The expected A$100m ($75m) increase in bad debts stems from funding to Australian and multi-national resources-related companies, which have come under pressure due to the fall in commodity prices, writes Peter Wells.

In its first-quarter trading update on February 17, ANZ said its total credit charge was expected to be 'over [A]$800m for the first half of 2016' as it flagged rising bad debts in its south-east Asian loan book.

But some of that was also due to loans extended to resources companies. That total figure is now expected to rise by "at least [A]$100m" the bank said in a statement to the ASX today, owing to the difficulties resources-related companies are now facing.

Graham Hodges, the bank's chief financial officer, said today:

> While the overall credit environment remains broadly stable, we are continuing to see pockets of weakness associated with low commodity prices in the resources sector and in related businesses.

ANZ's revised bad debt figure follows a string of bad news for the bank. This month Australia's corporate regulator brought legal action against the bank for alleged manipulation of the country's benchmark interbank borrowing rate.

FT   *Source*: Reproduced with permission from www.ft.com, 24 March 2016.

Questions relating to this news story can be found on page 98 ➡

About this chapter

Chapter 3 finished by showing you how to prepare a trial balance. The trial balance has two main purposes: (1) to confirm that all transactions have been entered correctly in the double-entry system; and (2) to provide the information necessary to prepare an entity's basic financial statements. Such statements usually include a calculation of profit which is known as the statement of profit or loss, a statement of retained earnings showing how much of that profit the owners are reinvesting in the business and a calculation of the net assets the business has at a point in time known as the statement of financial position.

In this chapter we show you how to prepare such statements for a trading entity. A trading entity is a fairly simple organisation so it enables us to demonstrate the basic procedures without too many complications. The knowledge and experience that you gain from working your way through this chapter will then give you the foundation necessary to study more complex organisations.

<table>
<tr><td>

Learning objectives

</td><td>

By the end of this chapter you should be able to:

- prepare a simple set of financial statements for a trading entity;
- make adjustments in sets of financial statements for inventory, depreciation, accruals and prepayments, and bad and doubtful debts;
- list the main defects of historical cost accounting;
- explain why accounting profit is not the same as an increase in cash.

</td></tr>
</table>

Why this chapter is important

This chapter is important for non-accountants for the following reasons:

1 *To distinguish between capital and revenue items.* This is often a matter of judgement and it is not one that is always easy to make. You should not leave the decision entirely to your accountants because it has a major impact on the profit that your entity makes. Make sure that you get involved in the decision

2 *To be aware of the impact of subjective judgements on the accounts.* Subjective judgements are involved in preparing annual (or periodic) accounts. The main adjustments are for inventory, depreciation, accruals and prepayments, and bad and doubtful debts. The decisions that are taken can have significant effect on how much profit you make. So once again, don't leave it to your accountants to decide what to do.

3 *To understand that cash is not the same as profit.* It is vital that you understand the difference between *cash* and *profit*. If you don't, your entity is likely to go bankrupt. Just because you have made a profit doesn't necessarily mean that you've got the same amount of money in the bank. All sorts of adjustments are made to the cash position before accountants arrive at what is called 'profit'. Profit is *not,* repeat **NOT**, therefore, simply the difference between cash received less cash paid.

News clip

Banks to face €61.5bn hit from new accounting rules

New accounting rules could force Europe's top banks to recognise an extra €61.5bn in loan losses, new analysis shows. Spain's Caixa, Italy's UBI and the United Kingdom's Standard Chartered are the most affected by the change in the IFRS 9 rules. Banks that would see the slightest impact include Credit Suisse, UBS, Virgin Money and Nordea. While the rules do not come into force until 2018, Barclays said some banks with excess capital might 'soften the one-off impact' by taking higher provisions in 2016 and 2017.

Source: Adapted from www.ft.com, 1 September 2015.

Preparing basic financial statements

In this section we are going to explain how to prepare a basic set of financial statements for a sole trader. Such a set is usually made up of the following:

(a) a calculation of annual profit, which is known as the statement of profit or loss (SPL);

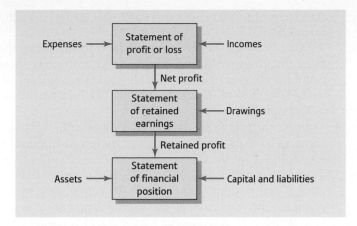

Figure 4.1 A trading entity's basic accounts

(b) a calculation of retained profit, which is known as the statement of retained earnings (SRE) and

(c) a statement showing the resources and sources of funding of the business at the year end known as the statement of financial position (SFP).

You can see how they relate to each other in Figure 4.1.

If an entity is trading in goods, a trading account may be used. The trading account is nothing more than the top section of the statement of profit or loss. There is no requirement to keep such an account, however. Sole traders are merely required to keep a record of all their incomes and expenses so that they can work out the profit on which they have to pay tax.

In order to keep our explanation simple, we are going to assume for the time being that once the trial balance has been prepared, no further adjustments are required. Then later on in the chapter we deal with a number of adjustments that usually have to be made at the period end (it is usually a year). In practice, the trial balance would normally be prepared before any adjustments are allowed for. They would then be entered in the books of accounts once everything has been agreed for that year.

We suggest that you adopt the following approach if you become involved in the year-end procedures:

1   Double-check that your trial balance (TB) balances.
2   Go through the TB line by line, inserting against each balance 'C' (for a capital item), 'R' (for a revenue item) and 'D' (for distributions to owners).
    2.1 R: Revenue expenditure is expenditure that is likely to provide a benefit for just one period, such as rent and electricity costs. Revenue income includes income from sales, bank deposits, dividends received and rents.
    2.2 C: Capital expenditure is expenditure that is likely to provide a benefit to the entity for more than one accounting period, such as the acquisition of its resources – the assets. Capital items also include the sources of funding – the finance provided by the owners and long-term debt funding such as loans. It is not always easy to make a distinction between capital and revenue items and some difficult decisions may have to be taken.
    2.3 D: If the TB has a line for drawings, mark that with 'D'. These represent distribution made to owners out of profits.
3   Insert the 'R' balances in the calculation of profit or loss (the so-called statement of profit or loss). This allows you to calculate the profit for the year:
    3.1 Calculate the gross profit (or loss) by deducting the cost of inventory sold from the trading income generated from selling it. Gross profit is the first subtotal in the

statement of profit or loss and some sole traders may choose to keep it as a separate calculation.

3.2 Calculate the net profit (or net loss) by deducting the rest of the entity expenses from the gross profit and adding any non-trading income. The balance is the net profit for the year (it could be a net loss). That bottom-line profit figure is transferred to the statement of retained earnings. The recommended layout (or format) is shown in Example 4.1.

4 Transfer the profit calculated above and the 'D' balance in the statement of retained earnings to work out how much of the profit is reinvested back in the business. See Example 4.1 for the format.

5 Transfer the retained earnings calculated above and the 'C' balances to the statement of financial position. Separate all the capital employed balances (including the net profit for the year) from all the capital expenditure items and classify them as shown in Example 4.1. Balance the statement of financial of position (which some in the United Kingdom refer to as 'the balance sheet' because it does indeed balance).

Activity 4.1		
(a)	Accounting profit = cash received less cash paid	*True/false*
(b)	Capital expenditure is normally the difference between cash received and cash paid.	*True/false*
(c)	Capital expenditure only provides a short-term benefit.	*True/false*

Example 4.1

Preparation of basic financial statements

The following trial balance has been extracted from Bush's books of account as at 30 June 2016:

Name of account		Dr (£)	Cr (£)
Cash at bank (1)	(C)	5000	
Capital (2)	(C)		11000
Cash in hand (3)	(C)	1000	
Drawings (4)	(D)	8000	
Motor vehicle (5)	(C)	6000	
Transport expenses (6)	(R)	2000	
Office expenses (7)	(R)	3000	
Purchases of inventory (8)	(R)	30000	
Trade payables (9)	(C)		4000
Trade receivables (10)	(C)	10000	
Sales (11)	(R)		50000
		65000	65000

Notes:
There were no opening or closing inventory.
R = Revenue items; C = Capital balances.

Required
Prepare Bush's statement of profit or loss account and statement of retained earnings for the year to 30 June 2016 and a statement of financial position as at that date.

Answer to Example 4.1

Bush
Statement of profit or loss for the year to 30 June 2016

	£	£
Sales (11)		50 000
Less: cost of goods sold:		
Purchases (8)		(30 000)
Gross profit		20 000
Less: expenses		
Transport expenses (6)	2 000	
Office expenses (7)	3 000	(5 000)
Net profit for the year		15 000

Bush
Statement of retained earnings for the year to 30 June 2016

Net profit for the year*	15 000
Less: Drawings (4)	(8 000)
Retained earnings	7 000

Bush
Statement of financial position at 30 June 2016

	£	£
Non-current assets		
Motor vehicles (5)		6 000
Current assets		
Trade receivables (10)	10 000	
Cash (1+3)	6 000	16 000
		22 000
Equity		
Capital (2)	11 000	
Retained earnings**	7 000	18 000
Current liabilities		
Trade payables (9)		4 000
		22 000

Notes:
 * Obtained from the statement of profit or loss.
 ** Obtained from the statement of retained earnings.

The bracketed number after each narration refers to the account number of each balance extracted from the trial balance.

Tutorial notes

1 The statement of profit or loss covers a period of time. In this example it is for the year *to* (or, alternatively, *ending*) 30 June 2016. The statement of financial position is prepared at a particular moment in time. It depicts the balances as they were at a specific date. In this example they are shown as at 30 June 2016. The statement of retained earnings shows a movement over a period of time (and in effect reconciles the position at two specific dates as we will see in more advanced examples later).

2 The statements are presented in what is called the *vertical* format, i.e. on a line-by-line basis starting at the top of the page and working downwards. In the past there was also a *horizontal* format which is now rarely used so you do not need to worry about it.

3 The last line of the statement of retained earnings shows a profit which is being retained or reinvested in the business of £7,000. This balance remains within the accounting system and so it will be carried forward to the next accounting period. It must, therefore, be included in the statement of financial position otherwise the statement of financial position would not balance. You will find the £7,000 towards the bottom of the statement of financial position.

4 The statement of financial position is divided into two main sections. The first section shows the resources of Bush – its assets worth £22,000 at 30 June 2016. It is split between *non-current assets* of £6000, i.e. those assets that are intended for long-term use in the business, and current assets, i.e. those assets that are constantly being turned over and replaced such as inventory, receivables and cash.

5 The second section shows how the £28,000 of assets has been financed, i.e. where the money has come from (do you remember the accounting equation that Resources = Sources of Funding?). There were two sources: equity and debt. £11,000 contributed by the owner as capital. £7000 is the profit left in the business – the £15,000 profit made for the year less £8000 taken out (in the form of cash or goods) by Bush during the year, presumably in anticipation that the entity would make a profit. The retained profit, which is worked out in the statement of retained earnings, represents the profit reinvested in the business, hence – a source of funding. Both capital and retained earnings are equity sources of funding (provided by the owners) In addition, there are *current liabilities* of £4000, which is a source of debt funding (or borrowing). Current liabilities are amounts owing to various parties that will be due for payment within the next 12 months.

6 In a more detailed example the expense section in the statement of profit or loss and the non-current assets, current assets, current liabilities and equity section in the statement of financial position would include many more balances. The statement of profit or loss balances would be grouped in sections, e.g. administrative expenses or distribution costs. In the statement of financial position, both non-current asset and current asset balances would be shown in reverse order of liquidity – meaning those assets which will take the longest to turn into cash being placed first, e.g. property before machinery and inventory before receivables. Similarly, liabilities would be listed in reverse order of when they are due for repayment – those that are going to be paid *last* being placed *first,* e.g. long-term loans would be shown before short-term loans and short-term loans would come before payables. If there are a number of capital balances, they too would be placed on 'a last should be first' basis, i.e. capital would come before retained profits.

| Activity 4.2 | In what order should the following balances be shown in a statement of financial position? |

(a) furniture and fittings; land; plant and machinery; property;

(b) cash; insurance paid in advance; other receivables; trade receivables; inventory;

(c) bank overdraft; electricity owing; other payables; trade payables.

Year-end adjustments

We can now move on to deal with a number of year-end adjustments. These are events that are normally only made at the end of the year when the financial statements are being prepared. We are going to deal with four of them. They involve allowing for opening and closing inventories, writing off some capital expenditure, dealing with outstanding receivables and payables and making an allowance for likely bad and doubtful debts (see Figure 4.2).

We begin with inventory.

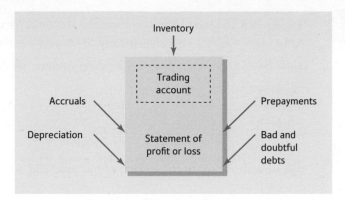

Figure 4.2 Main adjustments

Inventory

It is most unlikely that all the purchases that have been made during the year will have been sold by the end of it and so there will almost certainly be some goods still left in the stores. In accounting terminology, purchases still on hand at the period end are referred to as *inventory* (or *stock*).

When calculating the gross profit for the year, therefore, it is necessary to make some allowance for *closing* inventory, since we want to match the sales revenue earned for the period with the cost of goods sold and not the cost of all of those goods actually purchased during the year. This means that we have to check the quantity of inventory we have on hand at the end of the year and then put some value on it. In practice, this is an extremely difficult exercise. We shall be returning to it in a little more detail in Chapter 13. But we have another problem in dealing with inventory. Closing inventory at the end of one period becomes the opening inventory at the beginning of the next period so we have to allow for *opening* inventory as well. This means that the cost of goods sold is made up of three elements: opening inventory, purchases and closing inventory. Expressed as a formula, it is shown as:

> **Cost of goods sold = (opening inventory + purchases) − closing inventory**

By making an adjustment for opening and closing inventories, the top section of the statement of profit or loss (which some may show separately as a trading account) should now appear as in Example 4.2.

Example 4.2	**Example of a trading account with inventory adjustments**

	£	£
Sales		4 000
Less: Cost of goods sold		
Opening inventory	1 000	
Purchases	2 000	
	3 000	
Less: Closing inventory	(1 500)	(1 500)
Gross profit		2 500

<table>
<tr><td>Activity 4.3</td><td>Assume that Company A has a sales revenue of £10000 for the year. The opening inventory had a value of £2000 and during the year the company made purchases of £6000.

What would be the gross profit if the closing inventory was valued as follows?:

(a) £1500
(b) £2000
(c) £2500</td></tr>
</table>

We now move on to the second of our year-end adjustments: depreciation.

Depreciation

Expenditure that covers more than one accounting period is known as *capital expenditure*. Capital expenditure is not normally included in the statement of profit or loss but it would be misleading to exclude it altogether from the calculation of profit.

Expenditure on non-current assets (such as plant and machinery, motor vehicles and furniture) is necessary in order to help provide a general service to the business. The benefit received from the purchase of non-current assets must (by definition) extend beyond at least one accounting period. So the cost of the benefit provided by non-current assets ought to be charged to those accounting periods that benefit from such expenditure. The problem is in determining what charge to make. In accounting terminology, such a charge is known as *depreciation*.

News clip

Fractional ownership: appreciation of depreciation shapes an industry

Private flyers who are airborne at least 250 hours a year benefit from ownership of a whole aircraft. For those who fly between 50 and 250 hours – a part-ownership may be the way to go and NetJets, the global leader in long-term fractional ownership, caters for that market. But fractional ownership is expensive, not to mention that airplanes depreciate.

Source: Adapted from www.ft.com, 16 November 2015.

There is also another reason why non-current assets should be depreciated. By *not* charging each accounting period with some of the cost of non-current assets, the level of profit will be correspondingly higher and the owner would then be able to withdraw more profit from the business. If this happens, insufficient cash may be left in the business and the owner may then find it difficult to buy new non-current assets.

It is not easy to measure the benefit provided to each accounting period by some groups of non-current assets and most depreciation methods tend to be somewhat simplistic. The method most commonly adopted is known as *straight-line depreciation*. This method charges an equal amount of depreciation to each accounting period that benefits from the purchase of a non-current asset. The annual depreciation charge is calculated as follows:

$$\frac{\text{original cost of the asset} - \text{estimated residual value}}{\text{estimated life of the asset}}$$

The residual value is sometimes referred to as *scrap value*.

Another method that you might come across (although it is far less common than straight-line depreciation) is *reducing balance*. A percentage depreciation rate is applied to the original cost of the asset **after** deducting any depreciation charged in previous periods. Example 4.3 shows how both depreciation estimation calculations work.

The reducing balance method of calculating depreciation results in a much higher charge in the early life of the asset than does straight-line depreciation. So it is much more suitable for non-current assets such as vehicles because they tend to depreciate very quickly in the first two or three years.

You can see that in order to calculate the annual depreciation charge using either the straight-line method or the reducing balance method, it is necessary to work out (a) how long the asset is likely to last or be used by the business (known as its useful life) and (b) what it can be sold for.

It is customary to include non-current assets at their historic (i.e. original) cost in the statement of financial position but some non-current assets (such as property) may be revalued at regular intervals. If this is the case, the depreciation charge will be based on the revalued amount and not on the historic cost. It should also be noted that even if the asset is depreciated on the basis of its revalued amount, there is still no guarantee that it can be replaced at that amount. A combination of inflation and obsolescence may mean that the eventual replacement cost is far in excess of either the historic cost or the revalued amount. It follows that when the non-current asset eventually comes to be replaced, the entity may not have sufficient cash available to replace it.

Example 4.3	**Depreciating non-current assets**

A non-current asset bought on 1 January 2015 costs £1000. Assume that the residual value is nil and that the depreciation rate to be applied is 20%. The depreciation rate per year would then be as follows:

Straight-line method of depreciating non-current assets

Year		£
1. 01.15	Original cost	1000
31.12.15	**Depreciation charge for the year (20%)**	**(200)**
	Balance at end of year 2	800
31.12.16	**Depreciation charge for the year (20%)**	**(200)**
	Balance at end of year 2	600
31.12.17	**Depreciation charge for the year (20%)**	**(200)**
	Balance at end of year 3	400

Reducing balance method of depreciating non-current assets

Year		£
1.01.15	Original cost	1000
31.12.15	**Depreciation charge for the year (20%)**	**(200)**
	(Reduced) balance at end of year 1	800
31.12.16	**Depreciation charge for the year (20%)**	**(160)**
	(Reduced) balance at end of year 2	640
31.12.17	**Depreciation charge for the year (20%)**	**(128)**
	(Reduced) balance at end of year 3	512

Tutorial notes

1 Depreciation would be charged each year until eventually the original cost of the asset is written off completely. As you can see with the straight-line method, the same amount of depreciation is charged every year as the calculation is based on the original cost of the asset and is the same every time. With the reducing balance method the depreciation charge is different every year (and it is higher in the earlier years of the life of the asset) as the calculation is based on the reduced balance of the asset. That reduced balance is known as *net book value* (meaning the value of the asset net of depreciation for prior periods).

2 We have used a depreciation rate of 20% in this example in order to make it easier to follow. In practice, the depreciation rate would be calculated by using the formula:

$$r = 1 - \sqrt[n]{\frac{R}{C}}$$

where r = the depreciation rate to be applied; n = the estimated life of the asset; R = the residual (scrap) value and C = its historic cost.

Activity 4.4

The cost of a company's plant was £50,000. It was estimated that the plant would have a life of 20 years and that it could then be sold for £5000.

Using the straight-line method of depreciation, how much depreciation would you charge to the statement of profit or loss in Year 1?

The depreciation charge for the year is charged to the statement of profit or loss as an expense. The statement of financial position would include the following details for each group of non-current assets:

1 the historic cost (or revalued amount), i.e. the gross book value (GBV);
2 the accumulated depreciation;
3 the net book value (NBV).

In other words, line 1 minus line 2 = line 3.

These statements of financial position requirements are illustrated in Example 4.4.

Example 4.4

Statement of financial position: disclosure of non-current assets

Non-current assets	Cost	Depreciation	Net book value
	£	£	£
Buildings	100 000	(30 000)	70 000
Equipment	40 000	(25 000)	15 000
Furniture	10 000	(7 000)	3 000
	150 000	(62 000)	88 000
Current assets			
Inventory		10 000	
Receivables		8 000	
Cash		2 000	
			20 000
			108 000

Activity 4.5	What depreciation policy would you recommend? (a) straight-line for all assets; (b) reducing balance for all assets; (c) reducing balance for certain types of non-current assets and straight-line for all other assets; (d) other methods (state what).
	Your answer:
	Why?

Accruals and prepayments

The third of our last-minute adjustments relates to accruals and prepayments.

News clip

Profit overstating scandal sends shares sliding

Tesco has been plunged deeper into crisis after it was forced to suspend four senior executives and call in investigators following the discovery that its profits had been artificially inflated by £250m. More than £2bn was wiped off the value of Britain's biggest retailer on Monday after its new chief executive told the City that forensic accountants and lawyers had been drafted in to scrutinise its books in the wake of a warning from a whistleblower that payments from suppliers were being misbooked and business costs were being glossed over. Tesco said the changes had misleadingly boosted profits by £250m in the first six months of the year.

Source: Adapted from theguardian.com, 22 September 2014.

We will deal with each of these adjustments separately.

Accruals

An accrual is an amount owing for a service provided during a particular accounting period but still unpaid for at the end of it. For example, the entity may have paid the last quarter's electricity bill one week before the year end. In its accounts for that year, therefore, it needs to allow for (or *accrue*) the amount that it will owe for the electricity consumed during the last week of the year. The amount due will normally be settled in cash a few days after the year end.

The accrual will be based on an estimate of the likely cost of one week's supply of electricity or as a proportion of the amount payable (if it has already received the invoice).

The accrual will be included in the amount charged to the statement of profit or loss for the period as part of the cost of the service provided. The formula is as follows:

> (amounts paid during the year + closing accruals) − opening accruals

The closing accruals will be shown on the statement of financial position as part of the current liabilities.

Activity 4.6

You owed £500 to the telephone company at 31 December 2016. During the year to 31 December 2017 you paid the company £4000. At 31 December 2017, you owed the company £1000.

What amount for telephone charges would you charge to the statement of profit or loss for the year to 31 December 2017?

Prepayments

A prepayment is an amount paid in cash during an accounting period for a service that will be provided in a subsequent period. For example, assume a company's year end is 31 December. It buys a van halfway through 2016 and licenses it for 12 months, so half of the fee paid will relate to 2016 and half to 2017. It is necessary, therefore, to adjust 2016's accounts so that only half of the fee is charged in that year. The other half will eventually be charged to 2017's accounts.

Prepayments made during the year will be deducted from the amount charged to the statement of profit or loss. The formula is as follows:

(amount paid during the year + opening prepayments) − closing prepayments

The closing prepayments will be shown in the statement of financial position as part of the current assets.

Activity 4.7

Jill had paid £3000 in advance for insurance at 31 December 2016. During the year to 31 December 2017 she paid the insurance company £10,000. At 31 December 2017 she estimated that she had paid £2000 for insurance cover that related to the following year.

What amount for insurance charges should Jill charge to her statement of profit or loss for the year to 31 December 2017?

Bad and doubtful debts

News clip

Debts and defaults – is the oil and gas sector running out of steam?

2016 is set to see the first wave of corporate bankruptcies in the oil and gas sector.

Globally, the oil and gas industry has issued $1.4 trillion of bonds and taken out a further $1.6 trillion in syndicated loans, driving the sector's combined debt to $3 trillion.

Further to a depressant effect on oil prices, it could unleash a tidal wave of corporate bankruptcies in the world's largest economy.

The question exercising the minds of economists and investors is the extent to which this contagion could metastasise beyond the energy sector, as banks cut off credit access, loans turn bad and financial conditions enter a critical tightening phase.

Source: Adapted from *The Telegraph,* 17 April 2016.

The fourth main adjustment made in finalising the annual accounts involves making adjustments for bad debts and an allowance for bad and doubtful debts.

The realisation rule allows us to claim profit for any goods that have been sold, even if the cash for them is not received until a later accounting period. This means that we are taking a risk in claiming the profit on those goods in the earlier period, even if the legal title has been passed to the customer. If the goods are not eventually paid for, we will have overestimated the profit for that earlier period. Fortunately, there is a technique whereby we can build in an allowance for any possible *bad debts*, as they are called. This is quite a tricky operation and so we will need to explain it in two stages: first, how to account for bad debts and, second, how to allow for the possibility that some debts may be *doubtful*.

Bad debts

Once it is clear that a debt is bad (i.e. it is highly unlikely it will ever be paid), then it must be written off to the statement of profit or loss immediately as an expense. This means that we have to charge it to the current year's statement of profit or loss even though it may relate to an earlier period. This is because it is usually impractical to change accounts once they have been finalised because the owner may have already taken his profit out of the business in cash. On the statement of financial position we then show trade receivables *after* deducting any bad debts that have been written off.

Activity 4.8	Gibson's trade receivables at 31 December 2016 amount to £75,000. One of the trade receivables has owed Gibson £5000 since 2014. Gibson thinks that the receivable now lives abroad in exile.
	Should Gibson write off the £5000 as a bad debt to the statement of profit or loss for the year to 31 December 2016? If so, which account should be debited and which account should be credited? And what amount for trade receivables should be shown in Gibson's statement of financial position at 31 December 2016?

Allowance for doubtful debts

The profit in future accounting periods would be severely distorted if the entity suffered a whole series of bad debts. So it seems prudent to allow for the possibility that some debts may become bad. We can do this by setting up a *allowance for* doubtful debts (an allowance is simply an estimate of the impact of something that is highly likely to happen) and debiting an annual charge to a special account. In order to calculate the allowance for doubtful charge, it is necessary to estimate first the likely level of irrecoverable debts. The estimate will normally be based on the experience that the entity has had in dealing with irrecoverable debts in the past. In simple bookkeeping exercises, the allowance is usually expressed as a percentage of the outstanding trade receivables.

The procedure is illustrated in Example 4.5.

Example 4.5	# Accounting for bad and doubtful debts

You are presented with the following information for Maxximmo Ltd for the year to 31 March 2017:

	£
Trade receivables at 1 April 2016	20000
Trade receivables at 31 March 2017	33000
Allowance for doubtful debts at 1 April 2016	1000

Note:

One of the outstanding receivables has been declared bankrupt and it is now certain that Maxximmo Ltd will not be able to recover £3000 which is owed to it. An allowance for doubtful debts is maintained equivalent to 5 per cent of the trade receivables as at the end of the year.

Required:
(a) Calculate the increase required in the allowance for doubtful debts account for the year to 31 March 2017.
(b) Show how both the trade receivables and the allowance for doubtful debts account would be featured in the statement of financial position at 31 March 2017.

Answer to Example 4.5(a)

	£
Trade receivables as at 31 March 2016	33 000
Less: Specific bad debts to be written off to the statement of profit or loss for the year to 31 March 2017	(3 000)
	30 000
Allowance required: 5% thereof	1 500
Less: Allowance at 1 April 2016	(1 000)
Increase in the allowance for doubtful debts account*	500

Note:

* This amount will be charged to the statement of profit or loss for the year to 31 March 2017

Tutorial notes

The balance on the allowance for doubtful debts account will be higher at 31 March 2017 than it was at 1 April 2016. This is because the level of trade receivables is higher at the end of 2017 than it was at the end of 2016. The required increase in the provision of £500 will be *debited* to the statement of profit or loss. If it had been possible to reduce the provision (because of a lower level of trade receivables at the end of 2017 compared with 2016), the decrease would have been *credited* to the statement of profit or loss.

Statement of financial position extract at 31 March 2017

	£	£
Current assets		
Trade receivables	30000	
Less: Allowance for doubtful debts	(1 500)	
		28 500

As a non-accountant it is important for you to grasp just two essential points about the treatment of bad debts and doubtful debts.

- A debt should never be written off until it is absolutely certain that it is bad, because once it is written off, it is highly unlikely that any further attempt will ever be made to recover it.
- It is prudent to allow for the possibility of some doubtful debts. Nevertheless, it is perhaps rather a questionable decision to reduce profit by an arbitrary amount, e.g. by guessing whether it should be 3 per cent or 5 per cent of outstanding receivables. Obviously, the level that you choose can have a big effect on the profit for the period in question.

Activity 4.9	Watson keeps an allowance for doubtful debts account. It is maintained at a level of 3 per cent of his total outstanding trade receivables as at the end of the year. The balance on the allowance account at 1 January 2017 was £9000. His trade receivables at 31 December 2017 amounted to £250,000.
	What balance on his allowance for doubtful debts does he need to carry forward as at 31 December 2017? What amount does he need to write off to the statement of profit or loss for that year? And will it increase or decrease his profit?

A comprehensive example

In this section, we bring together the material covered in this chapter in a comprehensive example.

Example 4.6	## Example of basic accounting procedures

Wayne has been in business for many years. His accountant has extracted the following trial balance from his books of account as at 31 March 2017:

	£	£
Cash at bank	1 200	
Capital		32 000
Cash in hand	300	
Drawings	5 000	
Insurance	2 000	
Office expenses	15 000	
Office furniture at cost	5 000	
Office furniture: accumulated depreciation at 1 April 2016		2 000
Allowance for doubtful debts at 1 April 2016		500
Purchases	55 000	
Salaries	25 000	
Sales		100 000
Inventory at 1 April 2016	10 000	
Trade payables		4 000
Trade receivables	20 000	
	138 500	138 500

Notes:

The following additional information is to be taken into account:

1 Inventory at 31 March 2017 was valued at £15,000.

2 The insurance included £500 worth of cover which related to the year to 31 March 2018.

3 Depreciation is charged on office furniture at 10 per cent per annum of its original cost (it is assumed not to have any residual value).

4 A bad debt of £1000 included in the trade receivables balance of £20,000 is to be written off.

5 The allowance for doubtful debts is to be maintained at a level of 5 per cent of outstanding trade receivables as at 31 March 2017, i.e. after excluding the bad debt referred to in note 4 above.

6 At 31 March 2017, there was an amount owing for salaries of £1000.

Required:

(a) Prepare Wayne's statement of profit or loss and statement of retained earnings for the year to 31 March 2017.

(b) Prepare a statement of financial position as at that date.

Answer to Example 4.6

Wayne

Statement of profit or loss for the year to 31 March 2017

	£	£	(Source of entry)
Sales		100 000	(TB)
Less: Cost of goods sold:			
Opening inventory	10 000		(TB)
Purchases	55 000		(TB)
	65 000		
Less: Closing inventory	(15 000)	(50,000)	(QN 1)
Gross profit		50,000	
Less: Expenses:			
Insurance (2000 − 500)	1 500		(Wkg 1)
Office expenses	15 000		(TB)
c/f	16500	50,000	
Depreciation: office furniture (10% × 5000)	500		(Wkg 2)
Bad debt write off	1 000		(QN 4)
Increase in allowance for doubtful debts	450		(Wkg 3)
Salaries (25000 + 1000)	26 000		(Wkg 4)
		(44 450)	
Net profit for the year		5 550	

Wayne

Statement of retained earnings for the year to 31 March 2017

Net profit for the year	5 550	(SPl)
Less: Drawings	(55000)	
Retained Earnings	550	

Wayne
Statement of financial position at 31 March 2017

	£	£	£	(Source of entry)
Non-current assets	Cost	Accumulated depreciation	Net book value	
Office furniture	5 000	(2500)	2 500	(TB and Wkg 5)
Current assets				
Inventory		15 000		(QN 1)
Trade receivables (20 000 − 1000)	19 000			(Wkg 3)
Less: Allowance for doubtful debts	(950)	18 050		(Wkg 3)
Prepayment		500		(QN 2)
Cash at bank		1 200		(TB)
Cash in hand		300	35 050	(TB)
			37 550	
Financed by:				
Capital		32 000		(TB)
Retained earnings		550	32 550	(SRE)
Current liabilities				
Trade payables		4 000		(TB)
Accrual		1000	5 000	(QN 6)
			37 550	

Key:

TB = from trial balance;

QN = extracted straight from the question and related notes;

Wkg = workings (see below);

SPL/SRE = balance obtained from the statement of profit or loss/statement of retained earning.

Workings		£
1	Insurance:	
	As per the trial balance	2 000
	Less: Prepayment (QN 2)	(500)
	Charge to the statement of profit or loss	1 500
2	Depreciation:	
	Office furniture at cost	5 000
	Depreciation: 10% of the original cost	500
3	Increase in allowance for doubtful debts:	
	Trade receivables at 31 March 2017	20 000
	Less: Bad debt (QN 4)	(1 000)
		19 000

Workings

	Allowance required: 5% thereof	950
	Less: Allowance at 1 April 2016	(500)
	Increase in allowance: charge to profit and loss	450
4	Salaries:	
	As per the question	25 000
	Add: Accrual (QN 6)	1 000
		26 000
5	Accumulated depreciation:	
	Balance at 1 April 2016 (as per TB)	2 000
	Add: Depreciation for the year (Wkg 2)	500
	Accumulated depreciation at 31 March 2017	2 500

Accounting defects

In previous chapters of the book, we have emphasised that the calculation of accounting profit calls for a great deal of subjective judgement. Accounting involves much more than merely being very good at mastering some complicated arithmetical examples. So we think that it would be helpful (indeed, essential) if we summarised the major defects inherent in the traditional method of calculating accounting profit.

As a non-accountant, it is most important that you appreciate one vital fact: the method that we have outlined for calculating the profit for a period results in an *estimate* of what the accountant thinks the profit should be. You must not place too much reliance on the *absolute* level of accounting profit. It can only be as accurate and as reliable as the assumptions upon which it is based. If you accept the assumptions, then you can be fairly confident that the profit figure is reliable. You will then not go too far wrong in using the information for decision-making purposes but you must know what the assumptions are and you must support them. You should *always question accounting information before accepting it.*

The main reasons why you should not place too much reliance on the *actual* level of accounting profit (especially if you are unsure about the assumptions upon which it is based) are summarised below.

- Goods are treated as being sold when the legal title to them changes hands and not when the customer has paid for them. In some cases, the cash for some sales may never be received.
- Goods are regarded as having been purchased when the legal title to them is transferred to the purchaser, although there are occasions when they may not be received, e.g. if a supplier goes into receivership.
- Goods that have not been sold at the period end have to be quantified and valued. Counting inventory can be a complex operation and valuing it involves a considerable amount of subjective judgement.
- There is no clear distinction between capital and revenue transactions.

- Estimates have to be made to allow for accruals and prepayments.
- The cost of non-current assets is apportioned between different accounting periods using methods that are fairly simplistic and highly questionable.
- Arbitrary reductions in profit are made to allow for doubtful debts.
- Historic cost accounting makes no allowance for inflation. So the value of £100 (say) at 1 January 2016 is not the same as £100 at 31 December 2016. As a result, in periods when inflation is high, profit tends to be overstated largely because of low closing inventory values and low depreciation charges.

The defects of historic cost accounting as listed are serious but no one as yet has been able to suggest a better method of accounting. For the time being, therefore, all we can do is to take comfort in the old adage that 'it is better to be vaguely right than precisely wrong'.

We would like to emphasise one point before we leave this chapter. Many students are mystified when they begin their study of accounting why 'profit' is not the same as an increase in cash. Now that you have worked your way through this chapter you should be clear why this is not the case. So remember that:

> Accounting profit is not the same as an increase in cash.

Why? Most of the reasons are contained within the above list of accounting defects. We have also demonstrated the distinction pictorially in Figure 4.3. Basically, some cash items are excluded from the statement of profit or loss (e.g. capital expenditure) while some non-cash items are included in it such as a allowance doubtful debts. You can perhaps compile your own list of reasons by having a go at answering Activity 4.10.

Activity 4.10	List as many examples as you can of (a) cash transactions that are not normally included in a statement of profit or loss and (b) non-cash items that are usually included in such financial statements.

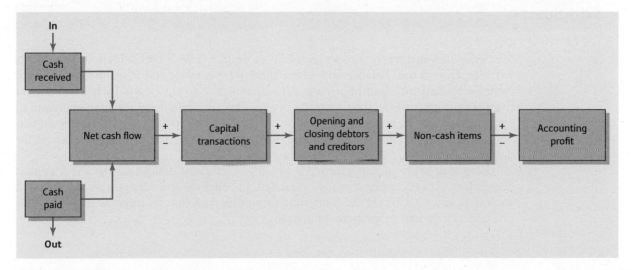

Figure 4.3 Cash vs accounting profit

Questions you should ask

It is important that as a non-accountant you should grasp the significance of this chapter. The decisions that your accountants will have taken in making a series of year-end adjustments to the financial accounts (particularly for inventory, depreciation, accruals and prepayment, and bad and doubtful debts) will have a considerable effect on the amount of profit that the entity reports for the year.

We suggest that you ask the following questions:

- What criteria have been used for distinguishing between capital and revenue items?
- Which items included in the financial statements may or may not be capital (or revenue)?
- What is the definition that you have used to determine revenue?
- Was a physical inventory check done at the year end?
- What method was used to value the closing inventory?
- What depreciation method has been used?
- Has historic cost been used to depreciate the non-current assets?
- If not, how has the cost of non-current assets been determined?
- How has the expected life of the assets been assessed?
- How do such lives compare with those used by our competitors?
- How have any residual values for the non-current assets been estimated?
- How have estimated values been determined for any accruals and prepayments?
- Have any bad debts been written off?
- How can we be certain that they are indeed bad?
- What basis is used to determine an appropriate level of allowance for doubtful debts?

Conclusion

We began this chapter by showing you how to prepare a basic set of financial statements working from a trial balance and where there were no year-end adjustments. We then went on to deal with four important adjustments that an entity usually has to make at the year end once the trial balance has been balanced. These four adjustments relate to opening and closing inventories, an allowance for depreciation on capital assets, adjusting for accruals and prepayments and writing off bad debts and making allowances for doubtful debts.

These four types of adjustment lead to many inherent deficiencies in the way that accounting profit is conventionally calculated. In concluding the chapter we summarised such deficiencies while at the same time reminding you that an increase in profit does not necessarily lead to an increase in cash.

Key points

1 A trial balance provides the basic data for the preparation of the financial accounts.

2 The basic financial statements of a trading entity normally include a statement of profit or loss, a statement of retained earnings and a statement of financial position. A trading account may be used by some manufacturing entities. The trading account is simply the top part of the statement of profit or loss.

3 Revenue balances are transferred to the statement of profit or loss, distribution to owners are transferred to the statement of retained earnings and capital balances to the statement of financial position.

4 The trading account, the statement of profit or loss and the statement of retained earnings form part of the double-entry system. The statement of financial position is merely a listing of the balances that remain in the ledger system once above statements have been prepared.

5 The basic financial accounts are nowadays normally presented in a vertical format.

6 Following the completion of the trial balance, some year-end adjustments have usually to be made to the financial statements. The main adjustments are made to inventory, depreciation, accruals and prepayments and bad and doubtful debts.

7 Accounting profit is merely an estimate. The method used to calculate it is highly questionable and it is subject to very many criticisms. Undue reliance should not be placed on the actual level of profit shown in the accounts. The assumptions upon which profit is based should be carefully examined and it should be viewed merely as a guide to decision-making.

8 Accounting profit is not the same as an increase in cash.

Check your learning

The answers to these questions can be found within the text.

1 Name two important functions of a trial balance.

2 What are the four financial statements that make up a set of basic accounts?

3 What are the three broad groups into which all transactions may be classified?

4 Name the two stages involved in preparing the basic accounts.

5 What term is given to the difference between sales revenue and the cost of goods sold?

6 What term is given to the difference between the total of all revenue incomes and the total of all revenue expenditures?

7 Which two formats may be used for the presentation of financial statements?

8 Which format is the one now commonly used?

9 What is meant by 'inventory'?

10 What is the term often used in the United Kingdom for inventory?

11 What is meant by 'opening inventory' and 'closing inventory'?

12 Which three items make up the closing inventory?

13 To which account are opening and closing inventories transferred?

14 Is opening inventory shown on the statement of financial position at the end of an accounting period?

15 Is closing inventory shown on the statement of financial position at the end of an accounting period?

16 What is depreciation?

17 Name two methods of depreciating non-current assets.

18 How are each of those methods calculated?

19 What is meant by the terms 'gross book value' and 'net book value'?

20 What amount for depreciation is shown on the statement of financial position?

21 What is (a) an accrual and (b) a prepayment?

22 Where are they normally disclosed in the statement of profit or loss?

23 Where are they to be found in the statement of financial position?

24 What is (a) a bad debt and (b) a doubtful debt?

25 What is a allowance for doubtful debts?

26 On what might the allowance be based?

27 List eight reasons why the calculation of accounting profit is an arbitrary exercise.

News story quiz

Remember the news story at the beginning of this chapter? Go back to that story and reread it before answering the following questions.

Yet again another alleged 'accounting irregularity' involving an inadequate allowance for bad debts.

Questions

1 Why are banks most affected by bad and doubtful debts?

2 What procedures do you think banks have in place to minimise their exposure to the risk of default by customers (which in turn impacts their own bad and doubtful debt charges)?

3 What do you think is an acceptable period of time for loans to be in arrears?

Tutorial questions

The answers to questions marked with an asterisk can be found in Appendix 4.

4.1 Explain why an increase in cash during a particular accounting period does not necessarily mean that an entity has made a profit.

4.2 'The differentiation between the so-called capital and revenue expenditure is quite arbitrary and unnecessary.' Discuss.

4.3 How far does a statement of financial position tell users how much an entity is worth?

4.4 'Depreciation methods and rates should be prescribed by law.' Discuss.

4.5 Explain why it is quite easy to manipulate the level of gross profit when preparing a trading account.

4.6 How far is it possible for an entity to build up hidden amounts of profit (known as *secret reserves*) by making some adjustments in the statement of profit or loss for doubtful debts?

4.7* The following trial balance has been extracted from Ethel's books of accounts as at 31 January 2017:

	Dr £	Cr £
Capital		10 000
Cash	3 000	
Payables		3 000
Receivables	6 000	
Office expenses	11 000	
Premises	8 000	
Purchases	20 000	
Sales		35 000
	48 000	48 000

Required:
Prepare Ethel's statement of profit or loss and statement of retained earnings for the year to 31 January 2017 and a statement of financial position as at that date.

4.8* Marion has been in business for some years. The following trial balance has been extracted from her books of account as at 28 February 2017:

	Dr £000	Cr £000
Cash at bank	4	
Buildings	50	
Capital		50

	Dr	Cr
	£000	£000
Cash in hand	2	
Payables		24
Receivables	30	
Drawings	55	
Heat and light	10	
Miscellaneous expenses	25	
Purchases	200	
Sales		400
Wages and salaries	98	
	474	474

Required:
Prepare Marion's statement of profit or loss and statement of retained earnings for the year to 28 February 2017 and a statement of financial position as at that date.

4.9 The following trial balance has been extracted from Jody's books of account as at 30 April 2016:

	Dr	Cr
	£000	£000
Capital (as at 1 May 2015)		30
Cash	1	
Electricity	2	
Maintenance	4	
Miscellaneous expenses	7	
Purchases	40	
Rent and rates	6	
Sales		85
Vehicle (at cost)	30	
Wages	25	
	115	115

Required:
Prepare Jody's statement of profit or loss and statement of retained earnings for the year to 30 April 2016 and a statement of financial position as at that date.

4.10 The following trial balance has been extracted from the books of Garswood as at 31 March 2017:

	Dr	Cr
	£	£
Advertising	2 300	
Cash at bank	300	
Capital		55 700
Cash in hand	100	

	Dr	Cr
	£	£
Discounts allowed	100	
Discounts received		600
Drawings	17 000	
Electricity	1 300	
Investments	4 000	
Investment income received		400
Office equipment	10 000	
Other payables		800
Other receivables	1 500	
Machinery	20 000	
Purchases	21 400	
Purchases returns		1 400
Sales		63 000
Sales returns	3 000	
Stationery	900	
Trade payables		5 200
Trade receivables	6 500	
Wages	38 700	
	127 100	127 100

Required:
Prepare Garswood's statement of profit or loss and statement of retained earnings for the year to 31 March 2017 and a statement of financial position as at that date.

4.11 Pete has extracted the following trial balance from his books of account as at 31 May 2016:

	Dr	Cr
	£000	£000
Cash at bank		15
Building society account	100	
Capital (as at 1 June 2015)		200
Cash	2	
Heat, light and fuel	18	
Insurances	10	
Interest received		1
Land and property (at cost)	200	
Long-term loan		50
Long-term loan interest paid	8	
Motor vehicles (at cost)	90	
Motor vehicle expenses	12	
Plant and equipment (at cost)	100	
Property maintenance	7	
Purchases	300	

	Dr	Cr
	£000	£000
Repairs to machinery	4	
Rent and rates	65	
Sales		900
Wages and salaries	250	
	1166	1166

Required:

Prepare Pete's statement of profit or loss and statement of retained earnings for the year to 31 May 2016 and a statement of financial position as at that date.

4.12* The following information has been extracted from Lathom's books of account for the year to 30 April 2016:

	£
Purchases	45 000
Sales	60 000
Inventory (at 1 May 2015)	3 000
Inventory (at 30 April 2016)	4 000

Required:

(a) Prepare Lathom's trading account for the year to 30 April 2016.
(b) State where the inventory at 30 April 2016 would be shown on the statement of financial position as at that date.

4.13 Rufford presents you with the following information for the year to 31 March 2017:

	£
Purchases	48 000
Purchases returns	3 000
Sales	82 000
Sales returns	4 000
Inventory at 1 April 2016	4 000

He is not sure how to value the inventory as at 31 March 2017. Three methods have been suggested. They all result in different closing inventory values, namely:

	£
Method 1	8 000
Method 2	16 000
Method 3	4 000

Required:

(a) Calculate the effect on gross profit for the year to 31 March 2017 by using each of the three methods of inventory valuation.
(b) State the effect on gross profit for the year to 31 March 2017 if Method 1 is used instead of Method 2.

4.14* Standish has been trading for some years. The following trial balance has been extracted from his books of account as at 31 May 2017:

	Dr £	Cr £
Capital		22 400
Cash	1 200	
Payables		4 300
Receivables	6 000	
Drawings	5 500	
Furniture and fittings	8 000	
Heating and lighting	1 500	
Miscellaneous expenses	6 700	
Purchases	52 000	
Sales		79 000
Inventory (at 1 June 2016)	7 000	
Wages and salaries	17 800	
	105 700	105 700

Note: Inventory at 31 May 2017: £12 000.

Required:
Prepare Standish's statement of profit or loss and statement of retained earnings for the year to 31 May 2017 and a statement of financial position as at that date.

4.15 Witton commenced business on 1 July 2015. The following trial balance was extracted from his books of account as at 30 June 2016:

	Dr £	Cr £
Capital		3 000
Cash	500	
Drawings	4 000	
Payables		1 500
Receivables	3 000	
Motor car at cost	5 000	
Office expenses	8 000	
Purchases	14 000	
Sales		30 000
	34 500	34 500

Additional information:

Inventory at 30 June 2016: £2000.

The motor car is to be depreciated at a rate of 20 per cent per annum on cost; it was purchased on 1 July 2015.

Required:
Prepare Witton's statement of profit or loss and statement of retained earnings for the year to 30 June 2016 and a statement of financial position as at that date.

4.16 The following is an extract from Barrow's statement of financial position at 31 August 2016:

Non-current assets	Cost £	Accumulated depreciation £	Net book value £
Land	200 000	–	200 000
Buildings	150 000	(60 000)	90 000
Plant	55 000	(37 500)	17 500
Vehicles	45 000	(28 800)	16 200
Furniture	20 000	(12 600)	7 400
	470 000	(138 900)	331 100

Barrow's depreciation policy is as follows:

(a) A full year's depreciation is charged in the year of acquisition, but none in the year of disposal.

(b) No depreciation is charged on land.

(c) Buildings are depreciated at an annual rate of 2 per cent on cost.

(d) Plant is depreciated at an annual rate of 5 per cent on cost after allowing for an estimated residual value of £5000.

(e) Vehicles are depreciated on a reduced balance basis at an annual rate of 40 per cent on the reduced balance, i.e. on the net book value as at the end of the previous year.

(f) Furniture is depreciated on a straight-line basis at an annual rate of 10 per cent on cost after allowing for an estimated residual value of £2000.

Additional information:

(a) During the year to 31 August 2017 new furniture was purchased for the office. It cost £3000 and it is to be depreciated on the same basis as the old furniture. Its estimated residual value is £300.

(b) There were no additions to, or disposals of, any other non-current assets during the year to 31 August 2018.

Required:

(a) Calculate the depreciation charge for each of the non-current asset groupings for the year to 31 August 2017.

(b) Show how the non-current assets would appear in Barrow's statement of financial position as at 31 August 2018.

4.17* Pine started business on 1 October 2015. The following is his trial balance at 30 September 2016:

	£	£
Capital		6 000
Cash	400	
Payables		5 900
Receivables	5 000	
Furniture at cost	8 000	
General expenses	14 000	
Insurance	2 000	
Purchases	21 000	
Sales		40 000
Telephone	1 500	
	51 900	51 900

The following information was obtained after the trial balance had been prepared:

1 Inventory at 30 September 2016: £3000.
2 Furniture is to be depreciated at a rate of 15 per cent on cost.
3 At 30 September 2016, Pine owed £500 for telephone expenses, and insurance had been prepaid by £200.

Required:
Prepare Pine's statement of profit or loss and statement of retained earnings for the year to 30 September 2016 and a statement of financial position as at that date.

4.18 Dale has been in business for some years. The following is his trial balance at 31 October 2016:

	Dr £	Cr £
Cash at bank	700	
Capital		85 000
Depreciation (at 1 November 2015): Office equipment Vehicles		14 000
		4 000
Drawings	12 300	
Heating and lighting	3 000	
Office expenses	27 000	
Office equipment, at cost	35 000	
Rates	12 000	
Purchases	240 000	
Sales		350 000
Inventory (at 1 November 2015)	20 000	
Trade payables		21 000
Trade receivables	61 000	
Vehicles at cost	16 000	
Wages and salaries	47 000	
	474 000	474 000

Additional information (not taken into account when compiling the above trial balance):

1 Inventory at 31 October 2016: £26 000.
2 Amount owing for electricity at 31 October 2016: £1500.
3 At 31 October 2016, £2000 had been paid in advance for rates.
4 Depreciation is to be charged on the office equipment for the year to 31 October 2016 at a rate of 20 per cent on cost and on the vehicles at a rate of 25 per cent on cost.

Required:
Prepare Dale's statement of profit or loss and statement of retained earnings for the year to 31 October 2016 and a statement of financial position as at that date.

4.19 The following information relates to Astley for the year to 30 November 2017:

Item	Cash paid during the year to 30 November 2016	As at 1 December 2015 Accruals/ Prepayments		As at 30 November 2016 Accruals/ Prepayments	
	£	£	£	£	£
Electricity	26400	5200	–	8300	–
Gas	40100	–	–	–	4900
Insurance	25000	–	12000	–	14000
Rates	16000	–	4000	6000	–
Telephone	3000	1500	–	–	200
Wages	66800	1800	–	–	–

Required:

(a) Calculate the charge to the statement of profit or loss for the year to 30 November 2016 for each of the above items.

(b) Demonstrate what amounts for accruals and prepayments would be shown in the statement of financial position as at 30 November 2016.

4.20 Duxbury started in business on 1 January 2017. The following is his trial balance as at 31 December 2017:

	Dr £	Cr £
Capital		40 000
Cash	300	
Delivery van, at cost	20 000	
Drawings	10 600	
Office expenses	12 100	
Purchases	65 000	
Sales		95 000
Trade payables		5 000
Trade receivables	32 000	
	140 000	140 000

Additional information:

1 Inventory at 31 December 2017 was valued at £10 000.

2 At 31 December 2017 an amount of £400 was outstanding for telephone expenses and the business rates had been prepaid by £500.

3 The delivery van is to be depreciated at a rate of 20 per cent per annum on cost.

4 Duxbury decides to set aside a allowance for doubtful debts equal to 5 per cent of trade receivables as at the end of the year.

Required:

Prepare Duxbury's statement of profit or loss and statement of retained earnings for the year to 31 December 2017 and a statement of financial position as at that date.

4.21 Beech is a retailer. Most of his sales are made on credit terms. The following information relates to the first four years that he has been in business:

	2014	2015	2016	2017
Trade receivables at 31 January	£60000	£55000	£65000	£70000

The trade is one that experiences a high level of bad debts. Accordingly, Beech decides to set aside a allowance for doubtful debts equivalent to 10 per cent of trade receivables as at the end of the year.

Required:
(a) Show how the allowance for doubtful debts would be disclosed in the respective statement of financial positions as at 31 January 2014, 2015, 2016 and 2017.
(b) Calculate the increase/decrease in allowance for doubtful debts transferred to the respective statement of profit or loss for each of the four years.

4.22 The following is Ash's trial balance as at 31 March 2017:

	Dr £	Cr £
Cash at bank		4 000
Capital		20 500
Depreciation (at 1 April 2016): furniture		3 600
Drawings	10 000	
Electricity	2 000	
Furniture, at cost	9 000	
Insurance	1 500	
Miscellaneous expenses	65 800	
Allowance for doubtful debts (at 1 April 2016)		1 200
Purchases	80 000	
Sales		150 000
Inventory (at 1 April 2016)	10 000	
Trade payables		20 000
Trade receivables	21 000	
	199 300	199 300

Additional information:
1 Inventory at 31 March 2017: £15 000.
2 At 31 March 2017 there was a specific bad debt of £6000. This was to be written off.
3 Furniture is to be depreciated at a rate of 10 per cent per annum on cost.
4 At 31 March 2017 Ash owes the electricity board £600, and £100 had been paid in advance for insurance.
5 The allowance for doubtful debts is to be set at 10 per cent of trade receivables as at the end of the year.

Required:
Prepare Ash's statement of profit or loss and statement of retained earnings for the year to 31 March 2017 and a statement of financial position as at that date.

4.23 Lime's business has had liquidity problems for some months. The following trial balance was extracted from his books of account as at 30 September 2016:

	Dr £	Cr £
Cash at bank		15 200
Capital		19 300
Cash from sale of office equipment		500
Depreciation (at 1 October 2015): office equipment		22 000
Drawings	16 000	
Insurance	1 800	
Loan (long-term from Cedar)		50 000
Loan interest	7 500	
Miscellaneous expenses	57 700	
Office equipment, at cost	44 000	
Allowance for doubtful debts (at 1 October 2015)		2 000
Purchases	320 000	
Rates	10 000	
Sales		372 000
Inventory (at 1 October 2015)	36 000	
Trade payables		105 000
Trade receivables	93 000	
	586 000	586 000

Additional information:

1 Inventory at 30 September 2016: £68 000.
2 At 30 September 2016, accrual for rates of £2000 and insurance prepaid of £200.
3 Depreciation on office equipment is charged at a rate of 25 per cent on cost. During the year, office equipment costing £4000 had been sold for £500. Accumulated depreciation on this equipment amounted to £3000. Lime's depreciation policy is to charge a full year's depreciation in the year of acquisition and none in the year of disposal.
4 Specific bad debts of £13 000 are to be written off.
5 The allowance for doubtful debts is to be made equal to 10 per cent of outstanding trade receivables as at 30 September 2016.

Required:
Prepare Lime's statement of profit or loss and statement of retained earnings for the year to 30 September 2016 and a statement of financial position as at that date.

Website
Further practice questions, study material and links to relevant sites on the World Wide Web can be found on the website that accompanies this book. The site can be found at www.pearsoned.co.uk/dyson

Company accounts

Assets finally landing on the balance sheet . . .

Accounting's big shake-up to bring more transparency

By Kate Burgess and Harriet Agnew

When Sir David Tweedie was chairman of the International Accounting Standards Board, he joked his life-long ambition was to fly in an aircraft that actually existed on an airline's balance sheet (aka statement of financial position).

Now, some six years later, his hope is becoming a reality. A new IASB financial reporting standard will force companies, including airlines, to include leasing obligations in annual statements of assets and liabilities, from 2019. And next month the US Financial Accounting Standards Board will publish its own version of the standard.

It is the third in a series of accounting reforms since the financial crash, aimed at making companies' accounts more transparent – the others govern revenue recognition and the valuation of financial instruments.

All will have an impact on investors, as they have the potential to affect lending arrangements, dividend policies, tax planning and share prices. They also represent a step up in regulatory co-operation between the US and international standard setters. Converging the different corporate reporting frameworks has been fraught. While the two regulators were largely able to agree on the revenue recognition and lease accounting standards, attempts to agree a common base for assessing financial instruments failed in 2014.

Revenue recognition – or how and when companies declare their sales – has been at the heart of many an accounting scandal. US computing group IBM, insurance software business Quindell and supermarket chain Tesco have all stumbled over the way they account for revenues prompting investors to call for clearer rules to prevent over-optimistic executives booking sales before netting out costs.

Now, 10 years since the process of converging US and European rules began, the IFRS 15 joint standard will require revenues to be matched to costs from 2018.

AIRLINES

(A) Total assets (50 companies)	(B) Future payments for off balance sheet leases	(B) / (A)
$527bn	$152bn	28.8%

FT   *Source*: Reproduced with permission from www.ft.com, 20 January 2016.

Questions relating to this news story can be found on page 126. ➡

About this chapter

In Chapter 4 we showed you how to prepare a set of basic financial statements for a sole trader entity. The management and organisation of such entities are not normally very complex, so we have been able to cover the overall procedures without becoming *too* bogged down in the detail (although this may rather surprise you).

Many non-accountants using this book are, however, likely to work for a *company*. There are many different types of companies but the most common ones are private limited liability companies and public limited liability companies (as we explained in Chapter 2). By law, all companies have to prepare a set of annual accounts and supply a copy to their shareholders. They also have to file a copy with the Registrar of Companies, i.e. send it to the Registrar. This means that the accounts are then open to inspection by the public. The amount of detail disclosed or published in company accounts (i.e. included) depends upon their type and size.

We shall be dealing with the disclosure requirements of companies in Chapters 8 and 9. In this chapter we explain how to prepare a company's financial accounts for the *internal* management. There are no legal requirements covering the presentation and contents of financial accounts for such a purpose, so a company can do more or less as it wants. Nevertheless, in order to cut down on the amount of work involved, most companies probably produce internal accounts that are similar to the ones required for external purposes, except that they are likely to be much more detailed.

Learning objectives

By the end of this chapter you should be able to:

- explain what is meant by limited liability;
- distinguish between private and public companies;
- describe how companies are organised;
- prepare a basic set of financial statements for a company.

! Why this chapter is important

This chapter is important for a non-accountant because it shows how the material covered in earlier chapters can be adapted for use in preparing company accounts. As many non-accountants work for a company (while others will have contact with one), this chapter will help them to do a better job if they know something about the origin, structure and operation of companies. They will be even better placed if they can then use the available accounting information to assess the past and future performance of their own company and compare it with its competitors. In order to be able to do so, it is necessary to know where the accounting information comes from, what it includes, how it has been summarised and any deficiencies that it may have. This can be best achieved by being able to prepare a simple set of financial statements for a company. This chapter provides non-accountants with that opportunity.

We start our study of company accounts with an explanation of what is meant by 'limited liability'.

Limited liability

There is a great personal risk in operating a business as a sole trader or as a partnership. If the business runs short of funds, the owners may be called upon to settle the business's debts out of their own private resources. This type of risk can have a damaging effect on the development of new businesses. So there is a need for a different type of entity that will neither make the owners bankrupt nor inhibit new developments. This need became apparent in the nineteenth century following the Industrial Revolution when enormous amounts of capital were required to finance new and rapidly expanding industries such as the railways and shipbuilding.

These sorts of ventures were undertaken at great personal risk. By agreeing to become involved in them many investors faced bankruptcy if the ventures were unsuccessful (as they often were). It became apparent that the development of industry would be hindered unless some means could be devised of restricting the personal liability of prospective investors.

So the concept of *limited liability* was born although it was not entirely an innovation of the nineteenth century. It eventually received legal recognition in 1855 when the Limited Liability Act was passed. The Act only remained in force for a few months before it was repealed and incorporated into the Joint Stock Companies Act 1856. By distinguishing between the private and public affairs of business proprietors, the 1855 Act effectively created a new form of legal entity. Since the 1850s, Parliament has passed a number of other Companies Acts, all of which have continued to give legal recognition to the concept of limited liability.

The important point about a limited liability company is that no matter what financial difficulties it may get into, its members cannot be required to contribute more than an agreed amount of capital, so there is no risk of its members being forced into bankruptcy.

The concept of limited liability is often very difficult for business owners to understand, especially if they have formed one out of what was originally a sole trader or a partnership entity (this point is illustrated in Figure 5.1). Unlike such entities, companies are bound by some fairly severe legal operating restrictions. The legal restrictions can be somewhat burdensome but they are necessary for the protection of all those parties who might have dealings with the company (such as payables and employees). This is because if a limited liability company runs short of funds the payables and employees might not get paid. It is only fair, therefore, to warn all those people who might have dealings with it that they run a risk in doing business with it. So companies have to be more open about their affairs than do sole traders and partnerships.

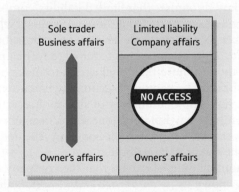

Figure 5.1 Access: sole trader vs limited liability company

Structure and operation

In this section we examine the structure and operation of limited liability companies. In order to make it easier to follow, we have broken down our examination into a number of subsections. A summary of the section is also presented in diagrammatic format in Figure 5.2.

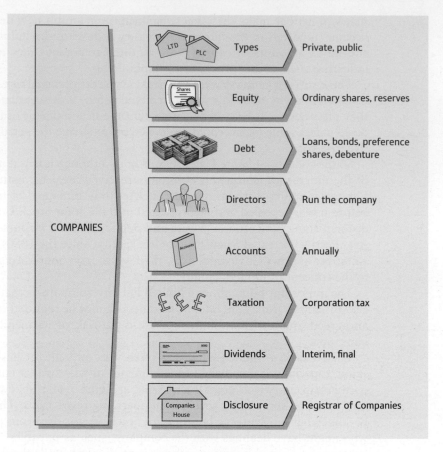

Figure 5.2 Structure and operation of companies

Equity

Although the law recognises that limited liability companies are separate beings with a life of their own, i.e. separate from those individuals who collectively own and manage them, it also accepts that someone has to take responsibility for promoting the company and giving it life. Only one person is required to form a private company and that person (or persons if there is more than one) agrees to make a capital contribution by buying a number of shares. The capital of a company is known as its *share capital*. The share capital will be made up of a number of shares of a certain denomination, such as 10p, 50p or £1. Members may hold only one share, or many hundreds or thousands depending upon the total share capital of the company, the denomination of the shares and the amount that they wish to contribute.

The maximum amount of capital that the company envisages ever raising has to be stated. This is known as its *authorised share capital,* although this does not necessarily mean that it will issue shares up to that amount. In practice, it will probably only issue sufficient capital to meet its immediate and foreseeable requirements. The amount of share capital that it has actually issued is known as the *issued share capital*. Sometimes, when shares are issued, prospective shareholders are only required to pay for them in instalments. Once all the issued share capital has been paid for, it is described as being *fully paid*.

There are two main types of shares: *ordinary shares* and *preference shares*. The holders of ordinary shares are the owners of the company. The holders of preference shares are payables to the company (more on those later).

Ordinary shares entitle the shareholder to a share of the profit made by the company, which is paid in the form of dividends. The specific level of dividend is an arbitrary decision made by managers. Managers may decide to pay all of the profit of the company to the shareholders as dividends, or none at all and reinvest all the profit, or they may pay some out as dividends to shareholders and keep the remainder (the so-called retained earnings that we saw in Chapter 4). The funds received by a company from ordinary shareholders in exchange for the issue of ordinary shares, as well as any profits retained as reserves in the business, are referred to as *equity* capital.

Despite being called 'shares', preference shares are debt, rather than equity, and are not ordinarily part of the share capital structure of a company. Preference shareholders are not owners of the company. They are payables. Preference shareholders are normally entitled to a fixed level of dividend (which is in effect like interest on a loan that was given to the company) and they have priority over the ordinary shareholders in receiving dividends as well their investment back if the company is liquidated. Sometimes the preference shares are classed as *cumulative;* this means that if the company cannot pay its preference dividend in one year, the amount due accrues until such time as the company has the profits to pay all of the accumulated dividends.

We show the types of shares that companies may have in Figure 5.3.

Types of companies

A prospective shareholder may invest in either a public company or a private company. A *public company* must have an authorised share capital of at least £50,000, and it becomes a public company merely by stating that it is a public company. In fact, most public limited companies in the United Kingdom have their shares listed on the London Stock Exchange and so they are often referred to as *listed* (or quoted) companies. As a warning to those parties who might have dealings with them, public companies have to include the term 'public limited liability company' after their name (or its abbreviation 'plc').

Any company that does not make its shares available to the public is regarded as being a *private company*. Like public companies, private companies must also have a stated amount of authorised share capital although no minimum amount is prescribed. Otherwise, their share capital requirements are very similar to public companies.

Private companies also have to warn the public that their liability is limited. They must do so by describing themselves as 'limited liability companies' and attaching the term 'limited' after their name (or the abbreviation 'ltd').

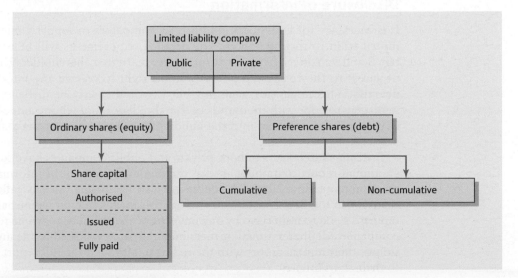

Figure 5.3 Types of shares

Limited liability companies have to disclose some information about their operations as well as putting 'limited' ('ltd') or public limited company ('plc') after their name in order to warn the public that their liability is limited.

Do you think that such safeguards are adequate? What more can be done? How far do you think that it is fair for individuals to set up businesses under the protection of limited liability? The business may then go into liquidation and the payables will be left without any means of getting their money back from the owners of the company. Is this acceptable if the concept of limited liability encourages new businesses to be formed?

Debt

Besides obtaining the necessary equity capital from their shareholders, companies often secure debt funding by borrowing money from banks or investors. In addition to ordinary loans which you are familiar with and the preference shares explained earlier, the company may issue bonds or *debentures*. A company may invite the public to loan it some money for a certain period of time (the period can be unspecified) at a certain rate of interest. A debenture loan in particular may be secured on specific assets of the company, on its assets generally or it might not be secured at all. If the loan is secured and the company cannot repay it on its due repayment date, the debenture holders may sell the secured assets and use the amount to settle what is owing to them.

Bonds and debentures, like shares, may be bought and sold freely on the Stock Exchange. The nearer the redemption date for the repayment for the bonds or debentures, the closer the market price will be to their nominal value, i.e. their face, or stated paper value. If they are to be redeemed at a premium, i.e. in excess of their nominal value, the market price may exceed the nominal value.

Debt holders are not shareholders of the company and they do not have voting rights. From the company's point of view, one further advantage of raising capital in the form of debt instruments is that, for taxation purposes, the interest can be charged as a business expense against the profit for the year (unlike dividends).

Disclosure of information

It is necessary for both public and private companies to supply a minimum amount of information to their members. The detailed requirements will be examined in Chapters 8 and 9. You might find it surprising to learn that shareholders have neither a right of access to the company's premises nor a right to receive any information that they demand. This might not seem fair but it would clearly be difficult for a company's managers to cope with thousands of shareholders, all of whom suddenly turned up one day demanding to be let into the building in order to inspect the company's books of account.

Instead, shareholders in both private and public companies have to be supplied with an annual report containing at least the minimum amount of information required by the Companies Act 2006. The company also has to file (as it is called) a copy of the report with the Registrar of Companies. This means that on payment of a small fee the report is open to inspection by any member of the public who wants to consult it. Some companies (defined as small or medium-sized) are permitted to file an abbreviated version of their annual report with the registrar, although the full report must still be sent to their shareholders.

The disclosure requirements are shown in summary form in Figure 5.4.

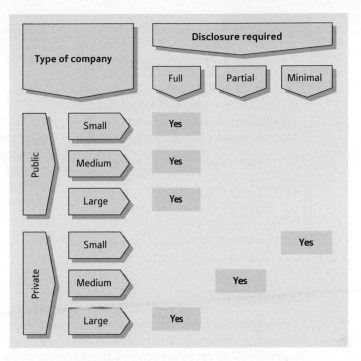

Figure 5.4 Disclosure of information

Accounts

Company accounts are very similar to those of sole traders. They do, however, tend to be more detailed and some modifications have to be made in order to comply with various legal requirements.

Directors

A limited liability company must always be regarded as a separate entity, i.e. separate from those shareholders who own it collectively and separate from anyone who works for it. This means that all those who are employed by it are its employees, no matter how senior they are. Nevertheless, someone has to take responsibility for the management of the company and so the shareholders usually delegate that responsibility to *directors*.

Directors are the most senior level of management. They are responsible for the day-to-day running of the company and they answer to the shareholders. Any remuneration paid to them as directors is charged as an expense of the business. They may also be shareholders but any dividends that they receive are regarded as being a private matter. They should not be confused with any payments that they receive as directors.

The distinction between employees and shareholder–employees is important even if the sole member of a private company works full-time in the business. The same requirement applies to public companies except that they must have at least two members. As we have emphasised throughout the chapter, in law, the company is regarded as being a separate entity. Even if there are just two shareholders who both work full-time for the company, the company is still treated as distinct from that of the two individuals who happen to own it. They may take decisions that appear to affect no one else except themselves but because they operate the company under the protection of limited liability they have certain obligations as well as rights. As a result they are not as free to run the company as they would be if it were (say) a partnership.

Dividend pay-out

Prudential brushed off fears of a slowdown in Asia as it revealed 2015 results that beat expectations and declared a special dividend alongside a rise in its regular payout.

Operating profits of £4bn came in 10 per cent ahead of expectations and were 26 per cent higher than 2014. The company announced a 5 per cent rise in the dividend to 38.8p. Citi had expected the payout to rise by 10 per cent, as it had the previous year. But Prudential said it would pay a 10p-per-share special dividend as a result of changes it had made ahead of the introduction of the EU's Solvency II rules. It is the first special dividend the company has paid since 1970.

Source: Adapted from ft.com, 9 March 2016.

Dividends

As we explained earlier, profits are usually distributed to shareholders in the form of a dividend. A dividend is calculated on the basis of so many pence per share. The actual dividend will be recommended by the directors to the shareholders. It will be based on the amount of net profit earned during the year and how much profit the directors want to retain in the business.

A dividend may have been paid during the year as an *interim dividend,* i.e. a payment on account. At the year end the directors may recommend a *final* dividend. The final dividend has to be approved by the shareholders at a general meeting.

Taxation

Taxation is another feature which clearly distinguishes a limited liability company from that of a sole trader entity. Sole traders do not have tax levied on them as entities. Instead, tax is levied on the amount of profit the owner has made during the year. The tax payable is a private matter and in accordance with the entity rule, it lies outside the boundary of the entity. Any tax that appears to have been paid by the entity on the owner's behalf is treated as part of the owner's drawings, i.e. an amount paid as part of the share of the profits.

Activity 5.2

Assume that you would like to start a small business of your own. You have heard that a limited liability company will not make you bankrupt if it is unsuccessful. So you decide to form a company.

List three advantages and three disadvantages in the table below of running your business as a limited liability company.

Advantages	Disadvantages
(1)	(1)
(2)	(2)
(3)	(3)

Companies are treated quite differently. They are taxed in their own right like individuals. They have their own form of taxation known as *corporation tax*. Corporation tax was introduced in 1965 and all companies are eligible to pay it. It is based on the company's accounting profit for a particular financial year. The accounting profit has to be adjusted, however, because some items are treated differently for tax purposes, e.g. the depreciation of non-current assets. Any corporation tax due at the year end is treated as a current liability.

Now that we have outlined the basic structure and operation of limited liability companies, we can begin to examine company accounts in some detail. We start with the statement of profit or loss.

The statement of profit or loss

As we suggested earlier, the preparation of a company's statement of profit or loss is basically no different from that of sole trader entities. Almost an identical format or structure may be adopted and it is only after the net profit stage that some differences become apparent – that is where corporation tax paid on profits it shown. An example of a company's statement of profit or loss is shown in Example 5.1. It is very similar to the sole trader example used in the previous chapter so that you can easily see the differences.

You can see from Example 5.1 that the company's net profit for the year is appropriated (or used) in three ways:

- to pay tax;
- to pay dividends;
- for retention within the business.

The appropriation of tax is shown as part of the statement of profit or loss. The other appropriations of profit are shown on a separate statement.

The statement of changes in equity

The contributions made by shareholders as well as payments to them are shown on a complex statement called the statement of changes in equity (SCE). For example, when a company issues new shares or cancels shares, the movement between share capital at the start and end of a period will be shown in that statement. The complexity of the statement of changes in equity is beyond the scope of this book but one part of it – the calculation showing how much of profits is distributed as dividends to shareholders and how much is retained in reserves – we have already seen in Chapter 4 (except that for sole traders we referred to these payments to the owners as drawings).

The statement of retained earnings

Small companies in the United Kingdom do not have to prepare the statement of changes in equity but they do still have to show how profits are appropriated. This is done in a statement of retained earnings (SRE) which really is just an extract from the statement of changes in equity.

Example
5.1

A company's statement of profit or loss and other statements

Cush Ltd.
Statement of profit or loss for the year to 30 June 2016

	£	£
Sales		50 000
Less: cost of sales		(30 000)
Gross profit		20 000
Less: Distribution costs (1)		(2 000)
Less: Administrative expenses (1)		(3 000)
Operating profit		15 000
Add: Interest income (2)		1 500
Less: Preference share dividends and other interest expense (2)		(1 000)
Net Profit for the year before tax		15 500
Less: Tax (3)		(500)
Profit after tax		15 000

Tutorial notes to Example 5.1

1 Company accounts have specific headings for groups of expenses, such as distribution costs and administrative expenses. Expenses such as, rent, advertising and fuel costs will be grouped under one of those headings.

2 In addition, separate headings are used specifically for the incomes from cash deposits and expenses related to servicing debt funding.

3 Finally, the appropriation of tax that the company as a separate legal entity has to pay to HMRC based on the profits made is also shown before the bottom line profit figure is reported.

(Option 1 – big companies)

Cush Ltd
Statement of changes in equity for the year to 30 June 2016

	Share capital	Retained earnings
Opening balance (on 1 July 2015)	10 000	10 000
Issue of new shares	1 000	
Profit for the year after tax*		15 000
Less: Dividends		(8 000)
Closing balance (on 30 June 2016)	11 000	17 000

(Option 2 – small companies)

Cush Ltd
Statement of retained earning for the year to 30 June 2016

Opening retained earnings (on 1 July 2015)	10 000
Profit for the year after tax*	15 000
Less: Dividends	(8 000)
Closing retained earnings (on 30 June 2016)	17 000

Activity 5.3	Complete the following equations:

(a) _____ − taxation = net profit for the year after taxation.

(b) Net profit for the year after taxation − _____ = retained profit for the year

The statement of financial position

News clip

Going, going . . .

British Home Stores (BHS), the department store chain sold by Sir Philip Green for £1, is seeking to offload a pension deficit worth £571m, about 10 per cent larger than it was three years ago. BHS executives believe that the removal of the pension liabilities, as well as deep cuts to the retailer's rent bill, is essential for the company to survive.

Source: Extracted from www.ft.com, 7 March 2016.

The structure of a limited liability company's statement of financial position is also very similar to that of a sole trader. The main difference arises because of the company's capital structure although there are some other features that are not usually found in non-company statements of financial positions.

The main features of a company's statement of financial position are shown in Example 5.2. It includes a number of tutorial notes which will help you as you work through the example.

Example 5.2	**A company's statement of financial position**

Exhibitor Ltd

Statement of financial position at 31 March 2017

	£000	£000
Non-current assets		
Property, Plant and Equipment		600
Investments (1)		100
Current assets		6000
		6700
Capital and Reserves (2):		
Ordinary shares of £1 each (3)	1500	
Capital reserves (4)	200	
Revenue reserves (5)	600	
Shareholders' funds (6)		2300
Non-current liabilities		
Loans (7)	100	
Preference shares of £0.50 each (5)	500	
		600

	£000	£000
Current liabilities		
Trade payables	2950	
Accruals	50	
Corporation tax (8)	300	
Dividend declared (9)	500	3800
		6700

Note

The number shown after each narration refers to the tutorial notes below.

Tutorial notes to Example 5.2

1 *Investments.* This item usually represents long-term investments in the shares of other companies. Short-term investments (such as money invested in bank deposit accounts) would be included in current assets. The shares may be either in public or private limited liability companies. The market price of the investments should be stated. A directors' valuation should be obtained if this is not available.

2 *Capital and reserves.* Details of the authorised, issued and fully paid-up share capital may be shown although ordinarily this is done in the notes to the accounts.

3 *Ordinary shares.* Details about the different types (if any) of shares that the company has issued should be disclosed.

4 *Capital reserves.* This section may include several different reserve accounts of a capital nature, i.e. amounts that are not available for distribution to the shareholders as dividend. It might include, for example, a share premium account (an extra amount paid by shareholders in excess of the nominal value of the shares). The premium does not rank for dividend but prospective shareholders are sometimes willing to pay it if they think that the shares are particularly attractive. Another example of a capital reserve is that of an asset that has been revalued. The difference between the original cost and the revalued amount will be credited to a *revaluation* reserve account.

5 *Revenue reserves.* Revenue reserve accounts are amounts that are available for distribution to the shareholders. Any profits retained in the business and not paid out to shareholders may be included under this heading. Retained profits are normally shown separately under the heading 'retained earnings.

6 *Shareholders' funds.* The total amount available to shareholders at the statement of financial position date is equal to the share capital originally subscribed plus all the capital and revenue reserve account balances.

7 *Non-current liabilities.* This section of the statement of financial position will include all the long-term loans and other debt obtained by the company, i.e. those loans that do not have to be repaid for at least 12 months, such as debentures and preference shares. The portion of long-term bank loans which are due for payment in more than 12 months from the year-end date will also be shown here, while any portion of the loans due for settlement as well as interest due on the loan in the next 12 months will be shown as current liabilities.

8 *Corporation tax.* This represents the outstanding tax due on the company's profits for the year.

9 *Dividend declared.* When a dividend is declared, it is a few days or weeks before the payment of the dividend is made. For interim dividends, both the declaration and the payment would have happened during the year and there would be no liability at the year end. For dividends declared after the year end, only a disclosure in the notes to the accounts is made. If a dividend declared exists as a liability at the year end that means that the declaration was made very shortly before the year end but the payment of the dividends is outstanding at the year end and will happen very shortly after the year end, and so a current liability is shown. This is rare.

Activity 5.4	State in which section of the statement of financial position you are likely to find the following items:

(a) Amount owing for corporation tax.
(b) Debentures
(c) Plant and machinery.
(d) Preference shares.
(e) Trade receivables.

A comprehensive example

Example 5.3 brings together the material covered in this chapter.

Example 5.3	**Preparation of a company's accounts**

The following information has been extracted from the books of Handy Ltd as at 31 March 2017:

	Dr £	Cr £
Cash at bank	2000	
Capital: 100000 issued and fully paid ordinary shares of £1 each		100000
50000 issued and fully paid 8% preference shares of £1 each		50000
Debentures (10%: repayable 2035)		30000
Debentures interest	3000	
Dividends received		700
Dividends paid: Ordinary interim	5000	
Preference	4000	
Freehold land at cost	200000	
Investments (listed: market value at 31 March 2017 was £11000)	10000	
Office expenses	47000	
Motor van at cost	15000	
Motor van: accumulated depreciation (at 1 April 2016)		6000
Motor van expenses	2700	
Purchases	220000	
Retained profits (at 1 April 2016)		9000
Sales		300000
Share premium reserve		10000
Inventory at cost (at 1 April 2016)	20000	
Trade payables		50000
Trade receivables	27000	
	555700	555700

Additional information

1 The inventory at 31 March 2017 was valued at historical cost of £40,000.

2 Depreciation is to be charged on the motor van at a rate of 20 per cent per annum on cost. No depreciation is to be charged on the freehold land.

3   The corporation tax for the year has been estimated to be £10,000.

4   The directors propose a final ordinary dividend of 10p per share.

5   The authorised share capital of the company is as follows:

   1   150,000 ordinary shares of £1 each and

   2   75,000 preference shares of £1 each.

Required

(a)   Prepare Handy Ltd's trading and statement of profit or loss and statement of retained earnings for the year to 31 March 2017.

(b)   Prepare a statement of financial position as at that date.

Answer to Example 5.3(a)

Handy Ltd
Statement of profit or loss for the year to 31 March 2017

	£	£
Sales		300000
Less: Cost of goods sold:		
Opening inventory	20000	
Purchases	220000	
	240000	
Less: Closing inventory	(40000)	(200000)
Gross profit		100000
Add: Other Income:		
Dividends received		700
Less: Distribution costs		
Motor van depreciation (1)	3000	
Motor van expenses	2700	(5700)
Less: Administrative Expenses		
Office expenses		(47000)
Profit before interest and tax		48000
Less: Interest		
Debenture interest	3000	
Preference dividend paid (8%)	4000	(7000)
Net profit for the year before tax		41000
Less: Corporation tax (2)		(10000)
Net profit for the year after tax		31000

Handy Ltd
Statement of retained earnings for the year to 31 March 2017

	£	£
Retained profits brought forward		9000
Net profit for the year after tax		31000
Less: Ordinary Share Dividends (3):		
Interim dividend paid (5p per share)	5000	
Final dividend declared	10000	(15000)
(10p per share)		
Retained profits carried forward (4)		25000

Answer to Example 5.3(b)

Handy Ltd Statement of financial position at 31 March 2017

	£	£	£
Non-current assets	Cost	Accumulated depreciation	NBV
Freehold land (5)	200000	–	200000
Motor van (6)	15000	(9000)	6000
Investments (7)	215000	(9000)	11000
			217000
Current assets			
Inventories at cost		40000	
Trade receivables		27000	
Cash		2000	69000
Total assets			286000
Capital and Reserves:			
Ordinary shares of £1 each (10)		100000	
Share premium reserve (11)		10000	
Revaluation reserve (7)		1000	
Retained profits (12)		25000	
Shareholders' funds (13)			136000
Non-current liabilities (14)			
10% debenture stock (repayable 2035)		30000	
Preference shares of £1 each (10)		50000	80000
Current liabilities			
Trade payables		50000	
Corporation tax payable (8)		10000	
Dividend declared (9)		10000	70000
			286000

Note:

The number shown after each narration refers to the following tutorial notes:

Tutorial notes

1 Depreciation has been charged on the motor van at a rate of 20 per cent per annum on cost (as instructed in question note 2).

2 Question note 3 requires £10,000 to be charged as corporation tax. To calculate tax in real life the relevant tax rate percentage as advised by HMRC is applied to the taxable profit and not to the accounting profit. The tax rate and the taxable profit have not been given in the question.

3 A proposed ordinary dividend of 10p has been included as instructed in question note 4.

4 The total retained profit of £25,000 is carried forward to the statement of financial position (see tutorial note 12 below).

5 Question note 2 states that no depreciation is to be charged on the freehold land.

6 The accumulated depreciation for the motor van of £9000 is the total of the accumulated depreciation brought forward at 1 April 2016 of £6000, plus the £3000 written off to the statement of profit or loss for the current year (see tutorial note 1 above).

7 Note that the investments have been revalued to reflect their current market value. The revaluation difference between what was paid for them and what they are now worth is shown in the revaluaiton reserve which in effect represents unrealised profit (i.e. the profit that could be made if the investments were sold).

8 The corporation tax charged against profit (question note 3) will be due for payment in 2017/18 (after the year end). The amount due is treated as a current liability.

9 The proposed ordinary dividend will be due for payment shortly after the year end and so it is also a current liability. The interim dividend and the preference dividend have already been paid, so they are not current liabilities.

10 Details of the authorised, issued and fully paid share capital are disclosed in the notes to the accounts rather than on the face of the statement.

11 The share premium is a capital account: it cannot be used for the payment of dividends. It will normally remain unchanged in successive statement of financial positions although there are a few highly restricted purposes for which it may be used.

12 The retained profits become part of a revenue account balance that could be used for the payment of dividends. The total retained profits of £25,000 is the amount brought in to the statement of financial position from the statement of retained earnings.

13 The total amount of shareholders' funds should always be shown.

14 Non-current and current liabilities, while sources of funding, are not part of shareholders' funds and so they need to be shown separately in the statement of financial position.

 ## Questions you should ask

Many of the questions that we have suggested in previous chapters that non-accountants should ask are of relevance in this chapter. For example, the various accounting rules adopted by the accountants in preparing the company's statement of profit or loss, the statement of changes in equity (for big companies) or the statement of retained earnings (for small companies) and the statement of financial position, especially those with a significant impact on revenue, inventory valuation, depreciation and allowance for doubtful debts.

The following questions relate particularly to this chapter:

• Can our accounting records disclose with reasonable accuracy (as the 2006 Companies Act requires) our financial position at any time?

• Do the accounting records contain entries for all money received and spent?

• Do they also contain a record of all assets and all liabilities?

• Do the accounting records include a statement of the inventory held at the financial year end?

• Are there details of inventory-taking from which the statement of inventory has been compiled?

• Is a record kept of all goods sold and purchased as well as all the buyers and sellers so that they can all be identified?

• Have all financial statements been prepared in accordance both with the requirements of the Companies Act 2006 and with recommended practice?

• Do the accounts genuinely represent a 'true and fair' view of the company's affairs?

Conclusion

This chapter has briefly examined the structure and content of limited liability company accounts using a number of simple examples. Although a great deal of information can be obtained from studying the annual accounts of a company, it is difficult to extract the most relevant and significant features. Some further guidance is needed, therefore, in how to make the best use of the financial accounting information presented to you. This will be provided in Chapters 7–10, but first we need to examine some other types of account. We do so in Chapter 6.

Key points	
	1 The financial statements of a company are similar in format (i.e. structure) to those of sole traders.
	2 The profits of a company are taxed separately (like an individual). The tax is based on the accounting profit for the year. Any tax due at the year end will be shown in the statement of financial position as a current liability.
	3 The net profit after tax may be paid to shareholders in the form of a dividend although some profit will normally be retained in the business. Dividends declared should be shown in the statement of financial position as a current liability.

Check your learning

The answers to these questions can be found within the text.

1 What is meant by 'limited liability'?

2 When was it first incorporated into company law?

3 Why was it found necessary to do so?

4 Distinguish among the authorised, issued and fully paid share capital of a company.

5 Name two main types of shares.

6 What is the basic difference between them?

7 What are the two main types of limited liability companies?

8 What is a debenture loan?

9 What is meant by 'disclosure of information'?

10 Why do companies have to let the Registrar of Companies have certain types of information?

11 What is a director?

12 What is a dividend?

13 Name two types of dividend.

14 What name is given to the tax that a company pays on its profits?

15 Name three ways in which a company's profits are appropriated.

16 List three types of assets.

17 Name three items that may be included under the heading of 'current liabilities'.

18 Distinguish between a capital reserve and a revenue reserve.

19 What is a share premium reserve?

20 What is meant by 'shareholders' funds'?

21 What is the difference between a current liability and non-current liability?

News story quiz

Remember the news story at the beginning of this chapter? Go back to that story and reread it before answering the following questions.

This is yet another report of how accounting rules evolve over time – what might have been an appropriate accounting treatment yesterday is not necessarily going to be the appropriate accounting treatment tomorrow. These changes in the 'rules of the game' of accounting have significant impact on the reported bottom line profits.

Questions

1 Do you think it makes sense not to record leased aircraft as assets in the accounts of airlines? What are the arguments pro and against treating them as assets of the lessee airline company?

2 What impacts do you think the absence of these assets has on the accounts? Can you think which balances in the financial statements would be materially affected?

3 Why do you think revenue (sales) is often at the heart of accounting scandals? What are the moral as well as legal responsibilities of managers with respect to reporting valid revenue accurately, completely and in the correct period?

Tutorial questions

The answers to question marked with an asterisk may be found in Appendix 4.

5.1 'The concept of limited liability is an out-of-date nineteenth-century concept.' Discuss.

5.2 Appleton used to operate her business as a sole trader entity. She has recently converted it into a limited liability company. Appleton owns 80 per cent of the ordinary (voting) shares, the remaining 20 per cent being held by various relatives and friends. Explain to Appleton why it is now inaccurate for her to describe the company as 'her' business.

5.3 How far do you think that the information presented in a limited liability company's financial statements is useful to the owners of a small business?

5.4* The following balances have been extracted from the books of Margo Ltd for the year to 31 January 2017:

	Dr £	Cr £
Cash at bank and in hand	5000	
Plant and equipment:		
At cost	70000	
Accumulated depreciation (at 31.1.17)		25000
Retained earnings (at 1.2.17)		15000
Profit for the financial year (to 31.1.17)		10000
Share capital (issued and fully paid)		50000
Inventory (at 31.1.17)	17000	
Trade payables		12000
Trade receivables	20000	
	112000	112000

Additional information:
1 Corporation tax owing at 31 January 2017 is estimated to be £3000.
2 Margo Ltd's authorised share capital is £75,000 of £1 ordinary shares.
3 A dividend of 10p per share is proposed.

Required:
Prepare Margo Ltd's statement of profit or loss and statement of retained earnings for the year to 31 January 2017 and a statement of financial position as at that date.

5.5* Harry Ltd was formed in 2003. The following balances as at 28 February 2017 have been extracted from the books of account:

	Dr £	Cr £
Administration expenses	65000	
Cash at bank and in hand	10000	
Distribution costs	15000	
Dividend paid (on preference shares)	6000	
Furniture and equipment:		
At cost	60000	
Accumulated depreciation at 1.3.17		36000
Gross profit for the year		150000
Ordinary share capital (shares of £1 each)		100000
Preference shares (cumulative 15% of £1 shares)		40000
Retained earnings (at 1.3.17)		50000
Share premium reserve		20000
Inventory (at 28.2.17)	130000	
Trade payables		25000
Trade receivables	135000	
	421000	421000

Additional information:

1 Corporation tax owing at 28 February 2017 is estimated to be £24,000.
2 Furniture and equipment are depreciated at an annual rate of 10 per cent of cost and they are all charged against administrative expenses.
3 A dividend of 20p per ordinary share is proposed.
4 All the authorised share capital has been issued and is fully paid.

Required:

Prepare Harry Ltd's statement of profit or loss and statement of retained earnings for the year to 28 February 2017 and a statement of financial position as at that date.

5.6* The following balances have been extracted from the books of Jim Ltd as at 31 March 2016:

	Dr £	Cr £
Advertising	3000	
Cash	11000	
Payables		12000
Receivables	118000	
Furniture and fittings:		
At cost	20000	
Accumulated depreciation (at 1.4.16)		9000
Directors' fees	6000	
Retained earnings (at 1.4.16)		8000
Purchases	124000	
Rent and rates	10000	
Sales		270000
Share capital (issued and fully paid)		70000
Inventory (at 1.4.16)	16000	
Telephone and stationery	5000	
Travelling expenses	2000	
Vehicles:		
At cost	40000	
Accumulated depreciation (at 1.4.16)		10000
Wages and salaries	24000	
	379000	379000

Additional information

1 Inventory at 31 March 2016 was valued at £14,000.
2 Furniture and fittings, and the vehicles are depreciated at a rate of 15 per cent and 25 per cent, respectively, on cost.
3 Corporation tax owing at 31 March 2016 is estimated to be £25,000.
4 A dividend of 40p per share is proposed.
5 The company's authorised share capital is £100,000 of £1 ordinary shares.

Required

1 Prepare Jim Ltd's trading and statement of profit or loss and statement of retained earnings for the year to 31 March 2016 and a statement of financial position as at that date.

2 Why would the business not necessarily be worth its net assets value as at 31 March 2016?

5.7 The following trial balance has been extracted from Carol Ltd as at 30 April 2016:

	Dr £	Cr £
Advertising	2000	
Bank overdraft		20000
Bank interest paid	4000	
Payables		80000
Receivables	143000	
Directors' remuneration	30000	
Freehold land and buildings:		
At cost	800000	
Accumulated depreciation at 1.5.16		102000
General expenses	15000	
Investments at cost	30000	
Investment income		5000
Motor vehicles:		
At cost	36000	
Accumulated depreciation (at 1.5.16)		18000
Preference dividend paid	15000	
Preference shares (cumulative 10% shares of £1 each)		150000
Retained Earnings (at 1.5.16)		100000
Purchases	480000	
Repairs and renewals	4000	
Sales		900000
Share capital (authorised, issued and fully paid ordinary shares of £1 each)		500000
Share premium account		25000
Inventory (at 1.5.16)	120000	
Wages and salaries	221000	
	1900000	1900000

Additional information:

1 Inventory at 30 April 2016 was valued at £140,000.

2 Depreciation for the year of £28,000 is to be provided on buildings and £9000 for motor vehicles.

3 An accrual of £6000 is required for the auditors' remuneration.

4 £2000 had been paid in advance for renewals.
5 Corporation tax owing at 30 April 2016 is estimated to be £60,000.
6 The directors propose an ordinary dividend of 10p per share.
7 The market value of the investments at 30 April 2016 was £35,000.

Required:
Prepare Carol Ltd's trading and statement of profit or loss and statement of retained earnings for the year to 30 April 2016 and a statement of financial position as at that date.

5.8 Nelson Ltd was incorporated in 2003 with an authorised share capital of 500,000 £1 ordinary shares, and 200,000 5 per cent cumulative preference shares of £1 each. The following trial balance was extracted as at 31 May 2016:

	Dr £	Cr £
Administrative expenses	257000	
Auditor's fees	10000	
Cash at bank and in hand	5000	
Payables		85000
Debentures (12%)		100000
Debenture interest paid	6000	
Receivables	225000	
Directors' remuneration	60000	
Dividends paid:		
Ordinary interim	20000	
Preference	5000	
Furniture, fittings and equipment:		
At cost	200000	
Accumulated depreciation at 1.6.16		48000
Investments at cost (market value at 31.5.16: £340000)	335000	
Investment income		22000
Ordinary share capital (issued and fully paid)		400000
Preference shares		200000
Retained earnings (at 1.6.16)		17000
Purchases	400000	
Sales		800000
Share premium account		50000
Inventory at 1.6.16	155000	
Wages and salaries	44000	
	1722000	1722000

Additional information:
1 Inventory at 31 May 2016 was valued at £195,000.
2 Administrative expenses owing at 31 May 2016 amounted to £13,000.
3 Depreciation is to be charged on the furniture and fittings at a rate of 12.5 per cent on cost.

4 Salaries paid in advance amounted to £4000.
5 Corporation tax owing at 31 May 2016 is estimated to be £8000.
6 Ordinary dividend was declared just before the year end of 1.25p per share. That remains to be paid.

Required:
Prepare Nelson Ltd's trading and statement of profit or loss and statement of retained earnings for the year to 31 May 2011 and a statement of financial position as at that date.

5.9 The following trial balance has been extracted from the books of Keith Ltd as at 30 June 2016:

	Dr £	Cr £
Advertising	30000	
Cash	7000	
Payables		69000
Debentures (10%)		70000
Receivables (all trade)	300000	
Directors' remuneration	55000	
Electricity	28000	
Insurance	17000	
Investments (quoted)	28000	
Investment income		4000
Machinery:		
At cost	420000	
Accumulated depreciation at 1.7.16		152000
Office expenses	49000	
Ordinary share capital (issued and fully paid)		200000
Preference shares		50000
Preference share dividend	4000	
Retained earnings (at 1.7.16)		132000
Allowance for doubtful debts		8000
Purchases	1240000	
Rent and rates	75000	
Sales		2100000
Inventory (at 1.7.16)	134000	
Vehicles:		
At cost	80000	
Accumulated depreciation (at 1.7.16)		40000
Wages and salaries	358000	
	2825000	2825000

Additional information:
1 Inventory at 30 June 2016 valued at cost amounted to £155,000.
2 Depreciation is to be provided on machinery and vehicles at a rate of 20 per cent and 25 per cent, respectively, on cost.

3 Accrual is to be made for auditors' remuneration of £12,000.

4 Insurance paid in advance at 30 June 2016 amounted to £3000.

5 The allowance for doubtful debts is to be made equal to 5 per cent of outstanding trade receivables as at 30 June 2016.

6 Corporation tax owing at 30 June 2016 is estimated to be £60,000.

7 An ordinary dividend of 10p per share is declared just before the year end.

8 The investments had a market value of £30,000 at 30 June 2016.

9 The company has an authorised share capital of 600,000 ordinary shares of £0.50 each and of 50,000 8 per cent cumulative preference shares of £1 each.

Required:

(a) Prepare Keith Ltd's trading and statement of profit or loss and statement of retained earnings for the year to 30 June 2016 and a statement of financial position as at that date.

(b) Explain why shareholders of Keith Ltd would not necessarily have been able to sell the business for its net assets value as at 30 June 2016.

Website

Further practice questions, study material and links to relevant sites on the World Wide Web can be found on the website that accompanies this book. The site can be found at www.pearsoned.co.uk/dyson

Other entity accounts

Who is watching the public purse . . . ?

Accountability to Parliament for taxpayers' money

The incentives on departmental Accounting Officers (usually the Permanent Secretary) to safeguard value for taxpayers' money are weak compared to those associated with the day-to-day job of satisfying Ministers, according to today's report from the National Audit Office.

Accounting Officers (AOs) have always had to balance the priorities, risks and pressures associated with these dual accountabilities, but, over time, the emphasis appears to have shifted in a way that potentially undermines accountability to Parliament. The NAO finds that AOs appear to lack confidence to challenge Ministers where they have concerns about the feasibility or value for money of new policies or decisions, not least because standing up to Ministers is seen as damaging to a civil servant's career prospects.

The creation of accountability system statements was [a] positive development, but they are not comprehensive and often are little more than a compliance exercise. The NAO concludes that ensuring the essentials of accountability in some areas of government still seems to be an afterthought. Furthermore, HM Treasury has not asserted its own key role in setting the overall framework for AO accountability and providing clarity about expectations on AOs.

Overall, the NAO concludes that a robust, accountable system of decision-making, which safeguards taxpayers' money effectively, needs much more transparency than is currently the case. Among the NAO's recommendations is that the Treasury should introduce a new requirement on AOs to provide positive, on-the-record assurance ahead of key implementation decisions. This would help ensure that appropriate, informed judgements are made before public resources are committed.

Accounting officers are responsible for the delivery of value for money – the economy, efficiency and effectiveness of public projects and programmes. In this they converge closely with the Committee of Public Accounts and, of course, the NAO. AOs have always had to balance this role against other duties to execute policy and support Ministers. I think that these ministerial and policy goals have come to weigh more and more heavily. The ever-increasing influence of Special Advisers, and Ministers' greater involvement in policy implementation and Civil Service appointments, is pressing down on the 'Ministerial' end of the see-saw further and further, while considerations of value for money and public value rise steadily into the air.

Source: Amyas Morse, head of the National Audit Office, 23 February 2016.

Source: Accountability to Parliament for taxpayers' money, National Audit Office, 23 February 2016.

Questions relating to this news story can be found on page 148. ➡

About this chapter

In previous chapters we have shown you how to compile a set of financial statements and explained what they tell you by using examples from private sector sole trader businesses and limited liability companies. However, we would be presenting an unbalanced and unhelpful view of accounting if we did not also refer to the many other types of private and public entities.

In a book of this nature we cannot possibly deal with every conceivable type of entity that you may come across but fortunately we do not need to. In broad terms, the accounting requirements are usually similar to those of sole traders and companies and all that is possibly required is some technical specialist advice, e.g. if the entity is an investment bank or an insurance company. The main difference is more in the way that their financial statements are presented rather than in their accounting methods.

By the time you get to the end of this book you will find that you will have gained sufficient knowledge and confidence to be able to find your way around almost any type of financial statement no matter whether it is in the private or the public sector and irrespective of its organisation, size and type.

This chapter is yet another step towards achieving that goal.

Learning objectives	By the end of this chapter you should be able to:

- prepare a simple manufacturing account;
- describe the type of financial statements required by service sector entities;
- compare and contrast financial statements in the profit-making sector with those in the not-for-profit sector and
- state why accounting procedures in the public sector may be different from those in the private sector.

Why this chapter is important

This chapter is important for non-accountants because it will give you a more balanced and a more well-rounded appreciation of accounting and the presentation of accounting information in different types of entities.

Most accounting textbooks concentrate on looking at accounting practices in the private profit-making sector, especially those relating to manufacturing and trading entities. However, the service sector now forms a significant element in the private sector, so it would be misleading to ignore the accounting procedures in that sector. Similarly, in the not-for-profit sector there are many types of entities (such as charities and voluntary bodies) that play an important part in the life of many people. The Government too has a major impact on economic life and so we must also have a brief look at its method of accounting.

The relatively few other types of entities that we cover in this chapter will give you an indication of how basic accounting practices are used (with some modification) in other kinds of entities. You will also find that if you are involved in such entities, you can adapt your accounting knowledge to suit the requirements of different entities. Many non-accountants, for example, will be members of various social and sporting clubs so the accounting knowledge that you have gained by working your way through this book will enable you to assess the financial position and future prospects of such entities with relative ease. Indeed, you may already have come across misleading statements prepared by club treasurers, such as calling a summary of cash received and cash paid a 'balance sheet'! Mistakes like this may not be very serious but they will certainly confuse the club members and give them a false impression of the club's assets and liabilities.

It is to be hoped that after reading this book in general, and this chapter in particular, you will not make such mistakes – or other, much more serious ones.

Manufacturing accounts

An organisation that purchases or obtains raw materials and converts them to a finished goods state is known as a *manufacturing* entity. The finished goods are then sold to customers. Manufacturing entities are normally to be found in the private sector and they may operate as sole traders, partnerships or companies.

Unlike the examples we have used in previous chapters, manufacturing entities are not likely to use a *purchases* account. This is because they normally buy raw materials and then process them before they are sold as *finished goods*. So before the top part of the statement of profit or loss (i.e. the trading account) can be compiled, it is necessary to calculate the cost of converting the raw materials into finished goods. The conversion cost is called the *manufacturing cost* and it is the equivalent of a trading entity's purchases.

In order to calculate an entity's manufacturing cost, we need to prepare a *manufacturing account*. A manufacturing account forms part of the double-entry system and it is included in the periodic financial statements. It normally contains only manufacturing *costs* since it is rare to have any manufacturing *incomes*.

Manufacturing costs are debited to the manufacturing account. They are usually classified into *direct* and *indirect* costs. Direct costs are those costs that can be easily and economically identified with a particular segment (economically means at the least possible cost). A segment may be a department, a section, a product or a unit. Indirect costs are those costs that cannot be easily and economically identified with a particular segment. Indirect costs are sometimes referred to as 'overhead' or 'overheads'.

The format of the manufacturing account is straightforward. Normally, it contains two main sections itemising the direct and the indirect costs. Each section is then analysed into what are called the *elements of cost*. The elements of cost include materials, labour and other expenses.

Example 6.1 illustrates the format of a typical manufacturing account. A detailed explanation of its contents follows.

Construction of the account

In this section, we are going to explain how to construct a manufacturing account. We use Example 6.1 to do so.

Example 6.1	**Format of a basic manufacturing account**

	£000	£000
Direct costs (1)		
Direct materials (2)	20	
Direct labour (3)	70	
Other direct expenses (4)	5	
Prime cost (5)		95
Manufacturing overhead (6)		
Indirect material cost (7)	3	
Indirect labour cost (7)	7	
Other indirect expenses (7)	10	
Total manufacturing overhead incurred (8)		20

	£000	£000
Total manufacturing costs incurred (9)		115
Work-in-progress (10)		
Opening work-in-progress	10	
Closing work-in-progress	(15)	(5)
Manufacturing cost of goods produced (11)		110
Manufacturing profit (12)		11
Market value of goods produced transferred to the trading account (13)		121

Notes

(a) The number shown after each item refers to the tutorial notes. The values have been inserted purely for illustrative purposes.

(b) The term 'factory' or 'work' is sometimes substituted for the term 'manufacturing'.

Tutorial notes to Example 6.1

1 *Direct costs.* The exhibit relates to a *company's* manufacturing account. It is assumed that the direct costs listed for materials, labour and other expenses relate to those expenses that have been easy to identify with the specific products manufactured by the company.

2 *Direct materials.* The charge for direct materials will be calculated as follows:

direct material cost = (opening inventory of raw materials + purchases of raw materials) − closing inventory of raw materials

The total of direct material cost is sometimes referred to as *materials consumed*. Direct materials will include all the raw material costs and component parts that have been easy to identify with particular products.

3 *Direct labour.* This will include all those employment costs that have been easy to identify with particular products.

4 *Other direct expenses.* Besides direct materials and direct labour costs, there are sometimes other direct expenses that are easy to identify with particular products, e.g. the cost of hiring a specific machine. Such expenses are relatively rare.

5 *Prime cost.* The total of direct material costs, direct labour costs and other direct expenses is known as prime cost.

6 *Manufacturing overhead.* Overhead refers to the total of all indirect costs, and so any manufacturing costs that are not easy to identify with specific products will be classified separately under this heading.

7 *Indirect material cost, indirect labour cost and other indirect expenses.* Manufacturing overhead will probably be shown separately under these three headings.

8 *Total manufacturing overhead incurred.* This item represents the total of indirect material cost, indirect labour cost and other indirect expenses.

9 *Total manufacturing costs incurred.* The total of prime cost and total manufacturing overhead incurred equals the total manufacturing costs incurred.

10 *Work-in-progress.* This represents the estimated cost of incomplete work that is not yet ready to be transferred to finished inventory. There will usually be some opening and closing work-in-progress.

11 *Manufacturing cost of goods produced.* This equals the total manufacturing costs incurred plus (or minus) the difference between the opening and closing work-in-progress.

12 *Manufacturing profit.* The manufacturing cost of goods produced may be transferred straight to the finished goods inventory account. The finished goods inventory account is the equivalent of the purchases account in a trading organisation. Sometimes a manufacturing profit is added to the manufacturing cost of goods produced before it is transferred to the trading account. The main purpose of this adjustment is to enable management to compare more fairly the company's total manufacturing cost (inclusive of profit) with outside prices (since such prices will also normally include some profit). The profit added to the manufacturing cost of goods produced may simply be an appropriate percentage or it may represent the level of profit that the industry generally expects to earn. Any profit element added to the manufacturing cost (irrespective of how it is calculated) is an internal book-keeping arrangement, because the profit has not been earned or *realised* outside the business. It is what accountants call a 'book entry'.

13 *Market value of goods produced.* As explained in note 12 above, the market value of goods produced is the amount that will be transferred (i.e. debited) to the trading account.

Activity 6.1	Do you think that the structure of a manufacturing account makes it easy to follow? Check that you are clear about the meaning of each individual item. What does the information tell you about the cost of manufacturing during the period in question?

Example 6.2	**Constructing a manufacturing account**

The following balances, *inter alia*, have been extracted from the Wren Manufacturing Company as at 31 March 2017:

	Dr (£)
Carriage inwards (on raw materials)	6000
Direct expenses	3000
Direct wages	25000
Factory administration	6000
Factory heat and light	500
Factory power	1500
Factory rent and rates	2000
Factory supervisory costs	5000
Purchase of raw materials	56000
Raw materials inventory (at 1 April 2016)	4000
Work-in-progress (at 1 April 2016)	5000

Additional information

1 The inventory of raw materials at 31 March 2017 was valued at £6000.

2 The work-in-progress at 31 March 2017 was valued at £8000.

3 A profit loading of 50 per cent is added to the total cost of manufacture.

Required
Prepare Wren's manufacturing account for the year to 31 March 2017.

Answer to
Example 6.2

Wren Manufacturing Company:
manufacturing account for the year to 31 March 2017

	£	£	£
Direct materials			
Raw material inventory at 1 April 2016			4000
Purchases		56000	
Carriage inwards (1)		6000	62000
			66000
Less: Raw material inventory at 31 March 2017			6000
Cost of materials consumed			60000
Direct wages			25000
Direct expenses			3000
Prime cost			88000
Other manufacturing costs (2)			
Administration		6000	
Heat and light		500	
Power		1500	
Rent and rates		2000	
Supervisory		5000	
Total manufacturing overhead expenses			15000
			103000
Work-in-progress			
Add: Work-in-progress at 1 April 2016		5000	
Less: Work-in-progress at 31 March 2017		(8000)	(3000)
Manufacturing cost of goods produced			100000
Manufacturing profit (50%) (3)			50000
Market value of goods produced (4)			150000

Tutorial notes

1 Carriage inwards (i.e. the cost of transporting goods to the factory) is normally regarded as being part of the cost of purchases.

2 Other manufacturing costs include production overhead expenses. In practice, there would be a considerable number of other manufacturing costs.

3 A profit loading of 50 per cent has been added to the manufacturing cost (see question note 3). The manufacturing profit is a debit entry in the manufacturing account. The corresponding credit entry will eventually be made in the statement of profit or loss.

4 The market value of goods produced will be transferred to the finished goods inventory account.

Links with the other accounts

Example 6.2 deals with the manufacturing account in isolation. However, once the manufacturing account has been prepared, it will then be linked with the trading account (and hence also the statement of profit or loss) by transferring either the *manufacturing cost* of the goods produced or the *market value* of the goods produced to the trading account. The manufacturing cost or the market value of the goods produced is, therefore, the equivalent of 'purchases' in the trading account of a non-manufacturing entity. Apart from this minor amendment, the preparation of a trading account for a manufacturing entity is exactly the same as that for a trading entity. This relationship is shown in an outline in Figure 6.1.

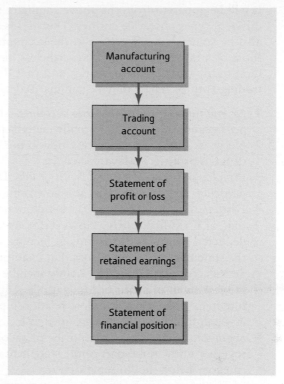

Figure 6.1 The relationship between the main accounts

Service entity accounts

The profit-making sector is made up of a great many other types of entities beside those that may be classified as manufacturing or trading. For convenience, we will describe them as *service entities*. Unlike manufacturing or trading entities, service entities do not normally deal in physical or tangible goods. Instead they offer advice and provide assistance to their customers, clients, patients or passengers. In recent years the manufacturing sector in the United Kingdom has declined and the service sector has become much more important.

The service sector is extremely diverse, but there are a number of recognisable categories. Some of the main ones are as follows.

- *Hotels and catering.* Such entities are generally regarded as being part of the service sector although the service they offer includes a physical or tangible element, e.g. the supply of food and drink.
- *Leisure and recreational activities.* Services included in this category include cinema, concerts and theatre productions, leisure and sports centres, and travel agencies.
- *Personal.* Examples of personal services include beauticians, hairdressing and manicures.
- *Professional.* The more common professional services include accounting, legal, architectural and medical (including chiropody and optical).
- *Transportation.* Transportation services include the movement of goods and passengers by air, land and sea.

| Activity 6.2 | Think of the main street in your own town or city. List six different types of service entities. |

It will be apparent from the above summary that there is an extremely wide variety of different types of service entities. This means that the accounts of different entities will also be somewhat different, e.g. the accounts of a beautician will not be identical to those of a railway company. Nevertheless, there are some basic features that are common to all service sector entities and that distinguish them from manufacturing and trading entities. These may be summarised as follows:

1 *No manufacturing and trading accounts.* These accounts are irrelevant in service entities because they do not normally manufacture products or trade in tangible goods.

2 *No gross profit.* As service entities do not prepare trading accounts, the calculation of gross profit is irrelevant.

3 *Primacy of the statement of profit or loss.* Details of the income and expenditure for a particular accounting period are shown almost entirely in the statement of profit or loss.

4 *Format.* The format of a service-sector statement of profit or loss is very similar to that of a trading entity. However, sometimes specific groups of expenditure are deducted from specific groups of income, the net amount then being highlighted in the statement of profit or loss. For example, suppose an entity sells food for £1000 and its cost was £600. The £1000 income *could* be shown in the income section of the statement of profit or loss with the £600 being shown separately as an expenditure item. But as there is a close relationship between the income and the expenditure, it is helpful to users if it is grouped as in Example 6.3.

5 *Segmentation.* Similar categories of income or expenditure are usually grouped together in the same part of the statement of profit or loss with the subtotal of each category being shown separately.

Example 6.3	**Extract from the statement of profit or loss**		
		£	£
	Income from sale of food	1000	
	Less: cost of provision	(600)	
			400

We illustrate the presentation of a set of financial statements for a service entity in Example 6.4. As you will see, the presentation of the statement of profit or loss, statement of retained earnings and the statement of financial position is very similar to the examples used in previous chapters.

Example 6.4	**A service entity account**		

Mei Loon: Educational training consultant
Statement of profit or loss for the year to 31 March 2017

	£	£
INCOME (1)		
Article fees	5000	
Author's licensing and collecting payments	2000	
Consultation fees	90000	
Lecture fees	30000	
Public lending right payment	1000	
Royalties	20000	148000

	£	£
EXPENDITURE (2)		
Computing	5000	
Depreciation : equipment (3)	2000	
: furniture (3)	500	
Heat and light	1000	
Insurances	600	
Photocopying	200	
Postage	100	
Rates	1500	
Secretarial	30000	
Stationery (4)	700	
Subscriptions	400	
Travelling	6000	(48000)
Net profit for the year (5)		100000

Statement of retained earnings for the year to 31 March 2017

	£
Opening retained earnings (12)	7000
Net profit for the year (13)	100000
Less: drawings (14)	(40000)
Closing retained earnings	67000

Statement of financial position at 31 March 2017

	£	
NON-CURRENT ASSETS (6)		
Office equipment	10000	
Less: accumulated depreciation	(4000)	6000
Office furniture	5000	
Less: accumulated depreciation	(1500)	3500
		9500
CURRENT ASSETS		
Inventory of stationery (7)	200	
Receivables (8)	15000	
Prepayments (9)	3000	
Cash at bank and in hand	52300	70500
		80000
CAPITAL AND RESERVES (12)		
Capital	10000	
Retained earnings	67000	77000
CURRENT LIABILITIES		
Payables (10)	2000	
Accruals (11)	1000	3000
		80000

Tutorial notes to Example 6.4

1 All six of the listed income items will have been compiled on an accruals and prepayments basis, i.e. the cash received during the period will have been adjusted for any opening and closing receivables.

2 Apart from depreciation, the expenditure items will have been adjusted for any opening or closing accruals and prepayments.

3 Mei Loon appears to be depreciating her office furniture by 10 per cent per annum on cost [($£500 \div £5000) \times 100\%$] and her office equipment by 20 per cent per annum on cost [($£2000 \div £10,000) \times 100\%$].

4 The stationery costs for the year have been reduced by the inventory at 31 March 2017 (see note 7).

5 The net profit for the year has been added to Mei Loon's capital at 1 April 2017 (see note 12).

6 The non-current assets are shown at their gross book value less the accumulated depreciation. The difference is known as 'net book value'.

7 Mei Loon has valued the inventory of stationery that she held at 31 March 2017 at £200.

8 The receivables entry probably represents what is owed to Mei Loon for various fees as at 31 March 2017.

9 The prepayments represent what she has paid in advance at the end of the year for various services, such as insurances or heat and light, from which she would expect to benefit in the year to 31 March 2018.

10 The payables represent what she owes at the end of the year for various goods and services supplied during the year.

11 The accruals are similar to the payables, but they probably relate to services such as insurances or heat and light (see note 9).

12 Mei Loon's capital balance is shown as £10,000. This is her original capital contribution. Previous years' profits of £7,000 that she had not drawn out of the business are reserves which are used in the retained earnings calculation. That should effect what addition investment (through reinvesting profits) has Mei Loon made since the inception of the business.

13 The net profit for the year is the balance on the statement of profit or loss.

14 Mei Loon has drawn £40,000 out of the business during the year for her own private use. Some of the £40,000 probably relates to previous years' profits that she has drawn out during the current year, along with various amounts drawn out in advance of this year's profits.

Activity 6.3

Refer to Example 6.4, examine Mei Loon's statement of profit or loss, statement of retained earnings and statement of financial position. What does the information tell you? How well has her consultancy done during the year to 31 March 2017? Is she likely to go bankrupt in the near future?

Not-for-profit entity accounts

News clip

Kids Company – the charity that failed

The trustees of Kids Company were 'negligent' and ignored repeated warnings about the organisation's financial health, MPs said as they outlined an 'extraordinary catalogue of failures' leading to the charity's collapse. Kids Company received £42m since it was set up in 1996 but was forced to close in August. In a report published on Monday, the MPs said trustees had neither the skills or experience to hold to account Kids Company's founder Camila Batmanghelidjh and allowed the charity's weak financial position to persist for years.

Source: Adapted from www.ft.com, 1 February 2016.

As the term suggests, not-for-profit entities are in business solely to provide some sort of service without necessarily needing to or wanting to make a profit. Examples include charities such as 'Save the Children', bridge clubs, music societies and sports organisations. It is possible that such bodies might be engaged in some sort of trading (or even manufacturing) but the profit motivation would not be their main consideration.

If not-for-profit entities have some manufacturing or trading activities, they will prepare manufacturing and trading accounts. The balance on the manufacturing account would be transferred to the trading account and the balance on the trading account (i.e. the gross profit) to a *statement of financial activities* (a sort of *income and expenditure account*). A statement of financial activities is in principle the same as a statement of profit or loss except that the balance on the account is described as the *excess of income* (or net expenditure) instead of *profit* (or *loss*) and (in the case of charities) it splits the incomes and expenses among *unrestricted funds, restricted funds* and *endowment funds*.

An example of a statement of financial activities and a statement of financial position for a social club is shown in Example 6.5. The preparation of such accounts is very similar to that for trading entities.

Example 6.5	**A social club's accounts**

Balli Social Club
Statement of financial activities for the year to 31 March 2017

	£	£
INCOME (1)		
Bar sales (2)	60000	
Less: purchases	(40000)	20000
Building society interest		200
Dances (2)	1600	
Less expenses	(900)	700
Food sales (2)	8000	
Less: purchases	(4500)	3500
Members' subscriptions		36200
		60600
EXPENDITURE (3)		
Accountants' fees	250	
Depreciation: furniture and fittings	3900	
Insurances	600	
Electricity	1400	
Office expenses	22000	
Rates	2000	
Salaries and wages	14000	
Telephone	3100	
Travelling expenses	13000	(60250)
Net income for the year (4)		350

Statement of financial position at 31 March 2017

	£ Cost	£ Accumulated depreciation	£ NBV
Non-current ASSETS (5)			
Club premises	18000		18000
Furniture and equipment	39000	(17900)	21100
	57000	17900	39100
CURRENT ASSETS (5)			
Inventory		1500	
Prepayments		200	
Members' subscriptions (in arrears)		7000	
Building society account		2700	
Cash		5500	16900
CURRENT LIABILITIES (5)			
Trade payables		2000	
Members' subscriptions (paid in advance)		800	
Accruals		1250	(4050)
			51950
ACCUMULATED FUND (6)			
Balance at 1 April 2016 (7)			51600
Net income for the year (8)			3 50
Balance at 31 March 2017 (9)			51950

Tutorial notes to Example 6.5

1 The income items will have been calculated on an accruals and prepayments basis.

2 Details relating to the bar, dances and food sales (and other similar activities) may require separate disclosure. If so, individual accounts would be prepared for these activities, the balance on such accounts then being transferred to the statement of financial activities.

3 Expenditure items would be calculated on an accruals and prepayments basis.

4 The balance on the account (the excess of income over expenditure for the year) is transferred to the Accumulated Fund account (see note 6).

5 None-current assets, current assets and current liabilities are calculated and presented similar to the way that they are for profit-making entities (although they are here netted off against each other to arrive at the net assets balance).

6 The Accumulated Fund is the equivalent of the capital element in the accounting equation. The total amount of £51,950 represents what the members have invested in the club as at 31 March 2017 and what could have been paid back to them (in theory) if the club had been closed down at that date. In practice, of course, the various items on the statement of financial position would not necessarily have been disposed of at their book values.

7 This was the balance in the Accumulated Fund at the beginning of the club's financial year.

8 This balance has been transferred from the statement of financial activities.

9 This is the balance in the Accumulated Fund as at the end of the club's financial year.

Activity 6.4

Referring to Example 6.5, how satisfactory do you think the Balli Social Club's financial performance has been during the year to 31 March 2017?

Government accounts

Public sector needs to do a better job with assets

The United Kingdom is also one of the world's leaders in preparing 'whole of government accounts' (WGA). These provide comprehensive and transparent information, similar to that required of private businesses. The 2016 Green Budget from the Institute for Fiscal Studies offers an interesting analysis. In the WGA, net liabilities have more than doubled, from £0.8tn on 31 March 2009 to £1.85tn five years later. This reflects a rise in public sector pension obligations, to £1.3tn, in addition to the near-doubling of public sector net debt from £0.7tn to £1.4tn. The picture may not be pretty, but it is more truthful.

Source: Extracted from www.ft.com, 15 April 2016.

Another important set of entity accounts relate to the government sector of the economy. Such accounts may generally be regarded as part of the not-for-profit service sector. There are three broad categories: central government accounts, local government accounts and quasi-governmental accounts.

Central government accounts incorporate the results of major departments such as defence, the environment, social security and trade and industry. Until a few years ago they were prepared on a cash basis, i.e. cash received for the year was matched with cash paid during that year but then the government switched to what it calls *resource* accounting. This is just another term for accounts prepared on an accruals and prepayments basis.

Resource accounting was introduced because government services needed to become more efficient, i.e. to offer a better service to the public for every pound spent. Cash accounting resulted in a lack of control of operations and projects. If a project was costing more than had been budgeted for it, for example, payments to suppliers would be delayed because this made the cash position look better.

Resource accounting has required government departments to adopt a different approach to the way that they manage their affairs. It involves setting objectives, laying down long and short-term plans, the tight management of funds and resources and statutory reporting similar to that required in the private sector.

Resource accounting involves producing sets of accounts that include operating cost statements. These are similar to statement of profit or loss and statement of financial positions. It is claimed that they have the following advantages:

- costs are charged to departments when they are incurred and not when they are paid for;
- distortions are removed between when goods and services are received, when they are paid and when they are consumed;
- departmental budgets are more realistic;
- it is much more difficult to disguise the overall cost of departmental activities and
- there is greater control over the safeguarding of non-current and current assets, e.g. inventory, and the monitoring of current liabilities such as payables.

These are substantial claims. Bearing in mind the difficulties that the commercial world has in dealing with 'accruals and prepayment' accounting, it is doubtful whether resource accounting is operating quite as smoothly as the government had expected.

Activity 6.5	Consider the benefits listed above that the switch to resource accounting was supposed to bring to government activities. How far do you think that they are being met? Is the absence of the profit motive in the not-for-profit sector a major difficulty?

An important part of the government sector is *local government*. Local government accounts include income and expenditure details relating to major services such as education, housing, police and social services. The annual budget (running from 1 April to 31 March) determines the amount of cash that the local authority needs to raise from its council tax payers in order to finance its projected expenditure for the forthcoming year. This is a highly political consideration and councillors are usually more concerned about the impact that a forthcoming budget may have on the electorate than about the expenditure that has already been incurred.

Another part of the government sector includes *quasi-government* bodies. They include those entities that are owned by the government but operated at arm's length (i.e. indirectly) through specially appointed authorities and councils. Examples include the British Broadcasting Corporation (BBC), secondary and tertiary education colleges and universities. Such entities are often heavily dependent on the government to provide a great deal of their operational income.

Overall, government accounting generally is a highly specialist activity, although the basics are similar to the procedures used in the private sector. As it is so specialised, we will not consider it any further in this book.

❗ Questions you should ask

This chapter covers a number of different types of entities so the following questions may not be relevant in all instances.

- How do you distinguish between 'direct costs' and 'indirect costs'?
- Why bother with manufacturing profit?
- How has the amount added for manufacturing profit been calculated?
- Are there any problems in deciding what income to take to the income and expenditure account?
- How have the depreciation rates for the non-current assets been arrived at?
- Should we allow for any bad debts or any doubtful ones? [A very important question in the case of social clubs.]
- What method has been used to estimate them?
- How have any accruals and prepayments been taken into account?

Conclusion

We began this chapter by describing the nature and purpose of manufacturing accounts and demonstrating how they may be compiled. We then moved the focus away from manufacturing and trading accounts towards other types of accounts used in the service sector and the not-for-profit sector.

You will have noticed that there is a great deal of similarity between manufacturing and trading accounts and the accounts of service sector entities. Manufacturing, trading and service sector entities all usually adopt an accruals and prepayments basis for preparing their financial statements and they are presented in the form of a statement of profit or loss (or equivalent) and a statement of financial position.

The main difference is in the detail. Non-manufacturing and trading entities have few (if any) raw material inventory, work-in-progress or finished goods and product costing is largely irrelevant. There are also a few differences in the way that information is presented in the statement of profit or loss (or the statement of financial activities) and the statement of financial position. So if you can work your way through a manufacturing entity's accounts, you should not have too much difficulty with non-manufacturing, non-trading and service sector accounts. Government accounts are, however, a different matter!

Key points

1 Entities that convert raw materials and component parts into finished goods may need to prepare a manufacturing account.

2 A manufacturing account is part of the double-entry system. Normally it will be prepared annually along with the other main financial accounts. It usually comes before the trading account.

3 The main elements of a manufacturing account include direct materials, direct labour, direct expenses and various indirect manufacturing costs.

4 A direct cost is a cost that can be easily and economically identified with a particular department, section, product, process or unit. An indirect cost is a cost that cannot be so easily and economically identified.

5 The type of manufacturing account described in this chapter would not be required if an entity had a management accounting system.

6 Service sector entities do not normally deal in physical or tangible goods or services. So they do not need to prepare a manufacturing or a trading account, their basic accounts consisting of a statement of profit or loss, a statement of retained earnings and a statement of financial position. The preparation of such financial statements is similar to that required for compiling manufacturing and trading entity accounts.

7 The accounts of not-for-profit entities are very similar to those of service entities, except that the statement of profit or loss is referred to as a statement of financial activities (or in some cases – income and expenditure account).

8 Government accounts are highly specialised although their basic structure is now similar to that adopted in the private sector.

Check your learning

The answers to these questions can be found within the text.

1   What is a manufacturing account?

2   What is (a) a direct cost and (b) an indirect cost?

3   What is meant by the term 'prime cost'?

4   How does an allowance for profit in the manufacturing account affect the cash position of the entity?

5   To which account is the 'market value of goods produced' transferred?

6   What is meant by the 'service sector'?

7   List five different groups of service sector entities.

8   Name four different types of businesses operating in the service sector.

9   What is meant by a 'not-for-profit' entity?

10   What terms are applied to its main financial statement?

11   Can a not-for-profit entity make profits?

12   What name is given to the balance that is transferred to the accumulated fund at the end of a financial period?

13   What is meant by an 'accumulated fund'?

14   What term does the government use to describe its method of accounting?

15   Name two types of local government activities.

16   Name two quasi-governmental entities.

News story quiz

Remember the news story at the beginning of this chapter? Go back to that story and reread it before answering the following question.

Government departments are required to prepare financial statements. The National Audit Office audits those as well as perform a range of value-for-money audits of how public money is spent.

Questions

1   While you may have never seen the complex accounts of government departments, how reassured you are that they are audited by the NAO? What is the benefit of audits to society?

2   As a taxpayer, what information do you want to see about how public money is spent?

3   What could be the implications for a business or a government department if more junior members of staff are reluctant to challenge the decisions of their superiors for fear of risking their career progression? As a manager, what kind of structures could you put in place to encourage transparency and participation in decision-making?

Tutorial questions

The answers to questions marked with an asterisk can be found in Appendix 4.

6.1 A direct cost has been defined as 'a cost that that can be easily and economically identified with a particular department, section product or unit'. Critically examine this definition from a non-accounting manager's perspective.

6.2 Although a manufacturing account may contain a great deal of information, how far do you think that it helps managers who are in charge of production cost centres?

6.3 It has been asserted that the main objective of a profit-making entity is to make a profit, while that of not-for-profit entity is to provide a service. Discuss this assertion in the context of the accounting requirements of different types of entities.

6.4* The following information relates to Megg for the year to 31 January 2017:

	£000
Inventory at 1 February 2016	
Raw material	10
Work-in-progress	17
Direct wages	65
Factory: Administration	27
Heating and lighting	9
Indirect wages	13
Purchases of raw materials	34
Inventory at 31 January 2017:	
Raw material	12
Work-in-progress	14

Required
Prepare Megg's manufacturing account for the year to 31 January 2017.

6.5* The following balances have been extracted from the books of account of Moor for the year to 28 February 2017:

	£
Direct wages	50000
Factory indirect wages	27700
Purchases of raw materials	127500
Inventory at 1 March 2016:	
Raw material	13000
Work-in-progress	8400
Inventory at 28 February 2017:	
Raw material	15500
Work-in-progress	6300

Required

Prepare Moor's manufacturing account for the year to 28 February 2017.

6.6 The following balances have been extracted from the books of Stuart for the year to 31 March 2017:

	£000
Administration: Factory	230
Direct wages	330
Purchases of raw materials	1123
Inventory at 1 April 2016:	
Raw material	38
Work-in-progress	29

Additional information:

Inventory at 31 March 2017:	
Raw material	44
Work-in-progress	42

Required

Prepare Stuart's manufacturing account for the year to 31 March 2017.

6.7 The following balances have been extracted from the books of the David and Peter Manufacturing Company as at 30 April 2017:

	£000
Direct wages	70
Factory equipment: at cost	360
General factory expenses	13
Heating and lighting (factory $\frac{3}{4}$; general $\frac{1}{3}$)	52
Purchases of raw materials	100
Inventory at 1 May 2016:	
Raw material	12
Work-in-progress	18
Rent and rates (factory $\frac{2}{3}$; general $\frac{1}{3}$)	42

Additional information

Inventory at 30 April 2017	£000
Raw material	14
Work-in-progress	16

The factory equipment is to be depreciated at a rate of 15 per cent per annum on cost.

Required

Prepare the David and Peter Manufacturing Company's manufacturing account for the year to 30 April 2017.

Website

Further practice questions, study material and links to relevant sites on the World Wide Web can be found on the website that accompanies this book. The site can be found at www.pearsoned.co.uk/dyson

Statement of cash flows

Is the end of cash near?....

Cash is king, says UK banknote printer De La Rue

Alan Tovey, Industry Editor for *The Telegraph*

You might not know the company's name, but you are definitely familiar with its biggest product – the £64bn of UK banknotes in circulation.

De La Rue is the company which produces the £5, £10, £20 and £50 notes for the Bank of England; and despite the rise of contactless payment and people's willingness to pay by plastic, it has no worries about the future of printed money.

'Even though we're using credit and debit cards more than ever, people still have cash in their wallet,' says chief executive Martin Sutherland. 'It's convenient, it's free at point of use, classless – not everyone has a bank account – and most of all, it's reliable. Cash is the payment mechanism of last resort, it will still work when there's a power cut or the card reader won't scan.' His confidence is backed up by data. Industry analyst Smithers Pira says the banknote market in Western Europe is growing at about 2.5% a year, with much higher rates in regions with more developed nations.

'We're focused on emerging economies where cash is king,' says Sutherland, adding that about 85% of De La Rue's business is for foreign markets, with the company involved in the design, production or issuing of banknotes in about 140 countries.

De La Rue is the biggest commercial printer of banknotes in the world – in some countries print works are state-owned – and it's also one of the most historic. The company has been printing banknotes for more than two centuries.

Just over a year ago De La Rue had its 10-year deal with the Bank of England – believed to be the company's biggest contract – renewed for another decade.

'We are generally seen as the leading designer of banknotes and passports but we have to be innovative about the security features we introduce because we are in an arms race with counterfeiters,' he says. 'The longer a particular feature is in circulation, the more time they have to work out how it is done and how to reproduce it, so we have to be constantly introducing new ideas. We're a counter-counterfeiting business.'

Source: Extract from *The Telegraph*, 30 December 2015.

Questions relating to this news story can be found on page 170. ➡

About this chapter

This chapter deals with cash flows and the financial statement that reports from them: the statement of *cash flows* (SCF). Cash is not static. It is nearly constantly in motion as it is used by individuals, businesses and governments every day. A statement of cash flows is a financial statement listing all the cash receipts and all the cash payments for a certain period of time. For over 25 years it has been considered to be one of the main financial statements. Preparation of the statement of cash flows is set out by International Accounting Standard 7 (IAS 7) *Statement of Cash Flows* which applies to UK listed companies and those UK companies which have elected to adopt International Financial Reporting Standards (IFRS). For all other UK companies, the preparation of the statement of cash flows is set out by FRS 102 *The Financial Reporting Standard Applicable in the UK and the Republic of Ireland (Section 7).* This standard has brought the requirements related to SCFs for non-listed companies in the United Kingdom much closer to IFRS than used to be the case.

Learning objectives

By the end of this chapter you should be able to:

- explain what is meant by cash and cash flows;
- explain what is meant by a statement of cash flows;
- describe its purpose;
- prepare a simple statement of cash flows;
- outline the main structure of a statement of cash flows in accordance with FRS 102 (Section 7) and IAS 7; and
- identify the main causes of a change in cash flows during an accounting period.

Why this chapter is important

This chapter is exceptionally important for non-accountants, especially those who are hoping to become senior managers in any entity, no matter its type or size. No entity can survive unless it takes in more cash than it is paying out and that applies both in the short term and in the long term. So all managers have to make sure that there is enough cash available (or that they can borrow enough) to meet their needs and settle their liabilities when they fall due. If they cannot do so, then their business will go bankrupt.

It follows that managers must monitor their cash position constantly. One way of doing this is for their accountants to give them a statement of cash flows (SCF) on a frequent and regular basis.

As a manager, an SCF will not mean much to you if you do not know where the information has come from, what it means and what you should do with it. This chapter gives you the knowledge to make full use of all that it will tell you.

News clip

Colt files for bankruptcy as cash is running out

Colt, the 179-year-old firearms manufacturer famous for making 'the gun that won the West', has filed for bankruptcy amid delayed government sales and stagnating demand. The company's cash reserves had dwindled to $11.1m by May 22. Last November, Colt borrowed $70m from Morgan Stanley to pay interest on its bonds, and in February 2015 said it might not have enough cash to make an interest payment by a June 2015 deadline.

Source: Adapted from The Financial Times, 15 June 2015.

What is cash?

You might think that there is no need to define what is meant by 'cash'. After all, everyone knows it is just notes and coins that you have in your pocket, tucked under the mattress or perhaps kept at the bank.

Within the context of accounting the definition is a little wider. It is as follows:

$$\text{Cash} = \text{cash on hand} + \text{demand deposits} + \text{overdrafts repayable on demand}$$

The definition of cash does indeed capture the coins and bank notes and cash at the bank (in both current and deposit accounts that give you instant access) as well as overdrafts which are repayable on demand. Strictly speaking, accounting rules also require for cash equivalents to be included. Cash equivalents are:

Short-term, highly liquid investments that are readily convertible to known amounts of cash and which are subject to insignificant risk of changes in value.

A maturity date of up to three months is usually taken as a guide to what is meant by 'short-term and highly liquid investments'.

For the rest of the chapter for simplicity we will only use cash to mean that which is in bank accounts and overdrafts repayable on demand.

Cash flow is an increase or decrease in cash during the period (*cash inflow* being when more cash is received than paid during a period; *cash outflow* being when more cash is paid than what received during a period).

Nature and purpose of the statement of cash flows (SCF)

News clip

A new era of cash-flow consciousness at electric car manufacturer

Tesla Motors Inc. signalled last week that a new era of cash-flow consciousness is underway at the electric car manufacturer. The newly hired CFO Jason Wheeler, formerly vice president of finance at Google, told analysts 'My mandate is clear: Cash is king.'

Wheeler said he sees $1 billion in cash as 'a nice comfort level' and that Tesla plans to draw upon an asset-backed revolving credit facility in 2016 to strengthen its cash position.

Source: Adapted from *Automotive News*, 14 February 2016.

An statement of cash flows (SCF) is a summary of all the cash that an entity has received for a period of account and all the cash payments that it has made during the same period.

Belton Limited
Statement of cash flows for the year to 31 December 2016

	2015	2016
	£000	£000
Receipts		
From Trade receivable (debtors)	1,410	1,990
Interest from cash deposits	–	400
	1,410	2,390
Payments		
To Trade payable (creditors)	720	1,400
Expenses	430	560
Development costs	20	250
Purchase of non-current assets	95	455
Repayment of loan	100	–
Tax paid	20	70
Dividends paid	30	60
	1,415	2,795
Net payments	(5)	(405)
Opening cash	10	5
Closing cash	5	(400)

Figure 7.1 Example of a statement of cash flows

The net balance is then usually added (or deducted) to the opening cash balance to arrive at the closing cash balance. An example of a simple SCF is shown in Figure 7.1.

A SCF is now considered to be one of the main financial statements along with the statement of profit or loss (SPL), the statement of changes in equity (SCE) and the statement of financial position (SFP). It is so because it provides vital information about an entity's cash position as reported in the SFP that is not disclosed in any of the other financial statements, i.e. **how** the entity got to its current cash position.

After working your way through this book so far, you might find this argument somewhat contradictory. You would have a point. In previous chapters we have emphasised just how important it is to show where the entity's *profit* has come from and now we are arguing for *cash*.

The truth is that both cash and profit are important: cash because an entity will not last overnight if it has not got the money to pay what it owes and profit because it will not survive in the long run if it does not make a profit.

In summary, remember that (1) cash received less cash paid is not the same as profit; (2) an entity needs enough cash to keep going; and (3) it has to make a profit in the long

News clip

Starting a new business: how to avoid failure

Businesses are most vulnerable during their early years of trading – half of all small businesses fail in the first couple of years, according to former *Dragon's Den* entrepreneur, Theo Paphitis. Theo explains that it's worth remembering the old business saying 'turnover is vanity, profit is sanity but cash is reality'. A shortage of cash is generally what sinks small businesses, so learning to monitor your cash flow is critical.

Source: Adapted from *The Guardian*, 22 March 2016.

run. Users of accounts need, therefore, information about an entity's cash position **AND** its profitability.

In the next section we explain how to prepare an SCF so that when you come across one, you will know where the information has come from, what it means and what you should do about it.

Activity 7.1	Go through Figure 7.1 identifying the main item that explains why a favourable cash balance of £5,000 has turned into a £400,000 overdraft.

Preparation

There are two recognised ways of preparing an SCF: the *direct method* and the *indirect method*. In the past, most companies opted for the indirect method but with the introduction of new accounting rules, the direct method is encouraged. During your career you might well come across both the direct and the indirect methods so we will show you both methods using the same example. First, the direct method.

The direct method

Under the direct method an SCF is prepared directly from entries made in the cash book (hence the name). It is a conceptually easy and simple way of preparing a SCF.

Example 7.1	**Preparation of a statement of cash flows**

The following information summarises all cash-related transactions for Durton Ltd in 2016:

1 Durton Ltd had £20,000 cash in its Barclays Bank account at the start of 2016.

2 On 1 January 2016 the company took out a £100,000 loan from Barclays Bank. The loan has an annual interest rate of 10%. The interest on the loan was paid on time in 2016.

3 Durton Ltd sells its products to customers on credit (the agreed credit term is 30 days). During 2016, it received £970,000 from customers in respect of sales of inventory made to them.

4 Durton Ltd purchases components for its products on credit (the agreed credit term is also 30 days). During 2016, it paid £680,000 to suppliers for purchases of components.

5 A new production line was acquired in the year at a cost of £150,000.

6 Salaries paid for the year amounted to £35,000. Various other operating expenses paid for by the business amounted to £100,000 for the year.

7 £30,000 was paid to shareholders as dividends.

8 Last year's tax liability to HMRC of £40,000 was settled in 2016.

The above transactions are posted to the cash book by the accountant. It looks like this:

Durton Ltd
Cash book summary for the year to 31 December 2016

Receipts	£000	Payments	£000
Balance b/f	20	Trade payables	680
10% loan	100	Salaries	35
Trade receivables	970	Operating expenses	100
		Loan interest	10

Cash Book (continued)

	£000			£000
		Taxation		40
		Dividends		30
		Non-current assets		150
		Balance c/f		45
	1 090			1 090

By closing the cash book it is possible to work out that the cash balance in the bank account of Durton Ltd at the end of the year is £45,000. There has been a cash inflow of £25,000 during 2016.

Required:
Prepare Durton's statement of cash flows for the year to 31 December 2016 using the direct method.

Answer to Example 7.1

Durton Ltd
Statement of cash flows for the year to 31 December 2016 using the direct method

	Tutorial notes	£000
Cash receipts		
From customers for sale of goods	1	970
10% loan	2	100
		1 070
Cash payments		
To suppliers for purchases of goods	3	(680)
Salaries	4	(35)
Operating expenses	4	(100)
Loan interest paid	5	(10)
Tax paid	6	(40)
Dividends paid	7	(30)
Non-current assets purchased	8	(150)
		(1 045)
Increase in cash during the year	9	25
Cash at 1 January 2016		20
Cash at 31 December 2016		45

Tutorial notes

Here are some of the reasons why the cash balance and the net cash flow are different from profit:

1 This amount has been received in cash from customers during the year for sales that were made by the company. Some of the payments relate to sales made in 2015. Equally, some payments for sales made in 2016 are still outstanding and will be settled in 2017. The figure here represents the actual cash received from customers in 2016 and will be different from the 2016 sales balance reported in the company statement of profit or loss for 2016.

2 The cash (asset) received from Barclays Bank as a loan (liability) will not be shown in the statement of profit or loss as only incomes earned and expenses incurred are shown there.

3 This amount is what has been paid to suppliers during the year for purchases that were made by the company. Some of the payments relate to purchases made in 2015. Equally, some payments for purchases made in 2016 are still outstanding and will be settled in 2017. The figure here represents the actual cash paid to suppliers in 2016 and will be different from the 2016 purchases balance reported in the company statement of profit or loss for 2016.

4   This amount is the aggregate for all expenses paid in 2016 (such as rent, advertising and salaries) even though the payments may be in respect of what was owed for 2015 or is prepaying for 2017.

5   As the loan has been taken out on 1 January 2016 £10,000 (10% on £100,000) is the total amount of interest for a full year. As all of it was paid in 2016, the amount will be the same as what is shown in the statement of profit or loss for 2016.

6   There is a time lag in the payment of taxation by companies. What is a liability to HMRC at the end of one accounting period is paid in the following one – here the 2015 liability was settled in 2016. The outstanding 2016 tax bill will be paid in 2017 (and there is no cash flow related to it in 2016).

7   The dividends may be the 2016 interim dividends or they could be a final dividend declared in 2015 and paid in 2016 or a combination of the two. Looking at the statement of financial position and statement of changes in equity (retained earnings) will explain which it is.

8   The cost of buying non-current assets would not be included in the statement of profit or loss as only incomes earned and expenses incurred are shown there (not assets).

9   The increase in cash during the year is the net of cash received and cash paid during 2016. Some of the cash received and cash paid relates to transactions entered into in 2015. Some may relate to payments for 2017 (e.g. part of the operating expenses paid may include a prepayment of rent, which covers the use of premises in 2017).

10   Hence neither the cash closing balance nor the net cash inflow balance will be the same as the reported profit.

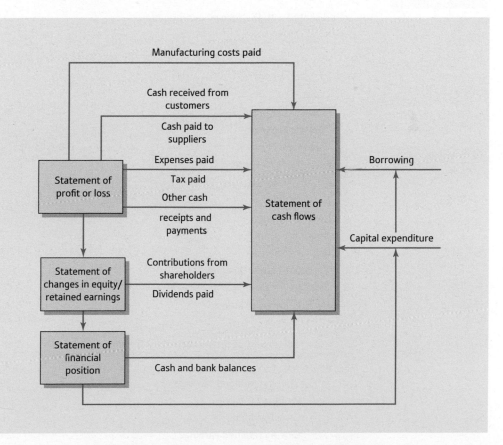

Figure 7.2 The interrelationship between the main financial statements

As you worked your way through Example 7.1 you probably found it fairly easy because you were given a highly summarised version of the cash book and this provided most of the information you needed. It would have been a little more difficult to prepare an SCF if you had to extract what you wanted from a poorly kept cash book, which is why keeping orderly accounting records is of paramount importance for any well-organised business.

Even though the SCF is fairly easy to prepare, the information provided is not independent of the other main financial statements: the SPL, the SRE and the SFP. The picture painted about a business would be partial if the financial statements are viewed in isolation as they all interrelate! This becomes more apparent if the indirect method is used even though it is perhaps a little more difficult to understand. We move now to the indirect method.

The indirect method

This method simply extracts and adapts where necessary the data included in the SPL, the SCE/SRE and the SFP. As a result, this method shows a clear link and a close relationship between the SCF and the other financial statements as Figure 7.2 demonstrates.

The indirect method is shown in Example 7.2 but it also includes the statement of retained earnings for 2016 and the statement of the company's retained earnings for both 2015 and 2016.

Example 7.2	**Preparation of a statement of cash flows using the indirect method**

You are presented with the following information:

Durton Ltd
Statement of profit or loss for the year to 31 December 2016

	£000	£000
Sales		1000
Less: Cost of goods sold		
Opening inventory	200	
Purchases	700	
Less: Closing inventory	(300)	
		(600)
Gross profit		400
Operating expenses		(240)
Operating profit		160
Interest expense		(10)
Net profit before taxation		150
Taxation		(50)
Net profit after taxation		100

Durton Ltd
Statement of retained earnings for the year to 31 December 2016

	£000
Opening retained earnings	200
Profit for the year	100
Less: Dividends	(60)
Closing retained earnings	240

Durton Ltd
Statement of financial position at 31 December 2016

	2015		2016	
	£000	£000	£000	£000
Non-current assets at cost	900		1 050	
Less: Accumulated depreciation	(150)	750	(255)	795
Current assets				
Inventory	200		300	
Trade receivables (debtors)	120		150	
Cash	20	340	45	495
		1 090		1 290
Capital and reserves				
Ordinary shares of £1 each	750		750	
Retained earnings	200		240	
		950		990
Non-current liabilities				
10% Loan (taken on 1 January 2016)		–		100
Current liabilities				
Trade payable (creditors)	70		90	
Taxation payable	40		50	
Dividend declared	30	140	60	200
		1 090		1 290

Required:
Prepare a statement of cash flows for the year to 31 December 2016 using the indirect method.

Answer to Example 7.2

Durton Ltd
Statement of cash flows for the year to 31 December 2016

	Tutorial notes	£000
Cash receipts		
From customers for sale of goods	1	970
10% Loan	2	100
		1 070
Cash payments		
To suppliers for purchases of goods	3	680
Salaries and other operating expenses	4	135
Loan interest paid	5	10
Taxation	6	40
Dividends	7	30
Purchases of non-current assets	8	150
		1 045
Increase in cash during the year 2016		25
Cash at 1 January 2016		20
Cash at 31 December 2016		45

Tutorial notes

Here is the explanation of how the cash flows were arrived at from information in the other financial statements:

1 Cash received from sale of goods = (opening debtors + sales) − closing debtors:
$$(1000 + 120) - 150 = 970.$$

2   Cash received when a loan was taken out in the current period: $100 - 0 = 100$.

3   Cash paid for purchases of goods = (opening creditors + purchases) − closing creditors:

$$70 + 700 - 90 = 680.$$

4   Operating expenses – depreciation: $240 - 105^* = 135$ [*accumulated depreciation balances: $255 - 150$]. Depreciation is an accounting adjustment and does not involve the payment of cash.

5   Loan interest: $10\% \times 100 = 10$. All of it has been paid as there is no outstanding liability in the SFP.

6   Taxation: 40. Only last year's has been paid as the taxation in the SPL for 2016 is the same amount shown in liabilities in the SFP for 2016, i.e. the current year's tax remains to be paid.

7   Dividends: 30. Only last year's dividend has been paid as the dividend in the SRE for 2016 is the same balance as the liability in the SFP for 2016, i.e. the final dividend declared remains to be paid. There does not appear to have been an interim dividend as the total dividend reported in the SRE is the same as what remains to be paid (hence the final dividend declared) which is a liability in the SFP.

8   Purchase of non-current assets: $1050 - 900 = 150$.

What is the SCF telling us?

As Example 7.1 and Example 7.2 show their respective SCFs are identical irrespective of the SCF is exactly the same regardless of whether the direct or indirect method was used.

We can now begin to work out what Durton's SCF is telling us. The statement of financial position shows that at 31 December 2015 the company had a cash balance of £20,000. By 31 December 2016, the cash balance was £45,000, an increase of £25,000. The retained earnings for the year of £40,000 were more than the £25,000 increase in cash during the year. We do not, of course, need to prepare an SCF to find out such information but we do need some help in determining why there is a difference. A SCF provides us with the evidence. Most of the cash received for the year came from sales and much of it was spent on buying goods, but if you look at the SCF a little more closely, you will also see that £100,000 was raised by taking out a loan and that £150,000 was incurred on purchasing some non-current assets. These items do not appear in the statement of profit or loss. There is probably a connection between them: the loan might have been taken to finance the purchase of the non-current assets. Certainly, without the loan, the cash position at the end of the year would have been very different, e.g. an overdrawn amount of £55,000 ($45,000 - 100,000$) instead of a favourable balance of £45,000. Similarly, if the taxation payable balance of £50,000 and the dividend declared of £60,000 at 31 December 2016 have to be paid early in 2017, the cash position would be extremely vulnerable. Durton Ltd would then have to depend on its trade receivables (£150,000 at 31 December 2016) settling their debts before it could pay its trade payables of £90,000.

Durton's SCF is a simplified example of a company's statement of cash flows. Nevertheless, it does enable the major cash items to be highlighted and to bring them to the attention of the managers and to the owners of the company. Although it is to be hoped that the cash position of Durton was being closely monitored during the year, an annual SCF enables the year's results to be put into context.

Activity 7.2

Durton Ltd retained earnings of £40,000 for the year to 31 December 2016 and yet its cash balance only increased by £25,000 from £20,000 at the beginning of the year to £45,000 at the end of it. The managing director (a salesperson) thinks that someone has defrauded the company of £15,000. Let him have a note (via email) explaining to him why this is not so.

The indirect method may appear to be a little more difficult to grasp (at least initially) than the direct method as the various cash flows are not as easy to trace. What is clear, however, is the very close relationship between the statement of profit or loss, the statement of retained earnings, the statement of financial position and the SCF.

Over time a layout for the SCF has evolved to show its close relationship with all financial statements. Both the FRC and the IASB have issued an accounting standard covering the preparation and presentation of SCFs: FRS 102 (Section 7) and IAS 7, respectively. IAS 7 is applicable for all listed companies in the United Kingdom and those who have elected to adopt IFRS. FRS 102 is applicable to the rest of the large and medium-sized companies in the United Kingdom. Small companies are exempt from preparing an SCF although they may choose to prepare one.

FRS 102 (Section 7) and IAS 7 are not absolutely identical but they follow the same principles. Overseas students (especially those from EU countries) are likely to use the IASB's version. However, UK students will probably come across both FRS 102 (Section 7) and IAS 7 so we will deal with each of them. First, FRS 102.

FRS 102 (Section 7) presentation

FRS 102 was last updated in September 2015. It is quite a complicated standard but only Section 7 deals with the statement of cash flows. We are also going to cover only the direct method as this is easier to grasp. Our discussion will be in two parts: (1) an example of a SCF as required by FRS 102 and (2) an explanation of some of its main features.

The main idea of a formal SCF is to show the cash inflows and outflows from a business in respect of three different aspects of a business: its operating activities, its investing activities and its financing activities. *Operating activities* are the principal revenue-generating activities of the entity, such as buying and selling inventory or the expenses incurred while generating revenues. The cash flows that relate to items that feature in the profit or loss calculation are included here. *Investing activities* relate to what a business does to invest for the future, such as buying a new property. *Financing activities* are activities that relate to how a business is funded, such as the issue of new shares or taking out a loan.

Layout

Figure 7.3 shows what a simple SCF could looks like under FRS 102 (Section 7) using the direct method.

There are a few other items that may be shown in a real company SCF but they are more advanced or relate specifically to banks so we will ignore them here for simplicity. There is also some choice about the presentation of interest and dividends which we will also omit. If you would like to find out all the details of the standard you will find FRS 102 on the FRC website.

When you prepare a SCF, headings may be omitted if no cash transaction has taken place either in the current period or in the previous period. They must be in the order listed. A subtotal should be included for each heading. The reconciliation at the bottom of the SCF is not always required but it is certainly helpful to users.

We will use Durton Ltd's accounts as our example once again because by now you should be familiar with the details.

The SCF looks very similar if the indirect method is used to prepare it, except for the operating cash flows section at the top. Under this method the statement starts with

Statement of cash flows for the year to 31 December 20xx

Cash receipts from customers	x
Cash payments to suppliers	(x)
Cash payments to and on behalf of employees	(x)
Cash payments for operating expenses	(x)
Interest paid or received	(x)/x
Dividends received	x
Cash payments or refunds of tax	(x)/x
Net cash in/(out)flow from operating activities	a
Cash payments to acquire non-current assets	(x)
Cash receipts from the sale of non-current assets	x
Cash payments to acquire investments (equity or debt instruments)	(x)
Cash receipts from the sale of investments (equity or debt instruments)	x
Net cash in/(out)flow from investing activities	b
Cash proceeds from issuing shares	x
Cash payments to owners	(x)
Cash proceeds from borrowings	x
Cash repayments of amounts borrowed	(x)
Net cash in/(out)flow from financing activities	c
Reconciliation of the cash position	
Cash in hand + deposits + overdraft at the start of the year	x
Net cash in/(out)flow for the year [a+b+c]	x
Cash in hand + deposits + overdraft at the end of the year	x

Figure 7.3 The statement of cash flow in accordance with FRS 102 (Section 7)

Example 7.3

Preparation of a statement of cash flows in accordance with FRS 102 (Section 7) using the direct method

Using the data from Durton Ltd, Example 7.1 on pages 155, prepare a statement of cash flows in accordance with FRS 102 (Section 7) using the direct method.

Durton Ltd
Statement of cash flows for the year to 31 December 2016

	£000
Cash receipts from customers	970
Cash payments to suppliers	(680)
Cash payments to employees	(35)
Cash payments for operating expenses	(100)
Interest paid	(10)
Cash payments of tax	(40)
Net cash inflow from operating activities	105
Cash payments to acquire non-current assets	(150)
Net cash outflow from investing activities	(150)
Cash payments to owners for dividends	(30)
Cash proceeds from borrowings	100
Net cash inflow from financing activities	70
Net cash inflow for the year [a + b + c]	25

	£000
Reconciliation of the cash position	
Cash at the start of the year	20
Net cash inflow for the year	25
Cash at the end of the year	45

operating profit as reported in the SPL which is reconciled to operating cash flows by adjusting operating profit for:

1 anything that went into the profit calculation as result of non-cash transactions (e.g. credit sales and purchases of inventory) and
2 the effect of accounting adjustments to profit done at the year end (such as depreciation, accruals and prepayments).

This is what the operating cash flow section would look like:

Statement of cash flows for the year to 31 December 20xx (extract)	
Operating profit	x
Add back depreciation and other accounting adjustments	x
(Increase)/decrease in inventory	(x)/x
(Increase)/decrease in trade receivables	(x)/x
Increase/(decrease) in trade payables	x/(x)
Interest (paid) or received	(x)/x
Dividends received	x
Cash (payments) or refunds of tax	(x)/x
Net cash in/(out)flow from operating activities	a

Figure 7.4 The operating cash flow section of the statement of cash flow in accordance with FRS 102 (Section 7) – indirect method

The above adjustments to the profit numbers would often be shown in the notes to the accounts rather than on the face of the SCF. The rest of the sections of the statement would look the same as under the direct method.

We will again use Durton Ltd's accounts as our example.

Example 7.4	**Preparation of a statement of cash flows in accordance with FRS 102 (Section 7) using the indirect method**

Using the data from Durton Ltd, Example 7.2 on pages 158, prepare a statement of cash flows in accordance with FRS 102 (Section 7) using the indirect method.

Durton Ltd
Statement of cash flows for the year to 31 December 2016

		£000
Operating profit	1	160
Add back depreciation	2	105
(Increase) in inventory	3	(100)
(Increase) in trade receivables	4	(30)

		£000
Increase in trade payables	5	20
Interest paid or received		(10)
Cash payments of tax		(40)
Net cash inflow from operating activities		**105**
Cash payments to acquire non-current assets		(150)
Net cash outflow from investing activities		**(150)**
Cash payments to owners		(30)
Cash proceeds from borrowings		100
Net cash inflow from financing activities		**70**
Net cash inflow for the year		**25**
Reconciliation of the cash position		
Cash at the start of the year		20
Net cash inflow for the year		25
Cash at the end of the year		45

Tutorial notes to Example 7.4

1 The operating profit of £160,000 has been obtained from the statement of profit or loss.

2 The depreciation charge has been obtained from the statement of financial position. It is the difference between the accumulated depreciation of £255,000 as at 31 December 2016 and £150,000 as at 31 December 2015.

3 The increase in inventory has been obtained from the two statements of financial positions. It is the movement between the two balances of £300,000 and £200,000. Note that an increase in inventory is the equivalent of a *reduction* in cash because more cash will have been paid out.

4 The increase in trade receivables of £30,000 represents the movement between the opening and closing trade receivables as obtained from the two statements of financial positions. An increase in trade receivables represents a *reduction* in cash because less cash has been received by the entity when sales were made on credit.

5 The increase in trade payables of £20,000 is again obtained from the statement of financial positions. The £20,000 represents an *increase* in cash because less cash has been paid out of the business when purchases were made on credit.

Main features

We hope that you have been able to work your way even so through Example 7.4 line by line and note by note without too much difficulty. We think that you will agree that it is not particularly easy to follow even if you are familiar with the data. We will now try to pull out some of the main features and difficulties in order to enable you to compile simple SCFs for yourself. If you can do that, then you should be able to cope with more complex presentations that you may come across in your job.

The reconciliation of operating profit to operating cash flows basically converts the traditional statement of profit or loss items prepared on an accruals basis back to a cash basis. We do this by adding to or deducting any increase or decrease in opening and closing receivable, prepayments, payable and accruals. If closing trade receivables, for example, are greater than the opening trade receivables, we *deduct* the increase from the operating profit. We do this because, other things being equal (*ceteris paribus*), less cash has been received during the year. If the closing trade receivables are less than opening ones, we *add* the decrease to the operating profit. Again we do this because, *ceteris paribus,* more cash has been received during the year.

This notion of adding or deducting the movement between the opening and closing current asset and current liability balances is sometimes quite difficult to grasp and so to work out. In order to make it much easier for you we have summarised the procedure in Table 7.1.

TABLE 7.1 The effect of working capital movements on cash flow

Item	Movement (closing less opening balance)	Effect on cash
Inventory	Increase	Down (more cash has been spent on inventory). Insert the movement in brackets
	Decrease	Up (less cash has been spent on inventory)
Trade receivable, other debtors and prepayments	Increase	Down (less cash has been received). Insert the movement in brackets
	Decrease	Up (more cash has been received)
Trade payables, other creditors and accruals (excluding taxation payable and dividends declared)	Increase	Up (less cash has been spent)
	Decrease	Down (more cash has been paid). Insert the movement in brackets

Activity 7.3

State whether each of the following statements is true or false.

(a) Operating activities reflect total cash inflows.   *True/false*
(b) Depreciation decreases the cash position.   *True/false*
(c) Tax paid decreases the cash position.   *True/false*
(d) A dividend declared increases the cash position.   *True/false*
(e) A decrease in trade receivables increases the cash position.   *True/false*
(f) An increase in trade payables decreases the cash position.   *True/false*

We now leave FRS 102 and in this section we explain how to prepare and present an SCF in accordance with IAS 7 which applies the same principles.

IAS 7 format

The process and principles are very similar to those explained for FRS 102 (Section 7). This is because the new FRS 102 was updated in September 2015 to bring it much closer to International Financial Reporting Standards than was previously the case.

Layout

A SCF prepared under IAS 7 has three main headings: *operating activities, investing activities* and *financing activities*. The operating activities include those incomes and expenses that you would normally find in the statement of profit or loss. If the indirect method is used, the adjustments that you need to make are identical to the ones we outlined for you in the previous section (see Table 7.1). Investing activities may include the purchases and sales of long-term assets and investments while financing activities include cash from the sale and purchase of the company's own shares, debentures and loans.

Walt Disney's cash flow in 2015

In 2015, Walt Disney Co increased its cash reserves by 24.79%, or $848m. The company earned $10.91bn from its operations for a cash flow margin of 20.79%. In addition, the company used $4.25bn on investing activities and also paid $5.51bn in financing cash flows.

Source: Adapted from www.ft.com, accessed 26 March 2016.

The standard allows a great deal of discretion about what to include under each heading but as with anything in accounting, once choices are made, they have to be applied consistently over time. There is a choice, for example, about where to show the cash flows related to interest and dividends and then received and paid may be classified as operating, investing or financing cash flows.

The direct method is the method encouraged by IAS 7 although an entity may choose to use the indirect method.

Real-life example

Here is what a SCF looks like for a real business: De La Rue (remember the business you read about at the start of the chapter, the company which prints out money?). The De La Rue group prepares its accounts under IFRS as adopted by the European Union and this is what its statement of cash flows looks like for the latest available accounting period (Figure 7.5).

De La Rue - Group Statement of Cash Flows for the period ended 28 March 2015	2015	2014
Cash flows from operating activities	£m	£m
Profit before tax	38.9	59.8
Adjustments for:		
Finance income and expense	11.9	12.0
Depreciation and amortisation	24.8	28.3
Decrease/(increase) in inventory	5.7	(6.1)
Decrease/(increase) in trade and other receivables	0.1	(11.5)
Decrease in trade and other payables	(5.4)	(0.9)
Decrease in reorganisation provisions	(0.3)	(6.0)
Special pension fund contributions	(18.6)	(11.5)
Loss/(profit) on disposal of property, plant and equipment and software intangibles	2.2	(4.0)
Asset impairment	3.8	14.2
Other non-cash movements	0.5	(0.4)
Cash generated from operating activities	63.6	73.9
Tax paid	(9.3)	(11.2)
Net cash flows from operating activities	54.3	62.7

De La Rue Group Statement of Cash Flows for the period ended 28 March 2015

Cash flows from investing activities		
Purchases of property, plant, equipment and software intangibles	(28.8)	(34.9)
Development assets capitalised	(5.1)	(4.7)
Proceeds from sale of property, plant and equipment	0.2	8.1
Net cash flows from investing activities	(33.7)	(31.5)
Net cash flows before financing activities	20.6	31.2
Cash flows from financing activities		
Proceeds from issue of share capital	0.4	3.8
(Repayments of)/proceeds from borrowings	(6.8)	47.2
Interest received	0.2	0.2
Interest paid	(4.8)	(4.6)
Dividends paid to shareholders	(36.8)	(42.2)
Dividends paid to non-controlling interests	(0.2)	(0.2)
Net cash flows from financing activities	(48.0)	4.2
Net (decrease)/increase in cash and cash equivalents in the period	(27.4)	35.4
Cash and cash equivalents at the beginning of the period	56.2	21.7
Exchange rate effects	0.1	(0.9)
Cash and cash equivalents at the end of the period	28.9	56.2
Cash and cash equivalents consist of:		
Cash at bank and in hand	28.6	55.7
Short-term deposits	2.2	2.2
Bank overdrafts	1.9	(1.7)
	28.9	56.2

Figure 7.5 De La Rue Statement of Cash Flow extracted from the group Annual Report 2015

As you can see, the statement of cash flows of a real business may be more complex than the simplified version we presented to you earlier in the chapter. Do not worry about not understanding all the extra terminology. What matters is that you get the idea of what a statement of cash flows is, how it is put together and what it tells you about a business.

Activity 7.4

Have a look at the De La Rue statement of cash flows above and answer the following questions:

(a) What constitutes cash for De La Rue?
(b) What method has the company used to prepare its SCF – the direct or indirect method?
(c) Where has De La Rue chosen to show the cash flows related to interest and dividends – in operating, investing or financing activities?
(d) Is De La Rue reporting a cash inflow or a cash outflow for 2015?
(e) What are the main reasons for that cash movement?

The differences between a SCF prepared under FRS 102 (Section 7) and one prepared under IAS 7 requirements are not particularly significant and its precise format does not really matter. What does matter is that as a manager: (a) you receive some sort of SCF; (b) that you know what it is and (c) and you know what action to take when you receive it. It could help to save your job and your company!

Spare a thought for governments as they also have to manage the cash receipts from taxes and the cash payments on government-funded services, such as roads maintenance, education, healthcare and many other competing priorities. The principles are exactly the same (although the detailed formats of government accounts differ from those of companies) and the repercussions of running out of cash are just as serious but on a far grander scale.

News clip

Greece debt crisis: Can new technology ease cash-flow issues?

As talks on Greece's future in the Eurozone drag on, the country's financial situation is close to collapse. Businesses and their customers are struggling to get hold of the money they need. Fans of Bitcoin say the virtual currency could be a way for Greeks to keep their money safe and avoid capital controls.

Source: BBC News Athens, 12 July 2015.

Questions you should ask

It is unlikely that as a non-accountant you will have to prepare statements of cash flows. Your accountants will do that for you and present you with them from time to time.

We will assume that after studying this chapter you know where the information comes from and what it means. But what questions should you ask? We suggest that the following may be appropriate:

- Why has there been an increase or a decrease in cash during the period?
- What are the main items that have caused it?
- Did we anticipate them happening?
- What caused them?
- What did we do about any likely problems?
- Are we going to be short of cash in the immediate period that follows?
- Will the bank support an extension of our overdraft?
- Can we borrow some funds from elsewhere?
- Might we need to borrow some on a long-term basis?
- How will that affect our future cash position?
- What impact will it have on our profitability?

Conclusion

A statement of cash flows contains some extremely useful information for management because it gives a lot more detail about the movement in the cash position. This is vital as it is possible for an entity to be profitable without necessarily having the cash resources to keep it going. Strict control over cash resources is absolutely essential, and a statement of cash flows can help in this respect.

1   Entities may have a long-term profitable future but in the short term they may be short of cash. This may curb their activities and in extreme cases they may be forced out of business.

2   To avoid this happening, owners and managers should be supplied with information about the cash movement and resources of the entity, i.e. about its liquidity. This can be done by preparing a statement of cash flows.

3   Listed companies in the European Union must use IAS 7 in preparing their *group* financial statements as they are required to adopt IASB requirements. Non-listed companies in the United Kingdom may use either IAS 7 or the FRS 102 (Section 7). Non-listed companies in other EU countries may have a similar arrangement.

4   Both IAS 7 and FRS 102 permit the use of either the direct method or the indirect method. The direct method is basically a list of the receipts and payments extracted from the cash book. The indirect method takes the respective balances from the statement of profit or loss and with the help of the information in the statement of financial position converts them back from an accruals basis to a cash basis. The direct method of presentation is encouraged, but the indirect method is acceptable.

Check your learning

The answers to these questions can be found within the text.

1   List five reasons why the accounting profit for a period will not necessarily result in an improvement in an entity's cash position.

2   Identify two statements of financial position items that may change an entity's cash position.

3   How does depreciation affect the cash balance?

4   What two methods may be used in preparing a SCF?

5   Which Financial Reporting Standards cover the preparation of SCFs?

6   What are SCFs?

7   Does an *increase* in (a) inventory, (b) trade receivables and (c) trade payables increase or decrease the cash position?

8   Does a *decrease* in (a) inventory, (b) trade receivables, and (c) trade payables increase or decrease the cash position?

9   What is cash?

10 Which International Accounting Standard covers the preparation of a SCF?

11 How many headings does this standard require?

12 What are they?

13 Which UK entities may adopt IAS 7?

14 What type of EU entity must adopt IAS 7?

15 List the assumptions and estimates that have to be made when compiling a SCF.

16 How reliable is a SCF?

17 What action would you expect a manager to take on receiving a SCF based on (a) historical data and (b) forecasted data?

News story quiz

Remember the news story at the beginning of this question? Go back to that story and reread it before answering the following questions.

Plastic cards (in the case of personal finances) and online banking (in the case of business finances) have been replacing the use of bank notes and coins in the United Kingdom and the Western World in the twenty-first century but access to cash in one form or another remains of paramount importance.

Questions

1 Why is access to cash so important to a business?

2 Why is access to cash particularly significant during a recession?

3 What factors may cause inefficient cash management during periods of boom?

4 How does the existence of counterfeit bank notes in an economy impact business?

Tutorial questions

The answers to questions marked with an asterisk can be found in Appendix 4.

7.1 'Proprietors are more interested in cash than profit.' Discuss.

7.2 Unlike traditional financial accounting, cash flow accounting does not require the accountant to make a series of arbitrary assumptions, apportionments and estimates. How far, therefore, do you think that there is a case for abandoning traditional financial accounting?

7.3 Does a statement of cash flows serve any useful purpose?

7.4* You are presented with the following information:

Dennis Limited

Statement of financial position at 31 January 2016

	31 January 2015		31 January 2016	
	£000	£000	£000	£000
Non-current assets				
Land at cost		600		700
Current assets				

	31 January 2015		31 January 2016	
	£000	£000	£000	£000
Inventory	100		120	
Trade receivables	200		250	
Cash	6	306	10	380
		906		1080
Capital and reserves				
Ordinary share capital	700		800	
Retained earnings	26	726	60	860
Current liabilities				
Trade payables		180		220
		906		1080

Required:

(a) Prepare Dennis Limited's statement of cash flows for the year ended 31 January 2016.

(b) Outline what it tells the managers of Dennis Limited.

7.5* The following statements of financial positions have been prepared for Frank Limited.

Statement of financial positions at:	28.2.16		28.2.17	
	£000	£000	£000	£000
Non-current assets				
Plant and machinery at cost	300		300	
Less: Depreciation	(80)		(100)	
		220		200
Investments at cost		–		100
Current assets				
Inventory	160		190	
Trade receivables	220		110	
Cash	–		10	
		380		310
		600		610
Capital and reserves				
Ordinary share capital	300		300	
Share premium account	50		50	
Retained earnings	30		40	
Shareholders' funds		380		390
Non-current liabilities				
Loans		–		60
Current liabilities				160
Trade payables	200	200		
	e/f	580		610

Statement of financial positions at:	28.2.16		28.2.17	
	£000	£000	£000	£000
	b/f	580		610
Bank overdraft		20		
		600		610

Additional information:
There were no purchases or sales of plant and machinery during the year.

Required:
(a) Prepare Frank Limited's statement of cash flows for the year ended 28 February 2017.
(b) What does it tell the managers of Frank Limited?

7.6 You are presented with the following information:

Starter
Statement of profit or loss for the year to 31 March 2017

	£	£
Sales		10000
Purchases	5000	
Less: Closing inventory	(1000)	(4000)
Gross profit		6000
Less: Depreciation		(2000)
Net profit for the year		4000

Statement of financial position at 31 March 2017

	£	£
Van	10000	
Less: Depreciation	(2000)	
		8000
Inventory	1000	
Trade receivables	5000	
Cash	12500	18500
		26500
Capital	20000	
Add: Net profit for the year	4000	24000
Trade payables		2500
		26500

Note:
Starter commenced business on 1 April 2016.

Required:
(a) Compile Starter's statement of cash flows for the year ended 31 March 2017.
(b) What does it tell the owners of Starter?

7.7 The following is a summary of Gregory Limited's accounts for the year ended 30 April 2017.

Gregory Limited
Extracts from the statement of profit or loss and statement of retained earnings
for the year ended 30 April 2017

	£000
Net profit before tax	75
Taxation	25
Dividend declared	50
Retained earnings for the year	40
	10

Gregory Limited
Statement of financial position at 30 April 2017

	30.4.16		30.4.17	
	£000	£000	£000	£000
Non-current assets				
Plant at cost	400		550	
Less: Depreciation	(100)		(180)	
		300		370
Current assets				
Inventory	50		90	
Trade receivables	70		50	
Cash	10		2	
		130		142
		430		512
Capital and reserves				
Ordinary share capital	200		200	
Retained earnings	132		142	
		332		342
Non-current liabilities		–		50
Current liabilities				
Trade payables	45		55	
Taxation	18		25	
Dividend declared	35		40	
		98		120
		430		512

Additional information:
There were no sales of non-current assets during the year ended 30 April 2017.

Required:
(a) Prepare Gregory Limited's statement of cash flows for the year ended 30 April 2017.
(b) Outline what it tells the managers of Gregory Limited.

7.8 The following summarised accounts have been prepared for Pill Limited:

Pill Limited
Statement of profit or loss for the year ended 31 May 2016

	2015	2016
	£000	£000
Sales	2400	3000
Less: Cost of goods sold	(1600)	(2000)
Gross profit	800	1000
Less: Expenses:		
Administrative expenses	(310)	(320)
Depreciation: vehicles	(55)	(60)
furniture	(35)	(40)
	400	420
Net profit before tax	400	580
Taxation	(120)	(150)
Net profit before tax	280	430

Pill Limited
Statement of retained earnings for the year ended 31 May 2016

	2015	2016
	£000	£000
Opening retained earnings	40	120
Net profit before tax	280	430
Dividends	(200)	(250)
Closing retained earnings	120	300

Pill Limited
Statement of financial position at 31 May 2016

	31.5.15		31.5.16	
	£000	£000	£000	£000
Non-current assets				
Vehicles at cost	600		800	
Less: Depreciation	(200)	400	(260)	540
Furniture	200		250	
Less: Depreciation	(100)	100	(140)	110
		500		650
Current assets				
Inventory	400		540	
Trade receivables	180		200	
Cash	320		120	
		900		860
c/f		1400		1510

	31.5.15		31.5.16	
	£000	£000	£000	£000
b/f		1400		1510
Capital and reserves				
Ordinary share capital	500		550	
Retained earnings reserve	120		300	
Shareholders' funds		620		850
Non-current liabilities				
Loans (10%)		190		40
Current liabilities				
Trade payables	270		300	
Corporation tax payable	170		220	
Dividends declared	150		100	
		590		620
		1400		1510

Additional information:
(a) There were no sales of non-current assets during the year ended 31 May 2016.
(b) The loans were paid back at the beginning of the year.

Required:
(a) Compile Pill Limited's statement of cash flows for the year ended 31 May 2016.
(b) What does it tell the managers of Pill Limited?

7.9 The following information relates to Brian Limited for the year ended 30 June 2016.

Brian Limited
Statement of profit or loss for the year to 30 June 2016

	£000	£000
Gross profit		230
Administrative expenses	76	
Loss on sale of vehicle	3	
Increase in allowance for doubtful debts	1	
Depreciation on vehicles	35	(115)
Net profit before tax		115
Taxation		(65)
Net profit after tax		50

Brian Limited
Statement of retained earnings for the year to 30 June 2016

	£000
Opening retained earnings	10
Net profit after tax for the year	50
Dividends	(25)
Closing retained earnings	35

Brian Limited
Statement of financial position at 30 June 2016

	2015		2016	
	£000	£000	£000	£000
Non-current assets				
Vehicle at cost	150		200	
Less: Depreciation	(75)		(100)	
		75		100
Current assets				
Inventory	60		50	
Trade receivables	80		100	
Less: Allowance for doubt-ful debts	(4)		(5)	
	76		95	
Cash	6		8	
		142		153
		217		253
Capital and reserves				
Ordinary share capital	75		75	
Retained earnings reserve	10		35	
		85		110
Current liabilities				
Trade payables	60		53	
Taxation	52		65	
Dividend declared	20	132	25	143
		217		253

Additional information:

1 The company purchased some new vehicles during 2016 for £75,000.
2 During 2016 the company also sold a vehicle for £12,000 in cash. The vehicle had originally cost £25,000, and £10,000 had been set aside for depreciation.

Required:
(a) Prepare a statement of cash flows for Brian Limited for the year ended 30 June 2016.
(b) Outline what it tells the managers of Brian Limited.

7.10 The following information is available for Carmen Limited.

The balance in the bank account of the business at 1 July 2016 was £30,000.

During the 12 months that followed the following transactions took place:

- New shares were issued by the company which raised an additional £10,000.
- Inventory was bought for £2,000.
- A loan of £13,000 was taken out from a lender.
- Interest expense of £1,000 was paid on the loan.
- A motor vehicle was purchased for £6,000.
- £5,000 was paid for various administrative expenses.

- £4,000 was paid to the tax authorities to settle last year's tax liability.
- The inventory was sold for £17,000.
- £1,000 of interest income was received on cash balances.
- Part of the loan was repaid: £9,000.
- A plot of land was purchased on credit from Summer Ltd and will be paid for in January 2018.
- £8,000 of dividends we paid to shareholders.

Required:

(a) Prepare a statement of cash flows for Carmen Limited for the year ended 30 June 2017, including the reconciliation between opening and closing bank balance.

(b) Outline what it tells the managers of Carmen Limited.

7.11 The following information is available for Zonka Limited.

The balance in the bank account of the business at 1 January 2017 was £30,000 overdrawn. During January 2017 the following transactions took place:

- New shares were issued by the company which raised an additional £100,000.
- Land was purchased for £60,000.
- A loan of £30,000 was taken out from a lender.
- Inventory was bought for £12,000 in cash.
- The inventory was sold for £27,000 in cash.
- £7,000 was paid for rent for the year.
- £6,000 was paid to the tax authorities to settle last year's tax liability.
- Half of the loan was repaid: £15,000.
- A motor vehicle was purchased for £1,500 on credit from Spring Ltd and will be paid for in February.
- Interest expense of £3,000 was paid on the loan.
- £17,000 was paid for consultant fees.

Required:

(a) Prepare a statement of cash flows for Zonka Limited for the month ended 31 January 2017, including the reconciliation between opening and closing bank balance.

(b) Outline what it tells the managers of Zonka Limited.

7.12 The following is a copy of the summary cash book of Tommy Hox Limited for 2017.

Tommy Hox Limited Summary cash book

	£		£
Balance b/d 1/1/17	88	Dividend	10
Capital	80	Loan	444
Sale of inventory	880	Factory	400
Loan	800	Interest	3
Land sale proceeds	808	Rent and Utilities	24
Interest Income	8	Taxation	6
		Purchase of inventory	666
		Balance c/d	1,111
	2,664		2,664

Required:

(a) Prepare a statement of cash flows for Tommy Hox Limited for the year ended 31 January 2017, including the reconciliation between opening and closing bank balance.

(b) Outline what it tells the managers of Tommy Hox Limited.

Website

Further practice questions, study material and links to relevant sites on the World Wide Web can be found on the website that accompanies this book. The site can be found at www.pearsoned.co.uk/dyson

Learning objectives

By the end of this case study you should be able to:

* identify the accounting rules adopted in preparing a set of accounts;
* evaluate the format and presentation of such accounts and
* suggest a more meaningful way of presenting them.

Background

Location   Bleasedale

Personnel   Alan Marshall: a member of the Calder Rambling Club
Wendy Hargreaves: Treasurer, Calder Rambling Club

Synopsis

Alan Marshall has recently joined the Calder Rambling Club, based in Bleasedale. A few months after joining he attended the annual general meeting.

Among the items on the agenda was the treasurer's report. Alan did not know a great deal about accounting and so he was somewhat mystified by the 'accounts' presented by the treasurer, Wendy Hargreaves. He took the opportunity to ask her a few questions but he did not understand the explanations. A copy of the accounts as presented at the meeting is shown in the appendix to this case study. They were described as a 'statement of financial position' and all the information was presented on one page.

After the meeting Alan learnt that Wendy had been in post for 25 years and the accounts had always been presented in that way. As long as the club had some money in the bank nobody else seemed concerned about them.

When he got home, Alan decided to write to Wendy asking for clarification about certain items contained in the 'statement of financial position'. She was very helpful and she provided him with more information. He was still not satisfied that the accounts presented a clear picture of the club's financial position for the year 2016/17. He also suspected that this was probably true for the preceding year as well. Alan's questions and Wendy's answers are shown below.

A: *What is 'Mr Smith's bequest'?*
W: A legacy left by ex-chairman Arthur Smith to the club some years ago.

A: *On the left-hand side, what does the item 'Cheques not through bank' mean?*
W: Cheques that had not gone through the bank at the end of the year.

A: *On the right-hand side what do the 'Deposits' mean?*
W: The New Year deposit relates to a booking made at a youth hostel for the forthcoming New Year. The Slide Show deposit is a payment to the hotel for the room booking for the slide show in December.

A: *On the right-hand side, what does the item 'Through bank' mean?*
W: Cheques that had not gone through the bank at the beginning of the year.

A: *Were any amounts paid in 2015/16 for 2016/17?*

W: Yes – a deposit of £88 paid to the rugby club for the Christmas party held in December 2016.

A: *Did we receive any money in 2015/16 that related to 2016/17?*

W: Yes – subscriptions of £50 in total from five members.

Required:

(a) Identify those accounting rules that the treasurer appears to have adopted in preparing the Calder Rambling Club's accounts and explain what each of them means.

(b) Giving your reasons, indicate what other accounting rules might be appropriate for the treasurer to adopt.

(c) Prepare the club's accounts in a format that you believe would more clearly present its financial performance and position during and at the end of the year.

Appendix

Calder Rambling Club
Statement of financial position of accounts for year 2016/17

	£		£
Bank balance at 13.9.16	4 365	Affiliation fees	20
Subscriptions	1 920	Rights of Way membership	150
Donations	5	Mountain Hut membership	30
Profits from:		Youth Hostel membership	6
Bus cancellation fees	406	Youth Hostel donation	100
Private buses	144	National Trust donation	50
Christmas party	173		
Cheese and wine	17	**Expenses:**	
		Printing and stationery	330
Mr Smith's bequest	96	Leaders' expenses	16
Bank interest (2015/16)	83	Recce expenses	1072
Subscriptions (2016/17)	30	Postage/telephones	6
		Secretary	131
		Treasurer	36
		Sundry items:	
		Hire of halls	285
		Insurance	88
		General	42
		Deposits:	
		New Year 2016/17	128
		Slide show 16.12.16	50
		Losses:	
		High tea	5
		Lecture	17
		Through bank	297
Cheques not through bank	841	Balance in bank 23.8.16	5 221
	£8080		£8080

Accounting policies

By the end of this case study you should be able to:

- outline the meaning of various conventional accounting policies used in preparing financial statements and
- explain the effect each policy has on the profit or loss for a particular period.

Background

Location	Aberdeen
Personnel	Clare Marshall: potential investor
	Kate Moorfield: chartered accountant

Synopsis

After leaving Birmingham University, Clare Marshall took up a marketing job in an Aberdeen oil firm. During her first five years with the company she earned a good salary and she was paid some highly satisfactory bonuses. She had managed to put a deposit down and take out a mortgage on a flat in Aberdeen, furnish it, buy a car and still have plenty of money left to take advantage of Aberdeen's amenities. She had also fallen in love with Scotland, and with a postgraduate student at Aberdeen University. So she was pretty certain that she would not be moving away from Scotland.

She had realised, however, that she might not always be earning a lot of money so she decided that she must start investing what little spare cash she had. She decided that as her future probably lay in Scotland she might as well invest in the country. Clare had taken a basic course in accounting when she was at university and her job gave her some knowledge of business life around the world, but she did not know very much about suitable companies in which to invest. So she decided to collect a number of Scottish companies' annual reports and accounts. She could have downloaded and printed them herself from the companies' websites but that was going to waste a lot of paper and printer cartridges so she ordered copies to be sent to her. They were delivered to her flat in dribs and drabs but eventually she was able to go through them all in detail.

It was hard going. Some of the reports were long and technical (especially and rather ironically, the oil company ones). However, one of the reports was from an Edinburgh-based construction company called J. Smart & Co. (Contractors) plc. Its 2016 report was only 69 pages long, so she started to go through it without feeling too daunted. Even so she found even this report hard going and she wished fervently that she had listened more carefully to her accounting lecturer when she was at university.

She got frustrated and bored, and so she decided to ring Kate Moorfield, one of the many new friends that she had made in Aberdeen. After they had discussed their respective boyfriends, Clare mentioned what she had been trying to do. Kate had recently passed her chartered accountancy examinations and she offered to go round to help Clare.

Kate was in her element. She took Clare through Smart's report pretty smartly, stressing what she said were two very important points:

- the preparation of accounting statements requires a great deal of individual judgement;
- apart from their relative brevity the format and content of Smart's accounts were no different from most other public companies.

Clare was reassured about the second point but concerned about accounts apparently needing a lot of 'individual judgement'.

'OK,' said Kate, 'let's look at Note 1 on pages 39–45. Rather interestingly they've called them accounting policies and *estimation* techniques. That makes my point. Apart from a few things that relate more to a construction company, they are pretty well what you will find in most reports.' Clare was beginning to feel a little less concerned.

Kate continued, 'If we go through a few of the policies, I can explain why some individual judgement is required and what impact the policies may have on the company's results.' 'How do you mean?' queried Clare. 'Are they flexible?' 'Oh yes,' replied Kate with the enthusiasm expected of a newly qualified chartered accountant. 'What do you mean exactly?' queried Clare rather anxiously. 'Now don't look so concerned,' said Kate, 'It's simply that depending on what accounting policies are adopted and what assumptions are made, it is possible to arrive at almost any figure for profit that you want. That is the case in the preparation of *any* accounting statement.'

Kate may have been overstating the point and Clare's face once more began to register alarm, so Kate began to explain the company's accounting policies while Clare listened very carefully. It wasn't long before they decided to go out for a coffee and it was several weeks later before Clare bought some shares in ... well, we'd better not say.

Required:
Some of Smart's accounting policies are outlined in the appendix to this case study.
(a) Explain what each of the accounting policies means.
(b) Demonstrate how the application of each of these policies can affect the level of accounting profit (or loss) for a particular period.

Appendix

J. Smart & Co. (Contractors) plc
Accounting policies and estimation techniques

Basis of preparation
The accounts have been prepared on a going concern basis and under the historical cost convention except where the measurement of balances at fair value is required as noted below for investment properties, available for sale of financial assets and assets held by defined benefit scheme.

The accounting policies set out below have been consistently applied to all periods presented in these accounts.

The preparation of financial statements requires management to make estimates and assumptions concerning the future that may affect the application of accounting policies and the reported amounts of assets and liabilities and income and expenses. Management believes that the estimates and assumptions used in the preparation of these accounts are reasonable. However, actual outcomes may differ from those anticipated.

Revenue
Revenue, which is stated net of value added tax, represents the invoiced value of goods sold, except in the case of long-term contracts where revenue represents the amounts received and receivable for work done in the year. The measurement and stage of

completion of long-term contracts are based on external valuations issued by third-party surveyors.

Profits on long-term contracts are calculated in accordance with International Financial Reporting Standards and do not relate directly to revenue. Profit on current contracts is only taken at a stage near enough to completion for that profit to be reasonably certain after making provision for contingencies, while provision is made for all losses incurred to the accounting date together with any further losses that are foreseen in bringing contracts to completion. The value of construction work transferred to investment properties is excluded from revenue.

Revenue from investment properties comprises rental income, service charges, insurance receivable and other recoveries, and is disclosed as other operating income in the Income Statement.

Rental income from investment property leased out under an operating lease is recognised in the Income Statement on a straight line basis over the term of the lease.

Revenue from private housing sales is recognised when transactions are legally completed. Revenue from private housing sales under shared equity scheme is accounted for at fair value.

Inventories and work in progress

Inventories are valued at the lower of cost and net realisable value. Land held for development is included at the lower of cost and net realisable value.

Work in progress other than long-term contract work in progress is valued at the lower of cost and net realisable value.

Cost includes materials, on a first-in first-out basis and direct labour plus attributable overheads based on normal operating activity, where applicable. Net realisable value is the estimated selling price less anticipated disposal costs.

Variations and claims are included in Revenue where it is probable that the amount, which can be measured reliably, will be recovered from the customer.

Long-term contracts

Amounts recoverable on contracts which are included in debtors are stated at cost as defined above, plus attributable profit to the extent that this is reasonably certain after making provision for maintenance costs, less any losses incurred or foreseen in bringing contracts to completion, and less amounts received as progress payments.

For any contracts where receipts exceed the book value of work done, the excess is included in trade and other payables as payments on account.

Depreciation

Depreciation is provided on all items of property, plant and equipment, other than investment properties and freehold land, at rates calculated to write off the cost of each asset over its expected useful life, as follows:

Freehold buildings – over 40–66 years

Plant and machinery – 25–33 1/3 % reducing balance

Office furniture and fittings – 20–33 1/3 % reducing balance

Motor vehicles – 33 1/3 % reducing balance.

Statement of cash flows

By the end of this case study you should be able to:

- identify the main features of a published statement of cash flows and
- evaluate the main reasons for changes in the cash position of an entity.

Location Sidmouth

Personnel   Edgar Glennie: a retired aircraft engineer
                James Arbuthnot: a retired chartered accountant

Edgar Glennie retired from his job as an aircraft engineer in the early part of 2017. He moved to Sidmouth on the south coast and he now spends most of his time playing golf and reading the papers. The financial and political news had not been good and he was worried about his pension. During the five years leading up to his retirement he had managed to invest some savings in a number of companies from which he earned a small income but the market had collapsed and his shares were worth much less than he had paid for them.

As a shareholder he was used to receiving a copy of the annual report and accounts from his various shareholdings. He very rarely bothered to open the envelopes, never mind read the contents. More recently, as a result of his concerns, he had vowed to pay more attention to the progress of the companies in which he had invested. One of the first documents that he received following his vow was the 2016 annual report and accounts from Liko plc.

Edgar opened the report fairly gingerly. He did not know much about accounting and he was certain that he would not understand a word of what it was trying to tell him. However, he knew enough to realise that if the company made a profit, he was likely to get a dividend but he also knew from the evidence of the recent period of recession that it had to have enough cash to keep going.

Liko's report was fairly thick – well over 100 pages. Page 1 was the 'Contents' which was useful. Where could he find out about the profit? There did not seem to be any mention of it so he turned over to the next page where there was some useful information but he still sought further detail. On page 1 he learned that Liko is the leading global provider of, mobile power solutions. It operates in around 100 countries worldwide. All of this was very interesting but where were the details about profit?

He flicked over more pages and more pages until he got to page 98. It appeared to be some sort of profit calculation but it was called a 'Group Income Statement'. It did give him the profit for the year: nearly £162 million compared with about £215 million for 2015. So profit had gone down, but at least it was still a profit! Good, now what about the dividend? There was no mention of it on that page.

He turned over to page 99: the 'Group Balance Sheet'. This was a much longer statement but he did find an amount called 'cash and cash equivalents' (whatever they were) of £48 million compared with the previous year of £37 million. He wondered where all the profit had gone!

Glancing at the opposite page he noticed that there was another statement called a 'Group Cash Flow Statement' but it showed 'cash and cash equivalents' of £32 million at the end of 2016 and £26 million at the end of 2015. How could that be? Why the discrepancy with the numbers on the previous page?

On pages 101 and 102 there was a very, very complex-looking table which spanned across the two pages. It was called Statement of Changes in Equity but it had so many columns that his eyes literally could not take all the information in.

Realising that his own knowledge of accounting was too limited for him to sort it all out, he decided to have a word with James Arbuthnot, a golfing friend of his. James had been a partner in a small firm of chartered accountants in Sidmouth until he had retired some years ago.

When Edgar telephoned James and told him what he had discovered, James said that of course he would be glad to help him. Some days later they got together in the golf club bar and James began to take him through Liko's report and accounts. He began close to where Edgar had left off – at the Group Cash Flow Statement...

Required:
(a) Liko's Group Cash Flow Statement for 2016 and the relevant notes to the accounts are shown in the appendix. Assume that you were James. Explain how a profit for the year after tax of £162 million only resulted in an increase in cash and cash equivalents of £14 million and why there appears to be a difference between the cash and cash equivalent balances on the Group Balance Sheet and the Group Cash Flow Statement.

Appendix

	2016 £ million	2015 £ million
Cash flow from operating activities		
Cash generated from operators	276	230
Tax paid	40	21
Net cash generated from operating activities	236	209
(1) Cash flow from inventory activities		
Acquisition (net of cash acquired)	(16)	–
Purchase of property, plant and equipment(PPE)	(265)	(181)
Proceeds from the side of PPE	9	8
Net cash used in inventory activities	(272)	(173)
Cash flow from financing activities		
Net proceeds from sale of ordinary shares	1	2
Increase in long-term loans	186	66
Replacement of long-term loans	(107)	(63)
Net movement in short-term loans	5	(7)
Interest received	1	2
Interest paid	(15)	(13)
Dividends paid to shareholders	(24)	(19)
Purchase of treasury shares	(13)	(4)
Sale of own shares by employee benefit trust	1	–
Net cash from/(used in) financing activities	35	36
Net decrease in cash and cash equivalents	(1)	(1)
Cash and cash equivalents at beginning of year	10	10
Exchange gain or cash and cash equivalents	2	–
Cash and cash equivalents at end of year		
	11	9

Relevant notes:

Notes	2016 £ million	2015 £ million
	2016 £ million	2015 £ million
Profit for years		
Adjustments for:		
Tax		
Depreciation		
Amortization of intangibles		
Finance income		
Finance cost		
Profit on sale of PPE (see below)		
Share-based payments		
Changes in working capital (excluding the effects of exchange differences on consolidation):		
Increase in inventories		
Increase in trade and other receivables		
Increase in trade and other payables		
Net movements in provision for liabilities and charges		
Net retirement benefit cost		
Cash generated from operations		

In the cash flow statement proceeds from sale of PPE comprises:

	2016 £ million	2015 £ million
Net book amount		
Proceeds from sale of PPE		

(2) Cash and cash equivalents

	2016 £ million	2015 £ million
Cost at bank and in hand	16	9
Short term bank deposits	1	1
	15	8
Cash and cash equivalents (as per the group balance sheet)	15	
Bank overdraft (as per the group balance sheet under borrowing)		

Source: Aggreko Plc Annual Report and Accounts 2015.

FINANCIAL REPORTING

In Part 3 we deal with the subject of *financial reporting*. The distinction between financial accounting (as covered in Part 2) and financial reporting is blurred. Indeed, at one time, no such distinction would be made. However, financial accounting is now regarded as a rather mechanical and technical process that ends with the preparation of the statement of profit or loss, the statement of retained earnings (or statement of changes in equity in the case of big/listed companies), the statement of financial position and the statement of cash flows. Financial reporting is more concerned with how accounting data can best be communicated to users of financial statements in accordance with legal and professional requirements.

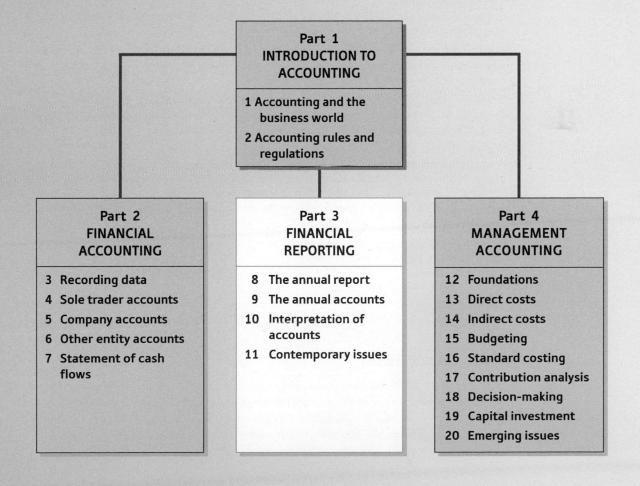

Yet more narrative

Brussels in corporate transparency push

Harriet Agnew

European companies may for the first time have to report on their environmental impact and diversity policy as part of new rules that are going to be voted on today in the European Parliament.

The directive, an important step to improve and standardise corporate transparency in the EU, also lays out the reporting of narrative and non-financial information by major companies.

The draft directive would force companies with more than 500 employees to disclose, where appropriate, a range of factors from workforce diversity to environmental impact and anti-corruption controls.

Frédéric Ichay, a Paris-based partner at Pinsent Masons, said the directive is designed to give more transparency, 'to give comfort to clients, counterparties and the general public' and to homogenise the European market.

The depth and quality of company reporting varied by country in Europe, with countries such as the United Kingdom Sweden and Denmark already addressing many of the issues, while others such as Poland and Greece lagged behind, said Mr Ichay. In the United Kingdom the practical impact of the directive may be less significant as a result of recent efforts by the government last year to improve narrative reporting.

A focus of the directive, which has been debated by member states for a number of years, is diversity, in its widest sense.

FT *Source*: Extracted from www.ft.com, 14 April 2014.

Questions relating to this news story can be found on page 206. ➡

About this chapter

The Companies Act 2006 requires companies to prepare accounts for each financial year. They are then obliged to send a copy of the accounts to every shareholder of the company. The Act also requires them to report on other aspects of their operations along with a number of legislative and professional requirements. The additional information is usually provided in report form. The reports and the accounts are then combined to form one document.

A copy of the report and accounts must also to be filed with the Registrar of Companies, i.e. sent to him; he then makes it available for public inspection. This process is what accountants mean when they talk about 'disclosure of information' or 'published accounts'.

Annual reports and accounts can be quite lengthy. Those for a relatively small plc, for example, can easily stretch to 50 pages while those for a large international plc may go well beyond 150 pages. So for shareholders there is an awful lot to read. In addition, much of the content is complex, highly technical and full of jargon. It is very difficult to believe that most annual report and accounts mean very much to the average shareholder and there is, in fact, some strong empirical evidence to suggest that very few are actually read.

In this book we have provided you with the necessary background information and knowledge that should enable to you make sense of a company's annual report and accounts. Nonetheless, you probably need some additional help in order to see how the material we have covered so far in this book relates to the published information. We provide that help in two chapters as the subject is too big to cover in one chapter. In this chapter we deal with 'reports' and in Chapter 9, the 'accounts'.

In both chapters we will be primarily concerned with the published reports and accounts of public limited liability companies and we will be making frequent references to examples extracted from such a source.

<table>
<tr><td>

**Learning
objectives**

</td><td>

By the end of this chapter you should be able to:

- list the types of reports found in a company's annual report and accounts;
- separate such reports from the accounts section;
- identify the introductory material;
- outline the contents of a chairman's report;
- explain what is meant by corporate governance;
- specify the nature of a business review;
- identify the main sections of a directors' report and
- summarise the contents of a directors' remuneration report.

</td></tr>
</table>

 ## Why this chapter is important

This chapter is important for non-accountants because at some time or other in whatever career you pursue you are going to come across company annual reports and accounts. Most entities of any size prepare such a document and by law companies are required to do so. As a result, published reports and accounts tend to act as a model for other types of entities irrespective of their nature and size.

It is highly likely that in your job you will be involved to a lesser or greater degree in the preparation of *the* annual report and accounts. And as you become more senior, you will have greater responsibility to ensure that your company complies with legal and professional requirements. Furthermore, given that the company has to produce such a document, you will want to make sure that as far as possible it is readable and understandable. That means you will need to have a good eye for presentation and an ability to spot what reads well and what does not. This chapter will help you to develop your knowledge and skill in what is required.

There is perhaps another reason why this chapter is important. In your private life you will probably want to become a shareholder in a company. One document at least that you will need to study before making an investment is its annual report and accounts; thereafter you will use it to monitor its progress. The chances are that once trained in the mysteries of annual reports and accounts, you will find them helpful when making your own personal investment decisions.

Activity 8.1	Obtain the annual report and accounts of three UK public limited liability companies.

Guidance: If some of your friends or relatives have shares in a company, they should automatically receive a copy of its annual report and accounts. See if they will let you have it. Otherwise write to the Company Secretary of each company. Most companies will let you have a set without any questions being asked. You are nowadays also able to download annual reports from the Internet. Choose commercial or industrial companies. Avoid banking and insurance companies as they have different reporting requirements.

Note: It is important that you do as requested above otherwise you will find it more difficult to work your way through both this chapter and the next one.

Overview

News clip

Too long and too 'complex'

Banks and other financial companies are publishing annual reports that are overly complicated and indigestible, prompted in part by regulatory requirements that have swelled the numbers of disclosures, analysts have complained.

Nearly two-thirds of analysts questioned by accountancy firm EY said they found annual reports and accounts to be 'too complex', while a similar proportion indicated the tomes being published by firms are hard to digest.

Reports from big lenders for 2013 confirmed the scale of the paper mountain, with HSBC publishing an annual report weighing in at nearly 600 pages while Barclays produced a document that was 444 pages. A decade ago, HSBC's annual report was half the current length.

Source: Extracted from www.ft.com, 8 June 2014.

You will find that with most annual reports and accounts it is relatively easy to separate the 'reports' from the 'accounts' no matter where they appear in the overall document or what they are called. The reports will usually come before the accounts and they will probably be put into various groupings although there is no statutory requirement to do so. The number of categories adopted can range from only two or three categories to as many as 10.

We will opt for a fairly broad approach in our discussion. As can be seen from Figure 8.1, we have decided to group the report section into three main categories: (1) introductory material; (2) corporate reporting and (3) shareholder information. What is reported in any report must not conflict with other reports.

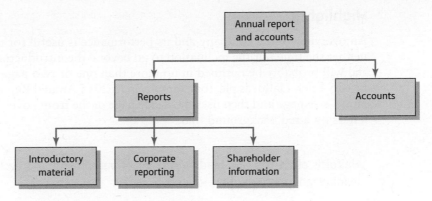

Figure 8.1 Annual reports: structure

We start our discussion with the introductory material section. You are likely to find it in the first few pages of any annual report and accounts.

Introductory material

The section is usually confined to the first few pages of the document (including sometimes the use of the inside page of the front cover). The information provided will probably tell you something about the company: what it does, where it has done it and how it was done, i.e. its history, location and a summary of its financial results.

The information that is likely to be disclosed may be broken down into four broad categories, as shown in Figure 8.2. They are: (1) highlights, i.e. specific matters to which the company particularly wants to draw attention; (2) a financial summary of the results for the year; (3) some promotional material and (4) the chairman's statement.

We will discuss each of these categories in turn starting with the 'highlights'.

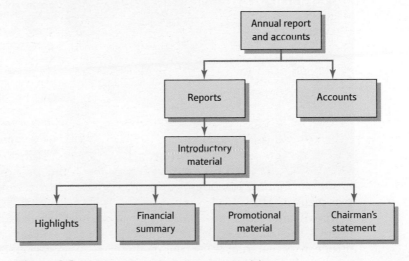

Figure 8.2 Annual reports: introductory material

Highlights

An overview of the company and its performance is useful for those readers who have neither the time nor the inclination to go beyond the introductory material. Such material will probably be outlined in no more than one or two pages but sometimes it may be very brief. Halfords plc, for example, in its 2015 Annual Report and Accounts adopts an A4-size page and then uses the inside page of the front cover to report in large white letters on a red background that:

> Halfords plc is the UK's leading retailer of automotive and cycling products, and the leading independent operator in auto repair.

A two-line sentence (in much smaller white letters) outlining the company's vision then follows (Figure 8.3). This in turn is followed by a summary of its three core principles and the elements of the strategy for each of the two segments of the business – retail and autocentres.

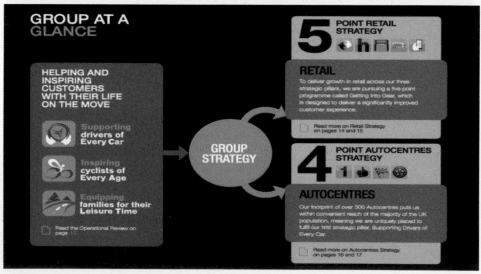

Figure 8.3 Introductory page

Source: Halfords plc, *Annual Report and Accounts*, 2015.

The contents of the Report and Accounts are then listed in small type on the next page.

The introductory section of the report includes on page 2 financial highlights and on page 3 a list of its activities. The introduction is then followed by the chairman's statement, followed by summaries of information about the marketplace, the business model and material issues. So in Halfords' case the highlights section is 12 pages long (including the inside cover). These are followed by just over 30 pages elaborating on the business's 'Strategy', 'Performance' and 'Risk'.

Similarly Aggreko's 2015 Annual Report and Accounts also uses A4-size pages. Page 1 lists the contents. Page 2 has also some performance highlights. Page 3 provides Operational overview. Pages 4 and 5 contain a note from the Chief Executive Officer, which covers 'Trading performance', 'Business Priorities', 'People and Culture', and 'Outlook'. Page 6 picks up on high-profile spectator events the company is involved with. Pages 8–53 are given over to the Strategic report (with sections for 'Business review', 'Performance review' and 'Sustainability review'.

Financial summary

Most companies usually give a brief financial summary of the group's performance for the year as part of the introductory section. This usually takes up no more than one page. Often it is a combination of numbers and graphs. Halfords' 2015 report is a good example. On page 2 under the heading 'Group Highlights' small bar charts are given showing data for five years: revenue, net profit before tax, earnings per share as well as some other performance indicators. Underneath some operational highlights are given – such as growth in cycling sales and growth in online retail sales.

Some of the information shown in Figure 8.4 will not mean much to you just yet so you can appreciate just how difficult it must be for those readers who have not had *any* training in accounting.

Promotional material

Many companies take the opportunity of promoting the company's products in their annual report and accounts. This makes sound business sense. Shareholders are also consumers and if there are thousands of them, the company might as well encourage them to buy its products.

A good example of how this can be done is A.G. Barr plc, the soft drinks manufacturer best known as the makers of *Irn Bru*. Its 2015 report and accounts is particularly striking. The 134-page report is full of vivid multi-colour display of its range of products.

By contrast, J. Smart & Co (Contractors) PLC, a much smaller company than Barr, has a very slim and sober presentation. Its 2015 report and accounts, which is only 69 pages in length, does not have any introductory material of any kind, still less any promotional material! This may be because construction companies are not into the mass consumer market.

| Activity 8.2 | Consult your copies of the three sets of annual reports and accounts that you obtained when completing Activity 8.1. Read through the introductory material. Write down the content of each company's material in just a few words in three adjacent columns. Then compare your results for the three companies. On a scale of 1–5 (5 being the highest), rate how informative you find each company's introductory material section. |

GROUP
HIGHLIGHTS

FINANCIAL HIGHLIGHTS

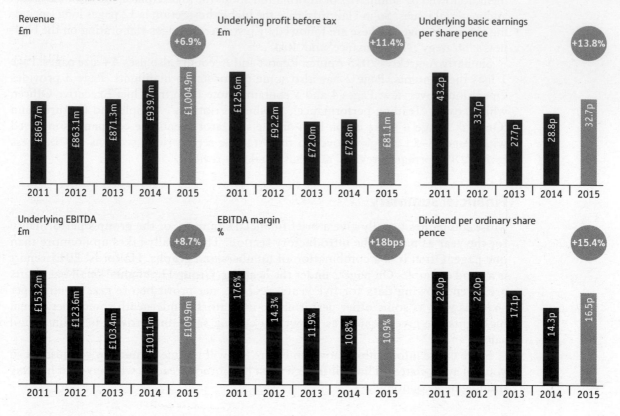

OPERATIONAL HIGHLIGHTS

72
STORES TRADING
UNDER REFRESHED
FORMAT

46%
RETAIL COLLEAGUES
THROUGH GEAR 2

77%
RETAIL NET
PROMOTER SCORE

+11.4%
GROWTH IN
CYCLING SALES

+14.3%
GROWTH IN ONLINE
RETAIL SALES

4
CYCLE REPUBLIC SHOPS
OPENED IN THE YEAR

Figure 8.4 Highlights page
Source: Halfords plc, *Annual Report and Accounts*, 2015.

Chairman's statement

Most company chairmen like to include a report or statement of their own in the annual report. There are no statutory, FRC/IASB or Stock Exchange requirements for chairmen to publish a report so the format and content will vary from company to company. A relatively brief chairman's report is shown in Figure 8.5.

You will probably find the chairman's statement in the first few pages of the annual report. You can expect it to be anything from one to four pages in length. It will be largely narrative in style although there will almost certainly be some quantitative

---

J. Smart & Co. (Contractors) PLC

CHAIRMAN'S REVIEW

ACCOUNTS
Headline Group profit for the year before tax, including an unrealised surplus in revalued property as required by the International Financial Reporting Standards was £3,752,000 compared with £3,544,000 last year. If the impact of revalued property is disregarded, then a truer reflection of Group performance emerges in the form of an underlying profit before tax for the year under review of £3,616,000 (including £186,000 profit from property sales) which compares with the figure for underlying profit last year of £3,755,000 (including £1,318,000 profit from property sales and joint venture property sales).

The Board is recommending a Final Dividend of 2.15p nett making a total for the year of 3.07p nett which compares with 3.02p nett for the previous year. After waivers by members holding over 50% of the shares, the Final Dividend will cost the Company no more than £421,000.

TRADING ACTIVITIES
Group construction activities carried out including private residential sales increased by 42%. Disregarding private residential sales Group construction activities increased by 2.3%. Own work capitalised increased by 125%. Group revenue increased by 39% and headline Group profit before tax increased by 6%. Underlying Group profit before tax excluding the unrealised surplus in revalued property decreased by 4%.

Turnover in contracting was more than last year and the loss was reduced. As forecast private residential sales were more than the previous year. Sales and profit in precast concrete manufacture increased.

The two large mixed social housing and private residential developments at Seafield Street and Pilton Drive, Edinburgh, continue to make satisfactory progress. A third phase of social housing at Pilton Drive and a further social housing contract at Fleming Place (adjacent to Seafield Street) have commenced.

Occupancy levels at our industrial estates continue to be satisfactory. A joint venture industrial development at Gartcosh near Glasgow is contemplated. Although interest in our commercial office premises has improved, take up of voids is still slow.

FUTURE PROSPECTS
Work in hand in contracting is slightly less than at this time last year and there is little prospect of more work in the short term. Accordingly, turnover in this sector will be down on last year. Prices remain competitive.

Private residential sales will be less than last year. It is by no means certain that current property valuation levels will be maintained at the end of the current financial year.

At this early stage it is difficult to make an informed forecast of the outcome for the current year. However, bearing in mind the foregoing circumstances and that the reduced turnover will impair the recovery of fixed overhead costs, it seems unlikely that the profit for the current year will match last year's profit.

JOHN M SMART

Chairman

15th November 2016

Figure 8.5 A chairman's statement

Source: J. Smart & Co. (Contractors) PLC, *Annual Report and Statement of Accounts,* 2016.

information. Research evidence suggests that chairmen's statements are the most widely read section of an annual report, perhaps because they are mainly narrative.

Chairmen tend to adopt an upbeat approach about the recent performance of the company and they are usually extremely optimistic about the future. You must, therefore, read their reports with some degree of scepticism and you should check their comments against the detailed results contained elsewhere within the overall annual report and accounts. Nevertheless, chairmen have to be careful that they do not become too optimistic. Their remarks can have a significant impact on the company's share price and they might have to answer to the Stock Exchange authorities if they publish misleading statements.

The contents of a typical chairman's statement could include the following items:

- *Results.* A summary of the company's results for the year covering turnover, pre- and post-tax profits, earnings per share and cash flow.
- *Dividend.* Details about any interim dividend paid for the year and any final dividend declared.
- *Prospects.* A summary of how the chairman sees the general economic and political outlook and the future prospects for the company.
- *Employees.* A comment about the company's employees including any notable successes, concluding with the Board's thanks to all employees for their efforts.
- *Directors.* A similar note may be included about the Board of Directors including tributes to retiring directors.

We now turn to what we have called the 'corporate reporting' section of a company's annual report and accounts.

Activity 8.3	Referring to your three sets of annual reports and accounts, find the chairman's statement and in each set go through them very carefully. Are there any items not included in the summary shown above? List the main contents of each chairman's statement.

Corporate reporting

Some companies call this section of the annual report and accounts 'the directors' report' but this can be a little confusing as the Companies Act uses the same term to refer to a much narrower type of report. We have, therefore, called this section 'corporate reporting' and classified it into three broad categories (as can be seen in Figure 8.6): (1) corporate governance; (2) the statutory directors' report and (3) the directors' remuneration report.

Corporate governance report

Strictly speaking, the Companies Act 2006 requires much of the material disclosed in this section to be included in a statutory directors' report although it is permitted to present it elsewhere within the overall report and accounts. Many companies do just that and we will do the same because it simplifies our discussion.

As far back as 1991, the accounting profession, the Financial Reporting Council and the London Stock Exchange set up a committee (known as the Cadbury Committee) to examine what has become to be known as 'corporate governance'. The term refers to

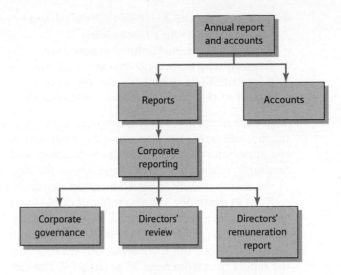

Figure 8.6 Annual reports: corporate reporting

the way the companies and other entities are controlled and managed. The Committee reported in 1992 and since that time there have been a number of other influential committees that have worked on the practice and development of 'corporate governance'.

While shareholders own companies, they appoint directors to run the companies for them. So it seems reasonable that the shareholders want to be assured that the directors know what they are doing, how they are going about it and how successful they have been. Nonetheless, Parliament has largely left the business and financial communities to deal with the matter and there has not been any detailed legislation. The specific requirements were laid down by the London Stock Exchange for all listed companies in a document called *The Combined Code*. This was replaced in September 2014 by *The UK Corporate Governance Code* ('*the Code*').

The Code *is* extremely detailed. It deals with both companies and institutional shareholders. In this chapter we are particularly interested in what the company and the directors have to disclose in their annual report and accounts. Corporate governance disclosure requirements are laid out in the Financial Conduct Authority Transparency Rules and Listing Rules and the Code itself. Schedule B of the Code: *Disclosure of corporate governance arrangements* captures all of the requirements. The schedule is five-pages long, so no doubt you will appreciate why this helps to increase the size (and weight) of annual reports and accounts. In summary, the main disclosure requirements are as follows.

- Application of the Code's principles.
- Compliance or not with all the Code's principles and if not, which, for how long and why.
- Details of the Board's operations, including the names of the chairman, deputy chairman, chief executive, senior independent director, independent non-executive directors and the names and members of the nomination, audit and remuneration committee members.
- The Chairman's comments along with any changes.
- Evaluation of the Board's performance, its committees and the directors.
- Ways the Board keeps in contact with shareholder opinion.
- Description of the work of the nomination committee (i.e. to the Board) and the (directors') remuneration committee.
- Directors' duties in the preparation of the accounts and the auditors' reporting responsibilities.

- Statement by the directors that the company is a going concern (this is particularly important in a time of recession).
- A review of internal control procedures.
- Reasons why there is no internal audit function (if that is so), duties and responsibilities of the audit committee, the appointment or otherwise of the external auditor and details of the external auditor's non-audit services.

There are also various clauses covering the disclosure of some additional information on the company's website about the nomination, remuneration and audit committees, the appointment of non-executive directors and the use of remuneration consultants. Similarly, additional information about the election of directors and the appointment of the external auditor has to be given in papers sent to shareholders.

Even in summary, the above list of disclosure requirements is formidable. In order to give you some ideas of what is required, Figure 8.7 shows the main headings used in the Governance section of the Halfords plc annual report and accounts as well as the headings within the Corporate Governance Report itself. The Governance section of the report runs from page 38 to page 74. The Corporate Governance Report itself starts on page 42 and is 8-pages long.

Activity 8.4	Once again, turn to your three sets of annual reports and accounts. Check whether there is a specific corporate governance statement or report. Read each one. Then copy the headings into adjacent columns, listing as far as possible similar items on the same line opposite each other.

CONTENTS OF THE HALFORDS PLC CORPORATE GOVERNANCE REPORT
- STATEMENT OF COMPLIANCE WITH UK CORPORATE GOVERNANCE CODE
- LEADERSHIP
  - BOARD COMPOSITION
  - BOARD RESPONSIBILITIES
  - BOARD MEETINGS AND ATTENDANCE
  - BOARD ATTENDANCE AT SCHEDULED MEETINGS
- COMMITTEES (NOMINATION, AUDIT, REMMUNIERATION)
  - KEY OBJECTIVES
  - MAIN RESPONSIBILITIES
- EFFECTIVENESS OF THE BOARD
  - INDEPENDENCE
  - SKILLS AND EXPERIENCE
  - DIVERSITY
  - APPOINTMENT TO THE BOARD
  - DIRECTORS' INDUCTION
  - TRAINING AND DEVELOPMENT
  - EVALUATION
  - RE-ELECTION
  - DIRECTORS AND THEIR OTHER INTERESTS
  - INTERNAL CONTROL AND RISK MANAGEMENT
- RELATIONS WITH SHAREHOLDERS

Figure 8.7 Corporate governance report: an example
Source: Halfords plc, *Annual Report and Accounts*, 2015.

Directors' report

The Companies Act 2006 (Strategic Report and Directors' Report) Regulations 2013 require company directors to prepare a report for each financial year. You will usually find the directors' report towards the end of the corporate governance section. The report is likely to be a very long one and to make up a high proportion of the overall annual report and accounts. No set format is required but it will probably be presented as a series of paragraphs under appropriate headings. The content of each paragraph will be mainly narrative but it is likely that some statistical information will also be included. The Secretary of State has the authority to put forward other requirements by way of 'regulations' so it is possible that over time this section, like any section in the annual report, will evolve as new issues arise. Some of the current requirements are as follows:

- The names of those persons who have been directors during the year.
- The likely future developments of the business (this may be shown in the Strategic Report instead).
- Quoted companies need to also include information on greenhouse gas emissions.
- If any of the required information has been shown in the Strategic Report, there should be an explanation in the Directors' Report explaining that and where the information can be found.

The 2006 Companies Act has six subsections dealing with matters that relate to the auditors. The following matters are of particular relevance:

- The directors' report must contain a statement that the directors are aware that all relevant information has been given to the auditors, i.e. all the information that they need in order to be able to complete their report.
- The directors have taken steps to be aware of all relevant information that the auditors might need and that the auditors in turn are aware of that information.

The statutory and listing disclosure information required in a directors' report is quite formidable. This part of the annual report and accounts can take up many pages. An example of what is included in the Halfords plc Directors' Report is shown in Figure 8.8.

Figure 8.8 Example content of a directors' report

Source: Halfords plc, *Annual Report and Accounts*, 2015.

Unless qualifying as 'small', companies must also include a strategic report, setting out a review of the company's operations. The strategic report is likely to follow or be part of the directors' report. Its purpose is to provide information to members of the company in order to help them assess how successful the directors have been in performing their duty in promoting the success of the company. Among the mandatory items to be included in the strategic report are the following:

- a fair review of the company's business;
- a description of risks and uncertainties facing it;
- a balanced and comprehensive analysis of its development and performance of the company's business during the year;
- a similar analysis of the company's business position at the end of the year;
- the main trends and factors likely to affect its future development, performance and position;
- the disclosure of information relating to the company's policies, the impact and effectiveness of such matters as the environment, the company's employees and social and community issues;
- information about persons who have essential contractual or other arrangements with the company;
- an analysis of the company's business incorporating key financial, environmental, employee and performance indicators;
- a reference to, and some additional explanations of, amounts included in the annual accounts;
- the steps taken to make sure that the auditors get all the information they need in order to prepare their report;
- information about environmental matters and
- the number of persons of each sex who are directors, senior managers and employees of the company.

Nomination committee report

This short report is about the process of appointment of the board of directors and its evaluation – its size and structure.

Audit committee report

This report is about the membership and remit of the Audit Committee – the committee of independent non-executive directors to whom the external and internal auditors report directly. As you would remember from an earlier chapter, the external auditors provide an independent examination of the financial statements and provide an opinion. They present their finding from the audit to the Audit Committee who in turn challenge the directors on the way they have been running the company and any significant issues picked up by the auditors. As the shareholders are not privy to these conversations, the audit committee report also provides a summary of any significant issues related to the financial statements.

Activity 8.5	Search through each of your three sets of annual reports and accounts. Find the section called 'Business Review' (or some such title). List the headings used in the review. Does it include all the requirements that we have listed in the above section? What is missing? If some items are missing, try to find them elsewhere in the respective report and accounts.

Directors' remuneration report

Since January 2016, all companies, except those which as 'small', are required to make certain disclosures about the aggregate remuneration of directors. Directors' remuneration is a hot topic in the corporate world. Shareholders hire directors to run the company on their behalf and thus outsource all operating decisions about the company. So in practice the directors determine their own pay although it has to be approved by the shareholders. What directors pay themselves is an expense for the company, which in turn reduces the profit that can be paid as dividends to shareholders. The higher the directors pay, the lower the dividends for shareholders.

The purpose of a directors' remuneration report, therefore, is to let shareholders know what their company is paying the directors to act on the shareholders' behalf. The total amount paid to the directors may be very large indeed. It will usually be made up of a complex package of fees, salaries, bonuses, pension contributions and share options.

News clip

FTSE 100 bosses face fresh revolt over pay

The temperature gauge on executive pay rose into the red zone this week as two FTSE 100 companies suffered defeats at the hands of shareholders.

On Thursday afternoon, 59 per cent of votes cast went against the pay package of BP chief executive Bob Dudley — the biggest protest against an FTSE 100 boss since Sir Martin Sorrell's defeat at WPP four years ago.

Hours later, the pay of Olivier Bohuon, chief executive of medical device group Smith & Nephew, was also rejected by 53 per cent of voting investors.

Not since 2012, when a number of chief executives were forced to resign amid shareholder revolt, has tension over pay been this high, say some investors. Although the votes were non-binding, the protests signal trouble ahead for others.

Source: Extracted from www.ft.com, 16 June 2016

For listed companies, the directors' remuneration requirements are significantly more. The remuneration report is split into two parts – a *historical remuneration report* showing how much did the directors get paid, and a *policy report* – which sets out the policy for future remuneration. The policy report part has to be put to shareholder vote every three years and is legally binding, a company will be in breach of the law if it paid its directors more than what is permissible in the policy.

The above requirements can lead to a very lengthy directors' remuneration report. For example, the Halfords' directors' remuneration report is 15-pages long. Directors' remuneration reports are presented mainly in a narrative style in paragraphs under relevant headings. There can, however, be some quantitative and statistical data and (as required) at least one performance graph.

The numbers in the remuneration report (such as each director's basic salary, bonus, benefits, share options and pension benefit) are subject to audit by the external auditor.

We do not have the space here to reproduce an actual directors' remuneration report but what we have done in Figure 8.9 is to extract the main headings used in Halfords' directors' remuneration report.

CONTENTS OF THE HALFORDS PLC DIRECTORS REMUNERATION REPORT

- REMUNERATION COMMITTEE CHAIRMAN'S LETTER
  - REMUNERATION POLICY
  - REMUNERATION STRUCTURE AND PHILOSOPHY
  - PERFORMANCE SHARE PLAN ('PSP')
  - SAVE AS YOU EARN SCHEME ('SAYE')
  - INCENTIVE / REMUNERATION REVIEW
  - CONCLUDING REMARKS
- REMUNERATION POLICY
- KEY ELEMENTS OF EXECUTIVE DIRECTORS' REMUNERATION POLICY
  - Base salary
  - Benefits
  - Pensions
  - Annual Bonus
  - Performance Share Plans
  - CEO Co-Investment Award
- KEY ELEMENTS OF NON-EXECUTIVE DIRECTOR REMUNERATION POLICY
- THE COMMITTEE
  - SUMMARY OF COMMITTEE ACTIVITY
  - STRUCTURE AND CONTENT OF THE REMUNERATION REPORT
  - ADVISORS
  - SHAREHOLDER DIALOGUE
  - VOTES IN RELATION TO THE ANNUAL REPORT ON REMUNERATION
- HOW WAS THE REMUNERATION POLICY IMPLEMENTED IN 2014/15 – EXECUTIVE DIRECTORS
  - Single remuneration figure
  - Salary
  - Annual Bonus
  - Performance Share Plans
  - Benefits
  - Pensions
- SHARE AWARDS GRANTED
- OUTSTANDING SHARE AWARDS (AUDITED)
- SHAREHOLDING GUIDELINES (AUDITED)
- PAYMENTS TO FORMER DIRECTORS (AUDITED)
- HOW WAS THE REMUNERATION POLICY IMPLEMENTED IN 2014/2015 – NON EXECUTIVE DIRECTORS
- HOW REMUNERATION POLICY WILL BE IMPLEMENTED FOR 2014/15 – EXECUTIVE DIRECTORS
- HOW REMUNERATION POLICY WILL BE IMPLEMENTED FOR 2015/16 – NON-EXECUTIVE DIRECTORS

Figure 8.9 Example content of a directors' remuneration report

Source: Halfords plc, *Annual Report and Accounts*, 2015.

Once more turn to your three sets of annual reports and accounts. Find the directors' remuneration report. Read through each one. List all the main headings in each report in three adjacent columns. Try to put similar headings opposite each other. Is there a regular pattern? Or are there some items that are specific to one company? Note the differences.

Shareholder information

Following on from the directors' remuneration report, you will then almost certainly come across the 'accounts'. We will come back to this section in the next chapter. After the accounts, you may then find some miscellaneous information that is of particular relevance to the shareholders. If it is not at the back of the report, then it may be included in the introductory section. The shareholder information is likely to include the following information: administrative matters; financial summary and glossary of terms.

Administrative matters

This may include notice of the annual general meeting, when the dividend may be paid, details about online shareholder services and share dealing, the names and addresses of the company officers and advisers, a financial calendar and a list of the principal companies of the group.

Financial summary

A summary of the financial results over the past five years (possibly 10) may be included in this part of the annual report and accounts. It will probably give some quantitative and statistical data and some graphs depicting the main results, covering such items as the revenue earned, profits, capital expenditure and number of employees. Such a summary is sometimes included in the accounts section of the overall annual report and accounts.

Glossary of terms

Some companies provide a list of the financial and technical terms used in their annual report and accounts.

List the shareholder information included in each of your three sets of annual reports and accounts. In most companies, this information will be at the back but some of it may be at the front. Are there any items not included in the text above? If so, add them to the list outlined in the text.

> ## 🔔 Questions you should ask
>
> In previous chapters we have stressed that the accounting information presented to you will have been prepared by your accountants and that you are unlikely to be involved in the detailed preparation. This chapter is different. The matters with which we have been dealing will be the responsibility of a large team of non-accountants with the assistance of the accountants. So what do you need to ask if you are involved in preparing your company's annual report? We suggest the following.
>
> - What information is legally and professionally required and where should it be shown?
> - What corporate governance information and other matters are we duty-bound to disclose and where is the best place to put it?
> - Are we sure that any statements made are in line with the financial data presented in the annual accounts?
> - Do we have some evidence to justify any predictions we make about our future prospects?
> - Are we presenting too much information to our shareholders and if so, can we cut it back?
> - Are the design, format and general content of the material likely to encourage users to read it?
> - Do the various reports contain any jargon and, if so, can we either cut it out or reduce it?
> - Are the publicity pages likely to annoy our shareholders?

Conclusion

A company usually publishes an annual report and accounts. It then supplies a copy to each shareholder (nowadays this may be an email with a link to a .pdf document on the company website) and files one with the Registrar of Companies for public inspection. In this chapter we have examined the annual *report* section of an annual report and accounts. The next chapter examines the annual *accounts* section.

In order to make our study of an annual report a little easier, we have suggested that it can be broken down into three main sections. The first few pages usually contain some introductory material about the company, such as its objectives and a summary of the financial year. In consumer-orientated companies there may also be many pages advertising the company's products. A chairman's report may be considered to be part of this section. You will probably find it towards the end of the introductory material. It will normally be narrative in style and upbeat in tone. The chairman usually summarises the financial performance for the year and reviews the prospects for the following year.

Following the introductory section, most annual reports and accounts contain what we have called a 'corporate reporting' section, although other terms are used. This section may be broken down into a number of categories. We have identified a number of reports in this section including the corporate governance report, the directors' report, the strategic report, the audit committee report and the directors' remuneration report. Much of the information disclosed in this section is now mandatory as part of the London Stock Exchange listing requirements but some of it is also a statutory requirement.

Thereafter there will almost certainly be a detailed section dealing with the 'accounts' (discussed in the next chapter) and, following the accounts, a brief section outlining some administrative matters that are of particular relevance for the shareholders. Such matters include company names and addresses, details of the AGM, a financial summary and sometimes a glossary.

Key points	
	1 A company's annual report and accounts contains a great many reports and statements, some of which are voluntary and some of which are mandatory. In this chapter we have dealt with annual reports.
	2 It is possible to identify three main sections of an annual report, although the detailed content and structure varies from company to company. The length of such reports also varies, depending partly on the size of the company and partly on its type, e.g. whether it is a manufacturing or a service-based company.
	3 The introductory section contains some details about the company, a summary of its financial results for the year, the chairman's statement contains details about the governance of the company and possibly some publicity material.
	4 The specific reports that follow include a directors' report and a directors' remuneration report.
	5 The annual accounts will normally then be presented followed by the last few pages of the overall document containing some miscellaneous information largely for the benefit of the shareholders.

Check your learning

The answers to these questions can be found within the text.

1 List three items that may be included in the introductory section of a company's annual report.

2 What mandatory requirement covers the contents of a chairman's statement?

3 List three items that will normally be included in a chairman's statement.

4 Identify three main sections under which the 'report of the directors' may be classified.

5 What is meant by corporate governance?

6 What is *The UK Corporate Governance Code*?

7 Name six of its provisions.

8 What three items should be included in the general contents section of a directors' report?

9 What is a strategic report?

10 Identify six items that it should include.

11 What information about the auditors should directors include in their report?

12 What is a directors' remuneration report?

13 Name six matters that should be included in it.

14 Identify three items that may be included in 'shareholder information'.

News story quiz

Remember the news story at the beginning of this chapter? Go back to that story and reread it before answering the following questions.

As you saw in this chapter, the length of the annual report runs over quite a number of pages already. Further requirements for environmental reporting (and other narrative reporting that may become the norm in future) will add to an already lengthy document.

Questions

1 What do you think are the needs of users of the annual report and accounts for narrative reporting? Think about the various user groups we have identified in an earlier chapter.

2 What might be the practical implications for companies and their managers from having to comply with new narrative reporting requirements? How might that impact your work as a manager?

3 How is comprehensive narrative reporting contributing to 'homogenising the European market'?

Tutorial questions

8.1 'A limited liability company's annual report should be made easier to understand for the average shareholder.' Discuss.

8.2 Examine the argument that annual reports are a costly irrelevance because hardly anyone refers to them.

8.3 Should companies be banned from including non-financial data in their annual reports?

Website

Further practice questions, study material and links to relevant sites on the World Wide Web can be found on the website that accompanies this book. The site can be found at www.pearsoned.co.uk/dyson

The annual accounts

Say what you think . . .

Toshiba says it inflated profits by nearly $2bn over seven years

Kana Inagaki in Tokyo

Toshiba said it had inflated profits by nearly $2bn over seven years as it assessed the fallout from an accounting scandal that has wiped more than a third off the company's share value.

Shares briefly rose nearly 6 per cent after Toshiba finally published its revised earnings on Monday before falling back to close up 1.8 per cent.

Investors said the company must do more to allay concerns about its nuclear and semiconductor businesses, which were the source of the large writedowns.

Masashi Muromachi, who took over as president in July, said the company would reconsider targets it had set earlier for sectors such as healthcare as it sought to restore confidence after disclosing what has become one of Japan's largest accounting scandals.

For the fiscal year to the end of March, the Japanese industrial group, which also makes televisions and laptops, reported a net loss of Y37.83bn ($318m). It recorded a profit of Y60.24bn a year earlier. Before the scandal broke, the company had expected a net profit of Y120bn.

Operating profit fell 34 per cent from the previous year to Y170bn, while revenue rose 2.6 per cent to Y6.66tn.

The company did not issue a forecast for the current financial year to March 2016, but it is scheduled to release its first-quarter earnings on September 14.

Toshiba had been unable to close its books since flagging accounting irregularities in April, but it had warned that it would swing to a full-year net loss as a result of related impairment charges.

An investigation found that senior executives had played a role in inflating profits over seven years, leading to a board shake-up and the resignation of Hisao Tanaka, its former chief executive.

The company missed two deadlines to report results, last week delaying its earnings release for the second time after discovering new accounting issues that required further investigation.

On Monday, Toshiba also said that it had revised down its pre-tax profit figures by Y225bn ($1.9bn) over a seven-year period dating back to 2008. On a net profit level, the downward revisions totalled Y155bn.

The amendments came after Toshiba wrote down the value of a nuclear project in south Texas, its semiconductor division and its consumer electronics businesses such as televisions and PCs.

FT   *Source*: Adapted from www.ft.com, 7 September 2015.

Questions relating to this news story can be found on page 224.

About this chapter

This chapter is a continuation of Chapter 8. In that chapter we dealt with the various reports that you will find in a listed company's annual report and accounts. In this chapter we are going to look at what may be found in its annual *accounts,* such as a statement of profit or loss and other comprehensive income, a statement of changes in equity, a statement of financial position and a statement of cash flows. Figure 9.1 gives you an overview of what we will be covering in this chapter.

By the end of this chapter you should be able to:

● list the six main reports and statements that are included in a public limited company's published annual accounts;

● outline what each of these reports and statements contains;

● locate additional information in the notes to the accounts;

● extract meaningful and useful information about the company's performance from the accounts;

● evaluate the significance of the auditor's report;

● locate information about the company's financial performance over the longer term.

Why this chapter is important

The various *reports* included in a company's published annual report and accounts are important for non-accountants because they provide a great deal of background information about the company and its operations. Much of this information is now mandatory either by statute or by professional requirements.

Apart from the periodic summary, most of the accounts section is mandatory. The information that it contains is considered vital because it tells shareholders and other users what profit the company has made, what its cash flow is like, what assets it owns and what liabilities it has incurred. Such information can provide the basis for a rigorous analysis of the company's performance in order to help assess its future prospects.

In Chapter 10 we shall explain how you can go about undertaking such an analysis. Accountants refer to it as 'interpreting the accountants', or as the man in the street might say, 'reading between the lines of the accounts'. This chapter provides you with the basic information that will enable you to interpret a set of accounts.

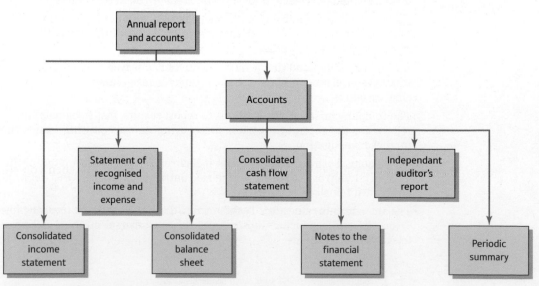

Figure 9.1 Annual accounts: structure

Activity 9.1	Turn to the three sets of the annual report and accounts that you used in Chapter 8. Find out what accounts are included in each of them and then list their titles in three adjacent columns.

Setting the scene

This section is divided into two parts. In the first part we give you a brief reminder of some of the material we covered in Chapter 2, while in the second part we explain what is meant by group accounts.

International financial reporting standards

Unlike most of the previous chapters in this book, in this one we are dealing with the *published* accounts of a limited liability company. If the accounts have been published, this probably means that if the company is *listed,* i.e. it is a public limited liability company (or a 'plc') and you can buy its shares on the Stock Exchange. We will also assume that it is incorporated in the United Kingdom but most of the points that we cover in this chapter are relevant even if the company is incorporated in one of the other 28 member countries of the European Union.

It is important that we make the above assumptions clear, particularly about the European Union. In the United Kingdom, the accounting requirements are included in the Companies Act 2006. As we mentioned in Chapter 2, the Act requires group listed companies to prepare accounts under IAS requirements. In this respect the Act simply incorporates EU law into British law. Other EU countries have had to do the same thing. This means that *all* group listed companies throughout the European Union have had to adopt IAS requirements. So perhaps apart from the language and the currency you should find that group listed company accounts throughout the European Union look similar in both content and presentation.

The main requirements affecting the presentation of published accounts under the IASB programme may be found in *IAS 1 (Presentation of Financial Information), IAS 7 (Statement of Cash Flows), IAS 28 (Accounting for Investments in Associates and Joint Ventures (2011)), IAS 34 (Interim Financial Reporting), IFRS 3 (Business Combinations) and IFRS 10 (Consolidated Financial Statements).* Old IASs will eventually be replaced by IFRSs but they remain valid until that happens.

IAS1 *Presentation of Financial Statements* prescribes the basis for *presentation* of financial statements so that comparability is ensured both with the financial statements of previous periods as well as the financial statements of other entities. To ensure comparability between periods, corresponding figures for the preceding year are included side by side with the current year figures. An entity is required to present at least:

- two statements of financial position;
- two statements of profit or loss and other comprehensive income;
- statements of cash flows;
- two statements of changes in equity and
- related notes for each of the above.

There are some other matters that will also be new to you when you come across a set of published accounts. They are:

- other names may be used as titles for the statements other than the ones listed above. The most common substitutions are 'income statement' for the statement of profit or loss and 'balance sheet' for the statement of financial position;

- the *statement of profit or loss and other comprehensive income* can be presented as one big statement or in two parts: one dealing with profit or loss and the other dealing with other comprehensive income;
- most published accounts will be for a *group* of companies.

We deal with group accounts in a little more detail below.

Group accounts

We referred to 'groups' in Chapter 2. A group of companies is like a family. One company (say, Company A) may buy shares in another company (say, Company B). When Company A owns more than 50 per cent of the voting shares in Company B, B becomes a *subsidiary* of A, *the parent company*. If A were to own more than 20 per cent but less than 50 per cent of the voting shares in B, B would be known as an *associate* of A. In effect, B is considered to be the offspring of A. Of course B might have children of its own, say, Company C and Company D. So C and D become part of the family, i.e. part of the A group of companies. An example of a group structure is shown in Figure 9.2.

The main significance of these relationships is that you can expect the published accounts to be those of the *group,* i.e. in effect, as though it were one entity (or 'family') so that any intergroup activities (such as sales between group companies or transfers of funds within 'the family') are ignored. This involves adding together all the accounts of the group companies, or *consolidating* them. Using IASB terminology, you can, therefore, expect a published set of accounts to include a *consolidated* statement of profit or loss and other comprehensive income, a *consolidated* statement of changes in equity, a *consolidated* statement of financial position and a *consolidated* statement of cash flows. Note that instead of using the term 'consolidated' some companies substitute 'group'. Such statements are now considered in turn in the following sections.

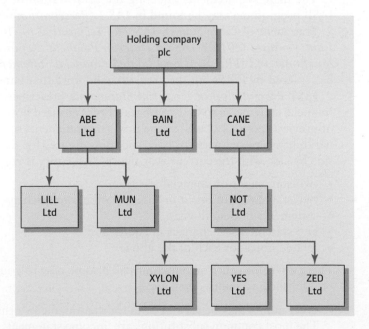

Figure 9.2 Example of a group company structure

Consolidated statement of profit or loss and other comprehensive income

We show a two-part consolidated statement of profit or loss and other comprehensive income prepared under IASB requirements in Example 9.1.

Example 9.1

A consolidated statement of profit or loss and other comprehensive income for a plc

Halfords plc
Consolidated statement of profit or loss (income statement) for the period to 3 April 2015

	Tutorial notes	£m
Revenue	1	1 025
Cost of sales	2	(479)
Gross profit	3	546
Operating expenses	4	(459)
Operating profit	5	87
Finance income	6	-
Finance costs	7	(4)
Profit before tax	8	83
Tax on profit	9	(18)
Profit attributable to equity shareholders	10	65
Earnings per share	11	
Basic earnings per share		33.8p
Diluted earnings per share		33.3p

Halfords plc
Consolidated statement of comprehensive income for the period to 3 April 2015

	Tutorial notes	£m
Profit for the period	10	65
Other comprehensive income for the period	12	2
Total comprehensive income for the period	13	67

Note:

References to the formal notes and the notes themselves have not been reproduced in the above example.

Tutorial notes

1 *Revenue.* The net invoiced sales value exclusive of value added tax of goods and services supplied to external customers during the year. It is common to also refer to this as *turnover.*

2 *Cost of sales.* No details were disclosed except that the amount does not include distribution costs and administration expenses (see Tutorial Note 4 below). It includes the cost of opening stock + the purchase or production cost of new stock – the cost of closing stock.

3 *Gross profit.* Gross profit is normally defined as the difference between sales revenue and cost of sales.

4 *Operating expenses.* These include selling and distribution costs and administrative expenses (such as salaries, electricity and advertising). It is possible that in some accounts this heading is followed by a separate heading for Other Operating Income in order to incorporate income from non-mainstream sources (e.g. when a business such as Sainsbury's sublets part of its stores to Starbucks and generates additional income).

5 *Operating profit.* This is the profit that the company has earned during the year on its normal manufacturing and selling activities. Sometimes that may be followed by a line of exceptional items (costs and income that are not expected to recur in the normal course of business).

6   *Finance income.* Interest income (received and receivable for the period).

7   *Finance costs.* Interest expense (paid and payable for the period).

8   *Profit before tax.* The profit made on the company's activities during the year before taking into account any taxation due on it.

9   *Tax on profit.* The tax amount will be mainly corporation tax payable on the profits for the year adjusted for amounts relating to other years.

10 *Profit attributable to equity holders.* This is the overall profit for the year after allowing for tax. In theory it could all be paid out to the shareholders.

11 *Earnings per share.* The basic earnings per share are the profit for the year attributable to equity holders divided by the weighted average number of ordinary shares in issue during the year. The diluted earnings per share are calculated similarly to the basic earnings per share except that an allowance is made for some shares that *might* be issued if the right to take them up is exercised.

12 *Other comprehensive income.* These are items of income and expense (including reclassification adjustments) that are not recognised in profit or loss as per IFRS – for example, complex items such as the fair value on cash flow hedges.

13 *Total comprehensive income.* This is the change in the owner's equity resulting from transactions and other events, other than with the owners in their capacity as owners. In other words, this represents what is sometimes referred to as the 'bottom line' and shows how much the value of the owner's equity has gone up (or down) as result of trading and operations. If incomes exceed expenses in a period, owners' equity has increased.

Halfords has presented its consolidated statement of profit and loss (which they have entitled consolidated income statement) by aggregating its expenses according to *function*, i.e. by itemising the cost of sales, distribution costs and administrative expenses. This is known as the *operational* format and most companies adopt it. An alternative format is to aggregate expenses according to their *nature* by itemising changes in inventories of finished goods and work in progress, raw materials and consumables, depreciation and amortisation expenses and other operating expenses. This is known as the *type of expenditure* format. The chances are that you will not come across this format very often. There is no difference in presentation between the two formats after the operating profit line.

Unusually Halfords' statement of profit or loss and statement of other comprehensive income cover a 53-week period. This is because the Halfords group prepares accounts for periods up to the Friday closest to 31 March each year. Ordinarily companies report their profits for a year (52 weeks).

Activity 9.2

Refer to your three sets of annual accounts and turn to the page that includes the consolidated statement of profit or loss (which some companies entitle as 'income statement'). Read down through the statement on a line-by-line basis. If you do not understand a particular item, look it up in the 'notes to the accounts'. Compare your three statements with Example 9.1 and list any significant differences between them.

Statement of changes in equity

IAS requires that a reconciliation is shown between the opening and closing position for each component of equity, separately disclosing:

- the movement in profit or loss;
- the movement in other comprehensive income and
- contributions and distributions to owners (e.g. from the issue of new shares or payment of dividends).

This is known as the *Statement of Changes in Equity*. It is a very complex-looking statement.

Example 9.2 shows Halfords' statement of changes in equity for 2015.

Example 9.2	A statement of changes in equity for a plc

Halfords plc

CONSOLIDATED STATEMENT OF CHANGES IN SHAREHOLDERS' EQUITY

	Attributable to the equity holders of the Company						
				Other reserves			
	Share capital £m	Share premium account £m	Investment in own shares £m	Capital redemption reserve £m	Hedging reserve £m	Retained earnings £m	Total equity £m
Balance at 29 March 2013	2.0	151.0	(13.2)	0.3	0.6	158.0	298.7
Total comprehensive income for the period							
Profit for the period	–	–	–	–	–	55.5	55.5
Other comprehensive income							
Cash flow hedges:							
Fair value changes in the period	–	–	–	–	(3.0)	–	(3.0)
Transfers to inventory	–	–	–	–	1.1	–	1.1
Transfers to net profit:							
Cost of sales	–	–	–	–	(0.1)	–	(0.1)
Income tax on other comprehensive income	–	–	–	–	0.8	–	0.8
Total other comprehensive income for the period net of tax	–	–	–	–	(1.2)	–	(1.2)
Total comprehensive income for the period	–	–	–	–	(1.2)	55.5	54.3
Transactions with owners							
Share options exercised	–	–	2.1	–	–	–	2.1
Share-based payment transactions	–	–	–	–	–	1.0	1.0
Income tax on share-based payment transactions	–	–	–	–	–	0.9	0.9
Dividends to equity holders	–	–	–	–	–	(27.7)	(27.7)
Total transactions with owners	–	–	(1.1)	–	–	(25.8)	(26.9)
Balance at 28 March 2014	2.0	151.0	(14.3)	0.3	(0.6)	187.7	326.1
Total comprehensive income for the period							
Profit for the period	–	–	–	–	–	65.8	65.8
Other comprehensive income							
Cash flow hedges:							
Fair value changes in the period	–	–	–	–	7.9	–	7.9
Transfers to inventory	–	–	–	–	(1.4)	–	(1.4)
Transfers to net profit:							
Cost of sales	–	–	–	–	(3.4)	–	(3.4)
Income tax on other comprehensive income	–	–	–	–	(1.2)	–	(1.2)
Total other comprehensive income for the period net of tax	–	–	–	–	1.9	–	1.9
Total comprehensive income for the period	–	–	–	–	1.9	65.8	67.7
Transactions with owners							
Share options exercised	–	–	0.7	–	–	–	0.7
Share-based payment transactions	–	–	–	–	–	1.4	1.4
Purchase of own shares	–	–	–	–	–	–	–
Income tax on share-based payment transactions	–	–	–	–	–	0.2	0.2
Dividends to equity holders	–	–	–	–	–	(28.4)	(28.4)
Total transactions with owners	–	–	0.7	–	–	(26.8)	(26.1)
Balance at 3 April 2015	2.0	151.0	(13.6)	0.3	1.3	226.7	367.7

Source: Halfords plc, *Annual Report and Accounts*, 2015.

You probably remember that in earlier chapters we referred to the moment between the retained earnings at the beginning and end of a period as the statement of movement in retained earnings. It showed how much profit from the current year is paid in dividends to shareholders and how much is added to reserves. In effect, that was an extract form the statement of changes in equity – the last column. As you can see, the same reconciliation is performed on all other reserves the company has (such as the share capital, the share premium, revaluation reserve, etc.).

Activity 9.3	Look up the statement of changes in equity in each of your three accounts. List all the various items in each statement in adjacent columns.

Consolidated statement of financial position

IAS1 does not strictly prescribe the format of the statement, so you can expect variations in the way that companies present the information that *must* be disclosed on the face of the statement of financial position. The standard requires the separation of current and non-current assets and liabilities (current being the ones which are expected to be sold/settled within the next 12 months).

The most common presentation order is:

- Resources and sources of funding approach: Assets (top) followed by Capital and Reserves, then Liabilities (bottom).

  Within that assets and liabilities can be listed first current then non-current or vice versa. Other possibilities are:

- Net assets approach: Assets − Liabilities (top) and Capital and Reserves (bottom).
- Long-term financing approach: Assets − Current Liabilities (top) and Non-Current Liabilities + Capital and Reserves (bottom).

If you remember what we said in an earlier chapter about the accounting equation, you will recognise that the statement of financial position *is* the accounting equation in any of its many possible forms!

- Assets = Capital and Reserves + Liabilities
- Assets − Liabilities (i.e. Net Assets) = Capital and Reserves
- Assets − Current Liabilities = Non-Current Liabilities + Capital and Reserves

The top and bottom parts of the statement should always be in balance just in the same way that the accounting equation is always in equality. Because of that balance, the statement is often referred to as the *balance sheet*.

The resources = sources of funding approach is the most common format. Some companies, especially in the United Kingdom still use an alternative net assets format of the accounting equation.

News clip

No accounting for complexity

Oh no, another useful accounting dodge blocked. From 2019, the full liability of operating leases must be put on the balance sheet. Financial leases are already there (as you know) since they are more like the hire-purchase agreements that put millions of washing machines into homes in the 1960s. Operating leases are the mainstay of shops, airlines and hotels, which frequently own little more than their logo. Now everyone will have to come clean.

Source: www.ft.com, 15 January 2016.

Example 9.3 is a reasonably simple presentation of a group statement of financial position although we have not included the previous year's statement of financial position or the formal notes relating to the current one.

Example 9.3	An example of a published consolidated statement of financial position for a plc

Halfords plc
Consolidated statement of financial position (balance sheet) as at 3 April 2015

	Tutorial notes	£m
Non-current assets		
Intangible assets	1	357
Property, plant and equipment	2	104
Deferred tax assets	3	4
		465
Current assets		
Inventories	4	150
Trade and other receivables	5	56
Derivative financial instruments	6	4
Cash and cash equivalents		22
		232
Total assets		697
Current liabilities		
Borrowings	7	(23)
Trade and other payables		(181)
Current tax liabilities		(12)
Provisions	8	(11)
		(227)
Non-current liabilities		
Borrowings	7	(61)
Accruals and deferred income	9	(32)
Provisions	8	(8)
		(101)
Net assets		369
Shareholders Equity		
Share capital	10	2
Share premium	11	151
Investment in own shares	12	(13)
Other reserves	13	2
Retained earnings	14	227
Total equity		369

Source: Halfords plc, *Annual Report and Accounts*, 2015.

Tutorial notes

1 Intangible assets are things such as brand name and trademarks, computer software and goodwill.

2 Shown at cost or valuation after allowing for additions, disposals and depreciation.

3 Deferred tax due from the tax authorities beyond the financial year.

4 Finished goods after write down to net realisable value.

5   These receivables are after an allowance for doubtful debts.

6   These are complex financial instruments linked to other financial instruments, for example, options on shares.

7   Loans and other borrowings are split between amounts payable in the next 12 months (current) and amounts payable beyond the next 12 months (non-current).

8   Provisions are estimates of losses and costs in the next 12 months (current) and beyond that. In the case of Halfords, they relate to things like sales returns, product liability and unused gift vouchers as well as provisions associated with vacant property costs.

9   Accruals are estimates of expenses not settled at the year end (e.g. rents and electricity).

10 200m ordinary shares (allotted, called up and fully paid) of 1p each. Represents the nominal value of shares.

11 Share premium represents the amount paid by shareholders in excess of the nominal value of the shares (in share capital).

12 Companies will sometimes buy their own shares without cancelling them with a view to selling them in the market if needed to raise cash quickly. These are referred to as *treasury shares*.

13 Other reserves could include revaluation of property reserves, capital redemption reserves resulting from the purchase of own shares and other types of complex reserves.

14 This is the profit retained within the business for future investment. The figure comes from the statement of changes in equity (the final column, which is much the same as what we had previously referred to as a statement of movement in retained earnings).

As you can see, Halfords has used the net asset approach to the presentation of its statement of financial position. In the top part, assets are shown in reverse order of *liquidity* (liquidity is a term to represent how long it will take to liquidate an asset and turn it into cash). Hence non-current assets are followed by the current assets to arrive at *total assets;* and property is shown above inventory, for example, because you would expect to sell inventory quickly and property takes a long time to liquidate and turn into cash. Cash is the most 'liquid' of all assets and is shown at the bottom of the assets list.

Activity 9.4

Referring to your set of three published accounts, work your way down each of the three consolidated statement of financial positions. If you do not understand what any of the items mean, consult the 'notes to the accounts'. Then compare Halfords' main section headings to those in each of your three statement of financial positions. Note any differences in the description of the headings and the order in which they are presented. Assuming that there are some differences between them, which format do you think is the easiest to follow?

Consolidated statement of cash flows

We dealt with statements of cash flows (SCFs) in Chapter 7 and we showed a real company example. Since we have been using the Halfords' accounts as an example in this chapter, and so that you can get a complete picture of published accounts for the same company, we show here in Example 9.4 the Halfords' statement of cash flows (without the 2014 comparative figures or the notes).

Activity 9.5	Turn to statement of the cash flows in each of your three accounts. Examine the terminology, the presentations and layout of each SCF along with Halfords' ones. Are there any substantial differences between the four SCFs? If there are, make a note of them. Then extract the two or three most significant items in each SCF that have resulted in an increase or a decrease in cash and cash equivalents during the year.

Example 9.4	**Example of a published statement of cash flows for a plc**

Halfords plc

CONSOLIDATED STATEMENT OF
CASH FLOWS

	53 weeks to 3 April 2015 £m
Cash flows from operating activities	
Profit after tax for the period, before non-recurring items	66.2
Non-recurring items	(0.4)
Profit after tax for the period	65.8
Depreciation — property, plant and equipment	20.2
Impairment charge	0.7
Amortisation — intangible assets	5.5
Net finance costs	3.5
Loss on disposal of property, plant and equipment	1.7
Equity-settled share based payment transactions	1.4
Fair value (gain)/loss on derivative financial instruments	(2.0)
Income tax expense	18.0
Decrease/(increase) in inventories	0.9
(Increase)/decrease in trade and other receivables	(3.0)
Increase in trade and other payables	27.2
Increase in provisions	0.5
Finance income received	0.1
Finance costs paid	(3.2)
Income tax paid	(17.1)
Net cash from operating activities	120.2
Cash flows from investing activities	
Acquisition of subsidiary, net of cash acquired	(14.0)
Purchase of intangible assets	(7.5)
Purchase of property, plant and equipment	(32.1)
Net cash used in investing activities	(53.6)
Cash flows from financing activities	
Net proceeds from exercise of share options	0.7
Purchase of own shares	—
Proceeds from loans, net of transaction costs	220.2
Repayment of borrowings	(254.0)
Payment of finance lease liabilities	(0.3)
Dividends paid	(28.4)
Net cash used in financing activities	(61.8)
Net increase/(decrease) in cash and bank overdrafts	4.8
Cash and cash equivalents at the beginning of the period	(4.7)
Cash and cash equivalents at the end of the period	0.1

NOTES TO CONSOLIDATED STATEMENT
OF CASH FLOWS

I. ANALYSIS OF MOVEMENTS IN THE GROUP'S NET DEBT IN THE PERIOD

	At 28 March 2014 £m	Cash flow £m	Other non-cash changes £m	At 3 April 2015 £m
Cash and cash equivalents at bank and in hand	(4.7)	4.8	—	0.1
Debt due after one year	(84.0)	33.9	(0.6)	(50.7)
Total net debt excluding finance leases	(88.7)	38.7	(0.6)	(50.6)
Finance leases due within one year	(0.3)	0.3	(0.6)	(0.6)
Finance lease due after one year	(10.6)	—	—	(10.6)
Total finance leases	(10.9)	0.3	(0.6)	(11.2)
Total net debt	(99.6)	39.0	(1.2)	(61.8)

Non-cash changes include finance costs in relation to the amortisation of capitalised debt issue costs of £0.6m (2014: £1.0m) and changes in classification between amounts due within and after one year.

Cash and cash equivalents at the period end consist of £22.4m (2014: £5.3m) of liquid assets and £22.3m (2014: £10.0m) of bank overdrafts.

Source: Halfords plc, *Annual report and accounts,* 2015.

Notes to the financial statements

The statement of profit or loss and other comprehensive income, the statement of changes in equity, the statement of financial position and the statement of cash flows are usually supported by a great deal of additional notes. These notes serve two main purposes:

- they avoid too much detail being shown on the face of the financial statements;
- they make it easier to provide some supplementary information.

IASB requirements specify what information *must* be disclosed on the face of the financial statements. This means that the notes can stretch to many pages. Halfords' 2015 notes to the accounts, for example, are 14 pages long (on A4 paper); the notes to Barclays Bank's 2015 accounts run to nearly 80 pages! This is an awful lot of information to plough through and you have to be a dedicated shareholder to do so. The *Statement of Principles for Financial Reporting* expected financial information to be understandable, but only if users had:

> a reasonable knowledge of business and economic activities and accounting and a willingness to study with reasonable diligence the information provided.

After studying the information in some financial statements (no doubt reasonably diligently), you could perhaps be forgiven if you felt that the FRC is being just a little bit too optimistic in its expectations.

Independent auditor's report

News clip

Auditors' fears increase over Hong Kong companies

Auditors have sharply increased their warnings over the financial health of Hong Kong companies at a time when investors fear the repercussions of China's slowing economy. A total of 149 companies have so far this year reported modified opinions for their financial accounts – as many as for all of 2014. Of those, 27 listed on the main board of the Hong Kong exchange carried 'disclaimers' where auditors sidestep giving a definitive opinion.

Source: Adapted from ft.com, 23 August 2015.

The independent (i.e. external) auditor's report is usually found before the financial statements. The independent auditor is required to do the audit and then to report to the shareholders in accordance with relevant legal and regulatory requirements. Most reports will be short – probably no longer than one page – and unless some highly unusual events have taken place, most auditors' reports will be very similar.

Halfords' independent auditors' report (note the plural) is reproduced in Figure 9.3. Read through it very carefully. The following features are of particular interest.

1 The independent auditors have audited not only the financial statements but also parts of the directors' remuneration report (as required).
2 There is quite a long statement explaining the respective responsibilities of the directors and of the auditors. Note what they are.
3 The audit has been conducted on the basis of international auditing standards (the United Kingdom and Ireland).
4 The auditors explain what was involved in doing the audit (basis of audit opinion).
5 The auditors confirm that the group financial statements give a 'true and fair' view for the period in question.
6 This opinion is in accordance with IFRS requirements as adopted by the European Union and the provision of the 2006 Companies Act) and IAS regulations.
7 The name of the most senior auditor from the audit firm is given.

Activity 9.6	Find the auditor's report in each of your three accounts. Read through them. Does the auditor state that the accounts represent a 'true and fair' view or are there any qualifications or reservations about something in the financial statements? If there are any qualifications (probably introduced by the phrase 'except for . . . '), list them.

Periodic summary

Many companies include a periodic summary as part of their accounts. The usual period covered is five years but sometimes it may be 10. The summary will usually be found after the 'notes to the accounts'.

As there are no IASB requirements to produce such a summary, companies are free to choose how it should be presented and what to put in it. Even so, the independent auditor is required to report 'on other information contained in the Annual Report' to ensure that 'it is consistent with the audited Group financial statements' (see Figure 9.3). So companies are not entirely free to publish just what suits them.

We suggest that in most periodic summaries you will find some details about the sales revenue, gross profit, profit before tax and dividends paid. You might also find some items extracted from the statement of financial position such as non-current assets, some non-current liabilities and the retained earnings.

Although periodic statements are limited in scope, they can help users to assess the company's performance over a much longer period than the two years that are legally required (the current year's result and the previous one). This is a significant point because conventional financial statements prepared on an annual basis may not suit some companies whose activities are much more oriented to the long term. As a result, the preparation of financial statements on such a short-term basis may be highly misleading. Periodic summaries may help, therefore, to give a much fairer picture of the company's affairs although there does not appear to be any current plans to make them mandatory. Nowadays, however, there are databases where financial statements going back many years are stored, so often investors would consult those rather than the published accounts for long-term trends in key financials.

Halfords' periodic summary is shown in Example 9.5.

INDEPENDENT AUDITOR'S REPORT'
TO THE MEMBERS OF HALFORDS GROUP PLC ONLY

OPINIONS AND CONCLUSIONS ARISING FROM OUR AUDIT
1. OUR OPINION ON THE FINANCIAL STATEMENTS IS UNMODIFIED

We have audited the financial statements of Halfords Group plc ("the Group") for the 53 week period ended 3 April 2015 set out on pages 77 to 111. In our opinion:

* the financial statements give a true and fair view of the state of the Group's and of the Parent Company's affairs as at 3 April 2015 and of the Group's profit for the 53 week period then ended;

* the Group financial statements have been properly prepared in accordance with International Financial Reporting Standards as adopted by the European Union (IFRSs as adopted by the EU);

* the parent company financial statements have been properly prepared in accordance with UK Accounting standards; and

* the financial statements have been prepared in accordance with the requirements of the Companies Act 2006 and, as regards the Group financial statements, Article 4 of the IAS Regulation.

2. OUR ASSESSMENT OF RISKS OF MATERIAL MISSTATEMENT

In arriving at our audit opinion above on the financial statements the risks of material misstatement that had the greatest effect on our audit were as follows.

VALUATION OF INVENTORY WITHIN THE RETAIL DIVISION (£147.8 MILLION)

Refer to pages 52 to 55 (Audit Committee Report), page 86 (accounting policy) and page 97 (financial disclosures).

* **The risk** – The Group holds a significant amount of inventory across a broad and diverse product range. Changes in consumer tastes and demands may mean that they cannot be sold or sales prices are discounted to less than the current carrying value. Estimating the future demand for, and hence the recoverable amount of, these products is inherently subjective.

* **Our response** – Our audit procedures in this area included testing the design and effectiveness of controls over identifying slow moving or discontinued products. We critically assessed the Group's provision for those product lines identified as slow moving or potentially slow moving, by obtaining an understanding of the Group's sales and purchasing plans for 2015/6, and the new product launches therein, as well as the level of expected discounting. We compared post year-end sales data to items within the Group's provision and to information provided by Category Managers responsible for each product category, in particular any product ranges that were forecast to be phased out or replaced, which were corroborated with the Group's purchasing plans. In addition, we compared inventory holding at the year end to past, and expected, sales performance to further identify potentially excess inventory lines.

We also considered the adequacy of the Group's disclosures about the degree of estimation involved in arriving at the provision.

VALUATION OF GOODWILL ASSOCIATED WITH THE NATIONWIDE AUTOCENTRES ACQUISITION (£69.7 MILLION)

Refer to pages 52 to 55 (Audit Committee Report), page 85 (accounting policy) and page 95 (financial disclosures).

* **The risk** – Following the acquisition of Nationwide Autocentres in 2010, the Group has held significant goodwill in the business. The business operates in a competitive market and commercial difficulties; such as loss of a significant customer, changes to market share or changes to the frequency with which customers replace their cars, may lead to a risk that the business does not meet the growth projections necessary to support the carrying value of the goodwill. Due to the inherent uncertainty involved in forecasting these cashflows, this is one of the key judgemental areas that our audit is concentrated on.

* **Our response** – Our audit procedures included, challenging the assumptions used around prospective trading levels, in light of the historical forecasting accuracy for newly opened Autocentres, given the proportion which have been opened in the past 2-3 years. We assessed the Group's performance against budget in the current and prior periods to evaluate the historical accuracy of overall forecasts. We used breakeven analysis to determine the key sensitivities within the budgeting model, which we considered to be the discount rate and the growth rate. The discount rate was determined by an independent third party. Further, we have critically assessed the various components of discount rate, by benchmarking the rate against external market data and the Group's financial position. We have assessed the continuing improvement in customer retention, a key factor in the growth rate, through reference to the Net Promoter Score (NPS) provided by an independent third party, and through our observation of a recent increase in customer-centric initiatives around the Group.

We considered the adequacy of the Group's disclosures about the sensitivity of the outcome of the impairment assessment to changes in key assumptions.

3. OUR APPLICATION OF MATERIALITY AND AN OVERVIEW OF THE SCOPE OF OUR AUDIT

The materiality for the Group financial statements as a whole was set at £4.0 million (FY14: £5.0 million), determined with reference to a benchmark of Group profit before tax, of which it represents 5.0% (FY14: 6.9%), a reduction from the prior period to ensure consistency with the industry peer group and other listed companies.

We report to the Audit Committee any corrected or uncorrected identified misstatements exceeding £0.2 million in addition to other identified misstatements that warranted reporting on qualitative grounds.

The Group audit team performed the audit of the Group as if it was a single aggregated set of financial information. The audit was performed using the materiality set out above and covered 100% of total Group revenue, Group profit before taxation, and total Group assets.

4. OUR OPINION ON OTHER MATTERS PRESCRIBED BY THE COMPANIES ACT 2006 IS UNMODIFIED

In our opinion:

* the part of the Directors' Remuneration Report to be audited has been properly prepared in accordance with the Companies Act 2006; and

* the information given in the Strategic Report and the Directors' Report for the financial year for which the financial statements are prepared is consistent with the financial statements.

➡

5. WE HAVE NOTHING TO REPORT IN RESPECT OF THE MATTERS ON WHICH WE ARE REQUIRED TO REPORT BY EXCEPTION

Under ISAs (United Kingdom and Ireland) we are required to report to you if, based on the knowledge we acquired during our audit, we have identified other information in the annual report that contains a material inconsistency with either that knowledge or the financial statements, a material misstatement of fact, or that is otherwise misleading.

In particular, we are required to report to you if:

* we have identified material inconsistencies between the knowledge we acquired during our audit and the directors' statement that they consider that the annual report and financial statements taken as a whole is fair balanced and understandable and provides the information necessary for shareholders to assess the Group's performance, business model and strategy; or
* the Audit Committee report, as set out on pages 52 — 55, does not appropriately address matters communicated by us to the Audit and Risk Committee.

Under the Companies Act 2006 we are required to report to you if, in our opinion:

* adequate accounting records have not been kept by the parent company, or returns adequate for our audit have not been received from branches not visited by us; or
* the parent company financial statements and the part of the Directors' Remuneration Report to be audited are not in agreement with the accounting records and returns; or
* certain disclosures of directors' remuneration specified by law are not made; or
* we have not received all the information and explanations we require for our audit.

Under the Listing Rules we are required to review:

* the directors' statement, set out on page 41, in relation to going concern;
* the part of the Corporate Governance Statement on pages 42 to 49 relating to the company's compliance with the 10 provisions of the UK Corporate Governance Code 2012 specified for our review.

We have nothing to report in respect of the above responsibilities.

SCOPE OF REPORT AND RESPONSIBILITIES

As explained more fully in the Directors' Responsibilities Statement set out on page 71, the directors are responsible for the preparation of the financial statements and for being satisfied that they give a true and fair view. A description of the scope of an audit of financial statements is provided on the Financial Reporting Council's website at www.frc.org.uk/auditscopeukprivate. This report is made solely to the company's members as a body and is subject to important explanations and disclaimers regarding our responsibilities, published on our website at www.kpmg.com/uk/auditscopeukco2014a, which are incorporated into this report as if set out in full and should be read to provide an understanding of the purpose of this report, the work we have undertaken and the basis of our opinions.

Peter Meehan (Senior Statutory Auditor)
for and on behalf of KPMG LLP, Statutory Auditor
Chartered Accountants
One Snowhill
Snow Hill Queensway
Birmingham
B4 6GH
4 June 2015

Figure 9.3 An example of an independent auditors' reportSource: Halfords plc, Annual Report and Accounts, 2015.

| Example 9.5 | **Example of a periodic summary** |

Halfords plc
Five-year record

	52 weeks to 1 April 2011 (audited) £m	52 weeks to 30 March 2012 (audited) £m	52 weeks to 29 March 2013 (audited) £m	52 weeks to 28 March 2014 (audited) £m	52 weeks to 27 March 2015 (proforma)* £m
Revenue	869.7	863.1	871.3	939.7	1,004.9
Cost of sales	(384.7)	(390.3)	(394.2)	(435.5)	(469.8)
Gross profit	485.0	472.8	477.1	504.2	535.1
Operating expenses	(364.4)	(373.7)	(400.0)	(426.4)	(450.5)
Operating profit before non-recurring items	128.1	97.2	78.1	77.8	84.6
Non-recurring operating expenses	(7.5)	1.9	(1.0)	(0.2)	(0.3)
Operating profit	120.6	99.1	77.1	77.6	84.3
Net finance costs	(2.5)	(5.0)	(6.1)	(5.0)	(3.5)
Profit before tax and non-recurring items	125.6	92.2	72.0	72.8	81.1
Non-recurring operating expenses	(7.5)	1.9	(1.0)	(0.2)	(0.3)
Profit before tax	118.1	94.1	71.0	72.6	80.8
Taxation	(34.7)	(24.8)	(18.2)	(17.0)	(17.4)
Taxation on non-recurring items	2.1	(0.9)	(0.1)	(0.1)	(0.1)
Profit attributable to equity shareholders	85.5	68.4	52.7	55.5	63.3
Basic earnings per share	40.7p	34.2p	27.2p	28.6p	32.5p
Basic earnings per share before non-recurring items	43.2p	33.7p	27.7p	28.8p	32.7p
Weighted average number of shares	210.4m	199.9m	194.3m	194.0m	194.2m

KEY PERFORMANCE
INDICATORS

	52 weeks to 1 April 2011	52 weeks to 30 March 2012	52 weeks to 29 March 2013	52 weeks to 28 March 2014	52 weeks to 27 March 2015
Revenue growth	+4.6%	-0.8%	+1.0%	+7.9%	+6.9%
Gross margin	55.8%	54.8%	54.8%	53.7%	53.2%
Operating margin	13.9%	11.5%	8.8%	8.3%	8.4%
Underlying Group EBITDA	£153.2m	£123.6m	£103.4m	£101.1m	£109.9m
Net debt	(£103.2m)	(£139.2m)	(£110.6m)	(£99.6m)	(£61.8m)

* The statutory 53-week period to 3 April 2015 comprises reported results that are non-comparable to the 52-week periods reported in other years. To provide a more meaningful comparison, the above tables include the proforma 52-weeks to 27 March 2015.

Source: **Halfords plc,** *Annual report and accounts,* 2015.

Questions you should ask

It is probably only at a very senior level that you would be in a position to ask questions about your company's draft annual report and accounts prepared for publication, but if you get the opportunity, the following ones might be pertinent.

- Are we absolutely confident that we have complied with the minimum statutory and mandatory accounting statements?

- Can we reduce the number of pages without missing out any essential information?

- Would it be possible to use different formats so that users not trained in accounting can follow them more easily?

- Can any item be left out to make it easier for users to understand?

- Could we avoid professional jargon and substitute terms that the layperson would understand?

Conclusion

In this chapter we have examined the accounts section of listed companies' annual report and accounts. We have suggested that it is possible to group the various types of financial statements into seven major categories:

- statement of profit or loss and other comprehensive income;
- statement of changes in equity;
- statement of financial position;
- statement of cash flows;
- notes to the accounts;
- auditor's report and
- periodic summary.

All these statements, except the periodic summary, are mandatory for the United Kingdom and other EU group listed companies. This now means that they have to be prepared in accordance with IASB requirements. When they are combined with the 'reports' (discussed in Chapter 8), they can form quite a formidable document especially for a very large international group of companies. Overall, the annual report and accounts is supposed to provide sufficient information for shareholders to be satisfied that their company is being managed effectively and efficiently. However, it may be that the sheer amount of information does not enable shareholders to be entirely reassured. There can be such a thing as 'information overload'!

Key points

1. An annual report and accounts contains a great many statements but those relating to the accounts (often referred to as the 'financial statements') may take up to about half of the entire contents.

2. The accounts section will include (always with comparatives) a statement of profit or loss and other comprehensive income, a statement of changes in equity, a statement of financial position and a statement of cash flows. These will be accompanied by the notes to the accounts, an auditor's report and often a periodic summary. If the accounts deal with a group of companies, the parent company's statement of financial position will also be given.

3. As a part of the European Union all UK group listed companies are required to adopt IASB standards in the preparation of their financial statements.

4. *IAS 1* specifies the format of the statement of profit or loss and other comprehensive income, the statement of changes in equity and the statement of financial position. *IAS 7* covers the statement of cash flows.

5. A minimum amount of information is usually shown on the face of the various statements with the remaining mandatory information being shown in notes to the accounts.

Check your learning

The answers to these questions can be found within the text.

1 What is meant by 'disclosure'?

2 What is a group of companies?

3 What are consolidated accounts?

4 Which main international accounting standard covers the presentation of accounts?

5 What is meant by the 'operational' and 'type of expenditure' formats for the presentation of the statement of profit or loss?

6 Which of the statements are prepared 'for a reporting period' and which are prepared 'as at the reporting period end'?

7 Name two items that you might find in a statement of changes in equity.

8 What is meant by the terms 'current' and 'non-current' in a company's statement of financial position?

9 Give an example of a non-current liability.

10 What international accounting standard covers the preparation of a listed company's statement of cash flows?

11 How many main headings are there in a listed company's statement of cash flows?

12 Why are 'notes to the accounts' used?

13 What opinion does an independent auditor usually express about a company's financial statements?

14 What mandatory requirements cover the publication of a periodic summary statement?

News story quiz

Remember the news story at the beginning of this chapter? Go back to that story and reread it before answering the following questions.

Questions

1 What do you think are the implications for Toshiba and its shareholders from the financial irregularities that were found to exist in its published accounts over a number of years?

2 What do you think are the implications for the auditors who signed off on those accounts in prior years?

3 Do you think accounts are worth the paper they are printed on, given what happened with Toshiba (and many other high profile corporate scandals in recent times)?

Tutorial questions

9.1 What items do you think could be taken out of a listed company's published statement or profit or loss and other comprehensive income and its statement of financial position without affecting the usefulness of such statements?

9.2 Describe what is meant by a 'qualified audit report' illustrating your answer with appropriate examples.

9.3 Suggest 10 items that should be disclosed in a listed company's periodic summary statement.

Website

Further practice questions, study material and links to relevant sites on the World Wide Web can be found on the website that accompanies this book. The site can be found at www.pearsoned.co.uk/dyson

Interpretation of accounts

So much data...

Investors mine Big Data for cutting-edge strategies

Robin Wigglesworth

Thinkunum is one of the many boutiques that specialise in providing non-traditional data that include everything from social media buzz to satellite images that can be mined by cutting-edge computer scientists for an investment edge.

Quarterly results, earnings calls, economic reports, executive meetings and expert industry insight have long been the bedrock of financial analysis, but the swelling world of 'Big Data' is starting to become increasingly important.

'It's a new age, this is the new way of doing analysis,' says Justin Zhen, a former hedge fund analyst and one of the founders of Thinknum. 'People want data. This is a high-growth area.'

Big Data are the simple, descriptive moniker given to the information explosion of recent years, powered by the online revolution. There are over 1bn websites with more than 10tn individual web pages, with 500 'exabytes' of data, according to Deutsche Bank. An exabyte is 1m terabytes or 1bn gigabytes. And the data deluge is growing every day. Over 100m websites are added to the Internet every year.

There has long been a lot of non-traditional data for innovative asset managers to mine, often using old-fashioned human graft. For example, some funds have sent junior analysts to stalk shopping malls and auto dealers for footfall and car sales estimates. But the size of the available data is expanding exponentially, and huge increases in computing power and algorithmic complexity allow digital data to be crunched automatically and near-instantaneously.

'The sheer magnitude and complexity of Big Data make it difficult for investment managers to use, process and understand. However, we strongly believe that portfolio managers who invest the time, resources and energy into Big Data and modelling will reap the benefits.'

'There's just so much data out there,' Mr Zhen says. 'Finance is behind most other industries. This is the future.'

FT   *Source: Adapted from Financial Times. 30 March 2016.*

Questions relating to this news story can be found on page 248. ➡

About this chapter

In this chapter we cover what accountants call the 'interpretation of accounts'. A set of accounts is like a book, which contains the story of a business. The numbers, disclosures and other information in the accounts tell part of the story but like any good book, there is also hidden meaning. The relationships between the numbers in the accounts help us to get to that hidden meaning and understand the full picture. You will often see, for example, a newspaper screaming in large headlines that Company X has made a profit of (say) £50 million. In absolute terms £50 million is certainly a lot of money but what does it mean? Is it a lot compared with what it took to make it? Is it a lot compared with other similar companies? How does it compare with previous years? Is it meeting investors' expectations?

The relationships between balances in the accounts help answer some of these questions. Others cannot always be answered directly from the financial statements themselves. The figures may have to be reworked and then compared with other similar data. So 'reading' the accounts and understanding the story of a business (in other words, interpreting accounts) is a type of detective work: you look for the evidence, you analyse it and then you give your verdict.

This chapter explains how you do the detective work. There are various ways of going about it but we will be concentrating on *ratio analysis*. This is one of the most common methods used in interpreting accounts and we shall be spending a lot of time on it.

Learning objectives

By the end of this chapter you should be able to:

- define what is meant by the 'interpretation of accounts';
- outline why it is needed;
- explain where and how one can get copies of company accounts;
- summarise the procedure involved in interpreting a set of accounts;
- explain the usefulness, importance and limitations of ratio analysis;
- calculate seven key accounting ratios that say a lot about the health of a business;
- explore the relationship between those ratios;
- explore other ratios that may be useful for non-accountants (ratios of interest to HR managers, bankers, marketing managers, production managers and others).

❗ Why this chapter is important

For non-accountants this chapter is one of the most important in the book. In your professional life you could rely entirely on your accountants to present you with any financial information that *they* think you might find useful. In time and with some experience you might understand most of it. The danger is that you might take the figures at their face value, just as you might when you read an eye-catching newspaper headline.

You could be misled by such headlines and then take what might turn out to be a most unwise decision, e.g. buying or selling shares or perhaps even making a takeover bid for a company! For example, an alleged £15 billion profit might be a record but how can we be certain that it is significant? The short answer is that we can't unless we relate it to something else, such as what sum of money it took to earn that profit or what profit other similar companies have made.

Accountants refer to the explanation process as the *interpretation of accounts*. After working your way through the chapter, you too will be able to interpret a set of accounts so that when you read a story in the newspaper or you come across some financial statements you can make much more sense of the information and you can put it into context, i.e. compare it with something meaningful. This is sometimes referred to as 'reading between the lines of the accounts'. We hope that by the end of the chapter you too can read between these lines. Such a skill is vital if you are to become a *really* effective manager.

Nature and purpose

In this section we explain what accountants mean when they talk about interpreting a set of accounts, why such an exercise is necessary and who might have a need of it.

Definition

The verb 'to interpret' has several different meanings. Perhaps the most common is 'to convert' or 'to translate' the spoken word of one language into another, but it also has other meanings such as 'to construe', 'to define' or 'to explain'. We will use the latter meaning. Our definition of what we mean by the *interpretation of accounts* may then be expressed as follows:

> A detailed explanation of the financial performance of an entity incorporating data and other quantitative and qualitative information extracted from both internal and external sources.

Information overload yet information is limited

By this stage of your accounting studies you will no doubt have realised that the amount of information contained in a set of accounts prepared for *internal* purposes is considerable. Even published accounts can be quite detailed. The 2011 Annual Report and Financial Statements of J Sainsbury's plc, a supermarket chain, covers 114 pages. The 2014 one covers 144 pages and the 2015 had 147 pages. That is a huge amount of information that shareholders are sent by the company every year and the number of pages has been rising over time!

Activity 10.1

Find the latest Annual Report and Financial Statements of J Sainsbury plc on the Internet (it would be available on the company corporate site under 'Investors-centre > Reports', rather than its customers-facing online shopping site).

(a) How many pages is the length of the document?
(b) What is included in it?

Source: extracts from the 2014 J Sainsbury's plc annual report and financial statements, http://annualreport2014.j-sainsbury.co.uk

Ordinarily an annual report and financial statements for a listed business like Sainsbury's will have the statement of the directors' responsibilities on 1 page, an independent auditors report on 1–3 pages, the primary financial statements on 6 or 7 pages, the notes to the financial statements on 50–60 pages and about 50–100 pages of other material (such as strategy and outlook, corporate social responsibility and environmental reports and information about the board of directors and their pay).

You would think that accounts of this length would provide you with all the information that you would ever want to know about the company but unfortunately this is not necessarily the case. There are three main reasons why this may not be so.

- *Structural.* Financial accounts are prepared on the basis of a series of accounting rules. Even financial accounts prepared for internal purposes contain a restricted amount of information and this is especially the case with published accounts. Only information that can be translated easily into quantitative financial terms is usually included, and also some highly arbitrary assessments have to be made about the treatment of certain matters such as valuation of assets such as inventory or investments, depreciation of non-current assets such as property or equipment, accruals for director bonuses and allowance for bad debts. Furthermore, financial accounts are also usually prepared on a historical basis so they may be out-of-date by the time that they become available, the details may relate at best to one or two accounting periods and probably no allowance will have been made for inflation.
- *Absolute.* The monetary figures are presented almost solely in absolute terms. For example, Sainsbury's reported a loss rather than a profit for 2014 (a loss of £166 million to be precise), yet it still paid a £330 million in dividend to its shareholders. So how, you might ask, can that be? Exactly. This is a good example of why we need to dig behind the figures; it's why we need to *interpret* them.
- *Contextual.* Even if you could grasp the size and significance of what a loss of £166 million meant, in isolation it does not tell us very much. In order to make them more meaningful they need to be put in context perhaps by comparing them with the previous years' results or with companies in the same industry.

Users

Company law concentrates almost exclusively on shareholders but as we explained in Chapter 2, there are many other user groups. We reproduce the seven main user groups listed in that chapter in Table 10.1. Beside each group we have posed a question that a user in each particular group may well ask and which it hopes to find the answer to in the accounts.

TABLE 10.1 Users of financial accounts and their questions

User group	Questions asked
Customers	How do its prices compare with its competitors?
Employees	Has it enough money to pay my wages?
Governments and their agencies	Can the company pay its taxes?
Investors	What's the dividend like?
Lenders	Will I get my interest paid?
Public	Is the company likely to stay in business?
Suppliers and other creditors	Will we get paid what we are owed?

The questions in Table 10.1 cannot always be answered directly from the financial statements. For example, investors asking the question 'What's the dividend like?' will find that the annual report and accounts gives them the dividend paid by the company in total as well as dividend per share for the current and the previous year in *absolute* amounts. Somewhere within the annual report and accounts the percentage increase may be given but that still does not really answer the question. Investors will probably want to know how their dividend relates to what they have invested in the company (what accountants call the 'yield'). As most investors probably paid different amounts for their shares, it would be impossible to show each individual shareholder's yield in the annual account, so investors have to calculate it for themselves.

Activity 10.2

Taking the seven user groups listed in Table 10.1, what other questions do you think that each user group would ask? List each user group and all the questions that you think each would ask. Then insert:

(a) where the basic information could be found in the annual report and accounts to answer each question and

(b) what additional information would be required to answer each question fully.

Procedure

In this section we outline the basic procedure involved in interpreting a set of accounts. The scale and nature of your investigation will clearly depend on its purpose so we can only point you in the right direction. For example, if you were working for a large international company proposing to take over a foreign company, you would need a vast amount of information and it might take months before you had completed your investigation. By contrast, if you were a private individual proposing to invest £1000 in Sainsbury's plc, you might just spend part of Saturday morning reading what the city editor of your favourite newspaper had to say about the company (although we would recommend you to do much more than that).

In essence, an exercise involving the interpretation of accounts involves four main stages:

- collecting the information;
- analysing it;
- interpreting it and
- reporting the findings.

Collecting the information

This stage involves you first conducting a fairly general review of the international economic, financial, political and social climate and a more specific one of the *country* in which the entity operates. In broad terms, you are looking to see whether it is politically and socially stable with excellent prospects for sound and continuing economic growth. Then you should look at the particular *industry* in which it operates. Ask yourself the following questions.

- Is the government supportive of the industry?
- Is there an expanding market for its products?
- Is there sufficient land and space available for development?

- Is there a reliable infrastructure, e.g. utility supplies and a transport network?
- Are there grants and loans available for developing enterprises?
- Is there an available and trained labour force nearby?

Once you have got all this macro- and micro-economic information, you will need to obtain as much information about the *entity* as you can get. This will involve finding out about its history, structure, management, operations, products, markets, labour record and financial performance. These days you should be able to obtain much of this information from the Internet, including press releases, trade circulars and analysts' reviews.

Finally, the entity financial statements is a very rich source of information. As we mentioned at the beginning – it is like a book that tells the story of a business, how it performed in the recent past and what its financial position is. There are three places you can look to find the accounts of companies you are interested in:

1 Companies are required to file their accounts at Companies House (the registrar of companies in the United Kingdom) and you are able to download company information, including accounts for the most recent and previous years, from the Companies House website.
2 Listed companies tend to also have a section on their own website dedicated to the needs of investors where they provide access to the accounts alongside other announcements related to the company.
3 Large financial databases of historical financial information exist for a whole range of companies. For example, Amadeus is one such database – it has 10 years of data for over half a million private and public European companies.

By the end of this early stage of your investigation you will probably already have a 'feel' or a strong impression about the entity but your work is not yet over. Indeed, there is still a great deal more work to do.

Analysing the information

Analysing the information involves putting together all the information you have collected and making sense of it. In this book as we are primarily concerned with the accounting aspects of business, so we will concentrate on how you can begin to make sense of the *financial* information that you have collected.

The main source of such information will normally be the entity's annual report and accounts. In order to make our explanation easier to follow we will assume that we are dealing primarily with public limited liability companies (although you will find that much of what we have to say is relevant when dealing with other types of entities).

There are four main techniques that you can use in interpreting a set of financial statements: horizontal analysis, trend analysis, vertical analysis and ratio analysis. Figure 10.1 depicts a diagrammatic representation of these different types of analyses. A brief description of each one is outlined below.

1 *Horizontal analysis.* This technique involves making a line-by-line comparison of the company's accounts for each accounting period chosen for the investigation. You may have noted, for example, that the sales for the year 2014 were £100m, £110m in 2015 and £137.5m in 2016. This type of comparison across a row of figures is something that we do naturally but such a casual observation is not very effective when we are faced with a great many detailed figures. In order to grasp what they mean, at the very least we would need to calculate the changes from one year to the next. Even then their significance might still be hard to take in. So we would probably have to calculate the *percentage* increases year by year (10 per cent for 2015 and 25 per cent in 2016 in the above example) and this could involve an awful lot of work with a pen, paper and a calculator, or preferably a spreadsheet.

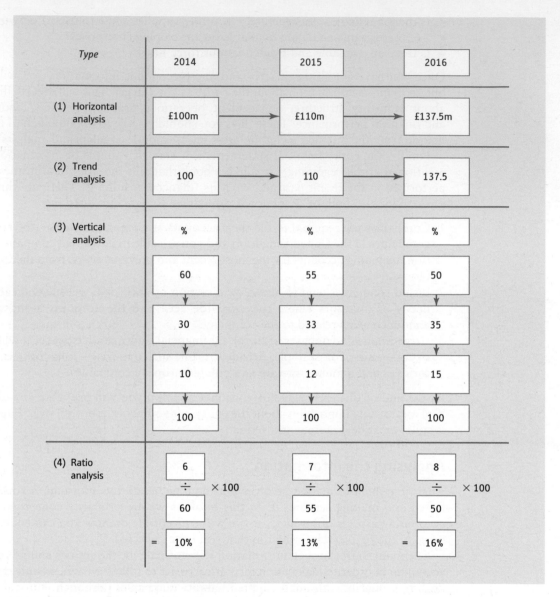

Figure 10.1 Interpreting accounts: main analytical techniques

2 *Trend analysis.* This is similar to horizontal analysis except that all the figures in the first set of accounts in a series are given a base line of 100 and the subsequent sets of accounts are converted to that base line. So if the sales for 2014 were £50m, £70 for 2015 and £85m for 2016, the sales of £50m for 2014 would be given a base line of 100; the 2015 sales would then become 140 (70 × 100/50) and the 2016 sales 170 (85 × 100/50). This method enables us to grasp much more easily the changes in the absolute costs and values shown in the financial statements. For example, if we told you that the sales were £202,956,000 for 2015 and £210,161,000 in 2016, it is not too difficult to calculate that they have gone up by about £7m but the figures are still too big for most of us to absorb. The changes that have taken place would be much easier to take in if they are all related to a base line of 100. In this example, the sales for 2015 would then be given a value of 100, with 103 (210 161 × 100/202 956) for 2016, an increase of about 3 per cent (it's actually 3.6 per cent). The figures then

begin to mean something because by converting in this way they relate more to our experience of money terms and values in our everyday life.

3 *Vertical analysis.* This technique requires the figures in each financial statement (usually restricted to the statement of profit or loss account and the statement of financial position) to be expressed as a percentage of the total amount. For example, assume that a company's trade receivables were £10m in 2015 and that net assets was £50m; in 2016, the trade receivables were £12m and the net assets total was £46m. Trade receivables would then be shown as representing 20 per cent of the net assets total (10 × 100/50) in 2015 and 26 per cent in 2016 (12 × 100/46). This would be considered quite a large increase so the reasons for it would need to be investigated. The modern practice of using lots of sectionalised accounts and subtotals means that it is not always easy to decide what *is* the total of a particular financial statement. If you come across this difficulty, we suggest that you use the sales revenue figure for the total of the statement of profit or loss and the total of net assets (or shareholders' funds, it should be the same figure!) for the total of the statement of financial position.

4 *Ratio analysis.* A ratio is simply the division of one arithmetical amount by another arithmetical amount expressed as a percentage or as a factor. Ratio analysis is a most useful means of comparing one figure with another because it expresses the relationship between lots of amounts easily and simply. If the cost of sales for 2015 was £12m, for example, and the sales revenue was £20m, we would express the relationship as 60 per cent (12 × 100/20) sales or 0.6 to 1 (12/20). Ratio analysis is such an important technique in the interpretation of accounts that we will be dealing with it in some detail a little later in the chapter.

Activity 10.3	State whether the following assertions are true or false:

(a) Ratio analysis is only one form of analysis that can be used in interpreting accounts.   *True/false*

(b) Ratio analysis aims to put the financial results of an entity into perspective.   *True/false*

(c) Ratio analysis helps to establish whether or not an entity is a going concern.   *True/false*

Interpreting the information

This is the third stage in a broad interpretative exercise. By this stage of your investigation you would have collected a great deal of information about the company you are investigating and you would have put that information into context by subjecting it to a whole battery of analyses. Now you have to use all the information that you have before you to interpret or to *explain* what has happened. Some of the questions you might ask yourself include the following:

- What does it tell me about the company's performance?
- Has the company done well compared with other financial periods?
- How does it compare with other companies in the same sector of the economy?
- Are the world economic, political and social circumstances favourable to trade generally?
- What are they like for this company's industry?
- What are the prospects for the region in which this company does its business?

Asking and answering such questions might seem a formidable task but like anything else, the more practice you get, the easier it becomes. In any case, by this time your initial research and your various analyses will have given you a strong indication about the company's progress and its future prospects. You will have realised that there are a number of obvious strengths and weaknesses and a variety of positive and negative factors and trends.

When you have come to a conclusion based on the evidence and the analysis that you have framed, you have one further task: report it to whoever asked you to do the study in the first place.

Reporting the findings

In most interpretive exercises of the type described in this chapter you will probably have to write a written report. Many people are fearful of having to commit themselves to paper and they find this part of the exercise very difficult. However, having to write something down helps you to think more clearly and logically. It may also throw up gaps in your argument, so regard this part of the exercise as more of an opportunity than a threat.

The format of your report will depend on its purpose but basically it should be broken down into three main sections. Your first section should be an *introduction* in which you outline the nature and purpose of your report including a brief outline of its structure. The second part should contain your *discussion* section in which you present your evidence and your assessment of what the evidence means. In the third *concluding* section summarise briefly the entire study, list your conclusions and state your recommendations. Business reports usually have a key fourth component which is usually written at the end but placed at the start of a business report – an *executive summary*. An executive summary is a one-page summary of all the key points made in your report.

In the next section we consider in much more detail one of the analytical techniques mentioned earlier in the chapter: *ratio analysis*.

Ratio analysis

We are now going to spend the rest of the chapter dealing with ratio analysis in some detail. Before we begin you should note the following points.

- There are literally hundreds of ratios that we could produce but most accountants have just a few favourites.
- Always check the definition of a particular ratio you come across because while the name may be familiar to you, the definition could be different from the one that you use.
- Strictly limit the number of ratios you adopt. If you use 20 different ratios, for example, and you are covering a five-year period, you have 100 ratios to calculate *and* to incorporate in your analysis. That's a lot to handle!

That is why in this book we are going to limit the number of accounting ratios that we cover in detail to just seven but some additional ones are referred to on the companion website if you wished to explore more.

Ratios are usually grouped into five broad categories (although there is some overlap between them):

- liquidity (solvency) ratios;
- profitability ratios;
- efficiency ratios;
- investment ratios and
- gearing (leverage) ratios.

Liquidity (solvency) ratios measure the extent to which an entity is able to settle its current liabilities and remain solvent. In other words, they try to assess how much cash the entity has available in the short term (this usually means within the next 12 months) and if assets can be turned into cash quickly in order to settle current liabilities.

Profitability ratios measure the extent to which an entity has been able to generate an adequate return in relation to the resources it had.

Efficiency ratios tell us how an entity has been managed, i.e. how well its resources have been looked after by those running the business.

Investor ratios relate to the market value of company shares and dividends and are of interest to investors in listed companies primarily.

Gearing (leverage) ratios provide information about the funding structure of a business and measure the extent to which an entity is able to settle its non-current obligations, i.e. repay its debt funders.

So let's have a look at how ratios are used by potential investors and others to judge a business. Have you ever watched an episode of the popular BBC2 TV programme *Dragons' Den?* It documents how potential investors (business angels) make decisions about whether to invest in start-up enterprises.

Activity 10.4	Watch the episode of *Dragons' Den* where Sarah Lu, a young entrepreneur, is pitching to secure some additional start up funding to grow her business – Youdoodoll. The video is available on the companion website or you can search for it on YouTube. Note down any accounting or financial terms the Dragons use in their interrogations. Then answer the following questions:

(a)   What are the Dragons doing while questioning the entrepreneur?
(b)   What are they not directly asking but working out for themselves?

Source: based on the BBC2 programme, *Dragons' Den*, Series 5, Episode 2, aired 22 October 2007.

In any episode that you watch you will see that the Dragons are asking questions, taking notes and making calculations on their note pads. The things the Dragons interrogate the entrepreneurs about include:

- *Market/Demand:* What is the size of the market (including overseas)? What is the quantity of the product sold (on average per, say, month)? Are there any bulk orders?
- *Revenue related:* What is the sale price?
- *Cost related:* What is the cost to produce?
- *Cash:* Who are the customers and how are they paying – in cash?
- *Patent protection:* Is the product patented?

These questions are asked so that the Dragons can work out for themselves some things such as:

- Revenue = Quantity Sold × Sale Price per item
- Cost of Goods Sold = Quantity Sold × Cost to Produce per item
- Revenue − Cost of Goods Sold = Gross Profit

You should remember that revenue, cost of goods sold and gross profit are all part of the statement of profit or loss of a business. If the business has only just started up and financial statements are not really available, investors will try to build those up themselves so that they can make an assessment of performance to date (even at an early stage).

The Dragons are particularly impressed with the fact that customers have pre-ordered the product and paid for it in cash up-front. Remember what we mentioned earlier – that 'revenue is vanity, profit is sanity but cash is reality'. They certainly seem to agree with that.

What they do next, and that's where their decision-making happens, is they calculate ratios. For example, relating profit to revenue gives them an idea of what is known as profit margin (a profitability ratio).

Illustrative examples

Profit margin ratio (an example profitability ratio)

The profit margin shows what percentage of every £1 of sales is profit.

$$\text{profit margin} = \frac{\text{profit}}{\text{revenue}} \times 100$$

This ratio is usually expressed as a percentage. The higher the margin, the better not only because there is more profit in absolute terms but because there is more of a buffer to absorb unfavourable economic or market events such as reduced customer demand or increased supplier costs. A business with a 1 per cent profit margin (i.e. which makes 1p profit out of every £1 of products sold) does not have much scope to manoeuvre to remain profitable and is in a worse-off position in comparison to a business with a 15 per cent profit margin (i.e. one which makes 15p profit out of every £1 of products sold). In capital-intensive businesses (those that require a lot of assets such as those in the manufacturing industry), the margins tend to be higher and in labour-intensive business they tend to be lower.

Return on capital employed (ROCE) ratio (an example efficiency ratio)

Relating profit to funding gives the potential investors an idea of how effective the business is in using its resources to generate profit. Funding, known as *capital employed,* is the sum of equity and debt funding. Equity funding comes from the equity investors, those who own the business. Debt funding comes from banks and other creditors – ordinary loans that may have been taken out by the business or bonds and preference shares against which the business has borrowed from the capital markets.

This is how return on capital employed is calculated:

$$\text{return on capital employed (ROCE)} = \frac{\text{profit}}{\text{capital employed}} \times 100$$

$$\text{ROCE} = \frac{\text{profit}}{\text{equity funding} + \text{debt funding}} \times 100$$

This ratio is usually expressed as a percentage. The higher ROCE the better. A business making £1 million in profit with only £100,000 of funding is a much better investment opportunity than a business that is making £1 million in profit with £500,000 of funding.

The Dragons are using their extensive knowledge of business to compare the proposed venture to other similar ventures and to make an assessment of the opportunity presented to them in comparison to others. The calculation of profit margin allows them to compare the profitability of the venture compared to other similar ventures. Return on capital employed allows them to compare whether investment in this venture is returning more when compared to other investment opportunities.

So we have looked at how ratios are used by potential investors to make decisions about investing in start-ups for which very little financial information may be available. Now let's look at assessing businesses that have a proven track record and a lot more financial information to go on.

We have mentioned already that there are many different ratios and many different ways of computing them. It can be quite an overwhelming task to try and discern what they are all pointing towards. Seasoned investors suggest that calculating just four ratios will give a potential investor enough of an idea about a business.

News clip

Health check

Here's an exercise to test a company's health. It is not comprehensive but it is useful and it only takes 30 minutes.

So how can we run a financial health check? We look in the company accounts and calculate key ratios to see whether a business needs excessive amounts of capital to generate its growth; whether it uses that capital efficiently; whether it can

generate growth internally (rather than depend too much on acquisitions) and – crucially – whether it can turn operating profits into cash.

The key ratios which tell us all of the above are capital turn, return on capital employed, profit margin and operating cash flow to operating profit.

Source: Adapted from *Investors Chronicle,* 1 March 2011.

Surprise, surprise – two of the key ratios identified for a quick company health check are the same two ratios the Dragons are using – ROCE and profit margin!

Profit margin we said is about assessing how much of all sales made is translated into profit. Notice how we have not been very specific about which profit line to use when calculating the ratios so far. If you remember the examples of financial statements we looked at, there are different profit subtotals in the statement of profit or loss, for example, there is gross profit, operating profit and profit after tax. Well, each one of those can be used to calculate the profit margin ratio. If the gross profit figure is used, then the ratio will be the gross profit margin ratio; if the operating profit is used, then the ratio will be the operating profit margin ratio and so on, and each will tell us something slightly different about how efficient management is in turning sales into profit.

Bottom-line profits belong to those who own the business, but if not paid up as dividends they are reinvested in the business and contribute to its growth over time without the need for external financing, hence the ratio gives an indication of whether growth is internally fuelled.

Capital turn ratio (another example of an efficiency ratio)

The third ratio that the 'Health Check' article suggests that we use is capital turn – a ratio that we had not mentioned before. It is calculated is follows.

$$\text{capital turn} = \frac{\text{revenue}}{\text{capital employed}}$$

This ratio is usually expressed as a factor, e.g. 3:1. The capital turn ratio gives an indication of how much sales were generated for every £1 of capital employed. The more revenue that is generated per £1 of funding, the better. For example, imagine that a business made £2 million in sales with £1 million of funding provided to it from equity and debt sources in year one. Imagine that in year two, with unchanged funding, it made

£10 million in sales. That clearly is a growing business, and an investment in a growing business is likely to be more promising!

Consistency in the ratio over time for the same company would mean that the management is able to achieve stable sales relative to capital employed regardless of how much or the type of funding that was available to the business. Capital-intensive business will tend to have a low capital turn ratio, and labour-intensive businesses, such as those in the service industries, will tend to have a high capital turn ratio, so it is important to compare like with like.

ROCE revisited (an example efficiency ratio)

As we explained above, ROCE is a measure of how effective the management has been in using the funding that was made available to the business – higher profits for the same capital employed representing more efficient use of resources. It turns out that ROCE is actually capital turn multiplied by profit margin. This relationship means that ROCE can be used for comparison across different types of businesses – both capital- and labour-intensive ones as capital-intensive businesses will tend to have a low capital turn but high profit margins and labour-intensive businesses – just the opposite.

$$\text{ROCE} = \frac{\text{revenue}}{\text{capital employed}} \times \frac{\text{profit}}{\text{revenue}}$$

As you know from working with fractions in maths, the revenue balances will cancel out to leave us with the earlier form of the ratio that we presented.

$$\text{return on capital employed (ROCE)} = \frac{\text{profit}}{\text{capital employed}} \times 100$$

Operating cash flow to operating profit ratio (an example liquidity ratio)

Do you remember that what made the Dragons stand up in their chairs when interrogating Sarah Lu from the start-up business we looked at earlier was that sales made were in exchange for cash? The customer had placed bulk orders and prepaid for them in cash. It looks like we have more evidence that there is truth in the sayings 'cash is king' and 'cash is reality, while sales are vanity and profit is sanity'.

The fourth ratio suggested for a quick health check is indeed about cash: the operating cash flow to operating profit ratio. In the calculation of this ratio we are very specific about the profit line to be used (unlike what we discussed about the profit margin ratio where different profit lines could be used). This is how to calculate it:

$$\frac{\text{operating cash flow}}{\text{operating profit}}$$

The operating cash flow to operating profit ratio gives an indication of how much cash is collected given the reported profits. This ratio is usually expressed as a factor, for example, 1:2 would mean that for every £1 in profit, 50p is collected in cash. A business can be profitable on paper but unless it has cash, it is vulnerable. Collecting cash from customers you have sold to is key in keeping a healthy business. The higher the ratio, the better, as it would mean most of the sales were cash sales or that if they were on credit, cash was collected from customers in a timely manner.

In summary – if the ratios point to:

1 *a healthy profit margin for its industry* – as a cushion against adverse events in the trading environment; also as an indication of potential for growth to be generated internally (if profits are reinvested);
2 *a stable or improving capital turn* – as an indication of consistent performance of the business: you give it capital, it turns it into sales at a consistent or improving rate rather than waste the resources invested in it;
3 *a good return on capital employed* – as an indication of efficient use of the resources given to it to generate what matters: profits and (crucially)
4 *profits being translated into cash promptly*

then it is safe to conclude that the business is in good health overall. These four key ratios alone can give us a pretty good indication about that.

There are three more very commonly used ratios that are worth mentioning here to complete the picture. These are the current ratio, the debt to equity ratio and the earnings per share (EPS) ratio – a liquidity, gearing and market ratio, respectively.

Current ratio (an example liquidity ratio)

The *current ratio* gives us an indication about a business's ability to pay its current liabilities as they fall due. The term 'current' means receivable or payable within the next 12 months (the same meaning as in the financial statements).

Cash is needed to pay liabilities. If someone has no cash, they can sell some assets to generate cash. The current assets are the ones intended for selling and turning into cash in the next 12 months anyway, so the current assets figure in relation to current liabilities is a good yardstick of a company's ability to meet obligations in the short run. The current ratio is calculated as follows:

$$\text{current ratio} = \frac{\text{current assets}}{\text{current liabilities}}$$

It is usually expressed as a factor, e.g. 3 to 1, or 3:1, although you will sometimes see it expressed as a percentage (300% in our example, i.e. $\frac{3}{1} \times 100$).

Note that the entity may not always have to settle all of its current liabilities within the next week or even the next month. Be careful before you assume that a factor of (say) 1:2 suggests that the company will be going into immediate liquidation. Some creditors, such as tax and dividends, may not have to be paid for several weeks. In the meantime, the company may receive regular receipts of cash from its debtors and it may be able to balance these against what it has to pay to its creditors. In other instances, some entities (such as supermarkets) may have a lot of cash trade and it is possible that they then may have a current assets ratio of less than 2:1. This is not likely to be a problem for them because they are probably collecting sufficient amounts of cash daily through the checkouts. In some cases, however, a current assets ratio of less than 2:1 may signify a serious financial position, especially if the current assets consist of a very high proportion of inventory.

In summary if a company has more current assets than current liabilities, it is in a good position as it has enough to turn into cash and pay its liabilities as they fall due over the next 12 months. If the ratio is below 1 (and even below 2, as we mentioned earlier), which signifies there is not enough to pay creditors in the short term, more borrowing may be needed or the business may be forced into liquidation.

Debt to equity ratio (an example gearing ratio)

The debt to equity ratio gives more information about how a business is funded.

$$\text{debt to equity} = \frac{\text{debt funding}}{\text{equity funding}}$$

A business that has borrowed a lot is said to be highly geared, as opposed to one which is funded primarily by shareholders. There is nothing wrong with borrowing money to expand operations or to cover a short-term cash flow problem but borrowing ties a company down into making fixed interest payments, which puts pressure on results. Big loans may often have covenants which, if breached, trigger the repayment of the loan in full at a time when the company may be struggling for cash. Generally speaking, a highly geared business is considered more risky especially if you are a banker who has been approached for yet more funding. It is also risky for a potential or existing shareholder – if something was to go wrong, the company would be closed down, its assets sold and creditors repaid. Equity investors, however, come last in the pecking order so they will only get their money back if there is something left after repaying creditors. This is very unlikely.

If the company is doing well though it is good news for an equity investor: they put a little bit of money in the business, the business borrowed most of its funding, it grew and now the equity investor is enjoying the upside – a share of the profits along with an increased share price (while the bankers will only ever get just the interest they have negotiated plus the loan repaid at the end of its term).

Earnings per share (EPS) ratio (an example investor ratio)

As we mentioned the share of profits we will finish with an example of an investor ratio. As referred to earlier company shareholders are entitled to the profits a company makes and they share it in proportion to their share of the company. Imagine that you and I jointly owned a company and you had 70 of the shares and I had 30 of the shares. Any profit the company made will be split between us in a 70:30 proportion. Earnings per share will tell us how much of the profit is attributed to each individual share so that we can each multiply that by our number of shares and work out how much we are entitled to in total.

This is how EPS is calculated:

$$\text{earnings per share (EPS)} = \frac{\text{profit after tax}}{\text{number of shares issued}}$$

If a company made £400,000 after all expenses and tax for the year have been netted off, and there are 2,000,000 shares held by investors, then each share will be entitled to receive a 20p dividend as a share of that profit. A 10 per cent investor who has 200,000 shares will be entitled to 200,000 × 20p = £40,000 as their 10 per cent share of the £400,000 profit. Of course there is no guarantee how much will be declared as dividends by management as they may decide to keep some or all of the profit in the business and grow the business.

There are many more ratios but presenting all of them here is both confusing and unnecessary as we have enough to work with to try and read the story of a business. If you would like to find out more about different ratios, you can access further material on the companion website.

Example 10.1

Imagine that you are a bank manager and Marks and Spencer plc have approached you for a £10 million loan to be paid back after 5 years with a 10 per cent annual interest. Can you review their latest published financial statements and make a lending decision?

Marks and Spencer plc
Consolidated statement of profit of loss for the years

	Notes	52 weeks ended 28 March 2015			52 weeks ended 29 March 2014		
		Underlying £m	Non-underlying £m	Total £m	Underlying £m	Non-underlying £m	Total £m
Revenue	2,3	10,311.4	–	10,311.4	10,309.7	–	10,309.7
Operating profit	2,3,5	762.5	(61.2)	701.3	741.9	(47.4)	694.5
Finance income	5,6	15.5	–	15.5	20.1	4.9	25.0
Finance costs	6	(116.8)	–	(116.8)	(139.1)	–	(139.1)
Profit before tax	4,5	661.2	(61.2)	600.0	622.9	(42.5)	580.4
Income tax expense	7	(124.8)	6.5	(118.3)	(117.1)	42.7	(74.4)
Profit for the year		536.4	(54.7)	481.7	505.8	0.2	506.0
Attributable to:							
Owners of the parent		541.2	(54.7)	486.5	520.0	4.8	524.8
Non-controlling interests		(4.8)	–	(4.8)	(14.2)	(4.6)	(18.8)
		536.4	(54.7)	481.7	505.8	0.2	506.0
Basic earnings per share	8	33.1p	(3.4p)	29.7p	32.2p	0.3p	32.5p
Diluted earnings per share	8	32.9p	(3.4p)	29.5p	31.9p	0.3p	32.2p

Marks and Spencer plc
Consolidated statement of financial position as at

	Notes	28 March 2015 £m	29 March 2014 £m
Assets			
Non-current assets			
Intangible assets	14	858.2	808.4
Property, plant and equipment	15	5,031.1	5,139.9
Investment property		15.6	15.7
Investment in joint ventures		12.2	12.7
Other financial assets	16	3.0	3.0
Retirement benefit asset	11	460.7	200.7
Trade and other receivables	17	283.3	313.5
Derivative financial instruments	21	75.8	40.6
Deferred tax assets		1.2	–
		6,741.1	6,534.5
Current assets			
Inventories		797.8	845.5
Other financial assets	16	11.6	17.7
Trade and other receivables	17	321.8	309.5
Derivative financial instruments	21	117.9	13.7
Cash and cash equivalents	18	205.9	182.1
		1,455.0	1,368.5
Total assets		8,196.1	7,903.0

Liabilities			
Current liabilities			
Trade and other payables	19	**1,642.4**	1,692.8
Partnership liability to the Marks & Spencer UK Pension Scheme	12	**71.9**	71.9
Borrowings and other financial liabilities	20	**279.4**	448.7
Derivative financial instruments	21	**7.7**	51.5
Provisions	22	**46.2**	44.8
Current tax liabilities		**64.0**	39.6
		2,111.6	2,349.3
Non-current liabilities			
Retirement benefit deficit	11	**11.7**	11.7
Trade and other payables	19	**319.7**	334.0
Partnership liability to the Marks & Spencer UK Pension Scheme	12	**441.0**	496.8
Borrowings and other financial liabilities	20	**1,745.9**	1,655.1
Derivative financial instruments	21	**20.0**	75.4
Provisions	22	**32.1**	31.4
Deferred tax liabilities	23	**315.3**	242.6
		2,885.7	2,847.0
Total liabilities		**4,997.3**	5,196.3
Net assets		**3,198.8**	2,706.7
Equity			
Issued share capital	24	**412.0**	408.1
Share premium account		**392.4**	355.5
Capital redemption reserve		**2,202.6**	2,202.6
Hedging reserve		**64.3**	(41.8)
Other reserve		**(6,542.2)**	(6,542.2)
Retained earnings		**6,670.5**	6,325.1
Total shareholders' equity		**3,199.6**	2,707.3
Non-controlling interests in equity		**(0.8)**	(0.6)
Total equity		**3,198.8**	2,706.7

Marks and Spencer plc

Consolidated statement of changes in equity for the period

Note the movement in Retained Earnings in the sixth column.

	Ordinary share capital £m	Share premium account £m	Capital redemption reserve £m	Hedging reserve £m	Other reserve[1] £m	Retained earnings[2] £m	Total £m	Non-controlling interest £m	Total £m
As at 31 March 2013	403.5	315.1	2,202.6	9.2	(6,542.2)	6,150.3	2,538.5	(19.0)	2,519.5
Profit/(loss) for the year	–	–	–	–	–	524.8	524.8	(18.8)	506.0
Other comprehensive (expense)/income:									
Foreign currency translation	–	–	–	(0.7)	–	(21.6)	(22.3)	–	(22.3)
Remeasurements of retirement benefit schemes	–	–	–	–	–	(85.3)	(85.3)	–	(85.3)
Tax credit on retirement benefit schemes	–	–	–	–	–	31.8	31.8	–	31.8
Cash flow and net investment hedges									
– fair value movements in other comprehensive income	–	–	–	(117.6)	–	7.7	(109.9)	–	(109.9)
– reclassified and reported in net profit[3]	–	–	–	36.4	–	–	36.4	–	36.4
– amount recognised in inventories	–	–	–	18.7	–	–	18.7	–	18.7
Tax on cash flow hedges and net investment hedges	–	–	–	12.2	–	–	12.2	–	12.2
Other comprehensive expense	–	–	–	(51.0)	–	(67.4)	(118.4)	–	(118.4)
Total comprehensive (expense)/income	–	–	–	(51.0)	–	457.4	406.4	(18.8)	387.6

Transactions with owners:								
Dividends	–	–	–	–	–	(273.6)	(273.6)	–	(273.6)
Transactions with non-controlling shareholders	–	–	–	–	–	(39.3)	(39.3)	37.2	(2.1)
Shares issued on exercise of employee share options	4.6	40.4	–	–	–	–	45.0	–	45.0
Credit for share-based payments	–	–	–	–	–	21.3	21.3	–	21.3
Deferred tax on share schemes	–	–	–	–	–	9.0	9.0	–	9.0
As at 29 March 2014	**408.1**	**355.5**	**2,202.6**	**(41.8)**	**(6,542.2)**	**6,325.1**	**2,707.3**	**(0.6)**	**2,706.7**
As at 30 March 2014	**408.1**	**355.5**	**2,202.6**	**(41.8)**	**(6,542.2)**	**6,325.1**	**2,707.3**	**(0.6)**	**2,706.7**
Profit/(loss) for the year	–	–	–	–	–	486.5	486.5	(4.8)	481.7
Other comprehensive (expense)/income:								
Foreign currency translation	–	–	–	(2.0)	–	(5.5)	(7.5)	–	(7.5)
Remeasurements of retirement benefit schemes	–	–	–	–	–	193.7	193.7	–	193.7
Tax charge on retirement benefit schemes	–	–	–	–	–	(40.2)	(40.2)	–	(40.2)
Cash flow and net investment hedges								
– fair value movements in other comprehensive income	–	–	–	210.9	–	10.3	221.2	–	221.2
– reclassified and reported in net profit[1]	–	–	–	(60.0)	–	–	(60.0)	–	(60.0)
– amount recognised in inventories	–	–	–	(21.6)	–	–	(21.6)	–	(21.6)
Tax on cash flow hedges and net investment hedges	–	–	–	(21.2)	–	–	(21.2)	–	(21.2)
Other comprehensive income	–	–	–	106.1	–	158.3	264.4	–	264.4
Total comprehensive (expense)/income	–	–	–	106.1	–	644.8	750.9	(4.8)	746.1
Transactions with owners:								
Dividends	–	–	–	–	–	(280.7)	(280.7)	–	(280.7)
Transactions with non-controlling shareholders	–	–	–	–	–	–	–	4.6	4.6
Shares issued on exercise of employee share options	3.9	36.9	–	–	–	–	40.8	–	40.8
Purchase of own shares held by employee trusts	–	–	–	–	–	(24.2)	(24.2)	–	(24.2)
Release of share-based payments	–	–	–	–	–	(1.1)	(1.1)	–	(1.1)
Deferred tax on share schemes	–	–	–	–	–	6.6	6.6	–	6.6
As at 28 March 2015	**412.0**	**392.4**	**2,202.6**	**64.3**	**(6,542.2)**	**6,670.5**	**3,199.6**	**(0.8)**	**3,198.8**

Marks and Spencer plc

Consolidated statement of cash flows for the period

	Notes	52 weeks ended 28 March 2015 £m	52 weeks ended 29 March 2014 £m
Cash flows from operating activities			
Cash generated from operations	26	1,349.1	1,175.5
Income tax paid		(71.1)	(45.9)
Net cash inflow from operating activities		**1,278.0**	**1,129.6**
Cash flows from investing activities			
Proceeds on property disposals		35.4	25.0
Purchase of property, plant and equipment		(521.8)	(440.1)
Purchase of intangible assets		(178.0)	(201.5)
Reduction/(purchase) of current financial assets		6.0	(1.7)
Interest received		9.3	3.4
Net cash used in investing activities		**(649.1)**	**(614.9)**

Cash flows from financing activities

Interest paid[1]	(115.3)	(132.7)
Cash (outflow)/inflow from borrowings	(165.7)	167.5
(Repayment)/drawdown of syndicated loan notes	(10.2)	154.1
Redemption of medium-term notes	–	(400.0)
Decrease in obligations under finance leases	(4.8)	(7.3)
Payment of liability to the Marks & Spencer UK Pension Scheme	(54.4)	(50.3)
Equity dividends paid	(280.7)	(273.6)
Shares issued on exercise of employee share options	40.8	44.2
Purchase of own shares by employee trust	(24.2)	–
Net cash used in financing activities	**(614.5)**	**(498.1)**
Net cash inflow from activities	14.4	16.6
Effects of exchange rate changes	(2.3)	(1.6)
Opening net cash	175.7	160.7
Closing net cash	**187.8**	**175.7**

1. Includes interest on the partnership liability to the Marks & Spencer UK Pension Scheme.

	Notes	52 weeks ended 28 March 2015 £m	52 weeks ended 29 March 2014 £m
Reconciliation of net cash flow to movement in net debt			
Opening net debt		**(2,463.6)**	**(2,614.3)**
Net cash inflow from activities		14.4	16.6
(Decrease)/increase in current financial assets		(6.0)	1.7
Decrease in debt financing		235.1	136.0
Exchange and other non-cash movements		(3.1)	(3.6)
Movement in net debt		**240.4**	**150.7**
Closing net debt	27	**(2,223.2)**	**(2,463.6)**

Marks and Spencer plc
Extract from the notes to the financial statements

27 ANALYSIS OF NET DEBT

A. Reconciliation of movement in net debt

	At 30 March 2014 £m	Cash flow £m	Exchange and other non-cash movements £m	At 28 March 2015 £m
Net cash				
Bank loans, overdrafts and syndicated bank facility (see note 20)	(445.7)	164.2	2.5	(279.0)
Less: amounts treated as financing (see below)	439.3	(175.9)	(2.5)	260.9
	(6.4)	(11.7)	–	(18.1)
Cash and cash equivalents (see note 18)	182.1	26.1	(2.3)	205.9
Net cash per statement of cash flows	175.7	14.4	(2.3)	187.8
Current financial assets (see note 16)	17.7	(6.0)	(0.1)	11.6
Debt financing				
Bank loans, and overdrafts treated as financing (see above)	(439.3)	175.9	2.5	(260.9)
Medium-term notes (see note 20)	(1,609.8)	–	(2.0)	(1,611.8)
Finance lease liabilities (see note 20)	(52.2)	4.8	(1.2)	(48.6)
Partnership liability to the Marks & Spencer UK Pension Scheme (see note 12)	(555.7)	54.4	–	(501.3)
Debt financing	(2,657.0)	235.1	(0.7)	(2,422.6)
Net debt	(2,463.6)	243.5	(3.1)	(2,223.2)

B. Reconciliation of net debt to statement of financial position

	2015 £m	2014 £m
Statement of financial position and related notes		
Cash and cash equivalents (see note 18)	205.9	182.1
Current financial assets (see note 16)	11.6	17.7
Bank loans and overdrafts (see note 20)	(279.0)	(445.7)
Medium-term notes – net of hedging derivatives	(1,652.0)	(1,649.0)
Finance lease liabilities (see note 20)	(48.6)	(52.2)
Partnership liability to the Marks & Spencer UK Pension Scheme (see notes 12 and 21)	(512.9)	(568.7)
	(2,275.0)	(2,515.8)
Interest payable included within related borrowing and the partnership liability to the Marks & Spencer UK Pension Scheme	51.8	52.2
Total net debt	**(2,223.2)**	**(2,463.6)**

Source: M&S Annual Report and Financial Statements 2015.

Tutorial notes

1   As a banker, to make a decision to lend you would be interested in making an assessment of how healthy this business is – will it survive to pay you back £10 million in five years time? If it defaults – that would be a big bad debt write-off for your bank. The business is reporting over £480 million in profits in its 2015 SPL. That's seems acceptable but absolute figures don't mean much in isolation. Also – profit is sanity but cash is reality.

2   You would also perhaps be interested if the business has enough cash to be able to service the debt – i.e. to pay you the interest when it falls due.

3   You can see in the SFP that the business has nearly £206 million in cash and cash equivalents at the end of the year. In addition, there has been £14 million net cash inflow during the year. This is all positive news to you.

4   The business, however, has an awful lot of borrowing already! More than £1.7 billion has already been borrowed – see non-current liabilities in the SFP. All of a sudden the outlook of the situation has changed. The business is highly geared – the ratio of debt to equity confirms that.

5   They do have enough current assets to cover their current liabilities – the current ratio is nearly 8:2. Also the operating cash flow to operating profit ratio is very healthy – they are indeed collecting a lot of cash, as you would expect of a retail business when customers pay at the point of sale. That's reassuring.

6   Finally, you may also be interested if enough assets exist in this business which are *de facto* collateral for the loan – if the business defaults and the company goes into liquidation, its assets will be sold and the creditors (including your lending bank) would recover some or all of its money. It does appear that the business has a very healthy property portfolio of over £5 billion which more than covers all the existing debt and more. Perhaps it should lend after all. There are of course always risks but they appear to be not too great. You may of course analyse the financial information in a lot more depth and come up with many more comments as part of your analysis.

Limitations of ratio analysis

News clip

Earnings management

A willingness to manipulate company earnings is key to success in corporate accounting, a study by the American Accounting Association has suggested.

According to the paper, presented at the association's annual meeting this week, the most successful corporate accountants are those most willing to manage earnings and are hired and promoted for that reason.

Source: www.accountancyage.com/news, 12 August 2015.

Ratios are an excellent way to interpret the results of companies and understand the story behind the numbers but they do have certain limitations. For example:

- Ratios are based on past historical information contained in the financial statements and as such refer to past performance. Past performance is not necessarily an indication of future performance.
- We have explained in this book so far a number of accounting adjustments and estimates that exist in the financial statements of companies – depreciation, allowance for doubtful debts and accruals. They have the potential to significantly change the numbers reported by companies.

- Sometimes the numbers in the financial statements are wrong even if audited – accounting scandals often discredit the numbers in the accounts of even the largest of companies.
- Companies have different year ends and may be subject to different accounting rules; US companies, for example follow different accounting rules to companies in the United Kingdom. This makes comparison between different companies difficult. You should only really compare like with like.
- We also saw that there are many options when calculating ratios – do we use gross profit, operating profit or profit after tax when computing profit margin or ROCE? Unless you understand which formula has been used to calculate a ratio and which lines from the financial statement were used, it would be impossible to interpret the result.

While ratio analysis is very useful it should be used in combination with other information when making decisions about investing in or lending to a company.

 Questions you should ask

As far as this chapter is concerned, there are two situations in which you might find yourself: either with a set of financial accounts that will have been interpreted for you or some that you might have to interpret for yourself. Irrespective of which situation you find yourself in, you might find it useful to ask (or ask yourself) the following questions.

- How reliable is the basic accounting information underpinning this information in front of me?
- Have consistent accounting policies been adopted throughout the period covered?
- If not, has each year's results been adjusted on the same accounting basis?
- Were there any unusual items in any year that may have distorted a comparative analysis?
- Was the rate of inflation significant in any year covered by the report?
- If so, should the basic accounting data be adjusted to allow for it?
- What are the three or four most significant changes in these accounts during the period they cover?
- Are there any apparent causal links between them, such as greater efficiency resulting in a higher level of profitability or higher profits causing cash flow problems?
- What are the most important factors that this report indicates about the company's progress during the period in question and its prospects for the future?

Conclusion

This chapter has explained how you can examine the financial performance of a company (or other entity) over a certain period of time. If a detailed examination is required, it may be necessary to examine the general business environment and economic sector in which it operates. Much information will also be collected about the company itself. One of the main sources of information will be its annual report and accounts.

While a great deal of information may be found in the annual reports and accounts, that information has to be put into context as the absolute numbers disclosed are often large, do not mean much in isolation and are often difficult to understand. This means that the accounts need to be analysed. There are four main types of analyses:

- *horizontal analysis,* involving a line-by-line inspection across the various time periods;

- *trend analysis*, in which all the data are indexed to a base of 100;
- *vertical analysis*, where each period's data is expressed as a percentage of a total and
- *ratio analysis*, which requires a comparison to be made of one item with another item expressing the relationship as either a percentage or a factor.

All of these four types of analyses rely primarily on the accounting data. Such data are subject to a number of reservations, such as the accounting policies and the methods used in preparing the accounts. These reservations must be allowed for when interpreting a set of accounts, especially when a comparison is made with other companies since accounting policies and methods are often different.

Ratio analysis is the most important of the four types of analyses. There are literally hundreds of ratios that could be calculated, plus some highly specialist ones that relate to particular industries. Ratios are usually grouped under five headings:

- *liquidity ratios*, which help to decide whether an entity has enough cash to continue as a going concern;
- *profitability ratios*, which measure the profit an entity has made;
- *efficiency ratios*, which show how well the entity has used its resources;
- *investment ratios*, which help to consider the investment potential of an entity and
- *gearing ratios*, which help to understand the funding structure of a business and associated risks.

In this chapter we have selected just seven common but important ratios with at least one representative from each of the above groups of ratios.

Irrespective of the category into which they fall, ratios should only be regarded as a signpost: in themselves they do not actually *interpret* the accounts for you. They are merely an arithmetical device that points you in the right direction and help you to assess what *has* happened and to predict what *might* happen. They provide you with the evidence, but you have to use that evidence to come to a verdict.

Key points	
1	The interpretation of accounts involves examining financial accounts in some detail so as to be able to explain what has happened and to predict what is likely to happen.
2	The examination can be undertaken by using a number of techniques, such as horizontal analysis, trend analysis, vertical analysis and ratio analysis.
3	Ratio analysis is a common method of interpreting accounts. It involves comparing one item in the accounts with another closely related item. Ratios are normally expressed in the form of a percentage or a factor. There are literally hundreds of recognised accounting ratios (excluding those that relate to specific industries) but we have restricted our study to just seven. More are available for independent study on the companion website.
4	Not all of the ratios are relevant for all entities. It is necessary to be selective in your choice of ratios.
5	When one item is related to another item in the form of a ratio, it is important to make sure that there is a close and logical correlation between the two items.
6	In the case of some ratios, different definitions can be adopted. This applies particularly to ratios referring to profit and capital employed (such as ROCE).
7	Assessing trends and calculating ratios are not the same as interpreting a set of financial accounts. Interpretation involves using a wide range of information sources as well as the incorporation of various types of analyses into a cohesive appraisal of an entity's past performance and its future prospects.

Check your learning

The answers to these questions can be found within the text and the supplementary material on the companion website.

1 What is meant by the term 'interpretation of accounts'?

2 Give three reasons why the absolute data shown in financial accounts may need to be interpreted.

3 List the users of accounts and suggest one piece of information that each user group may require from a set of financial accounts.

4 What is the difference between (a) horizontal analysis and (b) trend analysis?

5 What is vertical analysis?

6 What is (a) a ratio and (b) ratio analysis?

7 What five main categories may be used for classifying accounting ratios?

8 What does 'ROCE' mean and how may it be calculated?

9 What is the difference between the gross profit ratio and operating profit ratio?

10 Why might it be misleading to compare the net profit ratio of one entity with that of another entity?

11 Why is liquidity important and which ratios may be used for assessing it?

12 What is meant by 'EPS' and where might you find it in a set of published accounts?

13 What is capital gearing and how might it be calculated?

14 What is a possible link between the following types of ratios: (a) profitability and efficiency; (b) profitability and liquidity; (c) profitability and investment (d) efficiency and liquidity?

15 Outline the main steps you would take if you were asked to appraise the financial performance of a company using its annual report and accounts.

News story quiz

Remember the news story at the beginning of this chapter? Go back to that story and reread it before answering the following questions.

This is an interesting news story suggesting that other data and information not contained in the historical accounts may be more meaningful for understanding business and economic activity generally.

Questions

1 Do you think financial accounts or Big Data are more useful in assessing the performance and position of a business? Why?

2 What problems do you see with the use of financial accounts in assessing a business?

3 What problems do you see with the use of Big Data in assessing a business?

Tutorial questions

The answers to questions marked with an asterisk may be found in Appendix 4.

10.1 'Accounting ratios are only as good as the data on which they are based.' Discuss.

10.2 How far do you accept the argument that the return on capital employed ratio can give a misleading impression of an entity's profitability?

10.3 Is ratio analysis useful in understanding how an entity has performed?

10.4* The following information has been extracted from the books of account of Betty for the year to 31 January 2017:

Statement of profit or loss for the year to 31 January 2017

	£000	£000
Sales (all credit)		100
Less: Cost of goods sold:		
Opening inventory	15	
Purchases	65	
	80	
Less: Closing inventory	(10)	(70)
Gross profit		30
Administrative expenses		(16)
Net profit		14

Statement of retained earnings for the year to 31 January 2017

Opening retained earnings	0
Net profit for the year	14
Less: drawings	(6)
Closing retained earnings	8

Statement of financial position as at 31 January 2017

	£000	£000
Non-current assets (net book value)		29
Current assets		
Inventory	10	
Trade receivables	12	
Cash	3	25
		54
Capital and Reserves:		
Capital	40	
Retained earnings	8	48
Current liabilities		
Trade payables		6
		54

Required:
Calculate the following accounting ratios:
(a) gross profit ratio
(b) return on capital employed
(c) current ratio

10.5* You are presented with the following summarised accounts:

James Ltd
Statement of profit or loss for the year to 28 February 2017

	£000
Sales (all credit)	1200
Cost of sales	600
Gross profit	600
Administrative expenses	(500)
Loan interest	(10)
Profit on ordinary activities	90
Taxation	(30)
Profit after tax	60

James Ltd
Statement of retained earnings for the year to 28 February 2017

Profit for the year	60
Dividends	(40)
Retained profit for the year	20

James Ltd
Statement of Financial Position at 28 February 2017

	£000	£000	£000
Non-current assets (net book value)			685
Current assets			
Inventory		75	
Trade receivables		200	
			275
			960
Capital and reserves			
Ordinary share capital		600	
Retained earnings		20	
Shareholders' funds			620
Non-current liabilities			
10% Loans			100
Current liabilities			
Trade payables		160	
Bank overdraft		10	
Taxation payable		30	
Dividend declared		40	240
			960

Required:
Calculate the following accounting ratios
(a) return on capital employed
(b) gross profit
(c) capital turn
(d) debt to equity.

10.6 You are presented with the following information relating to three companies:

Statement of profit or loss for the year to 31 March 2017

	Mark Limited £000	Luke Limited £000	John Limited £000
Profit before tax	64	22	55

Statement of financial position (extracts) at 31 March 2017

	Mark Limited £000	Luke Limited £000	John Limited £000
Capital and reserves			
Ordinary share capital of £1 each	100	177	60
Share premium account	–	70	20
Retained earnings	150	60	200
Shareholders' funds	250	307	280
Non-current liabilities			
Cumulative 15% preference shares of £1 each	–	20	10
10% debentures loans	–	–	100
	0	2	110

Required:
Calculate the following accounting ratios:
(a) return on capital employed
(b) capital gearing.

10.7 The following information relates to Helena Limited:

Trading account year to 30 April 2017

	2013 £000	2014 £000	2015 £000	2016 £000	2017 £000
Sales (all credit)	130	150	190	210	320
Less: Cost of goods sold:					
Opening inventory	20	30	30	35	40
Purchases (all in credit terms)	110	110	135	145	305
Less: Closing inventory	(30)	(30)	(35)	(40)	(100)

	2013 £000	2014 £000	2015 £000	2016 £000	2017 £000
	(100)	(110)	(130)	(140)	(245)
Gross profit	30	40	60	70	75
Trade receivables at 30 April	45	40	70	100	150
Trade payables at 30 April	20	25	25	30	60

Required:
Calculate the following accounting ratios for each of the five years from 30 April 2013 to 2017 inclusive:
(a) gross profit
(b) mark-up
(c) stock turnover
(d) trade debtor collection period
(e) trade creditor payment period.

Note that you will need to refer to the additional ratios on the companion website to be able to do this question.

10.8 You are presented with the following information relating to Hedge public limited company for the year to 31 May 2016:

- The company has an issued and fully paid share capital of £500,000 ordinary shares of £1 each. There are no preference shares.
- The market price of the shares at 31 May 2016 was £3.50.
- The net profit after taxation for the year to 31 May 2016 was £70,000.
- The directors have declared a dividend of 7p per share for the year to 31 May 2016.

Required:
Calculate the following accounting ratios:
(a) dividend yield
(b) dividend cover
(c) earnings per share
(d) price/earnings ratio.

Note that you will need to refer to the additional ratios on the companion website to be able to do this question.

10.9 The following information relates to Style Limited for the two years to 30 June 2016 and 2017, respectively:

Statement of profit or loss for the years 2016 and 2017

	2016 £000	2016 £000	2017 £000	2017 £000
Sales (all credit)		1500		1900
Less: Cost of goods sold:				
Opening inventory	80		100	
Purchases (all on credit terms)	995		1400	
c/f	1075		1500	

	2016		2017	
	£000	£000	£000	£000
b/f		1500		1900
	1 075		1 500	
Less: Closing inventory	(100)	(975)	(200)	(1300)
Gross profit		525		600
Less: Expenses		(420)		(495)
Net profit		105		105

Statement of financial position as at 30 June 2017

	2016		2017	
	£000	£000	£000	£000
Non-current assets (net book value)		685		420
Current assets				
Inventory	100		200	
Trade receivables	375		800	
Cash	25	500	–	1000
		1185		1420
Capital and reserves				
Ordinary share capital (9,000,000 10p shares)	900		900	
Profit and loss account	205		310	
Shareholders' funds		1105		1210
Current liabilities				
Bank overdraft	–		10	
Trade payables	80	80	200	210
		1185		1420

Statement of cash flows (extract) for the years 2016 and 2017

	2016		2017	
	£000	£000	£000	£000
Operating cash flow		100		200
Investing cash flow		10		(80)
Financing cash flow		25		–
Nat cash flows		125		120

Required:
(a) Calculate the following accounting ratios for the two years 2016 and 2017:
   • gross profit
   • capital turn
   • return on capital employed
   • operating cash flow to operating profit ratio
   • current ratio
   • debt to equity ratio
   • earning per share.

(b) Comment on the company's performance for the year to 30 June 2016 and its health.

10.10 Imagine that you have £10,000 that you are willing to invest in shares. What follows are the 2014 financial statement of two supermarkets – Tesco plc and Sainsbury's plc.

(a) Calculate the seven key ratios discussed in the chapter using the above information and conclude which of the two companies would be a better investment.

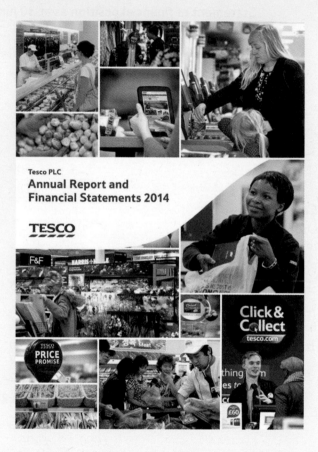

Tesco PLC
**Annual Report and
Financial Statements 2014**

TESCO

(b) List some of the limitations of the data that you used in answering part (a) of the question.

Year ended 22 February 2014	Notes	52 weeks 2014 £m	52 weeks 2013 (restated*) £m
Continuing operations			
Revenue	2	63,557	63,406
Cost of sales		(59,547)	(59,252)
Gross profit		4,010	4,154
Administrative expenses		(1,657)	(1,482)
Profits/losses arising on property-related items		278	(290)
Operating profit		2,631	2,382
Share of post-tax profits of joint ventures and associates	13	60	72
Finance income	5	132	120
Finance costs	5	(564)	(517)
Profit before tax	3	2,259	2,057
Taxation	6	(347)	(529)
Profit for the year from continuing operations		1,912	1,528
Discontinued operations			
Loss for the year from discontinued operations	7	(942)	(1,504)
Profit for the year		970	24

Tesco plc Consolidated statement of financial position as at

	Notes	22 February 2014 £m	23 February 2013 £m
Non-current assets			
Goodwill and other intangible assets	10	3,795	4,362
Property, plant and equipment	11	24,490	24,870
Investment property	12	227	2,001
Investments in joint ventures and associates	13	286	494
Other investments	14	1,015	818
Loans and advances to customers	17	3,210	2,465
Derivative financial instruments	21	1,496	1,965
Deferred tax assets	6	73	58
		34,592	37,033
Current assets			
Inventories	15	3,576	3,744
Trade and other receivables	16	2,190	2,525
Loans and advances to customers	17	3,705	3,094
Derivative financial instruments	21	80	58
Current tax assets		12	10
Short-term investments		1,016	522
Cash and cash equivalents	18	2,506	2,512
		13,085	12,465
Assets of the disposal group and non-current assets classified as held for sale	7	2,487	631
		15,572	13,096
Current liabilities			
Trade and other payables	19	(10,595)	(11,094)
Financial liabilities:			
Borrowings	20	(1,910)	(766)
Derivative financial instruments and other liabilities	21	(99)	(121)
Customer deposits and deposits from banks	23	(6,858)	(6,015)
Current tax liabilities		(494)	(519)
Provisions	24	(250)	(188)
		(20,206)	(18,703)
Liabilities of the disposal group classified as held for sale	7	(1,193)	(282)
Net current liabilities		(5,827)	(5,889)
Non-current liabilities			
Financial liabilities:			
Borrowings	20	(9,303)	(10,068)
Derivative financial instruments and other liabilities	21	(770)	(759)
Post-employment benefit obligations	26	(3,193)	(2,378)
Deferred tax liabilities	6	(594)	(1,006)
Provisions	24	(183)	(272)
		(14,043)	(14,483)
Net assets		14,722	16,661
Equity			
Share capital	27	405	403
Share premium		5,080	5,020
All other reserves		(498)	685
Retained earnings		9,728	10,535
Equity attributable to owners of the parent		14,715	16,643
Non-controlling interests		7	18
Total equity		14,722	16,661

Consolidated statement of cash flows for the years 2014 and 2015

Tesco plc

Year ended 22 February 2014	Notes	52 weeks 2014 £m	52 weeks 2013 £m
Cash flows from operating activities			
Cash generated from operations	29	4,316	3,873
Interest paid		(496)	(457)
Corporation tax paid		(635)	(579)
Net cash generated from operating activities		3,185	2,837
Cash flows from investing activities			
Acquisition/disposal of subsidiaries, net of cash acquired/disposed		(13)	(72)
Proceeds from sale of joint ventures and associates		–	68
Proceeds from sale of property, plant and equipment, investment property and non-current assets classified as held for sale		568	1,351
Purchase of property, plant and equipment, investment property and non-current assets classified as held for sale		(2,489)	(2,619)
Proceeds from sale of intangible assets		2	–
Purchase of intangible assets		(392)	(368)
Net decrease/(increase) in loans to joint ventures		61	(43)
Investments in joint ventures and associates		(12)	(158)
Net (investments in)/proceeds from sale of short-term investments		(494)	721
Net (investments in)/proceeds from sale of other investments		(268)	706
Dividends received from joint ventures and associates		62	51
Interest received		121	85
Net cash used in investing activities		(2,854)	(278)
Cash flows from financing activities			
Proceeds from issue of ordinary share capital	27	62	57
Increase in borrowings		3,104	1,820
Repayment of borrowings		(1,912)	(3,022)
Repayment of obligations under finance leases		(9)	(32)
Purchase of non-controlling interests		–	(4)
Dividends paid to equity owners	8	(1,189)	(1,184)
Net cash from/(used in) financing activities		56	(2,365)
Net increase in cash and cash equivalents		387	194
Cash and cash equivalents at beginning of the year		2,531	2,311
Effect of foreign exchange rate changes		(105)	26
Cash and cash equivalents including cash held in disposal group at the end of the year		2,813	2,531
Cash held in disposal group	7	(307)	(19)
Cash and cash equivalents at the end of the year	18	2,506	2,512

Consolidated statement of profit or loss for the year to 25 February
J Sainsbury plc

	Note	2014 £m	Restated 2013 £m
Revenue	4	**23,949**	23,303
Cost of sales		**(22,562)**	(22,026)
Gross profit		**1,387**	1,277
Administrative expenses		**(444)**	(462)
Other income		**66**	67
Operating profit	5	**1,009**	882
Finance income	6	**20**	19
Finance costs	6	**(159)**	(153)
Share of post-tax profit from joint ventures and associates	14	**28**	24
Profit before taxation		**898**	772

Consolidated statement of financial position as at the end of

J Sainsbury plc

		Group			Company	
	Note	2014 £m	Restated 2013 £m	Restated 2012 £m	2014 £m	2013 £m
Non-current assets						
Property, plant and equipment	11	**9,880**	9,804	9,329	**16**	17
Intangible assets	12	**286**	171	160	**–**	–
Investments in subsidiaries	13	**–**	–	–	**7,562**	7,316
Investments in joint ventures and associates	14	**404**	532	566	**6**	91
Available-for-sale financial assets	15	**255**	189	178	**37**	34
Other receivables	17a	**26**	38	38	**1,229**	1,264
Amounts due from Sainsbury's Bank customers	17b	**1,292**	–	–	**–**	–
Derivative financial instruments	29	**28**	47	37	**23**	41
Deferred income tax asset	21	**–**	–	–	**–**	1
		12,171	10,781	10,308	**8,873**	8,764
Current assets						
Inventories	16	**1,005**	987	938	**–**	–
Trade and other receivables	17d	**433**	306	286	**1,428**	1,254
Amounts due from Sainsbury's Bank customers	17b	**1,283**	–	–	**–**	–
Derivative financial instruments	29	**49**	91	69	**48**	72
Cash and bank balances	26b	**1,592**	517	739	**136**	351
		4,362	1,901	2,032	**1,612**	1,677
Non-current assets held for sale	18	**7**	13	–	**–**	–
		4,369	1,914	2,032	**1,612**	1,677
Total assets		**16,540**	12,695	12,340	**10,485**	10,441
Current liabilities						
Trade and other payables	19a	**(2,692)**	(2,726)	(2,740)	**(4,457)**	(4,571)
Amounts due to Sainsbury's Bank customers	19b	**(3,245)**	–	–	**–**	–
Borrowings	20	**(534)**	(165)	(150)	**(341)**	(24)
Derivative financial instruments	29	**(65)**	(65)	(88)	**(47)**	(65)
Taxes payable		**(189)**	(148)	(149)	**–**	(6)
Provisions	22	**(40)**	(11)	(9)	**(2)**	(1)
		(6,765)	(3,115)	(3,136)	**(4,847)**	(4,667)
Net current liabilities		**(2,396)**	(1,201)	(1,104)	**(3,235)**	(2,990)
Non-current liabilities						
Other payables	19a	**(204)**	(173)	(137)	**(863)**	(876)
Amounts due to Sainsbury's Bank customers	19b	**(302)**	–	–	**–**	–
Borrowings	20	**(2,250)**	(2,617)	(2,617)	**(394)**	(633)
Derivative financial instruments	29	**(21)**	(4)	(1)	**(10)**	(4)
Deferred income tax liability	21	**(227)**	(277)	(317)	**–**	–
Provisions	22	**(29)**	(39)	(63)	**(2)**	(2)
Retirement benefit obligations	30	**(737)**	(632)	(348)	**–**	–
		(3,770)	(3,742)	(3,483)	**(1,269)**	(1,515)
Net assets		**6,005**	5,838	5,721	**4,369**	4,259
Equity						
Called up share capital	23	**545**	541	538	**545**	541
Share premium account	23	**1,091**	1,075	1,061	**1,091**	1,075
Capital redemption reserve	24	**680**	680	680	**680**	680
Other reserves	24	**127**	140	111	**7**	11
Retained earnings	25	**3,560**	3,401	3,331	**2,046**	1,952
Equity attributable to owners of the parent		**6,003**	5,837	5,721	**4,369**	4,259
Non-controlling interests		**2**	1	–	**–**	–
Total equity		**6,005**	5,838	5,721	**4,369**	4,259

Consolidated statement of cash flows for the years 2014 and 2015

J Sainsbury plc

	Note	Group 2014 £m	Group 2013 £m	Company 2014 £m	Company 2013 £m
Cash flows from operating activities					
Cash generated from/(used in) operations	26a	**1,227**	1,268	**38**	(25)
Interest paid		**(148)**	(143)	**(73)**	(85)
Corporation tax paid		**(140)**	(144)	–	–
Net cash generated from/(used in) operating activities		**939**	981	**(35)**	(110)
Cash flows from investing activities					
Purchase of property, plant and equipment		**(916)**	(1,067)	–	–
Purchase of intangible assets		**(13)**	(26)	–	–
Proceeds from disposal of property, plant and equipment		**335**	205	–	–
Acquisition of subsidiaries net of cash acquired	37c	**1,016**	(21)	**(243)**	–
Increase in loans to joint ventures		**(7)**	(5)	–	–
Investment in joint ventures		**(13)**	(1)	–	–
Investment in subsidiaries		–	–	**(20)**	–
Proceeds from repayment of loan to joint venture		**4**	16	–	–
Interest received		**20**	19	**50**	117
Dividends received		–	18	**250**	250
Net cash generated from/(used in) investing activities		**426**	(862)	**37**	367
Cash flows from financing activities					
Proceeds from issuance of ordinary shares		**19**	17	**18**	16
Proceeds from short-term borrowings		**200**	–	**200**	–
Repayment of short-term borrowings		**(200)**	(50)	**(200)**	(50)
Proceeds from long-term borrowings		**250**	75	**200**	50
Repayment of long-term borrowings		**(206)**	(61)	**(122)**	(22)
Repayment of capital element of obligations under finance lease payments		**(25)**	(20)	–	–
Interest elements of obligations under finance lease payments		**(8)**	(7)	–	–
Dividends paid	10	**(320)**	(308)	**(320)**	(308)
Net cash used in financing activities		**(290)**	(354)	**(224)**	(314)

Website

Further practice questions, study material and links to relevant sites on the World Wide Web can be found on the website that accompanies this book. The site can be found at www.pearsoned.co.uk/dyson

Contemporary issues

Failing to meet standards

Ten UK companies fell short of FRC reporting standards

Harriet Agnew

Ten UK companies including WH Smith, Royal Bank of Scotland and Rolls-Royce have issued financial statements that failed to meet the accountancy watchdog's standard for clear reporting.

The Financial Reporting Council said in a report made public on Tuesday that it examined the accounts of 271 companies and approached 37 per cent of them for further information and explanation. Typically, correspondence from the FRC results in companies agreeing to make some change to their next reports and accounts.

Ten company reports fell short of the FRC's standards of reporting in various respects, although some of those issues related to previous accounting periods. The other seven companies in that group were Anglo-Eastern Plantations, Anglo Pacific Group, Eland Oil & Gas, Pendragon, GKN and the Co-Operative Bank.

Part of the FRC's mandate is to monitor compliance with the financial reporting requirements of the Companies Act 2006. In June, the FRC announced a 'clear and concise' initiative, building on the concept of cutting clutter from corporate reports.

In this year's corporate reporting review, the FRC devoted most of its attention to FTSE 350 companies, as these represent the major part of investment in theUK-listed companies. But the watchdog said that it continued to see a higher proportion of poorer quality accounts produced by smaller listed and AIM quoted companies.

In April, the FRC launched a three-year project to improve the quality of smaller companies' reporting. At the moment it is gathering evidence on the causes of some of the problems.

FT *Source: www.ft.com, 14 October 2014.*

Questions relating to this news story can be found on page 270. ➡

About this chapter

In this chapter we look at some recent events and debates within the business world related to topics we have discussed in previous chapters. We also make an attempt to look ahead over the next five years and beyond to see what changes may take place in financial accounting and reporting. As this is a book for non-accountants, we will not speculate about those possible developments that would be of particular concern to professional accountants. Instead we have identified three current issues that are of relevance to all managers irrespective of their discipline. They are: (1) fraud; (2) audit rotation and (3) changes to existing and the introduction of new, accounting standards.

By the end of this chapter you should be able to:

• explain what is financial statements fraud and name some recent high-profile accounting scandals and cases of alleged fraud;

• outline how recent changes to audit rotation requirements are likely to improve the quality financial statements of companies, and

• identify the major changes currently underway and others that are likely to take place in financial reporting practice in the next five years and beyond.

Why this chapter is important

Accounting is a dynamic discipline. It has to be in order to cope with a rapidly changing world. New problems and new issues arise and some way has to be found of dealing with them as quickly as possible. There may then be a need to report them to interested parties and in what form should the report take.

Accountants are expected to take a lead on the reporting issues. This is their expertise but non-accountants should also be heavily involved because the impact of many issues is far too wide-ranging to be left to just one group of specialists. For example, an accounting scandal can significantly impact on reputation, profit, the dividend a company is able to pay to its shareholder and on its share price – far-reaching repercussions with effects beyond just the accounts and the accounting department of an organisation.

Non-accountants need to know what new accounting and reporting issues are currently under discussion in the business, economic, financial and political worlds and what proposals are being suggested to deal with them. Space does not allow us to deal with all of them in this book but we can give you an indication of some of the changes that have recently come about as well as issues that are currently under discussion and likely to take place in the next five years.

We have chosen a small number of topical issues but you are encouraged to read the business and financial press regularly to keep up with emerging issues in business and financial reporting.

This chapter is particularly important for non-accountants for the following reasons.

• To be aware of the general business environment in which accounting operates both nationally and internationally.

• To be informed about some contemporary issues in financial accounting and reporting.

• To advise your senior manager of any changes that may affect your own sphere of responsibility.

• To take an active part in any debate on the effect of any proposed financial reporting changes in your own entity.

• To foster an attitude of professional scepticism and integrity in business.

Overview

In Chapter 10 we looked at how to interpret company accounts and read the story behind the numbers. In question 10.10 at the end of that chapter you were asked to compare the 2014 financial statements of two supermarkets (Tesco and Sainsbury's) with a view to deciding which one of the had been the better performer.

You certainly will not be very pleased if you went through that exercise only to be told that the information you based your judgement on was not reliable.

Tesco to be investigated by Financial Conduct Authority over accounting scandal

Last week, Tesco stunned investors by announcing that a whistleblower had alerted its most senior lawyer to over-optimistic accounting for payments from suppliers and business costs. The group admitted it had overstated its expected first-half profits by £250m. The statement came three weeks after a trading update that predicted first-half profit would be £1.1bn, down from £1.6bn a year earlier.

Tesco's shares have fallen every day since last Monday's announcement and have lost more than a fifth of their value in that time.

The UK's top financial regulator has launched a full-scale investigation into the £250m accounting scandal that has plunged Tesco into crisis.

Sainsbury's put further pressure on Tesco over the error by saying it was confident its own commercial revenues were properly recorded.

Source: Adapted from www.theguardian.com, 1 October 2014.

Fraud

As we explained in Chapter 10 analysing financial statements is a powerful means of understanding how a business works. However limitations still are one of which is that the analysis of the financial information still depends very much on the quality of that information. If the numbers in the accounts are not right, if they are materially misstate grossly inflate, understate or unit important information, then relying on the financial information is pointless. Instead of assisting users in making decisions, the financial information misleads and wrong decisions are made.

There have been numerous accounting scandals and aleged fraud cases in recent business history. Here is a list of some of the big ones:

- 2001 Enron – obscured large debts held 'off balance sheet'.
- 2002 Worldcom – inflated assets by billions.
- 2002 Tyco International – falsified income and millions were misappropriated by high-ranking officials for personal benefit.
- 2008 Lehman Brothers – disguised loans as sales.
- 2011 Olympus – covered up losses on bad investments over a period of approximately 20 years.
- 2014 Tesco – overstated revenues received from suppliers (note that this is where suppliers pay Tesco, rather than the other way round, for the privilege of being chosen as a supplier).
- 2016 Toshiba – overstated profits over a number of years.

Accounting scandals have the potential to bring down companies as happened to (Lehman Brothers) and even countries are not immune from the effects of corporate accounting scandals.

Japan government worries

The scandal at Toshiba has got Japan's government worried that investors will lose confidence in the country.

Source: www.theguardian.com, 21 July 2015.

Activity 11.1

Research more facts about any two of the accounting scandals listed above (or others that you may be aware of). What do you think was the motive behind the inappropriate accounting?

When accounting irregularities are found, questions are raised about the competence of the professionals qualified and tasked with applying the complex accounting rules in preparing the accounting information. Mistakes can happen for a variety of reasons – IT system failures, human error and incompetence but often at the root of accounting scandals is the intentional misrepresentation of the accounting information. It is intent that differentiates error from fraud.

This is how ICAEW defines fraud:

Fraud is usually taken to mean the gaining of an illicit advantage through deception and in particular the manipulation of financial information or accounting records.
Source: http://www.icaew.com

Managers in business are often under pressure to deliver results. In the case of listed entities – there is pressure to report high profits and pay dividends to shareholders. In addition, it is not uncommon for managers' remuneration (salaries and most notably, bonuses) to be linked to the reported performance. All that pressure leads in some cases to unethical behaviour and fraud.

Figure 11.1 shows is how the National Fraud and Cyber Crime Reporting Centre explains what accounting fraud is and the steps that managers could take to contribute that prevent fraud in the organisations that they work for (Figure 11.1).

There are other types of fraud also, not related to company financial statements – such as benefit fraud or identity fraud. As managers you will need to be aware of those types of fraud and the way they may impact your business, if any, but vigilance of accounting fraud will in all cases be of importance.

One mechanism which aims to improve the credibility of the numbers in the financial statements and reduce the incidences of accounting scandals is the audit of those financial statements. So now let's move on to look again at audit and in particular auditor independence and the need for audit rotation.

False accounting fraud

False accounting fraud happens when company assets are overstated or liabilities are understated in order to make a business appear financially stronger than it really is.

False accounting fraud involves an employee or an organisation altering, destroying or defacing any account; or presenting accounts from an individual or an organisation so they don't reflect their true value or the financial activities of that company.

False accounting can take place for a number of reasons:

- to obtain additional financing from a bank
- to report unrealistic profits
- to inflate the share price
- to hide losses
- to attract customers by appearing to be more successful than you are
- to achieve a performance-related bonus
- to cover up theft.

Whatever the reasons for false accounting, they are all motivated by the need to falsify records, alter figures or possibly keep two sets of financial accounts.

Protect yourself against false accounting fraud

Your organisation can take the following steps to help protect itself from false accounting:

- vet employees' CVs and references thoroughly
- put a whistleblowing policy in place
- control access to buildings and systems using unique identification and passwords
- restrict and closely monitor access to sensitive information
- impose clear segregation of duties
- consider job rotation
- use tiered authority and signature levels for payments
- reconcile bank statements and other accounts on a regular basis
- audit processes and procedures from time to time
- promote a culture of fraud awareness among staff
- adopt, and rigorously implement, a zero tolerance policy towards employee fraud
- have a clear response plan in place in case fraud is discovered.

Source: http://www.actionfraud.police.uk/fraud-protection/false-accounting-fraud, June 2016

Figure 11.1 False accounting fraud

Audit rotation

As mentioned in previous chapters an audit is an independent examination of the accounts by auditors.

Auditors are usually qualified accountants who specialise in checking financial statements and who are employed by a firm of chartered or certified accountants. Most firms of accountants are very small and they do not have either the staff or the experience to audit large public companies. Indeed, in the United Kingdom there are probably only about six firms of accountants capable of doing a very large audit for an international group of companies.

Auditor firms are appointed to examine balances in the accounts and underlying transactions on a sample basis and to provide an opinion on whether the financial statements are materially misstated or not. A misstatement (which can be a result of either error or fraud) is said to be 'material' if it would cause investors and potential investors to change their minds about the state of the company.

Not all companies require an audit although some may choose to have one even if not required by the law. The Companies Act 2006 sets the audit requirements. From 1 January 2016, only companies that meet any two of these criteria require an audit:

1 Turnover > £10.2m
2 Net assets > £5.1m
3 Employees > 50

Activity 11.2	What percentage of UK companies do you think do not require an audit?
	(a) 21 per cent;
	(b) 57 per cent;
	(c) 86 per cent.

According to government statistics based on 2014 data, a surprisingly high number of companies in the United Kingdom do not meet the audit thresholds and therefore do not require an audit: 1,398,400 of the UK non-dormant companies. That's 86 per cent of companies! Since the increase of the thresholds in 2016, the number of companies not requiring an audit is now probably much higher than it was at that time.

Nonetheless the relatively small percentage of the UK companies at the large end of the spectrum which do require and are subject to annual audits have not been spared their share of accounting scandals. One of the reasons why that is so relates to the difficulty in detecting fraud. By its very nature, fraud is intentional, which means that the perpetrators take great care to cover it up and make it difficult for auditors to detect. Another reason that has come to the forefront of debate is the actual independence of auditors. The problem of perceived decrease in auditor independence is not confined to the United Kingdom only.

News clip

Audit firms called to account for cosy tenures

A lot has changed in the past 125 years. Since 1890, the year in which Shredded Wheat, the popular breakfast cereal, was created and the fire alarm was invented, modern society has been transformed completely, from the discovery of antibiotics to the development of aeroplanes, television and the Internet.

But one thing has remained stubbornly constant: the accounting firm used by Procter & Gamble. P&G's relationship with Deloitte is coming under increasing pressure to end.

Source: www.ft.com, 14 June 2015.

New European Union Audit Directive and Regulations that came into force in June 2016 now require companies to tender the audit of their financial statements once every 10 years and to actually rotate their auditors at least every 20 years.

The law states that shareholders appoint the auditors of the company. In practice, they cannot do so because it is impossible for them all to get together and vote on the merits of the various firms. As a result it is usually left to the directors to select a firm and put the name forward to the shareholders at a general meeting for their formal approval. Shareholders rarely vote against the directors' recommendation, and so auditors are well aware that if they fall out with the directors they are likely to lose the audit. That is why auditors are not perhaps as independent as is sometimes believed.

The auditors' independence may also be compromised because of a number of other factors:

- They may become heavily dependent on the fee earned for a particular audit.
- The staff generally and the partner in charge particularly, may become too friendly with the directors.
- It is common for staff to leave an audit firm and take up a full-time position with the client company.
- Audit firms often do lucrative non-audit work for the company, such as management consultancy and tax advice.

Activity 11.3

(a) Should an independent body appoint company auditors? Yes/No
(b) Should auditors be allowed to do other work for their clients in addition to auditing? Yes/No
(c) Should auditors be allowed to take up full-time employment with a former client? Yes/No
(d) Should auditors be allowed to do an audit for only a limited period? Yes/No
  Why?

All these factors are of very real concern because they could compromise the audit firm's independence. If a company engages in dubious financial practice, therefore, then the auditors may be accused of not doing anything about it because 'they are in the directors' pockets'. The change in audit rotation rules aims to deal with this issue.

While it may be true that auditors have been complacent in some accounting scandals, a more likely cause is the *expectations gap* that we referred to in Chapter 1, i.e. the public think that the auditors are there to do one job, whereas in reality they are there to do an entirely different one. Their job is primarily to confirm that the accounts are true and fair view, not to discover if there has been any fraud.

News clip

Schroders dumps PwC as its auditor after 57 years

Schroders is to begin searching for a new auditor, three years after Europe's second-largest listed asset manager was forced to backtrack on an attempt to replace PwC as its accounting firm.

The London-based investment company's decision to end its 57-year relationship with PwC comes after a number of large investors raised concerns about the ability of audit firms to deliver independent advice when they have worked for the same company for decades.

Investors have intensified their focus on auditor independence in the aftermath of the financial crisis. Questions were raised about why the big four accounting firms — PwC, Deloitte, EY and KPMG — either failed to spot or failed to highlight mounting problems in the banking sector.

Source: www.ft.com, 27 March 2016.

Some of the decisions that both directors and auditors have to make when preparing or auditing the financial statements are complex and highly judgemental. It is sometimes complexity rather than intent to mislead that leads to irregularities in the financial information. Accounting standards evolve to assist with making these judgement calls. We now move on to look at recent and pending changes to the accounting standards.

Changing standards

In Chapter 2, we spoke about the various regulation and standards that the accountants have to comply with. These are not static and evolve over time as needs of users change or problems with the existing way of doing things become apparent. We cannot be absolutely certain what changes will take place in financial accounting and reporting over the next few years. Some changes that appear highly likely at the moment may be abandoned altogether, while others may be radically amended or delayed well into the long term. We can, however, be reasonably confident that:

- The International Accounting Standards Board (IASB) will continue to be the pre-eminent worldwide body responsible for setting accounting standards.
- Company annual reports and accounts will have become much longer and even more difficult to understand than they are now.

We hope that we are wrong on the last point. There are signs that the problem is recognised (see the news clip below) but we are certainly not confident that much will or can be done about it.

News clip

Will simpler also be better?

As the amount of information in financial statements has grown, 'simplification' and 'reducing complexity' have become themes in recent years for regulators and accounting standard setters. Standard setters and regulators are acutely aware that investors can be confused and preparers overwhelmed by the complexity of accounting standards and by the content and volume of information presented in financial statements.

Source: www.journalofaccountancy.com, 13 April 2015.

We now move on to a brief summary of some of the recent and current accounting standards projects.

IASB projects

In this section we are going to summarise the main projects that the IASB was working on or had just completed in the summer of 2016. This will give you a good idea of the changes that are likely to take place in financial reporting practice over the following five years. In the United Kingdom and the other EU countries its requirements will, of course, only be mandatory for publicly listed companies. Nonetheless, they will inevitably have an influence on other types of entities. Here is a summary of three of its main projects as taken from the IASB website:

Leases

The objective of the project was to develop a new *Leases* Standard that sets out the principles that both parties to a contract, i.e. the customer ('lessee') and the supplier ('lessor'), apply to provide relevant information about leases in a manner that faithfully represents those transactions. To meet this objective, a lessee is required to recognise assets and liabilities arising from a lease.

IFRS 16 *Leases* was issued by the IASB on 13 January 2016 and has a mandatory effective date of 1 January 2019.

Insurance contracts

The insurance industry is an important and increasingly international industry and insurance contracts expose entities to long-term and uncertain obligations. Today, the accounting for insurance contracts does not provide users with the information they need to understand the insurer's financial position, performance and risk exposure. In addition, IFRS does not address specific insurance issues and it is not obvious how insurers should deal with these issues under current IFRSs. Consequently, great diversity in the accounting practices of the insurance industry has developed over time.

The IASB is currently in the process of balloting the forthcoming insurance contracts Standard and aims to issue the final Standard towards the end of 2016.

Conceptual framework

The *Conceptual Framework* describes the objective of and the concepts for general purpose financial reporting. It is a practical tool that:

- assists the Board to develop IFRS Standards that are based on consistent concepts;
- assists preparers to develop consistent accounting policies when no IFRS Standard applies to a particular transaction or event, or when a Standard allows a choice of accounting policy and
- assists others to understand and interpret the Standards.

The objective of the *Conceptual Framework* project is to improve financial reporting by providing a more complete, clear and updated set of concepts. To achieve this, the Board is building on the existing *Conceptual Framework* – updating it, improving it and filling in the gaps instead of fundamentally reconsidering all aspects of the *Conceptual Framework*.

The consultation on this project is ongoing.

Activity 11.4	Log on to the IASB's website. Find the link relating to current projects. Identify those projects that do not appear in the above summary.

You will appreciate that some of the estimated publication dates indicated by the IASB for its various projects may well be put back. We can certainly expect some projects to be delayed as sudden urgent issues arise, unforeseen difficulties occur in dealing with some issues and some may even be abandoned as a result of political difficulties in some countries.

We now turn to have a look at standards set by the Financial Reporting Council in the United Kingdom.

FRC projects

Like the IASB, the Financial Reporting Council (FRC) has an active work programme. As a consequence of the changes to company law arising from the implementation of the EU Accounting Directive, it made amendments to UK accounting standards to ensure continued consistency between the revised legal frameworks and the financial reporting framework. These changes became effective from 1 January 2016.

Here is a brief summary of the new Financial Reporting Standards issued by the FRC:

FRS100 Application of financial reporting requirements

The standard sets out the applicable financial reporting framework for entities preparing financial statements in accordance with legislation, regulations or accounting standards applicable in the United Kingdom.

FRS101 Reduced Disclosure Framework

The standard introduces a new reduced disclosure framework enabling most companies to use the IFRS recognition and measurement bases in their financial statements, while being exempt from a number of disclosures required by full IFRSs.

FRS102 The Financial Reporting Standard Applicable in the United Kingdom and Republic of Ireland

This financial reporting standard is replacing old UK GAAP. It is single standard in place of a number of old standards. It is based on the IFRS for SMEs, with significant modifications to address company law requirements and incorporate additional accounting options.

FRS103 Insurance Contracts

A standard with specific accounting requirements for entities with insurance contracts.

FRS104 Interim Financial Reporting

The Standard is based on IAS 34 *Interim Financial Reporting*.

FRS105 The Financial Reporting Standard applicable to the Micro-entities Regime

FRS 105 is based on FRS 102, but its accounting requirements are adapted to satisfy the legal requirements applicable to micro-entities and to reflect the simpler nature and smaller size of micro-entities.

Activity 11.5	**Opportunity knocks**
	Log on to the FRC's website. Check through the list of projects. What are the new projects?

We can see from the above work programmes that the change to IASB requirements for listed companies in the European Union has had a major impact on UK GAAP standards issued by the FRC for smaller and unlisted entities. It appears that as UK standards become compatible with ISAB standards, the FRC will become, in effect, a sub-branch of the IASB albeit with special responsibility for acting on behalf of the United Kingdom. This might only be likely, however, if IASB requirements become mandatory for both private and public companies. They are not at present. They only apply to listed group companies so it would appear that for the time being the FRC still has a major role to play in developing and issuing accounting standards for entities not subject to the IFRS full regime.

> **❗ Questions you should ask**
>
> Allowing for changes that *may* have taken place since the book was published, you might like to pose the following questions.
>
> - Have we had to change our treatment of any accounting matters as a result of new IFRSs/ FRSs?
> - Has the FRC or the IASB published anything during this last year that affects us?
> - Are there any new accounting concepts that we have incorporated into our financial statements this year?
> - What methods do we use to recognise the amount of revenue we take to the profit or loss calculation?
> - Have our auditors raised any concern about our financial statements?

Conclusion

This chapter has looked at some current issues that affect financial accounting and reporting practices.

We examined some recent accounting scandals and considered what is the difference between error and fraud.

We also examined the role external auditors play in financial reporting and the importance of their independence, now strengthened by the new audit rotation rules.

Finally, we have reviewed the current work of both the IASB and the FRC as it was in the summer of 2016 and highlighted the major projects that are likely to result in changes to financial reporting over the next few years.

Key points

1 Errors in accounting information are unintentional. Fraud is intentional – a determined act of misrepresenting accounting information. Corporate history is full of examples of accounting scandals and cases of accounting fraud.

2 Auditors act on behalf of shareholders but they cannot afford to fall out with a company's directors. They also face difficult decisions about supporting the directors in the treatment of certain contentious accounting matters. Both of those are some of the reasons why auditor independence has been called into question and new audit rotation rules come into force in 2016.

3 Both the IASB and the FRC have an active development programme which should result in new standards coming on stream within the next five years. Most of their projects are highly technical and they are not of immediate relevance to non-accountants.

Check your learning

The answers to these questions can be found within the text.

1 What are the names of some big corporate fraud cases?

2 What are the most commonly misrepresented or falsified balances in the financial statements?

3 What is an audit?

4 What is an auditor?

5 What is an external auditor's basic job?

6 Give three reasons why an external auditor's independence may be compromised.

7 Give a reason why auditors need to be rotated often.

8 What are the disadvantages of audit rotation?

9 What do the initials IASB and FRC stand for?

10 When do IASB standards normally become effective?

News story quiz

Remember the news story at the beginning of this chapter? Go back to that story and reread it before answering the following questions.

Questions

1 What do you think are the reasons for the cases of financial reporting lacking clarity?

2 What could directors and managers do to improve the clarity of their company's reporting?

3 What could auditors do to improve the clarity of reporting?

Tutorial questions

11.1 Examine the prospects of one set of accounting standards being applicable on a worldwide basis.

11.2 Assess the likely future of the UK's Financial Reporting Council as a financial reporting standards setter?

11.3 Discuss the relationship between a company's external auditor and its directors.

11.4 Discuss the concept of 'independence'. Why is that so important for audits?

11.5 Design a possible fraud scheme. Consider what its impact would be on the financial statements and how auditors may uncover a similar fraud.

Website

Further practice questions, study material and links to relevant sites on the World Wide Web can be found on the website that accompanies this book. The site can be found at www.pearsoned.co.uk/dyson

The communication of financial information

After preparing this case study you should be able to:

- identify significant features in a company's statement of profit or loss account, statement of financial position and statement of cash flows;
- describe the financial performance of a company using the above statements;
- prepare a chairman's report based on the information extracted from the financial statements and from other sources.

Background

Location   Moodiesburn, Scotland

Company   Devro plc

Synopsis

Devro plc is a Scottish-based company with its headquarters at Moodiesburn near Glasgow. It is one of the world's leading producers of manufactured casings ('skins') for the food industry. It supplies a wide range of products along with technical support to manufacturers of sausage, salami, hams and other cooked meats. The company concentrates on producing edible collagen products. Collagen is a common form of animal protein. In recent years such products have been replacing gut casings in all of the company's markets.

Besides its operations in Scotland, Devro has production plants in Australia, the Czech Republic and the United States. It also services markets from appropriately located offices around the world and through agents and distributors.

The appendix to this case study includes some information about Devro's activities for the year ended 31 December 2015.

Required:

Based on the above information and that contained in the appendix, draft a chairman's statement covering the year to 31 December 2015.

Appendix

Board changes

Retirements: Simon Webb, Group Finance Director, will retire in March 2016. Successor: Rutger Helbing. The Board now has six directors: three executive and three non-executive directors. The last new director appointment was in 2013.

Dividend

	2015 £m	2014 £m
Final paid of 6.1 pence per share (2014: 6.1 pence)	10.2	10.2
Interim paid of 2.7 pence per share (2014: 2.4 pence)	4.5	4.5
	14.7	14.7

The directors propose a final dividend of 6.10 pence per share in respect of the financial year ended 31 December 2015 which will absorb an estimated £10.2m of shareholders' funds. It will be paid on 13 May 2016 to shareholders who are on the register at close of business on 29 March 2016.

Financial

Before exceptional items:	2015 £m	2014 £m
Revenue	230.2	232.3
Operating profit	33.3	30.3
Profit before tax	29.2	26.1
Profit after tax	25.6	22.9
Basic earnings per share	8.8p	2.6p
Exceptional items (See Below):		
Operating profit	(14.1)	(23.9)
Taxation	3.1	5.4
Cash and cash equivalents at 31 December	9.6	0.1

Exceptional items

The biggest exceptional items relate to:

Restructuring savings: The planned cost reductions have been realised following the restructuring of operations in Scotland in 2014, as the group closes its older and less-efficient capacity, alongside the outsourcing of hide preparation operations in Australia. Together these actions contributed £5.8 million of cost savings, which was slightly ahead of target.

Input costs: Input costs reduced £3.0 million during the year following a number of years of increases. The group benefited from lower raw material costs in the United States and Australia, alongside lower energy costs across all locations.

Operational

Sales to external customers *Geographical segmental revenue:*	2015 £m	2014 £m
Americas	64.0	57.8
Asia-Pacific	69.6	70.1
Europe	96.6	
		104.4
	230.2	232.3

Outlook

For current trading, some markets are positive and providing good opportunities for growth, while others face continuing economic and political pressures that limit demand. In China, Devro continues to pursue the strategy of supplying differentiated products for the premium sector, which is growing, whereas in the standard casings sector there has been a contraction in volumes recently along with high levels of availability leading to price erosion.

For Devro, in 2016, it is the timely and efficient commissioning of our new plants that will most significantly contribute to improved profitability and, while we anticipate inevitable challenges in this phase, we are confident in the ability of our local management teams to reach successful conclusions.

Our transformation will complete in 2016, after which Devro will be well positioned to supply all of our markets with competitive products from efficient manufacturing operations. The benefits from this transformation will begin to flow through to profits in 2016 and the long-term growth prospects are strong.

Note: For further information about Devro plc, log on to its website (www.devro.com).

Interpretation of accounts

**Learning
objectives**

After preparing this case study you should be able to:

- evaluate a set of financial statements for a large company;
- identify the main changes in the company's financial position over a period of time and
- summarise the information contained within such statements.

Background

Location   Denmark

Company   LEGO

Synopsis

The name 'LEGO' is an abbreviation of the two Danish words 'leg godt', meaning 'play well'. It is the company's name and its ideal.

The LEGO Group was founded in 1932 by Ole Kirk Kristiansen. The company has passed from father to son and is now owned by Kjeld Kirk Kristiansen, a grandchild of the founder.

It has come a long way over the past almost 80 years – from a small carpenter's workshop to a modern, global enterprise that is now one of the world's largest manufacturers of toys.

Access the company's 10-year financial information at http://www.thelegocasestudy.com/financial-information.html

Source: http://www.lego.com/en-gb/aboutus/lego-group/the_lego_history

Required:

Analyse the company's financial performance for the past 10 years.

MANAGEMENT ACCOUNTING

Part 4 deals with management accounting. Chapter 12 provides a foundation for a study of the subject. Chapters 13 and 14 covers some basic costing accounting matters; Chapters 15 and 16 with planning and control procedures and Chapters 17, 18 and 19 with some decision-making issues. Finally, Chapter 20 reviews a number of emerging issues in management accounting.

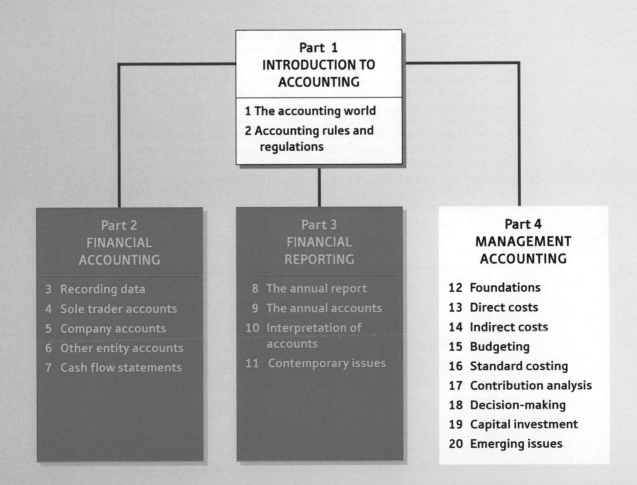

Part 1
INTRODUCTION TO ACCOUNTING

1 The accounting world
2 Accounting rules and regulations

Part 2
FINANCIAL ACCOUNTING

3 Recording data
4 Sole trader accounts
5 Company accounts
6 Other entity accounts
7 Cash flow statements

Part 3
FINANCIAL REPORTING

8 The annual report
9 The annual accounts
10 Interpretation of accounts
11 Contemporary issues

Part 4
MANAGEMENT ACCOUNTING

12 Foundations
13 Direct costs
14 Indirect costs
15 Budgeting
16 Standard costing
17 Contribution analysis
18 Decision-making
19 Capital investment
20 Emerging issues

Foundations

A well-paid profession

Salaries rise

Chris Warmoll

Management accountants are benefitting from salaries that are growing at twice the national average. That's the message from the Chartered Institute of Management Accountant (CIMA), whose latest annual survey shows that qualified members earn £62,791, a 1.6% growth on the 2014 figure.

The current UK average salary is £27,200 in comparison, just 0.7% up from the previous year, according to the Office for National Statistics. Even those still studying for their qualification reported a salary growth rate of 2.3% – earning an average annual base salary of £33,031 – 21% more than the national average. Then on top of base salaries, 58% of CIMA students in the United Kingdom received a bonus in 2015, with the average being 7% of annual salary. This increases to 8% of annual salary for qualified members, with 70% reporting a bonus in 2015.

Perhaps unsurprisingly, both members and students in the United Kingdom are positive about the future trend of their salary with 88% of members and 83% of students expecting a salary increase over the next 12 months. This is in line with the global average, with 90% of members and students expecting a pay increase over the next 12 months. The average pay increase was 5%.

Andrew Harding, managing director of CIMA, said: 'In contrast to the ongoing trend of weak wage growth nationally, the earning potential of our members has remained high, driven by the relevance and value of their skills to business. As we face ongoing economic uncertainty, we continue to see strong demand for management accounting skills as business seeks better support in decision-making. Businesses know the benefit of strong management accounting skills in driving value and managing risk and so management accountants are increasingly sought after – and receiving increased remuneration as a result.'

Source: Adopted from www.accountancyage.com/aa/news, 17 November 2015.

Questions relating to this news story can be found on page 289 ➡

About this chapter

In Parts 1–3 of this book we have concentrated on financial accounting and financial reporting. In Part 4 we turn to management accounting – one of the most important branches of accounting. In this chapter we outline the nature and purpose of management accounting, trace its historical development, describe its main functions and examine the impact it has on the behaviour of those coming into contact with it.

The chapter provides you with a foundation for the subject. It then makes it easier for you to deal with the eight other chapters that cover management accounting in some depth.

Learning objectives

By the end of this chapter, you should be able to:

- describe the nature and purpose of management accounting;
- trace its historical development;
- outline the six main functions of management accounting and
- assess its impact on human behaviour.

Why this chapter is important

The previous chapters in this book covered mainly financial accounting and financial reporting. It is logical to start a study of accounting in this way because financial accounting practices have strongly influenced the development of much else in accounting. This is especially true of management accounting. Nevertheless, until you become a senior manager it is unlikely that you will be involved to any great extent in the financial accounting and reporting requirements of an entity. This is not the case with management accounting. Even as a junior manager you are likely to have to provide information for management accounting purposes and to receive reports of your departmental or sectional performance.

At the very least, therefore, it is helpful to know what that information is for and what the various reports mean, especially when you are asked to act on them. It also suggests that all employees in an entity should know something about management accounting if they want to be really good at their jobs.

It follows that this chapter is important because it provides the foundation for a detailed study of management accounting.

Nature and purpose

News clip

Backward-looking

'Presenting management accounts to a board is a totally backward-looking process that talks about what we did last month, or year,' asserts Patrick Burrows, the Chief Financial Officer of London City Airports. 'What boards actually want to talk about,' he goes on to say, 'is "where are we going?" and "should we be expecting more or less?"'

Source: Economia, December 2015.

You will recall from reading Chapter 1 that accounting is a specialised service function involving the collection, recording, storage and summary of *data* (primarily of a financial nature) and the communication of *information* to interested specialised. It has six main branches, the two most prominent being financial accounting and management accounting. *Financial accounting* deals mainly with information normally required by parties that are *external* to an entity, e.g. shareholders or government departments. *Management accounting* has a similar role, except that the information supplied is normally for parties *within* an entity, e.g. management.

In Chapter 1 we also gave you CIMA's definition of management accounting. For convenience, we will repeat it here.

> *Management accounting is the application of the principles of accounting and financial management to create, protect, preserve and increase value for the stakeholders of for-profit and not-for-profit enterprises in the public and private sectors. (CIMA, Official Terminology, 2005)*

This is a fairly wide definition of management accounting. Its *primary* purpose is to supply accounting information for use *within* an entity but that information may also be of interest to external parties such as banks, credit rating agencies and the government. Clearly, therefore, in that respect at least it is very similar to financial accounting. However, we can distinguish many differences between financial accounting and management accounting. We summarise them for you below and they are also depicted in Figure 12.1.

- *Non-mandatory:* there are no statutory or mandatory professional requirements covering management accounting.

- *Data:* more quantitative data are normally incorporated into a management accounting system.

- *Qualitative data:* management accounting information increasingly includes a great deal of qualitative data.

- *Non-monetary:* data that cannot be translated into monetary terms is inserted into management accounting reports.

- *Forecasted and planned:* data of both a historic and a forecasted or planned nature is of considerable importance and relevance in management accounting.

- *Users:* management accounting is primarily concerned with providing information for use *within* an entity.

It follows from the above that unlike financial accountants, management accountants have considerably more freedom in providing the type of information that meets the specific requirements of interested parties. The main party will normally be the entity's managers.

Companies					
Management accounting		Main user	Financial accounting		
Management			Shareholders		
None		Regulations	Statutory		Professional
Non-monetary	Quantitative	Qualitative	Data	Financial	
Historical	Forecasted	Planned	Budgeted		

Figure 12.1 Management accounting vs financial accounting: main differences

Historical review

Until the eighteenth century, Britain was primarily an agrarian society and there were comparatively few recognisable industrial entities. Furthermore, most entities (of whatever type) were relatively small and they were financed and managed by individuals or their families. As a result, it was unnecessary to have formal documentary systems for planning, control and reporting purposes because the entities were small enough for the owners to assess these considerations for themselves on a day-to-day basis.

During the eighteenth century, Britain became the first country in the world to undergo an industrial revolution. In just a short period of time it changed from a predominantly agricultural society to an industrial one and by the late nineteenth century it had become a major industrial power in the world. There were two specific consequences of this development. First, the new industrial enterprises needed large amounts of money to get them. This could not be provided by just a few individuals.

It had to be sought from 'investors' whose interest in the enterprise was largely financial. Such investments were extremely risky and there was the strong possibility of personal bankruptcy. So Parliament intervened and introduced the concept of *limited liability* into company law. Second, the new enterprises needed specialist staff to operate and manage them. Such staff had often to be recruited from outside the immediate family circle.

These two consequences resulted in the ownership of the enterprise often being divorced from its management. A number of Companies Acts passed in the nineteenth and twentieth centuries gave shareholders in limited liability companies the right to receive a minimum amount of information annually, and auditors had to be appointed to report to them about the company's activities.

The complexity, scale and size of the new industrial enterprises meant that it was difficult for professional managers to exercise control on the basis of personal knowledge and casual observation. It became necessary to supply them with information that was written down. At first this revolved round the statutory annual accounts, but it soon became clear that such accounts were produced too late, too infrequently and in too little detail for effective day-to-day managerial control. As a result, a more detailed recording and reporting system gradually evolved during the period from 1850 to about 1900. We now refer to this as a *cost accounting system*. Its main purposes were to provide sufficient information for the valuation of closing stock, work-in-progress and finished goods, and for calculating the costs of individual products. In the early days it was common for financial accounting systems and cost accounting systems to run side-by-side but they eventually merged when it became clear that they used much of the same basic data. The development of management accounting is shown in Figure 12.2. Notice how the pace of development quickens after the eighteenth century.

The really major developments in management accounting occurred in the United States at the beginning of the twentieth century. By 1925 most of the practices and techniques used today had been established and few new developments in management accounting took place until towards the end of the twentieth century. The position has changed somewhat during the past 30 years or so and many new ideas have been put forward and incorporated into practice mainly by some large companies.

From the beginning of the twentieth century the new management accounting techniques were rapidly developed and practised fairly widely in the United States but progress was much slower in Britain. Apart from the largest industrial companies, the application of management accounting did not become common until about 1970. Even now, there is evidence that many smaller entities still depend on what is sometimes called 'back of the envelope' exercises for managerial planning and control purposes. It should

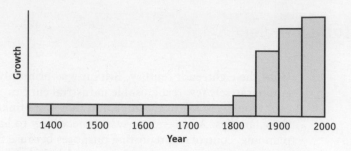

Figure 12.2 Management accounting: development

also be noted that over the same period, manufacturing industry in many industrial nations has given way to service industries. This means that many of the traditional management accounting techniques such as stock control and pricing, standard costing and product costing are of much less significance than they once were. Nevertheless, they are still of some importance and we will be covering them in subsequent chapters.

Main functions

News clip

Improving productivity

In a letter to the *Financial Times,* CIMA's Chief Executive indicates that management accounting does not just report on past performance but it takes into account all relevant information in order to produce forward-looking strategy. He argues that far from being the 'root cause' of the problem, 'management accounting is the professional service that can truly tackle the productivity challenge facing "UK plc"'.

Source: Adapted from www.cimaglobal.com/About-us/Press-office/Press releases/2015/CIMA-Chief Executive-outlines-how-manage.

The overall role of a management accountant is to provide information for management purposes. Six specific functions can be readily identified: planning, control, cost accounting, decision-making, financial management and auditing.

The interrelationship of these functions is shown in Figure 12.3 and we outline them briefly in the rest of this section.

Planning

Planning can be classified into two broad groupings: long term and short term.

Long-term planning

Long-term planning is commonly called *strategic planning* or *corporate planning*. We will refer to it as 'strategic planning' because this appears to be the most widely used term. *Strategy* is a military term meaning the ability to plan and organise manoeuvres in such a way that the enemy is put at a disadvantage. Over the past 20 years, strategic

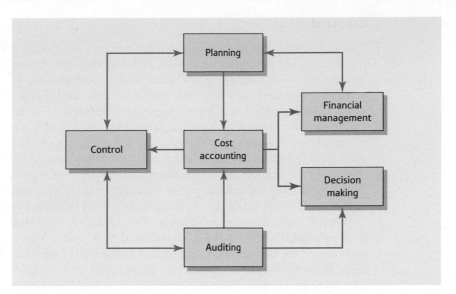

Figure 12.3 Management accounting: main functions

planning has become an important managerial function in both profit-making and not-for-profit entities. In essence, it involves working out what the entity wants to achieve in the long term i.e. beyond a calendar year, and how it intends to achieve it.

There are six basic steps involved in preparing a strategic plan. A summary is shown in Table 12.1.

Strategic planning is not just a management accounting function. The senior management of the entity will probably set up a multidisciplined strategic planning team that may include management accountants along with other specialists. The management accountants' major role will be to collect data and to provide information (mainly of a financial nature) required by the team.

Short-term planning

Accountants normally refer to short-term planning as *budgeting,* the 'short term' being regarded as being a period of up to a calendar year. Budgeting is covered in Chapter 15.

TABLE 12.1
Steps in preparing a strategic plan

Step	Action	Question to be asked
1	Establish the entity's main objective such as earning a minimum of 20% on capital employed)	*'Where do we want to be in x years' time?'*
2	Assess the entity's current position	*'Where are we now?'*
3	Evaluate the external factors (economic, financial, political and social) that will apply during the period of the plan	*'What is the outside world likely to be like?'*
4	Specify the differences between the current position and the required future one	*'What gaps are there between where we are now and where we want to be?*
5	Conduct a SWOT analysis	*'What are our strengths, weaknesses, opportunities and threats?'*
6	Put the strategic plan together	*'What do we have to do to get towards where we want to go?'*

Control

Unless an entity has a clear plan of what it wants to achieve, it is unlikely to be success-ful. An additional benefit of having a plan is that it can also form part of the control mechanism of the entity. What management accountants do is to measure what has actually happened over a certain period of time and then compare it with what was planned to happen. Any apparent significant differences (or *variances* as they are called) are investigated, and if they are not acceptable, then action is taken to ensure that future actual events will meet the agreed plan. It may be found, for example, that the actual price paid for some raw materials was £5 per kilo when the plan allowed for a payment of only £4.50 per kilo. Why was there a variance? Was it poor planning? Was it impos-sible to estimate the actual price more accurately? Was it inefficient purchasing? Were higher quality materials purchased and if so, was there less wastage?

Not all variances are unwelcome. For instance, 1000 units might have been sold when the plan only allowed for sales of 950 units. The reasons for this variance should still be investigated, and if this *favourable* trend were deemed likely to con-tinue then it would be necessary to ensure that additional resources e.g. production, administration, distribution and finance were made available to meet higher expected levels of sales.

Note that it would be the responsibility of the management accountants to coordinate the investigation of any variances and report back to the entity's senior management. *It would not be the management accountant's responsibility to take any form of disciplinary action.* This is a point that is not always understood by those employees who come into contact with management accountants!

Further aspects of control are covered in Chapters 15 and 16.

Activity 12.1

Planning involves working out what you want to happen. Control involves (a) looking at what has happened, then (b) taking action if the actual events are different from the planned events. The control element happens after the events so how can they be con-trolled? Why might it still be beneficial to review such events even after they have happened?

Cost accounting

Historically, cost accounting has been the main function of management accounting. It is now much less significant, and other functions, such as the provision of information for decision-making, have become much more important. The cost accounting function involves the collection of the entity's ongoing costs and revenues, the recording of them in a double-entry bookkeeping system (a task that these days is normally done by com-puter), the balancing of the 'books' and the extraction of information as and when required by management. Cost accounting also involves the calculation of *actual costs* of products and services for stock valuation, control and decision-making purposes.

We deal with cost accounting in Chapter 13.

Decision-making

The provision of information for decision-making is now one of the major functions of management accountants. Although actual costs collected in the cost accounting records may provide some guidance, decision-making information usually requires dealing with anticipated or expected future costs and revenues and it may include data that would not normally be incorporated in a traditional accounting ledger system.

Most decisions are of a special or 'one-off' nature and they may involve much ingenuity in obtaining information that is of assistance to managers in considering a particular decision. Note that it is the managers themselves who will (and should) take the decision, not the management accountants.

Various aspects of decision-making are covered in Chapters 17, 18 and 19.

Financial management

The financial management function associated with management accounting generally is again one that has become much more significant in recent years and it has almost become a discipline in its own right. Its main function is to seek out the funds necessary to meet the planning requirements of the entity as economically, effectively and efficiently as possible – (the three 'Es'). CIMA defines them as follows:

> **Economy:** Acquisition of resources of appropriate quantity and quality at minimum cost.
> **Effectiveness:** Utilisation of resources such that the output of the activity achieves the desired result.
> **Efficiency:** Achievement of either maximum useful output from the resources devoted to an activity or the required output from the minimum resource input.
>
> (CIMA: Official Terminology, 2005)

Auditing

Auditing involves the checking and verification of accounting information and accounting reports. There are two main types of audit: external and internal.

External auditing may be regarded as part of the financial accounting function, while internal auditing is more of a management accounting responsibility. External auditors work for an outside entity, while internal auditors are employees of the entity itself and they are answerable to its management. In practice, external and internal auditors work closely together. Internal auditors' remit may also be extended to assessing the economy, effectiveness and efficiency of management systems generally instead of concentrating almost exclusively on the cost and financial records.

Behavioural considerations

News clip

Strategic decision making

A recent report prepared by Dr Graham Pitcher of Nottingham Trent University, and sponsored by the Chartered Institute of Management Accountant, indicates that many management accountants are involved in formulating business strategy and that they make a valuable contribution to top-level decision making. By contrast, those businesses and public sector bodies that do not make full use of their management accountants' expertise tend to have a less clear idea of their business strategy.

Source: Adapted from www.cimaglobal/About-us/Press-release/2015/ more-can-be-done-in-strategic-decision-making.

Figure 12.4 The modern management accountant: a model diplomat

The collection of data and the supply of information are not neutral activities. They have an impact on those who are involved in supplying and receiving such material. The impact can be strongly negative and it can adversely affect the quality of the data or information. In turn, this may cause management to make some erroneous decisions because of unreliable data and biased information. This is a feature of the job that accountants are now trained to recognise, i.e. the *behavioural impact* that *they* may have on other employees. What relevance has this for non-accountants?

Much of the information collected and stored in a financial accounting system is backed by legislation and neither accountants nor non-accountants can ignore what is required regardless of their own personal views. The legal position puts financial accountants in a powerful position because if necessary they can *demand* what they want from other employees.

Management accountants cannot make such demands as there are no statutory requirements to produce management accounts or even any equivalent professional management accounting standards. Their power, as such, comes from the close working relationship that they have with the directors and other senior managers. There is no doubt that in practice this puts them in an extremely strong position.

However, irrespective of the source of the power that accountants may have in making demands on other employees, modern thinking suggests that it is unwise to exercise it too obviously. Accountants are now taught that they have a much better chance of obtaining what they want and when they want it by working *with* other employees rather than by ordering them around.

This approach to dealing with other staff works best, of course, if it is reciprocated. So as a non-accountant you too should regard accountants more as friends rather than as enemies, i.e. try to work with them rather than against them. Some non-accountants may find this hard to do especially if they have had some unfortunate confrontations with accountants in the past. However, remember that it is usually better to talk than to fight (*jaw jaw, rather than war war*) and that accountants are basically employed to provide a service for other employees.

In return for cooperating fully with your accountants and getting the service that you want and that they can provide, what approach can you expect them to adopt? We suggest that their behaviour towards you should be as follows:

- *Cooperative.* Treat you as an equal and make it clear that your work is just as important as what they do.
- *Non-autocratic.* Avoid being autocratic, condescending and superior.
- *Diplomatic.* Be courteous, patient, polite and tactful.
- *Informative.* Explain in some detail why, what and when some information is required and in what form.

- *Helpful*. Assist in digging out the information that they require.
- *Considerate*. Take into account your other responsibilities and give you a realistic amount of time to provide any information that they require.
- *Courteous*. Avoid threatening implicitly or explicitly any disciplinary action.
- *Instructive*. Guide you through the mechanics of the management accounting system that relate to your responsibilities.

In practice, the above requirements may be somewhat idealistic. Sometimes, for example, senior managers do not encourage a participative approach and they may not always be willing to provide appropriate training courses. The management accountants in the entity then have a responsibility to point out to the senior managers that the planning and control systems that operate in such an environment are not likely to be particularly successful.

It must also not be forgotten that the relationship between management accountants and non-accountants is not one-sided and that non-accountants have an equal responsibility to be cooperative. Clearly, management accountants will find it difficult to work with staff who adopt a resentful or surly manner and who try to make life difficult for them.

Activity 12.2	Suppose that as a departmental manager you received an e-mail from the chief management accountant containing the following statement:

> **I wish to inform you that you overran your budget by £10,000 for March 2016. Please inform me immediately what you intend to do about this overspend. Furthermore, I will need to know why you allowed this gross piece of mismanagement to occur.**

How are you likely to respond to such an e-mail? Write down your thoughts.

❗ Questions you should ask

Some entities impose a management accounting system on their managers and they are expected to do just as they are told. However, experience suggests that such an approach does not work. It is much better to involve staff in the detailed implementation and operation of information systems. What approach does *your* own organisation take? We suggest that you ask the following questions (but remember to be tactful!).

- Who wants this information?
- What is it for?
- What's going to happen to it?
- Will I get some feedback?
- What will I be expected to do about it?
- May I suggest some changes?
- How can I help to improve what is done?

Conclusion

This chapter has provided a foundation for a more detailed study of management accounting. Management accounting is one of the six main branches of accounting. Its main purpose is to supply information to management for use in planning and controlling an entity and in decision-making. It grew largely out of the simple financial accounting systems used in the late nineteenth century when it became apparent that such systems could not provide managers with the day-to-day information that such systems needed, e.g. for use in stock control and for product costing purposes. In the early part of the twentieth century management accounting came to be increasingly recognised as a useful planning and control mechanism. More recently it has become an integral part of overall managerial decision-making. The discipline now has six main recognisable functions: planning, control, cost accounting, decision-making, financial management and auditing.

There are no statutory or mandatory professional requirements that govern the practice of management accounting. Nevertheless, management accounting techniques are now regarded as being of considerable benefit in assisting an entity to achieve its longer term objectives. As a result, management accountants tend to hold senior positions in most entities and they may wield considerable power and influence. However, their work can be largely ineffective and the quality of the information that they provide poor if they do not receive the wholehearted support of their fellow employees. Unless this is forthcoming, the eventual decisions taken by management, based on the information provided by the management accountants, may possibly lead to problems in the running of the entity.

Key points	
	1 Management accounting is one of the six main branches of accounting.
	2 Its main purpose is to collect data and provide information for use in planning and control and for decision-making.
	3 Management accounting evolved in the late nineteenth century out of the simple financial accounting systems used at the time when more detailed information was needed for stock control and for production costing purposes.
	4 It began to be used as a planning and control technique in the early part of the twentieth century.
	5 In more recent years, management accounting techniques have become incorporated into managerial decision-making.
	6 Six main functions of modern management accounting can now be recognised: planning, control, cost accounting, decision-making, financial management and auditing.
	7 Management accounting practices can have a negative impact on both the providers and the users of information if management accountants adopt an autocratic and non-participative attitude.
	8 A negative approach to management accounting requirements may result in poor-quality information and erroneous decision-making.

Check your learning

The answers to these questions can be found within the text.

1 What is meant by 'management accounting'?

2 List six ways in which it is different from financial accounting.

3 Suggest two reasons why in pre-industrial times there was no need for entities to have a management accounting system.

4 For what purposes did nineteenth-century managers need a more detailed costing system?

5 What is meant by 'strategic planning'?

6 How does it differ from budgeting?

7 What are the six steps involved in preparing a strategic plan?

8 What is meant by 'control'?

9 Describe briefly the nature of cost accounting.

10 What is meant by 'decision-making'?

11 What is the main purpose of financial management?

12 To what extent are management accountants involved in auditing?

13 Why should management accountants be aware of the behavioural impact of information supply?

News story quiz

Remember the news story at the beginning of this chapter? Go back to that story and reread it before answering the following questions.

The news that management accountancy salaries had risen at twice the national average will be of interest to most students and especially to those who will shortly be looking for a well-paid job.

Questions

1 According to the article, what skills do management accountants need that may justify paying them such high salaries?

2 What sort of skills does business need in order to 'support' decision-making?

3 What is meant by the phrases 'driving value' and 'managing risk'?

Tutorial questions

The answers to questions marked with an asterisk can be found in Appendix 4.

12.1 Examine the usefulness of management accounting in a service-based economy.

12.2 The first step in preparing a strategic plan is to specify the entity's goals. Formulate three possible objectives for (a) a manufacturing entity and (b) a national charity involved in animal welfare.

12.3 Assess the importance of taking into account behavioural considerations when operating a management accounting system from the point of view of (a) the management accountant and (b) a senior departmental manager.

12.4* Distinguish between financial accounting and management accounting.

12.5* Describe the role of a management accountant in a large manufacturing entity.

12.6 Outline the main steps involved in preparing a strategic plan.

12.7 What is the difference between 'planning' and 'control'?

12.8 'Management accountants hold an extremely powerful position in an entity and this enables them to influence most of the decisions.' How far do you think that this assertion is likely to be true in practice?

Further practice questions, study material and links to relevant sites on the World Wide Web can be found on the website that accompanies this book. The site can be found at www.pearsoned.co.uk/dyson

Direct costs

Cost cutting

JLR problems

Andy Sharman

Jaguar Land Rover has launched an ambitious drive to cut costs by £4.5bn which it hopes to achieve by the end of the decade. This decision intention underlines the challenge that the British carmaker faces to offset declining sales in China and to meet tougher emissions targets.

Under its Indian ownership since 2008, JLR has blazed a trail of rapid growth, with turnover tripling and sales and employment both doubling since 2010. A second-quarter net loss unveiled by parent Tata Motors last Friday revealed a darkening picture – with three-month sales down 32 per cent for both brands. According to sources close to the decision the company has put in place a freeze on hiring new white-collar employees.

Taken together, the lackluster result and the austerity drive mark a stinging correction to the optimism that has accompanied JLR's rise as Europe's fastest growing large carmaker on the back of rampant Chinese demand for products such as Range Rover Evoque.

JLR's plans were formulated in the summer and they will come through its production processes so that multiple models can use the same basic building blocks. The company will also seek to cut back-office functions, squeeze procurement costs in the supply chain and streamline logistics. Material, employee and other costs amounted to almost £20bn in 2015 and a £3bn-plus research and development budget may be ring-fenced.

JLR wants to release 50 new or updated products over the next five years and plans to open a new plant in Slovakia as part of an attempt by chief executive Ralf Speth to catch up with his former employer BMW and the other large German premium carmakers.

FT *Source: Adapted from the Financial Times, 9 November 2015, p. 23.*

Questions relating to this news story can be found on page 303 ➡

About this chapter

In the previous chapter we explained something about the nature and purpose of management accounting, why and how it developed as a separate branch of accounting and what its main functions are today. One such function is *cost accounting*.

Cost accounting involves collecting detailed financial data about products and services, and the recording of that data. The data may then be extracted from the books of account, summarised and presented to the management of an entity. The managers will use the information presented to them for planning and control purposes. The information may take various forms depending on what it is to be used for. At the very least, managers are usually interested in knowing the profit or loss made by individual products or services. For convenience, we will call this process *product costing*.

Following the Industrial Revolution, the new type of managers in the nineteenth century attempted to base their selling prices on what products had cost to make. Unfortunately, the financial accounting systems at that time could not provide the information required, so a separate branch of accounting called *cost accounting* began to develop. In the twentieth century, cost accounting has been subsumed into a much broader branch of accounting now generally referred to as *management accounting*.

Even so, accountants still cost products using a technique that has hardly changed in over 100 years. This technique is known as *absorption costing*. In broad terms, absorption costing involves the following procedure:

- isolate those costs that can be easily identified with a particular product;
- apportion the non-identifiable costs.

Accountants describe the first stage as *allocating* the direct costs and the second stage as *absorbing* the indirect costs. In this chapter we cover the first stage and in the next chapter the second stage.

Learning objectives

By the end of this chapter, you should be able to:

- identify direct costs material, direct labour and other direct costs;
- describe three important methods of charging direct material costs to production and
- calculate prime costs.

 ## Why this chapter is important

This is the first of the two chapters covering the subject of cost accounting. As a non-accountant you may be puzzled why you need to know *anything* about cost accounting. It might seem reasonable to assume that you can safely leave that subject to your accountants. We do not think so.

There are two broad reasons why we hold this view. In order to be a really successful manager we think that you need to know something about cost accounting for two reasons: (1) to achieve greater control over the resources for which you are responsible and (2) to make better decisions. This chapter will help you do both of these things when dealing with material and labour costs and the price at which they should be charged to production. If managers get the pricing decision wrong it can have some serious and often adverse consequences for the survival of the company. So it is far too important a decision for you to delegate it entirely to your accountants. They will usually supply you with all the cost and financial information that you need but you will be in a much better position to assess its reliability and usefulness if you are familiar with its source, the assumptions made in preparing it and the methods used to compile it.

Responsibility accounting

A cost accounting system will normally be based on what is called 'responsibility accounting'. *Responsibility accounting* has a number of identifiable features. They are as follows:

- *Segments.* The entity is broken down into separate identifiable segments. Such segments are known as 'responsibility centres'. There are three main types:
  - (i) *Cost centres.* A cost centre is a clearly defined area of responsibility under the overall control of a designated individual to which the costs directly associated with the specified area are charged. There are two main types of cost centres: *production* cost centres where products are manufactured or processed, e.g. a machining department or an assembly area and *service* cost centres where a service is provided to other cost centres such as the personnel department or the canteen. Cost centres can take a number of forms e.g. departments, production lines, machines, products or sales areas.
  - (ii) *Profit centres.* A profit centre is similar to a cost centre except that both costs and revenues associated with the centre are charged to it. It is then possible to calculate the profit or loss for each profit centre. The oil division of a large chemical company is an example of a profit centre.
  - (iii) *Investment centres.* An investment centre is similar to a profit centre except that it is also responsible for all the major investment decisions that relate to that centre. A division of a large multinational company is an example of an investment centre.
- *Boundaries.* The boundaries of each segment will be clearly established.
- *Control.* A manager will be put in charge of each separate segment.
- *Authorisation.* Segmental managers will be given the independence to run their segments as autonomously as possible.

By identifying different segments within an entity, it is then possible to isolate the various costs and revenues associated with each segment. This means that segmental managers can then be made solely responsible for planning, budgeting and controlling all their segment's activities and for making any decisions that affect it. They will also, of course, be held responsible for whatever does or does not happen within it.

Classification of costs

While in theory a responsibility accounting system enables costs and revenues to be easily identified on a segmental basis (from now on we will refer to all responsibility centres as 'cost centres'), in practice it is not always easy to identify each cost with a particular cost centre because there are some costs that are so general and so basic that no one manager has control over them, e.g. factory rentals and business rates. Such costs are levied on a property as a whole and they do not relate directly to any particular cost centre.

Costs that are easily and economically identifiable with a particular segment are known as *direct costs*. So if it is possible to identify all the costs of the entity with particular cost centres, then there is no problem because by definition *all* costs must be direct costs. While this may be true at the cost centre level, it is usually not true at the product or unit level. Some costs will certainly be easy to identify with particular units (classed as *direct unit costs*) but there will be other costs (classed as *indirect unit costs*) where it is much more difficult to relate them to units of production, e.g. canteen costs or the wages department expenses. In what way, therefore, is it possible to charge some of the indirect costs to individual units? In practice, it is not easy but we explain how it might be done in the next chapter.

Irrespective of whether costs are classified into the direct or indirect categories, we also need to have some idea of their nature, so they are usually broken down into their *elements,* i.e. whether they are material costs, labour costs or other types of costs. The *elements of cost* are shown in diagrammatic form in Figure 13.1. This breakdown is similar to the one we adopted for manufacturing accounts in Chapter 6.

There are two particular points to note about Figure 13.1. First, in a competitive market, selling price can rarely be determined on a 'cost-plus' basis, i.e. total cost of sales plus a profit loading. If the entity's prices are higher than its competitors, then it is not likely to sell very many units. However, if its selling prices are lower than its competitors it might sell many units but the profit on each unit may be low. Its competitors are then likely to bring down their prices very quickly. So when the market largely determines selling prices, it is vital that the entity's total costs are strictly controlled and monitored so that the gap between its total sales revenue and its total cost of sales (i.e. its profit) is as wide as possible. Second, the classification shown will not necessarily be relevant for all entities. For example, an entity in the service sector (such as an insurance broker) is not likely to have any direct or indirect production costs.

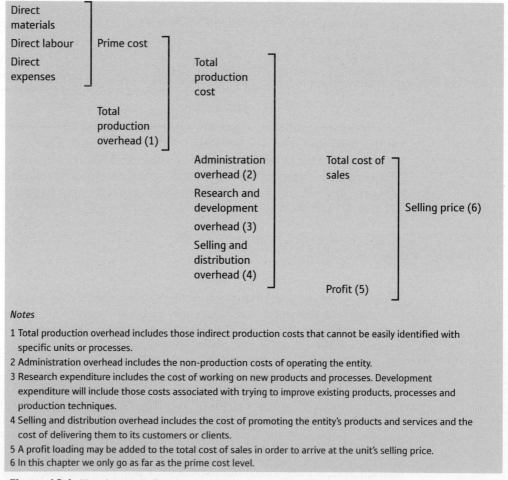

Notes

1 Total production overhead includes those indirect production costs that cannot be easily identified with specific units or processes.
2 Administration overhead includes the non-production costs of operating the entity.
3 Research expenditure includes the cost of working on new products and processes. Development expenditure will include those costs associated with trying to improve existing products, processes and production techniques.
4 Selling and distribution overhead includes the cost of promoting the entity's products and services and the cost of delivering them to its customers or clients.
5 A profit loading may be added to the total cost of sales in order to arrive at the unit's selling price.
6 In this chapter we only go as far as the prime cost level.

Figure 13.1 The elements of cost

Source: Based on Chartered Institute of Management Accountants (2005). CIMA Official Terminology. Oxford: CIMA Publishers.

Figure 13.1 is based on what is called *total absorption costing*. This is a method whereby *all* costs of the entity are charged to (or absorbed into) particular products irrespective of their nature. If only production costs are absorbed into product costs, the system is referred to simply as absorption costing.

There is also another important costing method known as *marginal* costing. This method involves classifying costs into their fixed and variable elements. Fixed costs are those that do not change irrespective of how many units are produced (i.e. regardless of output). Variable costs are those costs that do change and change directly proportionally to the number of units produced. We shall be dealing with marginal costing in Chapter 17.

We can now begin our detailed study of direct costs. We start with direct materials.

Activity 13.1	To which cost centre do you think a company's factory rent and business rates should be changed?

Direct materials

Inventory adjustments

Hanger Inc., an American company based in Austin, Texas, announced on 9 June 2015 that it was restating certain previously issued financial information. The restatement was due to errors identified with the implementation of new inventory valuation methods, processes and controls as well as with other previously disclosed errors.

Management has determined these adjustments to be material errors requiring restatements covering the financial years ending on 31 December 2009 to 2013, as well as the interim periods ending 31 March and 30 June 2014.

Source: www.prnewswire.com/news-releases/
hanger-announces-restatement-of-previously-issued-financial-statementre...28/12/2015.

Materials consist of raw materials and component parts. Raw materials are those basic ingredients that are incorporated into the production of a product, such as flour, sugar and raisins used in making cakes. Component parts include miscellaneous ready-made goods or parts that are purchased (or manufactured specially) for insertion into a main product such as a car radiator.

As we discussed earlier, a direct cost is one that can be easily and economically identified with a particular segment of an entity. However, there is a problem when dealing with materials. It might be easy and economic to identify them *physically* with a particular segment but it does not necessarily follow that it is then easy to attach a cost to them. There are two main problems. First, *size*. We might be able to identify a few screws used in assembling a chair, for example, but it would not be worthwhile costing them separately because their relative value is so small. Such costs would, therefore, be classified as *indirect* material costs. Second, *timing*. Materials may have been purchased at different times and at different prices, so it might not be possible to know whether 1000 kg of material held in stock had been purchased at £1, £2 or £3 per kilo. This problem applies particularly when materials that are purchased in separate batches are stored in the same containers, e.g. grains and liquids.

In such circumstances, it is necessary to determine an appropriate pricing method. Many such methods are available but as the price of materials charged to production also affects the value of closing stock, regard has to be had to the financial reporting requirements of the entity. In management accounting we are not bound by any statutory or mandatory professional requirements and so we are perfectly free to adopt any stock valuation method we wish. Unfortunately, if the chosen method is not acceptable for financial reporting purposes, we would have to revalue the closing stock for the annual accounts. This could be a very expensive exercise. We would, therefore, normally adopt a pricing method that is suitable both for the annual accounts and for management accounting purposes. This means adopting the requirements contained in *SSAP 9* (Stocks and long-term contracts). There are three preferred methods (assuming that the specific unit cost cannot be identified). We summarise each of them below. They are also shown in diagrammatic format in Figure 13.2.

- *First-in, first-out (FIFO)*. This method adopts the first price at which materials have been purchased.
- *Average cost*. An average cost may be calculated by dividing the total value of materials in stock by the total quantity. There are a number of acceptable averaging methods but we will be using the *continuous weighted average* (CWA) cost method.
- *Standard cost*. This method involves estimating what materials are likely to cost in the future. Instead of the actual price, the *estimated* or *planned* cost is then used to charge out the cost of materials to production. The standard cost method is usually adopted as part of a standard costing system. We shall not be considering it any further in this chapter because we will be dealing with standard costing in Chapter 16.

First-in, first-out

We will now use a calculative example to explain how the FIFO and the continuous weighted average pricing methods work. It is sensible to issue the oldest stock to production first, followed by the next oldest and so on, and this should be done wherever possible. This method of storekeeping means that old stock is not kept in store for very long, thus avoiding the possibility of deterioration or obsolescence. However, as some materials may be stored in such a way that they become a mixture of old and new stocks it is then not possible to identify each separate purchase. Nevertheless, in pricing the issue of stock to production there seems to be some logic in following the first-in, first-out procedure and charge production with the oldest price first, followed by the next oldest price and so on. The procedure is as follows:

1 Start with the price paid for the oldest material in stock and charge any issues to production at that price.

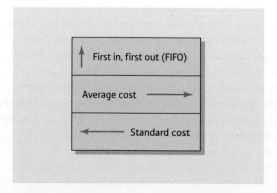

Figure 13.2 Direct material costing methods

2 Once all of the goods originally purchased at that price have been issued, use the next-oldest price until all of that stock has been issued.

3 The third-oldest price will be used next, then the fourth oldest and so on.

The use of the FIFO pricing method is illustrated in Example 13.1.

Example 13.1	**The FIFO pricing method of charging direct materials to production**

The following information relates to the receipts and issue of a certain material into stock during January 2015:

Date	Receipts into stores			Issue to production
	Quantity units	Price £	Value £	Quantity units
1.1.15	100	10	1000	
10.1.15	150	11	1650	
15.1.15			125	
20.1.15	50	12	600	
31.1.15				150

Required:

Using the FIFO method of pricing the issue of goods to production, calculate:

(a) the issue prices at which goods will be charged to production;

(b) the closing stock value at 31 January 2015.

Answer to Example 13.1

(a) The issue price of goods to production:

Date of issue	Tutorial note	Units	Calculation	£
15.1.15	(1)	100	units × £10 =	1000
	(2)	25	units × £11 =	275
		125		1275
31.1.15	(3)	125	units × £11 =	1375
	(4)	25	units × £12 =	300
		150		1675

(b) Closing stock:

	£
25 units × £12 =	300
Check:	
Total receipts (£1000 + £1650 + £600)	3250
Total issues (£1275 + £1675)	2950
Closing stock	300

Tutorial notes

1 The goods received on 1 January 2015 are now assumed to have all been issued.

2 This leaves 125 units in stock out of the goods received on 10 January 2015.

3 All the goods purchased on 10 January 2015 are assumed to have been issued.

4 There are now 25 units left in stock out of the goods purchased on 20 January 2015.

Although Example 13.1 is a simple one, it can be seen that if the amount of material issued to production includes a number of batches purchased at different prices, the FIFO method involves using a considerable number of different prices.

The advantages and disadvantages of the FIFO method may be summarised as follows.

Advantages

- The method is logical.
- It appears to match the physical issue of materials to production.
- The closing stock value is closer to the current economic value.
- The stores ledger account is arithmetically self-balancing and there are no adjustments that have to be written off to the profit and loss account.
- It meets the requirements of *SSAP 9*.
- It is acceptable for UK tax purposes.

Disadvantages

- It is arithmetically cumbersome.
- The cost of production relates to out-of-date prices.

Continuous weighted average

In order to avoid the detailed arithmetical calculations involved in using the FIFO method, it is possible to substitute an *average* pricing method. There are a number of different types but we are going to use the continuous weighted average (CWA) method. This method may require frequent changes to be made to the issue prices depending on the number of orders purchased. Although it appears very complicated, it is the easiest one to use *provided* that the receipts and issues of goods are recorded in a stores ledger account. An example of a manual stores ledger account is shown in Figure 13.3.

You will note from Figure 13.3 that the stores ledger account shows both the quantity and the value of the stock in store at any one time. The CWA price is obtained by dividing the total value of the stock by the total quantity. A new price will be struck each time new purchases are taken into stock.

The method is illustrated in Example 13.2. We use the same data as in Example 13.1 but we have taken the opportunity to present a little more information, so that we can explain more clearly how a CWA price is calculated.

The main advantages and disadvantages of the CWA method are as follows.

Advantages

- The CWA is easy to calculate, especially if a stores ledger account is used.
- Prices relating to previous periods are taken into account.
- The price of goods purchased is related to the quantities purchased.
- The method results in a price that is not distorted either by low or high prices, or by small or large quantity purchases.
- A new price is calculated as recent purchases are taken into stock and so the price is updated regularly.

Disadvantages

- A CWA price tends to lag behind current economic prices.
- The CWA price may not relate to any actual price paid.
- It is sometimes necessary to write-off any arithmetical adjustments in the stock ledger account to the profit and loss account.

We now move on to have a look at the other main type of direct cost: labour.

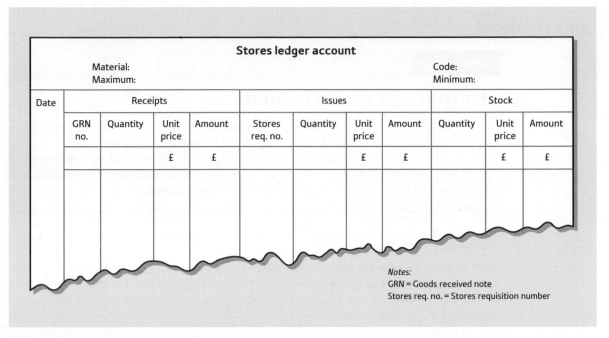

Stores ledger account										
Material: Maximum:								Code: Minimum:		
Date	Receipts				Issues				Stock		
	GRN no.	Quantity	Unit price	Amount	Stores req. no.	Quantity	Unit price	Amount	Quantity	Unit price	Amount
			£	£			£	£		£	£

Notes:
GRN = Goods received note
Stores req. no. = Stores requisition number

Figure 13.3 Example of a stores ledger account

Example 13.2

The CWA pricing method of charging direct materials to production

You are presented with the following information relating to the receipt and issue of a certain material into stock during January 2015:

Date	Receipts into stores			Issues to production			Stock balance	
	Quantity units	Price £	Value £	Quantity £	Price £	Value £	Quantity Units	Value £
1.1.15	100	10	1000				100	1000
10.1.15	150	11	1650				250	2650
15.1.15				125	10.60	1325	125	1325
20.1.15	50	12	600				175	1925
31.1.15				150	11.00	1650	25	275

Note:
The company uses the continuous weighted average method of pricing the issue of goods to production.

Required:
Check that the prices of goods issued to production during January 2015 have been calculated correctly.

Answer to Example 13.2

The issue prices of goods to production during January 2015 using the continuous weighted average method have been calculated as follows:

$$15.1.15 \quad \frac{\text{Total stock value at 10.1.15}}{\text{Total quantity in stock at 10.1.15}} = \frac{2650}{250} = \underline{£10.60}$$

$$25.1.15 \quad \frac{\text{Total stock value at 20.1.15}}{\text{Total quantity in stock at 20.1.15}} = \frac{1925}{175} = \underline{£11.00}$$

Direct labour

News clip

Employees undervalued

A survey of 513 senior decision-makers across industry has revealed that 97% believe that good management and investment in employees have a direct impact on business' performance, 57% are either unaware of or do not use any data on their human resources when deciding business strategy, and 94% said that they think poor management of employees can contribute to corporate failure.

Source: Adapted from www.cimaglobal.com/About-us/Press-office/Press-releases/2015/Companies-failing-to-value-employees-despite-...

Labour costs include the cost of employee salaries, wages, bonuses and the employer's national insurance and pension fund contributions. Wherever it is practical to do so labour costs will be charged to specific units. If it is impractical, then they will have to be treated as indirect costs.

The identification and pricing of direct labour are much easier than with direct materials. Basically, the procedure is as follows.

1 Employees working on specific units are required to keep a record of how many hours they spend on each unit.
2 The total hours worked on each unit is multiplied by the appropriate hourly rate.
3 A percentage amount is added to the total to allow for the employer's other labour costs, e.g. national insurance, pension fund contributions and holiday pay.
4 The total amount is then charged directly to that unit.

The procedure is illustrated in Example 13.3.

Example 13.3	**The charging of direct labour cost to production**

Alex and Will are the two employees working on Unit X. Alex is paid £10 an hour and Will £5. Both men are required to keep record of how much time they spend on each job they do. Alex spent 10 hours and Will 20 when working on Unit X. The employer has estimated that it costs him an extra 20 per cent on top of what he pays them to meet his contributions towards national insurance, pension contributions and holiday pay.

Required:
Calculate the direct labour cost of producing Unit X.

Answer to Example 13.3

Calculation of the direct labour cost:

	Hours		Rate per hour £		Total £
Alex	10	×	10	=	100
Will	20	×	5	=	100
					200
Employer's costs (20%)					40
Total direct labour cost					240

It should be made clear that in practice it is by no means easy to obtain an accurate estimate of the direct labour cost of one unit. Indeed, if it is very difficult to do so it will probably not be worthwhile. Even in those cases where there is no doubt that employees were working on a particular unit (as in Example 13.3), we depend on them keeping an accurate record. If you have ever had to do this in your own job you will know that this is difficult, especially if you are frequently being switched from one job to another, or you spend lots of time chatting in the corridor!

No matter what the difficulty, it is important that management should emphasise to employees just how important it is for them to keep an accurate record of their time. Labour costs may form a high proportion of total cost such as in service industries and so tight control is important. This is especially the case if tender prices are based on total unit cost. A high cost could mean that the company fails to get a contract, whereas too low a cost would reduce the amount of profit that the entity makes.

Other direct costs

Apart from material and labour costs, there may be other types of costs that can be relatively easily identified with specific units. These are, however, somewhat rare because unlike materials and labour, it is usually difficult to trace a direct physical link to specific units unless, for example, some specialist plant is hired to work on one particular job. It would then be possible to charge the hire cost specifically to that job.

Irrespective of the difficulties of identifying other expenses with production, it is important to make every effort to do so. Otherwise, the indirect charge just becomes bigger and bigger, and that then causes even greater distortions when it comes to estimating and pricing a new job.

❗ Questions you should ask

We suggest that you put the following questions to your management accountants.

- What is included in material costs?
- What criteria do you use for determining whether the costs are direct or indirect?
- What method do you use for charging them out to production?
- How do you determine whether labour costs are direct or indirect?
- What system is used to ensure that time spent on specific jobs is recorded accurately?
- Are there any other costs that could be classified as direct?
- What are they?
- What criteria can we use for charging them to specific units?

Conclusion

Responsibility accounting is a management control system that involves dividing an entity into segments and placing each segment under the control of a designated manager. Three main types of segments may be identified: cost centres (responsible for costs only), profit centres (responsible for costs and revenues) and investment centres (responsible for costs, revenues and investment decisions). Control is achieved by giving each manager complete responsibility for the costs incurred by his or her centre (and for any revenues received). Such costs (and revenues) can then be said to be *direct* to that centre. However, direct costs are normally defined as those that can be easily attributed to specific cost units. Those costs that cannot be easily attributed to specific cost units are known as *indirect* costs.

A direct cost is a cost that can be easily and economically identified with a specific cost centre and some costs can also be easily identified with specific units or products. Those that cannot be so identified are known as *indirect* costs.

Costs are usually classified into elements of cost. By building the costs up in layers, it is possible to determine a selling price, although market conditions have also to be taken into account when doing so.

Direct material costs include raw materials and component parts. If the cost of materials used in a particular product is known, then there is no problem in charging them out to products. The unit cost will be used. Otherwise, a pricing method has to be selected. The recommended ones are first-in, first-out, an averaging method or the standard cost. Direct labour costs are those costs that can be easily attributed to specific units. They are charged out on the basis of hours worked and the hourly rate paid plus an allowance for employer's employment costs, such as national insurance, pension contributions and holiday pay. There may be other direct costs that can also be attributed to specific units but these are relatively rare.

Key points	
	1 Product costing has three main purposes: stock valuation, the planning and controlling of costs and the determination of selling prices.
	2 The procedure involves isolating those costs that are easy and economic to identify with specific units. Such costs are described as *direct costs*. Those costs that are not easy or economic to identify with specific costs are known as *indirect costs*. The total of indirect costs is known as *overhead* (or *overheads*).
	3 Some material costs can be physically identified with specific units and their cost ascertained easily. In cases where it is difficult to isolate the cost of material used in production, e.g. where batches of materials are purchased at different prices and where they are stored collectively, an estimated price has to be determined. There are three acceptable methods for pricing materials (apart from being able to use the unit cost itself): first-in, first-out, average cost and standard cost. The average cost method recommended in this book is known as the *continuous weighted average* (CWA) cost method.
	4 Wherever possible, labour costs should be charged directly to specific units. Employees will need to keep time sheets that record the hours they have spent working on specific jobs. The amount charged to a particular unit will then be the time spent working on that unit multiplied by the respective hourly wage rate.
	5 Some other services may also be identifiable with specific units, e.g. the hire of a machine for a particular contract. The cost of such services should be charged directly to production if it can be easily and economically determined.

Check your learning

The answers to these questions can be found within the text.

1 What is meant by 'responsibility accounting'?

2 What is (a) a cost centre, (b) a profit centre and (c) an investment centre?

3 What is (a) a direct cost and (b) an indirect cost?

4 What is meant by the 'elements of cost'?

5 What is meant by 'prime cost'?

6 What are direct materials?

7 What four methods may be used for charging direct materials out to production?

8 What is meant by 'direct labour'?

9 How is it collected and charged out to production?

10 Give an example of a direct cost other than materials or labour.

News story quiz

Remember the news story at the beginning of the chapter? Go back to that story and reread it before answering the following questions.

The company now known as Jaguar Land Rover has a long history that stretches back to the beginning of the motoring era. Most students will be familiar with the name of the company, reflecting as it does two of the most famous and prestigious motor vehicles in the automobile industry. However, like many of its competitors, it is fighting a tough battle to survive in a highly competitive market.

Questions

1 Do you think that the selling price of Jaguar and Land Rover vehicles is a strong determining factor in being able to sell them?

2 Which of the various types of costs mentioned in the article would you identify as being a 'direct cost'?

3 How ambitious is the drive to cut costs by £4.5bn 'by the end of the decade', i.e. in about five years time?

Tutorial questions

The answers to questions marked with an asterisk can be found in Appendix 4.

13.1 Examine the argument that an arbitrary pricing system used to charge direct materials to production leads to erroneous product costing.

13.2* The following stocks were taken into stores as follows:

1.1.15 1000 units @ £20 per unit.
15.1.15 500 units @ £25 per unit.

There were no opening stocks.

On 31.1.15 1250 units were issued to production.

Required:

Calculate the amount that would be charged to production on 31 January 2015 for the issue of material on that date using each of the following methods of material pricing:

(a) FIFO (first-in, first-out)
(b) continuous weighted average.

13.3* The following information relates to material ST 2:

		Units	Unit price £	Value £
1.2.15	Opening stock	500	1.00	500
10.2.15	Receipts	200	1.10	220
12.2.15	Receipts	100	1.12	112
17.2.15	Issues	400	–	–
25.2.15	Receipts	300	1.15	345
27.2.15	Issues	250	–	–

Required:

Calculate the value of closing stock at 28 February 2015 assuming that the continuous weighted average method of pricing materials to production has been adopted.

13.4 You are presented with the following information for Trusty Limited:

2016	Purchases (units)	Unit cost £	Issues to production (units)
1 January	2 000	10	
31 January			1 600
1 February	2 400	11	
28 February			2 600
1 March	1 600	12	
31 March			1 000

Note: There was no opening stock.

Required:

Calculate the value of closing stock at 31 March 2016 using each of the following methods of pricing the issue of materials to production:

(a) FIFO (first-in, first-out)
(b) continuous weighted average.

13.5 The following information relates to Steed Limited for the year to 31 May 2017:

	£
Sales	500 000
Purchases	440 000
Opening stock	40 000

Closing stock value using the following pricing methods:

FIFO (first-in, first-out)	90 000
Continuous weighted average	79 950

Required:
Calculate Steed Limited's gross profit for the year to 31 May 2017 using each of the above closing stock values.

13.6 Iron Limited is a small manufacturing company. During the year to 31 December 2015 it has taken into stock and issued to production the following items of raw material, known as XY1:

Date 2015	Receipts into stock			Issues to production Quantity (litres)
	Quantity (litres)	Price per unit £	Total value £	
January	200	2.00	400	
February				100
April	500	3.00	1 500	
May				300
June	800	4.00	3 200	
July				400
October	900	5.00	4 500	
December				1400

Notes:
1 There were no opening stocks of raw material XY1.
2 The other costs involved in converting raw material XY1 into the finished product (marketed as Carcleen) amounted to £7000.
3 Sales of Carcleen for the year to 31 December 2015 amounted to £20,000.

Required:
(a) Illustrate the following methods of pricing the issue of materials to production:
  1 first-in, first-out (FIFO)
  2 continuous weighted average.
(b) Calculate the gross profit for the year using each of the above methods of pricing the issue of materials to production.

Further practice questions, study material and links to relevant sites on the World Wide Web can be found on the website that accompanies this book. The site can be found at www.pearsoned.co.uk/dyson

Indirect costs

Rolls Royce shake-up

Rolls Royce is to axe the company's two divisions in a sweeping management shake-up in an attempt by the new chief executive Warren East to revive the company's fortunes following five profit warnings.

The removal of a layer of top management is the first part of a programme to simplify processes at a group notorious for its unwieldy decision-making and hierarchical structure. The head of aerospace, Tony Wood, is also leaving the group as part of an overhaul that will lead to the abolition of the company's divisional structure. In place of two broadly defined divisions, the heads of the five units (civil aero-engines, defence, nuclear, marine and power systems) will now report directly to Mr East as part of the new management team. Next year a new chief operating officer will also be recruited and the company's operating system will be rewritten.

Mr East is tightening his oversight as he seeks to cut costs and accelerate decision making in the world's second biggest aero-engineering company. Although he has promised investors that there will be gross cost savings of £150m to £200m, he has not ruled out a sixth profit warning. Indeed, he has described Rolls-Royce as 'a company with £13bn of revenue, £10bn of product cost, and almost £4bn of other costs and not very much profit'. No wonder he believes some people in Rolls Royce have been insulated in the past 'from the realities of what's going on'.

FT   *Source: Based on a* Financial Times *article, 16 Dec. 2015, p. 1.*

Questions relating to this news story can be found on page 325 ➡

About this chapter

This is the second of two chapters in Part 4 that deal with *cost accounting.* We have split our study of cost accounting into two parts because the subject is too big to deal with in just one part. Chapter 13 dealt with direct costs while this one covers indirect costs. By the end of the chapter you will have been shown how accountants have traditionally gone about calculating product costs. In recent years the traditional method has been severely criticised, so we will also outline a relatively new technique for dealing with indirect costs (or overheads). This technique is called *activity-based costing* (ABC) and its proponents make great claims for it.

Learning objectives	By the end of this chapter, you should be able to:

- outline the nature of overheads, i.e. indirect production and non-production costs;
- calculate unit costs using absorption costing;
- assess its usefulness;
- explain what is meant by activity-based costing;
- summarise its advantages and disadvantages.

Why this chapter is important

In the previous chapter we suggested that you needed to know something about cost accounting for three main reasons:

- to achieve greater control over what you manage;
- to make better decisions;
- to get involved in the material pricing decision.

The first two reasons hold good for this chapter but there is another reason that relates directly to the contents of this chapter.

The treatment of indirect costs in product costing is fairly questionable and there is much controversy in accounting circles about its usefulness and reliability. You should not leave it entirely to the accountants to decide what to do. As a non-accountant and as a manager you have to get stuck right into the debate but you cannot do that if you don't know what the accountants are talking about.

This chapter will help you to talk to accountants at their level and enable *you* to decide what is best for *your* department when it comes to dealing with the 'overheads'.

Production overhead

News clip

Overhead reduction

As part of its cost management programme, Mondelez International has implemented Zero-Based Budgeting to reset spending, identify specific cost reductions and capture sustainable savings. The company's Executive Vice-President and Chief Finance Officer reports that eighteen months into its ZBB efforts, the company is delivering benefits faster than expected in all indirect cost packages.

Source: globenewwire.com/news-release/2015/09/10/767359/10148849/enMondelez-International-Details-Cost-Reduct.

In Chapter 12, we suggested that if management accounting is going to be used as part of a control system, it is necessary for all costs within an entity to become the direct responsibility of a designated cost centre manager. In this section we will examine how the *production* overhead gets charged to specific units. 'Production' relates to the output of any type of entity although it is more usually associated with those types of entities that manufacture a physical or a tangible product. 'Overheads' is a substitute term for indirect costs. An indirect cost is one that cannot easily be identified with a specific unit of output, a cost centre, a profit centre or an investment centre.

The charging of production overhead to specific units is rather a complicated procedure. It is known as *absorption costing*. In order to make it easier for you to follow we will take you through it slowly in three stages. As shown in Figure 14.1 the three stages are: (1) allocation; (2) apportionment; and (3) absorption. The figure shows the terms associated with the technique and also how costs are absorbed into one unit.

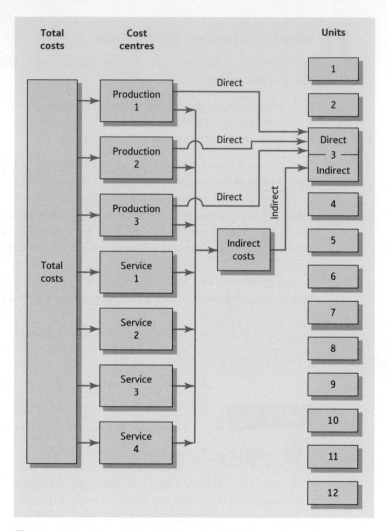

Figure 14.1 Absorption costing system: flow of costs

Stage 1: Allocate all costs to specific cost centres

Allocation is the process of charging the entire cost of an item to a cost centre (or a cost unit) without needing to apportion it or share it out in any way. It is essential that all costs are first allocated to a cost centre because they then become the responsibility of the manager of that centre. Some costs may be difficult to identify with a particular cost centre because they can be associated with a number of cost centres, e.g. factory rent or business rates. Nevertheless such costs should be charged to a specific cost centre and not a 'general' or a 'sundry' one (even though the relationship may be largely nominal). This requirement is very important because if it is not strictly applied some costs will not be monitored and they will then just spiral out of control.

After the costs have been allocated to a cost centre, the next step is to divide them into two broad categories: *production* cost centres and *service* cost centres. Production cost centres are those departments or sections where the product is manufactured or partly manufactured. *Service* cost centres are those sections or departments that provide a service to other cost centres (including other service cost centres).

Once we have classified the cost centres into 'production' and 'service' we can move on to Stage 2.

Stage 2: Share out the production service cost centre costs

There are two ways of sharing out the production service cost centre costs.

- A proportion of *each* cost is charged to all other cost centres that have benefited from the service provided.
- A proportion of the *total* of each production service cost centre's costs is charged to those other cost centres benefitting from the service provided.
- A proportion of is charged to those other cost centres benefiting from the service provided.

In practice a combination of both methods is usually adopted, i.e. some costs are charged out individually while the remainder are charged out in total.

Irrespective of which method is adopted the costs are usually shared out using some quantitative factor. A few of the more common methods are described below.

- *Numbers of employees.* This method would be used for those service cost centres that provide a service to individual employees, e.g. the canteen, the works manager's office and the wages office. Costs will then be apportioned on the basis of the number of employees working in a particular production department as a proportion of the total number of employees working in all production cost centres.
- *Floor area.* This method would be used for such cost centres as cleaning and building maintenance.
- *Activity.* Examples of where this method might be used include the drawings office (on the basis of drawings made), materials handling (based on the number of requisitions processed) and the transport department (on the basis of vehicle operating hours).

A problem arises in dealing with the apportionment of service cost centre costs when service cost centres provide a service for each other. The wages office, for example, will probably provide a service for the canteen staff, and in turn the canteen staff may provide a service for the wages staff. Before the service cost centre costs can be apportioned among the production cost centres, therefore, the service cost centre costs have to be charged out to each other.

Unfortunately, the problem becomes circular because it is not possible to charge some of the canteen costs to the wages office until the canteen has been charged with some of the costs of the wages office. Similarly, it is not possible to charge out the wages office costs until part of the canteen costs have been charged to the wages office. The problem is shown in diagrammatic form in Figure 14.2. The treatment of *reciprocal service costs* (as they are called) can become an involved and time-consuming process unless a clear policy decision is taken about their treatment. There are three main ways of dealing with this problem.

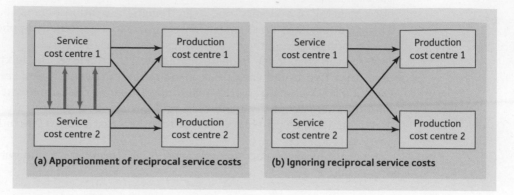

Figure 14.2 Service cost centre reciprocal costs

1 *Ignore interdepartmental service costs.* If this method is adopted, the respective service cost centre costs are only apportioned among the production cost centres. Any servicing that the service cost centres provide for each other is ignored.

2 *Specified order of closure.* This method requires the service cost centre costs to be closed off in some specified order and apportioned among the production cost centres and the remaining service cost centres. As the service cost centres are gradually closed off, there will eventually be only one service cost centre left. Its costs will then be apportioned among the production cost centres. Some order of closure has to be specified, and this may be quite arbitrary. It may be based, for example, on those centres that provide a service for the largest number of other service cost centres, or it could be based on the cost centres with the highest or the lowest cost in them prior to any interdepartmental servicing. It could also be based on an estimate of the benefit received by the other centres.

3 *Mathematical apportionment.* Each service cost centre's total cost is apportioned among production cost centres and other service cost centres on the basis of the estimated benefit provided. The effect is that additional amounts keep being charged back to a particular service cost centre as further apportionment takes place. It can take a very long time before there is no more cost to charge out to any of the service cost centres. However when that point is reached, all the service cost centre costs will then have been charged to the production cost centres. This method involves a great deal of exhaustive arithmetical apportionment. It is also very time-consuming, especially when there are a great many service cost centres. Although it is possible to carry out the calculations manually, it is only practical if done by computer.

In choosing one of the above methods it should be remembered that they all depend on an *estimate* of how much benefit one department receives from another. Such an estimate amounts to no more than an informed guess. It appears pedantic therefore, to build an involved arithmetical exercise on the basis of some highly questionable assumptions. We suggest, therefore, suggest that interdepartmental servicing charging should be ignored.

We have covered some fairly complicated procedures in dealing with Stages 1 and 2. So, before moving on to Stage 3, we use Example 14.1 to illustrate the procedure.

We can now move on to examine stage 3 of the absorption process.

Example 14.1	**Charging overhead to cost centres**

You are provided with the following indirect cost information relating to the New Manufacturing Company Limited for the year to 31 March 2016:

Cost centre:	£
Production 1: indirect expenses (to units)	24 000
Production 2: indirect expenses (to units)	15 000
Service cost centre A: allocated expenses	20 000
Service cost centre B: allocated expenses	8 000
Service cost centre C: allocated expenses	3 000

Additional information:
The estimated benefit provided by the three service cost centres to the other cost centres is as follows:
Service cost centre A: Production 1 50%; Production 2 30%; Service cost centre B 10%; Service cost centre C 10%.
Service cost centre B: Production 1 70%; Production 2 20%; Service cost centre C 10%.
Service cost centre C: Production 1 50%; Production 2 50%.

Required:
Calculate the total amount of overhead to be charged to cost centre units for both Production cost centre 1 and Production cost centre 2 for the year to 31 March 2016.

Answer to Example 14.1	*New Manufacturing Co. Ltd*

Overhead distribution schedule for the year to 31 March 2016

Cost centre	Production		Service		
	1	2	A	B	C
	£	£	£	£	£
Allocated indirect expenses	24 000	15 000	20 000	8 000	3 000
Apportion service cost centre costs:					
A (50 : 30 : 10 : 10)	10 000	6 000	(20 000)	2 000	2 000
B (70 : 20 : 0 : 10)	7 000	2 000	–	(10 000)	1 000
C (50 : 50 : 0 : 0)	3 000	3 000	–	–	(6 000)
Total overhead to be absorbed by specific units	44 000	26 000	–	–	–

Tutorial notes	1 Units passing through Production cost centre 1 will have to share total overhead expenditure amounting to £44,000. Units passing through Production cost centre 2 will have to share total overhead expenditure amounting to £26,000. The number of units passing through both departments may be the same. They might be assembled, for example, in cost centre 1 and packed in cost centre 2.
	2 The total amount of overhead to be shared amongst the units is £70,000 (44,000 + 26,000) or (£24,000 + 15,000 + 20,000 + 8000 + 3000). The total amount of overhead originally collected in each of the five cost centres does not change.
	3 This exhibit involves some interdepartmental reapportionment of service cost centre costs. However, no problem arises because of the way in which the question requires the respective service cost centre costs to be apportioned.
	4 The objective of apportioning service cost centre costs is to share them out among the production cost centres so that they can be included in the cost of specific units.

Stage 3: Absorb the production overhead

Once all the indirect costs have been collected in the production cost centres, the next step is to charge the total amount to specific units. This procedure is known as *absorption*.

The method of absorbing overhead into units is normally a simple one. Accountants recommend a single factor, preferably one that is related as closely as possible to the movement of overhead. In other words, an attempt is made to choose a factor that directly correlates with the amount of overhead expenditure incurred. Needless to say, like so much else in accounting, there is no obvious factor to choose!

There are six main methods that can be used for absorbing production overhead. They are all based on the same equation:

$$\text{Cost centre overhead absorption rate} = \frac{\text{total cost centre overhead}}{\text{total cost centre activity}}$$

The formulae for each of the six methods are as follows.

(1) Specific units

$$\text{Absorption rate} = \frac{\text{total cost centre overhead}}{\text{number of units processed in the cost centre}}$$

This method is the simplest to operate. The same rate is applied to each unit and so it is only suitable if the units are identical.

(2) Direct materials cost

$$\text{Absorption rate} = \frac{\text{total cost centre overhead}}{\text{cost centre total direct material costs}} \times 100$$

The direct material cost of each unit is then multiplied by the absorption rate.

It is unlikely that there will normally be a strong relationship between the direct material cost and the level of overheads. There might be some special cases, but they are probably quite unusual, e.g. where a company uses a high level of precious metals and its overheads strongly reflect the cost of safeguarding those materials.

(3) Direct labour cost

$$\text{Absorption rate} = \frac{\text{total cost centre overhead}}{\text{cost centre total direct labour costs}} \times 100$$

The direct labour cost of each unit is then multiplied by the absorption rate.

Overheads tend to relate to the amount of time that a unit spends in production and so this method may be particularly suitable since the direct labour cost is a combination of hours worked and rates paid. It may not be appropriate, however, where the total direct labour cost consists of a relatively low level of hours worked and of a high labour rate per hour because the cost will not then relate very closely to time spent in production.

(4) Prime cost

$$\text{Absorption rate} = \frac{\text{total cost centre overhead}}{\text{prime cost}} \times 100$$

The prime cost of each unit is then multiplied by the absorption rate. This method assumes that there is a close relationship between prime cost and overheads.

As there is probably no close relationship between either direct materials or direct labour and overheads, it is unlikely that there will be much of a correlation between prime cost and overheads. So the prime cost method tends to combine the disadvantages of both the direct materials cost and the direct labour cost methods without having any real advantages of its own.

(5) Direct labour hours

$$\text{Absorption rate} = \frac{\text{total cost centre overhead}}{\text{cost centre total direct labour hours}}$$

The direct labour hours of each unit are then multiplied by the absorption rate.

This method is highly acceptable, especially in those cost centres that are labour intensive because time spent in production is largely related to the cost of overhead incurred.

(6) Machine hours

$$\text{Absorption rate} = \frac{\text{total cost centre overhead}}{\text{cost centre total machine hours}}$$

The total machine hours used by each unit is then multiplied by the absorption rate.

This is a most appropriate method to use in those departments that are machine intensive. There is probably quite a strong correlation between the amount of machine time that a unit takes to produce and the amount of overhead incurred.

The various absorption methods are illustrated in Example 14.2.

Example 14.2

Calculation of overhead absorption rates

Old Limited is a manufacturing company. The following information relates to the assembling department for the year to 30 June 2017:

	Assembling department Total £000
Direct material cost incurred	400
Direct labour incurred	200
Total factory overhead incurred	100
Number of units produced	10 000
Direct labour hours worked	50 000
Machine hours used	80 000

Required:
Calculate the overhead absorption rates for the assembling department using each of the following methods:
(a) specific units
(b) direct material cost
(c) direct labour cost
(d) prime cost
(e) direct labour hours
(f) machine hours.

(a) Specific units:

$$\text{OAR} = \frac{\text{TCCO}}{\text{Number of units}} = \frac{£100\,000}{10\,000} = \underline{£10.00\text{ per unit}}$$

(b) Direct material cost:

$$\text{OAR} = \frac{\text{TCCO}}{\text{Direct material cost}} \times 100 = \frac{£100\,000}{400\,000} \times 100 = \underline{25\%}$$

of direct material cost incurred.

(c) Direct labour cost:

$$\text{OAR} = \frac{\text{TCCO}}{\text{Direct labour cost}} \times 100 = \frac{£100\,000}{200\,000} \times 100 = \underline{50\%}$$

of direct labour cost incurred.

(d) Prime cost:

$$\text{OAR} = \frac{\text{TCCO}}{\text{Prime cost}} \times 100 = \frac{£100\,000}{400\,000 + 200\,000} \times 100 = \underline{16.67\%}$$

of prime cost incurred.

(e) Direct labour hours:

$$\text{OAR} = \frac{\text{TCCO}}{\text{Direct labour hours}} = \frac{£100\,000}{50\,000} = \underline{£2.00\text{ per direct labour hour}}$$

(f) Machine hours:

$$\text{OAR} = \frac{\text{TCCO}}{\text{Machine hours}} = \frac{£100\,000}{80\,000} = \underline{£1.25\text{ per machine hour}}$$

Example 14.2 illustrates the six absorption methods outlined in the text. In practice, only one absorption method would normally be chosen for each production cost centre, although different production cost centres may adopt different methods, e.g. one may choose a direct labour-hour rate and another may adopt a machine hour rate.

The most appropriate absorption rate method will depend on individual circumstances. A careful study would have to be made of the correlation between (a) direct materials, direct labour, other direct expenses, direct labour hours and machine hours; and (b) total overhead expenditure. However it is generally accepted that overhead tends to move with time, so the longer a unit spends in production the more overhead it will incur. If this is the case, then benefit labour-intensive cost centres should use the direct labour hour method while machine-intensive departments should use the machine hour method.

A comprehensive example

At this stage it will be useful to illustrate overhead absorption in the form of a comprehensive example, although that does not mean that we are going to use hundreds of costs centres! The example chosen uses the minimum amount of information for us to bring together all the basic principles of overhead absorption.

Example 14.3

Overhead absorption

Oldham Limited is a small manufacturing company producing a variety of pumps for the oil industry. It operates from one factory that is geographically separated from its head office. The components for the pumps are assembled in the assembling department; they are then passed to the finishing department, where they are painted and packed. There are three service cost centres: administration, stores and work study.

The following information is relevant for the year to 30 June 2016:

Allocated cost centre overhead costs:	£000
Administration	70
Assembling	25
Finishing	9
Stores	8
Work study	18

Additional information:

1 The allocated cost centre overhead costs are all considered to be indirect costs as far as specific units are concerned.

2 35,000 machine hours were worked in the assembling department, and 60,000 direct labour hours in the finishing department.

3 The average number of employees working in each department was as follows:

Administration	15
Assembling	25
Finishing	40
Stores	2
Work study	3
	85

4 The stores received 15,000 requisitions from the assembling department, and 10,000 requisitions from the finishing department. The stores department did not provide a service for any other department.

5 The work study department carried out 2000 chargeable hours for the assembling department and 1000 chargeable hours for the finishing department.

6 One special pump (code named MEA 6) was produced. It took 10 machine hours of assembling time, and 15 direct labour hours were worked on it in the finishing department. Its total direct costs (materials and labour) amounted to £100.

Required:

(a) Calculate an appropriate absorption rate for:
  (i) the assembling department,
  (ii) the finishing department.

(b) Calculate the total factory cost of the special MEA 6 pump.

Answer Example 14.3(a)

Oldham Ltd
Overhead distribution schedule for the year to 30 June 2016

		Production		Service	
Cost centre	Assembling	Finishing	Administration	Stores	Work study
	£000	£000	£000	£000	£000
Allocated overhead costs (1)	25	9	70	8	18
Production					

Cost centre	Assembling £000	Production Finishing £000	Administration £000	Service Stores £000	Work study £000
Apportion administration:					
25 : 40 : 2 : 3 (2)	25	40	(70)	2	3
Apportion stores: 3 : 2 (3)	6	4	–	(10)	–
Apportion work study: 2 : 1 (4)	14	7	–	–	(21)
Total overhead to be absorbed	70	60	–	–	–

Tutorial notes

1   The allocated overhead costs were given in the question.

2   Administration costs have been apportioned on the basis of employees. Details were given in the question. There were 85 employees in the factory but 15 of them were employed in the administration department. Administration costs have, therefore, been apportioned on a total of 70 employees, or £1000 per employee. The administration department is the only service department to provide a service for the other service departments, so no problem of interdepartmental servicing arises.

3   The stores costs have been apportioned on the number of requisitions made by the two production cost centres, that is 15,000 + 10,000 = 25,000, or 3 to 2.

4   The work study costs have been apportioned on the basis of chargeable hours, i.e. 2000 + 1000 = 3000, or 2 to 1.

Calculation of chargeable rates:

1   Assembling department:

$$\frac{\text{TCCO}}{\text{Total machine hours}} = \frac{£70\,000}{35\,000} = £2.00 \text{ per machine hour}$$

2   Finishing department:

$$\frac{\text{TCCO}}{\text{Total direct labour hours}} = \frac{£60\,000}{60\,000} = £1.00 \text{ per direct labour hour}$$

It would seem appropriate to absorb the assembling department's overhead on the basis of machine hours because it appears to be a machine-intensive department. The finishing department appears more labour intensive and so its overhead has been absorbed on that basis.

Answer to Example 14.3(b)

MEA 6: Calculation of total factory cost

	£	£
Direct costs (as given in note 6)		100
Add: factory overhead:		
Assembling department (10 machine hours × £2.00 per MH)	20	
Finishing department (15 direct labour hours × £1.00 per DLH)	15	35
Total factory cost		135

Non-production overhead

News clip

Hornby shake-up

Model train maker Hornby reported a pre-tax loss of £4.5 million in the six months to September 30, 2015. This was caused by the introduction of a new stock monitoring distribution and logistics system which hit sales in July and August.

Source: Based on a *Financial Times* article, 9 Dec. 2015, p. 23.

In the previous section we concentrated on the apportionment and absorption of *production* overheads. Most companies will, however, incur expenditure on activities that are not directly connected with production activities. There could be for example selling and distribution costs, research and development costs and head office administrative expenses. How should these types of cost be absorbed into unit cost?

Before this question can be answered, it is necessary to find out *why* we would want to apportion them. There are three possible reasons:

- *Control.* The more that an entity's costs are broken down, the easier it is to monitor them. It follows that just as there is an argument for having a detailed system of responsibility accounting at cost centre level, so there is an argument for having a similar system at unit cost level. However, in the case of non-production expenses this argument is not a very strong one. The relationship between units produced and non-production overhead is usually so remote that no meaningful estimate of the benefit received can be made. The apportionment of non-production overhead is, therefore, merely an arithmetical exercise and no manager could be expected to take responsibility for costs charged to their cost centre in this way. From a control point of view, therefore, the exercise is not very helpful.
- *Selling price.* In some cases, it might be necessary to add to the production cost of a specific unit a proportion of non-production overhead in order to determine a selling price that covers all costs and allows a margin for profit. This system of fixing selling prices may apply in some industries, e.g. in tendering for long-term contracts or in estimating decorating costs. In most cases, however, selling prices are determined by the market and companies are not usually in a position to fix their selling prices based on cost with a percentage added on for profit (known as cost-plus pricing).
- *Stock valuation.* You might think that we need to include non-production overheads in valuing stocks but as *SSAP 9* does not permit them to be included they are usually ignored. This is largely because much more work will be involved if the management accounts had to be altered to suit the requirements of the financial accounts.

It is obvious from the above summary that there are few benefits to be gained by charging a proportion of non-production overhead to specific cost units. In theory, the exercise is attractive because it would be both interesting and useful to know the *actual* cost of each unit produced. In practice, however, it is impossible to arrive at any such cost, and so it seems pointless becoming engaged in a purely spurious arithmetical exercise.

The only real case for apportioning non-production overhead applies where selling prices can be based on cost. What can be done in those situations? There is still no obvious formula and an arbitrary estimate has still to be made. The easiest method is simply to add a percentage to the total production cost, perhaps based on this relationship between non-production overhead and total cost. This is bound to be a somewhat questionable method, since there can be no close relationship between production and non-production activities. It follows that the company's tendering or selling-price policy should not be too rigid if it is based on this type of cost-plus pricing.

Activity 14.1	You are a manager in a company that manufactures consumer products. Market prices are competitive and you need to keep down your costs in such a content does charging non-production overhead to unit costs serve any useful purpose?
	Explain Why.

Predetermined absorption rates

An absorption rate can be calculated on a historical basis i.e. after the event, or it can be predetermined i.e. calculated in advance.

As we have argued, there is no close correlation between fixed overhead and any particular measure of activity: it can only be apportioned on what seems to be a reasonable basis. However, if we know the total actual overhead incurred, we can make sure that it is all charged to specific units, even if we are not sure of the relationship that it has with any particular unit.

In order to do so we need to know the *actual cost of overheads* and the *actual activity level* (whether measured in machine hours, direct labour hours or on some other basis). In other words, we can only make the calculation when we know *what* has happened.

The adoption of *historical* absorption rates is not usually very practicable. We have to wait until the actual period is over before an absorption rate can be calculated, the products costed and the customers invoiced. It is therefore, preferable to use what is known as a *predetermined absorption rate*. This involves estimating the overhead likely to be incurred and the direct labour hours (or machine hours) that are expected to be worked. If one or other of these estimates turns out to be inaccurate, then we would have either undercharged our customers (if the rate was too low), or overcharged them (if the rate was too high).

This situation could be very serious for a company. Low selling prices caused by using a low absorption rate could have made the company's products very competitive, but there is not much point in selling a lot of units if they are being sold at a loss. Similarly, a high absorption rate may result in a high selling price. Each unit may then make a large profit but not enough units may be sold to enable the company to make an overall profit.

The difference between the actual overhead incurred and the total overhead charged to production (calculated on a predetermined basis) gives rise to what is known as a *variance*. If the actual overhead incurred is in excess of the amount charged out, the variance will be *adverse*, i.e. the profit will be less than expected. However, if the total overhead charged to production is less than was estimated, then the variance will be *favourable*. The effect of this procedure is shown in diagrammatic form in Figure 14.3. Other things being equal, a favourable variance gives rise to a higher profit, and an adverse variance results in a lower profit.

It is a cardinal rule in costing that variances should be written off to the profit and loss account at the end of the costing period in which they were incurred. It is not considered fair to burden the next period's accounts with the previous period's mistakes. In other words, we should start off the new accounting period with a clean sheet.

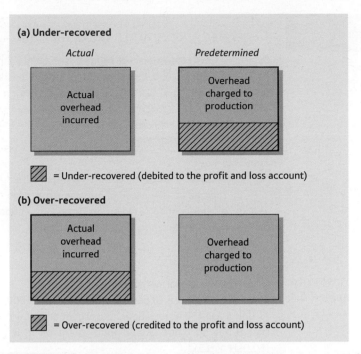

Figure 14.3 Predetermined rates under- and over-recovery of overhead

Throughout the preceding sections we have clearly expressed many reservations about the way in which accountants have traditionally dealt with overheads. In recent years, dissatisfaction about overhead absorption has become widespread, and now a different technique called *activity-based costing* is being advocated. We review it briefly in the next section.

Activity-based costing

As we have seen, the calculation of product costs involves identifying the *direct costs* of a product and then adding (or absorbing) a proportion of the *indirect costs* (i.e. the overheads) to the total of the direct costs.

This was the method used for most of the twentieth century. It was only in the 1980s that it began to be apparent that the traditional method of absorbing overhead was inappropriate in an advanced manufacturing environment. As it involves calculating the total cost of overheads in a particular cost centre and charging them out to particular units on a time basis, the total cost is *averaged* among those units that flow through that particular cost centre. The assumption behind this procedure is that the more time that a unit spends in production, the more overhead it will incur. This means that no distinction is made between fixed and variable overhead and that some units may be charged with a cost that they did not certain.

A comparison between the more traditional overhead absorption method and activity based costing is shown in Example 14.4.

Example 14.4 illustrates the potential unfairness of the traditional method of absorbing overhead. As the method *averages* the total cost among particular units, those units that do not benefit from a particular activity bear a disproportionate amount of the total cost. In the above example, Unit A should only be charged £180 of overhead (compared with £750 under the traditional method), whereas Unit B should be charged £820 (compared with £250 under the traditional method).

Example 14.4

Overhead absorption a fairer method

In Jasmine Ltd's production cost centre 1, two units are produced: Unit A and Unit B, the total overhead cost being £1000. This is made up of two costs: (1) machine set-up costs of £800; and (2) inspection costs of £200. Overhead is absorbed on the basis of direct labour hours. The total direct labour hours (DLH) amount to 200. Unit A requires 150 DLH and Unit B 50 DLH.

The machinery for Unit A only needs to be set up once whereas Unit B requires nine set-ups. Unit A and Unit B both require two inspections each.

Required:

(a) Calculate the total overhead to be charged to Unit A and to Unit B using:
   (i) the traditional method of absorbing overhead
   (ii) a fairer method based on set-up and inspection costs
(b) Prepare a table comparing the two methods.

Answer to Example 14.4

(a) (i) The traditional method

The absorption rate is £5 per direct labour hour (£1000 total overhead ÷ 200 direct labour hours). As Unit A has 150 direct labour hours spent on it, it will absorb £750 (150 DLH × £5) of overhead. Unit B has 50 direct labour hours spent on it; it will, therefore, absorb £250 of overhead (50 DLH × £5).

(a) (ii) A fairer method

Each set-up costs £80 [£800 ÷ 10 (1 set-up for A + 9 set-ups for B)].
Each inspection costs £50 [£200 ÷ 4 (2 inspections for A + 2 inspections for B)].
The total overhead charged to Unit A, therefore, would be £180: £80 for set-up costs (1 set-up × £80) plus £100 inspection costs (2 inspections × £50).
Unit B would be charged a total of £820: £720 of set-up costs (9 set-ups × £80) and £100 inspection costs (2 inspections × £50).
The fairer method illustrated here is known as *activity-based costing*.

(b) Comparing the two methods

The table below compares the two approaches to overhead absorption:

Jasmine Limited

Product	Overhead absorbed on a traditional basis £	Overhead absorbed on an activity basis £
A	750	180
B	250	820
Total	1 000	1 000

It follows that if the eventual selling price is based on cost, the traditional method would grossly inflate Unit A's selling price and deflate Unit B's selling price. Unit A's selling price would probably be highly uncompetitive and only a few units might be sold. Unit B's selling price would probably be highly competitive. A great many units of Unit B might be sold, therefore, but the total sales revenue may not be sufficient to recover all the overhead costs.

The fairer method that we have described is called activity-based costing (ABC). In order to illustrate the principles behind ABC, we have made reference to just one cost centre. However, in practice overheads for the whole of the entity (including both manufacturing and non-manufacturing overheads) would be dealt with collectively. They would then be allocated to *cost pools*, i.e. similar areas of activity. It is estimated that even in the largest entities a total of about 30 cost pools is the maximum number that it is practicable to handle. This means that some costs may be allocated to a cost pool where there is only a distant relationship between some of the costs. In other words, like the traditional method of absorbing overheads, ABC also involves some averaging of costs.

Once the overheads have all been allocated to an appropriate cost pool, a *cost driver* for each pool is selected. A cost driver is the main cause of the costs attached to that pool. Once again some approximation is necessary because some costs collected in that pool may only have a loose connection with the selected driver. By dividing the total cost in a particular cost pool by the cost driver, an overhead cost per driver can be calculated. For example, suppose the total overhead cost collected in a particular cost pool totalled £1000 and the costs in that pool were driven by the number of material requisitions (say 200), the cost driver rate would be £5 per material requisition (£1000 cost ÷ 200 material requisitions).

The final stage is to charge an appropriate amount of overhead to each unit benefiting from the service provided by the various cost pools. So if a particular unit required 10 material requisitions and the cost driver rate was £5 per material requisition, it would be charged £50 (£5 per material requisition × 10 requisitions). Of course, it may benefit from the services provided by a number of other cost pools, so it would collect a share of overhead from each of them as well.

The above procedures are illustrated in Example 14.5.

Example 14.5	**Activity-based costing (ABC)**

Shish Limited has recently introduced an ABC system. The following details relate to the month of March 2017.

1 Four cost pools have been identified: parts, maintenance, stores and administration.

2 The cost drivers that were identified with each cost pool are: total number of parts, maintenance hours, number of material requisitions and number of employees.

3 Costs and activities during the month were:

Cost pool	Total overhead £000	Activity	Quantity
Parts	10 000	Number of parts	500
Maintenance	18 000	Number of maintenance hours	600
Stores	10 000	Number of material requisitions	20
Administration	2 000	Number of employees	40

4 500 units of Product X3 were produced. This production run required 100 parts and 200 maintenance hours; 6 material requisitions were made and 10 employees worked on the units.

Required:
Using ABC, calculate the total amount of overhead absorbed by each unit of Product X3 in March 2017.

Answer Example 14.5

Shish Ltd

Cost pool	Overhead	Cost driver	Cost driver rate	Usage by Product X3	Overhead cost charged to Product X3
(1)	(2) £000	(3)	(4) £	(5)	(6) £
Parts	10 000	500 parts	20	100 parts	2 000
Maintenance	18 000	600 hours	30	200 hours	6 000

Cost pool	Overhead	Cost driver	Cost driver rate	Usage by Product X3	Overhead cost charged to Product X3
(1)	(2)	(3)	(4)	(5)	(6)
Stores	10 000	20 requisitions	500	6 requisitions	3 000
Administration	2 000	40 employees	50	10 employees	500
Total overhead to be absorbed by Product X3					11 500

1 Column (4) has been obtained by dividing the data in column (2) by the data in column (3).

2 The data in column (6) has been obtained by multiplying the data in column (4) by the data in column (5).

3 The total amount of £11,500 shown in column (6) is the total amount of overhead to be absorbed by Product X3.

Solution

The total amount of overhead to be absorbed by each unit of Product X3 would be £23 (£11,500 ÷ 500 units).

ABC is an attempt to absorb overhead on the demands that a particular unit in production makes of the various resources that it uses before it is completed and becomes part of the 'finished stock'. In traditional overhead absorption costing, a unit is charged with the *average* charge for overheads irrespective of what proportion relates to that specific unit. This means that some units are charged with more than their fair share of overheads while others are perhaps charged with much less.

There is no difference in principle between ABC and traditional overhead absorption costing. ABC simply looks for a closer relationship between individual activities and the relationship that they have with specific units of production, while the traditional method adopts a more general approach. However, ABC does not require any distinction to be made between production overhead and non-production overhead – an issue that is largely ignored in traditional overhead absorption.

❗ Questions you should ask

The topic covered in this chapter is one that should encourage non-accountants to ask some very searching questions. We suggest that you use the following as a starting point.

- Have you had any problems in identifying some costs with particular cost centres?
- If so, which?
- How did you decide which cost centre to charge them to?
- What methods have you used to charge service cost centre costs to production cost centres?
- Have you ignored any interservice cost centre charging?
- If not, how have you dealt with the problem?
- What activity bases have you used to absorb overheads into product costs?
- Have you worked out absorption rates on a historical or a predetermined basis?
- What have you done about non-production overheads?
- Is there a case for switching to activity-based costing?

Conclusion

In this chapter we have continued our study of cost accounting that we began in Chapter 13. In this chapter we have explained how production overheads are absorbed into product costs. In summary, the procedure is as follows.

1 Allocate all costs to appropriate cost centres.
2 Distinguish between production and service cost centres.
3 Examine the individual costs in each production service cost centre and, where possible, apportion them on some equitable basis to other cost centres.
4 Apportion the total of any remaining service cost centre costs either (1) to production cost centres or (2) to production cost centres as well as other service cost centres. If (2), continue to reapportion the service cost centre costs until they have all been charged to production cost centres.
5 Select an absorption method based on either the number of units flowing through a particular cost centre or on the time a unit spends in the cost centre based on direct labour cost, direct labour hours or machine hours.
6 Divide the total overhead in each production cost centre by the selected absorption factor.
7 Charge each unit with its share of overhead e.g. direct labour hours or machine hours × the absorption rate.
8 Add the amount calculated to the total direct cost of that unit.

It is also necessary to determine whether the above procedure should be done on a historical or a predetermined basis and whether non-production overheads should also be absorbed into product cost.

The above method has been in use for well over 100 years. Some academics and practitioners do not believe that it is suitable for modern manufacturing methods. In recent years a new method called *activity-based costing* has been adopted by some large companies. ABC is similar to traditional overhead absorption costing except that both production and non-production overheads are assigned to one of a number of identifiable cost pools. The main factor that causes those overheads to be incurred (known as a *cost driver*) is identified and a cost driver rate calculated (the pool overhead divided by the cost driver). Products are then charged with their share of each of the cost pool overheads.

Key points

1 In order to charge unit costs with a share of production overheads, *all* costs should first be identified with a specific cost centre.

2 Some cost centres provide a service to other cost centres. These are known as *service cost centres*. The various costs collected in the service costs centres should be shared out on an apportionment basis among the other cost centres. Some costs collected in the service cost centres may be apportioned separately; otherwise, the *total service cost centre cost* will be apportioned. An element of cross-charging arises when the service centres provide services for each other. This can be resolved either by ignoring any cross-charging, apportioning the total of the service centre costs in some specified order, or by mathematical apportionment.

3 Once the production cost centres have received their share of the service centre costs, an absorption rate for each production cost centre should be calculated. The

traditional method is to take the total of each production cost centre's indirect cost (i.e. its overhead) and divide it either by the actual (or planned) direct labour hours, or by the machine hours actually worked (or planned to be worked) in that particular cost centre.

4 The absorption rate calculated for each production cost centre is used to charge each unit passing through that cost centre with a share of the production overhead.

5 The total production cost of a particular unit can then be calculated as follows:

direct materials cost + direct labour cost + direct expenses +

share of production overhead = total production cost.

6 The absorption of non-production overhead (head office administrative expenses, selling and distribution costs and research development costs) is not recommended, except when it may be required for pricing purposes.

7 Absorption rates will normally be predetermined, i.e. they will be based on planned costs and anticipated activity levels.

8 The under-absorption or over-absorption of overhead should be written off to the profit and loss account in the period when it was spent.

9 In recent years a new way of dealing with the absorption of overheads called *activity-based costing* has been suggested. ABC involves charging overheads to common cost pools, identifying what main factor drives the costs in each of the respective pools, and then calculating a cost driver rate. Units are then charged with their share of each of the pool costs.

Check your learning

The answers to these questions can be found within the text.

1 What is (a) a production cost centre, (b) a service cost centre?

2 What do the terms 'allocate', 'apportion' and 'absorb' mean?

3 Suggest three ways that service cost centre costs may be charged to other cost centres.

4 What is meant by 'reciprocal service costs'?

5 Indicate three ways to deal with them.

6 What is the basic formula for absorbing production overheads into product costs?

7 List six methods of how this may be done.

8 What is non-production overhead?

9 How should it be absorbed into product costs?

10 What is a predetermined absorption rate?

11 What is meant by under- and over-recovery of overhead?

12 What do the initials 'ABC' mean?

13 What is a cost pool and a cost driver?

14 How does ABC differ from traditional absorption costing?

News story quiz

Remember the news story at the beginning of this chapter? Go back to that story and reread it before answering the following questions.

Rolls Royce is another famous British company struggling to compete in a highly competitive market. This article outlines some of the recent measures that it is taking after already making five profit warnings.

Questions

1 Why do you think that it has taken so many profit warning before any serious attempts were made to revive its financial fortunes?

2 Is it likely that a reorganisation of the company's managerial structure and divisional structure will make a significant difference to reducing its costs?

3 What would you identify as the major cause of the company's possible financial struggles?

Tutorial questions

The answers to questions marked with an asterisk may be found in Appendix 4.

14.1 'Arithmetical precision for precision's sake.' How far is this statement true of the traditional methods used in absorbing overheads into product costs?

14.2 Has total absorption costing any relevance in a service industry?

14.3 Some non-accountants believe that the technique of overhead absorption was devised simply to provide jobs for accountants. How far do you agree?

14.4 How should reciprocal service costs be dealt with when calculating product costs?

14.5 Assess the usefulness of activity-based costing in managerial decision making.

14.6* Scar Limited has two production departments and one service department. The following information relates to January 2016:

		£
Allocated expenses:		
Production department: A		65 000
	B	35 000
Service department		50 000

The allocated expenses shown above are all indirect expenses as far as individual units are concerned.

The benefit provided by the service department is shared among the production departments A and B in the proportion 60 : 40.

Required:
Calculate the amount of overhead to be charged to specific units for both production department A and production department B.

14.7* Bank Limited has several production departments. In the assembly department it has been estimated that £250,000 of overhead should be charged to that particular department. It now wants to charge a customer for a specific order. The relevant data are:

	Assembly department	Specific unit
Number of units	50 000	–
Direct material cost (£)	500 000	8.00
Direct labour cost (£)	1 000 000	30.00
Prime cost (£)	1 530 000	40.00
Direct labour hours	100 000	3.5
Machine hours	25 000	0.75

The accountant is not sure which overhead absorption rate to adopt.

Required:
Calculate the overhead to be absorbed by a specific unit passing through the assembly department using each of the following overhead absorption rate methods:

(a) specific units
(b) percentage of direct material cost
(c) percentage of direct labour cost
(d) percentage of prime cost
(e) direct labour hours
(f) machine hours.

14.8 The following information relates to the activities of the production department of Clough Limited for the month of March 2017:

	Production department	Order number 123
Direct materials consumed (£)	120 000	20
Direct wages (£)	180 000	25
Overhead chargeable (£)	150 000	
Direct labour hours worked	30 000	5
Machine hours operated	10 000	2

The company adds a margin of 50 per cent to the total production cost of specific units in order to cover administration expenses and to provide a profit.

Required:
(a) Calculate the total selling price of order number 123 if overhead is absorbed using the following methods of overhead absorption:
   direct labour hours;
   machine hours.
(b) State which of the two methods you would recommend for the production department.

14.9 Burns Limited has three production departments (processing, assembly and finishing) and two service departments (administration and work study). The following information relates to April 2018:

	£
Direct material	
Processing	100 000
Assembling	30 000
Finishing	20 000
Direct labour	
Processing (£4 × 100 000 hours)	400 000
Assembling (£5 × 30 000 hours)	150 000
Finishing (£7 × 10 000 hours) + (£5 × 10 000 hours)	120 000
Administration	65 000
Work study	33 000
Other allocated costs	
Processing	15 000
Assembling	20 000
Finishing	10 000
Administration	35 000
Work study	12 000

Apportionment of costs:

	Process %	Assembling %	Finishing %	Work study %
Administration	50	30	15	5
Work study	70	20	10	–

Total machine hours: Processing 25 000

All units produced in the factory pass through the three production departments before they are put into stock. Overhead is absorbed in the processing department on the basis of machine hours, on the basis of direct labour hours in the assembling department, and on the basis of the direct labour cost in the finishing department.

The following details relate to unit XP6:

	£	£
Direct materials		
Processing	15	
Assembling	6	
Finishing	1	22
Direct labour		
Processing (2 hours)	8	
Assembling (1 hour)	5	
Finishing	12	25
[(1 hour × £7) + (1 hour × £5)]		
Prime cost		47

XP6: Number of machine hours in the processing department = 6

Required:
Calculate the total cost of producing unit XP6.

14.10 Outlane Limited's overhead budget for 2019 is as follows:

	£000
Administration	100
Depreciation of machinery	80
Employer's national insurance	10
Heating and lighting	15
Holiday pay	20
Indirect labour cost	10
Insurance: machinery	40
property	11
	c/f 286

	£000
	b/f 286
Machine maintenance	42
Power	230
Rent and rates	55
Supervision	50
	663

The company has four production departments: L, M, N and O. The following information relates to each department.

Department	L	M	N	O
Total number of employees	400	300	200	100
Number of indirect workers	20	15	10	5
Floor space (square metres)	2 000	1 500	1 000	1 000

Department	L	M	N	O
Kilowatt hours' power consumption	30 000	50 000	90 000	60 000
Machine maintenance hours	500	400	300	200
Machine running hours	92 000	38 000	165 000	27 000
Capital cost of machines (£)	110 000	40 000	50 000	200 000
Depreciation rate of machines (on cost)	20%	20%	20%	20%
Cubic capacity	60 000	30 000	10 000	50 000

Previously, the company has absorbed overhead on the basis of 100 per cent of the direct labour cost. It has now decided to change to a separate machine hour rate for each department.

The company has been involved in two main contracts during the period, the details of which are as follows:

Department	Contract 1: Direct labour hours and machine hours	Contract 2: Direct labour hours and machine hours
L	60	20
M	30	10
N	10	10
O	–	60
	100	100

Direct labour cost per hour in both departments was £3.00.

Required:
(a) Calculate the overhead to be absorbed by both contract 1 and contract 2 using the direct labour cost method.
(b) Calculate the overhead to be absorbed using a machine hour rate for each department.

Budgeting

Who watches the policeman?

The FRC's 2015 budget

The Financial Reporting Council (FRC) published its Plan and Budget for 2015/2016 on 25 March 2015 The Plan confirms the FRC's mission, highlights progress on its three-year strategy and sets out its priorities for the coming year.

The budget for the FRC's core operating activities will increase by 6% to enable it to deliver its priorities and support the Department for Business, Innovation and Skills in preparing for the implementation of the new EU Audit Directive and Regulation. The amount raised through the preparers' levy will increase by 6.1%. In response to stakeholder feedback on the Draft Plan & Budget, the increase in the minimum levy will be limited to 3.2%. The levy payable by larger organisations will vary according to their market capitalisation (or, where applicable, turnover). The contribution from the accountancy professional bodies will increase by 2.5%.

The budget for audit quality reviews will increase by 12.5% in response to the Competition and Market Authority requirements.

Source: Based on www.frc.org.uk/News-and-Events/FRC-Press/Press2...

Questions relating to this news story can be found on page 347 ➡

About this chapter

This chapter explores the nature and purpose of a budget. It outlines the various types of budgets, how they all fit together and how they may be used to keep a tight control of an entity's operations. It also explains that budgets and budgetary control are not neutral techniques. They have an impact on human behaviour and this has to be taken into account when using them.

Learning objectives

By the end of this chapter, you should be able to:

- describe the nature and purpose of budgeting and budgetary control;
- list the steps involved in operating a budgetary control system;
- describe the difference between fixed and flexible budgets;
- outline the behavioural consequences of a budgetary control system.

Why this chapter is important

The more knowledge that you have as a manager, the more influence you will be able to exert. This applies particularly to budgeting so this chapter is important for the following reasons.

- Your job will probably involve you in supplying information for budgetary purposes. It is easier to supply what is needed if you know what it is for and how it will be used.
- You are likely to have to prepare a budget for your department. Obviously, it is easier to do this if you have had some training in how to do it.
- You may be supplied with various reports that show your budgeted results against actual results. You may then be asked what you are going to do to correct any variance. The impact that this will have on you will depend on a number of factors, such as how familiar you are with the way that the information has been compiled, what inherent deficiencies it may have and what reliability you can place on it.

Budgeting is not a process that is of interest only to accountants as it should involve all employees working in the entity. As a manager you will find that if you throw yourself wholeheartedly into the process it will help you to do your job more effectively.

Budgeting and budgetary control

News clip

Finance Manager appointment

Isle of Man Post Office has announced that as from May 2016 David Fayle has been appointed to the position of Finance Manager. David first joined the Post Office in 2008 as Management Accounts Clerk, which involved preparing financial management accounts for business unit managers and executive directors. In his new role David will have responsibility for the management accounting team within the Post Office. This includes looking after year-end accounting processes, budgeting and forecasting. He will also have responsibility for providing business information to management and the board.

Source: Based on www.iompost.com/out-news/press-releases/david-fayle-promoted-toisle-of-man-post-office-finance-manager/01/01/2016.

We start our analysis by explaining what we mean by a 'budget' and 'budgetary control'.

Budget

The term *budget* is probably well understood by the layman. Many people, for example, 'budget' for their own household expenses even if it is only by making a rough comparison between next month's salary and the next month's expenditure. Such a budget may not be very detailed but it contains all the main features of what accountants mean by a budget. There are as follows:

- *Policies:* budgets are based on the policies needed to fulfil the objectives of the entity.
- *Data:* they are usually expressed in monetary terms.
- *Documentation:* they are usually written down.
- *Period:* they relate to a future period of time.

Most entities will usually prepare a considerable number of what might be called sub-budgets. A manufacturing entity, for example, might prepare sales, production and administration budgets. These budgets would then be combined into an overall budget known as a *master budget*. A master budget is made up of a budgeted profit and loss account, a budgeted balance sheet and a budgeted cash flow statement.

Once a master budget has been prepared, it will be examined closely to see whether the overall plan can be accommodated. It might be the case, for example, that the sales budget indicates a large increase in sales. This will have required the production budgets to be prepared on the basis of this extra sales demand. The cash budget, however, might show that the entity could not finance the extra sales and production activity out of its budgeted cash resources, so additional financing arrangements will have to be made because obviously no entity would normally turn down the opportunity of increasing its sales.

Budgets are useful because they encourage managers to examine what they have done in relation to what they *could* do. However, the full benefits of a budgeting system only became apparent when it is used for *control* purposes. This involves making a constant comparison between the actual results and the budgeted results, and then taking any necessary corrective action. This procedure is called 'budgetary control'.

Budgetary control

When the actual results for a period are compared with the budgeted results and it is seen that there are material or significant differences (called variances), then corrective action must be taken to ensure that future results will conform to the budget. This is the essence of budgetary control, as can be seen in Figure 15.1. It has several important features.

- *Responsibilities:* managerial responsibilities are clearly defined.
- *Action plan:* individual budgets lay down a detailed plan of action for a particular sphere of responsibility.
- *Adherence:* managers have a responsibility to adhere to their budgets once the budgets have been approved.
- *Monitoring:* the actual performance is monitored constantly and compared with the budgeted results.
- *Correction:* corrective action is taken if the actual results differ significantly from the budget.
- *Approval:* departures from the budget are only permitted if they have been approved by senior management.
- *Variances:* those that are unaccounted for are subject to individual investigation.

Any variance that occurs should be investigated carefully. The current actual performance will then be immediately brought back into line with the budget if this is considered necessary. Sometimes the budget itself will be changed, e.g. if there is an unexpected increase in sales. Such changes may, of course, have an effect on the other budgets and so cannot be done in isolation.

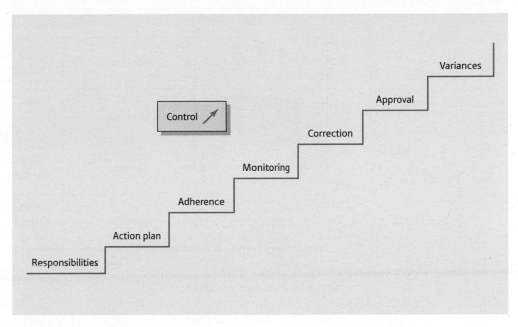

Figure 15.1 Budgetary control: features

Now that we have outlined the nature and purpose of budgeting and budgetary control, we are in a position to investigate how the system works.

Procedure

In order to make it easier for you to follow the budget procedure we will break it down into four main stages: (1) who administers it; (2) what they aim to do; (3) the length of the budget period; and (4) how the master budget is made up. These four stages are shown in pictorial form in Figure 15.2. We start by first examining the administration of the budget process.

Administration

The budget procedure may be administered by a special budget committee or it may be supervised by the accounting function. It will be necessary for the budget committee to lay down general guidelines in accordance with the company's objectives and to ensure that individual departments do not operate completely independently. The production department, for example, will need to know what the company is budgeting to sell so that it can prepare its own budget on the basis of those sales. However, the detailed production budget must still remain the entire responsibility of the production manager.

This procedure is in line with the concept of responsibility accounting (see Chapter 13). If the control procedure is to work properly, managers must be given responsibility for clearly defined areas of activity, such as their particular cost centre. They are then fully answerable for all that goes on there. Unless managers are given complete authority to act within clearly defined guidelines, they cannot be expected to account for something for which they are not responsible. This means that if the budgeting control system is to work, managers must help prepare, amend and approve their own cost centre's budget.

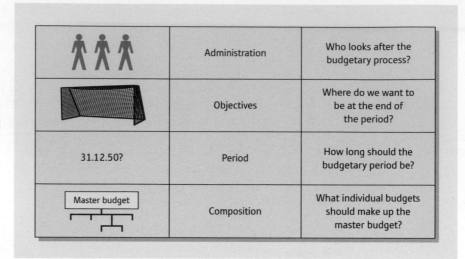

Figure 15.2 Budget procedure

Objectives

The budget procedure starts with an examination of the entity's objectives. These may be very simple. They may include, for example, an overall wish to maximise profits, to foster better relations with customers or to improve the working conditions of employees. Once an entity has decided on its overall objectives, it is in a position to formulate some detailed plans.

These will probably start with a *forecast*. There is a technical difference between a forecast and a budget. A forecast is a prediction of what is *likely* to happen, whereas a budget is a carefully prepared plan of what *should* happen.

Period

The main budget period is usually based on a calendar year. It could be shorter or longer depending on the nature of the product cycle. The fashion industry, for example, may adopt a short budget period of less than a year, while the construction industry may opt for a five-year period. Irrespective of the industry, however, a calendar year is usually a convenient period to choose as the base period because it fits in with financial accounting requirements.

Besides determining the main budget period, it is also necessary to prepare budgets for much shorter periods. These are required for budgetary control purposes in order to compare the actual results with the budgeted results on a frequent basis. The sub-budget periods for some activities may need to be very short if very tight control is to be exercised over them, e.g. the cash budget may be broken down into weeks, while the administration budget may only need to be broken down into quarters.

Composition

In order to give you as wide a picture of the budgeting process as possible we will assume that we are dealing with a manufacturing company in the private sector. In practice the structure and content is likely to be extremely complex but we have stripped it down to its bare minimum. Even so, if you look at Figure 15.3 you will see that it still looks very involved. There is no need to worry! Later on in the chapter we will be using a quantitative example to illustrate the process and then it should all click into place.

In commercial organisations, the first budget to be prepared is usually the sales budget. Once the sales for the budget period (and for each sub-budget period) have been determined, the next stage is to calculate the effect on production. This will then enable an agreed level of activity to be determined. The *level of activity* may be expressed in so many units or as a percentage of the theoretical productive capacity of the entity. Once the level of activity has been established, then departmental managers can be instructed to prepare their budgets on that basis.

Let us assume, for example, that 1000 units can be sold for a particular budget period. The production department manager will need this information in order to prepare his or her budget. This does not necessarily mean that the budget will be for a production level of 1000 units because allowance will also have to be made for the budgeted level of opening and closing stocks.

The budgeted production level will then be translated into how much material and labour will be required to meet that particular level. Similarly, it will be necessary to prepare overhead budgets. Much of the general overhead expenditure of the company (such as factory administrative costs, head office costs and research and development expenditure) will be fixed and it will not be affected by the activity level. One type of overhead, however, that may be affected by the activity level is the sales and distribution overhead budget because an increase in the number of units sold, for example, may involve additional delivery costs.

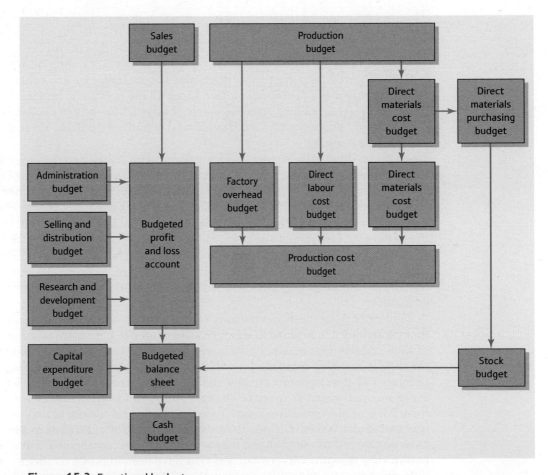

Figure 15.3 Functional budgets

Source: Adapted from Chartered Institute of Management Accountants (2005). CIMA Official Terminology, Oxford: CIMA Publishers.

Not all entities start the budget process with sales. Local authorities are a good example. They usually prepare a budget on the basis of what they are likely to spend. The total budgeted expenditure is then compared with the total amount of council tax needed to cover it after allowing for grants and other income. If the political cost of an increase in council tax appears to be too high, then the council will require a reduction in the budgeted expenditure. Once the budget has been set, and the council tax has been levied on that basis, departments have to work within the budgets laid down. However, since the budget will have been prepared on an estimate of the actual expenditure for the last two or three months of the old financial year, account has to be taken of any a surplus or shortfall brought forward into the current year. If the estimate eventually proves excessive, the local authority will have overtaxed for that year. This means that it has got some additional funds available to cushion the current year's expenditure. Of course, if it has undertaxed for any balance brought forward, departments might have to start cutting back in the current year.

Activity 15.1	A local authority has underestimated its expenditure for the last two months of the financial year to 31 March. What can it do to cover the deficit in the next financial year? Indicate what options are open to it.

This process is quite different in the private sector because the budgeted sales effectively determine all the other budgets. In a local authority it is the expenditure budgets that determine what the council tax should be and it is only the control exercised by central government and by the local authority itself that places a ceiling on what is spent. A budget prepared for a particular department, cost centre or any other responsibility centre is known as a *functional budget*. Once all the functional budgets have been prepared, they are combined into the *master budget*. The master budget is, in effect, a consolidated budgeted profit and loss account, a budgeted balance sheet and a budgeted cash flow statement.

An initial draft of the master budget may not be acceptable to the senior management of the company. This may be because it cannot cope with that particular budgeted level of activity, e.g. as a result of production or cash constraints. Indeed, one of the most important budgets is the *cash budget*. The cash budget translates all the other functional budgets (including that for capital expenditure) into cash terms. It will show in detail the pattern of cash inputs and outputs for the main budget period, as well as for each sub-budget period. If it shows that the company will have difficulty in financing a particular budgeted level of activity (or if there is going to be a period when cash is exceptionally tight), the management will have an opportunity to seek out alternative sources of finance.

This latter point illustrates the importance of being aware of future commitments, so that something can be done in advance if there are likely to be constraints (irrespective of their nature). The master budget usually takes so long to prepare, however, that by the time it has been completed it will be almost impossible to make major alterations (although IT developments are now making this less of a difficulty). It is then tempting for senior management to make changes to the functional budgets without referring them back to individual cost centre managers. It is most unwise to make changes in this way because it is then difficult to use such budgets for control purposes. If managers have not agreed to the changes, they will argue with considerable force that they can hardly take responsibility for budgets that have been imposed on them.

In the next section we use a comprehensive example to illustrate how all the functional budgets fit together.

A comprehensive example

It would be very difficult to follow the basic procedures involved in the preparation of functional budgets if we used an extremely detailed example. The example that we are going to work through cuts out much of the detail and only illustrates the main procedures. Nevertheless, there are still 14 steps to take!

Example 15.1

Preparation of functional budgets

Sefton Limited manufactures one product known as EC2. The following information relates to the preparation of the budget for the year to 31 March 2017:

1 Sales budget details for product EC2:
   Expected selling price per unit: £100.
   Expected sales in units: 10,000.
   All sales are on credit terms.

2 EC2 requires 5 units of raw material E and 10 units of raw material C. E is expected to cost £3 per unit, and C £4 per unit. All goods are purchased on credit terms.

3 Two departments are involved in producing EC2: machining and assembly.

The following information is relevant:

	Direct labour per unit of product (hours)	Direct labour rate per hour £
Machining	1.00	6
Assembling	0.50	8

4 The finished production overhead costs are expected to amount to £100,000.

5 At 1 April 2016, 800 units of EC2 are expected to be in stock at a value of £52,000, 4500 units of raw material E at a value of £13,500, and 12,000 units of raw materials at a value of £48,000. Stocks of both finished goods and raw materials are planned to be 10 per cent above the expected opening stock levels as at 1 April 2016.

6 Administration, selling and distribution overhead is expected to amount to £150,000.

7 Other relevant information:
   (a) Opening trade debtors are expected to be £80,000. Closing trade debtors are expected to amount to 15 per cent of the total sales for the year.
   (b) Opening trade creditors are expected to be £28,000. Closing trade creditors are expected to amount to 10 per cent of the purchases for the year.
   (c) All other expenses will be paid in cash during the year.
   (d) Other balances at 1 April 2016 are expected to be as follows:

	£	£
Share capital: ordinary shares		225 000
Retained profits		17 500
Proposed dividend		75 000
Fixed assets at cost	250 000	
Less: Accumulated depreciation	100 000	
		150 000
Cash at bank and in hand		2 000

8 Capital expenditure will amount to £50,000, payable in cash on 1 April 2016.

9 Fixed assets are depreciated on a straight-line basis at a rate of 20 per cent per annum on cost.

Required:

As far as the information permits, prepare all the relevant budgets for Sefton Limited for the year to 31 March 2017.

Answer to Example 15.1

In order to make it easier for you to become familiar with the budgeting procedure we will take you through it step by step.

Step 1: Prepare the sales budget

Units of EC2		Selling price per unit £		Total sales value £
10 000	×	100	=	1 000 000

Step 2: Prepare the production budget

	Units
Sales of EC2	10 000
Less: Opening stock	800
	9 200
Add: Desired closing stock (opening stock + 10%)	880
Production required	= 10 080

Step 3: Prepare the direct materials usage budget

Direct materials:

E: 5 units × 10 080	=	50 400 units
C: 10 units × 10 080	=	100 800 units

Step 4: Prepare the direct materials purchases budget

Direct materials:	=	E (units)	C (units)
Usage (as per Step 3)		50 400	100 800
Less: Opening stock		4 500	12 000
		45 900	88 800
Add: Desired closing stock		4 950	13 200
(opening stock + 10%)		50 850	102 000
		× £3	× £4
Direct material purchases	=	£152 550	= £408 000

Step 5: Prepare the direct labour budget

	Machining	Assembling
Production units (as per Step 2)	10 080	10 080
× direct labour hours required	× 1 DLH	× 0.50 DLH
	10 080 DLH	5 040 DLH
× direct labour rate per hour	× £6	× £8
Direct labour cost	= £60 480	= £40 320

Step 6: Prepare the fixed production overhead budget

Given:	£100 000

Step 7: Calculate the value of the closing raw material stock

Raw material	Closing stock* (units)		Cost per unit £		Total value £
E	4 950	×	3	=	14 850
C	13 200	×	4	=	52 800
					67 650

* Derived from Step 4.

Step 8: Calculate the value of the closing finished stock

	£	£
Unit cost:		
Direct material E: 5 units × £3 per unit	15	
Direct material C: 10 units × £4 per unit	40	55
Direct labour for machining: 1 hour × £6 per DLH	6	
Direct labour for assembling: 0.50 hours × £8 per DLH	4	10
Total direct cost		= 65
× units in stock		× 880
Closing stock value		= 57 200

Step 9: Prepare the administration, selling and distribution budget

Given: £150 000

Step 10: Prepare the capital expenditure budget

Given: £50 000

Step 11: Calculate the cost of goods sold

	£
Opening stock (given)	52 000
Manufacturing cost:	
Production units (Step 2) × total direct cost (Step 3) = 10 080 × £65	655 200
	707 200
Less: Closing stock (Step 8: 880 units × £65)	57 200
Cost of goods sold (10 000 units)	= 650 000
(or 10 000 units × total direct costs of £65 per unit)	

Step 12: Prepare the cash budget

	£	£
Receipts		
Cash from debtors:		
Opening debtors	80 000	
Sales	1 000 000	
	1 080 000	
Less: Closing debtors	150 000	930 000
(15% × £1 000 000)		
Payments		
Cash payments to creditors:		
Opening creditors	28 000	
c/f	28 000	930 000

		£	£
	b/f	28 000	930 000
Purchases [Step 4: (£152 550 + 408 000)]		560 550	
		588 550	
Less: Closing creditors (£560 550 × 10%)		56 055	532 495
Wages (Step 5: £60 480 + 40 320)			100 800
Fixed production overhead			100 000
Administration, selling and distribution overhead			150 000
Capital expenditure			50 000
Dividend paid for 2016			75 000
			1 008 295

	£
Net receipts	(78 295)
Add: Opening cash	2 000
Budgeted closing cash balance (overdrawn)	(76 295)

Step 13: Prepare the budgeted profit and loss account

	£	£
Sales (Step 1)		1 000 000
Less: Variable cost of sales (Step 8: 10 000 × £65)		650 000
Gross margin		350 000
Less: Fixed production overhead (Step 6)	100 000	
Depreciation [(£250 000 + 50 000) × 20%]	60 000	160 000
Production margin		190 000
Less: Administration, selling and distribution		
Overhead (Step 9)		150 000
Budgeted net profit		40 000

Step 14: Prepare the budgeted balance sheet

	£	£	£
Fixed assets (at cost)			300 000
Less: Accumulated depreciation			160 000
			140 000
Current assets			
Raw materials (Step 7)		67 650	
Finished stock (Step 8)		57 200	
Trade debtors (15% × £1 000 000)		150 000	
		274 850	
Less: Current liabilities			
Trade creditors			
[Step 4: 10% × (£152 550 + 408 000)]	56 055		
Bank overdraft (Step 12)	76 295	132 350	142 500
			282 500
Financed by:			
Share capital			
Ordinary shares			225 000
Retained profits (£17 500 + 40 000)			57 500
			282 500

Fixed and flexible budgets

Flexible budget disadvantages

Some businesses owners use flexible budgeting to adapt to change and to measure and adjust for inflation. They also use it to gain better control of business activities and evaluate performance so that they can respond appropriately to uncertainties. Business owners must weigh budgeting choices carefully because flexible budgets have some striking disadvantages. These include a lack of information, difficulties in categorizing expenses into their fixed, variable and semi-variable elements, making accurate adjustments for sales and costs, and the need for continuous monitoring of the business environment.

Source: Adapted from smallbusiness.chron.com/disadvantages-flexible budget-57384.htl

The master budget becomes the detailed plan for future action that everyone is expected to work towards. However, some entities only use the budgeting process as a *planning* exercise. Once the master budget has been agreed, there may be no attempt to use it as a control technique. This means that the budget may be virtually ignored and it may not be compared with the actual results. If this is the case, then the company is not getting the best out of the budgeting system.

As was suggested earlier, a budgeting system is particularly useful if it is also used as a means of control. Control is achieved by comparing actual performance with the budgeted performance. If there are any significant variances, these are then investigated and any necessary corrective action taken.

The constant comparison of the actual results with the budgeted results may be done either on a *fixed* or a *flexible* budget basis. A fixed budget basis means that the actual results for a particular period are compared with the original budgets. This is to be expected because the budget is a measure and a measure has to be rigid: some very misleading results would be obtained if an elastic ruler was used to measure distances! Similarly, an elastic-type budget might also give some highly unreliable results. In some cases, however, a variable measure is used in budgeting in order to allow for certain circumstances that might have taken place *since* the budgets were prepared. Accountants call this *flexing* the budget. A flexible budget is an original budget that has been amended to take account of the *actual* level of activity.

This procedure might appear somewhat contradictory. Surely changing a budget once it has been agreed is similar to using an elastic ruler to measure distances? This is not necessarily the case in budgeting.

As we explained earlier, in order to prepare their budgets, some managers (especially production managers) will need to be given the budgeted level of activity. This means that such budgets will be based on a given level of activity. If the *actual* level of activity is greater (or less) than the budgeted level, however, managers will have to allow for more (or less) expenditure on materials, labour and other expenses.

Suppose, for example, that a manager has prepared his budget on the basis of an anticipated level of activity of 70 per cent of the plant capacity. The company turns out to be much busier than expected and it achieves an actual level of activity of 80 per cent. The production manager is likely to have spent more on materials, labour and other expenses than originally thought. If the actual performance is then

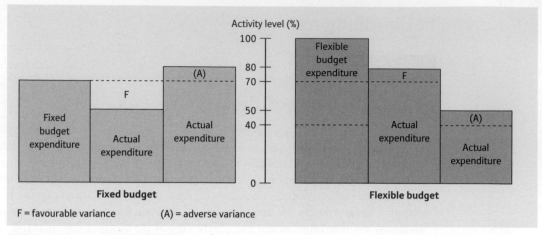

Figure 15.4 Flexing the budget

compared with the budget, i.e. on a fixed budget basis, it will look as though a great deal more had been spent than had been anticipated. Indeed it has although *some* of it, at least, must have been beyond the manger's control because of the increased activity. It is considered only fair, therefore, to allow for those costs that are not the responsibility of the manager. As a result there is a need to flex the budget, i.e. revise it on the basis of what it would have been if the manager had budgeted for an activity of 80 per cent instead of 70 per cent. The other assumptions and calculations made at the time the budget was prepared (such as material prices and wage rates) would not be amended. Figure 15.4 portrays this argument in pictorial form, which perhaps makes it easier for you to understand.

If a company operates a flexible budget system, the budgets may be prepared on the basis of a wide range of possible activity levels. This is a time-consuming method, and managers would be very lucky if they prepared one that happened to be identical to the *actual* level of activity. The best method is to wait until the actual level of activity is known before the budget is flexed.

The operation of a flexible budgetary system is shown in Example 15.2.

Example 15.2

Flexible budget procedure

The following information had been prepared for Carp Limited for the year to 30 June 2017.

Level of activity	Budget 50%	Actual 60%
	£	£
Costs:		
Direct materials	50 000	61 000
Direct labour	100 000	118 000
Variable overhead	10 000	14 000
Total variable cost	160 000	193 000
Fixed overhead	40 000	42 000
Total costs	200 000	235 000

Required:

Prepare a flexed budget operating statement for Carp Limited for the year to 30 June 2017.

Answer to Example 15.2

Carp Ltd

Flexed budget operating statement for the year 30 June 2017

Activity level	Fixed budget 50% £	Flexed budget 60% £	Actual costs 60% £	Variance (col. 2 less col. 3) favourable/(adverse) £
Direct materials	50 000	60 000	61 000	(1 000)
Direct labour	100 000	120 000	118 000	2 000
Variable overhead	10 000	12 000	14 000	(2 000)
Total variable costs	160 000	192 000	193 000	(1 000)
Fixed overhead	40 000	40 000	42 000	(2 000)
Total costs	200 000	232 000	235 000	(3 000)

Tutorial notes

1 All the budgeted *variable* costs have been flexed by 20 per cent because the actual activity was 60 per cent compared with a budgeted level of 50 per cent, i.e. a 20 per cent increase

$$\left(\frac{60\% - 50\%}{50\%} \times 100 \right)$$

2 The budgeted fixed costs are not flexed because, by definition, they should not change with activity.

3 Instead of using the total fixed budget cost of £200,000, the total flexed budget costs of £232,000 can be compared more fairly with the total actual cost of £235,000.

4 Note that the terms 'favourable' and 'adverse' as applied to variances mean favourable or adverse to profit. In other words, profit will be either greater (if a variance is favourable) or less (if it is adverse) than the budgeted profit.

5 The reasons for the variances between the actual costs and the flexed budget will need to be investigated. The flexed budget shows that even allowing for the increased activity, the actual costs were in excess of the budget allowance.

6 Similarly, it will be necessary to investigate why the actual activity was higher than the budgeted activity. It could have been caused by inefficient budgeting or by quite an unexpected increase in sales activity. While this would normally be welcome, it might place a strain on the productive and financial resources of the company. If the increase is likely to be permanent, management will need to make immediate arrangements to accommodate the new level of activity.

Behavioural consequences

News clip

Budget challenges

Budgets and budgetary control processes have become a mainstay in modern management accounting. A strong budget can bring both financial and operational benefits but the process is far from foolproof. Some of the major challenges include getting employees to support the budgetary process, setting a realistic goal, pinpointing individual responsibility for achieving performance goals, and ensuring that strict business ethics are applied throughout the entire budgetary process, especially when managers are specially rewarded for their performance.

Source: Adapted from smallbusiness.chron.com/challenges-budgeting-budgetary-control-59231.html

Budgeting and budgetary control systems are not neutral. They have an impact on people causing them to react favourably, unfavourably or with indifference. If managers react favourably then their budgets are likely to be accurate and relevant. Similarly, any information provided for them will be welcomed and it will be taken seriously. As a result, any necessary corrective action required will be pursued with some vigour.

Managers who react unfavourably or with indifference may prepare budgets that are inaccurate or irrelevant. Obviously such managers are not likely to take seriously any notice or any action based on suspect data.

It follows from the above that for a budgeting and budgetary control systems to work effectively, a number of important elements must be present. These are summarised below and they are also depicted in Figure 15.5.

- *Consultation.* Managers must be consulted about any proposal to install a budgeting or a budgetary control system.
- *Education and training.* Managers must undergo some education and training so that they are fully aware of the relevance and importance of budgeting and budgetary control systems and the part that they are expected to play.
- *Involvement.* Managers must be directly involved in the installation of the system and especially so in their own responsibility centre.
- *Independence.* Managers should prepare their own budgets (subject to some general guidelines) instead of having them imposed on them. Imposed budgets (as they are called) usually mean that managers do not take them seriously and they will then disclaim responsibility for any variances that may have occurred.
- *Non-disciplinary.* Managers should not be disciplined for any variances (especially if a budget has been imposed) unless they are obviously guilty of negligence. Budgetary control is a means of finding out *why* a variance occurred. It is not supposed to be a vehicle for disciplining managers.

With regards to the last point, if managers believe that the budgeting or budgetary control system operates against them rather than for them, they are likely to undermine it. This may take the form of *dysfunctional behaviour,* i.e. behaviour that may be in their own interest but not in the best interests of the company. They may, for example, act aggressively, become uncooperative, blame other managers, build a great deal of slack (i.e. tolerance) into their budgets, make decisions on a short-term basis or avoid making them altogether, and spend money unnecessarily up to the budget level that they have been given.

All of these points emphasise the importance of consulting managers and involving them fully in both the installation and operation of budgeting and budgetary control systems. If this is not the case, experience suggests that such systems will not work.

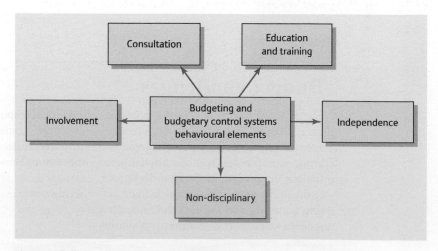

Figure 15.5 Budgeting: behavioural elements

Activity 15.2

As a departmental manager you budgeted to spend £10,000 in 2018. You spent £9000. You budgeted to spend £12,000 in 2019 but you were told you could only spend £11,000 as you had 'over-budgeted in 2018'. What are you likely to do when you come to prepare your budget for 2020?

❗ Questions you should ask

This is a most important chapter for non-accountants because you are likely to be involved in the budgetary process no matter what junior or senior position you hold. If your employer uses an imposed budgetary control system you may not have as much freedom to ask questions but you might want to point out as diplomatically as you can that there are problems with such systems. You might also like to put the following questions to the accountants and senior managers.

- How far is the time spent on preparing budgets cost effective?
- Do you think that budgets prepared for a calendar year is too long a period?
- Should those costs (and revenues) that relate to a longer timescale be apportioned to sub-budget periods?
- Is it appropriate to compare actual events with fixed budgets or should we use flexible budgets?
- Why can't I be responsible for preparing my own department's budget?
- Why do you alter my budget after I have prepared it?
- Do you expect me to be responsible for any variances that are outside my control?
- Why punish me and my staff when we were not responsible either for the budget or for what went wrong with it?

Conclusion

The full benefits of budgeting can only be gained if it is combined with a budgetary control system. The preparation of budgets is a valuable exercise in itself because it forces management to look ahead to what *might* happen rather than to look back at what *did* happen. However, it is even more valuable if it is also used as a form of control.

Budgetary control enables actual results to be measured frequently against an agreed budget (or plan). Departures from that budget can then be quickly spotted and steps taken to correct any unwelcome trends. There is a strong case for arguing that the comparison of actual results with a fixed budget may not be particularly helpful if the actual level of activity is different from that budgeted. It is recommended, therefore, that actual results should be compared with a flexed budget.

As so many functional budgets are based on the budgeted level of activity, it is vital that it is determined as accurately as possible, since an error in estimating the level of activity could affect the whole of the company's operational and financial activities. It is important, therefore, that any difference between the actual and the budgeted level of activity is investigated carefully.

Budgeting and budgetary control systems may be resented by managers and they might then react to the systems in such a way to protect their own position. This may not be of benefit to the entity as a whole.

Key points

1　A budget is a short-term plan.

2　Budgetary control is a cost control method that enables actual results to be compared with the budget, thereby enabling any necessary corrective action to be taken.

3　The preparation of budgets will be undertaken by a budget team.

4　Managers must be responsible for producing their own functional budgets.

5　Functional budgets are combined to form a master budget.

6　A fixed budget system compares actual results with the original budgets.

7　In a flexed budget system the budget may be flexed (or amended) to bring it into line with the actual level of activity.

8　A budgeting and budgetary control system is not neutral. It may cause managers to act in a way that is not in the best interests of the entity.

Check your learning

1　What is a budget?

2　List its essential features.

3　What is meant by 'budgetary control'?

4　List its essential features.

5　What is a variance?

6　What is a forecast?

7　How long is a normal budgeting period?

8　What is a sub-budget period?

9　What administration procedures does a budgeting system require?

10　In a commercial organisation, which budget is normally the first to be prepared?

11　What initial criterion is given to production managers before they begin to prepare their budgets?

12　What is meant by a functional budget?

13　List six common functional budgets.

14　What is meant by a fixed budget?

15　What is meant by a flexible budget?

16　Why is it desirable to prepare one?

17　List five desirable behavioural elements necessary to ensure a budgeting system is effective.

News story quiz

Remember the news story at the beginning of this chapter? Go back to that story and reread it before answering the following questions.

The Financial Reporting Council, the premier body in the United Kingdom responsible for financial reporting practises what it preaches and it too prepares a budget.

Questions

1 What is the difference between a plan and a budget?

2 What type of costs would an organisation like the FRC incur?

3 How do you think that the various levies mentioned in the news story have been determined?

Tutorial questions

The answers to questions marked with an asterisk can be found in Appendix 4.

15.1 The Head of Department of Business and Management at Birch College has been told by the Vice Principal (Resources) that his departmental budget for the next academic year is £150,000. What comment would you make about the system of budgeting used at Birch College?

15.2 Suppose that when all the individual budgets at Sparks plc are put together there is a shortfall of resources needed to support them. The Board suggests that all departmental budgets should be reduced by 15 per cent. As the company's Chief Accountant, how would you respond to the Board's suggestion?

15.3 Does a fixed budget serve any useful purpose?

15.4 'It is impossible to introduce a budgetary control system into a hospital because if someone's life needs saving it has to be saved irrespective of the cost.' How far do you agree with this statement?

15.5* The following information has been prepared for Tom Limited for the six months to 30 September 2016:

Budgeted production levels for product X

	Units
April	140
May	280
June	700
July	380
August	300
September	240

Product X uses two units of component A6 and three units of component B9. On 1 April 2016 there were expected to be 100 units of A6 in stock, and 200 units of B9. The desired closing stock levels of each component were as follows:

Month end 2016	A6 (units)	B9 (units)
30 April	110	250
31 May	220	630
30 June	560	340
31 July	300	300
31 August	240	200
30 September	200	180

During the six months to 30 September 2016, component A6 was expected to be purchased at a cost of £5 per unit, and component B9 at a cost of £10 per unit.

Required:
Prepare the following budgets for each of the six months to 30 September 2016:
(a) direct materials usage budget;
(b) direct materials purchase budget.

15.6* Don Limited has one major product that requires two types of direct labour to produce it. The following data refer to certain budget proposals for the three months to 31 August 2017:

Month	Production units
June	600
July	700
August	650

Direct labour hours required per unit:

	Hours	Budgeted rate per hour £
Production	3	4
Finishing	2	8

Required:
Prepare the direct labour cost budget for each of the three months to 31 August 2017.

15.7 Gorse Limited manufactures one product. The budgeted sales for period 6 are for 10,000 units at a selling price of £100 per unit. Other details are as follows:

1 Two components are used in the manufacture of each unit:

Component	Number	Unit cost of each component £
XY	5	1
WZ	3	0.50

2 Stocks at the beginning of the period are expected to be as follows:
4000 units of finished goods at a unit cost of £52.50.
Component XY: 16,000 units at a unit cost of £1.
Component WZ: 9,600 units at a unit cost of £0.50.

3 Two grades of employees are used in the manufacture of each unit:

Employee	Hours per unit	Labour rate per hour £
Production	4	5
Finishing	2	7

4 Factory overhead is absorbed into unit costs on the basis of direct labour hours. The budgeted factory overhead for the period is estimated to be £96 000.
5 The administration, selling and distribution overhead for the period has been budgeted at £275 000.
6 The company plans a reduction of 50 per cent in the quantity of finished stock at the end of period 6, and an increase of 25 per cent in the quantity of each component.

Required:
Prepare the following budgets for period 6:
(a) sales
(b) production quantity
(c) materials usage
(d) materials purchase
(e) direct labour
(f) the budgeted profit and loss account.

15.8 Avsar Limited has extracted the following budgeting details for the year to 30 September 2018:

1 Sales: 4000 units of V at £500 per unit
7000 units of R at £300 per unit

2 Materials usage (units):

	Raw material		
	O1	I2	L3
V	11	9	12
R	15	1	10

3 Raw material costs (per unit):

	£
O1	8
I2	6
L3	3

4 Raw material stocks:

	Units		
	O1	I2	L3
Opening stock	1300	1400	400
Closing stock	1400	1000	200

5 Finished stocks:

	Units	
	V	R
Opening stock	110	90
Closing stock	120	150

6 Direct labour:

	Product	
	V	R
Budgeted hours per unit	10	8
Budgeted hourly rate (£)	12	6

7 Variable overhead:

	Product	
	V	R
Budgeted hourly rate (£)	10	5

8 Fixed overhead: £193,160 (to be absorbed on the basis of direct labour hours).

Required:
(a) Prepare the following budgets:
    (i) sales;
    (ii) production units;
    (iii) materials usage;
    (iv) materials purchase; and
    (v) production cost.
(b) Calculate the total budgeted profit for the year to 30 September 2018.

15.9 The following budget information relates to Flossy Limited for the three months to 31 March 2019:

1   **Budgeted profit and loss accounts:**

Month	January	February	March
	£000	£000	£000
Sales (all on credit)	2 000	3 000	2 500
Cost of sales	1 200	1 800	1 500
Gross profit	800	1 200	1 000
Depreciation	(100)	(100)	(100)
Other expenses	(450)	(500)	(600)
	(550)	(600)	(700)
Net profit	250	600	300

2   Budgeted balance sheets:

Budgeted balances	December	January	February	March
	£000	£000	£000	£000
Current assets:				
Stocks	100	120	150	150
Debtors	200	300	350	400
Short-term investments	60	–	40	30
Current liabilities:				
Trade creditors	110	180	160	150
Other creditors	50	50	50	50
Taxation	150	–	–	–
Dividends	200	–	–	–

3 Capital expenditure to be incurred on 20 February 2019 is expected to amount to £470,000.
4 Sales of plant and equipment on 15 March 2019 is expected to raise £30,000 in cash.
5 The cash at bank and in hand on 1 January 2019 is expected to be £15,000.

Required:
Prepare Flossy Limited's cash budget for each of the three months during the quarter ending 31 March 2019.

15.10 Chimes Limited has prepared a flexible budget for one of its factories for the year to 30 June 2017. The details are as follows:

% of production capacity	30%	40%	50%	60%
	£000	£000	£000	£000
Direct materials	42	56	70	84
Direct labour	18	24	30	36
Factory overhead	22	26	30	34
Administration overhead	17	20	23	26
Selling and distribution overhead	12	14	16	18
	111	140	169	198

Additional information:
1 The company only expects to operate at a capacity of 45 per cent. At that capacity, the sales revenue has been budgeted at a level of £135,500.
2 Variable costs per unit are not expected to change, irrespective of the level of activity.
3 Fixed costs are also not likely to change, irrespective of the level of activity.

Required:
Prepare a flexible budget for the year to 30 June 2017 based on an activity level of 45 per cent.

Standard costing

A business strategy

Kevin Johnston

A manufacturing entity can adopt a strategy of establishing prices based on what its products cost to make. If a mark-up percentage is added to that cost, then it is possible to predict the selling price of the products and to know that it includes an allowance for profit. By keeping costs low, a strategy of competing on price can then be maintained. This strategy adds a number of internal and external advantages, but it requires vigilance to pull it off.

The production departments may not always meet the standard costs required of them. Labour costs may change if more or better trained workers are required and raw material costs may also rise as well. In such circumstances it is necessary to make personnel aware of what the

costs should be and compare them with the current costs. By setting objectives for raw materials and labour costs, it is possible to bring them into line with the standard cost targets. As a result, inefficiencies in the production process can be monitored and brought back into line with the pre-set standards.

A particular pitfall of standard costing is that the price of raw materials can fluctuate. This means that cost prices may have to be adjusted periodically and so actual prices then become a foundation for pricing. Similarly wages can increase over time, causing original cost estimates to be out of line with what was actually being spent. Standard costing only remains standard for so long – it has to be adjusted periodically.

Source: Adapted from http://smallbsiness.chron.com/stnadard-costing-business-str...

Questions relating to this news story can be found on page 371 ➡

About this chapter

This chapter examines *standard costing,* another planning and control technique used in management accounting. Like budgeting and budgetary control, standard costing involves estimating future sales revenue and product costs. Standard costing, however, goes into much more detail: the total *budgeted* cost is broken down into the elements of cost (direct materials, direct labour, variable overhead and fixed overhead) and these costs are then compared with the *actual* cost of those elements. The difference between the standard cost and the *actual* cost is known as a variance.

Variances are usually analysed into a volume variance and a price variance and sometimes these variances themselves are broken down into sub-variances. Significant variances are then investigated and immediate action is taken to correct any unexpected or unwelcome ones. The difference between budgeted sales and actual sales can also be analysed into volume and price variances.

Standard costing is of particular relevance in manufacturing industry where specific products or processes are produced repetitively.

Learning objectives

By the end of this chapter, you should be able to:

- describe the nature, purpose and importance of standard costing and variance analysis;
- identify the main steps involved in implementing and operating a standard-costing system;
- calculate three standard-costing performance measures;
- calculate sales, direct materials, direct labour, variable overhead and fixed overhead variances;
- prepare a standard-cost operating statement.

 ## Why this chapter is important

Standard costing is an important management accounting planning and control technique and you need to know what it is and how it works if you are to become a really effective and self-aware manager. This chapter is important, therefore, for three reasons:

- you could be required to provide information for standard-costing purposes;
- you may be presented with standard-costing operating statements;
- you need to know what action to take in order to control unexpected trends.

Operation

News clip

Enhancing efficiency

According to an article in *Automation World*, standard costing techniques enable managers in manufacturing enterprises to measure more efficiently the costs of goods sold, besides allowing for more effective budgeting and price setting on future jobs.

Source: http://www.automationworld.com/discrete-manufacturing/pr...

The operation of a standard-costing system requires virtually everyone in an entity to be involved. The system depends on the supply of a vast amount of information from every cost centre throughout the entity and the personnel who are best placed to supply it are those who work in the various cost centres. It is not, however, a one-way process. Once the information has been processed, it is fed back to those people who supplied it originally. They are then expected to use that information to deal with any significant variances.

If a standard-costing system is to work properly, it is vital that it is fully supported by those people it is supposed to help. If they do not think that it is of any benefit to them they are then likely to provide inaccurate information and to discount subsequent reports based on it. If this is how they do behave, then the system might as well be abandoned because it will result in ineffective planning and control.

Definitions

There are four important standard-costing terms you need to be familiar with:

1 *Standard: the amount or level set for the performance of a particular activity.*
2 *Standard cost: the planned cost for a particular level of activity.*
3 *Variance: the difference between the standard (or planned) cost and the actual cost.*
4 *Variance analysis: an investigation into and an explanation of why variances occurred.*

Uses

Four main purposes of standard costing can be identified:

- *Stock valuation.* The standard-cost method of stock valuation is the expected or planned price that the entity expects to pay for its materials. Its advantages are that it is simple to use and it can remain stable for some time. The main difficulties are in establishing a standard cost and in coping with significant differences between the actual costs and the standard costs.
- *Control.* By comparing in detail actual costs against the standard costs on a frequent basis swift action can be taken to correct any departures from what was planned.
- *Performance measurement.* Standard costing provides information that enables an entity to determine if it is meeting its objectives.
- *Pricing.* The information provided by a standard-costing system helps entities to set their selling prices.

Application

Standard costing is an extremely useful planning and control technique especially in those manufacturing companies where the production process is repetitive and identical units are constantly being turned out. This enables a general standard to be set that meets most situations. Non-repetitive operations do not enable a standard to be set very easily because by definition each operation tends to be different.

Standard costing is a development of the early twentieth century. By 1918 the basic equations that are still in use today had been devised. At the beginning of the twenty-first century manufacturing techniques are very different from those a hundred years ago, e.g. purchases are made to order and inventories are kept low. It might be thought, therefore, that standard costing would no longer be relevant. The research evidence available suggests that this is not so and that standard costing is still used quite widely.

Period

The standard-costing period will usually be the same as that for the main budget and sub-budget periods. Short periods are preferred so that the actual results can be compared frequently with the standard results. Corrective action can then be taken quickly before it is too late to do anything about any unexpected trends. Short standard-costing periods may also be necessary where market or production conditions are subject to frequent changes or where it is particularly difficult to prepare long-term plans.

Standards

The preparation of standard costs requires great care and attention. As each element of cost is subject to detailed arithmetical analysis, it is important that the initial information is accurate. Indeed, the information produced by a standard-costing system will be virtually worthless if subsequent analyses reveal that variances were caused by inefficient budgeting or standard setting.

In preparing standard costs, management will need to be informed of the level of activity to be used in preparing the standard costs, i.e. whether the entity will need to operate at, say, 80 per cent or 90 per cent of its theoretical capacity. An activity level should be chosen that is capable of being achieved. It would be possible to choose a standard that was *ideal*, i.e. one that represented a performance that could be achieved only under the most favourable of conditions. Such a standard would, however, be unrealistic, because it is rare for ideal conditions to prevail. An ideal standard is a standard that is attainable under the most favourable conditions and where no allowance is made for normal losses, waste and machine downtime.

A much more realistic standard is called an *attainable* standard. Such a standard is one that the entity can expect to achieve in reasonably efficient working conditions. In other words, it is accepted that some delays and inefficiencies, e.g. waste and machine downtime will occur, but it is also assumed that management will attempt to minimise them.

You may also come across the term *basic* standards. These are standards that are left unchanged over long periods of time. This enables some consistency to be achieved in comparing actual results with the same standards over a substantial period of time but they may become so out of date that meaningful comparisons are not possible.

Activity 16.1	Your company bases its standard costs on an ideal level of activity, i.e. no allowance is made for natural losses such as evaporation and the standard costs can only be achieved in entirely favourable conditions. As a cost centre manager, what would your reaction be when you received a report showing that your centre had a number of large unwelcome variances? What would you do about such variances?

Cost data

The cost data needed to operate a standard-costing system is considerable. The main requirements are as follows.

- *Direct materials:* types, quantities and price.
- *Direct labour:* grades, numbers and rates of pay.
- *Variable overhead:* the total variable overhead cost broken down into various categories, such as employee and general support costs.
- *Fixed overhead:* the total fixed overhead, likewise broken down into various categories such as employee costs, building costs and general administration expenses.

The above summary shows that the standard cost of a particular unit comprises four elements: direct materials, direct labour, variable overhead and fixed overhead. In turn, each element comprises two factors, namely quantity and price. In Example 16.1 we show you how the standard cost of a specific unit is built up.

Example 16.1	Calculation of the total standard cost of a specific unit using absorption costing

	£
● Direct materials	
Quantity × price (2 units × £5)	10
● Direct labour	
Hours × hourly rate (5 hours × £10)	50
● Variable overhead	
Hours × variable overhead absorption rate per hour (5 hours × £6)	30
● Fixed overhead	
Hours × fixed overhead absorption rate per hour (5 hours × £3)	15
Total standard cost per unit	105

Note: The example is based on fictitious data. It assumes that the unit cost is calculated on the basis of standard absorption costing. This is the most common method of standard costing. It is also possible to adopt a system of standard *marginal* costing (see Chapter 17).

Standard hours and the absorption of overhead

Standard absorption costing requires overhead to be absorbed on the basis of *standard* hours. In a non-standard costing system it is absorbed on the basis of *actual* hours. A standard hour represents the amount of work that should be performed in an hour assuming that it is done in standard conditions, i.e. in *planned* conditions. Each unit is given a standard time of so many hours in which the work should be done so the total standard time will be calculated as follows:

> **Number of units × standard hours per unit**

It is *not* calculated by multiplying the number of units by the *actual* hours per unit.

Sales

As well as calculating cost variances some companies do the same for sales although this is thought to be much less common. A detailed analysis of the budgeted sales is needed to obtain the number of each product to be sold and its selling price. Such information will be needed not just for the overall budget period but also for each sub-budget period.

There are a number of ways in which sales variances may be calculated. We could just deal with actual and budgeted sales revenue but in this book we are going to adopt a method based on *sales profit* as this method is thought to be of much greater interest and relevance to managers. Basically it involves taking the actual sales revenue and then deducting the *standard* cost of those sales (not the actual cost). The balance is then compared with the budgeted profit. Any difference between the actual cost and the standard cost is taken care of when the cost variances are calculated. We will explain how it works in a little more detail later in the chapter.

Performance measures

Management may find it useful if some performance measures are extracted from the standard costing data. Such measures pinpoint the level of efficiency of the entity, help managers to spot unfavourable trends and enable them to take immediate corrective action. There are three specific performance measures that we are going to cover in this chapter: the efficiency ratio, the capacity ratio and the production volume ratio (see Figure 16.1).

Referring to Figure 16.1, the actual hours are those direct labour hours actually worked. The budgeted direct labour hours are those that were expected or planned to be worked. Standard hours produced measure the actual output produced in standard direct labour hours. If each unit produced *should have* taken (say) five hours and 100 units were produced, the total hours produced would be 500 (5 DLH × 100). The budget might have been planned on the basis of 120 units, in which case the total standards labour hours would have been 600 (5 DLH × 120). In a machine-intensive cost centre, machine hours would be substituted for direct labour hours. The formula for each performance measure is outlined below.

The efficiency ratio

This ratio compares the total standard (or allowed) hours of units produced with the total actual hours taken to produce those units. The formula is:

$$\frac{\text{Standard hours produced}}{\text{Actual direct labour hours worked}} \times 100$$

Reminder:
The standard hours produced = the standard direct labour hours of production for the *actual* activity.

The efficiency ratio enables management to check whether the company has produced the units in more or less time than had been allowed.

The capacity ratio

This ratio compares the total actual hours worked with the total budgeted hours. It is calculated as follows:

$$\frac{\text{Actual direct labour hours worked}}{\text{Budgeted direct labour hours}} \times 100$$

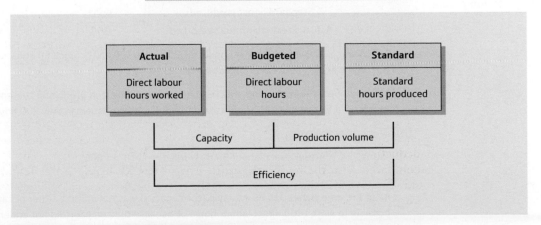

Figure 16.1 Three performance measures

The capacity ratio enables management to ascertain whether all of the budgeted hours (i.e. all the hours *planned* to be worked) were used to produce the actual units.

The production volume ratio

This compares the total allowed hours for the work actually produced with the total budgeted hours. It is calculated as follows:

$$\frac{\text{Standard hours produced}}{\text{Budgeted direct labour hours}} \times 100$$

The production volume ratio enables management to compare the work produced (measured in terms of standard hours) with the budgeted hours of work. This ratio gives management some information about how effective the company has been in using the budgeted hours.

In Example 16.2 we show you how to calculate these three ratios.

Example 16.2	**Calculation of efficiency, capacity and production volume ratios**

The following information relates to the Frost Production Company Limited for the year to 31 March 2016:

1 Budgeted direct labour hours: 1000
2 Budgeted units: 100
3 Actual direct labour hours worked: 800
4 Actual units produced: 90

Required:
Calculate the following performance ratios:
(a) the efficiency ratio
(b) the capacity ratio
(c) the production volume ratio.

Answer to Example 16.2

(a) **The efficiency ratio:**

$$\frac{\text{Standard hours produced}}{\text{Actual direct labour hours worked}} \times 100 = \frac{900^*}{800} \times 100 = \underline{112.5\%}$$

* Each unit is allowed 10 standard hours (1000 hours/100 units). Since 90 units were produced, the total standard hours of production must equal 900.

It would appear that the company has been more efficient in producing the goods than was expected. It was allowed 900 hours to do so but it produced them in only 800 hours.

(b) **The capacity ratio:**

$$\frac{\text{Actual direct labour hours worked}}{\text{Budgeted hours}} \times 100 = \frac{800}{1000} \times 100 = \underline{80\%}$$

All of the time planned to be available (the capacity) was not utilised, either because it was not possible to work 1000 direct labour hours or because the company did not undertake as much work as it could have done.

(c) **The production volume ratio:**

$$\frac{\text{Standard hours produced}}{\text{Budgeted hours}} \times 100 = \frac{900^*}{1000} \times 100 = \underline{90\%}$$

* As calculated for the efficiency ratio.

It appears that if 90 units had been produced in standard conditions, another 100 hours would have been available (10 units $\times$ 10 hours). Since the 90 units only took 800 hours to produce, at least another 20 units $\left(\dfrac{1000 - 800}{10}\right)$ could have been produced in standard conditions.

Comments

The budget allowed for 100 units to be produced and each unit was expected to take 10 direct labour hours to complete, a total budgeted activity of 1000 direct labour hours. However, only 90 units were actually produced. If these units had been produced in standard time, they should have taken 900 hours (90 units $\times$ 10 direct labour hours). These are the standard hours produced. The 90 units were completed in 800 actual hours. It appears, therefore, that the units were produced more efficiently than had been expected. The management will still need, of course, to investigate why only 90 units were produced and not the 100 units expected in the budget.

We can now move on to examine how standard cost variances may be calculated and whether they may be viewed as being either favourable or unfavourable. We do so in the next section.

Cost variances

News clip

Controlling and motivating

Studies have demonstrated that management and staff who do not have a target operate at a lower level than those staff who do have an achievable, motivational target. A standard costing target will help identify those managers not working as efficiently as they should be and help to reward those managers who do achieve those challenging standard costs. Managers may also be alerted to those areas of production that are not in control and where increased focus and supervision are necessary to bring the operation back into acceptable cost levels.

Source: http://www.bh-financial-tuition.co.uk/news/what-is-standard-costing-and-why-use-it

Structure

The difference between actual costs and standard costs may result in two main variances: price and quantity. These variances may either be favourable (F) to profit or adverse (A). This means that the actual prices paid or costs incurred can be more than anticipated (adverse to profit) or less than anticipated (favourable to profit). Similarly, the quantities used in production can result in more being used (adverse to profit) or less than expected (favourable to profit).

The standard production cost variances are shown in Figure 16.2. The formulae you need are shown below.

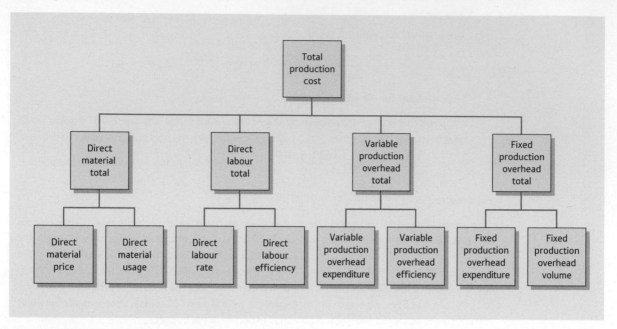

Figure 16.2 Main standard production cost variances

Direct materials

1 **Total** = (actual cost per unit × actual quantity used) − (standard cost per unit × standard quantity for actual production)

2 **Price** = (actual cost per unit − standard cost per unit) × total actual quantity used

3 **Usage** = (total actual quantity used − standard quantity for actual production) × standard cost

These relationships are shown in Figure 16.3.

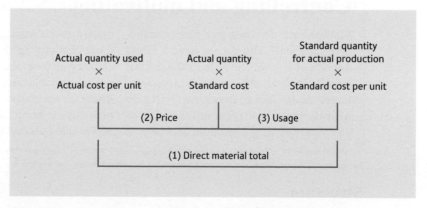

Figure 16.3 Calculation of direct material cost variances

Direct labour

1 **Total** = (actual hourly rate × actual hours) − (standard hourly rate × standard hours for actual production)

2 **Rate** = (actual hourly rate − standard hourly rate) × actual hours worked

3 **Efficiency** = (actual hours worked − standard hours for actual production) × standard hourly rate

These relationships are shown in Figure 16.4.

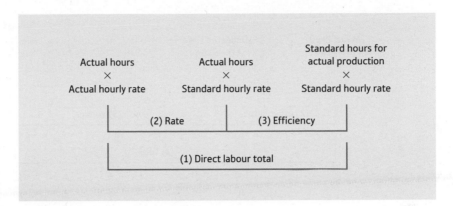

Figure 16.4 Calculation of direct labour cost variances

Variable production overhead

1 **Total** = actual variable overhead − [standard hours for actual production × variable production overhead absorption rate (VOAR)]

2 **Expenditure** = actual variable overhead − (actual hours worked × VOAR)

3 **Efficiency** = (standard hours for actual production − actual hours worked) × VOAR

These relationships are shown in Figure 16.5.

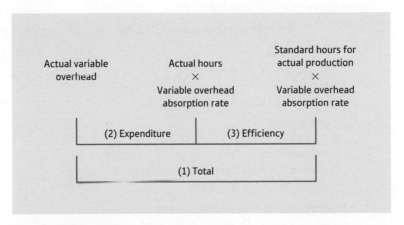

Figure 16.5 Calculation of variable production overhead variances

Fixed production overhead

1 **Total** = actual fixed overhead − [standard hours of production × fixed overhead absorption rate (FOAR)]

2 **Expenditure** = actual fixed overhead − budgeted fixed expenditure

3 Volume = budgeted fixed overhead expenditure − (standard hours for actual
production × FOAR)

These variances are shown in Figure 16.6.

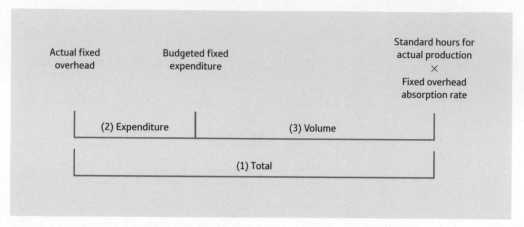

Figure 16.6 Calculation of fixed production overhead variances

A comprehensive example

We will now use a comprehensive example to illustrate the main cost variances. The
details are contained in Example 16.3.

Example 16.3	Calculation of the main cost variances

The following information has been extracted from the records of the Frost Production Company
Limited for the year to 31 March 2016:

Budgeted costs per unit:	£
Direct materials	30
(15 kilograms × £2 per kilogram)	
Direct labour	40
(10 hours × £4 per direct labour hour)	
Variable overhead	10
(10 hours × £1 per direct labour hour)	
Fixed overhead	20
(10 hours × £2 per direct labour hour)	
Total budgeted cost per unit	100

The following budgeted data are also relevant:

1 The budgeted production level was 100 units.
2 The total standard direct labour hours amounted to 1000.
3 The total budgeted variable overhead was estimated to be £1000.
4 The total budgeted fixed overhead was £2000.
5 The company absorbs both fixed and variable overhead on the basis of direct labour hours.

Actual costs:	£
Direct materials	2 100
Direct labour	4 000
Variable overhead	1 000
Fixed overhead	1 600
Total actual costs	8 700

Note: 90 units were produced in 800 actual hours, and the total actual quantity of direct materials consumed was 1400 kilograms.

Required:

(a) Calculate the direct materials, direct labour, variable production overhead and fixed production overhead total cost variances.

(b) Calculate the detailed variances for each element of cost.

Answer to Example 16.3(a)

In answering part (a) of this question the first thing that we need to do is to summarise the total variance for each element of cost for the actual 90 units produced:

	Actual costs	Total standard cost for actual production	Variance
	£	£	£
Direct materials	2 100	2 700 (1)	600 (F)
Direct labour	4 000	3 600 (2)	400 (A)
Variable production overhead	1 000	900 (3)	100 (A)
Fixed production overhead	1 600	1 800 (4)	200 (F)
Total	8 700	9 000	300 (F)

Notes:

(a) F = favourable to profit; A = adverse to profit.

(b) The numbers in brackets refer to the tutorial notes below.

Tutorial notes

1 The standard cost of direct material for actual production = the actual units produced × the standard direct material cost per unit, i.e. 90 × £30 = £2700.

2 The standard cost of direct labour for actual production = the actual units produced × standard direct labour cost per unit, i.e. 90 × £40 = £3600.

3 The standard variable cost for actual performance = the actual units produced × variable overhead absorption rate per unit, i.e. 90 × £10 = £900.

4 The fixed overhead cost for the actual performance = the actual units produced × fixed overhead absorption rate, i.e. 90 × £20 = £1800.

Comments on the answers to Example 16.3(a)

Example 16.3(a) shows that the total actual cost of producing the 90 units was £300 less than the budget allowance. An investigation would need to be made in order to find out why only 90 units were produced when the company had budgeted for 100. Although the 90 units have cost £300 less than expected, a number of other variances have contributed to the total variance. So assuming that these variances are considered significant, they would need to be carefully investigated in order to find out what caused them.

As a result of calculating variances for each element of cost, it becomes much easier for management to investigate why the actual production cost was £300 less than expected. However, by analysing the variances into their major causes, the accountant can provide even greater guidance. This is illustrated in part (b) of the example.

Answer to Example 16.3(b)

In answering part (b) of Example 16.3, we will deal with each element of cost in turn. As we do so we will take the opportunity to comment on the results.

Direct materials

1 **Price** = (actual cost per unit − standard cost per unit)

 × total actual quantity used

∴ the price variance = (£1.50 − 2.00) × 1400 (kg) = £700 (F)

The actual price per unit was £1.50 (£2100/1400) and the standard price was £2.00 per unit. There was, therefore, a total saving (as far as the price of the materials was concerned) of £700 (£0.50 × 1400). This was favourable (F) to profit.

2 **Usage** = (total actual quantity used − standard quantity for actual production)

 × standard cost

∴ the usage variance = (1400 − 1350) × £2.00 = £100 (A)

In producing 90 units, Frost should have used 1350 kilograms (90 × 15 kg) instead of the 1400 kilograms actually used. If this extra usage is valued at the standard cost (the difference between the actual price and the standard cost has already been allowed for), there is an adverse usage variance of £100 (50 (kg) × £2.00).

3 **Total** = price + usage:

∴ the total direct materials variance = £700 (F) + £100 (A) = £600 (F)

The £600 favourable total variance was calculated earlier in answering part (a) of the question. This variance might have arisen because Frost purchased cheaper materials. If this were the case then it probably resulted in a greater wastage of materials, perhaps because the materials were of an inferior quality.

Direct labour

1 **Rate** = (actual hourly rate − standard hourly rate) × actual hours worked

∴ the rate variance = (£5.00 − £4.00) × 800 DLH = £800 (A)

The actual hourly rate is £5.00 per direct labour hour (£4000/800) compared with the standard rate per hour of £4. Every extra actual hour worked, therefore, resulted in an adverse variance of £1 or £800 in total (£1 × 800).

2 **Efficiency** = (actual hours worked − standard hours for actual production) ×

 Standard hourly rate.

∴ the efficiency variance = (800 − 900) × £4.00 = £400 (F)

The actual hours worked were 800. However, 900 hours would be the allowance for the 90 units actually produced (90 × 10 DLH). If these hours were valued at the standard hourly rate (differences between the actual rate and the standard rate having already been allowed for when calculating the rate variance), a favourable variance of £400 arises. The favourable efficiency variance has arisen because the 90 units took less time to produce than the budget allowed for.

3 **Total** = rate + efficiency

∴ the total direct labour variance = £800 (A) + £400 (F) = £400 (A)

The £400 adverse total variance was calculated earlier in answering part (a) of the question. It arises because the company paid more per direct labour hour than had been budgeted, although this was offset to some extent by the units being produced in less time than the budgeted allowance. This variance could have been caused by using a higher grade of labour than had been intended. Unfortunately, the higher labour rate per hour was not completely offset by greater efficiency.

Variable production overhead

1 **Expenditure** = actual variable overhead − (actual hours worked × variable production overhead absorption rate)

$$\therefore \text{ the expenditure variance} = £1000 - (800 \times £1.00) = \underline{£200 \text{ (A)}}$$

2 **Efficiency** = (standard hours for actual production − actual hours worked) × variable production overhead absorption rate

$$\therefore \text{ the efficiency variance} = (900 - 800) \times £1.00 = \underline{£100 \text{ (F)}}$$

3 **Total** = expenditure + efficiency

∴ the total variable production overhead variance

$$= £200(A) + £100(F) = \underline{£100(A)}$$

The adverse variance of £100 (A) arises because the variable overhead absorption rate was calculated on the basis of a budgeted cost of £10 per unit. In fact the absorption rate ought to have been £11.11 per unit (£1000/90) because the total actual variable cost was £1000. There would, of course, be no variable production overhead cost for the ten units that were not produced. The £100 adverse total variance was calculated earlier in answering part (a) of the example.

Fixed production overhead

1 **Expenditure** = actual fixed overhead − budgeted fixed expenditure

$$\therefore \text{ the expenditure variance} = £1600 - £2000 = \underline{£400 \text{ (F)}}$$

The actual expenditure was £400 less than the budgeted expenditure. This means that the fixed production overhead absorption rate was £400 higher than it needed to have been if it had been the only fixed overhead variance.

2 **Volume** = budgeted fixed overhead − (standard hours of production × fixed production overhead absorption rate

$$\therefore \text{ the volume variance} = £2000 - (900 \times £2.00) = \underline{£200 \text{ (A)}}$$

As a result of producing fewer units than expected, £200 less overhead has been absorbed into production.

3 The fixed production overhead total variance was calculated earlier in answering part (a) of the question. The simplified formula is as follows:

Total = expenditure + volume

$$= £400 \text{ (F)} + £200 \text{ (A)} = \underline{£200 \text{ (F)}}$$

As the actual activity was less than the budgeted activity, only £1800 of fixed overhead was absorbed into production instead of the £2000 expected in the budget. However, the actual expenditure was only £1600 so the overestimate of expenditure compensated for the overestimate of activity.

Activity 16.2	In are sentence explain why (a) a favourable direct materials price variance can be offset by an adverse direct materials usage variance and (b) why might an adverse direct labour rate variance be offset by a favourable direct labour efficiency variance?

Sales variances

In an *absorption* costing system, a total sales variance would be classified into a selling price variance and a sales volume profit variance (see Figure 16.7).

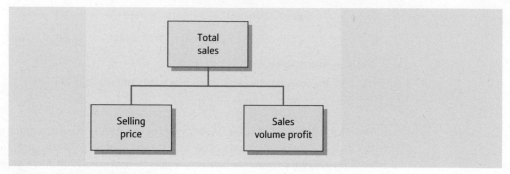

Figure 16.7 Main sales variances

The formulae are outlined below and they are also shown in diagrammatic form in Figure 16.8.

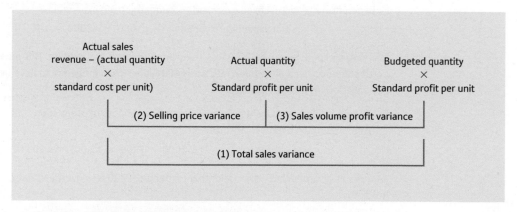

Figure 16.8 Calculation of sales profit variances

1 **Total sales variance** = [actual sales revenue − (actual sales quantity × standard cost per unit)] − (budgeted quantity × standard profit per unit)
2 **Selling price variance** = [actual sales revenue − (actual sales quantity × standard cost per unit)] − (actual quantity × standard profit per unit)

An alternative formula for the calculation of the selling price variance is as follows: (actual selling price per unit − standard selling price per unit) × actual sales quantity.

3 **Sales volume profit variance** = (actual quantity − budgeted quantity) × standard profit per unit

The use of sales variance formulae is illustrated in Example 16.4.

Example
16.4

Calculating sales variances

The following data relate to Frozen Limited for the year to 31 July 2016:

	Budget/standard	Actual
Sales (units)	100	90
Selling price per unit	£10	£10.50
Standard cost per unit	£7	–
Standard profit per unit	£3	

Required:
Calculate the sales variances.

Selling price variance = [actual sales revenue − (actual sales quantity × standard cost per unit)] − (actual quantity × standard profit per unit)

= [£945 − (90 units × £7)] − (90 units × £3) = (£945 − 630) − 270 = £45 (F)

The actual selling price per unit was £0.50 more than the standard selling price (£10.50–10.00) and so the variance is favourable. Other things being equal, the profit would be £45 higher than budgeted *for the actual number of units sold*.

Sales volume profit variance = (actual quantity − budgeted quantity) × standard profit per unit

The standard profit is £3 per unit.

(90 units − 100 units) = 10 × £3 = £30 (A)

The sales volume profit variance is £30 adverse because only 90 units were sold instead of the budgeted amount of 100 units. As a result, £30 less profit was made.

Total sales variance = [actual sales revenue − (actual sales quantity × standard cost per unit)] − (budgeted quantity × standard profit per unit)

The actual sales revenue = £945 (90 units × £10.50).

[£945 − (90 units × £7)] − (100 units × £3) = (£945 − 630) − 300 = £15 (F)

When the £45 favourable selling price is set off against the £30 adverse sales volume profit variance, there is a favourable total sales variance of £15 (£45 − 30).

Assuming that the demand for a certain product is elastic, what effect might a reduction in its selling price have on its sales volume profit variance?

Operating statements

Once all the variances have been calculated they may be summarised in the form of an operating statement. There is no standardised format for such a statement but the one used in Example 16.5 gives you a good idea of what one may look like.

The structure used in Example 16.5 is particularly helpful because it shows the link between the budgeted profit and the actual profit. This means that management can trace the main causes of sales and cost variances. In practice the statement would also show the details for each product.

Example 16.5	**Preparation of a standard cost operating statement**

Example 16.3 gave some information relating to the Frost Production Company Limited for the year to 31 March 2016. The cost data used in that example will now be used to illustrate the structure of a standard cost operating statement, along with some additional information.

Additional information:

1   Assume that the budgeted sales were 100 units at a selling price of £150 per unit.
2   90 units were sold at £160 per unit.

Required:
Prepare a standard cost operating statement for the year to 31 March 2016.

Answer to Example 16.5

Frost Production Company Limited. Standard cost operating statement for the year to 31 March 2016:

	(F) £	(A) £	£
Budgeted sales (100 × £150)			15 000
Budgeted cost of sales			10 000
(100 × £100)			
Budgeted profit			5 000
Sales volume profit variance (1)			(500)
Budgeted profit from actual sales			4 500
Variances: (2)			
Sales price (3)	900		
Direct materials usage		100	
Direct materials price	700		
Direct labour efficiency	400		
Direct labour rate		800	
Variable overhead efficiency	100		
Variable overhead expenditure		200	
Fixed overhead volume		200	
Fixed overhead expenditure	400		
	2 500	1 300	1 200
Actual profit			5 700

1 Sales volume profit variance = (actual quantity − budgeted quantity) × standard profit per unit

$$= (90 - 100) \times £50 = \underline{£500 \ (A)}$$

2 Details of the cost variances were shown in the answer to Example 16.3.

3 Selling price variance = (actual selling price per unit − standard selling price per unit) × actual sales quantity

$$= (£160 - £150) \times 90 = \underline{£900 \ (F)}$$

The operating profit statement will help management to decide where to begin an investigation into the causes of the respective variances. It is unlikely that they will all be investigated. It may be company policy, for example, to investigate only those variances that are particularly significant, irrespective of whether they are favourable or adverse. In other words, only *exceptional* variances would be investigated. A policy decision would then have to be taken on what was meant by 'exceptional'.

Activity 16.4

Suppose that you were the managing director of a medium-sized manufacturing company. Which managers do you think should be supplied with a copy of the company's four-weekly standard cost operating statement?

! Questions you should ask

The calculation of standard cost variances is a complex arithmetical exercise. As a non-accountant it is unlikely that you will have to calculate variances but it is important for you to have some idea of how it is done so that you are in a stronger position to find out what happened. You can then take any necessary corrective action.

What questions should you ask? We suggest that you can use the following as a basis for any subsequent investigation.

- Was the given level of activity accurate?
- Was the standard set realistic?
- Is there anything unusual about the actual events?
- Is the measure (i.e. the standard) reliable?
- Are there any particular variances that stand out?
- Are there any that are the main cause of any total variance?
- Is there a linkage between variances, e.g. between a favourable price variance and an unfavourable quantity/volume variance?
- Are there any factors that were not apparent at the time that the standards were set?

Conclusion

We have come to the end of a complex chapter. You may have found that it has been extremely difficult to understand just how standard cost variances are calculated. Fortunately it is unlikely that as a non-accountant you will ever have to calculate them for yourself. It is sufficient for your purposes to understand their meaning and to have some idea of the arithmetical foundation on which they are based.

Your job will usually be to investigate the *causes* of the variances and to take necessary action. A standard costing system is supposed to help managers plan and control the entity much more tightly than can be achieved in the absence of such a system. However, it can only be of real benefit if managers find that the information that they receive helps them do a better job.

Key points

1 A standard cost is the planned cost of a particular unit or process.

2 Standard costs are usually based on what is reasonably attainable.

3 Actual costs are compared with standard costs.

4 Corrective action is taken if there are any unplanned trends.

5 Three performance measures used in standard costing are the efficiency ratio, the capacity ratio and the production volume ratio.

6 Variance analysis is an arithmetical exercise that enables differences between actual and standard costs to be broken down into the elements of cost.

7 The degree of analysis will vary, but usually a total cost variance will be analysed into direct material, direct labour, variable overhead and fixed overhead variances and such variance will be sub-analysed into quantity and expenditure variances.

8 Sales variances may also be calculated, the total sales variance being analysed into a selling price variance and a sales volume profit variance.

9 The variances help in tracing the main causes of differences between actual and budgeted results but they do not *explain* what has actually happened – they are merely the starting point for a more detailed investigation.

Check your learning

1 Explain what is meant by the following terms: (a) a standard, (b) a standard cost, (c) a variance, (d) variance analysis.

2 List four uses of standard costing.

3 What type of entities might benefit from a standard costing system?

4 How long should a standard costing period be?

5 What is (a) a basic standard, (b) an attainable standard, (c) an ideal standard?

6 Name four types of information required for a standard costing system.

7 What is meant by 'a standard hour'?

8 Name three standard cost performance measures.

9 What are their respective formulae?

10 Complete the following equations:

    (a) direct materials total = _____ + _____

    (b) direct labour total = _____ + _____

    (c) variable production overhead total = _____ + _____

    (d) fixed production overhead total = _____ + _____

11 What is (a) an adverse variance, (b) a favourable variance?

12 Complete this equation: total sales variance = _____ + _____

13 Complete this statement: a standard cost operating statement links the budgeted profit to the _____ _____ for the period.

News story quiz

Remember the new story at the beginning of this chapter? Go back to that story and reread it before answering the following questions.

In a relatively short piece this news story suggests that standard costing is a *business strategy*. The basic procedures behind it appear to be fairly straightforward. However, as you worked your way through the chapter, you probably began to realise that there is a great deal more to standard costing than the piece suggests.

Questions

1 What is a 'business strategy'?

2 Can selling prices be based solely on what they *cost* to make?

3 Does this news story provide a reasonable summary of standard costing?

Tutorial questions

The answers to questions marked with an asterisk can be found in Appendix 4.

16.1 Is it likely that a standard-costing system is of any relevance in a service industry?

16.2 'Standard costing is all about number crunching and for someone on the shop floor it has absolutely no relevance.' Do you agree with this statement?

16.3 'Sales variance calculations are just another example of accountants playing around with numbers.' Discuss.

16.4* You are presented with the following information for X Limited:

Standard price per unit: £10.
Standard quantity for actual production: 5 units.
Actual price per unit: £12.
Actual quantity: 6 units.

Required:
Calculate the following variances:

(a) direct material total variance
(b) direct material price variance
(c) direct material usage variance.

16.5 The following information relates to Malcolm Limited:

Budgeted production: 100 units.
Unit specification (direct materials): 50 kilograms × £5 per kilogram = £250.
Actual production: 120 units.
Direct materials used: 5400 kilograms at a total cost of £32,400.

Required:
Calculate the following variances:

(a) direct material total
(b) direct material price
(c) direct material usage.

16.6* The following information relates to Bruce Limited:

Actual hours: 1000.
Actual wage rate per hour: £6.50.
Standard hours for actual production: 900.
Standard wage rate per hour: £6.00.

Required:
Calculate the following variances:

(a) direct labour total
(b) direct labour rate
(c) direct labour efficiency.

16.7 You are presented with the following information for Duncan Limited:

Budgeted production: 1000 units.
Actual production: 1200 units.
Standard specification for one unit: 10 hours at £8 per direct labour hour.
Actual direct labour cost: £97,200 in 10,800 actual hours.

Required:
Calculate the following variances:

(a) direct labour total
(b) direct labour rate
(c) direct labour efficiency.

16.8* The following overhead budget has been prepared for Anthea Limited:

Actual fixed overhead: £150,000.
Budgeted fixed overhead: £135,000.
Fixed overhead absorption rate per hour: £15.
Actual hours worked: 10,000.
Standard hours of production: 8000.

Required:
Calculate the following fixed production overhead variances:

(a) total
(b) expenditure
(c) volume.

16.9* Using the data contained in the previous question, calculate the following performance measures:

(a) efficiency ratio
(b) capacity ratio
(c) production volume ratio.

16.10 The following information relates to Osprey Limited:

Budgeted production: 500 units.
Standard hours per unit: 10.
Actual production: 600 units.
Budgeted fixed overhead: £125,000.
Actual fixed overhead: £120,000.
Actual hours worked: 4900.

Required:
Calculate the following fixed production overhead variances:

(a) total
(b) expenditure
(c) volume.

16.11 Using the data from the previous question, calculate the following performance measures:

(a) efficiency ratio
(b) capacity ratio
(c) production volume ratio.

16.12* Milton Limited has produced the following information:

Total actual sales: £99,000.
Actual quantity sold: 9000 units.
Budgeted selling price per unit: £10.
Standard cost per unit: £7.
Total budgeted units: 10,000 units.

Required:
Calculate:
(a) the selling price variance
(b) the sales volume profit variance
(c) the sales variance in total.

16.13 You are presented with the following budgeted information for Doe Limited:

Sales units	100
Per unit:	£
Selling price	30
Cost	(20)
Profit	10
Actual sales	120 units
Actual selling price per unit	£28

Required:

Calculate the sales variances.

16.14 The budgeted selling price and standard cost of a unit manufactured by Smillie Limited is as follows:

	£
Selling price	30
Direct materials (2.5 kilos)	5
Direct labour (2 hours)	12
Fixed production overhead	8
	25
Budgeted profit	5

Total budgeted sales: 400 units

During the period to 31 December 2017, the actual sales and production details for Smillie were as follows:

	£
Sales (420 units)	13 440
Direct materials (1260 kilos)	2 268
Direct labour (800 hours)	5 200
Fixed production overhead	3 300
	10 768
Profit	2 672

Required:

(a) Prepare a standard cost operating statement for the period to 31 December 2017 incorporating as many variances as the data permit.

(b) Explain what the statement tells the managers of Smillie Limited.

16.15 Mean Limited manufactures a single product, and the following information relates to the actual selling price and actual cost of the product for the four weeks to 31 March 2016:

	£000
Sales (50 000 units)	2 250
Direct materials (240 000 litres)	528
Direct labour (250 000 hours)	1 375
Variable production overhead	245
Fixed production overhead	650
	2 798
Loss	(548)

The budgeted selling price and standard cost of each unit was as follows:

	£
Selling price	55
Direct materials (5 litres)	10
Direct labour (4 hours)	20
Variable production overhead	5
Fixed production overhead	15
	50
Budgeted profit	5

Total budgeted production: 40 000 units.

Required:

(a) Prepare a standard cost operating statement for the four weeks to 31 March 2016 incorporating as many variances as the data permit.

(b) Explain how the statement may help the managers of Mean Limited to control the business more effectively.

Website

Further practice questions, study material and links to relevant sites on the World Wide Web can be found on the website that accompanies this book. The site can be found at www.pearsoned.co.uk/dyson

Chapter 17 Contribution analysis

Loss cut

Breakeven target

London Live, the local TV channel launched by Evgeny Lebedev's media company, has reduced its losses to £6m for the year to 30 September 2015 after going through a major restructuring and content strategy shift. It now aims to reduce its losses by £3m in 2016 and it is targeting breakeven in 2017.

Tim Kirkman, London Live's Chief Operating Officer said that he was really pleased with the progress that the business was making with over 100% year-on-year growth behind audience and revenues.

'The team is working really well together,' he commented, 'and the channel is now reaching more Londoners than well-established channels like Sky News, Sky Atlantic and Comedy Central.'

The channel is thought to have earned about £3m in revenues in 2016 and it is hoped to double this amount in 2017.

Source: Adapted from http://www.theguardian.com/media2015/oct/28/london-live-...04/01/2016.

Questions relating to this news story can be found on page 396 ➡

About this chapter

In the previous two chapters we have been concerned with the planning and control functions of management accounting. We now turn our attention to another important function of management accounting, *decision making*. In this chapter we explore a basic technique of decision making known as *contribution analysis*.

Contribution analysis is based on the premise that in almost any decision-making situation some costs are irrelevant, that is, they are not affected by the decision. They can, therefore, be ignored. In such circumstances management should concentrate on the *contribution* that a project may make. Contribution (C) is the difference between the sales revenue (S) of a project and the variable or extra costs (V) incurred by investing in that project. Other things being equal, as long as S − V results in C being positive then management should go ahead or continue with the project. If C is positive it means that something is left over to make a *contribution* to the fixed (or remaining) costs (F) of the entity. If the fixed costs have already been covered by other projects, then the contribution increases the entity's profit.

Learning objectives	By the end of this chapter, you should be able to:

- explain why absorption costing may be inappropriate in decision making;
- describe the difference between a fixed cost and a variable cost;
- use contribution analysis in managerial decision making;
- assess the usefulness of contribution analysis in problem solving.

Why this chapter is important

Of all the chapters in this book this is the most relevant and vital for non-accountants because whatever job you are doing and at whatever level, you will be required to make or to take decisions. Many of those decision will be straightforward day-to-day ones such as *'Do we order a week's or a month's supply of paper towels?* Other decisions will be more significant and long-term, for example *Should we increase our selling prices?* or *Do we buy this other company?*

While there is a cost implication in these sorts of decisions, it is unlikely that you would have to do the detailed calculations. Your accountants will do them for you and then present you with the results. However, in order to make sense of the information and to take an informed decision you need to know where the information has come from and how it has been compiled.

This is a valid point irrespective of the particular issue but it is especially valid for specific one-off decision making. If such decisions are based on absorbed costs you might make a spectacularly wrong decision because it would not be based on the project's *relevant* costs, i.e. those costs that are affected by that particular decision.

This chapter will help you to appreciate more clearly the nature of relevant costs and their importance in managerial decision making. As a result, you will be able take more soundly based decisions and be more confident about their eventual outcome.

Marginal costing

News clip

Fitch lowers corporate oil and gas price assumptions

London, 9 November 2015. Fitch Ratings has cut the oil and gas price assumptions it uses when rating energy-sector corporates. This decision reflects the continued imbalance between oil supply and demand, as well as its expectation that marginal costs will fall further in the medium term.

Source: https://www.fitchratings.com/site/fitch-home/pressrelease?id...03/01/2016

Chapters 13 and 14 dealt with cost accounting. The costing method described in some detail in those chapters is known as *absorption costing*. The ultimate aim of absorption costing is to charge out all the costs of an entity to individual units of production. The method involves identifying the *direct costs* of specific units and then absorbing a share of the *indirect costs* into each unit. Indirect costs are normally absorbed on the basis of direct labour hours or machine hours. Assuming that an overhead absorption rate is predetermined, i.e. calculated in advance, this method involves estimating the total amount of overhead likely to be incurred and the total amount of direct labour hours or machine hours expected to be worked. So the absorption rate could be affected by the total cost of the overhead, the hours worked or by a combination of cost and hours.

The total of the indirect costs (the overhead) is likely to be made up of a combination of costs that will change depending on how many units a department produces and those costs that are not affected by the number of units produced. Costs that change with activity are known as *variable costs*. It is usually assumed that variable costs vary directly with activity, e.g. if 1 kg costs £1, then 2 kg will cost £2, 3 kg will cost £3 and so on. Those costs that do not change with activity are known as *fixed costs*.

As we argued in Chapters 13 and 14, if we are attempting to work out the total cost of manufacturing particular units or if we want to value our stocks, it is appropriate to use absorption costing. Most cost bookkeeping systems are based on this method of costing but absorption costing is not normally appropriate in decision making as the fixed element inherent in most costs may not be affected by a particular decision.

Suppose that a manager is costing a particular journey that a member of staff is proposing to make to visit a client. The staff member has a car that is already taxed and insured, so the main cost of the journey will be for petrol (although the car may also depreciate slightly more quickly and it may require a service sooner). The tax and insurance costs will not be affected by one particular journey: they are *fixed costs,* no matter how many extra journeys are undertaken. The manager is, therefore, only interested in the *extra* cost of using the car to visit the client and he can then compare the cost of using the car with the cost of the bus, the train or going by air. Note that cost alone would not necessarily be the determining factor in practice; non-quantifiable factors such as comfort, convenience, fatigue and time would also be important considerations.

The extra cost of making the journey is sometimes described as the *marginal cost.* Hence the technique used in the above example is commonly referred to as *marginal costing.* Economists also use the term 'marginal cost' to describe the extra cost of making an additional unit (as with the extra cost of a particular journey). When dealing with production activities, however, units are more likely to be produced in batches. It would then be more appropriate to substitute the term *incremental costing* and refer to the *incremental cost,* meaning the extra cost of producing a batch of units. As the terms 'marginal costing' and 'marginal cost' are so widely used, however, we will do the same.

The application of marginal costing revolves round the concept of what is known as *contribution.* We explore this concept in the next section.

Activity 17.1

A business college has recently considered starting some extra evening classes on basic computing. The college runs other courses during the evening. The proposed course fee has been based on the lecturer's fee and the cost of heat, light, caretaking and other expenses incurred solely as a result of running the extra classes. However, the principal has insisted that a 25% loading be added to the fee to go towards the college's day-to-day running costs. This is in accordance with the college's normal costing procedures.

Why might the principal's requirement may be inappropriate when costing the proposed evening class lectures?

Contribution

In order to illustrate what is meant by 'contribution' we will use a series of equations. The first is straightforward:

$$\text{sales revenue} - \text{total costs} = \text{profit (or loss)} \qquad (1)$$

The second equation is based on the assumption that total costs can be analysed into variable costs and fixed costs:

$$\text{total costs} = \text{variable costs} + \text{fixed costs} \qquad (2)$$

By substituting equation 2 into equation 1 we can derive equation 3:

$$\text{sales revenue} - (\text{variable costs} + \text{fixed costs}) = \text{profit (or loss)} \qquad (3)$$

By rearranging equation 3 we can derive the following equation:

$$\text{sales revenue} - \text{variable costs} = \text{fixed costs} + \text{profit (or loss)} \qquad (4)$$

Equation 4 is known as the *marginal cost equation*. We will simplify it by substituting symbols for words, namely sales revenue $= S$, variable costs $= V$, fixed costs $= F$, and profit $= P$ (or loss $= L$). The equation now reads as follows:

$$S - V = F + P \qquad (5)$$

But where does contribution fit into all of this? Contribution (C) *is the difference between the sales revenue and the variable costs of that sales revenue.* So, in equation form:

$$S - V = C \qquad (6)$$

Contribution can also be looked at from another point of view. If we substitute C for $(S - V)$ in equation 5, the result will be:

$$C = F + P \qquad (7)$$

In other words, contribution can be regarded as being either the difference between the sales revenue and the variable costs of that sales revenue or the total of fixed cost plus profit.

What do these relationships mean in practice and what is their importance? The meaning is reasonably straightforward. If an entity makes a contribution, it means that it has generated a certain amount of sales revenue and the variable cost of making those sales is less than the total sales revenue ($S - V = C$). So there is a balance left over that can go towards contributing towards the fixed costs ($C - F$); any remaining balance must be the profit ($C - F = P$). Alternatively, if the contribution is insufficient to cover the fixed costs, the entity will have made a loss: $C - F = L$.

The importance of the relationships described above in equation format is important for two main reasons. First, fixed costs can often be ignored when taking a particular decision because, by definition, fixed costs will not change irrespective of whatever decision is taken. This means that any cost and revenue analysis is made much simpler. Second, managers can concentrate on decisions that will maximise the contribution, since every additional £1 of contribution is an extra amount that goes towards covering the fixed costs. Once the fixed costs have been covered, then every extra £1 of contribution is an extra £1 of profit.

Assumptions

The marginal cost technique used in contribution analysis is, of course, based on a number of assumptions. They may be summarised as follows:

- total costs can be split between fixed costs and variable costs;
- fixed costs remain constant irrespective of the level of activity;
- fixed costs do not bear any relationship to specific units;
- variable costs vary in direct proportion to activity.

The reliability of the technique depends very heavily on being able to distinguish between fixed and variable costs. Some costs may be semi-variable, i.e. they may consist of both a fixed and variable element. Electricity costs and telephone charges, for example, both contain a fixed rental element plus a variable charge. The variable charge depends on the units consumed or the number of telephone calls made. Such costs are relatively easy to analyse into their fixed and variable elements.

In practice, it may be difficult to split other costs into their fixed and variable components. The management accountants may need the help of engineers and work study specialists in determining whether a particular cost is fixed or variable. They may also have to draw on a number of graphical and statistical techniques. These techniques are somewhat advanced and beyond this book, so for our purposes we will assume that it is relatively easy to analyse costs into their fixed and variable components.

Format

In applying the marginal cost technique, the cost data are usually arranged in a vertical format on a line-by-line basis. The order of the data reflects the marginal cost equation $(S - V = F + P)$. This format enables the attention of managers to be directed towards the contribution that may arise from any particular decision. The procedure is known as *contribution analysis* and it is illustrated in Example 17.1.

Example 17.1	**A typical marginal cost statement**					

			Product			
	Symbol		A	B	C	Total
			£000	£000	£000	£000
Sales revenue (1)	S		100	70	20	190
Less: variable costs of sales (2)	V		30	32	18	80
Contribution (3)	C		70	38	2	110
Less: fixed costs (4)	F					60
Profit (5)	P					50

Notes:

- The number in brackets after each item description refers to the tutorial notes below.
- The marginal cost equation is represented in the 'symbol' column, i.e. $S - V = C$; $C = F + P$; and thereby $S - V = F + P$.

Tutorial notes

1 The total sales revenue would normally be analysed into different product groupings. In this example there are three products: A, B and 2.835 pt C.

2 The variable costs include direct materials, direct labour costs, other direct costs and variable overheads. Variable costs are assumed to vary *in direct proportion* to activity. Direct costs will normally be the same as variable costs, but in some cases this will not be so. A machine operator's salary, for example, may be fixed under a guaranteed annual wage agreement. It is a direct cost in respect of the machine but it is also a fixed cost because it will not vary with the number of units produced.

3 As explained above, the term *contribution* is used to describe the difference between the sales revenue and the variable cost of those sales. A positive contribution helps to pay for the fixed costs.

4 The fixed costs include all the other costs that do not vary in direct proportion to the sales revenue. Fixed costs are assumed to remain constant over a period of time. They do not bear any relationship to the units produced or the sales achieved. So it is not possible to apportion them to individual products. The *total* of the fixed costs can only be deducted from the *total contribution.*

5 The total contribution less the fixed costs gives the profit (if the balance is positive) or a loss (if the balance is negative).

Managers supplied with information similar to that contained in Example 17.1 may subject the information to a series of 'What if?' questions such as the following.

- What would the profit be if we increased the selling price of product A, B or C?
- What would be the effect if we reduced the selling price of product A, B or C?
- What would be the effect if we eliminated one or more of the products?
- What would happen if we changed the quality of any of the products so that the variable cost of each product either increased or decreased?
- Would any of the above decisions have an impact on fixed costs?

Application

News clip

Marginal costs will help utilities. . .

In the US, some utility companies are using marginal costing to explain how energy is flowing within distribution networks. The mapping of such flows can help utilities meet demand by planning how to regulate usage as well as incentivising customers to use power at times when more of it is available, such as from renewable energy sources.

Source: Adapted from http://www.onzo.com/marginal-costs-will-help-utilities-shift-...03/01/2016

As we have seen, the basic assumptions used in marginal costing are somewhat simplistic. In practice, they would probably only be regarded as appropriate when a particular decision was first considered. Thereafter each of the various assumptions would be rigorously tested and they would be subject to a number of searching questions such as: 'If we change the selling price of this product, will it affect the sales of the other products?' 'Will variable costs always remain in direct proportion to activity?' or 'Will fixed costs remain fixed irrespective of the level of activity?'

We will now use a simple example to illustrate the application of the technique. The details are shown in Example 17.2.

Example 17.2	**Changes in the variable cost**				
		One unit	Proportion	100 units	1000 units
		£	%	£	£
	Sales revenue	10	100	1000	10 000
	Less: variable costs	5	50	500	5 000
	Contribution	5	50	500	5 000

Tutorial notes to Example 17.2

1 The selling price per unit is £10, and the variable cost per unit is £5 (50% of the selling price). The contribution, therefore, is also £5 per unit (50% of the selling price).
2 These relationships are assumed to hold good no matter how many units are sold. So if 100 units are sold the contribution will be £500; if 1000 units are sold there will be a contribution of £5000, i.e. the contribution is assumed to remain at 50% of the sales revenue.
3 The fixed costs are ignored because it is assumed that they will *not* change as the level of activity changes.

Every extra unit sold will increase the profit by £5 per unit *once the fixed costs have been covered* – an important qualification. This point is illustrated in Example 17.3.

Example 17.3	**Changes in profit at varying levels of activity**					
	Activity (units)	1000	2000	3000	4000	5000
		£	£	£	£	£
	Sales	10 000	20 000	30 000	40 000	50 000
	Less: variable costs	5 000	10 000	15 000	20 000	25 000
	Contribution	5 000	10 000	15 000	20 000	25 000
	Less: fixed costs	10 000	10 000	10 000	10 000	10 000
	Profit/(Loss)	(5 000)	–	5 000	10 000	15 000

Tutorial notes to Example 17.3

1 The exhibit illustrates five levels of activity: 1000 units, 2000 units, 3000 units, 4000 units and 5000 units.
2 The variable costs remain directly proportional to activity at all levels, i.e. 50%. The contribution is, therefore, 50% (100% − 50%). The contribution per unit may be obtained by dividing the contribution at any level of activity level by the activity at that level, e.g. at an activity level of 1000 units the contribution per unit is £5 (£5000 ÷ 1000).
3 The fixed costs do not change, irrespective of the level of activity.
4 The contribution needed to cover the fixed costs is £10,000. As each unit makes a contribution of £5, the total number of units needed to be sold in order to break even, i.e. to reach a point

where sales revenue equals the total of both the variable and the fixed costs, will be 2000 (£10,000 ÷ £5).

5 When *more* than 2000 are sold, the increased contribution results in an increase in profit. For example, when 3000 units are sold instead of 2000 the increased contribution is £5000 (£15,000 − 10,000); the increased profit is also £5000 (£5000 − 0). Similarly, when 4000 units are sold instead of 3000, the increased contribution is another £5000 (£20,000 − 15,000) and the increased profit is also £5000 (£10,000 − 5000). Finally, when 5000 units are sold instead of 4000 units, the increased contribution is once more £5000 (£25,000 − 20,000), as is the increased profit (£15,000 − 10,000).

6 The relationship between contribution and sales is known (rather confusingly) as the *profit/volume* (or P/V) ratio. Note that it does not mean *profit* in relationship to sales but the *contribution* in relationship to sales.

7 Assuming that the P/V ratio does not change, we can quickly calculate the profit at any level of sales. All we need to do is to multiply the P/V ratio by the sales revenue and then deduct the fixed costs. The balance will then equal the profit at that level of sales. It is also easy to accommodate any possible change in fixed costs if the activity level moves above or below a certain range.

Example 17.2 and Example 17.3 are simple examples but we hope that they demonstrate just how useful contribution analysis can be in managerial decision making. While the basic assumptions may be somewhat questionable, they can readily be adapted to suit more complex problems.

Charts and graphs

Contribution analysis lends itself to the presentation of information in a pictorial format. Indeed, the $S - V = F + P$ relationship is often easier to appreciate when it is reported to managers graphically.

The most common format is in the form of what is called a *break-even chart*. A break-even chart is illustrated in Example 17.4 and it is based on the data used in Example 17.3.

Example 17.4 shows quite clearly the relationships that are assumed to exist when the marginal costing technique is adopted. Sales revenue, total costs and fixed costs are all assumed to be linear, so they are drawn as straight lines. Note also the following points:

- When no units are sold, the sales revenue line runs from the origin up to £50,000 when 5000 units are sold. It may then continue as a straight line beyond that point.
- The total cost line is made up of both the fixed costs and the variable costs. When there is no activity, the total costs will be equal to the fixed costs, so the total cost line runs from the fixed cost point of £10,000 up to £35,000 when 5000 units are sold. It may then continue beyond that point.
- The fixed cost line is drawn from the £10,000 point as a straight line parallel to the *x* axis irrespective of the number of units sold.

In practice, the above relationships are not likely to hold good over the range of activity indicated in the example. They are usually assumed to remain valid over only a small range of activity. This is known as the *relevant range*. In this example the relevant range may be from (say) 1000 to 3000 units. Above or below these levels the selling prices, the variable costs and the fixed costs may all change.

While this point might appear to create some difficulty, it should be appreciated that wide fluctuations in activity are not normally experienced. It is usually quite reasonable to assume that the entity will be operating in a fairly narrow range of activity and that the various relationships will be linear. It must also be remembered that the information is meant to be only a *guide* to managerial decision making and that it is impossible to be absolutely precise.

Example 17.4	**A break-even chart**

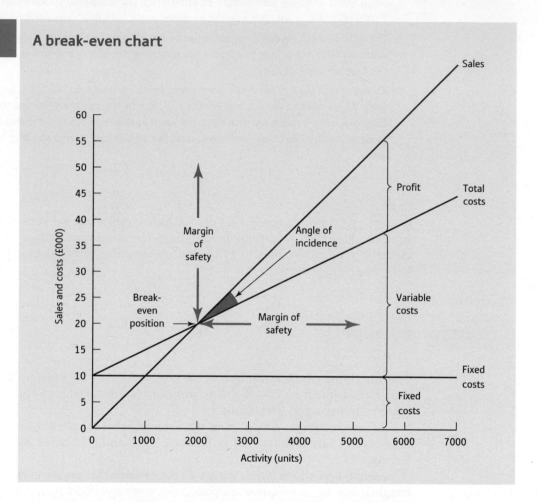

Tutorial notes to Example 17.4

1 The total costs line is a combination of the fixed costs and the variable costs. So it ranges from a total cost of £10,000 (fixed costs only) at a nil level of activity, to £35,000 when the activity level is 5000 units (fixed costs of £10,000 + variable costs of £25,000).

2 The angle of incidence is the angle formed between the sales line and the total cost line. The wider the angle, the greater the amount of profit. A wide angle of incidence and a wide margin of safety (see note 3) indicates a highly profitable position.

3 The margin of safety is the distance between the sales achieved and the sales level needed to break even. It can be measured either in units (along the *x* axis of the graph) or in sales revenue terms (along the *y* axis).

4 Activity (measured along the *x* axis) may be measured in units, as a percentage of the theoretical maximum level of activity or in terms of sales revenue.

The break-even chart shown in Example 17.4 does not show a separate variable cost line. This may be somewhat confusing, and so sometimes the information is presented in the form of a *contribution graph*. A contribution graph based on the data used in Example 17.4 is illustrated in Example 17.5.

 Example 17.5

A contribution graph

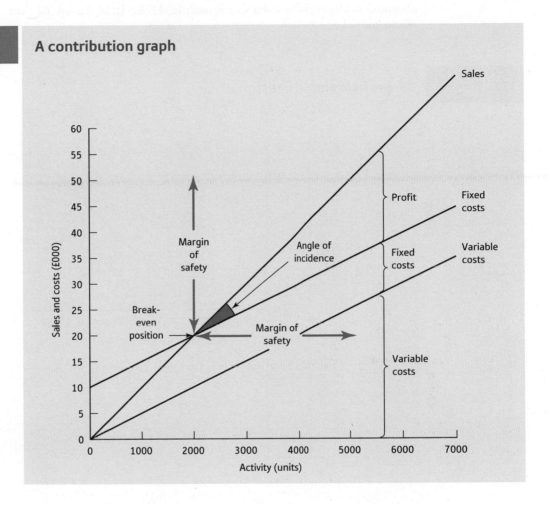

- The contribution graph shows the variable cost line ranging from the origin when there is no activity to £25,000 when 5000 units are sold. It then continues beyond that point in a straight line.
- The fixed cost line is drawn parallel to the variable cost line, i.e. higher up the *y* axis. As the fixed costs are assumed to remain fixed irrespective of the level of activity, the fixed cost line runs from £10,000 when there is no activity to £35,000 when 5000 units are sold. It is then continued as a straight line beyond that point.
- The fixed cost line also serves as the total cost line.

Apart from the above differences, the break-even chart and the contribution graph are identical. Which one should you adopt? There is no specific guidance that we can give since the decision is one largely of personal preference. The break-even chart is more common, but the contribution chart is probably more helpful since the fixed and the variable cost lines are shown separately.

One problem with both the break-even chart and the contribution graph is that neither shows the *actual amount of profit or loss* at varying levels of activity. So if you wanted to know what the profit was when (say) 4000 units were sold, you would have to use a ruler to measure the distance between the sales line and the total cost line. This is not very satisfactory so in order to get over this problem we can use a *profit/volume chart* (or graph).

A profit/volume chart shows the effect of a change in activity on profit. An example of such a chart is shown in Example 17.6. It is based on the data used in Example 17.3.

Example 17.6	**A profit/volume chart**

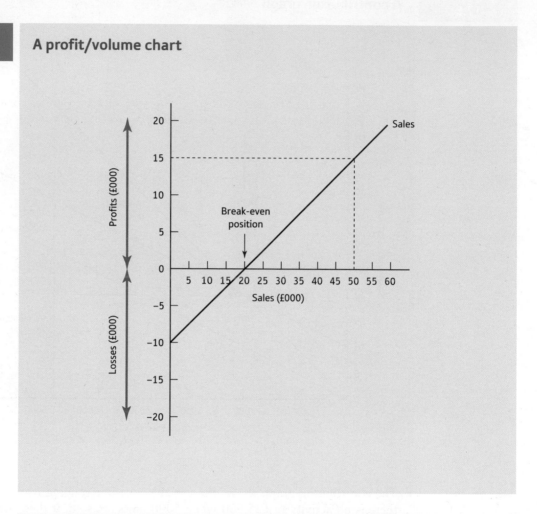

Tutorial notes to Example 17.6

1 The *x* axis can be represented either in terms of units, as a percentage of the activity level or in terms of sales revenue.

2 The *y* axis represents profits (positive amounts) or losses (negative amounts).

3 With sales at a level of £50,000, the profit is £15,000. The sales line cuts the *x* axis at the break-even position of £20,000 sales. If there are no sales, the loss equals the fixed costs of £10,000.

As can be seen from Example 17.6 the profit/volume chart only shows the entity's *total* profit or loss. It does not show the profit or loss made on individual products. It is possible to do so although as Example 17.6 shows the outcome is not altogether clear (see Example 17.7).

<table>
<tr><td>Example
17.7</td><td colspan="5">

Tilsy Limited

You are presented with the following information.
</td></tr>
</table>

Product	A	B	C	Total
	£	£	£	£
Sales	5 000	20 000	25 000	50 000
Less: variable costs	3 000	10 000	12 000	25 000
Contribution	2 000	10 000	13 000	25 000
Less: fixed costs				10 000
Profit				15 000

Additional information:
Assume that Tilsy first began manufacturing and selling Product A, then Product B and finally Product C. Its fixed costs remained constant at £10,000 irrespective of whether it was dealing with one, two or all three of these products.

Required:
Prepare a profit/volume chart showing the impact on its profit/(loss) of the individual product ranges.

Answer to
Example 17.7

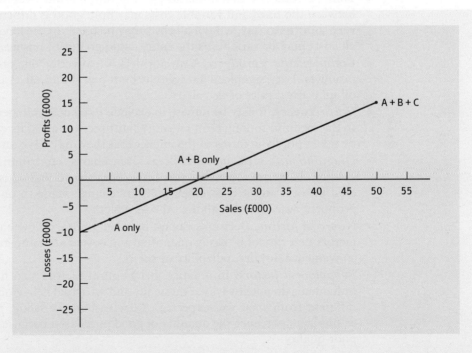

1 If Product A is the first product, the company makes a loss of £8000 (£2000 − 10,000). Once Product B is introduced a profit of £2000 is made [(£2000 + 10,000) − 10,000]. Then when Product C is added the profit becomes £15,000 [(£2000 + 10,000 + 13,000) − 10,000].

2 It would be possible to plot the three product ranges in a different order, e.g. Product B, then Product C, then Product A; or possibly Product C, then Product A, then Product B.

3 The disclosure of the impact of individual products on profit is useful because it can highlight the performance of a poorly performing product. Product A does make a small contribution of £2000 (£5000 − 3000) but this is not sufficient to offset the fixed costs of £10,000. It is only when Product B is introduced that the company begins to make a profit.

Reservations

The assumptions adopted in preparing marginal cost statements and their use in contribution analysis lead to a number of important reservations about the technique. The main ones are as follows.

- *Cost classification.* Costs cannot be easily divided into fixed and variable categories.
- *Variable costs.* Variable costs do not necessarily vary in direct proportion to sales revenue at all levels of activity. The cost of direct materials, for example, may change if supplies are limited or if they are bought in bulk. It is also questionable whether direct labour should be treated as a variable cost (as is often the case) since current legislative practice makes it difficult to dismiss employees at short notice.
- *Fixed costs.* Fixed costs are unlikely to remain constant over a wide range of activity. There is a good chance that they will change both beyond and below a fairly narrow range. They may perhaps move in 'steps', so that between an activity level of 0 and 999 units, for example, the fixed costs may be £10,000, be £12,000 between an activity level of 1000 and 2999 units, be £15,000 between an activity level of 3000 and 5000 units, and so on.
- *Time period.* The determination of the time period over which the relationship between the fixed and variable costs may hold good is difficult to determine. In the very short term (say, a day), all costs may be fixed. In the long term (say, five years), all costs may be variable as the entity could go out of business.
- *Complementary products.* A specific decision affecting one product may affect other products. For example, a garage sells both petrol and oil. A decision to stop selling oil may affect sales of petrol.
- *Cost recovery.* It may be unwise to exclude fixed costs altogether from the analysis. In the medium-to-long term an entity must recover all of its costs. Decisions cannot be taken purely in terms of the impact that they may have on contribution.
- *Diagrammatic presentations.* Break-even charts, contribution graphs and profit/ volume charts are somewhat simplistic. The sales of individual products are considered in total and it is assumed that any change made to one product will have a proportionate effect on all the other products.
- *Non-cost factors.* Decisions cannot be taken purely on the basis of cost. Sometimes factors that cannot be easily quantified and costed are more important, e.g. comfort, convenience, loyalty, reliability or speed.
- *Behavioural factors.* In practice, behavioural factors also have to be considered. Individuals do not always act rationally and an actual behaviour pattern may be quite different from what was expected. A decrease in the selling price of a product, for example, may reduce the quantity of good purchased because it is *perceived* to be of poor quality.

The factors listed above are all fairly severe reservations of the marginal costing technique and its use in contribution analysis. Nevertheless, experience suggests that it has still a useful part to play in managerial decision making provided that the basis on which the information is built is understood, its apparent arithmetical precision is not regarded as a guarantee of absolute certainty, and non-cost factors are taken into account.

With these reservations in mind, we can now move on to look at the technique in a little more detail. Before we do so, however, it would be useful to summarise the main formulae so that it will be easier for you to refer back to them when dealing with the various examples.

Activity 17.2	Reread the reservations outlined above. Which do you think are the three most significant weaknesses of the marginal costing approach?

Formulae

Earlier in the chapter we explained that marginal costing revolves around the assumption that total costs can be classified into fixed and variable costs. This then led us on to an explanation of what we called the *marginal cost equation*, i.e. $S - V = F + P$. This equation can be used as the basis for a number of other simple equations that are useful in contribution analysis. The main ones are summarised below.

Abbreviation:

- Sales − variable cost of sales = contribution $\qquad$ $S - V = C$
- Contribution − fixed costs = profit/(loss) $\qquad$ $C - F = P/(L)$
- Break-even (B/E)point = contribution − fixed costs $\qquad$ $C - F$
- B/E in sales value terms = $\dfrac{\text{fixed costs} \times \text{sales}}{\text{contribution}}$ $\qquad$ $\dfrac{F \times S}{C}$
- B/E in units = $\dfrac{\text{fixed costs}}{\text{contribution per unit}}$ $\qquad$ $\dfrac{F}{C \text{ per unit}}$
- Margin of safety (M/S) in sales value terms = $\dfrac{\text{profit} \times \text{sales}}{\text{contribution}}$ $\qquad$ $\dfrac{P \times S}{C}$
- M/S in units = $\dfrac{\text{profit}}{\text{contribution per unit}}$ $\qquad$ $\dfrac{P}{C \text{ per unit}}$

Example 17.8 illustrates the use of some of these formulae.

Example 17.8	**The use of the marginal cost formulae**

The following information relates to Happy Limited for the year to 30 June 2017.

Number of units sold: 10,000

	Per unit £	Total £000
Sales	30	300
Less: Variable costs	18	180
Contribution	12	120
Less: Fixed costs		24
Profit		96

Required:
In value and unit terms, calculate the following:
(a) the break-even position
(b) the margin of safety.

Answer to Example 17.8

(a) Break-even position in value terms:

$$\frac{F \times S}{C} = \frac{£24000 \times 300\,000}{120\,000} = \underline{£60\,000}$$

Break-even in units:

$$\frac{F}{C \text{ per unit}} = \frac{£24\,000}{12} = \underline{2000 \text{ units}}$$

(b) Margin of safety in value terms:

$$\frac{P \times S}{C} = \frac{£96\,000 \times 300\,000}{120\,000} = \underline{£240\,000}$$

Margin of safety in units:

$$\frac{P}{C \text{ per unit}} = \frac{£96\,000}{12} = \underline{8000 \text{ units}}$$

Tutorial note   Note the relationship between the sales revenue and the margin of safety. The sales revenue is £300,000 and £60,000 of sales revenue is required to break even. The margin of safety is, therefore, £240,000 (£300,000 − 60,000).

It would now be helpful to incorporate the principles behind contribution analysis into a simple example. Example 17.9 outlines a typical problem that a board of directors might well face.

Example 17.9

Marginal costing

Looking ahead to the financial year ending 31 March 2018, the directors of Problems Limited are faced with a budgeted loss of £10,000. This is based on the following data.

Budgeted number of units: 10,000

	£000
Sales revenue	100
Less: Variable costs	80
Contribution	20
Less: Fixed costs	30
Budgeted loss	(10)

The directors would like to aim for a profit of £20,000 for the year to 31 March 2018. Various proposals have been put forward, none of which require a change in the budgeted level of fixed costs. These proposals are as follows:

1 Reduce the selling price of each unit by 10 per cent.
2 Increase the selling price of each unit by 10 per cent.
3 Stimulate sales by improving the quality of the product, which would increase the variable cost of the unit by £1.50 per unit.

Required:
(a) For each proposal calculate:
   (i) the break-even position in units and in value terms;
   (ii) the number of units required to be sold in order to meet the profit target.

(b) State which proposal you think should be adopted.

Answer to Example 17.9

Problems Limited

(a) (i) and (ii)

Workings:	£
Profit target	20 000
Fixed costs	30 000
Total contribution required	50 000

The budgeted selling price per unit is £10 (£100 000/10 000). The budgeted variable cost per unit is £8 (£80 000/10 000).

The budgeted outlook compared with each proposal may be summarised as follows:

Per unit:	Budgeted position	Proposal 1	Proposal 2	Proposal 3
	£	£	£	£
Selling price	10	9	11	10.00
Less: Variable costs	8	8	8	9.50
(a) Unit contribution	2	1	3	0.50
(b) Total contribution required to break even (= fixed costs) (£)	30 000	30 000	30 000	30 000
(c) Total contribution required to meet the profit target (£)	50 000	50 000	50 000	50 000
Number of units to break even [(b)/(a)]	15 000	30 000	10 000	60 000
Number of units to meet the profit target [(c)/(a)]	25 000	50 000	16 667	100 000

(b) Comments

1 By continuing with the present budget proposals, the company would need to sell 15,000 units to break even or 25,000 units to meet the profit target. So in order to break even the company needs to increase its unit sales by 50% $\left(\dfrac{£15\,000 - 10\,000}{10\,000} \times 100\right)$ and by 150% $\left(\dfrac{£25\,000 - 10\,000}{10\,000} \times 100\right)$ to meet the profit target.

2 A reduction in selling price of 10% per unit would require unit sales to increase by 200% $\left(\dfrac{£30\,000 - 10\,000}{10\,000} \times 100\right)$ in order to break even and by 400% $\left(\dfrac{£50\,000 - 10\,000}{10\,000} \times 100\right)$ to meet the profit target.

3 By increasing the selling price of each unit by 10%, the company would only have to sell at the budgeted level to break even, but its unit sales would have to increase by 66.7% $\left(\dfrac{£16\,667 - 10\,000}{10\,000} \times 100\right)$ to meet the profit target.

4 By improving the product at an increased variable cost of £1.50 per unit, the company would require a 500% $\left(\dfrac{£60\,000 - 10\,000}{10\,000} \times 100\right)$ increase in unit sales to break even, or a 900% $\left(\dfrac{£100\,000 - 10\,000}{10\,000} \times 100\right)$ increase to meet the profit target.

Conclusion

It would appear that increasing the selling price by 10% would be a more practical solution for the company to adopt. In the short run, at least, it will break even and there is the possibility that sales could be sufficient to make a small profit. In the long run this proposal has a much better chance of meeting the profit target than do the other proposals. Some extra stimulus would be needed, however, to lift sales to this level over such a relatively short period of time. It is not clear why an increase in price would increase sales, unless the product is one that only sells at a comparatively high price, such as cosmetics and patent medicines. It must also be questioned whether the cost relationships will remain as indicated in the example over such a large increase in activity. In particular, it is unlikely that the fixed costs will remain entirely fixed if there were to be a 66.7% increase in sales.

Limiting factors

When optional decisions are being considered, the aim will always be to maximise contribution because the greater the contribution, then the more chance there is of covering the fixed costs and of making a profit. When managers are faced with a choice, therefore, between (say) producing product A at a contribution of £10 per unit or of producing product B at a contribution of £20 per unit, they would normally choose product B. Sometimes, however, it may not be possible to produce unlimited quantities of product B because there could be limits on how many units could either be sold or produced. Such limits are known as *limiting factors* (or key factors).

Limiting factors may arise for a number of reasons. It may not be possible, for example, to sell more than a certain number of units, there may be production restraints (such as shortages of raw materials, skilled labour or factory space), and the company may not be able to finance the anticipated rate of expansion.

If there is a product that cannot be produced and sold in unlimited quantities, then it is necessary to follow a simple rule in order to decide which product to concentrate on producing. The rule can be summarised:

choose the work that provides the maximum contribution per unit of limiting factor employed.

This sounds very complicated but it is easy to apply in practice. In outline, the procedure is as follows (we will assume that direct labour hours are in short supply).

1 Calculate the contribution made by each product.
2 Divide the contribution that each product makes by the number of direct labour hours used in making each product.
3 This gives the contribution per direct labour hour employed i.e. the limiting factor.
4 Select the project that gives the highest contribution per unit of limiting factor.

If we had to choose between two jobs, say, A and B, we would convert A's contribution and B's contribution into the amount of contribution earned for every direct labour hour worked on A and on B respectively. We would then opt for the job that earned the most contribution per direct labour hour. The technique is illustrated in Example 17.10.

Example 17.10

Application of key factors

Quays Limited manufactures a product for which there is a shortage of the raw material known as PX. During the year to 31 March 2017, only 1000 kilograms of PX will be available. PX is used by Quays in manufacturing both product 8 and product 9. The following information is relevant:

Per unit:	Product 8 £	Product 9 £
Selling price	300	150
Less: Variable costs	200	100
Contribution	100	50
P/V ratio $\left(\dfrac{£100}{300}\times 100\right)$ and $\left(\dfrac{£50}{150}\times 100\right)$	$33\frac{1}{3}$	$33\frac{1}{3}$
Kilograms of PX required	5	2

Required:
State which product Quays Limited should concentrate on producing.

Answer to Example 17.10

	Product 8 £	Product 9 £
Contribution per unit	100	50
	$\div$	$\div$
Limiting factor per unit (kg)	5	2
Contribution per kilogram	$= 20$	$= 25$

Decision:
Quays should concentrate on product 9 because it gives the highest contribution per unit of limiting factor.

Check:
Maximum contribution of product 8:

   200 units (1000kg/5) $\times$ contribution per unit $= 200 \times £100 = £20\,000$

Maximum contribution of product 9:

   500 units (1000kg/2) $\times$ contribution per unit $= 500 \times £50 = £25000$

In Example 17.10 it was assumed that there was only one limiting factor, but there could be many more. This situation is illustrated in Example 17.11. The basic data are the same as for Example 17.10.

Example 17.11

Marginal costing using two key factors

Information:

1 Assume now that it is not possible for Quays Limited to sell more than 400 units of product 9.
2 The company would aim to sell all of the 400 units because product 9's contribution per unit of limiting factor is greater than product 8's. The total contribution would then be £20,000 (400 × £50).

3 The 400 units would consume 800 units of raw materials (400 × 2 kilograms), leaving 200 (1000 − 800); kilograms for use in producing product 8.

4 Product 8 requires 5 kilograms per unit of raw materials, so 40 units (200kg ÷ 5kg) could be completed at a total contribution of £4000 (40 × £100).

Summary of the position:

	Product 8	Product 9	Total
Units sold	40	400	
Raw materials (kilograms used)	200	800	1 000
Contribution per unit (£)	100	50	
Total contribution (£)	4 000	20 000	24 000

Note: The £24,000 total contribution compares with the contribution of £25,000 that the company could have made if there were no limiting factors affecting the sales of product 9.

Questions you should ask

When you have a specific decision to take as a manager, it is almost certain that your accountants will do the detailed calculative work for you. They are likely to present you with a summary of their results and their recommendations.

We will assume that you have asked them for some guidance on a specific decision that you have to take. What should you ask them when you receive the information? The following questions are suggested, although you will, of course, need to adapt them depending on the circumstances.

- Where has the data come from?

- What estimates have you had to make in adapting the original data?

- Has the information been compiled on a contribution basis?

- If not, why not? What other method have you used? Why is the contribution approach not appropriate in this case?

- If the contribution approach has been used, how have the variable costs been separated from the fixed costs?

- Have you assumed that variable costs move in direct proportion to sales revenue?

- Over what timescale are the fixed costs fixed?

- Over what time period will the various cost relationships last?

- What impact will your recommendations have on other aspects of the business?

- What non-quantifiable factors have you been able to take into account?

- What non-quantifiable factors have been ignored?

- Generally, how reliable is the information that you have given me?

- What confidence can I have in it?

- Is there anything else that I should know?

Conclusion

Contribution analysis is particularly useful in short-term decision making but it is of less value when decisions have to be viewed over the long term. The system revolves around two main assumptions:

- some costs remain fixed irrespective of the level of activity;
- other costs vary in direct proportion to sales.

These assumptions are not valid over the long term but provided that they are used with caution then they can be adopted usefully in the short term.

It should also be remembered that the technique is only a *guide* to decision making and that non-cost factors have to be taken into account.

In Chapter 18 we use contribution analysis to deal with other managerial problems.

Key points

1 Total cost can be analysed into fixed costs and variable costs.

2 Fixed costs are assumed to be unrelated to activity. They may be ignored in making short-term managerial decisions.

3 A company will aim to maximise the *contribution* that each unit makes to profit.

4 The various relationships between costs can be expressed in the form of an equation: $S - V = F + P$, where S = sales, V = variable costs, F = fixed costs and P = profit.

5 It may not always be possible to maximise unit contribution because materials, labour, finance or other factors may be in short supply.

6 In the long run, fixed costs cannot be ignored.

Check your learning

The answers to these questions can be found within the text.

1 What system of costing is normally used for the costing of products and for stock valuation purposes?

2 Why is this system not suitable for specific decision making?

3 What is meant by 'decision making'?

4 What term is given to the extra cost of an event?

5 What is meant by 'incremental costing'?

6 What is (a) a fixed cost, (b) a variable cost?

7 What is meant by the term 'contribution'?

8 What is the marginal cost equation?

9 List four main assumptions that underpin marginal costing.

10 What is a break-even chart?

11 What is meant by the terms (a) 'break-even', (b) 'angle of incidence', (c) 'margin of safety'?

12 What is a contribution graph?

13 What is a profit/volume chart?

14 List six assumptions that are adopted when preparing a marginal cost statement.

15 What is the formula for calculating (a) the break-even position in sales value terms, (b) the break-even position in units, (c) the margin of safety in sales value terms, (d) the margin of safety in units?

16 What is meant by a 'limiting factor'?

17 Give three examples of limiting factors.

18 State the rule that is used when activity is restricted by the presence of a limiting factor.

News story quiz

Remember that news story at the beginning of this chapter? Go back to that story and reread it before answering the following questions.

This story relates to a UK television company that has been losing money. It now appears that it will not be long before it expects to achieve some much better results.

Questions

1 What is meant by the announcement that the company is 'targeting breakeven in 2017'?

2 Can you suggest some reasons why the company only *thinks* that it has made an operating loss of £6m in the year to the end of September 2015?

3 If the company is likely to break even in 2017, what will its costs be for that year?

Tutorial questions

The answers to questions marked with an asterisk can be found in Appendix 4.

17.1 'It has been suggested that although contribution analysis is fine in theory, fixed costs cannot be ignored in practice.' Discuss this statement.

17.2 'Contribution analysis described in textbooks is too simplistic and is of little relevance to management.' How far do you agree with this statement?

17.3 Do break-even charts and profit graphs help management to make more meaningful decisions?

17.4* The following information relates to Pole Limited for the year to 31 January 2016.

	£000
Administration expenses:	
Fixed	30
Variable	7
Semi-variable (fixed 80%, variable 20%)	20
Materials:	
Direct	60
Indirect	5
Production overhead (all fixed)	40
Research and development expenditure:	
Fixed	60
Variable	15
Semi-variable (fixed 50%, variable 50%)	10
Sales	450
Selling and distribution expenditure:	
Fixed	80
Variable	4
Semi-variable (fixed 70%, variable 30%)	30
Wages:	
Direct	26
Indirect	13

Required:
Using the above information, compile a contribution analysis statement for Pole Limited for the year to 31 January 2016.

17.5* You are presented with the following information for Giles Limited for the year to 28 February 2017:

	£000
Fixed costs	150
Variable costs	300
Sales (50 000 units)	500

Required:
(a) Calculate the following:
  (i) the break-even point in value terms and in units
  (ii) the margin of safety in value terms and in units.
(b) Prepare a break-even chart.

17.6 The following information applies to Ayre Limited for the two years to 31 March 2018 and 2019 respectively:

Year	Sales £000	Profits £000
31.3.2018	750	100
31.3.2019	1 000	250

Required:
Assuming that the cost relationships had remained as given in the question, calculate the company's profit if the sales for the year to 31 March 2019 had reached the budgeted level of £1,200,000.

17.7 The following information relates to Carter Limited for the year to 30 April 2017:

Units sold: 50,000	
Selling price per unit	£40
Net profit per unit	£9
Profit/volume ratio	40%

During 2018 the company would like to increase its sales substantially, but to do so it would have to reduce the selling price per unit by 20 per cent. The variable cost per unit will not change, but because of the increased activity the company will have to invest in new machinery which will increase the fixed costs by £30,000 per annum.

Required:
Given the new conditions, calculate how many units the company will need to sell in 2018 in order to make the same amount of profit as it did in 2017.

17.8 Puzzled Limited would like to increase its sales during the year to 3l May 2018. To do so, it has several mutually exclusive options open to it:

- reduce the selling price per unit by 15 per cent;
- improve the product resulting in an increase in the variable cost per unit of £1.30;
- spend £15,000 on an advertising campaign;
- improve factory efficiency by purchasing more machinery at a fixed extra annual cost of £22,500.

During the year to 31 May 2017, the company sold 20,000 units. The cost details were as follows:

	£000
Sales	200
Variable costs	150
Contribution	50
Fixed costs	40
Profit	10

These cost relationships are expected to hold in 2018.

Required:
State which option you would recommend and why.

17.9 The following information relates to Mere's budget for the year to 31 December 2018:

	Product			
	K	L	M	Total
	£000	£000	£000	£000
Sales	700	400	250	1350
Direct materials	210	60	30	300
Direct labour	100	200	200	500

		Product		
	K	*L*	*M*	*Total*
	£000	*£000*	*£000*	*£000*
Variable overhead	90	60	50	200
Fixed overhead	20	40	40	100
	420	360	320	1100
Profit/(loss)	280	40	(70)	250
Budgeted sales (units)	140	20	25	

Note: Fixed overheads are apportioned on the basis of direct labour hours.

The directors are worried about the loss that product M is budgeted to make and various suggestions have been made to counteract the loss, viz.:

- stop selling product M;
- increase M's selling price by 20 per cent;
- reduce M's selling price by 10 per cent;
- reduce its costs by purchasing a new machine costing £350,000, thereby decreasing the direct labour cost by £100,000 (the machine would have a life of five years; its residual value would be nil).

Required:
Evaluate each of these proposals.

Website

Further practice questions, study material and links to relevant sites on the World Wide Web can be found on the website that accompanies this book. The site can be found at www.pearsoned.co.uk/dyson

Decision making

Join the queue

Staff made redundant

The majority of the 450 staff at Fairline Boats have been made redundant after the luxury yacht maker went into administration last week. Administrators have kept on 69 workers to keep the business running and finish existing orders but the remaining 381 have been told not to return to work when they were sent home last Wednesday.

Most of the retained staff are at Fairline's factories in Corby and Oundle in Northamptonshire, where the 52-year-old company designs and manufactures a range of luxury boats under the Targa and Squadron brands, ranging in value from £350,000 to £2.5m. A few are still working at the boat testing site in Ipswich, Suffolk.

A supplier to the powerboat maker Fletcher, which is also owned by Fairline's private equity owner Wessex Bristol, told *The Guardian* that Fairline's suppliers had not been paid for three months, while many of Fletcher's suppliers were also waiting to be paid.

About 185 staff had already been suspended and encouraged to resign in recent weeks after Jon Moulton's private equity fund Better Capital sold Fairline to Wessex Bristol, for a deferred £2m in September.

At the end of March, the boat maker was still valued at £13.5m, but it has been hit by a slump in orders from wealthy Russians who have been affected by a deepening recession, falling commodity prices and a weak rouble.

Better Capital said it put Fairline into administration to protect its interests as a senior creditor after Wessex Capital failed to inject promised funds into the boat maker that were 'essential for it to function as a going concern'. Better Capital bought Fairline for £16.6m in 2011 and had invested a further £2.4m in the business.

The private equity fund said it had hoped that a 'sale to such an experienced and apparently well-funded buyer would secure the future of the business, but this had not been the case'.

Source: Adapted from http://www.theguardian.com/business/2015/dec/08/fairline-b...

Questions relating to this news story can be found on pages 416 ➡

About this chapter

In Chapter 17 we suggested that the use of absorption costing in many may lead to some unwise decision-making situations and that a contribution approach using marginal costing would perhaps be more appropriate. Marginal costing involves classifying costs on a fixed/variable basis, instead of on a direct/indirect basis as in absorption costing. There are, however, other ways of classifying costs and we outline some of them in this chapter.

The chapter also uses your overall knowledge of management accounting to examine some specific decision-making situations. We cover four main types of decision:

- those that involve determining whether to close or shut down a plant or a factory;
- those that involve deciding whether we supply or make our own materials and components;
- those that involve determining what price to charge for goods and services;
- those that involve deciding what price to charge for one-off or special orders.

Learning objectives

By the end of this chapter, you should be able to:

- outline the nature and purpose of decision making;
- list six ways of classifying costs for decision-making purposes;
- incorporate cost and financial data into specific decision-making situations.

! Why this chapter is important

The previous chapter was one of the most important in the book and this one is also very important. It tells you a little more about decision making and the classification of costs. It then uses some numerical examples to illustrate the particular direction that various decisions should take.

The chapter is heavily biased towards helping you as a non-accountant to make and to take effective decisions and so it is a very important one if you are to become an all-round first-class manager.

Nature and purpose

News clip

Making decisions

There are different ways to make decisions. Some work better than others, depending on the factors driving the decision and the people involved. The business size and structure may also affect the decision-making process.

Source: http://smallbusiness.chron.com/decision-making-processeso...2016

We start our examination of this important topic by examining the nature and purpose of decision making.

The term *decision* will be familiar to you in your everyday life. It means coming to a conclusion about a particular issue, e.g. when to get up in the morning, whether to have tea or coffee for breakfast, or choosing between a holiday and buying some new clothes. Similarly, in a managerial context, decisions have to be taken about whether or not to sell in particular markets, buy some new machinery or spend more money on research.

Management accountants will be involved in collecting data and supplying information for such decisions. While the information that they supply will be primarily of a financial nature, they will highlight other considerations that need to be taken into account before a final decision is made. The eventual decision will rest with the responsibility centre manager concerned. It may well be that non-cost factors turn out to be more important than measurable financial considerations. For example, an entity may buy components from an external supplier because they are cheaper. What happens if the supplier becomes unreliable? It might then be worth the extra cost of manufacturing the components internally in order to avoid the risk of any disruption to normal production.

The information required for decision-making purposes tends to be more wide-ranging and less constrained than that used in cost accounting. Its main characteristics are summarised below and depicted in Figure 18.1.

- *Forward looking.* While historical data may be used as a guide, information for decision making is much more concerned with what *will* happen rather than with what *did* happen. As so much of the information required is concerned with the future, considerable initiative and intuitive judgement is required in being able to obtain it.
- *One-off decisions.* Decision making often involves dealing with a problem that is unique, so a solution has to be geared towards dealing with that particular problem.
- *Data availability.* While some of the data required for decision making may be extracted from the cost accounting system, much of what is required may have to be obtained elsewhere.
- *Net cash flow.* Managers will be concerned with the impact that a decision may have on the expected net cash flow of a particular project, i.e. future cash receipts less future cash expenditure. The calculation of periodic profit and loss based on accruals and prepayments will be largely irrelevant.
- *Relevant costs.* Costs and revenues that are not affected by a decision are excluded from the analysis. Fixed costs, for example, would normally be ignored because they are not likely to change.
- *Opportunity costs.* Those benefits that would be foregone or lost as a result of taking a particular decision are known as *opportunity costs*. They form an important part of any decision-making analysis. You may decide, such as whether to look after your own garden yourself instead of doing some paid overtime. The opportunity cost would be the wages or salary you lose by not working overtime less the amount you save by not employing a gardener.
- *Probability testing.* Much of the information used in problem solving is speculative because it relates to the future and so it is advisable to carry out some probability testing. This is an extremely complex area and it goes beyond this book. In broad terms it involves calculating the *expected value* of a particular project or proposal. The basic idea is demonstrated in Example 18.1.

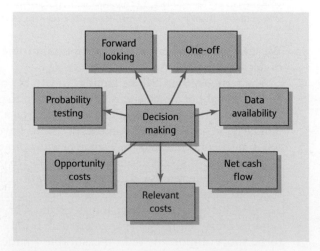

Figure 18.1 The nature of decision making

| Example 18.1 | **Probability testing** |

Company X sells one product codenamed A1. The marketing department has estimated that the sales of A1 for a forthcoming budget period could be £1000, £1500 or £2000. On further investigation it would appear that there is a 70 per cent chance that the sales will be £1000, a 20 per cent chance that the sales will be £1500 and a 10 per cent chance that the sales will be £2000.

Required:
Calculate the expected value of sales for product A1 during the forthcoming budget period.

Answer to Example 18.1

The question requires us to calculate the expected value of the sales of A1 for the forthcoming period. It might be easier for you to think of the expected value as the *weighted average*, which perhaps provides a clue to what is required. In order to calculate the expected values the budgeted sales figures are multiplied by their respective chances or probabilities. So:

Budgeted sales (1)	Probability (2)	Expected value (3)
£	%	£
1 000	70	700
1 500	20	300
2 000	10	200
	100	1 200

Tutorial notes

1 The expected value (or weighted average) of the sales for the forthcoming budget period is £1200 [as per column (3).]

2 The answer has been obtained by multiplying the three estimated levels of sales by their respective probabilities (column (1) multiplied by column (2)).

3 In this exhibit, the probabilities are expressed in percentage terms. When combined, they should always total 100%. Note that sometimes they are expressed in decimal terms; they should then total 1.0 (in our example 0.7 + 0.2 + 0.1 = 1.0).

4 The probabilities are estimates. They may be made partly on past experience, partly on an investigation of the market and partly on instinct. In other words they might be better described as 'guesstimates'.

5 Does the solution make sense? The expected value is £1200; this is £200 more than the lowest level of sales of £1000; the probability of this level being achieved is 70 per cent. The chance of the sales being at least £1000 is quite high. By contrast, there is only a 20 per cent probability that the sales could be as high as £1500 and only a 10 per cent chance that they could reach £2000. It seems reasonable to assume, therefore, that the sales are likely to be nearer £1000 than £1500 and that £1200 appears to be a reasonable compromise.

Cost classification

News clip

Storage costly

According to a survey by *Veritas*, most data retained by organisations are not identified or classified and gobble budget spent on storage, as well as being potentially non-compliant. A typical mid-size company wastes nearly a million pounds each year maintaining trivial files, including photos, music and videos.

The survey clearly demonstrates that there is a great need for some serious decision-making about what to store and what to keep in all sizes and types of entities.

Source: Adapted from http://www.computerweekly.com/news/450025609/Lack-of...

As we have explained in previous chapters, costs and revenues may be classified into various categories depending upon for what they are going to be used. In cost accounting, information is required mainly for product costing and stock valuation purposes, and so the most important category is the distinction between direct costs and indirect ones.

A direct/indirect cost classification is not normally appropriate in decision making. The preferred classification is that relating to fixed and variable costs but you will come across other cost classifications. We show the main ones used in decision making in Figure 18.2 along with a brief explanation of each classification.

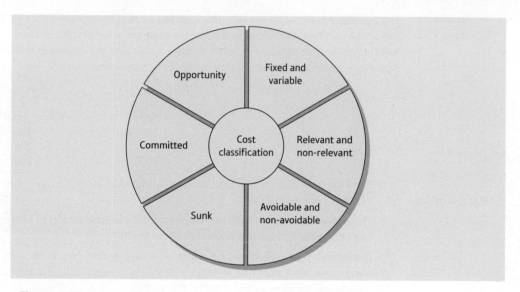

Figure 18.2 Cost classification

Fixed and variable costs

We covered such costs in the previous chapter. Fixed costs are those that are likely to remain unchanged irrespective of the level of activity. Variable costs are those that move directly proportional to activity – one unit results in £1 of variable cost, two units results in £2 of variable cost, three units in £3 of variable cost and so on.

In theory, those costs classified as 'fixed' will remain the same irrespective of whether the entity is completely inactive or if it is operating at full capacity. In practice, fixed costs tend to remain fixed only over a relatively small range of activity range and only in the short term.

The assumption that fixed costs remain unchanged means that they do not normally need to be taken into account. In other words, they can be ignored because they will not be affected by the decision and they are not relevant in any consideration of the issues.

Relevant and non-relevant costs

Relevant costs are those future costs that are likely to be affected by a particular decision. It follows that non-relevant costs are those that are *not* likely to be affected by the decision. This means that non-relevant costs, such as fixed costs, can be excluded from any cost analysis (although they are not always irrelevant).

Avoidable and non-avoidable costs

Avoidable costs are those that may be saved by not taking a particular decision. Non-avoidable costs will still be incurred if the decision is taken. Avoidable and non-avoidable costs are very similar to relevant and non-relevant costs and sometimes the terms are used synonymously.

Sunk costs

Sunk costs are those that have already been incurred as a result of a previous decision. They are not relevant as far as future decisions are concerned and they can be excluded from any decision-making analysis.

Committed costs

A committed cost arises out of a decision that has previously been taken although the event has not yet taken place. For example, a proposal to increase the capacity of a factory from 1000 to 1500 units per annum will result in increased capital expenditure. A decision to accept the proposal means that certain costs are *committed* and it only becomes a matter of time before there is a cash outflow. Once the proposal has gone ahead and it has been paid for, the costs become *sunk* costs. Committed costs (like sunk costs) are not relevant as far as *future* decisions are concerned.

Opportunity costs

We referred to opportunity costs in the previous section of this chapter. Just to remind you, an opportunity cost is a measure of the net benefit that would be lost if one decision is taken instead of another decision. Opportunity costs are not normally recorded in the cost accounting system because they are difficult to quantify so they may need to be estimated.

Activity 18.1

Carla Friar is a mature student at university. Her university fees and maintenance cost her £7000 a year. Carla gave up her job in a travel centre to become a full-time student. Her take-home pay was then £20,000 a year but she also lost various travel concessions worth £1000 a year. As a student she has little free time, she socialises infrequently and so she does not spend much. This saves her about £2000 a year but, of course, she misses her friends and her nights out.

What factors do you think that Carla should take into account in trying to work out the opportunity cost of being a student?

Types of decision

We now turn to some specific decisions that managers may have to take. They are shown in diagrammatic format in Figure 18.3. The figure is followed by an explanation of each decision. The purchase of capital assets is another important decision but we leave this topic to the next chapter as it needs to be considered in some depth.

Type	Question
Closure and shutdown	Will it be temporary or permanent?
Make or buy	Do we make our own or buy outside?
Pricing	Should it be market based or cost based?
Special orders	Will it be profitable?
Capital investment	How much will it cost?

Figure 18.3 Types of decision

Closure and shutdown decision

News clip

Teaching better decision making

According to Aron Pont, the Learning Solutions Architect at Sponge UK, better decision making comes through evaluation, exploration and experience. He believes that *elearning* games can improve and support such soft skills and so they support decision making in the workplace.

Source: Adapted from http://training pressreleases.com/news/sponge/2015/spo...

A common problem that managers may face from time to time is whether to close some segment of the enterprise, such as a product, a service, a department or even an entire factory. This is a *closure* decision, the assumption being that the closure would be permanent. A similar decision may have to be taken in respect of a temporary closure. This is known as a *shutdown* decision.

A closure decision sometimes needs to be taken because a segment within the overall entity may have become unprofitable, out of date or unfashionable and therefore no future is seen for it. A decision to close a segment of an entity temporarily would be taken when the segment's problems are likely to be overcome in the near future. A segment may be unprofitable at the moment but it perhaps could recover in (say) a year's time.

Closure and shutdown decisions are often required because a segment is regarded as being 'unprofitable'. The definition of 'unprofitable' has to be looked at very closely. A product, for example, may not be making a *profit* but it may be making a *contribution* towards the fixed costs of the company. Should it be abandoned? Great care would need to be taken before such a decision was taken. The abandonment of one product may have an impact on the sales of other products and it may be beneficial to sell the product below its variable cost (at least in the short term).

Closure and shutdown decisions are not easy to make because they often require staff to be made redundant. They cannot be determined purely on narrow cost grounds as other wide-ranging factors may need to be considered. We illustrate a relatively straightforward closure decision in Example 18.2.

| Example 18.2 | A closure decision |

A closure decision

Vera Limited has three main product lines: 1, 2 and 3. The company uses an absorption costing system. The following information relates to the budget for the year 2018.

Product line	1	2	3	Total
Budgeted sales (units)	10 000	4 000	6 000	
	£000	£000	£000	£000
Sales revenue	300	200	150	650
Direct materials	100	40	60	200
Direct labour	50	70	80	200
Production overhead	75	30	35	140
Non-production overhead	15	10	5	30
	240	150	180	570
Profit (Loss)	60	50	(30)	80

Additional information:

1 Both direct materials and direct labour are considered to be variable costs.
2 The total production overhead of £140,000 consists of £40,000 variable costs and £100,000 fixed costs. Variable production overheads are absorbed on the basis of 20 per cent of the direct labour costs.
3 The non-production overhead of £30,000 is entirely fixed.
4 Assume that there will be no opening or closing stock.

Required:
Determine whether product line 3 should be closed.

Answer to Example 18.2

Points

1 The first step in determining whether to recommend a closure of product line 3 is to calculate the *contribution* that each product line makes.
2 In order to do so, it is necessary to rearrange the data given in the question in a marginal cost format, i.e. separate the fixed costs from the variable costs.
3 If product line 3 makes a contribution then other factors will have to be taken into account before an eventual decision can be made.

Calculations

Product line	1	2	3	Total
Budgeted sales (units)	10 000	4 000	6 000	
	£000	£000	£000	£000
Sales revenue	300	200	150	650
Less: Variable costs:				
Direct materials	100	40	60	200
Direct labour	50	70	80	200
Variable production overhead (question note 2: 20% of direct labour cost)	10	14	16	40
c/f	160	124	156	440

Product line		1	2	3	Total
	b/f	160	124	156	440
Contribution		140	76	(6)	210
Less: Fixed costs:					
Production overheads					
(£140 − 40)					(100)
Non-production overheads					
(See question note 3)					(30)
Profit					80

Observations

It would appear that product line 3 neither makes a profit nor contributes towards the fixed costs. Should it be closed? Before such a decision is taken a number of other factors would have to be considered. These are as follows.

- Are the budgeted figures accurate? Have they been checked? How reliable are the budgeted data?
- What method has been used to identify the direct material costs that each product line uses? Is it appropriate for all three product lines?
- The question states that direct labour is a variable cost. Is direct labour really a variable cost? Is the assessment of its cost accurate and realistic?
- Variable production overheads are absorbed on a very broad basis related to direct labour costs. Does this method fairly reflect product line 3's use of variable overheads?
- Product line 3 appears to result in only a small negative contribution. Can this be made positive by perhaps a small increase in the unit selling price or by the more efficient use of direct materials and direct labour?
- Assuming that the cost data supplied are both fair and accurate, would the closure of product line 3 affect sales for the other two product lines or the overall variable costs?
- If closure of product line 3 is recommended, should it be closed permanently or temporarily? More information is needed of its prospects beyond 2018.

The decision

Clearly without more information it is impossible to come to a firm conclusion. Assuming that the cost accounting procedures are both accurate and fair, it would appear that *on purely financial grounds,* product line 3 should be closed. However, until we have more information we cannot put this forward as a conclusive recommendation.

Make or buy decisions

Make or buy decisions require management to determine whether to manufacture products internally or purchase them externally. Should a car company, for example, manufacture its own components or purchase them from specialist suppliers? Similarly, should a glass manufacturer concentrate on producing glass and purchase its packaging and safety equipment externally? In local government should a housing department employ its own joiners or contract outside firms to do the necessary work? In modern parlance these types of decisions are known as 'outsourcing'.

The theory beyond make or buy decisions revolves round the argument that entities should do what they are best at doing and employ others to undertake the peripheral activities. In other words, they should concentrate on their main objective and contract out or 'privatise' (in the case of governmental activities) all other essential activities.

A decision to contract out may often be taken simply because it appears to be cheaper (in monetary terms) to do so. This may be an unwise decision. There could be vital non-financial and non-quantifiable factors that are just as important as cost. For example, it may not be possible to obtain exactly what the company wants, or there could be delays in receiving some vital supplies. Both of these difficulties could cause a breakdown or hold-up to the company's own production. This might ultimately prove to be more expensive than manufacturing internally so when deciding to make or buy, *all* factors should be built into the analysis, even though it may be difficult to quantify some of them.

A simple make or buy decision is illustrated in Example 18.3.

Example 18.3

A make or buy decision

Zam Limited uses an important component in one of its products. An estimate of the cost of making one unit of the component internally is as follows.

	£
Direct materials	5
Direct labour	4
Variable overhead	3
Total variable cost	12

Additional information:

1 Fixed costs specifically associated with manufacturing the components are estimated to be £8000 per month.
2 The number of components normally required is 1000 per month.

An outside manufacturer has offered to supply the components at a cost of £18 per component.

Required:
Determine whether Zam Limited should purchase the components from the outside supplier.

Answer to Example 18.3

Points

Assuming that the cost data given in the question are accurate, the first step in answering the question is to calculate the cost of manufacturing the components internally. Although the variable cost of each unit is given, there may be some fixed costs directly associated with manufacturing internally and these have to be taken into account.

The fixed costs cause us a problem because the monthly activity levels may vary. However, we can only work on the data given in the question, i.e. 1000 units per month.

Calculations

Total cost of manufacturing internally 1000 units per month of the component:

	£
Total variable cost (1000 units × £12)	12 000
Associated fixed costs	8 000
Total cost	20 000
Total unit cost (£20 000 ÷ 1000)	£20

Tutorial notes

1 Assuming that Zam Limited requires 1000 units per month, it would be cheaper to obtain them from the external supplier (£20 compared with £18 per component).
2 The above assumption is based on purchases of 1000 units. The more units required, the cheaper they would be to manufacture internally. In order to match the external price, the

fixed costs can be no more than £6 per unit (the external purchase price of £18 less the internal variable cost of £12 per unit). If the fixed costs were to be limited to £6 per unit, the company would need to manufacture 1334 units (£8000 ÷ £6). The total cost would then be the same as the external cost (£24,000) but it would require a one-third increase in the activity level.

3 The cost data should be checked carefully (especially the estimated associated fixed costs) and the monthly activity level reviewed. It might then be possible to put forward a tentative recommendation.

The decision

Given the data provided in the question, it would be cheaper to purchase the components externally. This would free some resources within Zam Limited enabling it to concentrate on manufacturing its main product.

However, there are a number of other considerations that need to be taken into account. In particular the following questions would need to be asked.

● How accurate are the cost data?
● How variable is the monthly activity level?
● Is the external supplier's component exactly suited to the company's purposes?
● How reliable is the proposed supplier?
● Are there other suppliers who could be used in an emergency and at what cost?
● What control could be exercised over the quality of the components received?
● How firm is the quoted price of £18 per component and for what period will that price be maintained?
● How easy would it be to switch back to internal manufacturing if the supplier proved unreliable?

It follows that much more information (largely of a non-cost nature) would be required before a conclusive decision could be taken.

Pricing decisions

A very important decision that managers have to make in both the profit-making sector and the not-for-profit sector is that relating to pricing. Supermarkets, for example, have to price their goods, while local authorities have to decide what to charge for adult education, leisure centres and meals on wheels.

Two types of pricing decisions can be distinguished. The first relates to the prices charged to customers or clients external to the entity. We will refer to this type as *external* pricing. The second type relates to prices charged by one part of an entity to another part, such as when components are supplied by one segment to another segment. This type of pricing is known as *transfer* pricing. We will deal with each type separately.

External pricing

External selling prices may be based either on market prices or on cost. We will deal first with market-based prices.

Market-based pricing

Many goods and services are sold in highly competitive markets. This means that there may be many suppliers offering identical or near-identical products and they will be competing fiercely in respect of price, quality, reliability and service. If the demand for a product is *elastic,* then the lower the price the more units that will be sold. The opposite also applies and higher prices will result in fewer goods being sold. The demand for most everyday items of food, for example, is elastic.

It follows that when demand is elastic it is unlikely that individual sellers can determine their own selling prices so within narrow limits, they will have to base their selling prices on what is being charged in the market. Otherwise if they charge more than the market price their sales will be reduced. If they charge less than the market, then their sales will increase but the market will quickly adjust to a lower level of selling prices.

Where market conditions largely determine a supplier's selling prices, it is particularly important to ensure that tight control is exercised over costs. Otherwise the gap between total sales revenue and total costs (i.e. the profit) will be insufficient to ensure an adequate return on capital employed.

In some cases the demand for goods is *inelastic* – i.e. price has little or no effect on the number of units sold. The demand for writing paper and stationery, for example, tends to be inelastic, probably because it is an infrequent purchase and it is not a significant element in most people's budgets. This means that when the demand for goods is inelastic, suppliers have much more freedom in determining their own selling prices and they may then base them on cost.

Cost-based pricing

There are a number of cost-based pricing methods. We summarise the main ones below and the circumstances in which they are most likely to be used.

- *Below variable cost.* This price would be used:
  - when an entity was trying to establish a new product on the market;
  - when an attempt was being made to drive out competitors;
  - as a loss leader, i.e. to encourage other goods to be bought.
  A price at this level could only be sustained for a very short period (unless it is used as a loss leader) since each unit sold would not be covering its variable cost.
- *At variable cost.* Variable cost prices may be used:
  - to launch a new product;
  - to drive out competition;
  - in difficult trading conditions;
  - as a loss leader; price could be held for some time but ultimately some contribution will be needed to cover the fixed costs.
- *At total production cost.* This will include the unit's direct costs and a share of the production overheads. Prices at this level could be held for some time (perhaps when demand is low) but eventually the entity would need to cover its non-production overheads and to make a profit.
- *At total cost.* This will include the direct cost and a share of both the production and non-production overheads. Again such prices could be held for a very long period, perhaps during a long recession, but eventually some profit would need to be earned.
- *At cost plus.* The cost-plus method would either relate to total production cost or to total cost. The 'plus' element would be an addition to the cost to allow for non-production overhead and profit (in the case of total production cost) and for profit alone (in the case of total cost). In the long run, cost-plus prices are the only option for a profit-making entity. However, if prices are based entirely on cost, then inefficiencies may be automatically built into the pricing system and this could lead to uncompetitiveness.

Transfer pricing

In large entities it is quite common for one segment to trade with another segment. So what is 'revenue' to one segment will be 'expenditure' to the other. This means that when the results of all the various segments are consolidated, the revenue recorded in one segment's books of account will cancel out the expenditure in the other segment's books. Does it matter then what prices are charged for internal transfers?

The answer is 'Yes it does' because some segments (particularly if they are divisions of companies) are given a great deal of autonomy. They may have the authority, for example, to purchase goods and services from outside the entity. They almost certainly will do so if the price and service offered externally appears to be superior to any internal offer and this may cause them to sub-optimise, i.e. to act in *their* own best interest although it may not be in the best interests of the entity as a whole.

Let us suppose that segment A fixes its transfer price on a cost-plus basis, say at £10 per unit. Segment B finds that it can purchase an identical unit externally at £8 per unit. Segment B is very likely to accept the external offer. However segment A's costs may be based on *absorbed costs*. So *extra cost* (i.e. the variable cost) of meeting segment B's order may be much less than the external price of £8 per unit. In these circumstances it may not be beneficial for the *entity as a whole* for segment B to purchase the units from an outside supplier.

It follows that a transfer price should to be set at a level that will encourage a supplying segment to trade internally and to discourage a receiving segment to buy its goods externally. There are various transfer-pricing methods that can be adopted. We review the main ones below.

- *Market price.* If there are identical or similar goods and services offered externally, transfer prices based on market prices will neither encourage nor discourage supplying or receiving segments to trade externally.
- *Adjusted market price.* Market prices may be reduced in recognition of the lower costs attached to internal trading, e.g. advertising, administration and financing costs. This method encourages segments to trade with each other.
- *Total cost or total cost plus.* A transfer price based on total cost will include the direct costs plus a share of both production and non-production overhead. Total cost-plus methods allow for some profit. The main problems attached to the total-cost methods is that they build inefficiencies into the system as there is incentive to control costs little.
- *At variable cost or variable cost plus.* The variable cost method itself does not encourage a supplying segment to trade internally as no incentive is built into the transfer price. A percentage addition may provide some incentive since it enables some contribution to be made towards fixed costs. However transfer prices based on variable costs may be very attractive to *receiving* segments as the transfer price normally compares favourably with the external price. If the variable cost method is adopted it is recommended that it is based on the *standard* variable cost.
- *Negotiated price.* This method involves striking a bargain between the supplying and receiving segments based on a combination of market price and costs. As long as the discussions are mutually determined this method can be highly successful.
- *Opportunity cost.* This method may be somewhat impractical but if the costs can be quantified it is the ideal one to adopt. A transfer price based on the opportunity cost comprises two elements: first, the standard variable cost in the supplying segment, and second the entity's opportunity cost resulting from the transaction. It is the second element that is the hardest to determine.

Special orders

On some occasions an entity may be asked to undertake an order beyond its normal trading arrangement and to quote a price for it. Such arrangements are known as *special orders*. The potential customer or client would normally expect to pay a lower price than the entity ordinarily charges as well as possibly receiving some favourable treatment. What pricing policy should the entity adopt when asked to quote for a special order? Much will depend on whether it has some surplus capacity. If this is the case, it may be prepared to quote a price below variable cost if it wants to avoid a possible shutdown. However the minimum price that it would *normally* be willing to accept would be equal to the incremental (or extra) cost of accepting the order.

The incremental cost involved may be the equivalent of the variable cost. Prices based at or below the variable cost would be extremely competitive thereby helping to ensure that the customer accepted the quotation. The work gained would then absorb some of the entity's surplus capacity and help to keep its workforce occupied. There is also the possibility that the customer may place future orders at prices that would enable the entity to make a profit on them. But there is then the danger that in the meantime more profitable work has to be rejected because the entity cannot cope with both its normal orders and the special order.

A price in excess of the variable cost would make a contribution towards fixed costs and this would clearly be the preferred option. The quoted price would have to be judged very finely because the higher the price, the greater the risk that the customer would reject the quotation. The decision would involve trying to determine what other suppliers are likely to charge and what terms they would offer.

An indication of the difficulties associated with determining whether a special order should be accepted is demonstrated in Example 18.4.

The management accountant's main role in dealing with special orders would be to supply historical and projected cost data of the financial consequences of particular options. The eventual decision would be taken by senior management using a wide range of quantitative and qualitative information. The type of questions asked would be similar to some of the issues covered in the tutorial notes in the solution to Example 18.4.

Example 18.4	**A special order**

Amber Limited has been asked by a customer to supply a specially designed product. The customer has indicated that he would be willing to pay a maximum price of £100 per unit. The cost details are as follows.

Unit cost	£	£
Contract price		100
Less: Variable costs		
Direct materials	40	
Direct labour (2 hours)	30	
Variable overhead	10	80
Contribution		20

At a contract price of £100 per unit, each unit would make a contribution of £20. The customer is prepared to take 400 units, and so the total contribution towards fixed costs would be £8000 (400 units × £20). However, Amber has a shortage of direct labour and some of the staff would have to be switched from other orders to work on the special order. This would mean an average loss in contribution of £8 for every direct labour hour worked on the special order.

Required:
Determine whether Amber Limited should accept the special order.

Answer to Example 18.4	In order to determine whether Amber Limited should accept the special order, the extra contribution should be compared with the loss of contribution by having to switch the workforce from other orders. The calculations are as follows.

	£
Total contribution from the special order	8 000
(400 units × £20 per unit)	
Less: the opportunity cost of the normal contribution foregone	
[800 direct labour hours (400 units × 2 DLH) × £8 per unit]	6 400
Extra contribution	1 600

Before coming to a decision, the following points should also be considered. You will see that they range well beyond simple cost factors.

Tutorial notes

1   The costings relating to the special order should be carefully checked.

2   The customer should be asked to confirm in writing that it would be willing to pay a selling price of £100 per unit.

3   Determine whether the customer is likely to place additional orders for the product or not.

4   Check that the *average* contribution of £8 per direct labour hour, obtained from other orders applies to the workforce that would be switched to the special order, i.e. is the contribution from the other orders that would be lost more or less than £8 per direct labour hour?

5   Is it possible that new staff could be recruited to work on the special order?

6   Is more profitable work likely to come along in the meantime? Would it mean that it could not be accepted during the progress of the order?

Recommendation

Assuming that the points raised in the above notes are satisfied, then the recommendation would be to accept the special order at a price of £100 per unit. This would mean that Amber's total contribution would be increased by £1600.

Activity 18.2

The country is experiencing a deep recession. Trade is very bad. Then, rather unexpectedly, Company X is asked to supply one of its main products to a new customer but unfortunately at a price well below the product's variable cost. In adjacent columns list (a) all the reasons why it should accept the order; and (b) why it should be rejected. Overall, what would be your decision?

! Questions you should ask

The questions that you should put to your accountants about any specific decision-making problem will revolve round the robustness of the data that they have used and any non-quantitative factors they have incorporated into their recommendations. You could use the following questions as a guide.

- From where did you get the data?
- How reliable are the basic facts?
- What assumptions have you adopted?
- Have you included only relevant costs?
- Have you tested the results on a probability basis?
- What non-quantitative factors have you been able to identify?
- Is it possible to put any monetary value on them?
- Do you think that we should go ahead with this proposal?

Conclusion

An important function of management accountants in the twenty-first century is to assist in managerial decision making. In such a role their primary task is to provide managers with financial and non-financial information in order to help them make more effective decisions. Although the information provided may include much historical data, decision making often means dealing with future events, so the information provided consists of a great deal of speculative material. This means that management accountants needs to exercise considerable skill and judgement in collecting information that is both accurate and relevant for a particular purpose. Non-relevant information can be ignored as it only obscures the broader picture.

The significance of including only relevant data is seen when managers have to make special decisions, such as whether to close or shut down a segment of an entity, make or provide goods and services internally instead of obtaining them from an outside supplier, determine a selling price for the entity's goods and services, or whether to accept a special order and at what price. These are all-important and complex decisions and managers need reliable information before they can make them.

Key points	
1	Decision making involves having to resolve an outcome for a specific problem.
2	The information required relates to the future, it is specific to the problem, it may have to be collected specially for the task and it is geared towards estimating the future net cash flows of particular outcomes.
3	The information provided to management should include only relevant costs and revenues, with an estimate of any opportunity costs.
4	The data used in a management accounting information report should be subject to some probability testing.
5	The terms 'fixed and variable costs', 'relevant and non-relevant costs', 'avoidable and non-avoidable costs', 'sunk costs', 'committed costs' and 'opportunity costs' are all of special significance in decision making.
6	Closure and shutdown decisions should be based on the contribution earned or likely to be earned on the segment under consideration and compared with the likely closure or shutdown costs.
7	Generally it is more profitable to make goods or to provide services internally than to obtain them externally if their variable cost is less than or equal to external prices.
8	The pricing of goods and services for selling externally will normally be determined by the market price for similar goods and services. In some cases, however, selling prices can be based on cost. Depending on market conditions, the cost could be at or below variable cost, the absorbed or the total absorbed cost, with or without an addition for profit.
9	The internal transfer of goods and services should be based on market price or adjusted market price. Where this is not possible, any price at or in excess of the variable cost should be acceptable.
10	The ideal transfer price is one that is based on the standard variable cost in the supplying segment plus the entity's opportunity cost resulting from the transaction.

11 Special orders should be priced so that they cover their variable cost. There may be some circumstances when it is acceptable to price them below variable cost but this can only be a short-term solution. Any price in excess of variable costs helps to cover the entity's fixed costs.

12 Cost and financial factors are only part of the decision-making process. There are other factors of a non-financial and non-quantifiable nature (such as behavioural factors) that must be taken into account.

Check your learning

1 Define what is meant by a 'decision'.

2 List seven main characteristics of decision-making data.

3 Identify six ways of classifying costs.

4 What is an opportunity cost?

5 What is meant by a closure or a shutdown decision?

6 What is meant by a make or buy decision?

7 What is meant by a pricing decision?

8 What are the two main types of pricing decisions?

9 What is meant by a market price?

10 List six cost-based pricing methods.

11 What is the basic problem in determining pricing between segments within the same entity?

12 How might it be resolved?

13 What is meant by a special order?

14 How does it differ from the general pricing problem?

News story quiz

Remember the news story at the beginning of the chapter? Go back to that story and reread it before answering the following questions.

The news that a small UK manufacturing company has had to go into administration has featured in media reports many times during the last few years.

Questions

1 What action was taken by the directors of the company to safeguard its future in the months leading up to the time when it went into administration?

2 Bearing in mind the general economic climate at that time, were there any other measures that could have been taken?

3 How far do you think that the company's severe financial difficulties took the senior managers by surprise?

Tutorial questions

The answers to questions marked with an asterisk can be found in Appendix 4.

18.1 This chapter has emphasised that it is managers that make decisions and not management accountants. How far do you agree with this assertion?

18.2 Many of the solutions to the problems posed in this chapter depend on being able to isolate the variable cost associated with a particular decision. In practice, is it realistic to expect that such costs can be readily identified and measured?

18.3 Assume that you were an IT manager in a large entity and that the services that you provide are made available to both internal and external parties. Specify how you would go about negotiating an appropriate fee for services sought by other departments within the entity.

18.4* Micro Limited has some spare capacity. It is now considering whether it should accept a special contract to use some of the spare capacity. However, this contract will use some specialist direct labour that is in short supply. The following details relate to the proposed contract:

	£000
Contract price	50
Variable costs:	
Direct materials	10
Direct labour	30

In order to complete the contract, 4000 direct labour hours would be required. The company's budget for the year during which the contract would be undertaken is as follows:

	£000
Sales	750
Variable costs	(500)
Contribution	250
Fixed costs	(230)
Profit	20

There would be 50,000 direct labour hours available during the year.

Required:
Determine whether the special contract should be accepted.

18.5*Temple Limited has been offered two new contracts, the details of which are as follows:

Contract	(1)	(2)
	£000	£000
Contract price	1 000	2 100
Direct materials	300	600
Direct labour	300	750
Variable overhead	100	250
Fixed overhead	100	200
	800	1 800
Profit	200	300
Direct materials required (kilos)	50 000	100 000
Direct labour hours required	10 000	25 000

Note:
The fixed overhead has been apportioned on the basis of direct labour cost. Temple is a one-product firm. Its budgeted cost per unit for its normal work for the year to 31 December 2018 is summarised below.

	£
Sales	6 000
Direct materials (100 kilos)	700
Direct labour (200 hours)	3 000
Variable overhead	300
Fixed overhead	1 000
	5 000
Profit	1 000

The company would only have the capacity to accept one of the new contracts. Unfortunately, materials suitable for use in all of its work are in short supply and the company has estimated that only 200,000 kilos would be available during the year to December 2018. Even more worrying is the shortage of skilled labour, only 100,000 direct labour hours are expected to be available during the year. The good news is that there may be an upturn in the market for its normal contract work.

Required:
Calculate

(a) the contribution per unit of each limiting factor for
    (i) the company's normal work
    (ii) Contract 1
    (iii) Contract 2.
(b) The company's maximum contribution for the year to 31 December 2018, assuming that it accepts either Contract 1 or Contract 2.

18.6 Agra Limited has been asked to quote a price for a special contract. The details are as follows:

1 The specification required a quotation for 100,000 units.
2 The direct costs per unit for the order would be: materials £3, labour £15, distribution £12.
3 Additional production and non-production overhead would amount to £500,000, although £100,000 could be saved if the order was for less than 100,000 units.
4 Agra's normal profit margin is 20 per cent of total cost.

Required:
Recommend a minimum selling price if the order was for:

(a) 100,000 units
(b) 80,000 units.

18.7 Foo Limited has been asked to quote for a special order. The details are as follows:

1 Prices are to be quoted at order levels of 50,000, 100,000 and 150,000 units respectively. Foo has some surplus capacity and it could deal with up to 160,000 units.
2 Each unit would cost £2 for direct materials, and £12 for direct labour.
3 Foo normally absorbs production and non-production overhead on the basis of 200 per cent and 100 per cent respectively of the direct labour cost.
4 Distribution costs are expected to be £10 per unit.
5 Foo's normal profit margin is 20 per cent of the total cost. However, it is prepared to reduce this margin to 15 per cent if the order is for 100,000 units, and to 10 per cent for an order of 150,000 units.
6 The additional non-production overhead associated with this contract would be £200,000, although this would be cut by £25,000 if the output dropped below 100,000 units.

Required:
Suggest

(a) a selling price per unit that Foo Limited might charge if the contract was for 50,000, 100,000 and 150,000 units respectively;
(b) the profit that it could expect to make at these levels.

18.8 Bamboo Limited is a highly specialist firm of central heating suppliers operating exclusively in the textiles industry. It has recently been asked to tender for a contract for a prospective customer. The following details relate to the proposed contract.

1 Materials:
   - £20,000 of materials would need to be purchased.
   - £10,000 of materials would need to be transferred from another contract (these materials would need to be replaced).
   - Some obsolete stock would be used. The stock had originally cost £18,000. Its current disposable value is £4000.

2 The contract would involve labour costs of £60,000, of which £30,000 would be incurred regardless of whether the contract was undertaken.

3 The production manager will have to work several evenings a week during the progress of the contract. He is paid a salary of £30,000 per year, and on successful completion of the contract he would receive a bonus of £5000.

4 Additional administrative expenses incurred in undertaking the contract are estimated to be £1000.

5 The company absorbs its fixed overheads at a rate of £10 per machine hour. The contract will require 2000 machine hours.

Required:

Calculate the minimum contract price that would be acceptable to Bamboo Limited.

18.9 Dynasty Limited has been involved in a research project (code named DNY) for a number of months. There is some doubt as to whether the project should be completed. If it is, then it is expected that DNY will require another 12 months' work. The following information relates to the project.

1 Costs incurred to date are £500,000.

2 Sales proceeds if the project continues will be £600,000.

3 Direct material costs amount to £200,000. The type of material required for DNY had already been purchased for another project, and it would cost £20,000 to dispose of it.

4 Direct labour costs have come to £150,000. The direct labour used on DNY is highly skilled and it is not easy to recruit the type of staff required. In order to undertake DNY, some staff would have to be transferred from other projects. This would mean that there was a total loss in contribution from such projects of £350,000.

5 Research staff costs amount to £200,000. The staff would be made redundant at the end of project DNY at a cost of £115,000. If they were to be made redundant now, there would be a cost of £100,000.

6 The company can invest surplus cash at a rate of return of 10 per cent per annum.

7 Non-production overhead budgeted to be apportioned to DNY for the forthcoming 12 months amounts to £60,000.

Required:

Determine whether or not the DNY project should continue.

Website

Further practice questions, study material and links to relevant sites on the World Wide Web can be found on the website that accompanies this book. The site can be found at www.pearsoned.co.uk/dyson

Capital investment

Dividend protection

Capital spending slashed

Ed Crooks

Conoco Phillips, one of the largest oil and gas produces in the US, has announced another sharp cut in its capital spending as it seeks to protect its dividend, pointing to weaker output in the future. It has set a capital budget for 2016 of US Dollar 7.7bn, down 25 per cent from this year and less than half the amount that it spent in 2014.

Its move is the latest sign of how weak oil and gas prices are forcing companies to cut their investment, reducing future crude supplies and contributing to bringing the oversupplied market back into balance. Conoco's move echoes the announcement from Chevron, the second largest US oil group market capitalization, which said on Wednesday that it would cut capital spending by 24 per cent next year.

Conoco said yesterday that it expected oil and gas production growth of 1–3 per cent next year and did not give any projections for output beyond that, saying it would depend on what happened to prices. In the spring of 2014, before oil and gas prices slumped, it was projecting production growth of 3–5 per cent per year.

Ryan Lance, chief executive, told analysts: 'Despite the tough market, our dividend remains the highest priority use of our cash.' He added: 'We view the dividend level as a long-term decision and we've been in the current low price cycle for a relatively short period of time.' Mr. Lance said that the company had the flexibility to ramp up spending should prices improve, although it would be 'disciplined' in increasing investment in the event of an upturn, and would also strengthen its balance sheet.

Chevron also stressed that dividend payments were its 'top priority' in making capital expenditure reductions but two other energy companies, Kinder Morgan and Eni, have cut their dividends this year.

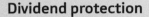 *Source*: Adapted and reproduced from the *Financial Times*, 11 December 2015.

Questions relating to this news story can be found on pages 440–441 ➡

About this chapter

This is another chapter in Part 4 of the book dealing with management accounting decision making. It explains how various calculative techniques can help management select a particular investment. Accountants call this exercise *capital investment appraisal*. The chapter also explores the main sources of external short-, medium- and long-term finance available for the financing of capital projects.

By the end of this chapter, you should be able to:

- describe what is meant by capital investment appraisal;
- identify five capital investment appraisal techniques;
- incorporate such techniques into quantitative examples;
- recognise the significance of such techniques;
- list the main external sources of financing capital investment projects.

 Why this chapter is important

Even as a junior manager you may be involved in capital investment decisions. At this stage of your career not much money will be involved and all you might be doing is deciding which one of two filing cabinets your section should buy. As you become more senior, the projects will become bigger and perhaps cost millions of pounds. You will have to decide which to go for and how they should be financed.

Such decision making will involve a consideration of various projects on both a quantitative and a qualitative basis. Your accountants will process the data for you and they may use one of the techniques discussed in this chapter. They will then present you with the results. It is extremely unlikely that you will be involved in the detailed number crunching but in order to make a decision about which project you should select you will need to question your accountants about their recommendations.

You will not be able to do so with any confidence unless you have some knowledge of their methods. This chapter provides you with the basic material. After studying it you will be in a much better position to make your own capital investment decisions and not just do what your accountants tell you to do.

Background

News clip

Press release

The directors of Norilsk Nickel, the leading global nickel and palladium producer, have approved the company's budget for 2016. The budget focuses on cost control but the company intends to continue investing in projects that will yield superior returns, as it is believed that the successful delivery of these projects will give the company a competitive advantage over its global peers. The 2016 budget will allow the company to maintain financial stability and give it access to long-term capital markets on favourable terms.

Source: Adapted from www.nornik.ru/en/press release, 14 December 2015.

Accountants make a distinction between *capital* expenditure and *revenue* expenditure. Expenditure of a capital nature provides a benefit to an entity for more than a year. Revenue expenditure has to be renewed if the benefit is to beyond one year.

Besides its long-term nature some other features of capital expenditure may be distinguished. They include the following:

- its purpose is to help the entity achieve its long-term objectives;
- it will often involve huge sums of money being spent on major projects;
- it may have a considerable impact on how many staff the entity employs and how they react;
- the benefits may be spread over very many years;
- it is difficult to assess precisely what those benefits will be.

All entities would find it difficult to survive if they did not invest in some form of capital expenditure from time to time, and they certainly would not be able to grow and to develop. Plant and machinery, for example will begin to wear out and become obsolete while in, the longer term, buildings will need to be replaced. In addition many entities have to set aside resources for projects that do not relate directly to their main business, such as the provision of leisure and social facilities for their employees.

All entities, whether public or private, usually have to select from a long list of possible capital investment projects because they certainly will not have either the time or the resources to do them all at once. Which projects should they choose and how should they be financed? This chapter deals with such questions.

Main methods

In this section we are going to examine the main methods used in capital investment (CI) appraisal. We will assume that we are dealing mainly with profit-making entities. Such entities will expect all their projects to make a profit except for those undertaken on health, social and welfare grounds (these types of project are particularly difficult to assess). There are five main techniques that accountants can use in CI appraisal. They are shown in diagrammatic form in Figure 19.1 and we examine each of them in the following sub-sections.

Payback

The payback method is an attempt to estimate how long it would take before a project begins to pay for itself. For example, if a company was going to spend £300,000 on

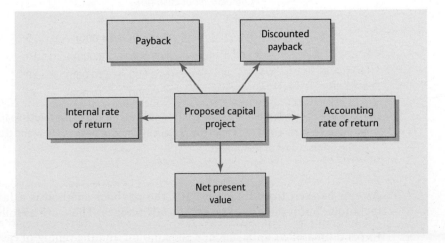

Figure 19.1 Capital investment appraisal methods

purchasing some new plant, the accountant would calculate how many years it would take before £300,000 had been paid back in cash. The recovery of an investment in a project is usually measured in terms of *net cash flow*. This is the difference between cash received and cash paid during a defined period of time. In order to adopt this method the following information is required:

- The total cost of the investment.
- The instalments payable on the investment.
- The accounting periods in which they will have to be paid.
- Details of any cash receipts and any cash payments connected with the project.
- The accounting periods in which they fall.

As the payback measures the rate of recovery of the original investment in terms of net cash flow, it follows that non-cash items (such as depreciation and profits and losses on sales of fixed assets) are not taken into account.

The payback method is illustrated in Example 19.1.

Example 19.1	**The payback method**

Miln Limited is considering investing in some new machinery. The following information has been prepared to support the project:

	£000	£000
Cost of machinery		20
Expected net cash flow:		
Year 1	1	
2	4	
3	5	
4	10	
5	10	30
Net profitability		10

Required:
Calculate the prospective investment's payback period.

Answer to Example 19.1	The payback period is as follows:

		£000
Cumulative net cash flow:		
Year 1		1
2	(£1 000 + £4 000)	5
3	(£5 000 + £5 000)	10
4	(£10 000 + £10 000)	20
5	(£20 000 + £10 000)	30

The investment will, therefore, have paid for itself at the end of the fourth year. At that stage £20,000 will have been received back from the project in terms of net cash flow and that sum would be equal to the original cost of the project.

As can be seen from Example 19.1 the payback method is a fairly straightforward technique but it does have several disadvantages. These are as follows:

- An estimate has to be made of the amount and the timing of cash instalments due to be paid on an original investment.

- It is difficult to calculate the net cash flows and the period in which they will be received.
- There is a danger that projects with the shortest payback periods may be chosen even if they are not as profitable as projects with a longer payback period. The payback method only measures cash flow: it does not measure profitability.
- The total amount of the overall investment is ignored and comparisons made between different projects may result in misleading conclusions. A project with an initial investment of £10,000 may have a shorter payback period than one with an initial investment of £100,000, although in the long run the larger investment may prove to be more profitable.
- The technique ignores any net cash flows received after the payback period.
- The timing of the cash flows is not taken into account: £1 received now is preferable to £1 received in five years' time. A project with a short payback period may recover most of its investment towards the end of its payback period while another project with a longer payback period may recover most of the original investment in the first few years. There is clearly less risk in accepting a project that recovers most of its cost very quickly than in accepting one where the benefits are deferred.

Irrespective of these disadvantages, the payback method has something to be said for it. While it may appear to be rather simplistic, it does help managers to compare projects and to think in terms of how long it takes before a project has recovered its original cost.

Discounted payback

The simple payback method ignores the timing of net cash receipts but this problem can be overcome by *discounting* the net cash receipts. You will probably be familiar with discounting in your everyday life. You know, for example, that if you put £91 into the building society and the rate of interest is 10 per cent per annum, your original investment will be worth about £100 [£91 + £9 (10% × £91)] at the end of the year. We could look at this example from another point of view. Assuming a rate of interest of 10 per cent per annum, what amount of money do you have to invest in the building society in order to have £100 at the end of the year? The answer is, of course, £91 (ignoring the odd 10p). In other words, £91 received now is about the same as £100 received in a year's time. This is what is meant by *discounting*. The procedure is as follows:

1 Calculate the future net cash flows.
2 Select an appropriate rate of interest.
3 Multiply the net cash flows by a discount factor.

The discount factor will depend on the cost of borrowing money. In the case of the building society example above, the discount factor is based on a rate of interest of 10 per cent. The factor itself is 0.9091, i.e. £100 × 0.9091 = £90.91. To check: take the £90.91 and add the year's interest, i.e. £90.91 × 10% = £9.091 + £90.91 = £100.00. You will not have to calculate discount factors as they are readily available in tables. We include one in Appendix 2 on page 479 of this book.

In order to confirm that you understand the point about discounting, turn to Appendix 2. Look along the top line for the appropriate rate of interest: in our case it is 10 per cent. Work down the 10 per cent column until you come to the line opposite the year (shown in the left-hand column) in which the cash would be received. In our example, the cash is going to be received in one year's time, so it is not necessary to go further than the first line. The present value of £1 receivable in a year's time is, therefore, 0.9091, or £90.91 if £100 is to be received in a year's time.

We can now show you how the discounted payback method works. We do so in Example 19.2.

Example 19.2	**The discounted payback method**

Newland City Council has investigated the possibility of investing in a new project, and the following information has been obtained:

	£000	£000
Total cost of project		500
Expected net cash flows:		
Year 1	20	
2	50	
3	100	
4	200	
5	300	
6	30	700
Net return		200

Required:

Assuming a rate of interest of 8%, calculate the project's overall return using the following methods:

(a) payback

(b) discounted payback.

Answer to Example 19.2

(a) Payback method

Year	Net cash flow	Cumulative net cash flow
	£000	£000
0	(500)	(500)
1	20	(480)
2	50	(430)
3	100	(330)
4	200	(130)
5	300	170
6	30	200

Calculation:

After 4 years the total cash flows received = £370,000 (£20,000 + 50,000 + 100,000 + 200,000). The £30,000 still necessary to equal the original cost of the investment (£500,000 − 370,000) will be met part way through Year 5, i.e. (£130,000 ÷ 300,000) × 12 months = 5.2 months. So the payback period is about 4 years and 5 months (41 months), assuming that the net cash flows accrue evenly throughout the year.

(b) Discounted payback

Year	Net cash flow	Discount factors	Present value at 8% [Column (2) × Column (3)]	Cumulative present value
(1)	(2)	(3)	(4)	(5)
	£000		£000	£000
0	(500)	1.0000	(500)	(500)
1	20	0.9259	19	(481)
2	50	0.8573	43	(438)
3	100	0.7938	79	(359)
4	200	0.7350	147	(212)
5	300	0.6806	204	(8)
6	30	0.6302	19	11

Calculation:
Using the discounted payback method, the project would recover all of its original cost during Year 6. Assuming that the net cash flows accrue evenly, this would be about the end of the fifth month because (£8000 ÷ 19,000) × 12 months = 5.1 months. The, therefore, discounted payback period is about 5 years 5 months (65 months).

The discounted payback method has the following advantages.

- Relatively easy to understand.
- Not too difficult to compute.
- Focuses on the cash recovery of an investment.
- Allows for the fact that cash received now may be worth more than cash receivable in the future.
- Takes more of the net cash flows into account than is the case with the simple payback method because the discounted payback period is always longer than the simple payback method.
- Enables a clear-cut decision to be taken, since a project is acceptable if the discounted net cash flow throughout its life exceeds the cost of the original investment.

Nonetheless, the simple payback method, it has some disadvantages.

- Sometimes difficult to estimate the amount and timing of instalments due to be paid on the original investment.
- Difficult to estimate the amount and timing of future net cash receipts and other payments.
- Not easy to determine an appropriate rate of interest.
- Net cash flows received after the payback period are ignored.

Irrespective of these disadvantages, the discounted payback method can be usefully and readily adopted by those entities that do not employ staff specially trained in capital investment appraisal techniques.

Accounting rate of return

The *accounting rate of return* (ARR) method attempts to compare the *profit* of a project with the capital invested in it. It is usually expressed as a percentage. The formula is as follows:

$$ARR = \frac{profit}{capital\ employed} \times 100$$

Two important problems arise from this definition.

- *Definition of profit*. Normally, the average annual net profit earned by a project would be used. However, as explained in earlier chapters, accounting profit can be subject to a number of different assumptions and distortions (e.g. depreciation, taxation and inflation) and so it is relatively easy to arrive at different profit levels depending on the accounting policies adopted. The most common definition is to take profit before interest and taxation. The profit included in the equation would then be a simple average of the profit that the project earns over its entire life.
- *Definition of capital employed*. The capital employed could be either the initial capital employed in the project or the average capital employed over its life.

Depending upon the definitions adopted the ARR may be calculated in one of two ways:

- Using the original capital employed:

$$ARR = \frac{\text{average annual net profit before interest and taxation}}{\text{initial capital employed on the project}} \times 100$$

- Using the average capital employed:

$$ARR = \frac{\text{average annual net profit before interest and taxation}}{\text{average annual capital employed on the project}^*} \times 100$$

$$^*\frac{\text{Initial capital employed} + \text{residual value}}{2}$$

The two methods are illustrated in Example 19.3.

Example 19.3

The accounting rate of return method

Bridge Limited is considering investing in a new project, the details of which are as follows:

Project life		5 years
	£000	£000
Project cost		50
Estimated net profit:		
Year 1	12	
2	18	
3	30	
4	25	
5	5	
Total net profit	90	

The estimated residual value of the project at the end of Year 5 is £10,000.

Required:
Calculate the accounting rate of return of the proposed new project using:
(a) the original capital employed
(b) the average capital employed.

Answer to Example 19.3

The accounting rate of return would be calculated as follows:
(a) *Using the initial capital employed:*

$$\frac{\text{Average annual net profits}}{\text{Cost of the investment}} \times 100$$

Average annual net profits = £18 000 (£90 000/5)

$$\therefore \text{Accounting rate of return} = \frac{£18\,000}{50\,000} \times 100 = \underline{36\%}$$

(b) *Using the average capital employed:*

$$\frac{\text{Average annual net profits}}{\text{Average capital employed}} \times 100$$

$$= \frac{£18\,000}{\frac{1}{2}\,(£50\,000\,+\,10\,000)} \times 100 = \underline{60\%}$$

Like the payback and discounted payback methods, the accounting rate of return method has several advantages and disadvantages.

Advantages

- Compatible with a similar accounting ratio used in financial accounting.
- Relatively easy to understand.
- Not difficult to compute.
- Draws attention to the notion of overall profit.

Disadvantages

- Net profit can be subject to different definitions, e.g. it might or it might not include the depreciation on the project.
- Not always clear whether the original cost of the investment should be used, or whether it is more appropriate to substitute an average for the amount of capital invested in the project.
- Use of a residual value in calculating the average amount of capital employed means that the higher the residual value, the lower the ARR. For example, with no residual value, the ARR on a project costing £100,000 and an average net profit of £50,000 would be 100%, i.e.:

$$\frac{£50\,000}{\frac{1}{2} \times (100\,000)\,+\,0} \times 100 = \underline{100\%}$$

With a residual value of (say) £10,000, the ARR would be 90.9 per cent, i.e.:

$$\frac{£50\,000}{\frac{1}{2} \times (100\,000\,+\,10\,000)} \times 100 = \underline{90.9\%}$$

The estimation of residual values is very difficult but it can make all the difference between one project and another.

- Gives no guidance on what is an acceptable rate of return.
- Benefit of earning a high proportion of the total profit in the early years of the project is not allowed for.
- Method does not take into account the time value of money.

Irrespective of these disadvantages, the ARR method may be suitable where very similar short-term projects are being considered.

Net present value

Unlike the payback and ARR capital investment appraisal methods, the net present value (NPV) method does take into account the time value of money. In summary the procedure is as follows.

1 Calculate the annual net cash flows expected to arise from the project.
2 Select an appropriate rate of interest, or required rate of return.
3 Obtain the discount factors appropriate to the chosen rate of interest or rate of return.
4 Multiply the annual net cash flow by the appropriate discount factors.
5 Add together the present values for each of the net cash flows.
6 Compare the total net present value with the initial outlay.
7 Accept the project if the total NPV is positive.

Example 19.4 illustrates this procedure.

Example 19.4	**The net present value method**

Rage Limited is considering two capital investment projects. The details are outlined as follows:

Project	1	2
Estimated life	3 years	5 years
Commencement date	1.1.01	1.1.01
	£000	£000
Project cost at year 1	100	100

Estimated net cash flows:

Year:	1	20	10
	2	80	40
	3	40	40
	4	–	40
	5	–	20
		140	150

The company expects a rate of return of 10% per annum on its capital employed.

Required:
Using the net present value method of project appraisal, assess which project would be more profitable.

Answer to Example 19.4

Rage Ltd

Project appraisal:

	Project 1			Project 2		
Year	Net cash flow	Discount factor	Present value	Net cash flow	Discount factor	Present value
(1)	(2)	(3)	(4)	(5)	(6)	(7)
	£	10%	£	£	10%	£
1	20 000	0.9091	18 182	10 000	0.9091	9 091
2	80 000	0.8264	66 112	40 000	0.8264	33 056
3	40 000	0.7513	30 052	40 000	0.7513	30 052
4	–	–	–	40 000	0.6830	27 320
5	–	–	–	20 000	0.6209	12 418
Total present value			114 346			111 937
Less: Initial cost			100 000			100 000
Net present value			14 346			11 937

Tutorial notes

1 The net cash flows and the discount factor of 10% (i.e. the rate of return) were given in the question.

2 The discount factors may be obtained from the discount table in Appendix 2.

3 Column (4) has been calculated by multiplying column (2) by column (3).

4 Column (7) has been calculated by multiplying column (5) by column 6.

Both projects have a positive NPV, but project 1 will probably be chosen in preference to project 2 because it has a higher NPV, even though its total net cash flow of £140,000 is less than the total net cash flow of £150,000 for project 2.

The advantages and disadvantages of the NPV method are as follows:

Advantages

- Use of net cash flows emphasises the importance of liquidity.
- Different accounting policies are not relevant as they do not affect the calculation of the net cash flows.
- Time value of money is taken into account.
- Easy to compare the NPV of different projects and to reject projects that do not have an acceptable NPV.

Disadvantages

- Difficulties may be incurred in estimating the initial cost of the project and the time periods in which instalments must be paid back (although this is a common problem in CI appraisal).
- Difficult to estimate accurately the net cash flow for each year of the project's life. This is a problem that is again common to most other methods of project appraisal.
- Not easy to select an appropriate rate of interest. The rate of interest is sometimes referred to as the *cost of capital*, i.e. the cost of financing an investment. One rate that could be chosen is that rate which the company could earn if it decided to invest the funds outside the business (the external rate of interest). Alternatively an internal rate of interest could be chosen. This rate would be based on an estimate of what return the company expects to earn on its existing investments. In the long run, if the internal rate of return is lower than the external rate then it would appear more profitable to liquidate the company and invest the funds elsewhere. A local authority does not have the same difficulty because it would probably use a rate of interest set by central government.

NPV is considered to be a highly acceptable method of CI appraisal. It takes into account the timing of the net cash flows, the project's profitability and the return of the original investment. However, a project would not necessarily be accepted just because it had an acceptable NPV as non-financial factors have to be allowed for. In some cases less profitable projects (or even projects with a negative NPV) may go ahead, for example if they are concerned with employee safety or welfare.

Internal rate of return

The internal rate of return (IRR) method is also based on discounting. It is very similar to the NPV method, except that instead of discounting the expected net cash flows by a *predetermined* rate of return, it estimates what rate of return is required in order to ensure that the total NPV equals the total initial cost.

In theory, a rate of return that is lower than the entity's required rate of return would be rejected but in practice the IRR would only be one factor to be taken into account in deciding whether to go ahead with the project. The method is illustrated in Example 19.5.

Example 19.5	**The internal rate of return method**

Bruce Limited is considering whether to invest £50,000 in a new project. The project's expected net cash flows would be as follows:

Year	£000
1	7
2	25
3	30
4	5

Required:

Calculate the internal rate of return for the proposed new project.

Answer to Example 19.5	**Bruce Ltd**

Calculation of the internal rate of return:

Step 1: Select two discount factors

The first step is to select two discount factors, and then calculate the NPV of the project using both factors. The two factors usually have to be chosen quite arbitrarily but they should preferably cover a narrow range. One of the factors should produce a *positive* NPV, and the other factor a *negative* NPV. In this question factors of 10% and 15% have been chosen to illustrate the method. In practice, you may have to try various factors before you come across two that are suitable for giving a positive and a negative result.

Year	Net cash flow	Discount factors		Present value	
(1)	(2)	(3) 10%	(4) 15%	(5) 10%	(6) 15%
	£			£	£
1	7 000	0.9091	0.8696	6 364	6 087
2	25 000	0.8264	0.7561	20 660	18 903
3	30 000	0.7513	0.6575	22 539	19 725
4	5 000	0.6830	0.5718	3 415	2 859
Total present values				52 978	47 574
Initial cost				50 000	50 000
Net present value				2 978	(2 426)

Notes:

1 Column (2) has been obtained from the question.
2 Columns (3) and (4) are based on the arbitrary selection of two interest rates of 10% and 15% respectively. The discount factors may be found in Appendix 2.
3 Column (5) has been calculated by multiplying column (2) by column (3).
4 Column (6) has been calculated by multiplying column (2) by column (4).

The project is expected to cost £50,000. If the company expects a rate of return of 10%, the project will be accepted because the NPV is positive. However, if the required rate of return is 15%, it will not be accepted because its NPV is negative. The maximum rate of return that will ensure a *positive* rate of return must, therefore, lie somewhere between 10% and 15%, so the next step is to calculate the rate of return at which the project would just pay for itself.

Step 2: Calculate the specific break-even rate of return

To do this, it is necessary to interpolate between the rates used in Step 1. This can be done by using the following formula:

$$\text{IRR} = \text{positive rate} + \left(\frac{\text{positive NPV}}{\text{positive NPV} + \text{negative NPV*}} \times \text{range of rates} \right)$$

*Ignore the negative sign and add the positive NPV to the negative NPV.

So in our example:

$$\text{IRR} = 10\% + \left(\frac{2978}{(2978 + 2426)} \times (15\% - 10\%) \right)$$

$$= 10\% + (0.5511 \times 5)$$

$$= 10\% + 2.76\%$$

$$= \underline{12.76\%}$$

The project will be profitable provided that the company does not require a rate of return in excess of about 13%. Note that the method of calculation used above does not give the precise rate of return (because the formula is only an approximation), but it is adequate enough for decision-making purposes.

Example 19.5 shows that the IRR method is similar to the NPV method in two respects:

- the initial cost of the project has to be estimated as well as the future net cash flows of the project; and
- the net cash flows are then discounted to their net present value using discount tables.

The main difference between the two methods is that the IRR method requires a rate of return to be estimated in order to give an NPV equal to the initial cost of the investment. The main difficulty arises in deciding which two rates of return to use so that one will give a positive NPV and the other will give a negative NPV. You will find that you may have to have many attempts before you arrive at two suitable rates!

The advantages and disadvantages of the IRR method may be summarised as follows.

Advantages

- Emphasis is placed on liquidity.
- Attention is given to the timing of net cash flows.
- Appropriate rate of return does not have to be calculated.
- Gives a clear percentage return on an investment.

Disadvantages

- Not easy to understand.
- Difficult to determine two rates within a narrow range.
- Method gives only an approximate rate of return.
- Gives some misleading results in complex CI situations, e.g. if there are negative net cash flows in subsequent years and where there are mutually exclusive projects.

As a non-accountant you do not need to be too worried about the details of such technicalities. All you need to know is that in practice the IRR method has to be used with some caution.

Selecting a method

Of the five capital investment appraisal methods we have covered, which one is the most appropriate?

We consider it important that the time value of money is taken into account in a CI appraisal since the profitability of a future project may be grossly optimistic if such a concept is ignored. The discounted payback method, the NPV method and the internal rate of return method all meet this requirement.

The internal rate of return method involves some complex calculations, although the overall result is relatively easy to understand. Nonetheless, it may be a little too sophisticated for most entities. The discounted payback method is simple to understand and it is intuitively appealing. Its main disadvantage is that net cash flow received after the payback period may be ignored. Almost by default, therefore, the NPV method would appear to be the most favoured method. The main difficulty with the NPV method is the selection of a suitable rate of return for a particular project. Great care needs to be taken, therefore before accepting or rejecting a project based on the NPV method because it is highly dependent on the arbitrary determination of a specified rate of return.

Activity 19.1	The text has covered five methods of capital investment appraisal. Which do you think is (a) the most useful and (b) the least useful?

Net cash flow

News clip

VW to prioritise cutting all planned investments

Volkswagen is cutting its capital spending by a modest 1bn Euro in 2016 as it tries to conserve cash to meet the cost of its diesel emissions scandal. Cutting investment marks an end to VW's vision of rapid growth, and becoming the world's largest carmaker by sales.

Source: Adapted and reproduced from the *Financial Times,* 22 November 2015.

Four of the capital investment appraisal methods that we have covered in this chapter require the calculation of a project's net cash flow (payback, discounted payback, NPV and IRR). This is obviously not an easy task because it requires making a great many assumptions and estimates of what might happen in the future – possibly for very many years ahead. There are two issues in particular that can cause a problem: the impact of inflation on future net cash flows and the treatment of taxation. We discuss each of these problems below.

Inflation

In simple terms, inflation means that in (say) a year's time £1 received *then* will not buy the same amount of goods and services as £1 received *now* (see Figure 19.2). So if we calculate future net cash flow on the basis of the currency's value *now* we are, in effect,

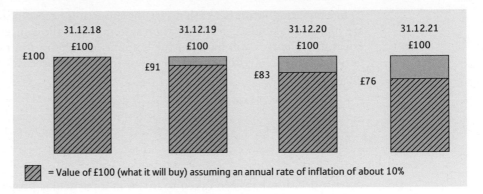

Figure 19.2 The impact of inflation

expecting to receive less cash in the future. In other words, we should estimate our future net cash flows on the basis of what it will take to purchase the equivalent of £1 of goods and services now. If prices have risen by 10 per cent in one year, for example, you will need to spend £1.10 in a year's time to buy exactly the same goods and services that you paid £1 for in the previous year.

There are two ways of allowing for inflation in capital investment appraisal: (1) indexing; and (2) adjustment of the rate of return. A brief explanation of each method is given below.

- *Indexing*. Future net cash flows may be indexed using a recognised price index. For example, assume that the net cash flow arising from a particular project will be £100 in Year 1, £150 in Year 2 and £200 in Year 3. The relevant current price index at the beginning of Year 1 is 100 but the index is expected to rise to an average level of 120 for Year 1, 140 for Year 2 and 175 for Year 3. In order to compare the net cash flows over the next three years more fairly, they need to be put on the same price base. If they are indexed, Year 1's net cash flow becomes £83 [(£100 × 100) ÷ 120]; Year 2's net cash flow becomes £107 [(£150 × 100) ÷ 140]; and Year 3's net cash flow becomes £114 [(£200 × 100) ÷ 175]. The adjusted future net cash flows of £83, £107 and £114 for Years 1, 2 and 3 respectively will then be incorporated into a CI exercise and discounted at the entity's cost of capital.
- *Adjusting the rate of return*. Instead of indexing, we could select a higher rate of return. The easiest approach would be to add the expected rate of inflation to the entity's cost of capital. So with inflation at a rate of 5 per cent per annum and a required rate of return of 10 per cent, £100 receivable in 12 months would be discounted at a rate of return of 15 per cent, i.e. £86.96 [(£100 × 100) ÷ 115, or using discount tables £100 × 0.8696].

Taxation

Corporation tax is based on the *accounting profit* for the year. In order to calculate the amount of *tax payable* for the year, the accounting profit is adjusted for those items that are not allowable against tax such as depreciation. There are also tax concessions that are not included in the calculation of accounting profit. Capital allowances, for example, are a tax allowance given when fixed assets are purchased. In essence, they are the equivalent of a depreciation allowance. Sometimes up to 100 per cent capital allowances are given so that the entire cost of purchase can be deducted from the profit in the year that a fixed asset was purchased. This means that in the year in the year of purchase, other things being equal, the amount of corporation tax payable will be low although in later years it will probably be higher.

In estimating future net cash flows, therefore, it is necessary to forecast what changes are likely to take place in the taxation system, what allowances will be available, what effect any changes will have on the amount of corporation tax payable and in what periods tax will have to be paid. Needless to say, the forecasting of such events is enormously difficult!

Sources of finance

Once a decision has been taken to invest in a particular project it is then necessary to search out a suitable method of financing it. There are a considerable number of available internal and external sources although they vary depending on what type of entity is involved. Both central and local government, for example, are heavily dependent on current tax receipts for financing capital investment projects, while charities rely on loans and grants. In this section we will concentrate on the sources of external finance available to companies. Such sources depend on the time period involved. For convenience, we will break our discussion down into the short term, the medium term, and the long term. The various sources of finance are shown in diagrammatic format in Figure 19.3 and we discuss each of them below.

Short-term finance

There are five major sources of external short-term finance.

- *Trade credit*. This is a form of financing common in all companies (and for all other entities). An entity purchases goods and services from suppliers and agrees to pay for them some days or weeks after they have been delivered. This method is so common

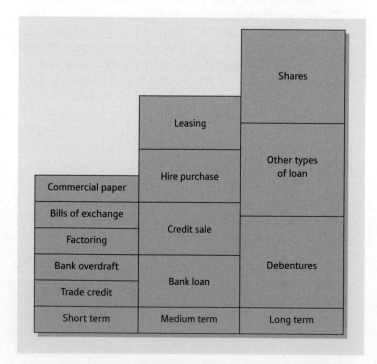

Figure 19.3 Sources of finance

that discounts are often given for prompt payment. By delaying the payment of creditors, the entity's immediate cash needs are less strained and it may be able to finance projects that otherwise could not be considered. However, it is clearly only a temporary method of financing projects (particularly long-term ones). The entity is also highly vulnerable to pressure from its creditors. This method often operates in tandem with a demand for debtors to settle their accounts promptly.

- *Bank overdraft.* This is a form of loan where the bank's customer is allowed to draw out more from the bank than has been deposited. An entity's overdraft may have to be secured by a *floating charge*. This means that the bank has a general claim on any of the entity's assets if the entity cannot repay the overdraft. There is usually an upper limit, the amount overdrawn can usually be called in at any time and the interest charge may be high. The main advantages of an overdraft are that it is flexible and that interest is normally only charged on the outstanding balance on a daily basis.
- *Factoring.* Factoring relates to an entity's debtors. There are two types of factoring: – recourse factoring, where an entity obtains a loan based on the amount of its debtor balances; and – non-recourse factoring, where the debtor balances are sold to a factor and the factor then takes responsibility for dealing with them.

Factoring is a convenient way of obtaining ready cash but either the interest rate on the loan or the discount on the invoices may be high.

- *Bill of exchange.* This is simply an invoice that has been endorsed (i.e. accepted) by a merchant bank. It can then be sold by the legal holder to obtain immediate finance. The interest charged depends on the creditworthiness of the parties involved, and if a company has a poor reputation then it will expect to pay more interest.
- *Commercial paper.* This is a form of short-term borrowing used by large listed companies. It is a bearer document, i.e. a person to whom the document is payable without naming that person.

Medium-term finance

There are four main types of external medium-term finance.

- *Bank loan.* Banks may be prepared to lend a fixed amount to a customer over a medium- to long-term period. The loan may be secured on the company's assets and the interest charge may be variable. Regular repayments of both the capital and the interest will be expected. Bank loans are a common form of financing but the restrictions often placed on the borrower may be particularly demanding.
- *Credit sale.* This is a form of borrowing in which the purchaser agrees to pay for goods (and services) on an instalment basis over an agreed period of time. Once the agreement has been signed, the legal ownership of the goods is passed to the purchaser and the seller cannot reclaim them. Sometimes very generous terms can be arranged, e.g. no payment may be necessary for at least 12 months but the basic cost of the goods may be far higher than other suppliers are charging.
- *Hire purchase.* HP is similar to a credit sale except that the seller remains the legal owner of the goods until all payments due have been completed. An immediate deposit may be necessary, followed by a series of regular instalments. Once the goods have been paid for the ownership passes to the purchaser. HP is usually an expensive method of financing the purchase of fixed assets.
- *Leasing.* This is a form of renting. A fixed asset (such as a car or a printing press) remains legally in the ownership of the lessor. In the case of some leases the asset may never actually be returned. In effect, the lessee becomes the *de facto* owner. Leasing can be expensive although if the lessor passes on what can sometimes be very generous tax allowances it can be a reasonably economic method of financing projects.

Long-term finance

External long-term finance can generally be obtained from three main sources.

- *Debentures.* These are formal long-term loans made to a company and they may be for a certain period or open-ended. Debentures are usually secured on all or some of an entity's assets. Interest is payable but because it is allowable against corporation tax debentures can be an economic method of financing specific projects.
- *Other types of loan:*
  - *Loan capital* is a form of borrowing in which investors are paid a regular amount of interest and their capital is eventually repaid. The investors are creditors of the entity but they have no voting rights.
  - *Unsecured loan stock* is similar to debenture stock except that there is no security for the loan. The interest rate tends to be higher than that on debenture stock because of the greater risk.
  - *Convertible unsecured loan stock* gives stockholders the right to convert their stock into ordinary shares at specified dates.
  - *Eurobond loan capital* can be obtained by borrowing overseas in the 'Euro' market. The loans are usually unsecured and they are redeemed at their face value on a certain date. Interest is normally paid annually. The rate depends partly on the size of the loan and partly on the particular issuer.
- *Shares.* Expansion of the company could be financed by increasing the number of ordinary shares available either on the open market or to existing shareholders in the form of a *rights issue*. An increase in an entity's ordinary share capital dilutes the holding of existing shareholders and all shareholders will expect to receive increasing amounts of dividend. Alternatively new or additional preference shares could be offered; preference shareholders would have an automatic right to a certain percentage level of dividend and so the issue of preference shares limits the amount of dividend available to ordinary shareholders.

Activity 19.2

You are in a small business as a sole trader. You want to purchase some new machinery costing £50 000.

main form of financing the project would you prefer?

(a) What form of financing would you use to purchase the machinery?
(b) Would you select a different method if you were is a partnership or you had limited liability?

❗ Questions you should ask

Capital investment appraisal is a most important decision-making function. The selection of a particular project and the most appropriate means of financing it are difficult decisions to make. As a senior manager you will receive some expert advice on what you can do but ultimately the final decision will be one for you. As far as the financial data are concerned, what questions should you put before your accountants? We suggest that the following may provide a framework for some detailed questioning.

- What capital appraisal method have you used?
- Why did you select that one?

- What problems have you encountered in calculating the net cash flow (or estimated net profit)?
- What allowances have you made for inflation and taxation?
- What rate of return have you used and why?
- What qualitative factors do you think should be taken into account?
- Are you able to put a monetary cost or value on them?

Conclusion

CI appraisal is a complex and time-consuming exercise. It is not possible to be totally accurate in determining the viability of individual projects but a valid comparison can usually be made between them.

Managers tend to be very enthusiastic about their own sphere of responsibility. As a result a marketing manager may be *sure* that additional sales will be possible, a production director may be *certain* that a new machine will pay for itself almost immediately and the data processing manager may be *convinced* that a new high-powered computer is essential.

In helping management to choose between such competing projects, accountants' the role is to try to assess their costs and to compare them with the possible benefits. Once a choice has been made they then have to ensure that the necessary finance will be available. CI appraisal should not be used as a means of blocking new projects. It is no different from all the other accounting techniques. It is meant to provide additional guidance to management and ultimately it is the responsibility of management to ensure that other factors are taken into account.

Key points

1 Capital investment appraisal forms part of the budgeting process.

2 There are five main methods of determining the viability of a project:
- payback
- discounted payback
- accounting rate of return
- net present value
- internal rate of return.

3 All the methods listed above have their advantages and disadvantages but the recommended methods are discounted payback and net present value.

4 Capital expenditure may be financed by a variety of external and internal sources. Sources of short-term finance for entities include trade credit, bank overdrafts, factoring, bills of exchange and commercial paper. Medium-term sources include bank loans, credit sales, hire purchase and leasing. Long-term sources include debentures and other types of loans, and share issues.

Check your learning

The answers to these questions can be found within the text.

1 What is the distinction between capital and revenue expenditure?

2 List five characteristics associated with capital expenditure.

3 What is meant by 'net cash flow'?

4 What is the payback method of capital investment appraisal?

5 What information is needed to adopt it?

6 List four disadvantages of the payback method.

7 What is the discounted payback method of capital investment appraisal?

8 What is meant by 'discounting'?

9 What does a discount factor depend on?

10 List four advantages and four disadvantages of the discounted payback method.

11 What is the accounting rate of return method of capital investment appraisal?

12 What formula should be used in adopting it?

13 And how should (a) the numerator and (b) the denominator be determined?

14 List three advantages and three disadvantages of the accounting rate of return method.

15 What is the NPV method of capital investment appraisal?

16 Outline seven steps needed to adopt it.

17 List three advantages and three disadvantages of the method.

18 What is the internal rate of return method of capital investment appraisal?

19 What is its basic objective?

20 What formula is used to determine the required rate of return?

21 List three advantages and three disadvantages of the method.

22 How may (a) inflation and (b) taxation be allowed for in capital investment appraisal?

23 List three main external sources of (a) short-term finance, (b) medium-term finance and (c) long-term finance.

News story quiz

Remember the news story at the beginning of this chapter? Go back to that story and reread it before answering the following questions.

Conoco Phillips' decision to reduce its capital spending while protecting its dividend would appear to be a somewhat questionable decision.

Questions

1 Do you think that protecting the dividend payment should be a higher priority than investing in capital projects?

2 What is the future for Conoco if it continues to sell less oil but it still protects its dividend?

3 What does the Chief Executive mean when he states that the company has the flexibility 'to ramp up spending should prices improve'?

Tutorial questions

The answers to questions marked with an asterisk can be found in Appendix 4.

19.1 'In capital expenditure appraisal, management cannot cope with any technique that is more advanced than payback.' How far do you think that this assertion is likely to be true?

19.2 'All capital expenditure techniques are irrelevant because:
(a) they cannot estimate accurately future cash flows;
(b) it is difficult to select an appropriate discount rate.'
Discuss.

19.3 Do any of the traditional capital investment appraisal techniques help in determining social and welfare capital expenditure proposals?

19.4 'We can all dream up new capital expenditure proposals', asserted the Managing Director, 'but where is the money coming from?' How might the proposals be financed?

19.5* Buchan Enterprises is considering investing in a new machine. The machine will be purchased on 1 January in Year 1 at a cost of £50,000. It is estimated that it will last for five years, and it will then be sold at the end of the year for £2000 in cash. The respective net cash flows estimated to be received by the company as a result of purchasing the machine during each year of its life are as follows:

Year	£	
1	8 000	(excluding the initial cost)
2	16 000	
3	40 000	
4	45 000	
5	35 000	(exclusive of the project's sale proceeds)

The company's cost of capital is 12 per cent.

Required:
Calculate:
(a) the payback period for the project
(b) its discounted payback period.

19.6* Lender Limited is considering investing in a new project. It is estimated that it will cost £100,000 to implement, and that the expected net profit after tax will be as follows:

Year	£
1	18 000
2	47 000
3	65 000
4	65 000
5	30 000

No residual value is expected.

Required:
Calculate the accounting rate of return of the proposed project.

19.7* The following net cash flows relate to Lockhart Limited in connection with a certain project that has an initial cost of £2,500,000:

Year	Net cash flow £000	
1	800	(excluding the initial cost)
2	850	
3	830	
4	1 200	
5	700	

The company's required rate of return is 15 per cent.

Required:
Calculate the net present value of the project.

19.8 Moffat District Council has calculated the following net cash flows for a proposed project costing £1,450,000:

Year	Net cash flow £000	
1	230	(excluding the initial cost)
2	370	
3	600	
4	420	
5	110	

Required:
Calculate the internal rate of return generated by the project.

19.9 Prospect Limited is considering investing in some new plant. The plant would cost £1,000,000 to implement. It would last five years and it would then be sold for

£50,000. The relevant profit and loss accounts for each year during the life of the project are as follows:

Year to 31 March		1 £000	2 £000	3 £000	4 £000	5 £000
Sales		2 000	2 400	2 800	2 900	2 000
Less: Cost of goods sold						
Opening stock		–	200	300	550	350
Purchases		1 600	1 790	2 220	1 960	1 110
	c/f	1 600	1 990	2 520	2 510	1 460
	b/f	1 600	1 990	2 520	2 510	1 460
Less: Closing stock		200	300	550	350	50
		1 400	1 690	1 970	2 160	1 410
Gross profit		600	710	830	740	590
Less: Expenses		210	220	240	250	300
Depreciation		190	190	190	190	190
		400	410	430	440	490
Net profit		200	300	400	300	100
Taxation		40	70	100	100	10
Retained profits		160	230	300	200	90

Additional information:
1 All sales are made and all purchases are obtained on credit terms.
2 Outstanding trade debtors and trade creditors at the end of each year are expected to be as follows:

Year	Trade debtors £000	Trade creditors £000
1	200	250
2	240	270
3	300	330
4	320	300
5	400	150

3 Expenses would all be paid in cash during each year in question.
4 Taxation would be paid on 1 January following each year end.
5 Half the plant would be paid for in cash on 1 April Year 0, and the remaining half (also in cash) on 1 January Year 1. The resale value of £50,000 will be received in cash on 31 March Year 6.

Required:
Calculate the annual net cash flow arising from the purchase of this new plant.

19.10 Nicol Limited is considering investing in a new machine. The machine would cost £500,000. It would have a life of five years and a nil residual value. The company uses the straight-line method of depreciation.

It is expected that the machine will earn the following extra profits for the company during its expected life:

Year	Profits £000
1	200
2	120
3	120
4	100
5	60

The above profits also represent the extra net cash flows expected to be generated by the machine (i.e. they exclude the machine's initial cost and the annual depreciation charge). The company's cost of capital is 18 per cent.

Required:

(a) Calculate:
   (i) the machine's payback period; and
   (ii) its net present value.
(b) Advise management as to whether the new machine should be purchased.

19.11 Hewie Limited has some capital available for investment and is considering two projects, only one of which can be financed. The details are as follows:

	Project	
	(1)	*(2)*
Expected life (years)	4	3
	£000	*£000*
Initial cost	600	500
Expected net cash flows (excluding the initial cost)		
Year		
1	10	250
2	200	250
3	400	50
4	50	–
Residual value	Nil	Nil

Required:
Advise management on which project to accept.

19.12 Marsh Limited has investigated the possibility of investing in a new machine. The following data have been extracted from the report relating to the project:

Cost of machine on 1 January Year 6: £500,000.
Life: four years to 31 December Year 9.
Estimated scrap value: Nil.
Depreciation method: Straight-line.

Year	Accounting profit after tax £000	Net cash flows £000	
6	100	50	(excluding the initial cost)
7	250	200	
8	250	225	
9	200	225	
10	–	100	

The company's required rate of return is 15%.

Required:

Calculate the return the machine would make using the following investment appraisal methods:

(a) payback
(b) accounting rate of return
(c) net present value
(d) internal rate of return.

Website

Further practice questions, study material and links to relevant sites on the World Wide Web can be found on the website that accompanies this book. The site can be found at www.pearsoned.co.uk/dyson

Emerging issues

Into the future

Facing challenges

The Association of Chartered Certified Accountants (ACCA) and the Institute of Management Accountants (IMA) have launched a new multi-year signature research initiative, focusing on the future of the accounting and finance profession. The initiative was launched on a new website in September 2015 and the report is the first joint ACCA/IMA project to be published.

This signature research initiative is intended to serve accounting and finance professionals by providing insights on what the future holds for the global profession. As explained by the ACCA's Chief Executive Helen Brand, the new platform aims to inform, educate and raise the debate about the future world of finance, business and accountancy. The new website similarly aims to engage senior business and finance leaders, academics and political decision-makers. The new futuretoday.com website will give a wider view of the issues that matter for the profession and for the broader global business community.

According to Jeff Thomson, the President and Chief Executive Officer of IMA, 'This new initiative ultimately is about serving the public interest and enhancing the capabilities of CFOs and their teams everywhere.' He believes that 'The accountancy profession has a responsibility to create and nurture stronger and more ethical organisations, and both the IMA and the ACCA are happy to be part of this change which will have a unique focus on future challenges and opportunities.'

Source: Adapted from http//www.imanet.org/abut-im/news-media-relations/ima-pre...

Questions relating to this news story can be found on page 468 ➡

About this chapter

In this the last chapter in the book we deal with some emerging issues in management accounting. Basic management accounting practice has changed very little over the last 100 years and although some new techniques were introduced as the twentieth century progressed there were few new development until about 1980. Since that time the discipline of management accounting has begun to be reviewed and reconsidered as a result of major developments in the commercial and industrial world.

This chapter explores some of the changes that have taken place in the business environment towards the end of the twentieth century and the impact that such changes are having on management accounting. We then review some of the developments that are gradually gaining wider acceptance as the twenty-first century progresses.

Learning objectives

By the end of this chapter, you should be able to:

- summarise the changes in the business environment during the last 40 years;
- explain why changes in the commercial and industrial environment have affected traditional management accounting practice;
- outline the nature and purpose of a number of recent developments in management accounting practice.

Why this chapter is important

This chapter is important for non-accountants for the following reasons.

- You will be able to judge the value of any management accounting information presented to you more effectively if you have some knowledge of its historical development.
- You will be able to contribute to any debate that involves examining whether or not traditional management accounting practices have a place in the new business environment.
- You will be able to question your accountants on the proposals that they may have for introducing new management accounting developments into the organisation in which you work.
- You will be able to determine whether the management accounting function could be reorganised in order to provide managers with a better service.

The business environment

The Second World War had a profound effect on the financial, economic, political and social life of the United Kingdom. The country had to be rebuilt. A great deal of damage had been done to the infrastructure, there had been a lack of investment in its traditional industries, and like many other countries in Europe the United Kingdom found it difficult to compete with emerging countries in overseas markets. Many of these countries had a large labour force and the United Kingdom found that they could sell their goods much more cheaply than it could. Furthermore, as they were able to create entirely new businesses it was much easier to introduce new ways of doing things. By contrast the United Kingdom had an industrial base rooted in the nineteenth century with a backward rather than a forward-looking approach to business.

The main country that heralded the new business era was Japan. Prior to the Second World War Japan had been a relatively unknown and somewhat primitive country. The impact of the war required it to be almost completely rebuilt and modernised without having the benefit of many indigenous raw materials. Japan's leaders realised that the country could only survive if it sold high-quality low-cost products to the rest of the world. It had to start from an almost zero industrial base but progress was helped by the close family traditions of Japanese culture and society. It took some time but eventually Japan was able to introduce the most modern practices into its industrial life.

These practices enabled the Japanese to be flexible in offering high-quality and reliable competitive products to its customers and deliver them on time. A detailed discussion of the managerial philosophy and various production techniques used by the Japanese is beyond this book but the following significant developments were pioneered in Japan.

- *Advanced manufacturing technology (AMT)*. AMT production incorporates highly automated and highly computerised methods of design and operation. It enables machines to be easily and cheaply adapted for short production runs, thereby enabling the specific requirements of individuals to be met.

- *Just-in-time (JIT) production*. Traditional plant and machinery were often time-consuming and expensive to convert if they needed to be switched from one product to another. Once the plant and machinery was set up long production runs were the norm. This meant that goods were often manufactured for stock and this increased the cost of storage. By contrast, AMT leads to an overall JIT philosophy in which an attempt is made to manufacture goods only when they have been specifically ordered by a customer. The JIT approach has implications for management accountants. As goods are only manufactured when ordered, raw materials and components are purchased only when they are required for a particular order. Stock pricing problems do not arise and stock control becomes less of an issue since stock levels are kept to a minimum.

- *Total quality management (TQM)*. Another approach that the Japanese have incorporated into their production methods is TQM. The basic concept reflects two basic objectives:

  (1) *Getting it right the first time*. Whatever task is being undertaken it should be done correctly the first time that it is attempted. This means that there should then be savings on internal failure costs as there is no wastage, reworking, re-inspections, downgrading or discounted prices. There will also be savings on external costs such as repairs, handling, legal expenses, lost sales and warranties. There could, however, be additional preventive costs e.g. planning, training and operating the system, as well as appraisal costs such as administration, audit and inspection.

  (2) *The quality of the output should reflect its specification*. In this context the concept of 'quality' should not be confused with the feeling of 'luxury'. A small mass-produced car, for example, may be regarded as a quality product (because its performance meets its specification) in exactly the same way that we equate a Rolls-Royce motor car with exceptional quality.

The industrial changes that had taken place in Japan were observed by other countries especially the United States and the new developments were subsequently adopted in many countries throughout the world albeit mainly in large international companies rather than in small domestic ones.

Other changes that took place after the end of the Second World War were more general. Among those that particularly affected the United Kingdom were the following:

- *Decline of manufacturing industry*. Traditional extractive and heavy manufacturing industries such as coal mining, iron and steel, shipbuilding and car manufacturing are now much less important and in some cases non-existent. Those manufacturing industries that do still exist are less in labour intensive than they used to be and labour costs themselves can no longer be regarded as a variable cost.

- *Growth of service industries*. There has been a growth of service industries such as finance services, entertainment, information supply and tourism. Service entities do not generally employ the thousands of employees that manufacturing industries used to employ. Nonetheless the service sector now forms a major part of the economy of the United Kingdom.

- *Organisation change*. Another noticeable development that has taken place in recent years in both the profit-making and not-for-profit sectors is the move to *outsourcing* or *privatisation*. This means that entities now concentrate on their core activities and everything else is either bought in or supplied from outside the entity. Firms that build bathrooms and kitchens, for example, may subcontract electricians, joiners and plumbers to do the basic work on a job-by-job basis while an industrial company may employ an outside organisation to look after its payroll.

- *Automation and computerisation.* Production processes and administrative backup is now intensively automated and computerised. Indeed, the impact of computerisation has been phenomenal. Most employees now have a personal computer on their desk giving them ready access to a vast internal and external data bank. This means that if they need (say) a report on a particular issue they can download it immediately without waiting for the accountants to do it for them. These developments are likely to become so significant that management accounting procedures in the near future will hardly be recognisable by today's practitioners.

Management accounting changes

News clip

Research funding available

The Chartered Institute of Management Accountants (CIMA) has launched a new research funding initiative. The Institute is committed to developing tomorrow's world-class management accounting researchers but it is aware that it is difficult for less-experienced researchers to obtain funding and advice through traditional channels. It is, therefore, offering funding of up to £5,000 for projects which explore issues in the field of management accounting that would be of interest to practitioners.

Source: Adapted from http://www.iaaer.orgpages/news-and-press-releases

The developments that have taken (and are still taking) place in business life in recent years have already had an effect on current management practices. Indeed since 1980 the pace has quickened and many entities have been keen to incorporate new ideas into their management accounting procedures. Such changes have tended to be mainly in medium- and large-scale industrial entities and the pace has been much less obvious in smaller service-based and not-for-profit entities.

We should not expect, therefore, a *revolution* to take place in management accounting practices over the next few years. We can expect more of a slow *evolutionary* process and it might take at least another 30 years before nineteenth-century management accounting practices are gradually phased out.

What changes can we expect? Although the pace will be slow, we suggest the following.

- The collection, recording, extraction and summary of data for information purposes will be performed entirely electronically. As a result the management accounting function will no longer need to be serviced by a large army of management accountants.

- As JIT procedures become dominant, stock control, materials pricing and stock valuation will become relatively insignificant tasks.

- Product costing will still be important but overheard absorption techniques will become more sophisticated and all the basic data will be processed by computer.

- Budgeting and budgetary control procedures will also become much more computerised and they will be capable of being subject to a variety of different possible outcomes.

- Standard costing is likely to become less significant in a TQM environment but if it does survive it will be possible to produce different standard costs for a variety of different outcomes.

- Management accountants will become more like business analysts specialising in the financial implications of decision making and they will use a wide variety of both internal and *external* data.

- Management accountants will constantly be having to develop and incorporate new techniques in order to cope with a commercial and industrial world that will be subject to rapid change.

It follows that if the above changes do take place, future non-accountants are likely to meet a very different type of management accountant from the one that they are familiar with today. Tomorrow's management accountant will be much more of a team player, less bound to the recording of past events and more involved in taking highly informed decisions about future events.

Allowing for the changing business environment and the need for management accounting to adapt to such changes, which of the newer *techniques* can we see management accountants developing over the next few years? We review some of the possibilities in the following sections but it must be remembered that progress is likely to be evolutionary rather than revolutionary. In the next section we explain how the topics we have chosen to discuss have been chosen.

Selected techniques

Although there were few new management accounting developments during much of the twentieth century these are now signs that the pace of change is beginning to quicken, possibly because of the rapid and enormous changes in taking place in information and production technology. An increase in the number of universities teaching and researching accounting has also possibly helped to awaken an interest in financial reporting and perhaps to a lesser extent in management accounting.

We have chosen ten relatively new management accounting techniques to discuss in this chapter. Our selection is somewhat arbitrary although it is based on some recent articles published in the accounting and financial press and on the changes taking place in the examination syllabi of the various professional accountancy bodies.

In order to simplify our discussion we will deal with the topics in alphabetical order so that it will be easier for you refer to them quickly if you need to check on a particular technique. They are: (1) activity-based management; (2) balanced scorecard; (3) benchmarking, (4) better and beyond budgeting; (5) environmental management accounting; (6) product life cycle costing; (7) strategic management accounting; (8) target costing; (9) throughput accounting; and (10) value chain analysis. These topics are also shown in that order in Figure 20.1.

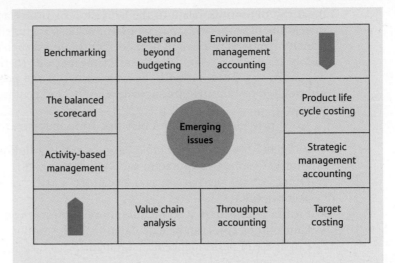

Figure 20.1 Emerging issues

Activity-based management

Activity-based management (ABM) is a relatively new management control technique. It involves the identification of all the production and non-production activities that take place within an entity, establishing the cost of each of those activities, and assessing how well they have been managed.

In Chapter 14 we discussed a similar fairly new management accounting technique called *activity-based costing* (ABC). ABC is used to determine how much of a manufacturing entity's *overhead* should be charged to individual products. ABM's potential is much greater because it can be applied in both manufacturing and non-manufacturing companies. It also it encompasses *all* costs and not just overheads.

The basic procedure is as follows.

1 Determine the key activities undertaken by the entity, e.g. purchasing materials, operating the machines, quality control.
2 Collect all the costs attached to each activity.
3 Charge them to appropriate cost pools.
4 Select a cost driver, i.e. identify the main factor that largely determines each activity.
5 Calculate the cost driver rate for each cost pool.

Sometimes the total cost in each cost pool is classified into core, support and diversionary activities or into value added or non-value added activities. If the diversionary or non-value added costs appear to be unacceptable, immediate steps would, of course, be taken either to reduce or eliminate them altogether.

It is also possible to calculate the ABM contribution. The concept is very similar to the one we met in marginal costing in Chapter 17. The ABM contribution formulae are as follows:

(i) *Sales revenue − activity pool costs = ABM contribution*
(ii) *ABM contribution − remaining costs = profit/(loss)*
(iii) *∴ Sales revenue − activity pool costs = remaining costs*

The activity pool costs include all the costs of making the products, providing the necessary services and delivering the products to the customer. The remaining costs must, by definition, relate to the provision of future activities (such as research and development) otherwise they would have been included in the pool costs. ABM proponents argue that it would be incorrect to regard such costs as part of current activities because they relate to a future time period. In financial accounting, research expenditure would normally be written off in the period in which it was incurred although in certain circumstances development expenditure may be deferred to a future period.

ABM provides a number of benefits. Among them are the following.

- Budgets become more reliable because a closer link is established between demand and the resources required to satisfy that demand.
- Diversionary activities can be more easily recognised and costs reduced accordingly.
- Profitability is improved because more accurate product costs are established.
- Unit output costs can be calculated (activity output costs/output volume) and these can assist in performance measurement.

However, as with most management accounting techniques there are some problems involved in operating an ABM system:

- It is difficult to reduce the number of activities to a practical level.
- The precise boundary between activities is often difficult to determine.
- The method causes resentment and jealousy as it cuts across traditional departmental structures.
- It is not always clear to the workforce who is in charge of a particular activity (as opposed to a department).

Not surprisingly, then, although ABM has been much discussed over the last 30 years it has not been widely adopted. That could be about to change as there are some signs that at least the more forward-thinking companies are considering implementing it.

The balanced scorecard

The balanced scorecard is a performance measurement device that aims to link an entity's objectives with its performance. The idea was put forward by two American academics, Kaplan and Norton, in a series of articles and books (see, for example Kaplan, R.S. and Norton, D.P. 'The Balanced Scorecard – Measures That Drive Performance', *Harvard Business Review,* January/February 1992).

An adapted version of Kaplan and Norton's balanced scorecard is illustrated in Figure 20.2. It has four *perspectives*. These relate to the organisational activity of the entity. Each perspective has a basic question linked to it:

1 *Financial*: how do we look to shareholders?
2 *Internal business process:* what must we excel at?
3 *Innovation and learning:* can we continue to improve value?
4 *Customer:* how do customers see us?

Each perspective then has a number of *objectives*. In turn each objective has a *measure* (such as the staff turnover ratio) and a *target* set for it (say 3 per cent per annum). In addition, managers are expected to come up with an initiative, i.e. what measures they would take to achieve each objective.

The model is flexible and can be adapted to individual circumstances so there could be any number of objectives attached to each perspective. However this would, increase the number of measures, targets and initiatives and this could lead to information overload.

	Objectives	Measures	Targets	Initiatives
Financial perspective 1 2 3				
Internal business process perspective 1 2 3				
Innovation and learning perspective 1 2 3				
Customer perspective 1 2 3				

Figure 20.2 A balanced scorecard

Source: Adapted from Kaplan, R.S. and Norton, D.P. (1996) 'Using the balanced scorecard as a strategic management system', *Harvard Business Review*, January/February. With permission from Harvard Business School Publishing.

Some academic observers suggest that the balanced scorecard idea has now become part of mainstream management practice. If that is so then you are highly likely to come across it when you become a manager in almost any type of entity. However, we would be cautious about just how widely it has been adopted. The idea might now be more than 25 years old but the evidence so far suggests that it is still an *emerging* issue.

Benchmarking

Benchmarking is one of many techniques used by accountants and other financial analysts to assess how well an entity is doing in achieving its objectives. The comparison of what happened with what was expected to happen is known as *performance measurement* and the comparison may be made using both financial and non-financial data from within the entity itself as well as with comparable data relating to other external entities.

According to the Chartered Institute of Management Accountants, benchmarking may take four different forms (CIMA 2005, p. 46). In brief, they are as follows:

1 *Internal*: a comparison is made between the entity's benchmarks and other entities within the *same* industry.
2 *Functional*: here comparisons are made with the *best* external practitioners irrespective of the type of industry in which they are engaged.
3 *Competitive*: the comparison in this case is made between the entity and its *direct competitors* in the same industry.
4 *Strategic*: the incorporation of comparable competitor benchmarks into the long-term planning of the entity.

It may not always be easy to obtain accurate and detailed information about the entity's competitors, especially when the exercise is extended to the strategic level. However, there is little doubt that when the benchmarks show quite clearly that the entity is not performing either as expected or as well as its competitors, then the results should encourage immediate and decisive action.

Better and beyond budgeting

In Chapter 15 we examined the nature and purpose of budgeting and budgetary control. Our discussion was strictly limited, however, to the traditional approach to the subject – one that has been widely adopted over very many years. This approach is known as *incremental* budgeting. In brief, incremental budgets are prepared by (a) taking last year's budget (it is usually for a year); (b) adjusting it for any expected changes during the forthcoming year; and then (c) increasing the costs and revenues by the expected rate of inflation during the budget period.

This method of budgeting has been increasingly subject to a great deal of criticism in recent years. Among them arise are the following.

- It is not related to the strategic aims of the entity.
- Budgets are prepared annually and they soon get out of date.
- The system is organised on a departmental basis.
- The budgets are based largely on last year's budget.
- Inefficiencies and inherent weaknesses are automatically built into the system.
- The focus is on financial outcomes and not on operational ones.
- Broad sweeping top-down changes are often made at the last minute, e.g. instruction from the managing director: *Knock 10% off everyone's budget.*
- Budgeting is a costly exercise in terms of time, energy and resources.

The above defects are just some of the criticisms that can be levelled against incremental budgeting but they should be sufficient for you to appreciate why there is now a demand for something better. Indeed, some accountants call it just that: 'better budgeting'. While other accountants are keen to go 'beyond budgeting'. It is not always clear what the difference is between these two approaches but perhaps the better budgeting movement is evolutionary while the beyond budgeting movement is more revolutionary.

Better budgeting

The demand for better ways of budgeting is not new but it has intensified in recent years owing to the enormous technological changes that have swept the westernised world. Some of the proposed changes that have been advocated over the last 30 years or so are summarised below.

- *Rolling budgets.* Budgets are still prepared on an incremental basis but as the year progresses the first month's budget is deducted and the first month of the next year is added. This procedure continues month by month as the year goes on. This method means that the budget is less out of date than is the case with a pure incremental budgeting system but otherwise it is still subject to all its other defects.
- *Zero-based budgeting (ZBB).* This method ignores last year's budget. Budgets are prepared on the basis of a complete new set of assumptions and outcomes that relate to the forthcoming year. So changed circumstances are taken into account but ZBB still suffers from most of the problems associated with incremental budgeting.
- *Activity-based budgeting (ABB).* This is a much more recent development following the recent interest in activity-based costing. Assuming that the activities of the entity have been grouped into cost pools and appropriate cost drivers selected, the budgets will be prepared on a cost pool and cost driver basis. ABC has not, as yet, been widely adopted in industry so it follows that ABB is at a very early stage of development. It is clearly an improvement on incremental budgeting but its major weaknesses are

that it is still being based largely on a non-strategic approach, it tends to be done only annually, it soon gets out of date, and it is firmly based on last year's budget.

Beyond budgeting

The beyond budgeting approach is a recognition that the world is very different from what it was in the nineteenth century. In recent years there has been an information technology revolution, plant and machinery have become more sophisticated, and companies are managed in a much more participative style than ever they were in Victorian times. Employees too are no longer as submissive as they used to be and their feelings need to be recognised and their recommendations should be taken seriously. All of these factors have encouraged the growth of the radical 'beyond budget' movement.

You might think that the term is rather a strange one. This is because its main proponents do not think that it is sufficient to merely have a radical overhaul of budgeting itself. They want a completely new management model albeit with budgeting at the heart of it. As they put it, they want to go *beyond* budgeting. We do not have the space here to explore this new management model in any depth so we will limit our discussion to some of the basic proposals.

It would be misleading to suggest that the movement is at the stage of being able to recommend a workable substitute for incremental budgeting but we can begin to identify some of the changes that are needed. They are as follows.

- Budgets should be related to the entity's strategy.
- They should cover a shorter period of time (perhaps as short as three months).
- Rolling forecasts based on various *outcomes* should be adopted instead of the traditional cost centre budgets.
- There should be a concentration on activities and processes rather than on departmental cost centres.
- Discretionary costs, such as advertising, marketing, research and training costs from the short-term forecasts, should be excluded.
- Non-financial as well as financial data should be included.
- Data relating to the company's competitors should also be included.
- Managers should be allowed greater autonomy when preparing their forecasts.
- Staff should be given bonuses for meeting the targets set for them.

The above requirements are far-reaching although some of them are beginning to be incorporated into many advanced manufacturing companies. What needs to happen now is for them to be welded together so that they form a workable comprehensive model that can replace incremental budgeting. We wait with interest to see how long it will take.

Environmental management accounting

News clip

Low carbon action needed

The global accountancy profession has urged world leaders to demonstrate determination and political will to achieve a low carbon, sustainable future ahead of the COP 21 Climate Change meeting in Paris.

Source: http://www.accountingforsustainability.org/abn-cop21-press-...

Environmental accounting (EA) is a relatively new branch of accounting involving the capture, recording, extraction, summary and reporting of financial and non-financial data that relates specifically to the environment. If such information is intended mainly for parties external to an entity it is usually referred to as *environmental reporting* (ER) and as *environmental management accounting* (EMA) if the information is primarily for internal management purposes.

A formal definition of environmental management accounting given by the CIMA is as follows:

> Identification, collection, analysis and use of two types of information for internal decision making: physical information on the use, flows and rates of energy, water and materials (including wastes); and monetary information on environment-related costs, earnings and savings. (CIMA, 2005, p.17)

EMA's primary aim is, therefore, quite simple: it is to provide information about what natural resources the entity consumes and how much they cost. Once such information is available action can be taken to reduce their consumption and provided them at a much lower cost.

EA is a relatively new branch of accounting. Its origins can be traced back to an influential report published in 1975 called *The Corporate Report*. This report broke new ground when it argued that companies had a wider responsibility to the community than simply reporting to shareholders. It identified six main user groups that have an interest in a company's performance (see Chapter 2). It argued that such groups are not just interested in having some financial information: they also want to know how the company fits in to the social, economic and political environment in which it operates. This suggestion was valid in 1975 but it is even more so today.

Over the last 25 years there has been a growing interest in and concern about the *physical* environment as the vast majority of scientists have given starker and starker warnings about its future, largely because of the apparent threat to the world caused by global warming. Some observers do not agree with this view but two almost indisputable facts are clear:

1 The world's population has got bigger and bigger.
2 There is a general clamour for living standards to rise.

As a result of these two phenomena a number of consequences arise:

- Natural resources become scarcer because some cannot be replaced as quickly as they are being consumed.
- The switch from a largely agrarian world to an advanced technological one has resulted in considerable air, land and water pollution.
- The climate does appear to be changing as more and more carbon is released into the atmosphere.
- It becomes more difficult to find the means of disposing of huge amounts of human waste without spoiling huge tracts of land and polluting water supplies.

No doubt as you worked your way through school you became very well aware of these problems. You probably feel very concerned about them and you might possibly be campaigning to get something done to stop them happening. By contrast to the attitude of young people, it has taken accountants, at least in their professional role, some time to accept that there is a problem. Credit is due in part to a number of academic accountants who have produced a great deal of research on this subject. The various professional accountancy bodies eventually began to support them and now EA is a common feature in many of their syllabi.

In the meantime, many companies had also begun to collect data about environmental matters. Then in 2006, the Companies Act of that year gave statutory backing to the disclosure of such information. It became a requirement for directors of quoted companies to include in their annual report those environmental matters that may have an impact on the company's business. As might be expected, the amount disclosed depends upon the nature of the company's business. A food processing company, for example, may only need a few lines to comment on 'Greenhouse Gas Emissions' whereas a chemical manufacturing conglomerate may need several pages to explain how it deals with such matters.

As the public become more concerned about environmental matters, many companies have set up an environment management team. Until recently accountants were not generally members of such a team although that is now beginning to change. What part do they play in the work of such a team? We can identify four specific responsibilities:

1 Converting the environmental implications of proposed projects into financial terms.
2 Providing financial data identifying environmental benefits and costs of ongoing projects.
3 Preparing both financial and non-financial environmental performance measures.
4 Ensuring that all environment reports comply with statutory and professional accounting requirements.

A traditional accounting system would not and could not identify those costs and revenues that we might now describe as being 'environmental'. When an EMA system is introduced into an entity the existing accounting system needs to be adapted so that it provides the required information about environmental costs and possible benefits. What are such costs and benefits? We will deal first with the costs.

Some environmental costs will be tangible such as direct materials and direct labour costs. Other costs will be intangible such as the costs of dealing with the opposition to a proposed addition to a factory. Once it has been agreed what is 'environmental', the accountants should not have undue difficulty in identifying the tangible costs but it is highly likely that it will be much more difficult to quantify the intangible ones. Once all the costs have been isolated they may then be classified under appropriate headings. The US Environment Protection Agency has suggested the following classification. We have also included some examples of what might be included in each category.

- *Conventional company costs:* capital equipment, materials, salvage value.
- *Upfront:* site preparation, R&D, installation.
- *Regulatory:* monitoring, training, pollution control.
- *Voluntary:* community outreach, annual reports, landscaping.
- *Back-end:* closure, disposal of inventory, site survey.
- *Contingent:* penalties and fines, personal injury damage, natural resource damage.
- *Image and relationship costs:* corporate image, relationship with workers, relationship with host communities.

We now turn to examine some environmental benefits. Among them are the following:

- *Capital cost savings:* these may arise from better project design resulting in increased production, less pollution and less wastage.
- *Revenue savings:* such savings could come through more efficient use of resources, e.g. materials, energy, water and the sale of waste products.
- *Intangible savings:* these may be very difficult to identify and to put a monetary value on them but environmental considerations may result in better labour relations, improved corporate image and enhanced acceptance of the brand image.

As far as accountants are concerned the collection, recording and reporting of the possible recognisable costs and revenues are what accountants are skilled at doing but as we have indicated, many (if not most) of the environmental costs and revenues are difficult to quantify and so to cost in financial terms. A move towards environmental management accounting and environmental reporting generally takes accountants into almost unknown territory but it is a journey that should be just as exciting as it is important.

Product life cycle costing

Product life cycle costing is a costing technique that captures, records and reports on the cost of making a product from the very first moment that it is conceived until the day that it is no longer made or sold. The essence of this form of costing is captured in its description as 'cradle to grave' costing (see Figure 20.3).

In those entities that do not manufacture a physical product it is known simply as 'life cycle costing'. It should be noted that although it might be thought of as a costing *method* its primary purpose is cost *management*. We start with a brief description of a product's 'life cycle'.

Just as humans go through various stages during their life (childhood, adolescence, adulthood, youth, middle age, old age) so do products. We can distinguish three main phases that most products go through. They are as follows.

1 *Development*. An initial idea is worked up into a design, a prototype is built and then tested. If successful the prototype goes into production. In many advanced technological industries this phase can account for up to 80 per cent of the overall cost.
2 *Manufacturing*. The product is manufactured and goes on to the market. Some products have a short life, perhaps only a few days, whereas others may last for decades. Irrespective of the length of their life it is possible to recognise at least four distinct stages. As Figure 20.3 shows there is: (a) an introductory period when it takes some time before the product begins to take off; (b) a growth period as sales begin to climb; (c) a period of maturity when sales are at their height; and (d) finally a period of decline as sales begin to fall off (sometimes quite rapidly).
3 *Disposal*. The product is eventually taken off the market and it is no longer manufactured. The product line has to be dismantled, the plant and possibly the building demolished, and any left-over materials and waste products are disposed of safely although, alas, that is not always the case.

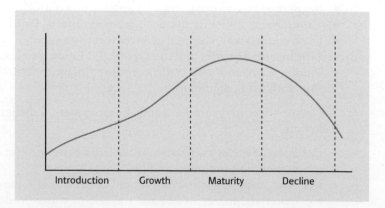

Figure 20.3 The product life cycle

Source: Fox, H. (1973) 'A framework for functional coordination', *Atlanta Economic Review*, 23(6): 8–11. With permission from the Federal Reserve Bank of Atlanta.

All of these phases incur costs but in a traditional costing system some costs such as research and development expenditure and disposal costs would be written off in the period in which they were incurred. This means that units that are eventually manufactured are undercharged and any profit that is made on them is overstated. The American defence industry in the early 1960s is credited with being the first organisation to address this basic cost accounting deficiency and it led eventually to the development of what is we now refer to as *product life cycle costing*.

Proponents of product life cycle costing argue that this method of cost accounting gives a much more accurate assessment of product profitability because it takes into account *all* the costs of making a product, beginning with its initial development and ending when it eventually goes out of production.

The perceived benefits of product life cycle costing may be summarised as follows:

- The technique minimises the possibility that a product will be manufactured regardless of whether it will make a profit during its lifetime.
- Much more emphasis is placed on the impact of the cost of a product at every stage of its development (from cradle to grave).
- A more realistic assessment is given of what profit a product is likely to make during its entire lifetime.
- Management pays much more attention to a product's eventual disposal costs.

There are, however, some obvious problems in incorporating product life cycle costing into even a well-established management accounting system. The main ones are:

- Good ideas might be stifled at an early stage because of their apparent lifetime cost.
- It is difficult to estimate the lifetime of an entirely new prospective product.
- It is even more difficult to determine the four phases (introduction, growth, maturity and decline) that a product may go through.

It is only fair to point out that although product life cycle costing is included in the syllabus of the various accountancy bodies, it has not as yet been widely adopted in practice. It is perhaps difficult to understand why this is the case. Accountants are well used to estimating the cost of making products over at least a two- or three-year period so in principle there should be no reason why this cannot be done for a product's entire life.

Strategic management accounting

News clip

SMA Research Project

A new research project led by Dr Graham Pitcher of Nottingham Trent University has been launched to investigate and enhance understanding of what is meant *strategic management accounting*. The term began to be adopted in the 1980s. It was then taken to mean 'the provision and analysis of management accounting data about a business and its competitors for use in monitoring business strategy'. However, there is still little agreement about this definition and the term is not widely used by practising accountants.

Source: Adapted from http://www.cimaglobal.com/Thought-leadership/Research-to-...

Strategic Management Accounting (SMA) is a more recent development of management accounting. Its main objective is to help an entity compare its performance with that of its competitors. In order to obtain a fair, meaningful and useful comparison between different entities, both internal and external financial and non-financial data are incorporated into the analysis.

The term has been generally used since about 1981 after it was introduced to a wider audience by Simmonds in a magazine article (*Management Accounting*, 59, pp. 26–29). Strictly speaking, SMA is not new but the formalisation of an exercise that some management accountants had been doing for many decades. SMA has the potential to change current management accounting procedures quite dramatically, especially as modern computer technology now allows large amounts of data to be processed without too much difficulty. It also means that management accountants of the future are likely to become more involved in the external activities of an entity as they search for more information about their competitor company's performance.

In summary, three distinct differences between traditional management accounting practice and SMA can be distinguished. They are as follows.

1 Much more emphasis is placed on the *strategy* of the entity, i.e. its long-term planning.
2 Non-financial data are included in the assessment of the entity's activities.
3 Comparable data relating to the entity's competitors form an integral part of the reporting practice.

Recent accounting literature is full of references to 'strategy'. Strategy is usually described in terms of its military usage. A workable dictionary definition is as follows:

> The science and art of conducting a military campaign by the combination and employment of means on a broad scale for gaining advantage in war.
> *Source:* Funk, C.E., Editor (1946) *New Standard Dictionary of the English Language.* New York: Funk and Wagnall's Company.

Or perhaps more relevant for our purposes:

> The use of stratagem or artifice in business or politics.
> *Source:* Funk, 1946.

If we apply these definitions to education you will probably find that your module has probably got an aim (*what are we trying to do in this module?*) and a number of objectives (*how are we going to achieve that aim?*). Similarly the aim of a profit-making business might be (say) to make a minimum return of 20 per cent on capital employed per annum. The management would then have to work out how to achieve that aim. It might, for example, plan to do so by working towards achieving a gross profit of 50 per cent per annum and attempt reducing overheads by 5 per cent per annum.

In simple terms it means that if an entity has adopted an SMA approach, the management accountants would have provided information that compares the actual results with the set objectives. They might have reported for example that *We aimed for a reduction in overheads of 5 per cent over the year as a whole but we are only achieving a level of 3 per cent*. Under a conventional management accounting system the accountants would compare (say) the 3 per cent reduction this year with last year's 2 per cent. The company is clearly doing better this year than it did last year but it is not meeting its objective, i.e. reducing overheads by 5 per cent over the year as a whole. This point might be further emphasised, or course, if the external competitors were reducing their overheads by 7 per cent.

Just as in education, where lecturers set module aims and objectives which force them into thinking deeply about what they are trying to do and how they are going to go about it so in business. That is a useful exercise in itself, but it is even more useful if you then compare how the business is doing with what you wanted it to do. In that sense the past is irrelevant: what has gone has gone. It is the future that matters.

Unfortunately SMA is not easy to put into practice. Setting aims and objectives should be fairly easy, as is the collection of internal data. The difficult bit is in obtaining comparable information about the entity's competitors. Nonetheless even if this is a problem there is no reason why an SMA approach should not be tried. Comparing actual data with data based on objectives is still a highly valuable way to control costs and to take better decisions. Management accounting is slow to change and as yet there is little evidence to suggest that SMA has been widely adopted.

Target costing

Target costing is a relatively new costing technique that has attracted much interest in the management accounting world. It was developed in Japan's automobile industry in the 1990. Its main objective was to bring new high-quality products onto the market that customers would want and at a price that they would be prepared to pay.

The conventional method of determining the selling price of goods is to estimate what they cost to make and then add an additional amount to allow for profit. This method is relatively easy to apply in practice, although as we have discussed in previous chapters, it is not without its difficulties. Target costing adopts an alternative approach. If it to be widely adopted, it would turn conventional costing methods upside down.

The first step in target costing is to set the *selling price* of goods. The second step is then to deduct the *desired* profit that the company wishes to make from selling those goods. The difference between the selling price and the desired profit determines the *maximum* amount that can be spent on manufacturing, marketing, selling and distributing the goods. This then becomes the *target* cost. The above relationships can be put in an equation format:

Target selling price − desired profit = target cost

By comparison, the traditional absorption method similarly expressed as a formula looks much more complicated:

*Direct material costs + direct labour costs +
overheads + desired profit = selling price.*

While the target pricing method may look very simple when expressed in an equation, the selling price of products cannot always be determined in this way because the price that competitors are charging for similar products has to be taken into account. If their prices are much lower than the entity's target price, then both the target selling price and the desired profit level would have undergo a most rigorous reappraisal process.

While the setting of target costs is similar to the more traditional method, it is much more intensive and inclusive as it involves adopting a team approach involving employees, suppliers and customers. In order to illustrate this point we will assume that a company which we will call Tarco Limited is preparing to launch a new product code-named tingal. After some sophisticated market research it is believed the tingals could be sold at a price of £10 each and Tarco aims to achieve a profit of £1 for every tingal sold. This means that no more than £9 per unit can be incurred in making, selling and distributing the unit. The initial cost estimates made, however, suggest the total cost of making and selling tingals would be £11 per unit.

If the Tarco management team were adamant that £1 must be made on each tingal sold, then a rigorous pruning exercise would have to be undertaken to reduce the apparent unit cost. Such an exercise would involve examining every stage of a tingal's life cycle, starting with its original design right up to the time when it was eventually taken off the market. The product's design cost, the manufacturing, selling and distribution, and the administration and finance costs associated with the product would all have to be re-examined to ascertain whether they could be reduced or even cut out altogether.

The basic target costing procedure described appears to be plain and simple: determine the selling price of a product and then deduct an amount for profit. The balance is then the maximum amount that can be incurred on making and selling that product. This means that all employees in the company have to work closely together to ensure that the total cost of making and selling the product does not go beyond what has been agreed, i.e. its target cost. The basic objective of target costing is, therefore, very clear and very easy to understand and it also has some other benefits, Among them are the following:

- Cost reduction becomes a major objective throughout the entire life cycle of the product.
- Valuable information about the entity's customers is incorporated into the costing system.
- Closer co-operation between the entity's staff is enhanced.
- Continuous product and process improvement is applied throughout the company.
- Staff are encouraged to suggest new ideas for making and selling the product.
- The design and development of new products are speeded up.

There are, of course, some problems to overcome in operating the system successfully, just as there are with most other procedures. In particular:

- assessing likely market conditions for the product;
- forecasting changes in technological developments;
- obtaining reliable knowledge about customer desires and needs;
- estimating the product's share of non-production overheads;
- predicting competitors' responses;
- determining what is an acceptable profit margin to add to the product's total cost.

The key to make sure that a target costing work will work effectively and efficiently depends largely on whether customers are prepared pay to the target selling price. If it appears to be somewhat high, then it might be possible to lower the desired profit. However, if the new price appeared to be still too high, the only way to stimulate the market would be lower the price and cut the costs. It may well be, for example, that the method of charging overheads to the new product turns out to be grossly unfair. Otherwise the only other solution might be to have a significant pruning of the entire target cost.

Such procedures may not always work but they do help to make the case for target costing. Compared with absorption costing, target costing clearly involves giving much great attention to the cost of making products and in the management of them.

Throughput accounting

Origin

Throughput accounting (TA) is a recent accounting development encouraged to a considerable extent by the arguments put forward in a book called *The Goal* by Goldratt and Cox, first published in 1984. In that book, the authors vividly demonstrated in the form of a novel that all companies are restricted at some time of other by *constraints* and *bottlenecks*. A constraint is some sort of limit that stops something being done, such as machine capacity or skilled labour shortage. A bottleneck is a limit or a delay in the production process, such as one machine being dependent on another much slower machine.

Goldratt and Cox's argument was expressed in an unusual fictional style but it was sufficiently convincing for it to receive a favourable response. Since it was published, much discussion about the argument advanced in the book has taken place. One feature in particular has come to be widely recognised as being particularly significant: the importance of measuring the input of direct materials as they are fed through the production system, i.e. the *throughput,* as it has become to be known. It soon became apparent that in order to turn management's attention much closer to this potentially important performance indicator, a new form of accounting was required. It did not take long before one suggestion in particular began to receive some serious attention: the one now referred to as *throughput accounting* (TA).

Format

It should be emphasised that throughput accounting is not a new cost accounting *method*. It is just a different way of preparing and reporting exactly the same data that are used to prepare absorption and marginal costing statements. Furthermore, like absorption costing, total costs are classified into their fixed and variable elements and similarly as with marginal costing they are presented in a marginal costing format (see Figure 20.4).

The main differences between the a marginal cost statement and a throughput accounting statement are that, in a TA system, only direct material costs are deducted from sales revenue and all other costs are treated as fixed costs. This means that even direct and indirect labour costs are treated in this way, i.e. as fixed costs. Until more recent times, this would have been unthinkable but there is now a strong argument for doing so. In the past it was easy to split labour costs between those employees who worked directly on production activities and those who provided a more general service

Marginal cost statement		Throughput accounting statement	
	£		£
Sales revenue	20000	Sales revenue	20000
Direct materials	6000	Direct materials	6000
Direct labour	3000		
Other direct expenses	1000		
	10000		
Contribution	10000	Throughput contribution	14000
Fixed costs	5000	Operating expenses	9000
Profit	5000	Profit	5000

Figure 20.4 Simplified marginal cost and throughput accounting systems

for the company. The wages of the 'direct' employees could easily be identified with various production processes and usually, if they did not work, they would not be paid. In accounting terminology their wages were considered to be both 'direct' and 'variable'.

In more modern times that classification and the idea that 'no work means no pay' are no longer valid. Modern employment conditions and legal requirements mean this it is very difficult to lay off staff at a moment's notice when there is no work and not pay them any wages when they are not working. This means that the conventional distinction between direct and indirect labour costs has become largely irrelevant. It is, therefore, now unrealistic to differentiate between those employees who work *directly* on manufacturing the product and those who provide support services for the company as a whole.

The traditional form of absorption costing did recognise that some costs besides labour should be treated as 'direct costs'. Such costs, however, tended not to be *material,* i.e. significant, so it did not really matter whether they were treated as direct or indirect costs. Such costs are treated similarly in throughput accounting and so they too are usually treated as 'fixed' costs.

Advantages

Throughput accounting has a number of advantages. The main ones are as follows:

- Sales revenue and direct material costs are relatively easy to identity.
- The concept of TA is not difficult to understand and to implement.
- No major changes to the accounting system are required
- The classification of costs into direct and indirect elements is largely avoided.
- Direct material costs can easily be identified and their relevance and importance highlighted.
- Direct labour costs do not have to be identified and costed.
- All other types of cost are treated as fixed costs.
- More attention is given to overcoming constraints and eliminating bottlenecks.

Disadvantages

Throughput's disadvantages include the following:

- Emphasis on increasing material input may result in overproduction.
- Less attention may be given to controlling operating expenses.
- Concentrating on throughput contribution may draw attention away from overall profitability.

Summary

The basic concept underpinning throughput accounting can be put quite simply. It is based on two fundamental assertions: (1) in the current economic and political circumstances, only materials can be realistically classified as a *direct* cost; and (2) concentration on material costs gives more attention to any possible production constraints and bottlenecks.

Value chain analysis

Value chain analysis (VCA) is an investigatory technique used to assess the value added to a product as it goes through a number of processes, beginning with the development stage and ending when the product is eventually delivered to the customer. This sequence of events is known as the *value chain* (see Figure 20.5).

VCA was developed in a book called *Competitive Advantage: Creating and Sustaining Superior Performance* written by M.E. Porter, published in 1985. The title of the book gives a clear indication clue to the technique's basic objective. It is asserted that by determining the value added to the product at every stage of the manufacturing process, a company can gain an advantage over its competitors. Porter distinguished between *primary* activities (such as operations, marketing and sales) and *support* activities (such as procurement and human resource management).

A value chain analysis involves six basic steps. In summary, they are as follows:

1 *Units.* The entity is broken down into basic strategic business units (SBUs). An SBU is a section of an entity that is responsible for a defined activity, such as planning, development, production and marketing. In service industries, the value chain will not be as long as in manufacturing entities.

2 *Identification.* Identify those activities within each SBU that are considered to add some value. Such activities will be similar to the ones depicted in Figure 20.5.

3 *Allocation.* Allocate revenue, costs and assets to each value-creating activity. This procedure is similar to the one that accountants use to set up cost centres.

4 *Division.* Divide each cost centre's cost by the main factor that causes or drives the costs incurred in each cost centre.

5 *Comparison.* Compare the results for each value added activity and isolate those activities that appear to add little value. If that is the case, then it will be necessary to determine whether the activity can be eliminated altogether, improved or outsourced, i.e. bought-in.

6 *Action.* The sixth stage will probably be the most difficult because it involves obtaining comparable information from the entity's competitors. Nonetheless it is helpful if it can be done because it will either give some reassurance to the entity or it will encourage them to make perhaps some major improvements to their own processes.

You may have spotted that the above procedure is very similar to activity-based costing. Perhaps the major difference is basically between the way that the costs and revenues are classified: ABC classifies them into activity cost pools while VCA puts them into stages or sequences.

VCA is a complicated exercise. It involves identifying and distinguishing between different 'sequences' and then costing them. The next step then involves selecting just one factor that drives the activity in each sequence. Although there may be some

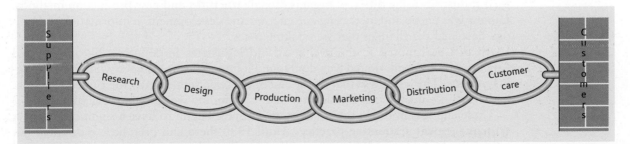

Figure 20.5 A production company's value chain
Source: Based on Porter, M.E. (1985) *Competitive Advantage: Creating and Sustaining Superior Performance.* New York, NY: Free Press.

difficulties in putting VCA into practice, it is probably a worthwhile exercise since non-value adding activities can be quickly spotted. Thereafter something has to be done about such activities and that certainly will not be easy.

> ## ❗ Questions you should ask
>
> This chapter has outlined some of the changes that have begun to take place in management accounting since about 1980. Progress has, however, been slow. You might like to check what changes your own company (or any other entity) has experienced or is proposing to make. We suggest that you ask the following questions.
>
> - Are our management accountants now expected to become business managers rather than number crunchers?
> - If so, are they going to be decentralised and located in separate operating units?
> - Are we going to be able to access accounting reports and statements direct from our PCs instead of waiting for the accountants to contact us?
> - Are we moving towards a more strategic management approach?
> - Can we expect to receive as much non-financial as well as financial information and will it include details about our competitors?
> - Are we proposing to replace our costing system with one that is more up to date and if so, what will take its place?
> - Are we going to put as much emphasis on environmental reporting as we do on financial reporting?

Conclusion

Part 4 of this book has dealt with management accounting. The emphasis has been on traditional management accounting techniques and their usefulness for managers. Most of those techniques originated in the late nineteenth and early twentieth centuries and they have hardly changed at all during the last 100 years.

In the meantime great changes have taken place in economic activity, especially since the Second World War ended in 1945. The main developments first took place in the Far East in countries that were not bound by past practices. They were able to build up their industries using different organisational structures and new production methods. Labour was cheap and increasing automation and development in information technology hastened the changes that were taking place.

All of this resulted in the decline of old industries in countries like the United Kingdom. Indeed, the United Kingdom found it impossible to compete with these emerging nations. The result was that by the end of the twentieth century the United Kingdom had very little manufacturing industry and its economy was largely serviced based.

These changes in the business environment have begun to have a significant impact on management accounting practices. Until 1980 there had been little movement but gradually the 'old world' began to realise that it too had to accept some fundamental changes to business life. If it were to be able to compete successfully with the 'new' world. Orders were hard to get, customers were more demanding, prices were competitive, costs had to be controlled more rigorously, goods and services had to be of the highest quality and an efficient aftercare service was vital.

Traditional management techniques could not cope with the requirements that were needed so some change was necessary. Perhaps the most significant one has been a move towards *activity-based costing* (see Chapter 14) subsequently extended to *activity-based management*. Even so, only large industrial companies have taken much interest in either ABC or ABM and much work still needs to be done in encouraging medium and small industrial entities as well as some service entities of their usefulness.

There are also some other issues that are not necessarily new (such as better budgeting and performance measurement) which are now receiving greater attention. Perhaps one emerging issue above all else is the attention currently being given to environmental matters. Many companies appear to be taking it very seriously and some of them are even publishing their own reports. It cannot be long now before the accountancy profession issues an environmental accounting standard.

We should not expect major changes to take place in management accounting practice very quickly or on any extensive scale. Such developments take a long time to become known and to become accepted. Progress will be slow and it will certainly be evolutionary rather than revolutionary.

Key points

1 Management accounting developed as a main branch of accounting towards the end of the nineteenth century.

2 By 1925 most management accounting techniques used today were in place and there was little further development until about 1980.

3 The decline of old industries in the Western world and the emergence of new economies in the Far East (particularly Japan), the introduction of new management philosophies (such as total quality management and just-in-time procedures), and new technologically based industries have together necessitated the development of more relevant management accounting techniques.

4 We can expect a slow movement towards incorporating these relatively new management accounting techniques into practice over the next few years. A more strategic management accounting approach is likely, involving comparing actual results with their set objectives, more non-financial data and comparative studies of competitors' results.

5 Activity-based management will probably become more widespread, and better (if not beyond) budgeting procedures will be devised.

6 One almost certain development will be a move towards environmental costing, accounting and reporting.

7 Throughput accounting, target costing, product life cycle costing, and value chain analysis will all probably be increasingly adopted by large technology-based companies.

Check your learning

The answers to these questions can be found within the text.

1 What were the main causes of industrial change after the Second World War?

2 What do the following initials mean: AMT, JIT, TQM?

3 List four major causes of the change in the UK economic environment over the last 30 years.

4 Identify four implications for management accounting of such changes.

5 What do the initials ABM and ABCM stand for?

6 What is the difference between ABC and ABM?

7 List the four stages in an ABM exercise.

8 What is the difference between better budgeting and beyond budgeting?

9 List five ways by which traditional budgeting practices could be improved.

10 What is environmental accounting?

11 What is performance measurement?

12 What is benchmarking?

13 What is a balanced scorecard?

14 What is meant by strategic management accounting?

15 What is the main feature that distinguishes strategic management accounting from traditional management accounting?

16 What are the four perspectives into which it may be classified?

17 What is a target cost?

18 List six links that make up a production company's value chain.

News story quiz

Remember the news story at the beginning of this chapter? Go back to that story and reread it before answering the following questions.

Questions

1 How will a proposed 'new multi-year research initiative' benefit the development of the accountancy, business and finance professions?

2 In what ways can these professions raise the debate about the future world of the accountancy profession?

3 What do you think is meant by the statement that the project aims to 'serve accounting and finance professionals by providing *insights* on what the future holds for the global profession'?

Tutorial questions

20.1 'Ugh!' snorted the chairman when confronting the chief accountant. 'Strategic management accounting is another of those techniques dreamed up by you and your mates to keep you all in a job.' Could the chairman have a point?

20.2 'Activity-based management is fine in theory but impossible in practice.'

Discuss.

20.3 How far do you think that short budget forecasts would be more useful than budgets tied in with the traditional annual financial reporting system?

20.4 Do you think that environmental management accounting is of any benefit to a company?

20.5 Do you think that target costing serves any useful purpose in a service entity?

20.6 Compare and contrast each of these management accounting techniques and then, giving your reasons, select the one that in your opinion is most likely to be useful to a non-accounting manager: product life cycle costing; throughput accounting and value chain analysis.

Website

Further practice questions, study material and links to relevant sites on the World Wide Web can be found on the website that accompanies this book. The site can be found at www.pearsoned.co.uk/dyson

After preparing this case study you should be able to:

- distinguish between fixed and flexible budgets;
- evaluate a budgetary control variance report;
- indicate what action should be taken to deal with any reported variances.

Background

Location:	Larkhill, Central Scotland
Company:	Larkhill Products Limited
Personnel:	Robert Jordan, Product Manager
	Dave Ellis, Management Accountant

Synopsis

Robert Jordan recently joined Larkhill Products Limited as a product manager. The company manufactures, distributes and sells a range of popular card games. At the end of his first month in post, Robert received the following statement from the management accountant.

Larkhill Products Limited
Monthly variance report: January 2018

	Original budget		Flexed budget	Actual	Quantity variance	Price variance	Total variance
	Per unit	Units	Units	Units			
Sales volume		20 000	18 000	18 000			2 000 (A)
Production volume		20 000	18 000	18 500			1 500 (A)
	£	£000	£000	£000	£000	£000	£000
Sales	40	800	720	648	–	72(A)	72(A)
Direct material	18	360	324	360	45(F)	81(A)	36(A)
Direct labour	12*	240	216	270	90(F)	144(A)	54(A)
	30	600	540	630	135(F)	225(A)	90(A)
Contribution	10	200	180	18			162(A)
Fixed costs		150	150	140		10(F)	(10)(F)
Profit/(loss)		50	30	(122)	135(F)	287(A)	152(A)

*3 DLH × £4.

Robert left school at the age of 18 with a couple of GCE Advanced Level passes. He had started his career promoting double glazing for a local company before moving into selling central heating systems. He was good at persuading people to buy and for the first ten years of his career he rarely stayed in one job for longer than two years. His ability and experience enabled him to gain promotion to more senior positions in sales and marketing.

He was never interested in going to college or university and he was far too busy to think of studying part-time for some sort of qualification. When he joined Larkhill he knew a great deal about selling but little about the other functional activities of the company, e.g. accounting, distribution, human relations and production. His interview had not been handled particularly well but Robert was good at dealing with people so he had been able to give the impression that he had a wide knowledge of business.

Robert panicked when he received the management accountant's statement. What was it? What did it mean? What was he supposed to do with it? Dare he ask anybody to help him?

After thinking about the problem overnight he decided to tackle it head on. The next morning he telephoned Dave Ellis, the management accountant. Robert was very authoritative and at the same time apologetic. 'Sorry about this, Dave,' he wheedled, 'as you know, I'm new here and my other companies had different ways of doing things. I'd appreciate it if you would do me a position paper about the monthly variance report.' He then indicated in more detail what he wanted. Dave agreed to supply him with some more information.

Robert was pretty sure that he had not convinced Dave about the reason why he wanted a 'position paper'. Nevertheless, he was confident that charm and warm words would see him through an embarrassing problem – as it always had.

Required:
Prepare an explanation for Robert Jordan, explaining what the monthly variance report means and what action is needed.

Standard cost operating statements

Learning objectives

After preparing this case study you should be able to:

- describe the nature and purpose of a standard cost operating statement;
- evaluate the information presented in such a statement;
- suggest ways in which that information may be enhanced.

Background

Location: Burnley, Lancashire

Company: Amber Textiles Limited

Personnel: Ted Finch, Managing Director

Synopsis

Amber Textiles Limited is a small textile processing company based in Burnley in Lancashire. It is one of the few remaining such companies in the United Kingdom but it too is struggling to survive as a result of intense competition from the Far East.

The board of directors has been well aware for some time that if the company is to continue in business, it must retain its customer base by being extremely competitive. There is little scope to increase selling prices and so costs have to be controlled extremely tightly.

The Board has done everything possible to do so. It had recently introduced for example an 'information for management' (IFM) system. The system involves using budgets for control purposes but it also produces standard costs for each of the company's main product lines. A firm of management consultants installed the system with the assistance of the company's small accounting staff.

The new IFM system seemed to involve an awful lot of paperwork and Ted Finch, the managing director, was struggling to cope with the sheer volume of reports that mysteriously appeared on his desk almost every day. By profession, Ted was a textile engineer. He had little training in numerical analysis and none related to accounting.

One morning, shortly after the new system was up and running, he found the following statement on his desk.

Amber Textiles Limited
Standard Cost Operating Statement

Period: Four weeks to 31 March 2017

	£	£	£
Budgeted sales			700 000
Budgeted cost of sales			(490 000)
			210 000
Sales volume profit variance			17 600
Budgeted profit from actual sales			227 600
Variances	Favourable	Adverse	
Sales price		20 000	
Direct material price	6 700		
Direct material usage	15 400		
Direct labour rate		17 600	
Direct labour efficiency	20 800		
Variable production overhead expenditure		3 140	
Variable production overhead efficiency	2 600		
Fixed production overhead expenditure		30 000	
Fixed production overhead volume	12 000		
	57 500	70 740	(13 240)
Actual profit			214 360

Ted studied the statement carefully. What was it? How had it been produced? What did it mean? What was he supposed to do with it?

He was still somewhat puzzled after studying it for some time so he decided to telephone the management consultants responsible for installing the IFM system. They referred him to a manual that they had prepared, a copy of which lay untouched on top of Ted's bookshelf. Sure enough the manual contained an explanation and an example of a 'standard costing operating statement'.

After studying the relevant section, Ted felt a little more confident about what he was supposed to do with the standard cost operating statement. Nevertheless, he thought that it might be useful to take some advice so he contacted his chief accountant and asked him to prepare a written report reviewing the statement. He stressed that he wanted to know precisely what action he should take (if any) to deal with its contents.

Required:

(a) Prepare the section of an *Information for Management* manual dealing with standard cost operating statements. The section should include an outline of the nature and purpose of such a statement, an explanation of its contents and the action management should take on receiving it.

(b) With regard to the specific standard cost operating statement for the four weeks to 31 March 2017, prepare a report explaining what the data mean, what inter-relationship there may be among the variances, and what specific action Ted Finch might expect his line managers to take in dealing with it.

(c) Outline what additional information might be useful to include in a standard cost operating statement.

Pricing

After preparing this case study you should be able to:

- distinguish between an absorption costing approach and a marginal costing approach;
- prepare a quotation for a customer using a number of different costing approaches;
- identify a number of other factors that must be considered when preparing a quotation.

Background

Location:	Dewsbury, West Yorkshire
Company:	Pennine Heating Systems Limited
Personnel:	Ali Shah, Managing Director
	Hugh Rodgers, Production Manager

Synopsis

Pennine Heating Systems Limited is a small heating and ventilation system company located in the West Yorkshire town of Dewsbury. It provides customer-designed systems for small businesses. The systems are designed, manufactured and installed specially for each customer. This means that each individual contract has to be priced separately.

The company had expanded rapidly in recent years but as it had done so its overhead costs had continued to increase. The managing director, Ali Shah, had always insisted that contracts should be priced on an absorption cost basis. This was not a problem in the early days of the company. There was then a considerable demand for what Pennine Systems was able to offer and customers almost always accepted whatever was quoted.

More recently, however, the demand for heating and ventilation systems had become less strong, competitors had come into the market, the national economy was in recession and customers were much more conscious about their costs than they used to be when the economy was expanding.

Although Pennine's reputation was good it had to be particularly sensitive about the price that it charged for its orders. Indeed, Ali sensed that the company was beginning to lose some business because its quotations were too high. He wondered whether he should review the pricing system in order to make sure that the company attracted sufficient business.

Ali was reminded of what he had intended to do late one Friday night when a request for a quotation landed on his desk. On the Monday, he asked Hugh Rodgers, his production manager to cost and to price it. He had the results on the Wednesday morning. Hugh's calculations were as follows.

	£
Direct materials	14 000
Direct labour	41 500
Prime cost	55 500
Factory overhead	11 100
Factory cost of production	66 600
Administration overhead	6 660
Selling and distribution overhead	9 990
Total operating cost	83 250
Profit	16 650
Suggested contract price	99 900*

*say £100 000.

Note:

Factory overhead, administration overhead, and selling and distribution overhead are added to the factory cost of production at rates of 20 per cent, 10 per cent and 15 per cent respectively. A profit loading of 20 per cent is then added to the total operating cost.

Ali suspected that a contract price of £100,000 may be too high to gain the contract but he wondered whether the company could afford to accept a much lower price. He asked Hugh to conduct an intensive investigation of the cost build-up and other matters relating to the contract. Hugh did so and he discovered, *inter alia*, the following information.

1 All the overheads include a share of the fixed costs of the company. 75 per cent of the factory overhead, 80 per cent of the administration overhead and 60 per cent of the selling and distribution overhead are fixed costs.

2 Hugh has been informed privately that a number of other companies have been asked to quote for the contract and that three other companies are being considered at contract prices of £70,000, £75,000 and £95,000 respectively.

Required:

(a) Advise Ali Shah what price Pennine Heating Systems Limited should quote for the contract.

(b) Outline what factors other than price Ali should take into account before offering a firm quotation.

Further Reading

This book contains sufficient material for most first-year modules in accounting for non-accounting students. Some students may require additional information, however, and it may be necessary for them to consult other books when attempting exercises set by their tutors.

There are many very good accounting books available for *accounting* students, but they usually go into considerable technical detail. *Non-accounting* students must use them with caution, otherwise they will find themselves completely lost. In any case, non-accounting students do not need to process vast amounts of highly technical data. It is sufficient for their purpose if they have an understanding of where accounting information comes from, why it is prepared in that way, what it means and what reliance can be placed on it.

Bearing these points in mind, the following books are worth considering.

Financial accounting

Elliott, B. and Elliott, J. (2015) *Financial Accounting and Reporting,* 17th edn, Harlow: Pearson. This is an excellent textbook that is now into its seventeenth edition. It should be a very useful reference book for non-accounting students.

Holmes, G.,Sugden, A. and Gee, P. (2008) *Interpreting Company Reports,* 10th edn, Pearson or its ebook alternative, Holmes, G.,Sugden, A. and Gee, P. (2011) *Interpreting Company Reports and Accounts,* 10th edn, Harlow: Pearson. A well-established text that deals with company financial reporting in some detail.

Wood, F. and Sangster, A. (2015) *Business Accounting,* Volumes 1 and 2, 13th edn, Harlow: Pearson. Wood is the master accounting-textbook writer. His books can be recommended with absolute confidence.

Management accounting

Arnold, J. and Turley, S (1996) *Accounting for Management Decisions,* 3rd edn, Harlow: Financial Times Prentice Hall. This book is aimed at first- and second-year undergraduate and professional courses. Non-accounting students should be able to follow it without too much difficulty.

Drury, C. (2015) *Management and Cost Accounting,* 9th edn, London: Cengage Learning. This book has become the established British text on management accounting. It is a big book in every sense of the word. Non-accounting students should only use it for reference.

Hopper, T., Scapens, R.W. and Northcott, D. (eds) (2007) *Issues in Management Accounting,* 3rd edn, Harlow: Prentice-Hall Europe. This book will be useful for those students who are interested in current developments in management accounting.

However, be warned! It is written in an academic style and some of the chapters are very hard going. It is also now somewhat dated.

Horngren, C.T., Foster, G., Datar, S. and Rajan, M. (2015) *Cost Accounting: International Version: A Managerial Emphasis.* 15th edn, Harlow: Pearson. Horngren is a long-established American text. It will be of benefit to non-accounting students mainly for reference purposes.

Smith, J.A. (ed.) (2007) *Handbook of Management Accounting,* 4th edn, Oxford: CIMA Publishing/Elsevier, This handbook contains 54 chapters on an extremely wide range of management accounting topics. It should be useful for non-accounting students when preparing essays or reports on issues in management accounting.

Note:
From time-to-time a new edition of each of the above books may be published. Always make sure that you are using the latest edition.

Discount Table

Present value of £1 received after *n* years discounted at *i* %

i *n*	1	2	3	4	5	6	7	8	9	10
1	0.9901	0.9804	0.9709	0.9615	0.9524	0.9434	0.9346	0.9259	0.9174	0.9091
2	0.9803	0.9612	0.9426	0.9246	0.9070	0.8900	0.8734	0.8573	0.8417	0.8264
3	0.9706	0.9423	0.9151	0.8890	0.8638	0.8396	0.8163	0.7938	0.7722	0.7513
4	0.9610	0.9238	0.8885	0.8548	0.8227	0.7921	0.7629	0.7350	0.7084	0.6830
5	0.9515	0.9057	0.8626	0.8219	0.7835	0.7473	0.7130	0.6806	0.6499	0.6209
6	0.9420	0.8880	0.8375	0.7903	0.7462	0.7050	0.6663	0.6302	0.5963	0.5645

i *n*	11	12	13	14	15	16	17	18	19	20
1	0.9009	0.8929	0.8850	0.8772	0.8696	0.8621	0.8547	0.8475	0.8403	0.8333
2	0.8116	0.7929	0.7831	0.7695	0.7561	0.7432	0.7305	0.7182	0.7062	0.6944
3	0.7312	0.7118	0.6931	0.6750	0.6575	0.6407	0.6244	0.6086	0.5934	0.5787
4	0.6587	0.6355	0.6133	0.5921	0.5718	0.5523	0.5337	0.5158	0.4987	0.4823
5	0.5935	0.5674	0.5428	0.5194	0.4972	0.4761	0.4561	0.4371	0.4190	0.4019
6	0.5346	0.5066	0.4803	0.4556	0.4323	0.4104	0.3898	0.3704	0.3521	0.3349

Chapter 1	**1.2**	Many answers are possible – 7 sheep; or 5 (alive) sheep and a ram; or 2 sheep, 1 ram and 3 lambs. The answer will depend on the arbitrary rules about categories we choose to use when counting.

1.3

Type of entity	*Advantage*	*Disadvantage*
(a) Sole trader	The owner has total control of the business and can make autonomous decisions	Unlimited liability; It may be difficult to obtain sufficient finance
(b) Partnership	Can pool funds to start up; shared workload (if partners are all active in the running of the enterprise)	Unlimited liability for the partners. If the business is unsuccessful, the partners may go bankrupt (unless it is an LLP – Limited Liability Partnership)
(c) Limited liability company	Limited liability for the owners/shareholders – they are not liable to settle business debts. The most they will ever lose is what they invested in the business to start with.	A bigger administrative burden (submission of accounts and returns to Companies House, in some cases – audit, etc.)

Chapter 2	**2.1**	Some regulations that might be applicable are 'Health and Safety' rules and regulations; or Fair Dealing with customers; or protection of client's money – to name but a few. In all cases, rules and regulations aim to protect or not mislead the public. Similarly with accounting rules and regulations, they have evolved over time to protect investors by ensuring information is made available in a consistent manner about what happened to the money invested in a business.

2.2 *Advantages*
Easy to compare this year's events with those that happened a year ago.
Annual comparisons are commonly made in other spheres and therefore acceptable.
A year reflects the normal climatic seasonal pattern.

Disadvantages

It is an artificial period of time.

It is either too short or too long for certain types of businesses.

Some of the information included in the annual accounts could be well over 12 months old by the time it is reported and it may by then be out of date.

2.3 Revenue should ordinarily be recognised when the risks and rewards related to owning a Porsche pass to the customer – the risk or the value of the asset depreciating, the need to insure it in case of accident, etc. Placing an order is ordinarily not sufficient to recognise a sale (as the customer may cancel the order). The timing of the payment is irrelevant (as often nowadays items are purchased on credit and payments made in instalments while the customer already is in possession of the asset). Delivery of the asset to the customer is ordinarily when risk and rewards pass and therefore a sale and a debtor can be recorded (if the asset is not paid for at that point).

Chapter 3 3.1 (a) A record of a certain event or transaction.

(b) A logbook in which records (or accounts) are kept (a book of account).

(c) As a verb: To receive something or the value received. To record an entry on the left-hand side of a ledger page. As a noun: Assets, expenses and dividends/drawings are known as 'debit' items.

(d) As a verb: To give something or the value given. To record an entry on the right-hand side of a ledger page. As a noun: Liabilities, income, capital and reserves are known as 'credit' items.

3.2 (a) Cash account; sales account.

(b) Rent paid account; cash at bank account.

(c) Wages account; cash account.

(d) Purchases account; cash at bank account.

(e) Ford's account; sales account.

3.3 The entries are on the wrong side.

3.4

Debit	*Credit*
(a) Suppliers	Cash
(b) Office rent	Cash at Bank
(c) Cash	Sales
(d) Cash at Bank	Dividends received (income)

3.5 A debit balance on an account means that the total on the debit side is greater than the total on the credit side. A credit balance is the opposite.

3.6 (a) no; (b) yes; (c) no.

Chapter 4 4.1 (a) false; (b) false; (c) false.

4.2 (a) Land; property; plant and machinery; furniture and fittings.

(b) Inventory; trade receivables; other receivables; insurance paid in advance; cash.

(c) Bank overdraft; trade payables; other payables; electricity owing.

4.3 (a) £3500 [£10000 less (2000 + 6000 − 1500)]

(b) £4000 [£10000 less (2000 + 6000 − 2000)]

(c) £4500 [£10000 less (2000 + 6000 − 2500)]

4.4 £2250 (£50000 − 5000 = 45000 ÷ 20)

4.6 £4500 [£4000 + 1000 − 500]

4.7 £11000 [£3000 + 10000 − 2000]

4.8 Probably yes. Debit the bad debt write-off (which reduced the profit in the statement of profit or loss) and credit Gibson's account (which reduced the trade receivables balance shown in the year-end statement of financial position): £70000 (£75000 − 5000).

4.9 £1500 [£9000 − (250000 × 3%)]. It will increase his profit by £1500.

4.10 (a) Issue of share capital, receipt of cash from loans and other borrowing, capital expenditure (when buying assets).

(b) Provisions, depreciation, allowance for bad debts.

Chapter 5 **5.2**

Advantages	Disadvantages
Free from personal bankruptcy	Formal accounting records to be kept
The business carries on in perpetuity	The Companies Act 2006 accounting requirements apply
Gives some status in the community	Disclosure of information to the public

5.3 (a) net profit for the year before taxation; (b) dividends.

5.4 (a) current liabilities; (b) non-current liabilities; (c) non-current assets; (d) non-current liabilities; (e) current assets.

Chapter 6 **6.3** The business is profitable, has cash and asset exceed liabilities – there is no sign of financial distress.

Chapter 7 **7.1** Payment of trade payables.

7.3 (a) false; (b) false; (c) true; (d) false; (e) true; (f) false.

7.4 (a) cash at bank and in hand + short-term deposits − bank overdrafts; (b) indirect method; (c) cash flows from financing activities; (d) cash outflow; (e) property purchased and dividends paid in the year exceeded the cash flow generated from trading operations.

Chapter 10 **10.3** (a) true; (b) true; (c) true.

Answers to tutorial questions

Chapter 1

1.4 The information that is collected can help non-accountants to do their job more effectively because it provides them with better guidance on which to make decisions. Any eventual decision is theirs and it would often be based on accounting information presented to them by the accountants. Furthermore, all managers must be aware of the statutory accounting obligations to which their organisation has to adhere if they are to avoid committing unlawful acts.

1.5 (a) To collect and store detailed information about an entity's activities.
(b) To abstract and summarise information in the most effective way for the requirements of a specified user or group of users.

1.6 None. The preparation of management accounts is for the entity to decide whether they serve a useful purpose.

1.8 Statutory obligations are contained in the Companies Act 2006. In addition, listed companies have to abide by certain mandatory professional requirements.

Chapter 2

2.4 (a) Matching
(b) Historic cost
(c) Quantitative
(d) Periodicity
(e) Reliability
(f) Going concern

2.5 (a) Relevance
(b) Entity
(c) Comparability
(d) Materiality
(e) Historic cost
(f) Realisation

2.6 (a) Entity
(b) Reliability
(c) Periodicity
(d) Reliability
(e) Dual aspect
(f) Realisation

Chapter 3 **3.4** Adam's books of account:

Account

Debit	Credit
(a) Cash	Capital
(b) Purchases	Cash
(c) Van	Cash
(d) Rent	Cash
(e) Cash	Sales
(f) Office machinery	Cash

3.5 Brown's books of account:

Account

Debit	Credit
(a) Cash at Bank	Cash
(b) Cash	Sales
(c) Purchases	Cash at Bank
(d) Office expenses	Cash
(e) Cash at Bank	Sales
(f) Motor car	Cash at Bank

3.10 Ivan's ledger accounts:

Cash account

		£			£
1.9.16	Capital	10000	2.9.16	Cash at Bank	8000
12.9.16	Sales	3000	3.9.16	Purchases	1000

Capital account

		£			£
			1.9.16	Cash	10000

Cash at Bank account

		£			£
2.9.16	Cash	8000	20.9.16	Roy	6000
30.9.16	Norman	2000			

Purchases account

		£			£
3.9.16	Cash	1000			
10.9.16	Roy	6000			

Roy's account

		£			£
20.9.16	Cash at Bank	6000	10.9.16	Purchases	6000

Sales account

		£			£
			12.9.16	Cash	3000
			15.9.16	Norman	4000

Norman's account

		£			£
15.9.16	Sales	4000	30.9.16	Cash at Bank	2000

3.11 Jones's ledger accounts:

Cash at Bank account

		£			£
1.10.16	Capital	20000	10.10.16	Petty cash	1000
			25.10.16	Lang	5000
			29.10.16	Green	10000

Capital account

		£			£
			1.10.16	Cash at Bank	20000

Van account

		£		£
2.10.16	Lang	5000		

Lang's account

		£			£
25.10.16	Cash at Bank	5000	2.10.16	Van	5000

Purchases account

		£		£
6.10.16	Green	15000		
20.10.16	Cash	3000		

Green's account

		£			£
28.10.16	Discounts received	500	6.10.16	Purchases	15000
29.10.16	Cash at Bank	10000			

Petty Cash account

		£			£
10.10.16	Cash at Bank	1000	22.10.16	Miscellaneous expenses	500

Sales

		£			£
			14.10.16	Haddock	6000
			18.10.16	Cash	5000

Haddock's account

		£			£
14.10.16	Sales	6000	30.10.16	Discounts allowed	600
			31.10.16	Cash	5400

Cash account

		£			£
18.10.16	Sales	5000	20.10.16	Purchases	3000
31.10.16	Haddock	5400			

Miscellaneous Expenses a/c

		£		£
22.10.16	Petty cash	500		

Discounts Received account

		£			£
			28.10.16	Green	500

Discounts Allowed account

		£		£
30.10.16	Haddock	600		

3.13 (a), (b) and (c) Pat's ledger accounts:

Cash account

		£			£
1.12.16	Capital	10000	24.12.16	Office expenses	5000
29.12.16	Fog	4000	31.12.16	Grass	6000
29.12.16	Mist	6000	31.12.16	Seed	8000
			31.12.16	Balance c/d	1000
		20000			20000
1.1.17	Balance b/d	1000			

Capital account

		£			£
			1.12.10	Cash	10000

Purchases account

		£			£
2.12.16	Grass	6000			
2.12.16	Seed	7000			
15.12.16	Grass	3000			
15.12.16	Seed	4000	31.12.16	Balance c/d	20000
		20000			20000
1.1.17	Balance b/d	20000			

Grass's account

		£			£
12.12.16	Purchases returned	1000	2.12.16	Purchases	6000
31.12.16	Cash	6000	15.12.16	Purchases	3000
31.12.16	Balance c/d	2000			
		9000			9000
			1.1.17	Balance b/d	2000

Seed's account

		£			£
12.12.16	Purchases returned	2000	2.12.16	Purchases	7000
31.12.16	Cash	8000	15.12.16	Purchases	4000
31.12.16	Balance c/d	1000			
		11000			11000
			1.1.17	Balance b/d	1000

Sales account

		£			£
			10.12.16	Fog	3000
			10.12.16	Mist	4000
			20.12.16	Fog	2000
31.12.16	Balance c/d	12000	20.12.16	Mist	3000
		12000			12000
			1.1.17	Balance b/d	12000

Fog's account

		£			£
10.12.16	Sales	3000	29.12.16	Cash	4000
20.12.16	Sales	2000	31.12.16	Balance c/d	1000
		5000			5000
1.1.17	Balance b/d	1000			

Mist's account

		£			£
10.12.16	Sales	4000	29.12.16	Cash	6000
20.12.16	Sales	3000	31.12.16	Balance c/d	1000
		7000			7000
1.1.17	Balance b/d	1000			

Purchases Returned account

		£			£
			12.12.16	Grass	1000
31.12.16	Balance c/d	3000	12.12.16	Seed	2000
		3000			3000
			1.1.17	Balance b/d	3000

Office Expenses account

		£			£
24.12.16	Cash	5000			

Tutorial note
It is unnecessary to balance off an account and bring down the balance if there is only a single entry in it.

(d) Pat's trial balance:

Pat
Trial balance at 31 December 2016

	£ Dr	£ Cr
Cash	1000	
Capital		10000
Purchases	20000	
Grass		2000
Seed		1000
Sales		12000
Fog	1000	
Mist	1000	
Purchases returned		3000
Office expenses	5000	
	28000	28000

3.14 (a) Vale's books of account:

Cash at Bank account

		£			£
31.12.16	Fish	45000	31.12.16	Dodd	29000
31.12.16	Cash	3000	31.12.16	Delivery van	12000
			31.12.16	Balance c/d	12000
		53000			53000
1.1.17	Balance b/d	12000			

Capital account

		£			£
			1.1.16	Balance b/f	20000

Cash account

		£			£
1.1.16	Balance b/f	1000	31.12.16	Purchases	15000
31.12.16	Sales	20000	31.12.16	Office expenses	9000
31.12.16	Fish	7000	31.12.16	Cash at Bank	3000
			31.12.16	Balance c/d	1000
		28000			28000
1.1.17	Balance b/d	1000			

Dodd's account

		£			£
31.12.16	Cash at Bank	29000	1.1.16	Balance b/f	2000
31.12.16	Balance c/d	3000	31.12.16	Purchases	30000
		32000			32000
			1.1.17	Balance b/d	3000

Fish's account

		£			£
1.1.16	Balance b/f	6000	31.12.16	Cash at Bank	45000
31.12.16	Sales	50000	31.12.16	Cash	7000
			31.12.16	Balance c/d	4000
		56000			56000
1.1.17	Balance b/f	4000			

Furniture account

		£		£
1.1.16	Balance b/f	10000		

Purchases account

		£			£
31.12.16	Dodd	30000			
31.12.16	Cash	15000	31.12.16	Balance c/d	45000
		45000			45000
1.1.17	Balance b/d	45000			

Sales account

		£			£
			31.12.16	Cash	20000
31.12.16	Balance c/d	70000	31.12.16	Fish	50000

		70000			70000
			1.1.17	Balance b/d	70000

Office Expenses account

		£			£
31.12.16	Cash	9000			

Delivery Van account

		£			£
31.12.16	Cash at Bank	12000			

(b) Vale's trial balance:

Vale
Trial balance at 31 December 2016

	Dr	Cr
	£	£
Cash at Bank	12000	
Capital		20000
Cash	1000	
Dodd		3000
Fish	4000	
Furniture	10000	
Purchases	45000	
Sales		70000
Office expenses	9000	
Delivery van	12000	
	93000	93000

Chapter 4 **4.7** Ethel's accounts:

Ethel
Statement of profit or loss account for the year to
31 January 2017

	£
Sales	35000
Less: Purchases	20000
Gross profit	15000
Less: Expenses:	
Office expenses	11000
Net profit (retained)	4000

Ethel
Statement of financial position at 31 January 2017

		£	£
Non-current assets			
Premises			8000
Current assets			
Receivables		6000	
Cash		3000	
	c/f	9000	8000

	£	£
Non-current assets		
b/f	9000	8000
Less: Current liabilities		
Payables	3000	6000
		14000
Financed by:		
Capital		
Balance at 1 February 2016		10000
Net profit retained for the year		4000
		14000

4.8   Marion's accounts:

Marion
Statement of profit or loss account for the year to
28 February 2017

	£000	£000
Sales		400
Less: Purchases		200
Gross profit		200
Less: Expenses:		
Heat and light	10	
Miscellaneous expenses	25	
Wages and salaries	98	133
Net profit		67

Marion
Statement of retained earnings for the year to
28 February 2017

Net profit for the year	67
Less: Drawings	(55)
Retained profit	12

Marion
Statement of financial position at 28 February 2017

	£000	£000
Non-current assets		
Buildings		50
Current assets		
Receivables	30	
Cash	6	
	36	
Less: Current liabilities		
Payables	24	12
		62
	£000	£000
Financed by:		
Capital		
Balance at 1 March 2016		50

Non-current assets	£000	£000
Retained profit for the year		12
		62

4.12 (a) Lathom's trading account:

Lathom
Trading account for the year to 30 April 2016

	£	£
Sales		60000
Less: Cost of goods sold:		
Opening inventory	3000	
Purchases	45000	
	48000	
Less: Closing inventory	4000	44000
Gross profit		16000

(b) The inventory would be shown under current assets, normally as the first item.

4.14 Standish's accounts:

Standish
Trading, statement of profit or loss for the year
to 31 May 2017

	£	£
Sales		79000
Less: Cost of goods sold:		
Opening inventory	7000	
Purchases	52000	
	59000	
Less: Closing inventory	12000	47000
Gross profit		32000
Less: Expenses:		
Heating and lighting	1500	
Miscellaneous	6700	
Wages and salaries	17800	26000
Net profit		6000

Standish
Statement of financial position at 31 May 2017

	£	£
Non-current assets		
Furniture and fittings		8000
Current assets		
Inventory	12000	
Receivables	6000	
Cash	1200	
	19200	

	£	£
Less: Current liabilities		
Payables	4300	14900
		22900
Financed by:		
Capital		
Balance at 1 June 2011		22400
Net profit for the year	6000	
Less: Drawings	5500	500
		22900

4.17 Pine's accounts:

Pine
Statement of profit or loss for the year to 30 September 2016

	£	£
Sales		40000
Less: Cost of goods sold:		
Purchases	21000	
Less: Closing inventory	3000	18000
Gross profit		22000
Less: Expenses:		
Depreciation: furniture (15% × £8000)	1200	
General expenses	14000	
Insurance (£2000 − 200)	1800	
Telephone (£1500 + 500)	2000	19000
Net profit		3000

Pine
Statement of financial position at 30 September 2016

	£	£	£
Non-current assets			
Furniture		8000	
Less: Depreciation		(1200)	6800
Current assets			
Inventory		3000	
Receivables		5000	
Prepayments		200	
Cash		400	
		8600	
Less: Current liabilities			
Payables	5 900		
Accrual	500	6400	2200
			9000
Financed by:			
Capital			
At 1 October 2015			6000
Net profit for the year			3000
			9000

| Chapter 5 | **5.4** | Margo Limited's accounts: |

Margo Limited
Statement of profit or loss for the year to 31 January 2017

	£000
Profit for the financial year	10
Tax on profit	3
Profit after tax	7

Margo Limited
Statement of profit or loss for the year to 31 January 2017

Profit for the year	7
less: dividends*	(0)
Retained profit for the year	7

Note: * ordinary dividends declared after the year end are not accounted for.

Margo Limited
Statement of financial position at 31 January 2017

Non-current assets	£000 at cost	£000 Less: Accumulated depreciation	£000 NBV
Plant and equipment	70	(25)	45
Current assets			
Inventory	17		
Trade receivables	20		
Cash	5	42	
Less: Current liabilities			
Trade payables	12		
Taxation	3	15	22
			67

Capital and reserves	Authorised	Issued and fully paid
	£000	£000
Share capital (ordinary shares of £1 each)	75	50
Statement of profit or loss (£15 + 2)		17
		67

5.5   Harry Ltd's accounts:

Harry Limited
Statement of profit or loss for the year to 28 February 2017

	£000	£000
Gross profit for the year		150
Administration expenses	71	
[£65 + (10% × £60)]		
Distribution costs	15	(86)
Profit before interest and tax		64
Preference share dividends (interest expense)		(6)
Profit before tax		58
Taxation		(24)
Profit after tax		34

Harry Limited
Statement of retained earnings for the year to 28 February 2017

Retained earnings (at 1.3.16) 50	50
Profit for the year	34
Retained earnings (at 28.2.17)	84

Note ordinary dividends declared after the year end are not accounted for.

Harry Limited
Statement of financial position at 28 February 2017

	£000	£000	£000
Non-current assets	at cost	Depreciation	NBV
Furniture and equipment	60	42	18
Current assets			
Inventory		130	
Trade receivables		135	
Cash		10	275
Less: Current liabilities			
Trade payables		25	
Taxation payable		24	(49)
Less: Non-Current liabilities			
Cumulative 15% preference shares of £1 each			(40)
			204

	Authorised, Issued and fully paid
Capital and reserves	
	£000
Ordinary shares of £1 each	100
Share premium account	20
Retained earnings	84
	204

5.6 Jim Limited's accounts:

(a)

Jim Limited
Statement of profit or loss for the year to 31 March 2016

	£000	£000	£000
Sales			270
Less: Cost of goods sold:			
Opening inventory		16	
Purchases		124	
		140	
Less: Closing inventory		(14)	(126)
Gross profit			144
Less: Expenses:			
Advertising		3	
Depreciation: furniture and fittings	3		
(15% × £20)			
vehicles (25% × £40)	10	13	
Directors' fees		6	
Rent and rates		10	
Telephone and stationery		5	
Travelling		2	
Wages and salaries		24	(63)
Net profit			81
Corporation tax			(25)
Net profit after tax			56
Retained profit for the year			

Jim Limited
Statement of profit or loss for the year to 31 March 2016

Opening retained earnings	8
Profit for the year	56
Less: ordinary dividends	(0)
Closing retained earnings	64

Jim Limited
Statement of Financial Position at 31 March 2016

	Cost £000	Depreciation £000	Net book value £000
Non-current assets			
Vehicles	40	(20)	20
Furniture and fittings	20	(12)	8
			28
Current assets			
Inventory		14	
Receivables		118	
Cash		11	143
Less: Current liabilities			
Payables		12	
Taxation payable		25	(37)
			134

	Authorised	Issued and fully paid
	£000	£000
Capital and reserves		
Ordinary shares of £1 each	100	70
Retained earnings		64
		134

(b) According to Jim Limited's Statement of Financial Position as at 31 March 2016, the value of the business was £134,000. This is misleading. Under the historic cost convention the Statement of Financial Position is merely a statement listing all the balances left in the double-entry bookkeeping system after the preparation of the statement of profit or loss.

It would be relatively easy, for example, to amend the balance of £134,000 by adjusting the method used for calculating depreciation and for valuing inventory. Furthermore, when a business is liquidated, it does not necessarily mean that the balances shown in the Statement of Financial Position for other items (e.g. non-current assets, receivables and payables) will be realised at their Statement of Financial Position amounts. There will also be costs associated with the liquidation of the business.

Chapter 6   **6.4**   Megg's accounts:

Megg
Manufacturing account for the year to 31 January 2017

	£000	£000
Direct materials:		
Inventory at 1 February 2016	10	
Purchases	34	
	44	
Less: Inventory at 31 January 2017	12	
Materials consumed		32
Direct wages		65
Prime cost		97
Factory overhead expenses:		
Administration	27	
Heating and lighting	9	
Indirect wages	13	49
		146
Work-in-progress at 1 February 2016	17	
Less: Work-in-progress at 31 January 2017	14	3
Manufacturing cost of goods produced		149

6.5   Moor's accounts:

Moor
Manufacturing account for the year to 28 February 2017

	£	£
Direct materials:		
Inventory at 1 March 2016	13000	
Purchases	127500	
	140500	
Less: Inventory at 28 February 2017	15500	125000
Direct wages		50000
Prime cost		175000
Factory overheads		27700
		202700
Work-in-progress at 1 March 2016	8400	
Less: Work-in-progress at 28 February 2017	6300	2100
Manufacturing cost of goods produced		204800

Chapter 7   **7.4**   (a)

Dennis Limited
Statement of cash flows for the year ended 31 January 2016

	£000	£000
Cash flows from operating activities		
Profit before taxation (£60 − 26)	34	
Adjustments for:		
Increase in trade and other receivables	(50)	
(£250 − 200)		
Increase in inventories (£120 − 100)	(20)	
Increase in trade payables (£220180)	40	
Cash generated from operations	4	
Net cash from operating activities		4
Cash flows from investing activities		
Purchase of property, plant and equipment	(100)	
(£700 − 600)		
Net cash used in investing activities		(100)
Cash flows from financing activities		
Proceeds from issue of share capital	100	
(£800 − 700)		
Net cash used in financing activities		100
Net increase in cash and cash equivalents		4
Cash and cash equivalents at 1 February 2015		6
Cash and cash equivalents at 31 January 2016		10

(b) Dennis Limited generated £4000 cash from its operating activities during the year to 31 January 2016. It also increased its cash position by that amount during the year. However, it did invest £100,000 in purchasing some tangible non-current assets during the year, but this appeared to be paid for out of issuing another £100,000 of ordinary shares.

The cash from operating activities seems low. It probably needs to examine its inventory policy and its debtor collection arrangements because both inventory and receivables increased during the year. Its payables also increased. Taken together, these changes might indicate that it is beginning to run into cash flow problems.

7.5 (a)

Frank Limited
Statement of cash flows for the year ended 28 February 2017

	£000	£000
Cash flows from operating activities		
Profit before taxation (£40 − 30)	10	
Adjustments for:		
Depreciation (£100 − 80)	20	
	30	
Decrease in trade and other receivables	110	
(£110 − 220)		
Increase in inventories (£190 − 160)	(30)	
Decrease in trade payables (£160 − 200)	(40)	
Cash generated from operations	70	
Net cash from operating activities		70
Cash flows from investing activities		
Purchase of shares	(100)	
Net cash used in investing activities		(100)
Cash flows from financing activities		
Proceeds from long-term borrowings (£60 − 0)	60	
Net cash used in financing activities		60
Net increase in cash and cash equivalents		30
Cash and cash equivalents at 1 March 2016		(20)
Cash and cash equivalents at 28 February 2017		10

(b) The cash flow statement for the year ended 28 February 2017 tells the managers of Frank Limited that the company has increased its cash position by £30,000 during the year. Its operating activities generated £70,000 in cash. This was supplemented by issuing £60,000 of debentures making the total increase in cash £130,000. However, £100,000 of cash was used to purchase some investments.

More tests would need to be done but on the limited evidence available, the company's cash position as at the end of the year looked healthy.

7.10 Statement of cash flows of Carmen Limited for the year ended 30 June 2017

	£ 000	£000
Operating activities		
Cash received from customers	17	
less: cash paid to suppliers	(2)	
less: operating expenses	(5)	
Interest received	1	
Interest paid	(1)	
Tax paid	(4)	
Net cash inflow from operating activities		6
Investing activities		
Purchase of non-current assets	(6)	
Net cash outflow from investing activities		(6)

Financing activities		
Issue of share capital	10	
New Borrowing	13	
Repayment of long-term loans	(9)	
Dividends paid	(8)	
Net cash inflow from financing activities		6
NET CASH INFLOW		6
Reconciliation:		
Opening cash balance		30
Closing cash balance		36
Increase in cash for the year		6

Note:
Interest and dividend could have been grouped within any of the other cash flows.

7.11 Statement of cash flows of Zonka Ltd for the month ended 31 January 2017

	£000	£000
Operating activities		
Cash from customers	27	
less: cash paid to suppliers	(12)	
less: operating expenses (£ 7000 + 17000)	(24)	
Interest paid	(3)	
Tax paid	(6)	
Net cash inflow from operating activities		(18)
Investing activities		
Purchase of non-current assets	(60)	
Net cash outflow from investing activities		(60)
Financing activities		
Issue of share capital	100	
New Borrowing	30	
Repayment of long-term loans	(15)	
Net cash inflow from financing activities		115
NET CASH INFLOW		37
Reconciliation:		
Opening cash balance		(30)
Closing cash balance		7
Increase in cash for the year		37

Note:
Interest could have been grouped within any of the other cash flows.

7.12 Statement of cash flows of Tommy Hox Ltd for the year ended 31 December 2017

	£000	£000
Operating activities		
Cash from customers	880	
less: cash paid to suppliers	(666)	
less: operating expenses	(24)	
Interest received	8	
Interest paid	(3)	
Tax paid	(6)	
Net cash inflow from operating activities		189
Investing activities		
	c/f	189

	b/f		189
Sale of non-current assets		808	
Purchase of non-current assets		(400)	
Net cash outflow from investing activities			408
Financing activities			
Issue of share capital		80	
New Borrowing		800	
Repayment of long-term loans		(444)	
Dividends paid		(10)	
Net cash inflow from financing activities			426
NET CASH INFLOW			1,023
Reconciliation:			
Opening cash balance			88
Closing cash balance			1,111
Increase in cash for the year			1,023

Chapter 10 **10.4** Betty's accounting ratios year to 31 January 2017:

(a) Gross profit ratio:

$$\frac{\text{Gross profit}}{\text{Sales}} \times 100 = \frac{30}{100} \times 100 = \underline{30\%}$$

(b) Return on capital employed:

$$\frac{\text{Net profit}}{\text{Capital}} \times 100 = \frac{14}{48} \times 100 = \underline{29.2\%}$$

(c) Current ratio:

$$\frac{\text{Current assets}}{\text{Current liabilities}} = \frac{25}{6} = \underline{4.2 \text{ to } 1}$$

10.5 James Limited's accounting ratios year to 28 February 2017:

(a) Return on capital employed:

$$\frac{\text{Net profit before taxation and dividends}}{\text{Shareholders'funds}} \times 100 = \frac{90}{620} \times 100 = \underline{14.5\%}$$

(b) Gross profit:

$$\frac{\text{Gross profit}}{\text{Sales}} \times 100 = \frac{600}{1200} \times 100 = \underline{50\%}$$

(c) Capital turn

$$\frac{\text{Revenue}}{\text{Capital Employed}} \times 100 = \frac{1200}{(620 + 100)} \times 100$$

(d) Debt to equity

$$\frac{\text{debt funding}}{\text{equity funding}} \times 100 = \frac{100}{620} \times 100 = 16\%$$

equity funding 620

Chapter 12 **12.4** The main function of *accounting* is to collect quantifiable data, translate it into monetary terms, store the information and extract and summarise it in a format convenient for those parties who require such information.

Financial accounting and management accounting are two important branches of accounting. The main difference between them is that financial accounting specialises in supplying information to parties *external* to an entity, such as shareholders or governmental departments. Management accounting information is mainly directed at the supply of information to parties *internal* to an entity, such as the entity's directors and managers.

12.5 A management accountant employed by a large manufacturing entity will be involved in the collecting and storing of data (largely, although not exclusively, of a financial nature) and the supply of information to management for planning, control and decision-making purposes. Increasingly, a management accountant is seen to be an integral member of an entity's management team responsible for advice on all financial matters.

Depending on seniority, the management accountant may be involved in some routine and basic duties such as the processing of data and the calculation of product costs and the valuation of inventories. At a more senior level, the role may be much more concerned with advising on the financial impact of a wide variety of managerial decisions, such as whether to close down a product line or determine the selling price of a new product.

Chapter 13 **13.2** Charge to production:

(a) FIFO

		£
1000 units	@ £20 =	20000
250 units	@ £25 =	6250
Charge to production		26250

(b) Continuous weighted average:

Date	Units		Value
			£
1.1.15	1000	@ £20	20000
15.1.15	500	@ £25	12500
	1500		32500

$$\text{Average} = \frac{£32500}{1500} = £21.67$$

Charge to production on 31.1.15 = 1250 × £21.67 = £27088

13.3 Value of closing inventory

Material ST 2

	Inventory	Units	Total inventory value £	Average unit price £
1.2.15	Opening	500	500	1.00
10.2.15	Receipts	200	220	
		700	720	1.03
12.2.15	Receipts	100	112	
		800	832	1.04
17.2.15	Issues	(400)	(416)	

25.2.15	Receipts	300	345	
		700	761	1.09
27.2.15	Issues	(250)	(273)	
28.0.15	Closing inventory	450	488	

Chapter 14 **14.6** Scar Limited's overhead:

Scar Limited
Overhead apportionment January 2016

	Production Department		Service Department
	A	B	
	£000	£000	£000
Allocated expenses	65	35	50
Apportionment of service department's expenses in the ratio 60:40	30	20	(50)
Overhead to be charged	95	55	–

14.7 Bank Ltd's assembly department – overhead absorption methods:

(a) Specific units:

$$\frac{\text{Total cost centre overhead}}{\text{Number of units}} = \frac{£250\,000}{50\,000} = \underline{£5 \text{ per unit}}$$

(b) Direct materials:

$$\frac{\text{Total cost centre overhead}}{\text{Direct materials}} \times 100 = \frac{£250\,000}{500\,000} \times 100 = 50\%$$

Therefore, 50% of £8 = $\underline{£4 \text{ per unit}}$

(c) Direct labour:

$$\frac{\text{Total cost centre overhead}}{\text{Direct labour}} \times 100 = \frac{£250\,000}{1000\,000} \times 100 = 25\%$$

Therefore, 25% of £30 = $\underline{£7.50 \text{ per unit}}$

(d) Prime cost:

$$\frac{\text{Total cost centre overhead}}{\text{Prime cost}} \times 100 = \frac{£250\,000}{1530\,000} \times 100 = 16.34\%$$

Therefore, 16.34% of £40 = $\underline{£6.54 \text{ per unit}}$

(e) Direct labour hours:

$$\frac{\text{Total cost centre overhead}}{\text{Direct labour hours}} = \frac{£250\,000}{100\,000} = £2.50 \text{ per direct labour hour}$$

Therefore, £2.50 of 3.5 DLH = $\underline{£8.75 \text{ per unit}}$

(f) Machine hours:

$$\frac{\text{Total cost centre overhead}}{\text{Machine hours}} = \frac{£250\,000}{25\,000} = £10 \text{ per machine hour}$$

Therefore, £10 of 0.75 = $\underline{£7.50 \text{ per unit}}$

Chapter 15 **15.5** Direct materials budget for Tom Limited:

Number of units

Month	30.4.16	31.5.16	30.6.16	31.7.16	31.8.16	30.9.16	*Six months to 30.9.16*
(a) Direct materials usage budget:							
Component:							
A6 (2 units for X)	280	560	1 400	760	600	480	4 080
B9 (3 units for X)	420	840	2 100	1 140	900	720	6 120
(b) Direct materials purchase budget:							
Component A6							
Material usage (as above)	280	560	1 400	760	600	480	4 080
Add: Desired closing inventory	110	220	560	300	240	200	200
	390	780	1 960	1 060	840	680	4 280
Less: Opening inventory	100	110	220	560	300	240	100
Purchases (units) ×	290	670	1 740	500	540	440	4 180
Price per unit =	£5	£5	£5	£5	£5	£5	£5
Total purchases	£1450	£3350	£8700	£2500	£2700	£2200	£20900

Number of units

Month	30.4.16	31.5.16	30.6.16	31.7.16	31.8.16	30.9.16	*Six months to 30.9.16*
Component B9							
Material usage (as above)	420	840	2 100	1 140	900	720	6 120
Add: Desired closing inventory	250	630	340	300	200	180	180
	670	1 470	2 440	1 440	1 100	900	6 300
Less: Opening inventory	200	250	630	340	300	200	200
Purchases (units)	470	1 220	1 810	1 100	800	700	6 100
Price per unit	£10	£10	£10	£10	£10	£10	£10
Total purchases	£4700	£12200	£18100	£11000	£8000	£7000	£61000

15.6 Direct labour budget for Don Limited:

Quarter

Grade:	30.6.17	31.7.17	31.8.17	*Three months to 31.8.17*
Production (units) ×	600	700	650	1950
Direct labour hours per unit =	3	3	3	3
Total direct labour hours	1800	2100	1950	5850
Budgeted rate per hour (£) ×	4	4	4	4
Production cost (£) =	c/f 7200	8400	7800	23400
Production cost (£) =	b/f 7200	8400	7800	23400

Finishing (units)	600	700	650	1950
Direct labour hours per unit ×	2	2	2	2
Total direct labour hours =	1200	1400	1300	3900
Budgeted rate per hour (£) ×	8	8	8	8
Finishing cost (£) =	9600	11200	10400	31200
Total budgeted direct labour cost (£)	16800	19600	18200	54600

Chapter 16 **16.4** Variances for X Limited:

(a) *Direct material total variance:* £

Actual price per unit × actual quantity 72
= £12 × 6 units

Less: Standard price per unit × 50 (A)
standard quantity for 22
actual production = £10 × 5 units

(b) *Direct material price variance:*
(Actual price − standard price) × £12 (A)
actual quantity = (£12 − 10) × 6 units

(c) *Direct material usage variance:*
(Actual quantity − standard quantity) × £10 (A)
standard price = (6 − 5 units) × £10

16.6 Variances for Bruce Limited:

(a) *Direct labour total variance:*

	£	£
Actual hours × actual hourly rate = 1000 hrs × £6.50	6500	6500
Less: Standard hours for actual production × standard hourly rate = 900 hrs × £6.00	5 400	
	£1100	(A)

(b) *Direct labour rate variance:*
(Actual hourly − standard £500 (A)
hourly rate) × actual hours =
(£6.50 − 6.00) × 1000 hrs

(c) *Direct labour efficiency variance:*
Actual hours − standard hours £600 (A)
for actual production) ×
standard hourly rate = (1000
hrs−900) × £6.00

16.8 Overhead variances for Anthea Limited:

(a) *Fixed production overhead total variance:*

	£
Actual fixed overhead	150000
Less: Standard hours of production × fixed production overhead absorption rate = (8000 hrs × £15)	120000
	30000 (A)

(b) *Fixed production overhead expenditure variance:*

£

Actual fixed overhead − budgeted fixed   (150000 − 135000)

15000   (A)

(c) *Fixed production overhead volume variance:*

Budgeted fixed overhead − (standard hours   15000   (A)
of production × fixed production
overhead absorption rate) = [£135000 −
(8000 × £15)]

16.9 Performance measures for Anthea Ltd:

(a) Efficiency ratio:

$$\frac{\text{SHP}}{\text{Actual hours}} \times 100 = \frac{8000}{10\,000} \times 100 = \underline{80\%}$$

(b) Capacity ratio:

$$\frac{\text{Actual hours}}{\text{Budgeted hours}^{\text{w}}} \times 100 = \frac{10\,000}{9000} \times 100 = \underline{111.1\%}$$

(c) Production volume ratio:

$$\frac{\text{SHP}}{\text{Budgeted hours}^{\text{w}}} \times 100 = \frac{8000}{9000} \times 100 = \underline{88.9\%}$$

$$^{\text{w}}\frac{135000}{15}$$

16.12 Selling price variance for Milton Ltd:

(a) Selling price variance:

[Actual sales revenue − (actual quantity×standard cost per unit)] £9000 (F)

− (actual quantity × standard profit per unit) = [£99000 − (9000 × £7)]

− (9000 × £3^{w}) −

^{w}£10 − 3

(b) Sales volume profit variance:

(Actual quantity − budgeted quantity) × standard

profit = (9000 units − 10000) × £3 = £3000 (A)

(c) Sales variance = £9000 (F) + 3000 (A) = £6000 (F)

Chapter 17 **17.4** Contribution analysis statement for Pole Ltd:

Pole Limited

Marginal cost statement for the year to 31 January 2016

	£000	£000
Sales		450
Less: Variable costs:		
Direct materials	60	
Direct wages	26	
Administration expenses: variable (£7 + 4)	11	
Research and development expenditure: variable (£15 + 5)	20	
Selling and distribution expenditure: variable (£4 + 9)	13	130
		320
Contribution		
Less: Fixed costs:		
Administration expenses (£30 + 16)	46	
Materials: indirect	5	
Production overhead	40	
Research and development expenditure (£60 + 5)	65	
Selling and distribution expenditure (£80 + 21)	101	
Wages: indirect	13	270
Profit		50

17.5 Break-even chart for Giles Limited:

(a) (i) *Break-even point:*

In value terms:

$$\frac{\text{Fixed costs} \times \text{sales}}{\text{Contribution}} = \frac{£150\,000 \times 500}{(500 - 300)} = £375\,000$$

In units:

	£
Selling price per unit (£500 ÷ 50)	10
Less: Variable cost per unit (£300 ÷ 50)	6
Contribution per unit	4

$$\frac{\text{Fixed costs}}{\text{Contribution per unit}} = \frac{£150\,000}{4} = £37500 \text{ units}$$

(ii) *Margin of safety:*

In value terms:

$$\frac{\text{Profit} \times \text{sales}}{\text{Contribution}} = \frac{£50\,000 \times 500}{200} = £125\,000$$

In units:

$$\frac{\text{Profit}}{\text{Contribution per unit}} = \frac{£50\ 000}{4} = \underline{\underline{12\ 500\ \text{units}}}$$

(b) *Break-even chart:*

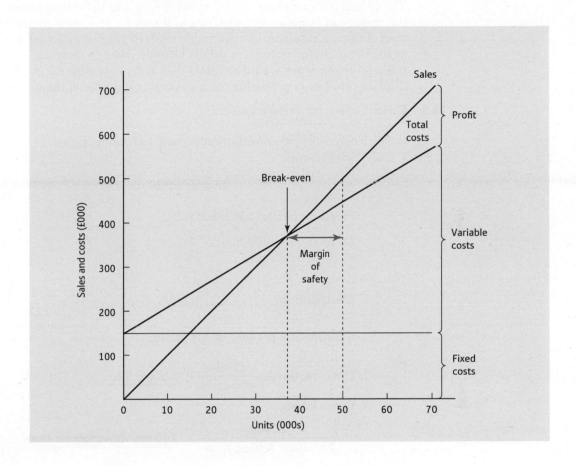

Chapter 18   **18.4**   A special contract for Micro Limited:

Budgeted contribution per unit of limiting factor for the year:

$$\frac{£250\ 000}{50\ 000} = \underline{\underline{£5\ \text{per direct labour hour}}}$$

Contribution per unit of limiting factor for the special contract:

	£	£
Contract price		50000
Less: Variable costs:	10000	
Direct materials		
Direct labour	30000	40000
Contribution		10000

Therefore contribution per unit of limiting factor:

$$\frac{£10\ 000}{4\ 000\ DLH} = \underline{\underline{£2.50\ \text{per direct labour hour}}}$$

Conclusion:
The special contract earns less contribution per unit of limiting factor than does the *average* of ordinary budgeted work. It may be profitable to accept the contract if either it displaces less profitable work or surplus direct labour hours are available. A careful assessment should be undertaken to ascertain whether much more profitable work would be found than is the case with the contract if it will displace other more profitable contracts that could arise in the near future.

18.5 Contributions for Temple Limited:

(a) Calculation of the contribution per unit of limiting factor
  (i) Normal work:

	£
Sales	6000
Direct materials (100 kilos)	700
Direct labour (200 hours)	3000
Variable overhead	300
	4000
Contribution	2000

Contribution per unit of key factor:

Direct materials: $\dfrac{£2000}{100\ \text{kilos}} = \underline{\underline{£20\ \text{per kilo}}}$

Direct labour:

$$\frac{£2000}{200\ \text{direct labour hours}} = \underline{\underline{£10\ \text{per direct labour hour}}}$$

  (ii) and (iii) Calculation of the contribution per unit of limiting factor for each of the proposed two new contracts:

	Contract 1	Contract 2
	£000	*£000*
Contract price	1000	2100
Less: Variable costs		
Direct materials	300	600
Direct labour	300	750
Variable overhead	100	250
	700	1600
Contribution	300	500
Contribution per unit of key factor:		
Direct materials	£300	£500

		50 kilos	100 kilos
	=	£6 per kilo	£5 per kilo
Direct labour		£300	£500
		10 DLH	25 DLH
	=	£30 per DLH	£20 per DLH

Summary of contribution per unit of limiting factor:

	Direct materials	*Direct labour*
	£	£
Normal work	20	10
Contract 1	6	5
Contract 2	30	20

(b) Calculation of the total maximum contribution

Contract 1

If Contract 1 is accepted, it will earn a total contribution of £300,000. This will leave 150,000 kilos of direct material available for its normal work (200,000 kilos maximum available, less the 50,000 used on Contract 1). This means that 1,500 units of ordinary work could be undertaken (150,000 kilos divided by 100 kilos per unit).

However, Contract 1 will absorb 10,000 direct labour hours, leaving 90,000 DLH available (100,000 DLH less 10,000 DLH). As each unit of ordinary work uses 200 DLH, the maximum number of units that could be undertaken is 450 (90,000 DLH divided by 200 DLH). Thus the maximum number of units of ordinary work that could be undertaken if Contract 1 is accepted is 450 and NOT 1500 units if direct materials were the only limiting factor. As each unit makes a contribution of £2000, the total contribution would be £900,000 (450 units × £2000).

The total maximum contribution, if Contract 1 is accepted, is therefore, £1,200,000 (£300,000 + 900,000).

Contract 2

If Contract 2 is accepted, only 100,000 kilos of direct materials will be available for ordinary work (200,000 kilos maximum available less 100,000 required for Contract 2). This means that only 1000 normal jobs could be undertaken (100,000 kilos divided by 100 kilos required per unit).

Contract 2 would absorb 25,000 direct labour hours, leaving 75,000 available for normal work (100,000 maximum DLH less the 25,000 DLH used by Contract 2). As each unit of normal work takes 200 hours, only 375 units could be made (75,000 DLH divided by 200 DLH per unit). If this contract is accepted, 375 is the maximum number of normal jobs that could be undertaken. This would give a total contribution of £750,000 (375 units multiplied by £2000 of contribution per unit).

If Contract 2 is accepted, the total maximum contribution would be £1,250,000, i.e. Contract 2's contribution of £500,000 plus the contribution of £750,000 from the normal work.

The decision
Accept Contract 2 because the maximum total contribution would be £1,250,000 compared with the £1,200,000 if Contract 1 was accepted.

Tutorial notes
1 The various cost relationships are assumed to remain unchanged at all levels of activity.
2 Fixed costs will not be affected irrespective of which contract is accepted.
3 The market for Temple's normal sales is assumed to be flexible.
4 Contract 2 will absorb one-half of the available direct materials and one-quarter of the available direct labour hours. Would the company want to commit such resources to work that may be uncertain and unreliable and that could have an adverse impact on its normal customers?

Chapter 19   **19.5**   Payback for Buchan Enterprises:

(a) Payback period:

Year	Investment outlay £	Cash inflow £	Net cash flow £	Cumulative cash flow £
1	(50000)	8000	(42000)	(42000)
2	–	16000	16000	(26000)
3	–	40000	40000	14000
4	–	45000	45000	59000
5	–	37000	37000	96000

Net cash flow becomes positive in Year 3. Assuming the net cash flow accrues evenly, it becomes positive during August: $(26/40 \times 12) = 7.8$ months. The payback period, therefore, is about 2 years 8 months.

(b) Discounted payback period:

Year	Net cash flow £	Discount factor @ 12%	Discounted net cash flow £	Cumulative net cash flow £
0	(50000)	1.0000	(50000)	(50000)
1	8000	0.8929	7 143	(42857)
2	16000	0.7929	12686	(30171)
3	40000	0.7118	28472	(1699)
4	45000	0.6355	28598	26899
5	37000	0.5674	20994	47893

Discounted net cash flow becomes positive in Year 4. Assuming the net cash flow accrues evenly throughout the year, it becomes positive in January of Year 4 $(1699/28,598 \times 12 = 0.7)$. Discounted payback period therefore equals 3 years 1 month. This value is in contrast with the payback method, where the net cash flow becomes positive in August of Year 3 (i.e. 2 years 8 months).

19.6 Lender Ltd's accounting rate of return:

$$\text{Accounting rate of return (APR)} = \frac{\text{average annual net profit after tax}}{\text{cost of investment}} \times 100\%$$

$$= \frac{\frac{1}{5}(\pounds18\ 000 + 47\ 000 + 65\ 000 + 65\ 000 + 30\ 000)}{100\ 000} \times 100\%$$

$$= \frac{45\ 000}{100\ 000} \times 100\%$$

$$= \underline{45\%}$$

Note: Based on the average investment, the ARR

$$= \frac{\pounds45\ 000}{\frac{1}{2}(100\ 000) + 0} \times 100\%$$

$$= \underline{90\%}$$

19.7 Net present value for a Lockhart project:

Year	Net cash flow £000	Discount factor @15%	Present value £000
1	800	0.8696	696
2	850	0.7561	643
3	830	0.6575	546
4	1200	0.5718	686
5	700	0.4972	348
Total present value			2919
Initial cost			2500
Net present value			419

Index